Also by Brooke Kroeger

The Suffragents:
How Women Used Men to Get the Vote

Undercover Reporting:
The Truth About Deception

Passing:
When People Can't Be Who They Are

Fannie:
The Talent for Success of Writer Fannie Hurst

Nellie Bly:
Daredevil, Reporter, Feminist

UNDAUNTED

UNDAUNTED

HOW WOMEN CHANGED
AMERICAN JOURNALISM

Brooke Kroeger

Alfred A. Knopf | New York 2023

THIS IS A BORZOI BOOK
PUBLISHED BY ALFRED A. KNOPF

www.aaknopf.com

Library of Congress Cataloging-in-Publication Data
Names: Kroeger, Brooke, 1949– author.
Title: Undaunted : how women changed American journalism /
Brooke Kroeger.
Description: New York : Alfred A. Knopf, 2023. |
Includes bibliographical references and index.
Identifiers: LCCN 2022031484 (print) | LCCN 2022031485 (ebook) |
ISBN 9780525659143 (hardcover) | ISBN 9780525659150 (ebook)
Subjects: LCSH: Women in journalism—United States—History. |
Women journalists—United States—Biography.
Classification: LCC PN4784.W7 K76 2023 (print) |
LCC PN4784.W7 (ebook) | DDC 070.4082—dc23/eng/20221028
LC record available at https://lccn.loc.gov/2022031484
LC ebook record available at https://lccn.loc.gov/2022031485

Manufactured in the United States of America

First Edition

For Alex Goren

1940–2021

Though in the Authors' Pantheon no niche obscure
Your waning names can hold forever fast,
The seeds of Truth ye blew afar are sure
To spring and live at last.

—MARY CLEMMER
From her poem "The Journalist," requested and
read before the New York Press Association in
Utica, June 8, 1881

CONTENTS

PREFACE   XI

PART ONE: FIRST WAVE
1840s–1880s

1   The Asterisk   3
2   The She Lot   23

PART TWO: EXPERTS, STUNTS, SOBS,
FRONT PAGES, AND AMAZONS
1880s–1920s

3   The Breakout   41
4   From Cuba to the Far East   63
5   New Thought   81
6   Janus-Faced   103

PART THREE: GLOBAL CRISES
1930s–1940s

7   Practice War   123
8   Depressionistas   137
9   Home Front   151
10 Sidebars   162

PART FOUR: ADVANCES AND SETBACKS
1950s–1970s

11	Bridges	185
12	Foment	205
13	Supernovas	214
14	Vietnam	231
15	Collective Action	242
16	Star Power	252

PART FIVE: REALIGNMENT
1980s–1990s

17	Not Quite	269
18	Power Coupling	291
19	Moving Up	303
20	Moving On	326

PART SIX: STATE OF PLAY
2000s–EARLY 2020s

21	Assessment	337
22	The More Things Change	350
	Epilogue #MeToo, You, Too	368
	ACKNOWLEDGMENTS	391
	NOTES AND SOURCES	397
	INDEX	539

PREFACE

Undaunted makes no claim to being all-inclusive. Rather, it seeks to share in a representative way how women have fared at the top of American journalism, a profession that men have dominated in the 180 years since mass media began.

To arrive at the best way to tell the story, I began with two search terms, "women" and "journalism," applied together, decade by decade, to every relevant database from 1840 to the present. The approach was hardly scientific but provided consistency. It also gave me a good sense of the conditions that governed the presence and place of women as journalists, the ideas about them that prevailed in each period, and how those ideas changed, or did not change, over time. It became possible to identify the individuals whose achievements received the most attention. I considered how and why some women attracted publicity and if and how their stories fit into the wider context of women's advancement. Then came the winnowing.

The telling is chronological. It gives precedence to the episodes that dealt with or dovetailed with the most significant news events and trends of each period. That meant leaving out many stories and people I would have liked to include.

Twelve questions guided me. Which stories best illustrated what women were up against in their professional lives? How or why did the most successful women first get in the door? Who were the true trailblazers and pioneers? Assuming talent and hard work, how much did background, privilege, strategy, charisma, style, looks, advocacy, connections, or luck figure in their ascent? How well did women manage their successes and failures, their celebrity and censure? Were they "womanly" or "manly" in their reporting and writing or in their editorial vision? What impact did they have on the nation's news diet and on the profession? Whom among women has the wider journalism community chosen to honor? Which qualities and characteristics fairly or unfairly attributed to women brought condemnation? Which brought respect? How did newsroom politics figure? Have women made a difference?

I could not resist including some related anecdotes that were too good to omit, but in the interest of a reasonable page count I removed many names, including bylines that deserved to be in the text. If readers find themselves asking, "But what about ____?," the notes section contains many of those answers.

I found value in highlighting great friendships and tracing the way some outstanding careers were built over decades. I endeavored to fairly praise men who gave deserving women an opportunity when it was not fashionable or usual to do so. Some of them might well have met a #MeToo-like fate had such a movement existed in their day. Others, because of the timing, did. The epilogue briefly details the social and cultural currents roiling in the early 2020s as my work on this book came to an end. It surprised me that the intertwining of gender and race would be such an unbroken through line and that the industry's economic crises, manpower shortages, and battered prestige at various points have proved as effective as changes in the law for creating opportunity for woman journalists, especially in the most coveted jobs.

In trying to understand the chances women seized on and the impediments they overcame, I have at times used a twenty-first-century lens to reflect on attitudes, impressions, and policies that stood unquestioned in their own day. Although the all-too-recurring theme right up to the present is progress followed by setback, it does make the triumphs seem all the sweeter.

In writing the biographies of Nellie Bly and Fannie Hurst and the history of undercover reporting, I engaged with many of the memoirs, biographies, archives, articles, oral histories, and studies that anchor this book. (Bly lived from 1864 to 1922; Hurst, from 1885 to 1968.) Journalism has been the world I've lived in, worked in, studied, written about, and taught for more than fifty years. Yet only for

Undaunted did I find myself considering the place of journalism's most successful women as one long continuum. I hope that comes through in the pages that follow.

Against daunting odds, women have always found chairs at the most important tables of this vital profession, seats that often proved hard to keep. Very few of the woman journalists in these pages, alas, have legacies that endured or will endure much beyond their own moment. This is as expected. It is worth pointing out that this is just as true for a great proportion of the profession's outstanding men.

The stories of the remarkable women included here provide a trove of still-sound career advice and some cautionary tales. Beyond that, we know now that it takes an ample mix of ages, races, genders, ethnicities, and political and cultural views to do American journalism's essential tasks most effectively. We also know that journalism's propensity to exclude—addressed repeatedly over the years, but never vanquished—has made us all the poorer. Within that context, our primary focus here is the impact women have had on journalism and journalism's impact on them.

—*Brooke Kroeger*
July 2022

PART ONE

FIRST WAVE

1840s–1880s

CHAPTER 1

The Asterisk

A history of journalism's women, the ones who have succeeded at the level of journalism's most admired men, needs to begin with the bookish Margaret Fuller, who, at thirty, happened into one of the most enviable careers of the past two centuries. Ingeniously, Fuller unstuck the gate that otherwise barred women of the 1840s from like achievements. Then she eased it open with generous intercession from the wives of two great men, the adoring forbearance of friends in high places, and a mad intellectual crush on Ralph Waldo Emerson.

She did not represent, as often claimed, an actual or ostensible "first." Woman writers were commonplace by 1840, as were women in the workforce at large. The Industrial Revolution put a tenth of the country's women in jobs outside the home in the decade that followed, typically in factories or as midwives, wet nurses, or domestic employees. Uncounted other women helped their families maintain a shop or did piecework at home. Educated women most often taught school. Nursing became another professional alternative in the 1860s, by which time the aggregate percentage of women in the workforce grew to 15 percent and has increased steadily ever since.

Women in the roles of writers, editors, publishers, and printers stretch back to colonial days. By the mid-nineteenth century, talented writers could turn to book publishing and the rapidly expanding world of magazines. They found places for their work, especially their stories and poetry, in general interest publications or those with a feminine or juvenile focus. The best known of the women's editors of the day was Sarah Josepha Hale, whom Louis Antoine Godey hired in 1837 to run his *Godey's Lady's Book*. Hale was a force in publishing until her retirement forty years later at eighty-nine.

As nonfiction writers, women were limited in what they could successfully bring to market. With few exceptions, what sold best were offerings bound up in the "women's sphere" of church, kitchen, children, husband, and home. The travelogue also passed muster in these years; its template allowed leeway into more controversial subject matter, a way for women to offer up pieces of wider interest.

Self-styled entrepreneurial journalistic ventures provided another outlet, as did the place women carved out for themselves in the advocacy press. These publications took up the great social and political currents of the age: temperance, religion, and abolition, soon to be joined by the movement for women's suffrage, which gained force near the end of the 1840s. They gave women a platform from which to showcase their intellect and range.

Although slavery was the undisputed scourge of the age, the denied rights of women, who represented half of the population, needed redress, too. Laws varied from state to state, but women in general had limited rights to property, inheritance, participation in court proceedings, and divorce. They had no say in determining what those laws would be or which city, county, state, or federal officials would represent them in elected posts. Not until the ratification of the Fourteenth Amendment in 1868 did African American women join African American men as citizens of the United States. All women, however, remained disenfranchised.

In these years, Lydia Maria Child, like Fuller, was among the few women who managed to squeeze into the realms claimed by men in journalism's most desired positions. Jane McManus Storm Cazneau was another, an annexationist who wrote from North Africa in 1841 and covered politics and the Mexican-American War of 1846–48 for several New York publications. Cornelia Walter's opportunity arrived by alternate means; she simply glided into her late brother's seat as editor of the *Boston Evening Transcript* and performed credibly as its editor from 1842 until she married in 1847. For women with the luck of marriage or birth lines as convenient as Walter's, the nepotistic route to top positions would long continue to be the quickest, but this does not diminish her place as the first woman to run a U.S.

daily newspaper in a major city. In the cases
of these women and a few others, opportunity derived from ability, awareness,
and insight into the era's major political, social, and cultural currents, and
the help of influential friends—or
relatives, in Walter's case. Their talents stood out enough for a few editorial overlords to ignore convention
just enough to land them prominent
jobs, assignments, or attention well
beyond what ladies of the era had been
conditioned to expect.

Cornelia Walter
(Historic New England)

As journalists, the sagas of Lydia Child,
Jane Cazneau, and Cornelia Walter survive primarily in the published research
of scholars. Yet all are convincing examples of mid-nineteenth-
century women who succeeded beyond their era's expectations. The
lives of Fuller and Child intertwine enough to tell a larger story of
how, in the 1840s, a few women found ways out of their designated
sphere to write about what they wanted to write about. That often
included the condition and rights of women, but only as one of a
broad range of topics they explored. Fuller takes center stage in this
quartet as much for what she accomplished as for the astonishing
level of respect she commanded then and continues to command 180
years later. Her story also has all the dimensions of a German fairy
tale for grown-ups.

In 1835, she was twenty-five and at the midpoint of a two-year
quest to know "in private" the man she believed to possess "the most
powerful of any American mind," Ralph Waldo Emerson. That year
she lost her mentor, her father, Timothy Fuller, a self-made honors
graduate of Harvard, an attorney, a distinguished orator, and a congressman from Massachusetts. His death left his family in severe
financial straits. Margaret had only about five years of formal schooling, mostly at academies for Victorian ladies-in-training—charm
schools, really—ill-suited to the needs and intellectual passions
of a prodigy. Her father's exacting tutelage groomed the oldest of
his nine children, his "bright and ugly" daughter, as she described

Margaret Fuller

*(Library of Congress, loc.gov/
item/2002712183/)*

herself, to move with extreme confidence among exceptional men. Horace Greeley called her, "mentally, the best instructed woman in America." As founder, editor, and publisher of the *New York Tribune*, the largest-circulation daily newspaper of the day, he would become the third most important man in Fuller's life after her father and Emerson.

Fuller's journals trace the way she almost stalked Emerson, seeking the right chance to connect. She enlisted one mutual friend to talk up her "excelling genius" and another to lend him a copy of her unpublished translation of Goethe's *Tasso*. Emerson resisted the overtures, put off by reports of Fuller's arrogance, her "overweening sense of power," her "slight esteem of others," and the biting satire that came with her erudition. "The men thought she carried too many guns," Emerson later wrote; other women felt she looked down on them. The sliver of an opening came from his observation that most of the men and women in his circles who at first found her "disagreeable" in time became her closest friends. This would include Nathaniel Hawthorne.

Emerson relented in the summer of 1836, prompted by "a little diplomatizing in billets by the ladies." Ten months into his second marriage to Lidian Jackson, Lidian invited Fuller to spend a fortnight at the family's home in Concord, Massachusetts. Lidian, too, had brains and culture, "a soaring Transcendentalist full of sensibility," as one new acquaintance described her, "yet as independent in her mind as—who shall I say—Margaret F." Emerson, Hawthorne, Henry David Thoreau, Greeley, and Fuller all had associations with each other and with the avant-garde transcendental movement and its Brook Farm experiment in communal living, which was just beginning. Lidian was thirty-two, her husband a year younger, and Fuller, twenty-six.

At first, Fuller's mannerisms repelled Emerson, as did her "extreme plainness," her nasal voice, and her "trick of incessantly opening and shutting her eyelids." Fuller was undeterred. Her most universally admired strength was her gift of discourse, a talent that would provide her income for several years after short, unsatisfying stints as a teacher. Under the title "Conversations," she organized seminars in and around Boston. They began on November 6, 1839, with a group of twenty-five women brought together in a friend's bookshop to debate topics Fuller chose from her vast knowledge of literature and the arts. For women, the social and legal clamps around their sphere had begun to chafe, even for the privileged women in Fuller's set. Fuller had a pressing need to earn but also described the underlying aim of "Conversations" to be her desire to help women "systematize" the precision and clarity of their thought processes. She attributed the deficiency to how rarely society called upon mid-nineteenth-century women to "test and classify" their knowledge. The exercise, she felt, would help women in a position to choose to divine what their most suitable engagements might be, given the walls of societal discouragement their times imposed. Fuller focused on how women might better layer "the life of thought upon the life of action." For the women who would aspire to careers in journalism over the decades to come, Fuller had put her finger on what had already hardened into a persistent barrier to their ability to advance. Over and over again, well into the twentieth century, men in charge would accuse women of lacking this basic competency, as if the deficit were part of the very nature of womankind.

Lydia Maria Child was among the original attendees of Fuller's "Conversations." Child had been an established writer since the 1820s, when Fuller was still in her mid-teens. Despite their age difference, these two kindred spirits became fast friends. Fuller, at fifteen, called Child "a new stimulus." When Fuller was sixteen and Child twenty-four, they set out together to read John Locke as their introduction to English metaphysics. They had a plan to follow up with study of the work on Locke's system by a woman they both idolized, the political theorist of the French Revolution Madame Germaine de Staël. Both Fuller and Child at different points and for different reasons would invite comparisons to the great "first woman of the republic." Child in time would become one of de Staël's biographers.

Child also became Fuller's earliest local model of a woman who wrote for a living. Child did so in part because her husband and collaborator, the attorney David Child, kept the two of them in constant debt. Child built her reputation as a writer, and a living for her and David, on what would sell. Women's-interest narratives and practical advice on domestic themes form the bulk of her earliest work. Beginning in 1826, Child also wrote, edited, and published *The Juvenile Miscellany*, considered the country's first children's magazine, a money-generating idea others would copy.

Namelessly, Child lives in common memory for her poem turned song, "Over the River and Through the Woods," but far more noteworthy is the way she found to exit the home-children-family universe that she inhabited as a writer for two decades. In 1830, she and her husband brought out the *Massachusetts Journal*. The newspaper failed two years later. The wide distribution of her domestic advice manual, *The Frugal Housewife*, published the year before, helped sustain the couple and continued to sell briskly both in England and in the United States until 1833, the publication year of her bold, comprehensive, eight-chapter polemic, *An Appeal in Favor of That Class of Americans Called Africans*, which changed everything. The book promoted the immediate emancipation of the enslaved with no compensation to the owners. As if to soften the blows the text would deliver to the slaveholders and self-satisfied among northerners and southerners alike, the title page incongruously, almost comically, touts her previous totally unrelated successes as "By Mrs. Child, Author of *The Mother's Book, The Girls' Own Book, The Frugal Housewife*, Etc."

"I am fully aware of the unpopularity of the task I have undertaken," she declared in the preface to *An Appeal*, accurately anticipating the ridicule and censure it quickly brought, enough to shatter her reputation. Friends and family shunned her; the literati and reading public blacklisted her for a decade. So many appalled parents canceled their subscriptions to *The Juvenile Miscellany* that it went bankrupt. Sales slowed even for her perennials like *The Frugal Housewife*. A month before *An Appeal* appeared, the editors of the *North American Review*, the nation's premier literary journal, had published a warm, twenty-five-page-long appreciation of Child's vast oeuvre. The essay declared that no other woman outranked her as a writer of useful books of prose, poetry, and practical advice with a consistent tone in fact and in fiction of "healthy morality" and "good sense." Because of

An Appeal, the magazine did an about-face a couple years later, its un-named critic asking how a writer so useful and agreeable could stray so far from what she did best. *The Literary Journal* went further, accusing Child of "inculcating doctrines and principles" that were neither popular nor "in every respect of the best moral tendency," and took more direct aim at Child's call to end the prohibition against marriage between Blacks and whites, something that "cannot, ought not to be tolerated in any decent community." As she became more deeply involved with antislavery work, the damage to her literary reputation increased her stock with the abolitionists. In 1829, four years before *An Appeal* appeared, William Lloyd Garrison, the editor of *The Liberator,* had already declared her another "first woman of the republic."

When Fuller was compared to de Staël, it would be to empha-size the parallels in their lives and talents, especially their legendary prowess with the spoken word. This is what made Fuller's "Con-versations" so successful between 1839 and 1844. In New England, her reputation as a luminescent conversationalist preceded her, even though she had never taken to the lecture circuit, as Emerson had. Locally, she already had star power; people wanted to hear her speak. Emerson, however, at least at the start of that first visit in 1836, was less impressed with her repartee than most everyone else. He found it too laden with personal history and gossip. Beyond that, he bristled at the calculated way she had studied his tastes and at her flagrant efforts to ingratiate. She made no secret of how deeply she admired him, how much she sought to please.

It took the rest of those first two weeks in Concord for her to wash away Emerson's initial negative impressions. He discovered that Fuller "piqued and amused" him, that he liked the way she chal-lenged his frankness with her own. In the end, he wrote later, her "urgent assault" became impossible to resist. "We like her," Lidian Emerson wrote to a mutual friend about the visit, "—she likes us."

Fuller's visit in 1836 became the first of many to the Emerson home over the next seven years and the start of an intense, con-tinuous, lifelong correspondence. Emerson would describe Fuller as that rare kind of friend who "never confounded relations, but kept a hundred fine threads in her hand without crossing or entangling any. An entire intimacy . . ."

Lidian Jackson Emerson and Ralph Waldo Emerson

(Lidian Jackson Emerson [Concord Mass. Free Public Library] and Ralph Waldo Emerson lithograph by Leopold Grozelier [Library of Congress, loc.gov/item/2003688869/])

In July 1840, Emerson launched *The Dial,* a quarterly magazine of "literature, philosophy, and religion" that he envisioned as "broad and great in its survey," an absolute "must read." Although Fuller was not his first choice, he named his "vivacious friend" of four years the magazine's first editor, promising an annual salary of $200 that revenues from its tiny circulation surely never produced. Fuller held the post for two of the four years Emerson published the magazine and continued to write for it after she stepped down as editor in Emerson's favor. For *The Dial,* she signed her long essays, poems, and translations with the single initial "F.," or not at all.

The convention of women keeping their names out of print except at birth, marriage, and death was well established and remained so for decades, inviting the aliases that became a nineteenth-century trend. Neither Fuller nor Child nor Walter adopted the practice, although Jane Cazneau in print at different times called herself "Josephine," "Cora Montgomery," or "MONTGOMERY."

Fuller's work for *The Dial* positioned her as an editor and essayist several cuts above all others. No other American woman invited such huge attention as a thinker and as a writer. Greeley had quickly grasped the powerhouse Fuller was becoming from his trips to the Boston area to visit Emerson and other friends. Greeley devoured every issue of *The Dial.* He saw it as "manna in the wilderness" for

a readership he doubted ever surpassed two thousand people. He
thought Emerson and Fuller were
its greatest asset, "these two rarest, if not ripest, fruits of New England's culture and reflection in the
middle of the Nineteenth Century."
The magazine inspired Greeley to
elevate the offerings of his *New York
Tribune* with *Dial*-like gestures. This
distinguished it from the tawdrier,
more sensationalistic competitors
like *The Sun* and *The New York Herald,* which also sold for a penny. He
operated from the premise that his

Jane McManus Storm Cazneau
(Kean Collection, Getty Images)

more than thirty thousand New York City readers, plus the thousands more who read the *Tribune*'s weekly national edition, would
delight in some finer fare.

In 1841, David and Lydia Maria Child moved to New York City.
David turned down an offer to became editor of the financially
strapped *National Anti-Slavery Standard,* a job Lydia promptly won
for herself. She took charge of the four-page weekly, whose aim was
winning converts to the abolition cause. In the two years she ran the
paper, in addition to other changes, she introduced her extremely
popular "Letters from New York" columns. The general concept of
a woman writing from afar was not new. The solo entrepreneurial
efforts of the feisty Anne Newport Royall, born in 1769, are a gos-
sipier early instance of this style of reporting. As a widow denied
dower, pension, or inheritance rights to her husband's large estate,
Royall spent ten years vagabonding across the country, collecting
local stories that she self-published and sold by subscription. In her
early sixties, she replicated the process in Washington, D.C., making
the city's politicians and elected officials her targets, much to their
annoyance, until she died at eighty-five in 1854.

Child's approach to the "letters" format favored reflective, fact-
based observations presented in narrative form. As editor, she preferred to insinuate her abolitionist and other messaging on social
reform rather than bludgeon readers with it, and during her tenure

Lydia Maria Child

*(Portraits of American Abolitionists,
Massachusetts Historical Society)*

the paper's primarily dwindling circulation increased, from twenty-five hundred to five thousand readers. But this neither sufficiently improved the paper's financial state nor won Child support among those who wanted the *Standard* to have a far more vociferous voice. Child resigned under some duress in 1843.

By then, she had other options. *The Dial* published her essay "What Is Beauty?" in April of that year, just before a collection of her "Letters from New York" appeared as a book. *The Dial* reviewed it favorably; other critiques were mixed. The book, which Child self-published rather than agree to cuts requested by established imprints, became a surprisingly strong seller.

Far more propitious than Child's essay on beauty, or anything else *The Dial* published in 1843, was Fuller's opus "The Great Lawsuit: Man Versus Men. Woman Versus Women," which set off a national conversation. Fuller framed her argument around what women of the nineteenth century thought they needed; what women had; what they did not or could not have; what men thought women were capable of being; what men thought women were capable of having; and if men were ready to see the condition of women improve. The essay called for equality in vocational and educational opportunity and stopped just short of an appeal for the right to vote.

Greeley's *Tribune* praised "Lawsuit" for its brilliance and beauty of expression along with the justice of its striking, elevating "thoughts and noble sentiments," if not the clarity of its arguments. The recognition Fuller had already attained was such that the *Tribune*'s lead paragraph identified the essay's author as "the only woman in America who could have written it," without mention of her name. The essay so impressed Greeley that he published a lengthy excerpt and encouraged Fuller to expand it to book length for his own imprint to publish.

Now the wife of Horace Greeley, Mary Young Cheney Greeley,

entered the life of Margaret Fuller in a significant way. Mary, who often traveled to Boston, was a devotee of Fuller's "Conversations." She, Greeley, and Fuller were all about the same age. By 1844, Mary had become so intent on finding ways to get closer to Fuller that she persuaded her husband not only to hire her as the *Tribune*'s new literary editor and second front-page columnist—his column being the first—but to bring her into their home in New York to live. Greeley had been publishing the *Tribune* for about three years at that point. He was no fiery feminist but wide open to ideas that could generate publicity, engage his readers, and attract others. Child, for instance, was already an occasional *Tribune* contributor, and Jane Cazneau had been in Greeley's sights since 1840, when his earlier literary weekly, *The New-Yorker*, published her "Josephine" pieces from North Africa and elsewhere.

Most of Fuller's friends expressed disdain for what they considered her down-market career move to the penny press. Emerson scoffed she had forsaken literature for the "treadmill." The salary, $10 a week, was certainly a draw. It was on par with the newspaper's other three full-time staff members, all men. Beyond that, Fuller said she saw the job as a chance to "produce something excellent" in popular education.

Mary Cheney Greeley and Horace Greeley
*(Mary Greeley, New Castle [Chappaqua, N.Y.] Historical Society,
photo by William Kurtz; Horace Greeley, Library of Congress,
photo by Mathew B. Brady, loc.gov/item/2004663966/)*

The Greeleys had just moved into a spartan, ramshackle old house on a romantic property in Turtle Bay, about where the United Nations headquarters now stands. Before Fuller took up residence with them around November, she spent the earlier part of the fall about seventy miles upstate in the town of Fishkill Landing, working on what she called her "pamphlet on women," the book version of "The Great Lawsuit." Fishkill was close enough to Sing Sing for Fuller to visit its woman inmates, mostly prostitutes, whose journals a friend had shared. The women were in a rehabilitation program run by the prison's women's director. Fuller's cousin the Reverend William Henry Channing preached on occasion to the men at Sing Sing and encouraged Fuller in this new interest. Her observations about the Sing Sing women found their way into her manuscript, along with more of Fuller's reflections on the perplexities of marriage, the nature of women, and those among them who were raising their voices against slavery.

Fuller found the Turtle Bay property "entirely charming" and settled in. Her first *Tribune* column, signed with an asterisk instead of the "F." of *The Dial,* appeared on December 1, 1844. In her first month on staff, she critiqued social reform in France, a new book of Emerson's essays, and a new poem by William Hosmer, the abolitionist author, editor, and pastor. She mused about Thanksgiving in a December 12 piece, oddly timed. She offered belated reflections on a monument to her adored Goethe in Frankfurt, Germany, erected two months earlier. On December 18, Fuller's presumed hand was in the *Tribune*'s prominent announcement that Child's book *Letters from New York* had gone into its third printing and that a second volume would soon be published. Two days later, in coproduction with the *Boston Courier* and featured in Fuller's customary slot in the left-hand column of the front page, the *Tribune* began serializing the first Child letters book with a column headlined "Kindness to Criminals: The Prison Association." The article's placement and Fuller's promotional blurb about Child and her books speak to the support the women gave each other.

Not two weeks later, Fuller positioned herself to take on the first of two new journalistic roles by adding social reform and the suffering of the underclass to her menu of topics. On New Year's Eve, she wrote to her cousin William Channing to ask when they could begin visiting public institutions. She requested they start on Blackwell's Island, the sliver of land in the East River now known as Roosevelt Island, where the almshouse, prisons, and asylums all were housed. "Now is the time for me to write about these things," she wrote.

Greeley, enthusiastic at the prospect of Margaret Fuller as urban reporter, gave her free rein. She was realistic about how little suffering she would be able to alleviate. The prostitutes were her greatest concern. "I have always felt great interest in those women who are trampled in the mud to gratify the brute appetites of men," she said, "and wished I might be brought, naturally, into contact with them. Now I am so."

Greeley's 1868 memoir devoted an entire chapter to Fuller, the only person other than the statesman Henry Clay to command such extended treatment in six hundred pages of reminiscences. In this paean, Greeley is as forthright about her deficiencies as he is about her gifts. He started with a long quotation from Emerson's insulting first impression of her and how she managed to bring him around. Greeley offered his own blunt criticism of her writing style and her slow delivery of articles. Her debilitating headaches frustrated him, as did her insistence on an escort for assignments around the city, even in daylight. This he found particularly irksome from the woman who declared in "The Great Lawsuit" that women should be free to be and do whatever they wished. "Let her be a sea captain, if she will," she wrote.

In overtaxed, understaffed newsrooms, providing women with escorts for their safety or the protection of their reputations was an annoyance and an unwanted expense. It joined a litany of reasons why editors excluded women from desirable assignments. But these never applied to Margaret Fuller. Despite all the things Greeley found so exasperating about her, he accommodated her needs. She elicited the support, tolerance, friendship, and devotion of a brilliant, busy editor and most everyone else she encountered at a time when women had no established place, no standing, in the work of a metropolitan daily. To Greeley, Fuller became a fearless and unselfish champion of the underserved. He left evaluation of her later writings to others but felt bound to commend her commitment to truth and her adherence to the public's need to know.

Fuller's first reporting on the city's disadvantaged appeared in the

Tribune on March 19, 1845, during her third month on staff, under the headline "Our City's Charities." The article chronicled her trip to Blackwell's Island, where she found the almshouse cleaner, more comfortable, and with a kinder staff than she expected. But she denounced the "great evil" of giving those it served nothing to do except raise vegetables and wash clothes. "There should be instruction," she urged, "both practical and in the use of books, opening to a better intercourse than they can obtain from their miserable homes, correct notions as to cleanliness, diet and fresh air." The asylum had twice as many patients as its space could properly accommodate. Compared with New York Hospital's private Bloomingdale Asylum, "insanity appeared in its more stupid, vile, or despairing forms," with patients crouched in corners, with "no eye for the stranger, no heart for hope, no habitual expectation of light."

Fuller did not originate eyewitness reporting on the city's neglected citizens. Both Child and Charles Dickens had visited and written about the downtrodden of Blackwell's Island in 1841. But Fuller's columns gave the genre new significance. "I doubt," Greeley wrote, "that our various benevolent and reformatory associations had ever before, or have ever since, received such wise, discriminating commendations to the favor of the rich, as they did from her pen during her connection with the *Tribune.*"

Fuller's book, retitled *Woman in the Nineteenth Century,* an expanded version of "The Great Lawsuit," came out to great fanfare in February 1845, a month before her first piece on the city's charities. At a slim 164 airily spaced pages, it was three times as long as the original article. That May, Lydia Child published her second *Letters from New York* volume. Child and Fuller, friends and so often companions, used their celebrated positions to trade praise in print for each other's new books. Conflict of interest was clearly not a concept among mid-nineteenth-century editors and book reviewers.

Child reviewed Fuller's book without reference to her own groundwork-laying history of the condition of women, published a decade earlier, or to Sarah Grimké's *Letters on the Equality of the Sexes, and the Condition of Woman,* which followed Child's history in 1838. Instead, prompted by the hard questions Fuller raised in her book, Child posed a series of her own. "Is love a mockery, and marriage a sham?" she asked. "What is woman's true mission? What is the harmonious relation of the sexes?" She underscored one of Fuller's core convictions, that "this extending murmur of the human heart, this increasing conviction that woman should be the friend, the companion, the real partner of man in all his pursuits, rather than the mere ornament of his parlor, or the servant of his senses, cannot be silenced." At this point, Lydia and her husband were mostly apart.

Edgar Allan Poe's *Broadway Journal* published two reviews of Fuller's book, the second of which by Charles Frederick Briggs did not come from the pen of a pal. The mildest of Briggs's rebukes was that Fuller could have cut the length by two-thirds and lost nothing. Other reviews were less harsh. Poe himself weighed in on Fuller in a series of profiles of New York's top literati that ran between May and October 1846 in *Godey's Lady's Book*. Most of the authors Poe wrote about were poets and periodical writers, and interestingly, ten of the thirty-nine writers he profiled were women. These included Lydia Child in brief and Fuller at length, with a great deal of attention to the latter's facial movements and crisp enunciation, evincing the common wonderment at her personal appeal. Perhaps his inclusion of so many women reflected the bias of the publication, whose prime audience was women, but it testified nonetheless to the acceptance of women as major authors and poets at this early date. Among those he included, only Fuller was on the staff of a daily newspaper.

Poe was quick to disavow Briggs's "silly, condemnatory criticism" of *Woman in the Nineteenth Century* and offered his opinion that although a few other American women could have written the book, only Fuller, given her independence and "unmitigated radicalism," would have published it. Greeley, while aware of the book's hazy clarity and logic, considered it "the loftiest and most commanding assertion yet" of women's rights in society and under the law. The book remains an important founding document of the feminist movement and is often considered Fuller's seminal work among the three books she published, the last of which was a two-volume collection of essays and miscellany. Fuller's columns often called out the national shame of slavery. In one published on the Fourth of July 1845, she wrote,

> This year, which declares that the people at large consent
> to cherish and extend Slavery as one of our "domestic

institutions," takes from the patriot his home. This year, which attests their insatiate love of wealth and power, quenches the flame upon the altar.

Fuller's "magnetic sway" was essential to her rise among men, but so were the strategic alliances she forged with other women. They started with Lidian Emerson and Mary Greeley, who opened the doors to the warm, deep, and useful relationships she then cultivated with their influential husbands, men who could transform a plain New England lady intellectual with as many off-putting quirks as gifts into a great national presence. Such support would often be essential for women who followed her into the profession.

In August 1846, Fuller "modified" her employment with the *Tribune*. She set out for Europe with the idea, affirmed by Greeley, of sending back columns from her travels, mostly for the *Tribune*'s front pages, where again she signed with an asterisk, a "star," as she called it. She remained in Europe for four years, ultimately caught up in the popular uprisings that erupted across the Continent, especially the Italian revolution of 1848. She enmeshed herself in the movement, even volunteering at a field hospital for the revolutionaries during the shelling of Rome. One scholar of the period considered this her finest journalist work. She wrote so movingly of the failed republican movements of the two Giuseppes, Garibaldi and Mazzini, that other scholars heard echoes of her dispatches in the poetry of Walt Whitman, particularly "Resurgemus," which first appeared in the *Tribune* June 21, 1850. It reappeared six years later in *Leaves of Grass* as "Poem of the Dead Young Men of Europe, the 72d and 73d Years of These States." Gone in the latter version is its original second stanza:

> *God, 'twas delicious!*
> *That brief, tight, glorious grip*
> *Upon the throats of kings.*

Fuller's work for America's leading daily newspaper as an essayist, social reform reporter, and foreign correspondent has placed her firmly at the forefront of woman journalists over the past two centuries. If there was another woman who thrived in the 1840s or earlier with anything approaching Fuller's free choice of assignments, her all-star status, or the unisex regard in which she was so widely held, she left no trace. Lydia Maria Child holds a distant second place to Fuller among women of the 1840s who gained the freedom to write for the major mainstream newspapers and magazines of the day outside their prescribed women's sphere. Jane Cazneau has been relegated to passing notice.

As the decade closed, the clamor for change in the status of women grew louder. Literary critics noticed the position women had begun to occupy in American literature. "Throughout Christendom woman has assumed new offices and achieved new and unlooked-for triumphs," wrote Rufus Wilmot Griswold in his 1847 *Prose Writers of America*. He cited Child and Fuller, among others, in saying of the women of his era, "In fifty years, she has done more in the domains of intellect than she had done before in five centuries." By 1848, six months before the first women's rights convention at Seneca Falls, New York, Fuller embodied the journalistic version of the woman sea captain she envisioned four years earlier in "The Great Lawsuit." Her impact was enormous. In January 1848, the aptly named *Harbinger*, the magazine of the transcendentalists' Brook Farm, declared, however prematurely, that women had left behind their "degrading position" to occupy the one where they should always have been, "equal in rank and dignity."

Charles Capper, among the most admired of Fuller's more than two dozen biographers, considered her the best-known intellectual of her day, her era's most important literary critic and cultural leader, and "the first woman in America to establish herself as a dominant figure in highbrow culture at large." Greeley availed her to the masses to produce work that was never meant to last but does.

Fuller's instinctive ability to turn friendship into a tool of personal advancement never seemed to come off as craven. Yet it's hard to imagine that her irregular charm offensive would have yielded such excellent results had she not possessed singular talent. The people in her thrall, those she cultivated as friends, were also in the best position to ignore convention and to provide her with rare opportunities. Few women of the period were this well positioned.

In May 1850, Fuller boarded the *Elizabeth* at Livorno, Italy, bound for New York, along with the husband and infant son she had kept secret from family and friends until after the baby was born. Gossip circulated about the order in which the marriage and the birth took place. If there had been an official marriage to the much younger, penniless, unschooled, but noble Giovanni Angelo Ossoli—no record survived—it seems to have taken place well after baby Angelo's conception. As a result, close friends worried about the cold reception this unlikely threesome would encounter once back in the United States.

As the ship approached the coast of Long Island at Fire Island, a hurricane ran it aground. Fuller, forty years old, her husband, and her baby, still in arms, all drowned. Horace Greeley wrote the *Tribune*'s obituary. It called for those closest to Fuller to "lose no time in selecting the fittest person to prepare a Memoir with a selection from her writings for the press," for never before had the country produced a woman of such "mental endowments and acquirements." Twenty-two years later, he had not changed his mind; she remained for him "the loftiest, bravest soul that has yet irradiated the form of the American woman."

On hearing the news of Fuller's death, Greeley, Thoreau, and others went immediately to Fire Island in hopes of recovering the bodies, to no avail. Emerson got to work on the memoir. Tributes in poetry and prose poured into the *Tribune* office. "No event has occurred here for a long time that has excited more general sensation, and more heartfelt expressions of sorrow," wrote the *Southern Literary Messenger*. "This lady for several years past had filled so conspicuous a place before the public, and had excited so much both of admiration and of reproach for the bold expression of her opinions." Fuller's last published piece appeared that month in *The United States Magazine and Democratic Review*, where Jane Cazneau also wrote. (Cazneau has sometimes been credited with coining the term "manifest destiny," which first appeared in the magazine.) Fuller's piece, "Recollections of the Vatican," described the place in Rome where Fuller spent her fondest hours. The magazine's obituary honored her "vigor of mind, depth of insight, the extent of her attainments, and varied culture," adding, "She has certainly left behind her, in this country, no superior."

When Child died in 1880 at seventy-eight, obituaries were neither long nor prominently placed, but they did acknowledge her "much distinguished" career and her important voice against slavery.

Cazneau, by coincidence, also died at sea, but news of the tragedy in 1878 prompted no known published outpouring of admiration or grief.

In these three cases, exceptional talent inspired men positioned to do so to give women high-profile assignments at which they then excelled. This in every case was as much a product of the women's gumption, intellect, guts, persistence, social and political awareness, and passions as their real and urgent need to make money. Not much could have happened for Fuller without the coven of transcendentalists who supported her so fiercely and who happened to include not one but two major publishers in Emerson and Greeley, men ready to see her rise as much for their own purposes as hers. Garrison's admiration of Child advanced her standing as an abolition thinker, a woman who had far more to offer than the children's stories and household hints that had kept her and David fed for so many years. Cazneau had as her advocate the proprietor of *The Sun,* Moses Yale Beach, who was also her business partner in Texas land speculation.

In Fuller's case, clearly, neither personal beauty nor writing style made the difference. No one ever described her work as "sprightly," the adjective of choice for the work of most woman journalists who followed her into prominence over the next forty years. Her unqualified intellect was vital to her success, as were her ability to generate a wide response to bold ideas and arguments and her focus on subjects that reflected or heralded the great social currents of the day.

How extraordinary for a woman of her time to have had the likes of Greeley and Emerson not only as her champions in life but as the passionate guardians and shapers of her legacy in death. In February 1852, publication of *Memoirs of Margaret Fuller Ossoli* rekindled the Fuller story in a two-volume chronological pastiche that included letters to and from Fuller, reminiscences from those closest to her, and selections from her writings. It appeared under Fuller's name as author with editor credit to Emerson, William Channing, and the theologian and author James Freeman Clarke, another Boston friend. Reviews were mixed. Among the most critical, the critic for *The Athenaeum* found the work "tawdry, whimsical and injurious to the cause which it was meant to magnify," and one of Fuller's admirers at *The United States Magazine and Democratic Review* wished out loud she had lived long enough to have saved herself from her friends.

Nevertheless, the book sold a thousand copies its first day out and by year's end had gone back to press four times.

"How can you describe a Force?" the poet and author Samuel G. Ward said in declining Emerson's request that he write Fuller's biography. And yet in every decade since her death in 1850, at least one new book, if not several, has had her name in its title, from the biographies to collections of her writings, to the six volumes of her letters, and reams of scholarship and literary and journalistic analyses and comparisons. Perhaps not surprisingly, as often as not, the authors are men, although the 2014 Pulitzer Prize for biography went to Megan Marshall for her book *Margaret Fuller: A New American Life*.

Together, Fuller, Child, Cazneau, and Walter demonstrated that woman journalists could have high-profile, well-paid careers. Did their example clear a path for their successors at the mass-circulation newspapers and magazines? It did, but only for a select few. Editors confined all the others to writing fluff.

CHAPTER 2

The She Lot

The woman journalists whose reputations soared at high-end publications of the early 1850s stayed on top until well into the 1880s with compensation to match. Reports of their earning power as journalists enticed other women to try to match their success. Even at their pinnacle in the 1870s, Grace Greenwood, Gail Hamilton, and Mary Clemmer Ames had not escaped the "As a Woman Sees It" tag, although they did avoid being reduced to chatty chroniclers of the Washington social scene, the demand editors made of other women on the capital beat. By 1879, Washington had a score of woman correspondents, up from four when that decade began. Originality, distinctive voice, and insight set the Greenwood-Hamilton-Clemmer trio apart. They had the magnetism of Margaret Fuller and the tirelessness of Lydia Maria Child. Their bylines were household names.

Grace Greenwood's real name was Sara Jane Clarke Lippincott. Gail Hamilton, known to friends and family as Abby, was born Mary Abigail Dodge. They came on the scene a decade apart, Greenwood first. Mary Clemmer was about Hamilton's age and rose to prominence in her thirties, after the annulment of a marriage urged upon her when she was seventeen. Greenwood and Hamilton seemed to follow Lydia Maria Child's strategy in gaining notice for themselves by going to work for the abolition press. They took cues from Margaret Fuller by going to live in the home of their boss, in their case Gamaliel Bailey, editor of *The National Era*. The Bailey home provided a nexus of Washington social life as alive with people to know as the Greeley home was in New York City. Although Bailey's popular

Gamaliel Bailey
(Historic New England)

Grace Greenwood
*(George Eastman Museum, photo
by Albert Sands Southworth)*

weekly established Greenwood and Hamilton as writers, the magazine is best remembered as the first to publish in serial form the most read book of the nineteenth century after the Bible, *Uncle Tom's Cabin* by Harriet Beecher Stowe. Greenwood likened Stowe to a prima donna who "stands in front, and with one surpassing voice reaches and satisfies all hearts."

Grace Greenwood worked by day as an assistant editor at *Godey's Lady's Book* while she gained prominence as a writer for the *Era.* In two years, she had enough articles for a book, *Greenwood Leaves,* published early in 1850. Her publisher at *Godey's,* Louis Antoine Godey, aided in her publicity effort. On the cover of his December 1849 issue, in large bold type, the magazine identified Greenwood as its coeditor. *The Daily Telegraph* of Columbia, South Carolina, appalled that the ostensibly apolitical *Godey's* had an abolitionist in a prominent role on its masthead, urged its readers to cancel their subscriptions. *The Daily South Carolinian* responded by defending Godey and calling out its in-town competitor for "dragging the question of slavery into everything." The damage to *Godey* and his southern subscriber list, however, was done.

Godey groveled. Without having seen the item in either newspaper, he wrote to the *Telegraph,* insisting that never in twenty years had *Godey's* ever cast aspersions on a southern institution in any way. Greenwood was soon out of work.

The controversy was perfect for the abolition press. Even the mainstream *Independent* bored in against Godey's "monstrous meanness" and lauded Greenwood for how little involvement she had with the magazine's abhorrent editorial policies. "Are these the men who are to direct the reading of our children?" *The Independent* asked. "Are our publishers to emasculate every transatlantic book until it will pass current at the South?" Both Greenwood and the abolition press condemned her firing. The publicity for Godey, and for his editor Sarah Josepha Hale, was terrible. *The National Era* republished his letter to the *Telegraph,* as well as the screed in *The Independent,* adding its own comment about Godey: "Let him try which is the better paymaster, Freedom or Slavery."

For Greenwood, it was all a useful burst of attention that led Gamaliel Bailey to hire her as the *Era*'s assistant editor. The publisher of *Greenwood Leaves* advertised the book regularly. Reviews might have been sparse and thin, but all the ancillary notice helped to get her pieces placed in *The New York Times* and *The Saturday Evening Post.* Her second *Greenwood Leaves* volume attracted greater attention than the first and her reputation grew. *Harper's Magazine* admired it as "a sincere, genial, thoroughly individualistic production," replete with "exuberant gayety," touches of "bitter sadness," and "occasional specimens of sharp-shooting, though the polished, nimble arrows are never dipped in poison." That became Greenwood's signature style.

Most other women who entered the profession in these years wrote florid, poignant, or pithy prose sketches and poems aimed at the growing audience of woman readers. A few women found assistant editor positions as Grace Greenwood had at *Godey's.* Others went to work full time at general interest magazines, and fewer still joined the staffs of newspapers. Piecework at the papers was always possible for women, but full-time jobs remained scarce, even though New York City alone had fifteen daily papers by the fall of 1851, most with columns expressly for women and, soon, full pages. Horace Greeley said that of the thousand talented writers in town from the 1840s to the 1870s, not more than fifty could earn a living by pen alone.

Throughout the 1850s, woman journalists as a class, or as the producers of the new revenue-generating women's pages, were largely ignored in the memoirs of the great editors of the period as well as in the lengthy, sweeping contemporaneous articles about the state of the U.S. press. Their growing presence went largely unacknowledged.

The invisibility only underscores how significant the breakthroughs of Greenwood, Hamilton, and Clemmer were as journalists freed from the women's sphere. All of them had high school educations and middle- to upper-middle-class New England or Middle Atlantic backgrounds. Like their most able predecessors, they were talented, savvy networkers who craved recognition, needed to earn, and figured out how to connect with those who could help make both happen. Grace Greenwood and Gail Hamilton as journalists sashayed from Bailey's *Era* into prestige general interest venues. While Greenwood grew in popularity, Gail Hamilton started writing for *The Atlantic,* an affiliation that lasted for decades. She, like Greenwood, regularly published collections of her work.

Census figures for 1860 put the combined annual circulation of newspapers and magazines at nearly a billion copies nationwide. By then, practically every newspaper in the country had a women's department where women filled pages with fashion trends and new elixirs, gossip, social notes, and advice. By 1863, women's collective presence began to get some attention, including the suggestion in *Vanity Fair* that they become known as the "She lot."

Mary Clemmer's story is worth recalling for the high pay she commanded; for her Civil War experiences, both as a journalist and as one of the many women across the country who put their domestic skills to use as essential wartime volunteers; and for her era-typical reflections and judgments—as damaging as they were helpful—on a career in journalism as women experienced it or should experience it.

At thirty-one, Clemmer bristled in print at the restrictions around what women were being allowed to write for publication. From Washington, in 1862, she responded to a request from an old editor friend in Springfield, Massachusetts, Samuel Bowles, to write for the *Republican* about her life in the capital. Their relationship went back to her high school days at the nearby Westfield Academy, when the school's principal sent Bowles a poem of Clemmer's that the newspaper published. She let Bowles know how stupid his request was: Near the end of a lengthy article padded out heavily with "inflated descriptions of things—people," Clemmer offers what read like an open letter to any future editor who dared to make a similar request of her or any woman journalist. She accused Bowles of wanting to "doom me to gossip," to make her "abandon myself ad libitum to the undisputed specialty of the true 'lady correspondent'" with her "flimsy letters with the most attenuated stuff." Editors never want women to cover current events, she groused. No wonder so much of what they write begins with "Last evening, the most brilliant affair of the season . . ." Bowles, to his credit, published Clemmer's attack in full.

That fall, she succeeded at more substantive reporting for New York's *Evening Post*. From the hillsides surrounding the house she shared unhappily with her husband, the Reverend Daniel Ames, she witnessed enough of the Battle of Harpers Ferry to write about it at length. Reports of the engagement by regular war correspondents appeared in near-real time from September 12 to September 15, 1862, when General

Mary Clemmer
(Frontispiece, Clemmer's Ten Years in Washington: Life and Scenes in the Nation's Capital, As a Woman Sees Them *[Hartford, Ct.: A.D. Worthington, 1874])*

Stonewall Jackson and his rebel forces showed up right behind Clemmer's home at "the only spot where he could besiege our stronghold" in what was then the Maryland Heights of Virginia. Her story did not appear until October 15, but she detailed the run-up to the fighting, the battle under the Union's general Dixon S. Miles, whom both soldiers and townspeople blamed squarely for what all considered an unnecessary surrender. Miles died of his injuries the following day. Clemmer's description of the cannonade:

> The rebel batteries opened upon us together. The windows rattled, the house shook to its foundations. Heaven and earth seemed collapsing. The roar rolling back to the mountains died and the deeper roar bursting upon their summits. One of our batteries on Camp Hill was directly in the rear of this house, behind the garden fence.
>
> The rebel batteries on Loudon faced us. Thus this loyal little domicile was under the heaviest fire. I intended to finish eating a piece of pie dancing on the plate before me, but

the shock of tremendous cannon behind the house sent me off my chair in defiance of my aspiration after a sublime courage. I am not a hero; I very much wish to be one, but I am not. It is exceedingly mortifying amid a stupendous occasion to find yourself unequal to its sublimity. With profound humility, oh Evening Post, I confess, that to escape the earthquake above, I went down into the cellar. I concluded, as a woman cannot command a battery, she should have the privilege of trying to save her head, though of no material use to anyone but herself.

The headline is revelatory: "The Battle of Harper's Ferry as a Woman Saw It." The month's delay did not stand in the way of its wide republication in papers across the country.

As the battles ended, editors began to reconsider the social concerns the war years had reduced to insignificance. "Women's Right to Labor," read a headline in *The Independent* in 1864 over a letter to the editor from Clemmer, sent from Armory Square Hospital, a military facility for the Union's wounded in the capital. Clemmer was volunteering at the facility to help with nursing. In the letter, she urged the professions to open their doors to women, all except the military, which, she said, should remain the exclusive province of men. Here was Clemmer, a woman of growing success and popularity, expressing a well-meant, ingrained attitude that worked against the efforts of women to advance. "We believe women naturally dependent," she added, "inclined to lean, disposed to seek a sheltered nook, to choose their occupations within narrower limits, where home and the affections are less interrupted; but still just as much entitled to the privileges and the rewards of labor, on the paths they honestly choose, as men." Real change, she went on, without explaining her reasoning, would only come when wealthy women grasped the importance of earning their own money. Only then would women who wanted to be merchants, doctors, lawyers, preachers, or editors not have to "take up a cross in assuming a profession."

Clemmer spent some time living in New York with the sister poets Alice and Phoebe Cary, whose joint biography she would later write. Through them, she made her way into the literati and got to know the city's publishers, among them Henry C. Bowen, who owned both *The Independent* and Brooklyn's *Union.* In March 1866, her marriage over, Bowen hired her to write letters from Washington for his publications, an arrangement that established her reputation as a journalist and continued until 1871. At that point, *Harper's Bazaar* reported, Bowen was paying her a handsome $5,000 a year, more, the writer suspected, than any man in a similar position was being paid. The *Tribune* was publishing Grace Greenwood's pieces "for which she obtains her own price."

Gail Hamilton's earnings were competitive with those of Greenwood and Clemmer. "Dear Sirs," she wrote to one publication in response to their request for a piece, "two hundred dollars an article, without limit as to length. Free range as to themes over this world and the next." Shortly before her death at sixty-three in 1896, she would lay out for a friend her philosophy about compensation, one most woman writers of future decades have struggled to adopt: "One ought not to *write* for money but I consider it a first duty after one has written to exact the highest possible price. It is not a matter which concerns only the writer, but all writers."

Over the years, gossipy personal items in the popular newspapers and magazines tracked their social, literary, and civic comings and goings, their coups at negotiating blockbuster contracts, and the cleverest gambits that they or their publishers concocted to promote their work. They remained visible in the culture at large and as successful in their day as their counterparts who were men. Top newspapers and magazines generated syrupy profiles about all three of them while they lived and warm tributes when they died.

That said, as time has shown, the bona fide national celebrity appeal they enjoyed during their lifetimes was fleeting, not enduring like Margaret Fuller's, which is not to diminish their importance. They matter because of the *way* readers of the period responded to them. The unqualified success of these three women demonstrated the wide popularity that a few women of the mid-nineteenth century could command for pursuing subjects generally believed to be beyond every woman's ken. It was work for which they were handsomely paid because they were worth it, because they were good for business. And yet Mary Clemmer understood the fate that awaited her and most everyone else, man or woman, who engaged in the journalistic enterprise. The work offered little room for immortality. As she put it in a poem, "Quick read, quick lost."

Alongside these major stars of the 1850s and 1860s whose careers stretch well into the 1880s are Jane Grey Swisshelm and Mary Ann Shadd Cary, whose impact as journalists and publishers aided the abolition movement. Swisshelm, who was white, copublished with her husband the antislavery weekly the *Saturday Visiter* in Pittsburgh and later, on her own, in St. Cloud, Minnesota. Cary, the daughter of prominent Black merchants, freeborn Pennsylvania abolitionists, left her teaching post in New York City and went to Canada to support Black migration north after passage of the 1850 Fugitive Slave Act. She soon became the copublisher of the *Provincial Freeman,* an important abolition paper. As a speaker and a writer, a colleague once wrote, Cary was formidable in appearance and "quick to take advantage of the weak points of her opponent, forcible in her illustrations, biting in her sarcasm, and withering in her rebukes."

Reprints of Swisshelm's columns on everything from kissing to horsewhipping found their way into the mainstream press as well as the *Freeman.* The bigger moment for Swisshelm came in 1850, when Horace Greeley agreed to hire her for the *Tribune* at $5 a column to write a weekly "Mrs. Swisshelm's Letter" from Washington. The first column ran not long after Margaret Fuller's tragic death. Cary was an important figure in Black abolition circles, but because the worlds in which she and Swisshelm moved were so separate, she would not have had so wide an avenue to the recognition Greeley opened for Swisshelm. For women of color, the limited opportunities a few white woman journalists were able to exploit at the top of the mainstream press of the 1850s were not in reach. That would remain the case for more than a hundred years.

In April 1850, the first of Swisshelm's "tart and spicy" columns for Greeley brought her so much new "social distinction" that, she said, even pro-slavery senators went out of their way to show respect. That stopped abruptly a few weeks later when, in her own paper but not the *Tribune,* she attacked Senator Daniel Webster for calling slavery a fixed historical reality in his "Seventh of March" speech. Her words were so personal, so vicious, and so potentially libelous that Greeley fired her. During the short month Swisshelm spent in the capital, she managed to persuade Vice President Millard Fillmore to

Jane Grey Swisshelm and Mary Ann Shadd Cary

(Jane Grey Swisshelm, Minnesota Historical Society;
Mary Ann Shadd Cary, Library and Archives Canada / C-029977)

change policy and seat her in the Senate press gallery, where women had long been barred. Others would, but she never got the chance to claim that chair.

Gail Hamilton not only followed Grace Greenwood onto the pages of *The National Era* and into Gamaliel Bailey's life and home but also became his household's governess for a time. (It's hard to imagine what the equivalent task a young man with journalistic ambitions in the 1850s might have undertaken to ingratiate himself with an editor he wanted to work under, but likely nothing as arduous as the care of six children.) To know Hamilton, Greenwood would later say, "is a large and brilliant and varied social experience." The benefits of Hamilton's close relationship with Bailey, and later with the statesman James G. Blaine, would in time become the two-sided coin of her career. An *Atlantic* colleague, writing of her eventual earning power, would say that she was well worth the cost. "Gail Hamilton in her prime was, in the fullest sense of the term, a personage, a brilliant, original, delightful, unforgettable individual" who had "the power to go on spinning indefinitely an iridescent thread out of her own mental substance." And yet, by twenty-seven, she had already been put in the unusual position "of being beset by deferential publishers and flattering journalists who wanted to exploit [her] for their own profit" and having "succumbed to their blandishments."

By April 1868, even with women in the field becoming harder to ignore, a national committee of journalists barred women from

Gail Hamilton
(Hamilton [Mass.]
Historical Society)

the dinner it hosted at Delmonico's in New York City to honor the visiting Charles Dickens. This was especially irksome to Jane Cunningham Croly, whose husband was to attend the banquet as a representative of *The World,* where she worked as the fashion editor. Croly's well-meaning articulation of the evolving role of women in the profession, like Clemmer's, did as much to emphasize the limitations of her vision of how to improve conditions as it did to explain the issues. Pioneer of the women's page that Croly was, one could ask what she meant in 1854 by saying, only two years after the Fuller memoir appeared and four years since her death, that what the Asterisk accomplished "seemed to be altogether lost." A long time later, she would dismiss Fuller as a role model, calling her "a scholar and a talker," not a "ready writer" nor "in any sense a journalist." Did Croly define "woman journalist" in her own image only? Croly said Fuller only became a journalist because the limitations on women in her day precluded the chance to be a college professor or president. "The difficulty of her whole life," Croly said, "was that she was a woman instead of a man."

Croly's disgruntlement over the Dickens dinner made the press. "Jane writes pretty good fashion letters," *The Pittsburgh Gazette* said, "but when she tries invectives she talks as if breeding was not part of her education." Six days later came the gentle countermove of the profession's women in New York: a "new society of literary and artistic women," the Order of the Pen. They quickly changed the name to the Blue Stocking Club, "bluestocking" being a moniker for literary women, and then to Sorosis, the first women's club in the United States. Its only stated intention was to meet once a month and, as the *Detroit Free Press* teased, to "vigorously exclude 'horrid men.'" Croly was named vice president and the poet Alice Cary, president. Mary Clemmer was among the first to join, and Gail Hamilton was one of the out-of-towners proposed for honorary membership. By August, the club announced a vague twofold mission: "to remove in some degree barriers which custom and etiquette place in the way

of friendly intercourse and united action" and to open discussion
of "such facts and principles as promise to exert an important influence on the welfare of women and on society." Croly had already
convened the first woman's congress in 1856 and did the same for the
second one in 1869. She led Sorosis after Cary and in 1889 founded
the New York Women's Press Club. Her 1901 obituary in *The New
York Times* declared her "the best-known woman journalist in America." It ran on page 3.

In 1870, a writer for *Galaxy* jokingly bemoaned the sorry situation of editors at the various New York weeklies who had to reject
the legions of earnest eighteen-year-old girls besieging their offices
with essays, editorials, poems, and travel and regular newspaper correspondence every bit as polished as what was making print. In 1872,
at around the time twenty-one-year-old Nelly Mackay Hutchinson
began to cover the women's movement for the *Tribune, Galaxy* published her detailed look at the prospects for women in journalism.
Of a newspaperwoman like herself, Hutchinson had an optimistic
view. "Right or wrong, she is there," she wrote, "and physical and
psychological differences are considered only in so far as they influence her journalistic availability. There is no bar to intellectual labor
set up against her; *within her natural limits* [my italics], she is free."
She went on to assert that a woman was unequipped to become a
managing editor or lead editorial writer "no matter how brilliant
her genius, how thorough and acute her business talent, how perfect
her organization." In Hutchinson's view, the long, late hours, the
"unexpected anxieties," the emergencies, and the stress made both
positions physically untenable for women, along with what she considered the known propensity of womankind to be "blindly impul-
sive and one-sided." For high-end opportunities ever to become a
possibility, she wrote, women would need to change more than their
social position and inadequate training. They would need to change
their very nature.

She then zigzagged to emphasize the positions at which woman
journalists excelled. Some unspecified editorial writing was on her
list along with the short, quippy, paragraph-long items that ran in
a stream as a column. Book reviewing worked, in her view, for the
women who didn't gush, as did some unidentified kinds of reporting.
She did acknowledge the great success of the special correspondents,

noting that by 1870 almost every newspaper had a wannabe Grace Greenwood or Gail Hamilton in its pay. Hutchinson thought the chief faults of the newer "Letters From" brigade were "haste and carelessness." Of woman journalists in general, she criticized the "slovenliness and spitefulness" that emanated from their almost universal lack of "a keen, exact habit of reasoning." Too many women were too much like Shakespeare's Lucetta in *Two Gentlemen of Verona,* she said, with her "I think him so because I think him so." Hutchinson attributed this "jelly like inaccuracy of thought and expression" to the lack of training, the same lack of training that Fuller had divined thirty years earlier when she started her Boston Conversations. But Hutchinson prophesied that rectification was at hand. "Human nature and journalistic genius are the same, whether clad in coat or petticoat," she wrote, contradicting the limitations on women she said only a change in their very nature could eliminate. After that flip-flop, her prediction that in time the best of the profession would be found "in no greater and no less degree in the wise and saintly blue-stockings of the future" sounded like a sop.

All the same, there were portents of change. By January 1873, reporters at other papers started to notice how many "feminine literary lights" the *Tribune* employed. Not long after, a writer for *The Atlantic* pondered how strange Margaret Fuller and Lydia Maria Child would have found the 1870s, with women crowding into the field "by the thousands." The correct figure was in the hundreds, but that was far greater than at any point in the past. Moreover, disparity in pay had not yet set in. Hutchinson went so far as to say that earnings for journalists at the time were "wholly impartial."

Bazaar about the same time speculated as to why the woman journalists in Washington earned so handsomely. "Aside from their ability," the writer said, "they attend very closely to their duties, do not pervade places where much Bourbon, late night, and bad cigars are consumed, and do not indulge in 'sinful games.'" More likely, the capital gossip the woman reporters mostly trafficked in sold copies. As the woman reporters based in Washington grew into a minor force, Mary Clemmer railed once again in 1870, as she had eight years earlier in the *Springfield Republican,* against the frothy social notes so many of them were obliged, or chose, to produce. In her column about this in *The Independent,* she was just as disdainful of those who ran around the capital "with pencils in her mouth and pens in her ears," invading the congressional reporters' galleries only to make themselves conspicuous. Unhelpfully again, Clemmer said woman reporters should only go where they would be received as ladies.

There was no known contemporaneous response, no challenge, to the contradictions, bogus assumptions, and faulty predictions in the public critiques of Clemmer and Croly, two of the profession's top woman exponents, or to those of the younger Hutchinson, not far behind them in garnered respect. There was no known call for proposals that could address the deficiencies they pinpointed, no push for ideas that could improve the lot of woman journalists generally and, by extension, the entire profession. What prompted the flawed pronouncements is not known. Perhaps it derived from the pseudoscience, popular at the time, that ascribed its ideas about "fixed nature" and "fixed natural abilities" to the sexes as well as to race. Perhaps the tenacious hold of the women's sphere on the popular imagination got in the way, with its set duties, cherished values, and vital significance. Whatever the reasons, and however understandable they might have been in their day, the defective response did not advance the discourse; an opportunity to stimulate progress was lost.

Throughout the 1870s, Mary Clemmer, Grace Greenwood, and Gail Hamilton ranged the widest and most effectively in their Washington letters, although friends thought Hamilton lost the needle on her journalistic compass by becoming too close to James G. Blaine, acting as his ersatz political adviser and aide. Even though *The New Century for Woman,* a publication of the Women's Centennial Committee of 1876, equated the words "Washington correspondent" with "suspicion of intrigue and unclean hands," it praised Greenwood's letters from the capital as "gay in their humor, incisive in their criticism, vigorous in tone without taint of fear or reproach upon their womanliness or honor." Of Hamilton's work over so many years, an *Atlantic* colleague would write, "We have had more weighty and more urbane writers among us than she was, but few more original and racy, and very few indeed so characteristically American. Her popularity was immense at one time; her *verve* seemed inexhaustible; her production was rapid and deservedly remunerative." The *Boston Traveller* remembered Mary Clemmer as "a potent force in the shaping of national issues by their power to influence public opinion," a person who "ennobled journalism by her profound conviction of its moral significance." These were feelings Clemmer expressed in a twenty-one-stanza poem requested by the New York Press Association for its meeting in Utica, New York, on June 8, 1881. Her words exhorted those assembled to exalt in their great purpose and ignore the disparagements that poets, novelists, literary figures, and statesmen hurled their way:

> *To serve thy generation, this thy fate:*
> *"Written in water," swiftly fades thy name;*
> *But he who loves his kind does, first and late,*
> *A work too great for fame.*

Too great for lasting fame, in any event. Clemmer continued to write poetry, letters, novels, and other books until close to the time of her death from a brain hemorrhage at fifty-three in 1884.

In 1875, Jane Croly counted sixty U.S. newspapers where women worked "as editors, editorial writers, and the like" and were "fully as successful as the average man." She also predicted—accurately, although it would take another century to come to fruition—that as coverage of social and domestic life became a more important part of the news diet, women would "find a large place" in what she called so revealingly "the field of regular journalism."

However, in 1875, most of the women at newspapers were doing "a large amount of work for small pay because their general and special culture has not fitted them for the best places." Croly's words again. Apprenticeship, the lone training system in those years, was available only to young men poised to be "bullied and shoved into acquiring respectable proficiency in the profession." With no standard mechanism for advancement, women had no recourse beyond what they could absorb by office osmosis. There was no formal opportunity to develop the specialized skills that paid best, and no men were working to change that, especially none who felt annoyed or even oppressed by the presence of woman workers in their midst. Croly pointed out that the same men who tolerated carelessness, negligence, and drunkenness in the men they worked with were quick to prejudge women on little if any evidence. Then there was the problem of night work. Respectable Victorian ladies were not to be seen prowling the streets alone after dark—going to evening meetings, returning to the office to file, making their way home alone after midnight. She urged woman hopefuls to think beyond any rosy visions they might harbor of money and fame; newspapers are "very hard workshops," she said, "and no woman should venture into the field who is not prepared to accept this fact." She encouraged women to recognize in themselves or acquire the skills that editors noticed, such as unique expertise or compelling big ideas, or exquisite news sense, qualities that would make them a "valuable acquisition." That was the best and only unassailable advice she gave. "Journalism must want something they can give," Croly said. In other words, women needed to make themselves needed.

Of course, Croly's own handprint was on where she had made herself useful and needed. In interviews, she credited herself with mothering the newspaper women's page in the mid-1850s with her columns: "Gossip with and for Ladies" and then "Parlor and Sidewalk Gossip." In 1875, Croly, who built her career as a fashion writer and women's magazine editor, said she could see that conditions for women had improved but not nearly enough. Emblematic of the attitude that still prevailed six years later was a response to news that a London newspaper had a woman war correspondent in Africa. "We shall now learn what the women there wear," *The Saturday Evening Post* quipped.

Croly ended her comments with a tired platitude that looked backward as much as forward. "The one thing to hope for now is that with the new education, the new ambitions and the new work, the new woman will cling fast to the best part of the old, the tender womanhood, wifehood and motherhood that the world cannot do without." Her expressed hope for new education, new ambitions, and new kinds of work for women offered no practical plan to achieve them, no plan for addressing the contradictions the new imposed on the old. There was no known effort by, say, the women's clubs to create an alternative training construct for women when editors would not. The future that Croly hearkened to had very narrow confines. Her words presaged all the subtle and overt contradictions that continued to go unchallenged, accepted as facts by women as well as men, for far too long.

PART TWO

EXPERTS, STUNTS, SOBS, FRONT PAGES, AND AMAZONS

1880s–1920s

CHAPTER 3

The Breakout

Prosperity, lost in the worldwide depression that followed the panic of 1873, came "back with a whoop" in the 1880s. As Ida Tarbell would later recount, the "wanton speculation" and "reckless overbuilding of railroads" heaved disorder. Factories and mills shut down, and the decade "dripped in blood." Yet plenty of men "struggled to get at causes, to find corrections, to humanize and socialize the country," she wrote, "for then as now there were those who dreamed of a good world although at times it seemed to them to be going mad."

In the newsrooms, supremely talented woman journalists like Tarbell gained traction, but most others rarely had the chance to engage directly in coverage of the major stories of the day. The few opportunities were at the magazines or in the women's news and features sections that flourished at the metropolitan dailies. Some papers featured woman columnists, and literary departments sometimes provided openings for women to rise as editors. It always seemed to attract attention when a woman journalist did well in an unexpected post.

Still, the most reliable high-prestige, reputation-building, out-in-the-world position for women off the women's pages remained the lone lady correspondent, one per publication and available only to a select few. Mary Clemmer, Grace Greenwood, and Gail Hamilton held on to their visibility until they died, Greenwood in 1904. By then, Mary Ann Shadd Cary had long since moved on to work in other ways on behalf of her people. In 1862, she returned to the

United States to help recruit Black soldiers to fight in the Civil
War. After the conflict, she engaged in efforts to capitalize on the
legislative victories that the Thirteenth, Fourteenth, and Fifteenth
Amendments to the Constitution portended for Black Americans.
She taught in Washington, D.C., for a time, and in 1878–79 served on
the executive committee of the National Woman Suffrage Association, where the need for political support from the South created one
of the earlier examples of race-gender cooperation marred by the
tensions between suffragists Black and white. In 1883, at the age of
sixty, Cary earned her bachelor's degree in law from Howard University, the second African American woman to do so. She died in 1893.

The number of woman journalists in the field continued to rise. At
the newspapers especially, the page space that department store ads
made available for women's-interest items was an important factor
in the creation of new jobs, but in pigeonholes from which woman
journalists rarely emerged. In February 1887, Jane Croly was able to
repeat the same deprecating broad-brush analysis she had offered
twelve years earlier: women still lacked training, she said again;
women had yet to demonstrate the "exactness and accurate habits
of mind" that journalism at its most challenging demanded.

In August of that year, Charles Dana, the editor and part owner
of the New York *Sun*, did not comment on the training deficit but
furthered the belittling perception that women were too loose with
facts. For newspapers, accuracy trumped writing ability, and women,
he said, "find it impossible not to exaggerate." On top of that, there
were plenty of first-rate men to choose from without having to resort
to the limited utility of women, whom he would never send out on
assignment after dark.

Dana's remarks appeared in a widely recirculated article in *The
Pittsburg Dispatch* that included the views of most of New York City's
top newspaper editors about the prospects for women in journalism.
Foster Coates of *The Mail and Express,* which employed more women
than any other New York daily, said their "very dress, constitution
and habits of life" left them ill-equipped for routine work. Robert G.
Morris of *The Evening Telegram* commented on the inappropriateness
of street-length skirts and petticoats. How could a woman dressed in
such a way slide down a banister or bound up three flights of stairs
four steps at a time, as competitive assignments so often required?

In the city room, men still considered women a nuisance. George Hepworth of James Gordon Bennett's *New York Herald* spoke of the unease men felt taking off their suit coats or propping their feet up on their desks with women in the room. He didn't mention the spittoons. What a shame that women balked at doing the kind of reporting they excelled at—society events, charitable endeavors, gossip, fashion, food. Colonel John Cockerill of *The World* boasted that his paper had two women on its full-time staff, although he did not say what they did, nor did he mention their limited prospects.

Had Whitelaw Reid of the *New York Tribune* been among those interviewed, he could have pointed to Nelly Mackay Hutchinson, his women's suffrage movement reporter, a sterling example of possibility on his full-time staff. In 1872, as a cub, Hutchinson wrote the *Galaxy* piece that said women would have to change their very nature to succeed in journalism's higher ranks. At the time, she was one of seven women among the newspaper's twenty-four editorial staff members. The city desk, the most desired place to work, had an additional twenty-six reporters, all men. In 1879, Hutchinson's seventh year on staff, Reid promoted her to establish and run the paper's sixteen-page Sunday supplement, which she did successfully. He then named her to succeed John R. G. Hassard as literary editor in Margaret Fuller's old post.

Hutchinson's legacy is no match for Fuller's, but Hutchinson was no less respected than the equally forgotten men who preceded and succeeded them both. For Hutchinson's obituary, colleagues recalled her imagination, loyalty, and formative contributions "as a pioneer in the broader field and as a brilliant writer in her chosen specialty." As accomplished as she had become by 1886, a New Orleans gossip columnist described her in the belittling manner so many accomplished women would be subjected to for decades to come—in Hutchinson's case, as "the pug-nosed poetess."

Of the editors whose comments appear in the *Dispatch* story, only Charles Ransom Miller, the editor of *The New York Times,* could point to a woman reporter on his staff, Midy Morgan, who had been "unsurpassed"—for seventeen years—on a presumed man's beat. Morgan, like Hutchinson, embodied the way expertise and prior training could transform a smart, talented woman's prospects in the field.

Amazingly, Midy Morgan, forty years old, with no prior journalism experience, landed her post at the *Times* within weeks of her move to the metropolis in the summer of 1869. Morgan, born in Cork, Ireland, was over six feet tall, blue-eyed, and charming. She arrived after a four-year "spree" in Rome and Florence with letters of introduction to Horace Greeley and to Henry J. Raymond, an owner of the *Times,* from George Perkins Marsh, Abraham Lincoln's minister to the kingdom of Italy and an early environmentalist.

Morgan's extended Italian sojourn stemmed in part from the death of her father in 1865, when the bulk of his "large estates," as she described the family holdings, passed to her brother. In Rome, she befriended many American expatriates, including Charlotte Cushman, the actress, contralto, and racy bon vivant. Cushman made many useful introductions.

In New York, Raymond died before Morgan could arrange to meet him, so she first approached Greeley, who did not look up from the papers on his desk as she entered his office nor even ask her to sit down. He barely glanced at Marsh's letter. He even suggested she forget journalism and take up growing mushrooms. Morgan was an expert equestrian, and one of her connections from the horse world, the financier Leonard Jerome, introduced her to Manton Marble, then the editor of *The World.* Marble assigned her to report on the upcoming races at Saratoga Springs. The legend holds that Marble double-teamed her with his regular racing reporter without letting him know and that Morgan's stories were good enough to make the paper over his. "An Irish Lady's Opinion of an American Watering Place—What She Thinks of American Gentlemen—the Races," reads a page 1 headline over the paper's Saratoga season ender, unsigned.

That September, the *Times* named a great friend of Raymond's, John Bigelow, interim editor. Perhaps the Marsh letter held more sway with Bigelow, who briefly served as U.S. minister to France, than it had with Greeley; perhaps Morgan's particular know-how was enough on its own. Either way, the *Times* hired her to fill an opening as its livestock markets reporter, a position she held for more than twenty years.

After only a couple of months in New York, she was ensconced enough among the New York elite to have been spotted in Central Park on one of the saddle horses of Mrs. August Belmont, wife of

Midy Morgan
(Courtesy of The New
York Times/*Redux)*

the multimillionaire. By then Morgan was well into a ten-month-long investigation of animal abuse at the city's cattle markets. Beyond the intolerable way the creatures were being treated, she emphasized the risk that inhumane animal practices posed to human beings. In June 1870, long before Upton Sinclair's *The Jungle,* she urged members of the American Institute's Farmers' Club to act in self-defense. "Nine times in ten we eat diseased meat at our hotels and restaurants," she told them. "It cannot be otherwise." Other attention-getting livestock investigations followed.

Morgan came to the fore while Grace Greenwood, Gail Hamilton, and Mary Clemmer were in their heyday. All four of them attracted publicity over the years, but contemporaneous lists of the most important woman journalists of the period tend to put Morgan first. In 1886, seventeen years after her foray to Saratoga Springs, Britain's *Pall Mall Gazette* would judge her the most successful woman reporter in America.

Perhaps Morgan's serious, though uninviting, subject matter saved her from the vicious jealous attacks that other celebrated woman journalists of the period sometimes experienced from their colleagues. The many writers who profiled Morgan described her towering presence, her good humor and conversation, her steel-rimmed spectacles, the dull, dark-colored waterproof dress she never seemed to change, her sensible man-styled boots, the waders she favored on muddier days, and the gloves of soft leather "that cover the little hands so plainly showing 'good blood.'" All her finery from those earlier European revelries she kept stored away. One sketch reported that she carried a revolver; another, that she seemed to have secrets. Various reports put her income equal to Mary Clemmer's.

At Morgan's death at sixty-three in 1892, *The Atlanta Constitution* offered the most far-reaching tribute. Morgan's career had demonstrated beyond doubt that "a woman can do anything on a newspaper that a man can do." Her inspiring, applause-worthy success, however, did not initiate a newswomen stampede to the stockyards. Nor did the reporting expeditions of Helen Campbell into the New York City slums, at least not right away. Campbell, eleven years Morgan's junior, had devoted her early writing years to fiction and children's literature. Her turn to investigative work came in her early forties, inspired by her membership in Jane Croly's Sorosis. She began by volunteering in New York City's gang-ridden Five Points neighborhood to help those "conceived in sin and shapen in iniquity" whom "the gospel of development scarcely promises to reach." She chronicled her encounters for magazines and then turned much of this material into books. At the same time, she became involved with the home economics movement, with its aim of making women more efficient household managers. Her sociological novel, *Mrs. Herndon's Income,* published in 1886, so effectively addressed the question of poor woman wage workers that Whitelaw Reid assigned her to investigate their lives and homes in New York for a twenty-one-part series for the *Tribune.* It ran as "Prisoners of Poverty" from October 1886 to March 1887, aiming to let readers into the lives of New York City's 200,000 such women at their most restless and discontent. Critics of the book had their complaints but acknowledged that she had captured "the condensed cry" of the women's anguish. This and her subsequent investigations led to her appointment as a lecturer at the University of Wisconsin and then, in 1896, to the directorship of a new Chicago settlement house. Her accomplishments were great but never drew attention to her as a personality, unlike Morgan or the most popular lady correspondents. Ida Tarbell, however, clearly grasped the significance of what Campbell had achieved. *The Chautauquan,* while Tarbell was editor, described Campbell's reports as so true to their subjects they bound their pitiful tales to the reader's mind "with an iron clasp."

In April 1887, Tarbell wrote a long piece about women in journalism, interviewing many who worked or had worked in the field. Campbell was not among Tarbell's interviewees, but in the story Tarbell singled her out once again for writing "thrilling pictures" of the poor, this time as Tarbell's springboard to a prophecy about the direction journalism needed to take: "No means can be more effective and far-reaching than that which Mrs. Campbell is using." That same year, Tarbell countered the assertion of another woman writer, whose story, also in *The Chautauquan,* claimed that women had yet to distinguish themselves as inventors. Tarbell analyzed U.S. Patent Office records to find six times more inventions by women than the earlier story reported, and not for trivial designs.

By 1890, women made up 20 percent of the nation's total workforce but, at a total of 888, less than 5 percent of the 21,849 editors and reporters. The business side also produced a couple of outstanding examples of women at the top of the masthead. And by September 1887, something like a dozen women had the top jobs at various magazines, several of those publications "serious."

Ida Tarbell
(Library of Congress, photo by Harris & Ewing, loc.gov/item/2004670771/)

Both Tarbell and Ida B. Wells would claim their most enduring recognition closer to either side of the century's turn, after Wells became editor and part owner of the *Memphis Free Speech and Headlight,* and Tarbell joined Lincoln Steffens and Ray Stannard Baker in the muckraker triad they created at *McClure's.* However, the careers of both Idas were well under way by the mid-1880s. They were educated women with disciplined minds, both well schooled in how to build an argument and support it with data. They earned their respected place in journalism by practicing serious, hard-hitting, research-driven reportage. Wells's most important work was done in the mid-1890s, Tarbell's, a few years later, and both gained even greater recognition and expanded their popularity through their lecture dates in the United States and abroad.

Tarbell was born in 1857 in the western Pennsylvania oil town of Titusville, where her father was an independent oil producer and refiner whose fortunes rose and fell with the impact of monopolistic practices. Wells was born to enslaved parents in Holly Springs, Mississippi, in 1862. Her father, a carpenter, was well respected. Both women came out of strong Methodist and Methodist-Episcopal backgrounds and left teaching behind to pursue journalism. The Tarbell home was a hospitality stop for clergy and presiding church elders. Through this connection, Tarbell knew the Reverend Theodore L. Flood, who enlisted her to help once he took charge of *The*

Chautauquan, the magazine of the popular Chautauqua adult education movement. She readily accepted the offer, given that Chautauqua "had been almost as much a part of my life as the oil business." The office was thirty miles away, in Meadville, where Tarbell was the only woman to graduate from Allegheny College in the class of 1880. She soon started writing articles and doing investigations, and before long she became the magazine's editor, a position she held for eight years, never paid more than $100 a month, a poor salary even then. She then went off to Paris for several years and studied at the Sorbonne.

Ida B. Wells attended a hometown industrial and normal school now known as Rust College. Her father was on the school's first board of trustees. In 1878, a local yellow fever epidemic killed both of her parents and the youngest of their eight children, but spared Wells, who was away visiting her grandmother. The 1880 U.S. census lists Wells at eighteen as head of household. Around that time, a dispute with the school's president led to her expulsion from Rust, a contretemps she later blamed on her own tempestuousness. Not long after, she moved to Memphis with two of her younger siblings to live with an aunt while she commuted to her teaching post some miles away. She took summer courses at Fisk University in Nashville and in 1884, in Memphis, began to write professionally for the weekly *The Living Way* under the pen name Iola. Other African American papers across the country picked up her reports, starting with her outrage at the forced ejections of Black women from ladies' railroad cars. She filed several lawsuits in protest; one resulted in a settlement in court that was lost on appeal. By 1889, she reigned in Black editorial circles as the "Princess of the Press" and in the mainstream trade magazine *The Journalist,* in the words of a Black woman colleague, as the person who "struck harder blows at the wrongs and weakness of the race" than anyone else.

Ida B. Wells, 1893
*(New York Public Library,
digitalcollections.nypl.org/
items/8694185c-b326-f40b-
e040-e00a1806638a)*

Oddly, there was no known mutual admiration expressed between Tarbell and Wells, who were peers in so many ways save the deep ravine that separated the races. Nor is there evidence that either of them directly acknowledged the explosion of attention that Nellie Bly, their contemporary if not exactly their peer, precipitated from her first assignment for *The World.*

Bly was a twenty-three-year-old upstart from the tiny hamlet of Cochran's Mills in Armstrong County, Pennsylvania, about a hundred miles due south of Titusville. Her higher education consisted of one uncompleted semester at a nearby normal school when she was fifteen. Born Elizabeth Jane Cochran in 1864 (she later added a final *e* to Cochran for flourish), she entered into journalism at *The Pittsburg Dispatch,* defying the common assumption that top-level work required education and training. Bly had a strong will and impeccable instincts for what would play big in newsprint. With her move to New York two years after she started at the *Dispatch,* Bly was basking in the limelight as if a stage star and had carved out a new and glamorous place in journalism for the daring young woman, "the New American Girl," the consummate "girl reporter." By contrast, although Wells's stature was firm and growing in the Black community at the same time, it would not spill into the mainstream until 1892, with her reports on the horrors of lynching. Ida Tarbell established literary credentials in the mid-1890s with well-received biographies of Napoleon Bonaparte, Abraham Lincoln in four volumes, and Madame Roland, the French political activist and writer Marie-Jeanne "Manon" Roland de la Platière. *McClure's* published Tarbell's greatest journalistic work between November 1902 and October 1904, her nineteen-part "History of Standard Oil." Although all three women were within a few years of one another in age, no one at any point would have called either of the two Idas "girl reporter."

The editorial announcement for the oil series consumed five pages, emphasizing the "painstaking reading and study" it required for Tarbell to master "the bewildering mass" of oil-company-related documents, and how her childhood in oil country enhanced the effort. She had imbibed the development of the oil business "with the very air she breathed." When the book version came out, *The Austin Statesman* counted Tarbell among the very few women ever to have attained "such authority and eminence in letters." In other words, Margaret Fuller terrain.

Tarbell told an interviewer that when she was fourteen, the fight of her father and other oilmen against special privileges had convinced her that for a local oilman to take a rebate from oil barons like John D. Rockefeller was as wrong as telling a lie. Once Rockefeller's Standard Oil came to town, she said, "going over" to the oil giant, succumbing to its unethical practices as it pushed to secure a monopoly for itself, was seen as an even greater mark of disgrace. Her work as a historian caused her to rethink what she had witnessed, to broaden her view, and her opus had major impact. It tarnished Rockefeller's reputation, influenced the U.S. Supreme Court in its decision to break up the multinational trusts, and established a new high-water mark in the emerging methods of investigative reporting that still resonates.

The *Memphis Free Speech and Headlight* waged a militant crusade against white efforts to upend the legal gains of Reconstruction, the same mission Mary Ann Shadd Cary engaged in after her return from Canada. Wells, as the paper's editor from 1889 to 1892, did not hesitate to call out members of her own community like Booker T. Washington, or the unacceptable state of Black schools, or a minister for consorting with a congregant. She even went after her business partner the Reverend Taylor Nightingale when he tried to misuse the newspaper to get back at members of his church who opposed him. Nightingale ended up in another imbroglio that put him in jail for eighty days. That enabled Wells and their third partner, J. L. Fleming, to buy out Nightingale's stake in the newspaper and drop *Headlight* from its name.

Wells took on lynching with a vengeance. On Saturday, May 21, 1892, she reported on eight men lynched the previous week in Arkansas, Alabama, Louisiana, and Georgia. "Nobody in this section of the country believes the old thread-bare lie that Negro men rape white women," her editorial concluded. "If Southern white men are not careful, they will overreach themselves and public sentiment will have a reaction; a conclusion will then be reached which will be very damaging to the moral reputation of their women." A few days later, white marauders broke into the *Free Speech* office and ransacked it, destroying its press. They ran Fleming out of town and warned Wells, who happened to be on vacation in New York, to stay away or risk bodily harm.

In New York, in virtual exile, Wells connected with the editor and publisher Timothy Thomas Fortune, who thought she was as "sharp as a steel trap" and "one of the few of our women who handle a goose-quill with diamond point as easily as any man in newspaper work." Fortune started *The New York Globe* in 1880, changed its name to *The New York Freeman* in 1884, and changed it again in 1887 to *The New York Age*. While in the city, Wells wrote "Southern Horrors: Lynch Law in All Its Phases," which Fortune published in the *Age* on June 25, 1892, and reprinted as a pamphlet. "Since my business has been destroyed," Wells wrote, "and I am an exile from home because of that editorial, the issue has been forced, and as the writer of it I feel that the race and the public generally should have a statement of facts as they exist."

In six thousand words, she covered the attraction of white women to Black men; individual murders across the country; the subversion of African American freedom by Ku Klux Klan raids and other terrors; malicious untruths in the white press; the position of southern leaders; and what African Americans could do to counter the lethal attacks. She pushed for Black men to use the boycott, emigration, and the press to stamp out lynch law, "that last relic of barbarism and slavery." In 1895, Wells, by then living in Chicago and married to the journalist, lawyer, and civil rights activist Ferdinand Lee Barnett, hyphenated her surname to Wells-Barnett. She continued her research and compiled it into a hundred-page pamphlet, *A Red Record: Tabulated Statistics and Alleged Causes of Lynchings in the United States, 1892–1893–1894*. In 2020, eighty-nine years after her death in 1931, the Pulitzer Prize board honored her with a rare special citation for her "outstanding and courageous reporting," accompanied by a prize of $50,000, recipients not immediately announced, in support of her mission.

There is no ready explanation for why the wide attention showered on women like Midy Morgan, Ida Tarbell, Ida B. Wells, and Nellie Bly did not end the concerns of editors about the stamina and acumen of woman reporters, their ability to keep themselves safe, or their suitability for the profession. But the half-life of negative

impressions, the stubborn tendency of men to prejudge the capabilities of all women from their unhappy experiences with a few, or
maybe with only one, or none, was boundless. On top of that was
the seeming inability of most woman aspirants to grasp the field's
exacting demands, to get beyond their overly romanticized notion of
what the work was really like. Tarbell understood this well. "There
is, perhaps, no profession whose requirements are less understood
by women than that of journalism," she wrote in her *Chautauquan*
piece. Women seeking jobs in the field were still confusing their
ability to dash off a decent essay with a journalist's "complicated,
many-sided labor." To succeed, she said, a woman had to be ready
to fit in with the organization's needs and perform any task better
than anyone else, whether that meant editing five thousand words
down to two thousand or writing an advertising circular. "The halo
which surrounds it," she said of the field, "is largely fictitious." This
sound advice from Tarbell curiously came with her questionable
and unexplained assumption that women might never be suitable
for the crime or morgue beats. She did, however, hedge her blanket
statement by saying that in the end the key determinant of whether
women could excel at the gritty work would depend on ability, in
and of itself. Tarbell did not mention sports, but as with crime and
death and war, a few women were about to find their way onto these
beats, too.

Very soon after Tarbell's article appeared, Nellie Bly was not finding it easy to land the kind of position she dreamed of on Park Row,
where all of New York's major dailies had their headquarters. She
thought surely her two prominent rookie years as Nellie Bly for
The Pittsburg Dispatch, including six months of headlines that regularly shouted "NELLIE IN MEXICO," had amply demonstrated her
readiness for the competitive New York City scene. To keep herself,
her mother, and her sister afloat in the summer of 1887, she freelanced for the *Dispatch*. On the strength of a letter of introduction,
she met with Joseph Howard Jr., a longtime city reporter and editor,
who by then was writing a column he circulated widely. He suggested she interview New York City's top newspaper editors—not
other woman journalists as Tarbell had done—on the prospects for
women in their newsrooms. The article that made their dispiriting
views public was Bly's. It prepared the ground for her biggest break,

not only because it enabled her to meet the men in their offices, but because what she learned both attracted wide attention and guided what she did next.

In Bly's piece, Foster Coates of *The Mail and Express* said he found the work of the women on his staff invaluable, so long as they confined their efforts to fashion, society, and gossip; dramatic and musical criticism; domestic, charitable, and religious news; book reviewing; and interviewing, which was the newest addition to the women's limited portfolio. A woman reporter was only useful to attract woman readers. "Women are always anxious to read what women write," he ventured, "and the knowledge that a woman has charge of some special department" sparked interest in the work that appeared on those pages, enhancing the paper's circulation goals. Nevertheless, he acknowledged how cemented the prejudice against women had become, adding, "Until they are tried it will never be removed." He said nothing about being willing himself to give them a try, nor anything about the women like Hutchinson, already working effectively in positions other than those he named.

Bly, so eager to be tried, asked John Cockerill of *The World* if he thought the time might come when women would be permitted to do more on newspapers than was currently on offer. "Not unless the public taste demands different news," he said. "I don't think women journalists will ever be in great demand in New York." He seemed to agree with Coates that the feeling against women came less from experience with them than from the lack of it. "We want originality and brightness, and I don't think it would be refused if found in a woman," Cockerill said. But then he added that same old canard: "Yet no editor would like to send a woman out in bad weather or to questionable places for news."

Coates and Cockerill had unconsciously provided Bly with ideas for how to get herself hired: Offer something to change the public taste. Be original and bright. Show indifference to bad weather and dangerous locales. Produce showstopping work. Once Bly gained access to Cockerill's office at *The World* again, she proposed an idea that checked all those boxes. With so many immigrants flooding the city, she asked him to send her alone, steerage, from Europe to America to document the experience. Cockerill judged the idea too risky and costly, but in that conversation it was agreed that Bly would feign insanity and become a patient at the women's insane asylum on Blackwell's Island so she could investigate its conditions and rumors of patient abuse. The plan was for her to remain inside until the paper could arrange her release.

The idea went considerably beyond the reporting of Charles Dickens, Lydia Maria Child, or Margaret Fuller on Blackwell's Island in the 1840s, but it was somewhat like an escapade of Julius Chambers, a reporter for the *New York Tribune*. In August 1872, Chambers entered the private Bloomingdale Asylum in the guise of an insane person. The subsequent stories he wrote do not include his byline, but he was clearly the author. Both he and Bly were in their early twenties when they made their respective forays. Bly's ruse and exit were as successful as Chambers's, and what they both witnessed was awful. Chambers and Bly both generated national attention and triggered an investigation into dubious asylum practices. Of the two investigations, only Bly's has had lasting impact. Bly's *Ten Days in a Mad-House* is the book version of her articles. Both begin in the style that made Bly so famous:

> On the 22d of September I was asked by the *World* if I could have myself committed to one of the asylums for the insane in New York, with a view to writing a plain and unvarnished narrative of the treatment of the patients therein and the methods of management, etc. Did I think I had the courage to go through such an ordeal as the mission would demand? Could I assume the characteristics of insanity to such a degree that I could pass the doctors, live for a week among the insane without the authorities there finding out that I was only a "chiel amang 'em takin' notes"? I said I believed I could. I had some faith in my own ability as an actress and thought I could assume insanity long enough to accomplish any mission intrusted [*sic*] to me. Could I pass a week in the insane ward at Blackwell's Island? I said I could and I would. And I did.

Her first big exposé led straight to the next. Week after week in her first year on staff, she produced feature after feature for *The*

Nellie Bly

*(Library of Congress, photo
by J. J. Myers, loc.gov/
item/89711961/)*

World, mostly exposés. She wrote first-person reports on working alongside the "white slaves" in a paper box factory, went through the application process at the city's matrimonial agencies, danced with ballerinas, posed as a sinner to investigate a home for unfortunate women, joined a chorus line to learn what drew women to the stage, interviewed woman prisoners at police court, and got a mind healer to teach her new ways to think.

With every mention of Nellie Bly in a headline—in fact, her name appeared in the headline of almost every story she ever wrote—she was fully aware of her contribution to *The World*'s growing circulation. When her paychecks did not reflect the value that she knew she brought, her friend Joe Howard came to her rescue. "The great successes of the past year in New York journalism have been made by Nellie Bly," he wrote in his "Howard's Letter" column of August 15, 1888. It appeared just shy of Bly's first anniversary at *The World*. He contested any colleague who suggested that her madhouse investigation was nothing more than a redux of the one Chambers did. He had gained entry as a patient not with a convincing performance of insanity, as Bly did, but by providing affidavits from two witnesses. Besides that, Howard wrote, he had not duped the management, as Bly had done. In Chambers's case, the asylum's director not only was party to the subterfuge but proposed it. Bly orchestrated her own arrest, caused days of fevered speculation in all the city's newspapers over the mysterious insane girl who showed up at police court, at Bellevue Hospital, and on the dreaded island, spurred by a mad scene that so alarmed the matron of the boardinghouse where she had billeted that the woman called the police to take Bly away. To get Bly released, *The World* sent a lawyer and the newspaper's sketch artist, Walt McDougall, to retrieve her. She had been inside for ten days.

Howard enumerated Bly's points of impact. Every major paper in the country had reprinted her stories. Extracts appeared in French and German publications, and medical journals took note of her exposé. He did not mention that the city responded by increasing its budget appropriation for the facility but that happened, too. Howard said he did not know any man, including himself, who had the brains to think out such a plot or the pluck to enact it. And even if one had, that man would have expected to be paid at least $100 a column. Given the length of Bly's two-part series over a pair of Sundays, that would amount to somewhere between $2,000 and $2,500. But "oh, she is a woman," Howard wrote. "She got nothing like it." At some point between the 1870s and the end of the 1880s, stardom for women had ceased to mean equal or even better pay.

Howard, well informed by Bly, went on about her subsequent triumphs and how little support *The World* had given her to execute them. He mentioned the corrupt Albany lobbyist she exposed by posing as a woman with a bribe to dispense, and the Central Park lecher she outsmarted by "placing herself in the very hand of the dirty dog." Were there other Nellie Blys? "I doubt very much if there are many women so compactly organized in mind, body, and estate as she, for this particular branch of our arduous work," he said. "But nevertheless, by her illustrious example she shows her sisters what women can do." In fact, the can-do, would-be Nellie Blys were writing for newspapers across the country—Annie Laurie in San Francisco, Eva Gay in Minneapolis, Polly Pry in Denver, and Nell Nelson in Chicago, just to name a few. Under Bly's nose, there were even imitators in the pages of *The World,* various women in their own or assumed names along with those who masqueraded as Meg Merrilies, the all-purpose byline the newspaper assigned to whoever performed a stunt.

Howard ended his column with kind words for the publicity-averse Nelly Mackay Hutchinson, who, by then, in addition to the important literary chair she occupied at the *Tribune,* had been named coeditor of the eleven-volume *Library of American Literature.* Howard compared the disparate career paths of Bly and Hutchinson and concluded that both clearly demonstrated what women with ability could accomplish in the field. "Girls, go in," he urged in closing, "and, being in, win."

The journalism of verification gave Tarbell and Wells their lofty standing. Both women "made the significant interesting" and compelling, a long-cherished principle of the profession. Bly did the same but through an impressionistic, sexier approach based on eyewitness narrative accounts of the amazing exploits of this consummate "Miss Push-and-Get-There." Counting her two years in Pittsburgh, her full-time career lasted less than five years. But unlike most of her many imitators, the national attention she sparked in her first two and a half years working full time at *The World* gave her a celebrity aura that endured, in and out of journalism, for the rest of her life and, so far, for a century beyond it. Her greatest claim is as the mother of investigative and immersion reporting presented in the sensational persona that was of a piece with her times, absent the gravitas that the work of Tarbell and Wells so readily displayed.

The stunt work that Bly made famous did lift a select group of women off the women's pages, but only to put them in another women's ghetto that played out from overexposure by the mid-1890s. Well before it did, Bly brought her own early journalism career to a reverberating climax between November 1889 and the end of January 1890 with a triumphant race around the world to beat the fictional eighty-day record of Jules Verne's Phileas Fogg in *Around the World in Eighty Days*. Once again, she demonstrated her bravura and independence, traveling alone without a chaperone for two and a half months with a single alligator tote bag instead of the usual "round dozen trunks." She completed her journey in seventy-two days, six hours, and eleven minutes. Newspapers across the country covered the trip every single day from myriad angles. Her fan following crescendoed, spawning board games, poems, trading cards, caps, lamps, and racehorses, all branded in her name. Adding to the journey's excitement, *Cosmopolitan* had sent Elizabeth Bisland in the other direction in a failed bid to beat Bly, who was oblivious to the challenge until her return. The national and international response for Bly was simply tumultuous.

When Joseph Pulitzer declined to reward her with a bonus for the sensation her trip around the world became, she quit. She toured the country giving lectures, signed a lucrative contract to write dime novels for *The New York Family Story Paper* (eleven serial stories that ran between 1889 and 1895), and, at thirty-one, married a man forty years her senior who she thought was richer than he turned out to be.

From time to time, journalism would draw her back. "Nellie Bly Returns," *The World* trumpeted in 1893 in the house ad that ran before her exclusive jailhouse interview with the anarchist Emma Goldman appeared. Women "will be made to feel prouder of woman's ability, man will realize his smallness," the ad proclaimed. Her "numerous and insignificant rivals may proceed to tremble."

Her success with the interview helped solidify the format as an important new woman's province. Among her subjects were the accused murderer Eva Hamilton, the aging suffrage leader Susan B. Anthony, and the governor of Illinois, John Peter Altgeld, at the height of the violent railway union strike outside Chicago against the Pullman train car company. Her coverage was distinct and exceptional in its focus on the plight of the workers' families instead of the brawling. Her clear-eyed, un-fawning coverage of a women's suffrage convention bored in on the dowdiness of the leaders as a missed opportunity to take advantage of the weapon of attractive appearance. Yet the suffragists honored her as a herald on horseback dressed in "stunning" emerald-green togs to match her eyes at their grand 1913 parade in Washington, D.C. It might have been a coincidence that the suffragist leaders started to dress more fetchingly after she chided them in print for their strategic misstep.

Critical to Bly's success was the support, admiration, and promotion that Arthur Brisbane never stopped providing, both as a colleague and section editor at *The World* and later as her boss at the *New York Evening Journal*. Until days before her death at fifty-seven in 1922 from a pneumonia-induced heart attack, she continued to attract choice assignments by being in the right place at the right time, by needing money, or just by being Nellie Bly. The astounding abiding success of Elizabeth Jane Cochrane Seaman followed no pattern and broke every rule.

As Bly moved offstage, the views of Foster Coates of New York's *Mail and Express* changed, increasingly influenced by the more recent accomplishments of women in the field. In a column he was writing regularly for *Ladies' Home Journal* in the early 1890s, he took up the question of women's chances in journalism more than once. No longer did he think women should be confined to fashion and "women's news" as he had expressed just three years earlier. His experiences had shown him that women "could do some kinds of reporting far better than men," although he cautioned against sending any reporter out without the right background and preparation. He understood the obstacles women had to overcome. "Most editors give women a chance by being unfair to them," he said, adding that women did not have the habit of men to gather in hotels, cafés, and clubs to discuss the matters of the day. A young woman reporter in London who failed to find work on Fleet Street nailed the issue: "A man meets other men at his club; he can be out and about at all hours; he can insist without being thought bold and forward; he is not presumed to be capable of undertaking only a limited class of subjects, but is set to anything."

Foster Coates showed prescience. He foresaw a distant day "when women will do a large proportion of newspaper reporting. In nearly all the big cities, they are now doing a little of it." Among them was Susette La Flesche, who was writing for the *Omaha World-Herald* as Inshata Theumba, or Bright Eyes, and being republished widely across the country. She projected a no-nonsense, just-the-facts authority from the Pine Ridge Reservation in South Dakota in late 1890 and early 1891, reporting on the massacre by U.S. soldiers of the Oglala Lakotas at Wounded Knee. La Flesche, a member of the Omaha tribe of Nebraska, told front-page readers of the *World-Herald* that she was "the only Indian speaking to the public through the press for the Indians, and I demand in the name of the race and for their welfare that it shall be done."

Susette La Flesche, 1879
(National Portrait Gallery Collection, photo by José María Mora, npg.si.edu/object/ npg_NPG.2013.3)

In 1895, *The Washington Post* took note of the new twenty-eight-year-old baseball columnist at *The Baltimore Telegram* with the byline "S.K.M." Although Sadie Kneller Miller is mostly forgotten, it is hard to imagine many women of this period who in time would come to have a more complete turn-of-the-century man's-world success story. Miller graduated from Western Maryland, now McDaniel College, in her hometown of Westminster, about forty miles northwest of Baltimore. She married her baseball-playing college sweetheart, Charles R. Miller, who was on his way to becoming an important Baltimore attorney and trust company executive. As the *Post* writer said in an eye-roll-producing way, this "bright, pretty, accomplished little lady" was probably the first in this line of work, having trained herself to be "always unbiased" as she said "a whole lot of clever, readable things," which, to her credit, other papers found valuable enough to liberally quote. Miller's "well enough" mastery of the game's finer points "opens another field for the lady journalist, and it may be expected that others will soon follow her example." For Miller, the baseball beat was only the start.

By 1900, no doubt thanks to the impact of women like Bly, Tarbell, and Wells, the number of woman journalists had nearly doubled from ten years before. The practice of paying women less was convenient for proprietors and quickly became entrenched. Pay equity, though practiced in Horace Greeley's day and somewhat after, was long gone if occasionally remarked upon. Given the available alternatives, there is only one plausible explanation for why paying women less became standard practice: the willingness of women who wanted journalism careers to accept what they were offered or forgo the chance. By an 1891 estimate, the top men in the profession received annual earnings of anywhere from $5,000 to $15,000. For women the following year, the estimate was $520 a year at the bottom to just over $4,000 a year at the top. The going rate for freelance columns by women—two thousand words was the usual length—ranged from $5 to $10 per piece, something like $140 to $280 today. "There is, I know, such a distinction," Foster Coates admitted, adding his profoundly mistaken prediction that "the future may be depended on to wipe that out. Women of brains and ability who have something to say and know how to say it, have no reason to fear."

Interest in journalism careers became so keen among girls that

editors began commissioning advice articles and books to guide
them and their worried parents. Yet once in the door, women still
rarely received promotions. Coates acknowledged that the chances
for career advancement were "not very good," unless a woman
was exceptionally talented. The practice of putting men in charge
remained firm, he said, a relic of the "old hypothesis" that men were
more reliable than women and more able to work hard for longer
hours. This "order of things" would die out, he said, "if women themselves want to change it. Let them first deserve promotion by good
work, and then enforce their claim."

In the British newspaper *The Independent,* the editor W. T. Stead
distilled his advice to woman journalists into five "don'ts": don't pre-
sume upon your sex; don't stand on your dignity; don't demand a
chaperone; don't be paid at first; and don't forget to read the papers.
Tarbell refined her advice in 1890, when Bly was at her pinnacle, suggesting that women who wanted to be journalists should first undertake at least two years of "thorough study" in political economy at a
top university, even if it cost them their entire patrimony. Without
preparation, she said, luck might ease the way in, but once in, would
provide little satisfaction.

In September 1894, Margaret Welch, *The New York Times*'s Saratoga correspondent and "Her Point of View" columnist, addressed
the American Social Science Association on the impact of newspaper
work on women's health. She said the work had sent a dozen or more
of her acquaintances into nervous exhaustion, five more into total
breakdowns, and two others to an early grave. In other cases, she
said, the culprit was a difficult home life, not journalism. As for the
recently deceased Midy Morgan "of revered memory," she was said
to have died at the end of a long and splendid newspaper career, but
not because of it. Welch decried the tendency of woman journalists
to eat poorly and dress stupidly, what she called "the handicaps of
their own making," emphasizing that a woman needed the physical
equipment for the opportunities at hand. "With it," she said, "the
work is not beyond her in any respect."

In 1898, a British author published *Journalism for Women: A Practical
Guide,* with the aim, as one British reviewer put it, of teaching women
to be journalists, not woman journalists, who are treated separately,

held to a lower standard, with a "premium on mediocrity." Even after so many years, and the many superb successes that should have changed men's minds when they took up the subject of the woman journalist and her place in the profession, all but Coates seemed to hold fast to their preconceptions and prejudices.

CHAPTER 4

From Cuba to the Far East

Nellie Bly and her would-be regiment
(*New York* World, *March 8, 1896, illustration by R. F. Outcault)*

Early in March 1896, shortly after Congress declared support for the Cuban rebellion against four hundred years of Spanish rule, Joseph Pulitzer's *World* delivered a scoop. Nellie Bly was preparing to go to Cuba not as a reporter but to lead a regiment that would join the local insurgents in their fight for independence. On March 8, Commander Bly strutted over half of a full page of the Sunday feature section in a uniform of her own design: a fashion-forward above-the-knee skirt, over-the-knee spats, and epaulets, her head topped in a plumed billed cap. Richard F. Outcault, creator of the *Yellow Kid* comic series that gave yellow journalism its name, sketched her with a sword held aloft in her right hand and her left elbow crooked, pressing her other hand into the side of her tiny cinched waist. Several lengths behind her, rows of soldiers, all men, marched in full dress as a crowd of hat-waving onlookers cheered. An unnamed interviewer, a man, caught up with Bly as she scurried around town, attempting to recruit troops and raise funds through a committee she hoped to form from members of the elite men's clubs. Women were braver than men, Bly told him, and had more of the qualities a military leader needed. Besides, she said, "do you think a company or a regiment of men soldiers, led by a woman, would ever dare run away? Do you think that if a woman were watching them any man of them would flinch? Do you think if a woman drew her sword and said, 'Come on!' there would be a single soldier in the whole army who would not 'come on' until his wounds made it impossible for him to crawl any further?"

Over the coming days and weeks, dozens of newspapers across the country republished the story. Others chose only to comment in short items, the so-called paragraphs, the briefs often composed unsigned by one of the few women on staff. The *Toledo Blade* asked if Spain might now want to recall for his own protection its commander-general in Cuba, Valeriano Weyler y Nicolau, "the Butcher," as he came to be known. To send Bly to Cuba was unfair, said the *Oberlin Herald* from Kansas: "Why frighten Weyler by such threats?" *The Galveston News* wondered how Bly's husband felt about so many men following his wife. *The Arizona Republic* offered, "Cuba has been stricken with war and pestilence, and now is about to undergo the saddest experience of all. Nellie Bly is going there." *The Argus* of Salt Lake City pierced even deeper: with Bly off to Cuba, "it's to be regretted that the Spaniards are such poor shots."

Of course, the whole business turned out to be hokum, and *The World* never mentioned it again. Six days later, however, Joseph Pulitzer's new rival, the *New York Evening Journal,* owned by William Randolph Hearst, popped up with a feminine-inspired Cuba sensation of its own, a real one.

The *Journal* had a good team on the ground in Cuba, headed since early February by Murat Halstead, a distinguished Civil War and Franco-Prussian War correspondent, then sixty-six, the former editor and a part owner of the *Cincinnati Commercial Gazette.* When he had sailed for Cuba on January 26, the *Journal* announced his departure with a couple of paragraphs under a little headline down a middle column on page 5. On March 14, a two-column, front-page sketch over a full column of text that continued on the next page introduced the paper's newest correspondent in Havana:

WEYLER TALKS
TO A WOMAN

———

The Butcher Tells Many
Interesting Things to
Kate Masterson

———

Cuban Women Who Fight in
Men's Clothes and Wield
Machetes

———

One of the Modern Amazons Is Now
Held a Prisoner in Morro
Castle

———

Tries to Make Out a Case

———

Denies That Cruelty Is Practiced to Prisoners
and Generally Ignores the
Facts as Described by
Correspondents

———

Kate Masterson had an impressive résumé. While she was still in convent school in Brooklyn, *Judge* and *Puck* published her popular verse and humor sketches under the pen name Kittie K. At twenty, in 1891, she originated the *Dramatic Mirror*'s popular "Matinee Girl" column and wrote it for a decade. In 1893, she went to work on the women's desk at *The New York Herald*, but soon left to do "special work of a less confining nature." This was a delicate way to describe the burdensome woman's lot in U.S. journalism by 1893, when the number of women working full time on newspapers numbered only in the high hundreds. Elizabeth Jordan described what she and other woman journalists experienced at the time: "Her sex will hinder one hundred times to once that it helps her; the air castles she has spent months in erecting may be demolished by a word; her best work will be taken as a matter of course, and anything less than her best as a deliberately planned and personal injury."

When Masterson joined the *Journal* staff early in 1896, the year Hearst set up shop in New York City, the Sunday editor sent her off to produce full-page illustrated features; one was set in the lab of Thomas Alva Edison in New Jersey, another in Newfoundland, where she talked with some of the province's starving fishermen.

None of these credits pass for war zone preparation, but the likely reason the *Journal* added Masterson to its Cuba roster soon became clear. Ten days earlier, *The World* published its exclusive interview with Commander-General Weyler. How better for the *Journal* to recoup from such a stinging competitive besting than with one of its own that packed more zing? Masterson even broke news. Weyler confirmed to her that machete-wielding women were among the rebel fighters and told her one of them was under arrest. Masterson questioned him about his draconian press censorship edicts and about his reputation for cruelty. She asked if the sounds from Cabanos Prison each morning were from rebels being shot. "War is war," he told her in the interview's most widely republished quotation. "You cannot make it otherwise, try as you will." Masterson and the *Journal* had managed to one-up *The World*.

Weyler also flirted with her. She included the exchanges in her story as dialogue, much in the style Bly developed to showcase the sassy charm she used to extract information. Masterson asked Weyler to permit her to go to the front. Impossible, he replied, it was unsafe, not because of the rebels, but because his own soldiers would all fall in love with her. What about letting her see the prison at Morro Castle? No again. Weyler did, however, lead her on a tour of his private quarters, through a secret door to his bedchamber. He spoke warmly of his children as he showed her their photographs. He invited her to dinner. He even allowed her to cable to the New York office all six thousand words she wrote without interference from his censors.

As a reporter, Masterson's femininity and Weyler's reaction to it provided distinct short-run advantages, the kind woman reporters in conflict situations right up to the present are quick to acknowledge as assets. Woman reporters by 1896 were well accustomed to access points forbidden to women but available to men. To submit to the "as a woman saw it" frame, and to be able to execute it with skill, gave a select group of women a way onto the front pages for major stories and a genuine chance to shine. Would a man have asked about the presence of woman fighters? Would Weyler have shown him his bedroom? Titillating details, which the yellow press favored in the late 1880s, added a dash of prurient spice. In the short run, this approach broke through a few barriers and enhanced a few careers. But this style of reporting—an easy target for ridicule, especially against a deadly backdrop—would accomplish little in the broader quest for professional parity.

Masterson broke more news before she left Cuba. She interviewed a wounded American survivor of the Spanish massacre at the Dolores plantation, and she snuck into Cabanos Prison to interview jailed insurgents. To gain entry, she adapted another ploy from the Bly playbook. "A Journal Woman in a Spanish Dungeon in Cuba," the headline blared, "She Visits the Cuban Patriots at the Risk of Her Life." Masterson had disguised herself in local dress as the wife of a Cuban prisoner. For another story, she reported at length on the plight of Cuba's women and children, including the rebel woman fighters. She even found time for a women's page softy about the cabinets where Cuban mothers stored baby clothes.

On March 28, as Masterson returned to New York, *The Cincinnati Commercial Gazette* announced that Josephine Miles Woodward was bound for Havana "fully supplied with credentials." The newspaper's society editor, a married, thirty-five-year-old mother of two sons, was to report "on the social, military, and political situation," with the requisite mandate, through "a woman's eyes." It is not clear if the idea had been planted by Murat Halstead, who hired Woodward when he was still the Cincinnati paper's editor, or if Kate Masterson's successful splash inspired it, or if Bly's concoction supplied the spark. Yet for some reason, several newspapers around the Midwest responded to the Woodward assignment as if it were news. This included the *Chicago Tribune*, which had just reprinted Masterson's major Cuba pieces for the *Journal* on its own front pages.

Another of Ohio's major papers, *The Columbus Dispatch*, wrote at greater length about what to expect from Woodward. The writer cautioned readers against thinking she could ever be fair and impartial, a posture that is second nature to trained men, the writer asserted. A woman's "naturally quick sympathies" will make her an "unconscious partisan of the oppressed," unable to separate feelings from facts. "Womanly sympathy" was bound to color her accounts. The irony in a pronouncement so tinctured with the writer's own bias was surely lost.

Woodward used her real name for the Cuba assignment, but in Cincinnati she wrote advice columns, features, and social notes under the name Margaret Kent. She attended the University of Kansas in her hometown of Lawrence, class of 1882, nine years before the university offered its first journalism course. Unlike Kate Masterson, Woodward had a derivative military background. Her father, Colonel John DeBras Miles, spent his career as a government agent, assigned at various points to the Cheyenne, Arapaho, and Kickapoo tribes in Oklahoma, Texas, Mexico, and Kansas. Drawing on her childhood experiences, Woodward sometimes lectured about Native American culture and customs.

Much as the *Journal* had done for Masterson, the *Commercial Gazette* promoted the arrival of "OUR WAR CORRESPONDENT" as soon as Josephine Woodward got to Tampa. The *Journal*'s two-column sketch of Masterson's face emphasized her youth; Woodward's made her look haughty, commanding. Woodward, too, landed an interview with Weyler, including the same peek through the secret door. Her piece is heavier on atmospherics than Masterson's, with a poignant mention of the "long line of weeping women leading little children, whom Weyler's edicts threatened to make fatherless." She devoted many paragraphs to the commander-general's facial expression and courtliness and shared with readers her delight in his saying he held her in "highest regard." More vintage Bly. The downbeat in Kate Masterson's interview is the hard news she broke; Josephine Woodward's story runs four columns, news-free. One Ohio paper found it remarkable that the Butcher had not eaten her. Another was more positive, saying her readable articles contained information other reporters missed and then declaring, "The question of whether a woman can be a war correspondent may be regarded as settled."

Halstead, on his return to New York from Havana, published a quickie book, *The Story of Cuba.* In it, he does not mention Josephine Woodward, his onetime protégée, but includes almost in full Kate Masterson's Weyler interview and her feature about the war's impact on Cuba's women. All the same, to keep perspective, no reporting by anyone from the Cuban War of Independence, 1895 to 1898, has had the staying power of stories like "The Death of Rodríguez" by Richard Harding Davis.

The assumptions that underlie *The Columbus Dispatch* editorial about what to expect from Josephine Woodward in Cuba underscored the attitudes and the expectations that a woman journalist of the 1890s was up against if she got to leave the women's page. Centuries of everyone's gender conditioning were still in play, so discordant with the pull of new ideas and ways circulating in the wider culture about what women could be and do. The protections, courtesies, and concessions that the gentlemanly embrace provided were not easy for women to cast off. Add to that the entrenched negative attitudes about woman reporters that editors and publishers kept expressing so openly and the market forces that kept the "As a Woman Saw It" construct alive. The women who used the template did so because they liked it, because they were good at it, or because it offered more interesting and challenging reporting opportunities than they could expect otherwise. Push; pull. The template also had the potential, as Bly had shown as a girl with derring-do, to lead to magazine and book deals, the lecture circuit, money, and fame.

The Columbus editorialist started by saying Woodward's assignment opened "an entirely new avenue of work for women," which, as we've seen, was untrue. Among other women who ventured afar in this particular period was Margherita Arlina Hamm. Two years earlier, in 1894, she was open about the privilege her status as the wife of a U.S.

Kate Masterson and Josephine Miles Woodward
(Kate Masterson, New York Evening Journal, *March 14, 1896;*
Josephine Miles Woodward, Cincinnati Commercial Gazette,
April 5, 1896)

diplomat in Asia accorded her and the access it provided to inside information from governmental, diplomatic, or military sources. In repeated interviews over several years, Hamm insisted that she was the first woman war correspondent ever and the first journalist to tell anyone in the United States and Europe about the Sino-Japanese War. The first woman war correspondent she was not, and her claim to have broken the news of the war's outbreak may or may not be true.

Hamm's case offers a granular example of how such a claim could gain or lose credence. Hamm was a well-known figure, both in Canada, where she was born in 1871, and in the United States, where she moved as a child. She studied at Boston's Emerson College and later at New York University. In 1891, she attracted major attention for a story from Bar Harbor, Maine, about the health of the former U.S. senator James G. Blaine. It brought firm denials from the political reporters she scooped and then their own admissions that she was right. As she sued the *Boston Herald* for libel, *The San Francisco Call* dismissed her as "a pretty girl of erratic habits and a love of notoriety" and "an adventuress, prevaricator, and consorter with disreputable characters." Hamm also wrote the popular "Among the Newspaperwomen" column for *The Journalist,* the must-read journalism trade magazine of the day. In October 1893, she married William E. S. Fales, a well-known writer twenty years her senior who spoke several Chinese dialects. Three months later, in late January 1894, the couple was off for China so Fales could begin his second tour of duty as the U.S. vice-consul to Amoy, in Fujian Province. By some point that June, however, they left China bound for the United States. On August 7, they boarded the SS *China* at Yokohama for its record-breaking time of twelve days and some hours to San Francisco, arriving on August 19. The couple's last weeks in East Asia coincided with the outbreak of the Sino-Japanese War.

Margherita Arlina Hamm, 1899

(New York Public Library Digital Collections, digitalcollections.nypl.org/ items/a01c7d44-32c9-b659- e040-e00a18066683)

Once back in the United States, as the couple made their way across the continent, reporters in Salt Lake City, Denver, and Chicago interviewed them during stopovers, as did Brooklyn's *Standard Union* once they got home to New York. If Hamm, a woman, had so recently been singularly responsible for breaking the news of war in East Asia, not to mention her claim to being the first woman ever to do such reporting, it is more than a little surprising that this would not warrant more attention in the stories produced by the reporters asking the questions. Yet only the *Rocky Mountain News* and Chicago's *Inter Ocean*, with which she was affiliated, even mentioned it. The *Chicago Tribune* reporter said dismissively, "She says she has been correspondent for the *Weekly Times* of London and several American papers." Fales, as a diplomat, said little on the trip cross-country, except that he and Hamm were in Nagasaki for twenty-four hours during and just after the first naval battle and that they met some of the officers involved.

For years, Hamm stuck to her version of events. *The Journalist* published an article as soon as she returned to New York City. Headlined "The Only Woman War Correspondent," and signed "J.C.C." (Jane Cunningham Croly?), it listed ten newspapers for which Hamm "corresponded regularly" in the United States and abroad and pressed all claims to an experience "wholly unique and unheard of. She is the only woman to have intercourse with the Empress Dowager of China, and the Queen of Corea, and this was gained through consular influences." Subsequent published profiles assert that Hamm beat every other reporter on the scene to provide "the first authentic news" of the war and that she used "cable and telegraph lines throughout Japan and China" to send news of the attacks on the palace in Seoul, the sinking of the Chinese steamship the SS *Kowshing*, which left some eight hundred soldiers dead, and an assassination attempt on the life of Korea's queen. Newspaper archives make clear that the first news of the attacks came in a July 24 exclusive from the Associated Press, which cited as its source "an alleged private dispatch." Perhaps she sent that cable; the attribution is unclear, but subsequent reports in the following days have datelines not in Asia and attribution to diplomatic sources.

In January 1895, five months after the couple's return to New York, Hamm clarified what she said had transpired. "After gathering the news I could at the time," *The Atlanta Constitution* reported her saying, "we sailed for America, going, of course, to San Francisco. I had my war story ready—enough matter to make a whole page in one of the New York papers. No information of the trouble had reached Europe or America. As soon as I arrived I offered my story to the highest bidder. The World paid $300 for it and published it in full, and also cabled it to London." Today, $300 would have the purchasing power of $9,000. What seems likely is that Hamm produced a fuller account of events, akin to how Mary Clemmer reported the Battle of Harpers Ferry so many years earlier. The lack of worshipful plaudits for Hamm, beyond those she generated herself, could reflect the lag to publication of the report in *The World,* its lack of a confirming byline, and her evident reliance on a diplomat husband's access and know-how. Or, if her claims were true, it could have been no more than an unwillingness to credit a woman like Hamm with such a major newsbreak.

Generally, it is not pretty, but puffed-up wartime exploits are an occupational hazard for journalism's men as well as its women. The propensity to fuse and confuse details or to exaggerate the extent of actual experiences has many mothers. Bouts of aggressive self-promotion, a deep desire to be taken seriously, the intended or inadvertent haze of unreliable, unverifiable memory offered in repeated lectures or interviews all play their part. Faulty recollections from family, friends, and colleagues are often contributors, especially because they provide obituary writers with details of long-ago events the reporters learn about secondhand. The greatest culprits are erroneous passages contained in the stacks of earlier clips pulled from archives and morgues. Successive generations of writers rely on them, not always with time or inclination to check further, thus they recycle the same errors, inadvertently or sloppily, and turn factoids into purported facts.

In the case of women, it is not hard to see how the impetus to aggrandize or distort wartime experiences could grow out of a desire to be taken seriously, or, how *not* being taken seriously might cause an actual achievement to be diminished or ignored. By the 1890s, war reporting by women was still considered unconventional, even though it was not. In this time of transition, stories of women's bravado were also inspirational, especially when difficult to refute. Mythmaking spoke to a desire to model individual women as standard-bearers, as agents of change. "Energy rightly applied will accomplish anything" was Bly's motto. Self-promotion surely figured in the exaggerations, especially while the suffrage and feminist movements were gaining momentum and needed to provide examples of women's resilience, versatility, and valiance.

Hamm's story aside, published tributes to woman journalists who have genuinely distinguished themselves in the field are valuable, but not if they are exaggerated and not when they make erroneous claims to a "first." Women are likely to have blazed those trails long ago. Their successors might have *felt* like pioneers because they trudged through the same muck and mud as their forebears, making triumphs in every generation continue to feel like breakthroughs. But every time a headline misidentifies a Joanie-come-lately in such a way, it distorts and reduces a long, rich historical record that deserves to be preserved.

Who creates the record, who promotes it, and who wins recognition all matter, as do the arbiters, the people who make the selections. For example, the earliest journalism historians overlooked, ignored, forgot, lessened, or discounted most of the early women of the field, even as these same scholars generously name-checked hundreds of utterly minor figures now long forgotten among the men. No wonder that in 1884, the publishing house of A. D. Worthington chose twenty eminent woman writers of the day to profile in a book titled *Our Famous Women: An Authorized Record of the Lives and Deeds of Distinguished American Women of Our Times.* These were a group of nineteenth-century paragons that included Clara Barton, Susan B. Anthony, Elizabeth Cady Stanton, and Harriet Beecher Stowe. Four journalists made the publisher's cut: Margaret Fuller, Lydia Maria Child, Mary Clemmer, and Mary L. Booth, the first editor in chief of *Harper's Bazaar.* "All over the land," the preface read, "women are conscious of a ferment and disturbance of thought which is the prophecy of better things. Everywhere they are asking, 'What can *I* do to hasten the New Day?'"

In 1897, Frances Willard and Mary A. Livermore, both suffragists, set out to "supply a vacant niche" with their encyclopedia of the nineteenth century's American woman achievers in all occupations. They started with fourteen hundred women and increased the number to fifteen hundred for their next edition. Their choices ranged from obvious to arbitrary to unavoidable, like the collegially reviled Nellie Bly. As for reporters who worked from conflict zones before 1896, the authors include Fuller's work from Europe but exclude entirely the anti-suffragist Jane Cazneau. Mary Clemmer's profile highlights her Civil War reporting from Harpers Ferry; Hamm's profile, notably, leaves out any mention of Asia. The authors omit Susette La Flesche at Wounded Knee and others who did early conflict reporting. They also ignore the splashy Cuba forays of Kate Masterson and Josephine Woodward, which might well have come too late in the publishing cycle for the authors to be aware of these exploits. Yet given the criteria they applied to the woman journalists they do include—Hamm, for example—Masterson and Woodward, who are not in the book, had careers more than significant enough to warrant entries even before Cuba.

The encyclopedia's omissions and exclusions were telling in other ways, too. Bias and discrimination, unconscious or deliberate, cuts all ways. For generations, it influenced reporters and sources, editors and colleagues, readers, fans, friends, and enemies. Willard and Livermore appear to have left out mention of any woman of color in any field. No Mary Ann Shadd Cary or Gertrude B. Mossell, who wrote for major mainstream publications as well as Black outlets, or Ida B. Wells. Not even Ida Tarbell rated a mention, perhaps because she had not embraced the suffrage movement; there is no other plausible explanation. All that is by way of saying that given the shaky frames early journalism historians so often erected, sometimes women who deserved a platform for their achievements did not get one, even when other women did the carpentry.

Neither Kate Masterson nor Josephine Woodward returned to Cuba. Nellie Bly never got there. No U.S. newspapers or magazines sent women to cover the Cuban insurgency against Spanish rule throughout the rest of 1896 or in 1897, although several would arrive soon after. In May 1897, when the *Journal* sent Stephen Crane to Greece to cover its war with Turkey, he brought along his common-law wife, Cora Stewart Taylor Crane, the onetime wife of an English baronet. She had since become a brothel owner and used the pen name Imogene Carter. In its house ads, the *Journal* included her as one of the eight reporters it sent to Greece. Several of them besides Crane also had household name recognition. On April 30, the newspaper ran four overwrought paragraphs signed by Imogene Carter in the top center of the front page. She wrote that she had been flatly refused any letters of introduction to "the people at the front," but that was not going to stop her.

Ten days later, her byline surfaced on the *Journal*'s third page:

Imogene Carter's Pen Picture
of the Fighting at Velestino

———

WITH THE HOWITZERS

———

Last of the Writers to Go; Shells
Screamed About Her as She Left the Field

———

HER BRAVERY AMAZES SOLDIERS

———

Journal's Woman War Correspondent
Has a Narrow Escape from the
Missiles of Death—Train Shelled on the Way to Volo

———

Only 120 words followed, adding nothing beyond what the head-line had already shouted. Carter looked ridiculous. What isn't known is if the few words the paper published were all that she had sent "by courier from the front" or if the editors turned a longer missive into a brief. Sacramento's *The Weekly Bee* slammed the "few lines of slush" and mocked Carter further by reprinting her little story in full. "What Imogene means by having 'one narrow squeak' is some-thing beyond our ken," the *Bee* writer sneered. "As to what these few words of a feminine scream have to do with the battle proper, or the campaign itself, is something which could scarcely be explained even with the aid of a diagram." During the monthlong hostilities, the *Journal* published only a couple of inconsequential paragraphs from her on the editorial page, titled, of course, "War as Seen Through a Woman's Eyes."

A few months later, the insurgency in Cuba was escalating. Riots broke out at the end of 1897 as Spain's commander-general Ramón Blanco replaced Weyler, who resigned. The situation became so tense that the United States anchored the battleship USS *Maine* in Havana harbor, an action said to be for the protection of U.S. citizens on the island. To allay Spanish wariness of the ship's intimidating presence, its enlisted men stayed on board. On February 15, 1898, as sailors rested and slept at the front of the vessel, a major explosion blew up that part of the ship, killing 266. A later investigation showed that a mine had exploded underneath the front of the ship, igniting five tons of powder charges intended for the ship's big guns. The sinking of the *Maine* accelerated the failure of diplomatic efforts, and although the attacker was never officially named, the yellow press accused Spain. On April 25, the United States declared war. Every major U.S. newspaper and magazine, led by *The World* and the *Journal*, mobilized.

By the time of the *Maine*'s destruction, William Randolph Hearst had managed to lure many of Joseph Pulitzer's top editors and report-ers onto his staff at the *Journal*. These included Arthur Brisbane, who was in place running the newspaper by April 21, 1898, just days before the U.S. invasion. Brisbane assembled a juggernaut of hardened stars and stylists to cover the war, again, men with known bylines, some, like Julian Hawthorne, the son of Nathaniel Hawthorne, with a liter-ary touch. For newspapers, Brisbane later said, nothing else mattered for the next four months, not even the latest silent movie or greatest football star. Obviously it was an exaggeration because just as the war wound down, *The Evening World* rolled out a six-part undercover investigation of the growing issue of underpaid, exploitative women's wage work from the shops to the factories to the chorus line. Journalism by this point had also joined that list.

Meanwhile, more woman reporters lined up for Cuba duty. If no assignment from a publication was forthcoming, they used their ingenuity to find a way to go, setting up work-arounds that women would deploy for decades to come. Arthur Brisbane might have championed Nellie Bly and soon the editor Eleanor "Cissy" Patterson, but as he prepared the paper for Cuba coverage with near-military precision, he was adamant about a policy of No Girls Allowed:

> Every beautiful newspaperwoman declared that of all mankind she was best adapted to enter Havana in disguise, interview Blanco, get his views on the war and on the enterprise of her newspaper, and return unscathed. Many tears were shed and much deep, indignant breathing was done by those heroic female reporters because no important newspaper would allow women to risk their lives even for the sake of newsgetting.

This was not even remotely true. By the scholar Carolyn Edy's count, at least a dozen women had credentials for Cuba among 129 accredited correspondents. It appears that most, however, never made it across the Gulf of Mexico unless they went as nurse volunteers. Margherita Hamm, for example, got credentials with an official designation as inspector for a volunteer women's auxiliary, which served several U.S. regiments and other units. She does not seem to have done much reporting. *The Washington Post* carried one story under her name about the soldiers in camp at Fernandina, Florida, and a poem under the Cuba dateline of La Quasina, near Santiago de Cuba, a brief ode to "freedom's poorest blade" she titled "The Song of the Machete." Hamm was one of two woman reporters who won subsequent recognition for their nursing work with Clara Barton, but not as correspondents.

Stephen Crane was in Cuba for the *Journal,* but this time without his wife. James Creelman had been with the Cranes in Greece, clearly taken with the couples-at-war phenomenon. In his view, men who brought their wives to battle zones had a distinct advantage, beyond the utility of an extra set of hands and legs to dash copy off to the cable head. "The swish of the journalistic petticoat on the edge of the military camp meant the bidden leaking of news," Creelman wrote, "and a correspondent with a clever wife beside him was a man to be dreaded by his rivals. For a woman, when she cannot drag forth the secrets of an army by strength, will make a sly hole in some man's discretion, and the news will run out of itself."

The two woman standouts in Cuba came without escort—Kit Coleman, a veteran correspondent from the *Toronto Mail and Empire,* and twenty-three-year-old Anna Northend Benjamin, who wangled the backing of the pictorial magazine *Leslie's Weekly* on the strength of a short stack of published stories that went back less than a year. She had managed in that short time to place her travel writing from Alaska and several light features in publications like *The Outlook,* the *Los Angeles Times,* and *The Boston Globe.*

Initially, a U.S. ban on woman correspondents at the war front officially blocked both women from getting to Cuba, and with so

many soldiers and top reporters needing transport, the women were a low priority in any event. Until Benjamin could find a way, she filed stories from Tampa for the *Los Angeles Times, Leslie's, Munsey's,* and *The Churchman.* Without the customary girlish signifiers, she wrote about the army's horses and mules, and about a worrisome case of yellow fever in Key West.

Benjamin got to Cuba by cajoling the captain of a collier to let her ride along on his coal cargo ship. From Guantánamo Bay on July 15 and from Siboney on July 16, she filed on the preparations for a ship's return to Florida after the Battle of Santiago, a story that appeared under a headline that would have irritated her,

Anna Northend Benjamin

(Obituary, New York Tribune, *Jan. 22, 1902)*

touting "A Woman's Point of View." To get home, she was allowed to hitch a ride on one of the departing transports. Naturally, it fell to Benjamin to help nurse the sick and wounded on board.

Once back in New York, Benjamin wrote more about Cuba for *The Independent* and *The Outlook* and lectured for months on "Tampa, Key West, and Cuba During the War," projecting her photographs with a stereopticon. She made a point in these appearances of disassociating herself from Clara Barton, informing her audiences that she was "not connected with the Red Cross. She went to Cuba as a war correspondent and tells of what she saw while there." A year later she was reporting from the Philippines for *Leslie's* and the *San Francisco Chronicle,* having arrived from San Francisco aboard the *Sheridan,* a new army transport that carried her and two thousand soldiers to Manila.

James Creelman told the story of reporters getting ready for the thirty-mile advance of General Arthur MacArthur's single division toward Emilio Aguinaldo's estimated twenty thousand to thirty thousand troops in the insurgent capital at Malolos. The correspondents were "examining their cameras, chatting with their field couriers, or laughing at the young woman correspondent who had just appeared," who was said to have arrived from San Francisco to do occasional work for a California paper. Despite what lay ahead, with "coquettish" refusal, Creelman wrote, the unnamed woman stayed put. "She had come to see the battle open with the dawn," Creelman went on, "and nothing could induce her to go back to Manila." The young woman's determination seemed unshakable, despite there being no place for her to sleep and nothing for her to eat, save a lump of chocolate she had brought. "The place was full of tropical fever— she brought forth some quinine pills, and took a sip of brandy from a dainty cut-glass flask." Creelman consumed many pages with his colleagues' pleas for her to leave, along with his own warnings of how horrific the sights of battle were going to be. In the end, he wrote, the rats drove her away.

Up to a point, Anna Benjamin, with her oft-described softness, quiet determination, and California credentials, might fit Creelman's description, but the details do not. When MacArthur moved on Malolos, for instance, Benjamin was still on her lecture tour in New England.

Perhaps Creelman's recollections were conflated, reconstituted images from the blur of a quick succession of battlefronts in Cuba, Greece, Cuba again, Puerto Rico, the Philippines, and Korea. Perhaps he was referring to actual woman reporters and wives who were not Americans. Details aside, his reflections do provide the perceptions of a man with firsthand experience assessing the presence of women at war. In 1901, Creelman professed to having "seen women war correspondents on the firing line more than once," and unlike the woman en route to Malalos, they rarely showed signs of "timidity or shockability." Sometimes, he wrote, they had to be restrained from trying to leave the trenches and dash onto the field during military engagements. "They are as eager as men to see the slaughter pressed," he said. But then he added what he thought women lacked as war reporters: "I have never read an account of a battle written by a woman that had anything of the ring and dash of the real fighting." He surely missed Mary Clemmer reporting the Battle of Harpers Ferry out of her kitchen window in 1862.

Anna Benjamin reported from the Philippines for several months, then moved on to Japan, Korea, and China, where she arrived with "no more sense of impending danger than if I had stepped into the train for Boston in the Grand Central Station in New York." It turned out to be the eve of the Boxer Rebellion in November 1899, an uprising against foreigners, Christians, and imperialists in the country. The danger was great, so she left almost immediately, first for Korea and then to take the Trans-Siberian Express to Russia. Everywhere, she kept reporting, mostly for soft features that began to appear in the months following her return to the United States in August 1900. A year later, she was off again, this time to Europe, where from France came a report cabled back to the United States in late January 1902 that "the effects of a tumor" had caused her death at the Château de Lalande outside Paris. She was twenty-seven. Her obituary in the *Tribune* described her as "slight and girlish in appearance," "quiet and retiring to the point of apparent timidity." It said she had none of the self-assertiveness "some might expect in a woman war correspondent." Her femininity must have been an asset, the obituary said, for army officers were glad to help her. She was not, after all, the "pushing, belligerent type." Her last story appeared in *The Atlantic* after her death.

CHAPTER 5

New Thought

Early in the twentieth century, the new American woman became enough of a public presence for pundits to draw a collective portrait of "her who is now always with us." In the view of *The Atlantic*, her "unapproachable prototype" was not Nellie Bly but the late Gail Hamilton, a "splendid" "*sport*," a "clever, high-spirited, self-sufficing, irreproachable," "not too womanly woman."

This new version of womanhood caused all manner of cultural response. In 1900, *The Arena* said "a whole volume of thought in the study of social economics" could revolve around the jealousy men had begun to exhibit toward women whose work matched their own in quality and output at poorer pay. Other articles focused on the women who were becoming journalists, puncturing the prevailing idea that this was glamorous work. There were repeated warnings about the corrupting influence of newsroom testosterone on youthful femininity and the stark contrast between the lives of real woman journalists and their romantic depiction in short stories and novels.

Early in the century's first decade, *The Ladies' Home Journal* asked one hundred top editors of the day—split evenly between men and women, most of them married—if they would favor newspaper careers for their daughters. Forty-two of the women responded and thirty of the men. Of the women, only three said they would want their daughters to follow them into the field; of the men, none. The women cited the impermanence of news work as publications came and went, the constant nervous strain it caused, the tendency of women who did the work to suffer breakdowns, and the disagreeable duties that made it hard to stay high-minded. "It lowers her," one respondent said, "she does it at continual cost." Another pointed out the unwholesome impact of the careless behavior of men in a newspaper office, "the most appalling moral eye-opener imaginable." She described newsrooms as a place where a woman grows "flippant and unwomanly in her desire to be regarded favorably by members of the staff." From one of the men: "I would rather see my daughter starve." In the newsroom, he said, a woman loses her refinement, her gentleness, her womanliness, and her sweetness. An editor in the West expressed satisfaction in having reduced the number of women on his staff from twelve to two. As a group, he said, they had "disorganized our reportorial force, and some had been caught turning in work as their own that their men colleagues produced for them. This may have been gallantry," he wrote, "but it was not business." Another editor had eighteen women on staff over a period of two years. He said four were okay, four got married and left, six broke down, two ended up in a sanitarium, and two others exhibited far too much swagger to represent his paper.

The survey's compiler was the magazine's editor at the time, Edward Bok, who stood against many of New York's more progressive editors and writers who became committed public allies of the suffrage movement as members of the Men's League for Woman Suffrage. Never before or since have influential men been so involved and instrumental as an organized force in a perceived women's cause. The major newspapers and magazines regularly covered the suffrage and anti-suffrage movements, which created substantive news reporting positions for women and significant mainstream attention for an often-despised cause.

At the decade's midpoint, Kate Masterson, the *Journal*'s Cuba pacesetter, idealized this new image of womanhood as an outgrowth of the late-nineteenth-century spiritual movement known as the New Thought. Masterson said women at last had developed the ability to impose reason over their "impressionable, emotional, imaginative, illogical" urges. They had learned not to worry or nag. They had figured out how to vanquish their colds, headaches, and the blues by ignoring them. "She grows more masculine in her way of looking at things, but never more masculine in speech, or manner, or dress,"

Masterson wrote. "She is not readily deceived, nor easily cast off her balance. She ceases to talk about luck as a factor of life."

What did it take for this newly reconstituted woman to make it in journalism? Remember that by 1900, more than 2,000 women had figured that out. Together, they made up just over 7 percent of the nation's 30,038 reporters and editors, but the growth of their numbers since the 1890s was nearly 150 percent. A couple of years earlier, Masterson weighed in on this subject as well. She said the most successful women at the newspapers had evolved beyond the early days of the women's pages and the "volcano of sensational feats" that was stunt work. They had become intelligent, cultured, ambitious, earnest journalists, women with high ideals who understood how the conditions in the field and "the tendency of the times" had made including them "an absolute necessity."

As evidence, Masterson pointed to the many women holding important positions in all facets of the work since the century's turn. She cited their adeptness as interviewers and the edge their tendency to be obedient (!) gave them with editors. A genuine acceptance of women in the field had finally happened, she said, thanks to the "enforced exit" of stunt work, which she called "downright freakish." In its place, women had undertaken important overseas assignments, had become drama critics and art editors, and had represented their papers during the wars in Cuba and the Philippines. No more was the woman journalist a "frivolous and agreeable absurdity" destined to disappear. All the same, Masterson warned women against the entrapment of "egoistic inspiration" or fascination with seeing their names in print. "There are no butterflies among the leading women writers of the day," she said. "But there are many splendid broad-minded women viewing life as it is with a clear vision."

Like Masterson, others who provided advice in the early years of the twentieth century held to the same received wisdom that men and women in the business had been doling out for thirty years. Sharp critical thinking remained essential, a need at last starting to be met by rigorous, full-service women's colleges and academic journalism programs at big state universities. Accuracy, news sense, originality, and discipline were still paramount, along with a thick skin, strong stomach, and indifference to the city room behavior of

Gertrude Bustill Mossell

(Penn Archives Digital Collection, photo by C. M. Gilbert, dla.library.upenn. edu/dla/archives/image. html?id=ARCHIVES_ 20140310004)

men. Other advice givers called for taste and refinement, courteousness, and a high sense of honor. Endurance and excellent health were essential, as was keen eyesight that could withstand the strain of sleeplessness, "exhausting toil," and long hours under artificial light. For women, businesslike clothes were an absolute must.

Gertrude Mossell, in her 1908 advice book for young African American women, prescribed subservience for those who wanted to get ahead in journalism, as she herself had managed to do. "Begin at the lowest round," she advised, "and try to learn each department of work well. Be thankful for suggestions and criticism, make friends, choose if possible your editor." Mossell wrote as G. B. Mossell or Mrs. N. F. Mossell for both Black and large-circulation newspapers and magazines. As early as 1888, she was the only Black member of the Women's National Press Association. For its time, her ability to cross over was uncommon if not unheard of, and she believed the opportunities she had won would come for others, but not until white editors and reporters stopped seeing Black people as a "novelty to be dreaded." She shared Kate Masterson's sense that women had an advantage over men in landing and conducting interviews, a province she predicted women would eventually own. Not once in seven years as a reporter had anyone, man or woman of either race, refused Mossell her request for an interview. "If at first for some reason they declined," she said, "eventually I gained my point."

No known barrier or challenge deterred the women who heard the call. Not the arduousness nor the drudgery, not the insulting way editors spoke about the women on their own staffs, nor the treacly descriptors like "pretty" and "little" inevitably attached to their names. The number of women in the field just kept growing.

Always, it seemed, there were new antagonisms to confront. In 1902, Rheta Childe Dorr, a Nebraskan by birth, returned to New York from Seattle, divorced with a toddler son. She went to work for

The Evening Post and proved her worth breaking news about laboring women in the immigrant communities who by then teemed the city's Lower East Side. In need of more money, Dorr appealed to her managing editor for a raise. He refused without apology, saying that it might be "rough justice" to say so, but women could never expect to be paid like men. Women were "mere accidents" in the workforce, not "permanent industrial factors," and besides that, young men needed to save for the day they would have children to support. Dorr argued back; the hypothetical circumstances the young men of the profession might one day experience were already her own. He then assigned her some book reviews and extra assignments for the Sunday supplement. In other words, in lieu of a raise, he gave her the opportunity to earn more by putting in extra time on top of her already long hours. Nonetheless, Dorr stayed at the paper for four years and left only when he made it clear there was no future for her at the *Post*. She went to Europe to freelance and then built her career on both sides of the ocean.

All the same, there were manifestations of the new dawn Kate Masterson predicted. Virginia Woolf had declared 1910 the demarcation point of the modern era, the moment "when human character changed," when relations shifted between "masters and servants, husbands and wives, parents and children. And when human relations change," she wrote, "there is at the same time a change in religion, conduct, politics and literature."

Jessie Tarbox Beals
(Schlesinger Library, Harvard Radcliffe Institute)

In journalism, the number of briefs where women found acceptance broadened, adding sports to the list and photojournalism for those who could wield a camera. Sadie Kneller Miller, the baseball writer in Baltimore, and Anna Northend Benjamin, in her work from Cuba and the Philippines, stand out in this period. Jessie

Tarbox Beals often gets the ever dubious "first" woman photojournalist credit for her staff job on the *Buffalo Courier,* starting in 1902.
However, that was seven years after Miller started writing baseball
and taking photos for *The Baltimore Telegram* and four years after
Anna Benjamin traveled to the world's war zones with her camera.
National recognition for Beals came in 1904 with her photos from
the St. Louis World's Fair. Some of the most arresting ones appeared
in *Leslie's,* which was among the earliest of the photo-rich weekly
general interest newsmagazines that were receptive to publishing
women's work.

In March 1900, Sadie Kneller Miller entered *Leslie's* weekly ama-
teur photo contest with a candid shot she had taken at Annapolis,
Maryland, at some point in 1898, after the end of the Spanish-
American War. It showed a group of imprisoned but cheerful-looking
Spanish officers captured after the fleet sank at Santiago de Cuba.
The *Telegram* was so proud of the national spotlight this scoop put
on its lady baseball writer that it carried an item of its own, praising
her "clever, impromptu snapshot" of a "rare and valuable scene."
Miller did not win the $5 first prize that week, but *Leslie's* took her
on board. For the next seventeen years, the magazine regularly featured her articles and photographs, dozens of them, from wherever
she went. Her nearly open access, as well as many exclusives at the
U.S. Naval Academy in Annapolis and other military installations,
was one of her curious advantages, highly unusual for a woman journalist of the day. She also had an arrangement in which she gave the
navy copies of the photographs she took under its auspices with
permission for the navy to reuse them for noncommercial purposes.
This remarkable advantage might well have come through her well-
connected husband, Charles R. Miller, who had an appointment as a
day inspector for the Port of Baltimore under Edwin Warfield, who
later would become Maryland's governor. Before that, at the trust
company where they both worked, Warfield was Miller's boss.

At work for *Leslie's,* Miller changed her byline to Mrs. Charles R.
Miller, or Mrs. C. R. Miller. At one of the suffrage conventions she
covered, a woman asked her why she did not use her own name.
"Because," she replied, "I am still prouder to show people I have a
husband of my own." In fact, many of Miller's assignments for *Leslie's* seemed to grow out of the couple's ample vacation and business

travel, opportunities Miller handily double serviced for publication. From 1900 to 1908 she wrote about or photographed everything from static pictures of new monuments to summer beach life on the New Jersey shore, major U.S. political party conventions, and the sites of Europe. She covered the World's Fair in St. Louis and the gold rushers of Alaska and the Klondike, the U.S. Army during the pacification of Cuba, developments in Mexico, a leper colony in Hawaii, and events in Morocco, Russia, and the Balkans. She ventured into danger without hesitation. For weeks, she covered the impact of the Great Baltimore Fire of February 7–8,

Sadie Kneller Miller
(Keith Richwine Collection, McDaniel College)

1904, documenting some of the fifteen hundred buildings the blaze destroyed and the $100 million in damage it caused.

On February 8, 1904, nearly seven thousand miles to the east, territorial negotiations between Russia and Japan broke down. At Port Arthur, in China's Liaodong Peninsula, the Japanese navy attacked Russia's Pacific Fleet. The woman who covered the conflict for *Leslie's* was Eleanor Franklin, another young writer in the magazine's stable. Franklin was born in Indiana, sent to a children's home when her mother died, and then adopted by a family in Kansas City, where she married a man twenty years her senior. Divorced, she moved to New York to pursue an acting career in 1898, when she was twenty-one. By 1902, she had become a regular drama critic for the magazine.

Martin Egan was a New York–based special correspondent for the *San Francisco Chronicle*, where he gained distinction covering the war in the Philippines in 1899 and the Boxer Rebellion in 1900. He initially developed his Asia expertise running a sideline syndicate, the Oriental News Service, which he started while working in British Columbia for the *Victoria Times*. He even found time to earn a law degree. The Associated Press hired him in 1903.

Just before the conflict in Asia broke out, the AP sent Egan to Japan to open the agency's first bureau in Tokyo. His most stunning feat on-site was his deft enabling of the transmission to New York of the AP's report by Richmond Smith on the siege of Port Arthur on November 4, 1904. Seconds or minutes were the usual time for a major wire service victory over the competition, but this story ran days ahead of any other. For the siege story, Egan had negotiated and orchestrated the sending of a government-provided junk to carry Smith's copy to the telegraphers. The feat was so extraordinary that the following day *The New York Times* devoted a separate article to what it called "one of the notable achievements in the annals of American journalism." The boat sailed under a white flag with only the red initials "M.E." on it. More than a decade later, Melville Stone, the AP's then president, said the relations Egan managed to establish with the Japanese government remained unparalleled, "easily more intimate than that of any other journalist."

Eleanor Franklin arrived in Japan early that summer of 1904 with no commensurate preparation. Week after week, as she got to know the country, *Leslie's* published her features. While Egan was arranging his grand stealth maneuver, Franklin's offering in *Leslie's* was "Tobacco's Prominent Part in Japan's Social Life." She got to know Egan, who, dining one night with Japan's prime minister, Count Kōshaku Katsura Tarō, let the Japanese leader know that a woman correspondent had arrived in Tokyo who needed credentials for the war front. The military granted the request. Over time, Franklin's stories from Japan developed a more authoritative air. By May 1905, one of the newspapers that carried her reports bragged that she was "the only woman newspaper correspondent with whom the Japanese war department has ever come in contact." Not "ever," as we have seen. A decade earlier, when Japan

Eleanor Franklin Egan
(Martin Egan Papers, Morgan Library Collection)

was at war with China, Margherita Arlina Hamm could have claimed that distinction for the courtesies extended to her via her diplomat husband when Japan and China were at war.

In 1905, Franklin and Egan became engaged in April or May and wed in Tokyo—or in other reports, Yokohama—on July 19. Four days earlier, with peace negotiations between the envoys of Russia and Japan about to start, Franklin landed an exclusive interview with Prime Minister Katsura. Newspapers across the United States carried her story, most describing her as their own "special correspondent." She broke news. An italicized editor's note to readers above the story as it appeared in *The Boston Globe* announced that "a bright American girl"—Franklin was twenty-eight at the time—had interviewed the prime minister at a point when "any slight hint of what Japan may demand is of intense interest." Katsura told her that in the current fight over the two empires' conflicting ambitions in southern Manchuria and Korea, Japan had taken up arms reluctantly and had overestimated Russia's strength as much as Russia had underestimated Japan's. "However," he said, "our victory does not alter the issue over which hostilities were begun."

Sadie Kneller Miller, too, had her big moments. In 1908, she covered the "great commotion" in the Balkans when Austria attempted its territorial grab on Turkey, and she reported from "unsanitary" czarist Russia during its cholera epidemic. In 1909, she was in Barcelona to report on the city's undercurrents of seething antigovernment anger, and she was on the firing line in Melilla for Morocco's second campaign against Spain. Miller's North Africa coverage, however, did not impress a writer for the *Army and Navy Journal*, who denounced the very notion of woman correspondents at the warfront. They reminded him of the trouble that unprepared, ill-equipped men who reported from the battlefronts had caused the military during the Civil War. He said he wept for any future officers "who shall have their deeds mentioned in the emotional chronicles of a female war correspondent" as she pours "into the agonized ears of the home folk the 'pitiful' tales of discontented privates, who suddenly discover that field rations are not like what mother used to cook."

In social notes, the Baltimore papers followed Sadie's career, as did her hometown paper in Westminster, Maryland, and both Millers as they came and went, reporting in 1911 that Sadie was laid up for a time for surgery. She nevertheless managed a photo essay from a swamp in North Carolina that year before she and Charles left for England to attend the coronation of King George V. Future assignments took her to Havana and to Guantánamo Bay, to the Panama Canal, to Helgoland in the North Sea, and to the Balkans. One of her biggest scoops came in late February 1914—her exclusive interview with General Francisco "Pancho" Villa, the guerrilla leader and most prominent figure of the Mexican Revolution. In an editor's note, *Leslie's* described Miller's interview as "the first time that this striking figure has been pictured to the people of the United States through the medium of a woman's keen intuitive powers." Villa had a message for *Leslie's* readers. "I am fighting for my country, the country that I love," he told her. "I am a soldier not a talker, but if I can make the people of your country understand better what the Constitutionalists of Mexico are fighting for, I shall be glad."

Franklin's career parallels Miller's in their common time frame, their fearlessness, their travels, their affiliations with *Leslie's,* and the respect they both earned on merit for the quality of their work. Yet, as with Hamm, the diplomat's wife, it is difficult to ignore the benefit they derived from husbands who were as supportive as they were positioned to help. Effective partnerships such as these would become a familiar scenario, an obvious benefit, although the edge it provided came with the downside of eyebrows raised over the women's genuine achievements. Still, it should be said that upstanding reporters take advantage of whatever ethically acceptable help they can muster, be it birth, ethnicity, race, connections, affiliations, old flames, clubs, chums, personal charisma, or a ready bank account. The competitive edge that involves money or sex inevitably invites the most scrutiny.

One would think the specter of so many woman journalists on assignment across the globe, accomplishing what had once seemed unimaginable, would have made the practice feel commonplace. Yet as women prepared to cover the major conflicts to come, the press continued to treat their presence as novel, as if the idea of women reporting from battle zones had come out of nowhere.

———

Early in 1907, and again in 1908, "The Trial of the Century" was under way, the first of several explosive twentieth-century courtroom dramas to win that distinction. Henry K. Thaw shot Stanford White to death over the ruination of Evelyn Nesbit, a series of events that created what seemed to be a terrific new arena where woman journalists could again break out of the women's pages, not for staged sensations that involved testing bulletproof vests or feigning insanity, but to cover major breaking news. What could be juicier for the yellow press than the murder of a world-famous architect (with a kinky penchant for underage girls) by a jealous husband (an obsessed, aging, cocaine-addicted millionaire), incensed over the ravaging of his young (arrestingly beautiful heartthrob of a model-actress) wife, whose mother's avarice stole her innocence and made her prey to the whims of older men of means? The courtroom proceedings were rich with accusations of sordid sex and rape and suggestions of hypnosis and insanity, not to mention the April–November liaisons encouraged by the woman whose daughter was awash in tears on the witness stand. Day after day, four major women's page writers provided schmaltz-smeared sidebars in return for gigantic name-in-the-headline story display, often in the news pages of the papers. Writing for William Randolph Hearst's empire and various agencies were Dorothy Dix, the doyenne of advice columnists, and Winifred Black of San Francisco and Ada Patterson, the latter two known earlier in their careers as West Coast Nellie Blys. The up-and-coming Nixola Greeley-Smith represented Joseph Pulitzer's *World*.

At around the same time, what seems in retrospect like a counteroffensive gained ground from woman reporters who opposed this embarrassing new trend. Sadie Kneller Miller, for *Leslie's*, motored through Cuba's interior with a woman friend to demonstrate it was safe. Rheta Childe Dorr led the cover of *Harper's Weekly* with her report "Bullying the Woman Worker." Gertrude Mossell completed her book and called it *The Work of the Afro-American Woman.* Martin and Eleanor Franklin Egan joined the rest of elite Washington in the East Room of the White House for one of the winter dinners Theodore Roosevelt hosted annually as tributes to the various branches of government, this one in honor of Congress. And the "strong," "dashing," "sparkling" Kate Masterson won published praise for all the scoops she had nabbed with "nerve and ingenuity that neither man nor woman had been able to procure."

Nixola Greeley-Smith built an amazing reputation on the women's page of *The World* almost from her first assignments in 1901. She quickly became known among colleagues as an interviewer of transcendent skill, someone who, in fluent French, German, or English, could "get at" anybody, who could " 'break in' where angels feared to tread." In 1902, she did not hesitate to publish her conversation with the never-before-interviewed Mrs. John Jacob Astor. The reporter got to meet with New York society's reigning queen on the strength of her own name and a letter of introduction from the U.S. senator Chauncey Depew. But when Greeley-Smith returned to the Astor home as a courtesy to confirm she could quote from their conversation, Mrs. Astor sent her maid to the door to refuse Greeley-Smith a second audience. She had the maid hand the reporter a $2 bill to compensate the young wage worker for the time she wasted in making the fruitless trip. Greeley-Smith, not quite twenty-two at the time, had arrogance to match Mrs. Astor's. She handed the money back to the maid with a request that she remind her employer that while Mr. Astor was still skinning rabbits, Greeley-Smith's grandfather was publishing the *New York Tribune*. And with that, the interview became the cover of *The Sunday World* "Extra Magazine" of March 9, 1902, signed by "Nixola Greeley-Smith, Granddaughter of Horace Greeley." Its revelations were innocuous enough. Mrs. Astor said it took a college degree for a man to qualify as a gentleman, that she only met people who came with worthy letters of introduction, especially foreigners, and that

Nixola Greeley-Smith
(The Day Book *[Chicago]*,
Oct. 30, 1913)

she disdained the millionaire arrivistes from the West now crowding Newport.

Nevertheless, in *The World*'s rivalry with the *Journal,* Greeley-
Smith's "get" in and of itself was gargantuan. A Maryland paper playfully reported that it had driven several of Hearst's "big chiefs" to
utter "language not found in the Koran" and dissolved Hearst himself
into an anger both "picturesque and sublime." All the *Journal* could
muster in response was to ponder the who-is-a-gentleman question.
Mark Twain did the same in a column of his own. "To be told to my
face, and in cold type, that I am no gentleman?" Twain huffed. "And
all because I was not fortunate enough to have a rich father to send
me to college?"

In 1906, the year before the Thaw trial, Greeley-Smith told an
interviewer from the rival *New York Herald* that she thought of herself not as a yellow journalist but as "cream-colored," and that she
liked the work she was doing. "My 'Hints and Helps for Lovers,' my
'Safe Advice to Distressed Husbands and Wives,' all the things I have
done in my five years of work on the New York World I personally consider worthwhile," she said. The *Herald* reporter asked what
her grandfather, the great innovator, the mighty champion of the
great Margaret Fuller, might say about her choice of subject matter.
Greeley-Smith said she felt sure he would be pleased. As for Fuller,
she added, she would have made a great editor for Greeley-Smith's
"Betty's Balm for Lovers" columns. "She would find that people are
much more interested in every day [*sic*] things," she said, "in things
that intimately affect their lives and their mundane happiness, than
they are in transcendentalism and other dull things she wrote about
in the Tribune fifty odd years ago."

Greeley-Smith's main courtroom competitors, Dorothy Dix, Winifred Black, and Ada Patterson, all at least twenty years her senior,
had reputations so fixed in the national consciousness that one editorial writer wondered about the shame they were bound to feel once
the Thaw trial ended since it seemed to hypnotize them and cost
them their sensibility. Dix had written that despite all the evidence of
Thaw's alleged insanity, his devotion to his wife stood out as the "one
true, sweet note," "the one beautiful and noble thing in the whole
sordid history." That same week, Ada Patterson defended the editors
who sent woman writers like herself into the courtroom to supply

what the public demanded: "that woman shall supplement man in the world's work." Supplement, she emphasized, not supplant. This was another of those subordinating shoot-yourself-in-the-foot attitudes, long ago accepted by women as well as men, a frame of mind that would help impede women's progress in the workplace for decades to come. Winifred Black that week compared Nesbit to a bedraggled kitten faced down by a killer bulldog. "I wonder," she mooned, "how many hard working absolutely faithful, unselfish, devoted wives who live but for one thing—to please their husbands—are blessed with such loyalty as I saw written on the face of big, stupid Harry Thaw." Greeley-Smith's reporting claimed the better part of page 3 of *The Sunday World* that week. Page 1, of course, went to the newspaper's unnamed man on the scene and would throughout the trials. Greeley-Smith's story decried the cross-examination of Nesbit by the U.S. district attorney William Travers Jerome under the headline "The Vivisection of a Woman's Soul." It sent Greeley-Smith and several more of the half a dozen woman reporters out of the courtroom, unable to bear the scene as he "tore the veil."

After the Thaw trials, "sob sister" became the derisive slur for any reporter writing on any topic whose prose aimed to pierce the heart. It is always associated by inference with utterly laughable qualities considered feminine in nature. Soon, the label became so fully embedded in the culture that even sportswriters chose it to describe a colleague or a manager or a teammate who went weepy over an injury or a defeat. More than a decade later, a woman reporter for the *New York Tribune* would describe as sisters of the sob the woman reporters who "prowl around at night writing up murders, if there are any, and instigating them if there are not," who "make friends with the millionaire's butler and write up the costume ball," or who "appear in the movies in $100 suits (alas!) with a neat notebook and a gold-tipped pencil. Didn't the movie director ever see the wads of copy paper stuffed in our pockets and that scrubby yellow newspaper pencil that is the undying earmark of the trade?" Actually, her description fused sob sisters with stunt girls and with the women's page writers who traded in gossip. In other words, a sweeping dismissal of the prevailing image of women's work.

The writer's point was to contrast the still-limited expectations of women in the field with a novel development in New Jersey, where an all-women staff of suffragists had assumed the running, editing, and writing of Atlantic City's daily newspaper, the *Evening Union.* "In a world where women are still used in newspapers to get the 'woman's angle' (very often an obtuse angle)," she wrote, "that's quite a move up." Within six months, however, the paper had been sold and its leadership ousted. The deposed editor, Mary North Chenoweth, protested any suggestion that the women had failed. The change, she said, simply reflected the desire of the new owners to be free from any political party or movement.

The sob sister influence was so pervasive in the early 1920s that authors of short stories, plays, and silent films continued to make it their theme. ("Mary Miles Minter in 'The Heart Specialist': A Pretty 'Sob Sister' on a Big New York Newspaper and Tired of Writing Other People's Love Stories.") In 1921, the *Los Angeles Times* columnist Ed O'Malley dismissed the women who wrote in this vein as yellow journalism's "natural offspring" and lamented that they seemed to have come to stay. He described them as women who "throw Noah Webster into a meat chopper" and turn the mutilated remains into "a handful of literary chop suey" that they string together and then shout, "Copy."

Helen Johns Kirtland with a group of Italian soldiers
near Italy's Piave River, 1918
(Library of Congress, loc.gov/item/2016652127/)

Soon, a tiny vanguard of women began to win full-dress reporter positions on big city papers. "Front-page girls" they became known as, a term they embraced. Starting in 1914, another group of American woman reporters, at least forty of them by the best estimates, got themselves sent or just up and sent themselves "over there" to cover World War I.

Shortly before Austria-Hungary declared war on Serbia on July 28, *Leslie's* ran several of Sadie Kneller Miller's photographs from Belgrade, although they appear to be from her trip the year before. Thereafter, the magazine relied far more heavily on the news agencies for the many photos and stories it published. It did, however, feature the work of the husband-and-wife team of Helen Johns Kirtland and Lucian Swift Kirtland, with some pages bylined by Helen alone.

Forty women surely count as a substantial presence for U.S. woman journalists on-site in Europe from 1914 to 1919. Yet the earliest historians of the period do not mention them among the correspondents, not even the 1918 *American Women and the World War,* which appropriately focused on women's exemplary organization and relief work. President Woodrow Wilson presented the essentiality of the women's war effort, which would have included the journalists, as the reason for his eleventh-hour decision to support the Nineteenth Amendment to the U.S. Constitution and push for its passage to give women the vote. Ratification came in 1920. In 1936, Ishbel Ross, in her six-hundred-page history of journalism's (white) women up to that point, labeled "marginal" the significance of women as war correspondents. Given her book's publication date, that would mean their contributions during World War I and the conflicts that preceded it. "There have been no great war correspondents," she states flatly in *Ladies of the Press: The Story of Women in Journalism by an Insider.* By implication, the highly respected Ross dismissed every woman reporter who had ventured into or found herself in a war zone during the eighty-six years before her book appeared.

Abroad during World War I, among the "no great war correspondents" were high-profile woman reporters like Bly and Egan along with those who worked piecemeal for the feature syndicates and the wire services and those who represented small regional papers with limited reach. When their articles were not tied to specific, time-sensitive events, which was most common, they mailed their stories home to appear with or without bylines if they appeared at all. Yet in these lesser groups were several women with an impressive penchant for self-promotion. After the war, they lectured, they produced memoirs or sat for interviews with oral historians or the press, and they deposited collections of their work and personal papers in university or library archives. This ready availability of resource material has facilitated the efforts of scholars whose own work has brought these women to wider attention than they otherwise might have had. With the exceptions noted, Ross was not entirely wrong in 1936. At that point, the war work of woman journalists attracted notice mostly for the women as women instead of being men. Attention focused on their pluck, their would-be and actual "firsts," or their narrow escapes. Curiosity about woman correspondents in war zones abides, even though its novelty should have worn off by the end of the Spanish American War.

As for the women who wrote for the wire services, their daily straight news stories might have gotten wider and more significant play than their syndicate counterparts, and might even have included scoops, but by design they are usually brief, often colorless, and just as often presented to the public unsigned. When these women produced bylined features, which they often did, client or member papers were free to strip out their names before publication. Editors or staff correspondents on-site representing client or member papers also had the option of melding wire service reporting into their own bylined articles, sometimes with attribution to the original source, but as often without it.

United Press made a woman, Alice Rohe, its wartime bureau manager in Rome. Roy Howard, president of the E. W. Scripps Company, which owned UP, was her sister's husband, although he professed genuine respect for Rohe as a journalist. He once described her as "the best newspaperman in America who never wore pants." Smaller client

Alice Rohe
(Library of Congress, loc.gov /item/2020630659/)

papers granted bylines to many of Rohe's feature stories, and she was successful in the post despite having to learn Italian after she arrived. Twice, she faced accusations of espionage. (This also happened once to Sadie Kneller Miller.) One aspersion against Rohe might have had to do with her friendship with George Creel, whom she knew from their earlier reporting posts in Kansas City, Denver, and New York City. In April 1917, as the United States entered the war, President Woodrow Wilson named Creel to run the Committee on Public Information, the government's war propaganda and censorship arm. Creel, writing after the war, described Rohe as a "valuable volunteer by reason of her intimate knowledge of Italy." In the second instance, Rohe aroused suspicion by taking too many photographs while on assignment in the principality of San Marino.

Edith Wharton, Mary Roberts Rinehart, and Gertrude Atherton, the novelists who went to war, got the attention they expected and earned it, writing for the weeklies and monthlies and then turning their collections of stories into books. The suffrage leader Inez Milholland wrote a handful of pieces from London and Rome for the *New York Tribune*. This was after the captain of the ship she arrived on told her a German U-boat had followed them across the ocean. The Italians soon expelled her for her pacifist stance. The reporters who had established national followings before they went overseas, those whose names endure, commanded equivalent star treatment. Nellie Bly arrived in Austria just as the war broke out in 1914. She made headlines across America over her multipart series for Arthur Brisbane at the *Evening Journal,* syndicated as "Nellie Bly on the Firing Line." Within two months of her arrival in Vienna, she had received accreditation to visit the line that separated the Austrian forces from the Russians to the northeast and the Austro-Hungarian front with Serbia to the south. She was fifty. Three other correspondents, all men, were on that trip, two Italians and an American reporter for United Press.

Two weeks before Bly left for the front on October 22, Rohe filed from Vienna about the once-gay city's gloom in a story promoted as "the first to reach America from an actual eye-witness in Austria." Rohe was said to be "the first American-trained newspaper woman to enter the zone of hostilities." Bly, though, was certainly ahead of any American woman who reported from the battlefields of the eastern front. Her writing from the Polish-Czech border is vintage Bly, never about the wider situation but focused on her visceral reactions to what she encountered: the dirty café tables in Przemyśl and the same rag that the cleaner used to wipe both table and floor; the sensations and sights in the trenches; the soldiers dying of cholera; the weight of her far-too-heavy fur coat. Brave, brazen, and often inane. It was an approach that kept her stories fresh despite the wartime delays to publication.

Eleanor Franklin Egan also covered the war. She was by then a seasoned internationalist. In 1908, she and her husband, Martin, went to the Philippines to coedit *The Manila Times*. They did so for several years until Egan took on a more remunerative position running publicity at J. P. Morgan and Company, where he was valued as a confidant to the firm's top executives. The Egans were players. In 1916, the *San Francisco Examiner* listed Eleanor's forays into Serbia, Montenegro, Turkey, Greece, and Egypt to say that she had gone "further into the war zone than any other English-speaking woman has gone since the hostilities began."

At the behest of President Wilson, Ida Tarbell went to Paris in 1917 to take part in the Women's Committee of the Council of National Defense. She found time to profile the Belgian cardinal Désiré Mercier for *The Red Cross Magazine*. Rheta Childe Dorr, ever more radicalized, headed straight to Russia to report on the revolution as it began that same year. Louise Bryant, with her husband, John Reed, did the same.

Back home, in October 1918, the month before the armistice, Genevieve Forbes, later Genevieve Forbes Herrick, would become one of the original "front-page girls" on the staff of the *Chicago Tribune*. She was a Northwestern graduate in politics and economics with a master's degree from the University of Chicago. World War I largely created the opportunity, as the departures of men who became soldiers allowed her to move "up" to assistant exchange editor ("an amoebic form of journalistic life" involving "shears and pastepots," she called it) and then to cover the outlying police districts as her predecessor left for France. ("Give the new girl a crack at it.") When the regular reporter returned, he did not "pry me out of my job," she said, "because of course he didn't want my job." Instead, he got promoted to a better position and she stayed put.

In March 1919, Nixola Greeley-Smith died at thirty-eight from an acute attack of appendicitis. The occasion prompted *The World* to muse about how much the journalistic universe had changed since her grandfather gave women "greater opportunity than any other editor of his day." In a grand, premature overstatement, the newspaper said Greeley-Smith's too-brief career had seen "the final triumph of the woman journalist in occupying a new profession," adding that it was not because woman journalists had been called upon to fill in for soldiers during the war, as was the case in so many other lines of work. Women were prevailing in journalism, *The World* declared, because their status in the field had already been established. It was at least a hopeful view.

Sadie Kneller Miller spent the war in failing health and died at fifty-three after a week's illness in November 1920. Obituaries were ample in the Baltimore area. *The New York Times* carried only fourteen words after her name, describing her as a former foreign correspondent, photographer, and special writer for *Leslie's*. *The New York Herald* recalled her coverage of the national political conventions—during which she was made a sergeant at arms "to facilitate her work, an office never before conferred on a woman, it is said." It also noted her reporting from Morocco and her Pancho Villa interview "at the time of the trouble on the Mexican border when other correspondents were afraid to seek the bandit." *Leslie's* offered no notice of its own.

Bly was in Vienna because she fled New York to escape prosecution over the business failings of her late husband's company, which she was running. She was still in Austria as the war ended, with friends in high places. After her press trips at the start of the war, she turned her attention to more neutral turf, reporting on the country's war widows and orphaned children. She pressed the *Journal*'s readers to send them aid even after the United States entered the war on the opposing side. She returned to New York in 1919 via the peace talks at Versailles, where no one in President Wilson's circle nor among the military intelligence officers paid the least attention to the clarion warnings about the rise of the Bolsheviks from the "hatty" lady who used to be world famous.

With Bly nearly penniless from the legal disputes, Brisbane gave her a regular column next to his own on the *Journal*'s back page.

Recurrent themes were her opposition to capital punishment, the plight of American seamen who were losing their jobs to foreign workers, and the needs of children whose parents could not keep them. During the two and a half years the column ran, Brisbane also called on her for front-page coverage of executions and kidnappings. She always obliged. The new crop of woman reporters took no notice. To them, the matronly lady in the chenille-dotted veil was more legend than person. "If this was bitter to her, no one knew it," recalled Ishbel Ross, who then was in her mid-twenties and on the ascendant at the *Herald Tribune*. Bly, she said, "had never cared for the opinion of her colleagues. Her eyes had always been fastened on the larger audience. In any event, she was tired and ill, and her main preoccupation was with her abandoned children."

Bly, at fifty-seven, died of pneumonia in January 1922. Brisbane crafted a memorial tribute column that pronounced his old friend and colleague all in caps, "THE BEST REPORTER IN AMERICA," without a gender exclusion. Eleanor Franklin Egan died three years later at forty-seven. The stories about her funeral were almost as long as her obituary. J. P. Morgan was among the distinguished mourners. Her pallbearers included Herbert Hoover and George Horace Lorimer, her editor throughout World War I at *The Saturday Evening Post*. This included her time in Serbia in 1916 for the Sanitary Commission of the Red Cross. The *New York Herald Tribune* summarized her many credits, including her appointment by the late president Warren G. Harding as a member of an advisory committee to the American delegation to the conference on arms limitation. "She was in London when the Zeppelins were bombing the city," the newspaper said. "She was in Mesopotamia when the English were fighting their way toward Baghdad; she traversed the Mediterranean when vessels by the hundreds cowered at Gibraltar in fear of the U-boats. She waited in the Hall of Mirrors while the peace treaty was signed at Versailles. She was a traveler in Bolshevik Russia and in India before and after the recent period of unrest there. She wrote of the after-war days in Japan." *The New York Times* reported that after the funeral a grief-stricken Martin Egan, so instrumental in her journalistic evolution, could not bring himself to leave the church for a good ten minutes.

During World War I, Kate Masterson would not become an

editor's choice to interview foreign commandants. After Cuba, most of her published work was fiction or essays on soft women's themes. Around 1915, her life took a difficult turn. Her troubles became obvious from a series of inflamed letters she sent to public officials. She became so delusional that her brother, the New York Supreme Court justice William J. Kelly, had her committed to an asylum. When she died at fifty-six in 1927, only a few papers published an obituary. The *Brooklyn Eagle* recalled that she had been "at one time one of the best known newspaper women of New York." The *Times* and the *New York Herald Tribune,* which both reported her breakdown, ignored her death. The president of the Woman's Press Club of New York City sent the *Herald Tribune* a poignant tribute that the newspaper published as a letter to the editor. "The tragic events of her life demanded heavy toll," the club president wrote. "She is well remembered by a circle of the older newspaper set, in which she shone as a particular star."

CHAPTER 6

Janus-Faced

Social upheaval in Europe in the 1920s and 1930s shaped several of the most prominent careers of woman journalists in the twentieth century. Dozens if not hundreds of "front-page girls" took the one or two places allowed them in newspaper city rooms large and small across America. They gained respect doing "men's work," often still with women's-interest coloration, but their successes created a slender opening for others who could demonstrate like ability. The grumbling for parity grew louder, but only by a few decibels, and in a newsroom atmosphere still rife with denigration, disparagement, discrimination, and diminution. Some of this, it must be said, was self-inflicted.

In 1921, as young women poured out of the nation's colleges, newspapers and magazines were so stingy with opportunity that a Vassar professor steered the aspiring writers at his all-women college toward careers in publicity or advertising. Editors, he reasoned, still clung to the belief that woman reporters lacked the versatility for all-purpose staff positions. The statistics told the story. Between 1920 and 1930, the number of women in the profession had indeed doubled yet again, but in the following decade their presence in the field grew only slightly, rising between 1930 and 1940 from 11,924 women to 14,750; the Depression was surely a factor. As late as 1926 in New York City, where the most ambitious women thronged, their opportunities were so limited that no more than a couple dozen women had jobs at all thirteen daily newspapers combined.

Men as reporters and editors had the freedom to flit from publication to publication. Not the women. For those who managed to find work at mainstream outlets, the safest course was to stay put, even in the drudge-filled jobs available to them. "We already have a woman" was the far too familiar refrain. This did not stop the director of Columbia's graduate journalism school from glowing as he spoke of the talented women the school had graduated in its first thirteen years. Pressed in 1925 to articulate what still stood in their way, he faulted the women themselves. They focused too much on what they could do over how well they could do it. "Women are usually the originators," he said, "and yet they let the men get ahead of them."

Fannie Hurst, inevitably described as the country's "highest paid short story writer" until her death in 1968, dabbled in journalism as so many fiction writers did, mostly for the highest-paying magazines. She was among the woman writers who traveled to Russia in the 1920s to report on how its people were faring in the grand, alluring socialist experiment with its progressive stance on women's equality. "Main Street-Russia" was Hurst's three-part series, for which *McCall's* paid her $10,000 and published in the first three months of 1925. Her Russian-born, Russian-speaking husband, a concert pianist, served as her interpreter.

Hurst, of the generation of feminists born in the mid-1880s, was a major but now forgotten voice for women's rights and advancement, a true but unrecognized prophet of the second wave of feminism not yet in clear view. The magazine *Vital Speeches* included a 1934 talk she gave repeatedly in which she urged vigilance against societal conditions set to erase the gains women had been making for nearly a century. She blamed the Depression, the "calamity of 1929," for fostering some of these dangerous counterforces, exacerbated by the policies of Adolf Hitler in Germany and Benito Mussolini in Italy, who had "successfully demoted fifty percent of their respective populations back into the kitchen." Both in the United States and in Europe, women were "being jammed down like jacks-into-boxes," she said. Further jeopardy came from the gold diggers among them. Apparently, Hurst's message had not gotten to the organizers of the "Ideal American College Girl" competition in 1938 when they asked her to be a judge. On learning that contestants could profess no career interest other than housewife, she told the hopefuls, "If this is the younger generation—ugh."

Among Hurst's contemporaries and friends were some of the most outstanding woman journalists of the century's first half, those born in the years from the mid-1880s to 1910: Hurst's great friend the British writer Rebecca West, in 1892, and Dorothy Thompson, in 1893. Among the thousands of woman reporters across the country or those working from abroad in these years, some rose to prominence as ingenues and then flamed out early; some died young or moved on to different pursuits. Others stayed relevant in careers that started out in high school or college and lasted well into the century's second half. Still others started late but lost no ground: Charlotta Spears Bass, born in 1874; Anne O'Hare McCormick in 1880; Marvel Cooke in 1903; and Alice Allison Dunnigan in 1906.

Intelligence and talent were the common attributes of the woman journalists who had success after the opportunity-stricken years of the Depression, as well as for the best of those who filled in for the reporters who became soldiers. Some of the women benefited, as always, from the advantages of pedigree, connections, privilege, whiteness, and mobility eased by financial comfort. Beauty, personal charisma, and a spectacular life force figured for a few. Others advanced on little more than their own determination and grit, outlasting the setbacks the Depression caused and surmounting any other forces that conspired to keep them down.

Catharine Brody soured completely on the prospects for women in daily journalism by the time she turned twenty-six. In *The American Mercury,* she offered a harsh critique of the way things were, larding her piece with examples from her own bitter experience. She dismissed the persistent claim of editors that their reluctance to hire women stemmed from a gentlemanly intention to keep them out of harm's way, where the work so often led. Yet Brody said editors had sent her on late-night scouting expeditions to the far ends of Brooklyn and Staten Island, obliged her to walk miles before dawn to catch streetcars in strange cities, and assigned her to accost total strangers for man-in-the-street quotations. Her first assignment eight years earlier, as a girl of eighteen, was women's night court. She argued that even editors at the stuffiest papers gladly took freelance articles from the women who roamed the globe's danger spots, so why such a hypocritical pretext at home? Why claim the worn-out excuse of protectiveness when the real point was to keep women under de facto quota?

Brody, born Katia Borodowko, the child of Orthodox Jews from Aknīste, Latvia, arrived in the United States in 1904, shortly before her fourth birthday, and became a naturalized U.S. citizen a decade later. Her stealth move to land a job was to impress the city editor of *The Globe,* her instructor for a New York University journalism course he taught in the paper's city room. A couple of years later, in 1921, Brody felt secure enough of her place on the staff to take a six-month leave to go to Paris with an arrangement to file stories back to the paper twice a week. When she returned, someone else was sitting at her desk.

Brody moved on to *The World.* In 1923, she persuaded her editors to let her set out on an assignment of her own making, at her own expense. In a $6 dress with a small handbag for luggage and $10 in her purse, she took factory and odd jobs in twenty cities, each for a week at a time. Her fourteen-part series ran in *The World* from December to March 1924 with significant republication in other papers, solidifying Brody's reputation as a writer. As a narrative construct, this immersive, experiential method was effective for drawing attention to emerging and intractable social problems and became a favorite of reporters, regardless of gender.

As she expressed in her *American Mercury* piece, Brody felt the quest to change the centuries-old mindset of men in her profession was hopeless. But she had not taken into account what the events in Europe had begun to mean for the exceptional career trajectories of Dorothy Thompson and Anne O'Hare McCormick, and would soon mean for other standouts of her generation and the next. Brody did observe with cynicism what she saw as the work-around woman journalists at home had started to enact in their efforts to get ahead. Out went the dowdy clothes and sensible shoes. Long gone were daredevil stunts as a means of winning the attention of the public and an editor's respect. In their place, woman reporters started to attack with their looks and "the susceptibility of men" to their appearance and blandishments. The ploys seemed to be working, Brody said. She could not quite tell if homely girls had stopped trying to get newsroom jobs or if editors had weeded them out.

"I am no Freud and so cannot delve into the sinister subconscious of the newspaper man," Brody wrote, although she did have a three-pronged theory. At bottom, the attitude of editors reflected either a "degenerated, sickly and half apprehended chivalry," the sentimental notion that nice girls should not become "hard-boiled reporters," or a sense that if women felt compelled to forsake the home for journalism, they should tuck themselves away in the women's pages. In Brody's view, prospects were not much better for the woman who did manage to land a city room metro reporting job. For assignments, women could expect "nothing but the crumbs" of unimportant stories, stuck with "the 'woman's angle'" and poor pay to match.

Exceptions aside, Brody surmised that the most insidious issue of all was the unstated, underlying presumption of editors that women lacked the physical and mental capabilities of men, that they simply were not good enough. "The more high-minded the journal," Brody said, "the more pronounced the superstitions." To date, she said, the net effect of the prejudice was how few truly outstanding woman reporters the country had produced. "Perhaps the only real personality so far developed in America was Nellie Bly," Brody wrote, "and she is dead."

Brody's published call summoned a response from the columnist Marguerite Moors Marshall, who lambasted woman reporters for undermining their own prospects. She called out those who never let an assignment interfere with a dinner date, who concocted interviews they never conducted, or who bragged that they could get their editors to ignore their mistakes by complimenting the pattern on the men's ties. Marshall said such behavior left all women vulnerable to a coat of tar from the unreliability brush. Those who did

Ishbel Ross
(Publicity photo, Historic Images)

not behave in such a way were forced to prove repeatedly that the accusations did not apply to them.

With such an attitude prevailing among men and precious few women in positions of authority to challenge it, effective advocacy was unlikely to emanate from the newsrooms. Redress, when the insulting treatment got too horrid, required other approaches. An episode outside the office of Charlie Chaplin's divorce lawyer in 1927 inspired such a move. Chaplin's second wife of just over two years was Lita Grey, the mother of two of his children. Their first son was born six months after their marriage when Grey was fifteen. Chaplin divorcing his child bride was top news everywhere.

At least half a dozen woman reporters were on hand when the comedian emerged from a "war council," a planning meeting with his divorce attorney. Among the stories that ran the next day was one in the *New York Daily News* that devoted the better part of a page to a sympathetic rendering of Chaplin's tale of woe. The story had co-exclusive quotations obtained by two reporters, both men, who traveled from Los Angeles on Chaplin's train. One of their stories described the scene outside the attorney's office where "the feminine among the scribes besought the comedian for his view on women and life." The women had pressed the actor hard about his proclivity for underage girls. Inexplicably, to a woman reporter at least, the men on the train with Chaplin during all those hours in transit left this aspect of the story unexplored. Instead of raising the issue in his story, the *Daily News* reporter chided his woman colleagues for pursuing such a discomfiting line of questioning. He described them without their names as "one young thing," "a flapper-esque chronicler," "a Greenwich Village maiden with the short bob," a "woman who had seen something of life," "the dame with the eye to the practical," and the "lady who had already started to pull out the gray ones."

Three of the woman reporters present appealed to the trade magazine *Editor & Publisher* through one of its columnists for "protection from the gibes and jeers of the mere male reporters." Irene Kuhn of New York's *Daily Mirror* led the charge with Margery Rex of the *New York Evening Journal* and Ishbel Ross, secure in her position at the *Herald Tribune* and highly respected by everyone as the "front-page girl" nonpareil. "The three of us," Kuhn said, "all reporters with years of experience, were expanded with elastic license into a bevy of 'flapperesque sob sisters' and 'giggling girlies' shuddering and cowering as the flashlights went off." She found it "poor journalistic policy to hold up to the reading public's ridicule the women who write for the papers, the success of the play 'Chicago' to the contrary, notwithstanding." She was referring to the courtroom and jailhouse sob sister "Mary Sunshine" in Maurine Dallas Watkins's 1926 Broadway success. (It took another fifty years to become the Bob Fosse musical.) Watkins, as playwright, based her script on the few months she spent in 1924 as one of the women who covered courts, crime, and "Murderess Row" for the *Chicago Tribune*.

The women did not name the culprit at the *Daily News* but argued to the *E&P* columnist that his offensive depictions eroded reader confidence in woman reporters "merely to satisfy the deadline quavers of some reporter who can't construct a good story in any other way." Kuhn said that although city editors by this point in 1927 had shown "whole-hearted" acceptance of women as news gatherers (an exaggeration, to be sure), a minority of men still exhibited their antagonism. "Nobody ever heard of a woman reporter panning a man in a story on which they had worked together," she said. "And it's not because they haven't had reasons. But personal opinions of working qualities hardly belong in a news story."

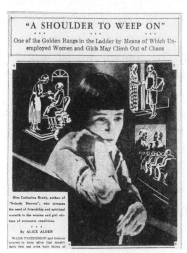

Catharine Brody

(Publicity photo, Harrisburg Evening News, *Jan. 13, 1933)*

Catharine Brody got so much attention from her "Newspaper Girls" piece for *The American Mercury* that she doubled back on the topic four years later, in 1930, for the *North American Review*. This time, her focus was money. She dismissed any claims that women had financial parity with men. Women, she groused, hit their highest earning potential in their early twenties and at the very top never earned more than $50 a week. "No matter how often she may change jobs thereafter her salary will remain about the same," Brody wrote.

Over the next eight years, Brody established a reputation as a magazine writer. She tried her hand at a novel, inspired by that newspaper series for *The World* nearly a decade earlier. More than a score of publishers rejected the manuscript before Longmans, Green said yes. *Nobody Starves,* published in 1932, became a best seller with four printings in its first year. British and French editions would follow. Its book jacket featured blurbs from Lincoln Steffens, Upton Sinclair, and the Nobel laureate Sinclair Lewis, who effused about its literary and social importance, how it "brought to life real men and women working in real factories"; how it transcribed their "fear of unemployment, which is more terrible than war, tragic love, or any of the stock situations of classic literature." Lewis called it "a real proletarian novel." A full year after publication amid a growing crowd of era-themed novels, it still received notice as "the outstanding novel of the depression."

Brody spent a great deal of time in the Ozarks, where her good friend Rose Wilder Lane's parents settled after they left South Dakota, where Rose's mother, Laura Ingalls Wilder, wrote her *Little House on the Prairie* series. The local press made a point of noting Brody's comings and goings, and the 1940 U.S. census has her listed as resident in both Springfield, Missouri, and New York City. "Everyone in 'these parts' will await with interest Miss Brody's new book," an item in *The Springfield Press* declared in June 1934, "because it is confidently expected that this book will repeat the success of 'Nobody Starves.'" Neither of her next two books did, but in 1938 a Boston librarian still placed Brody among the younger Jewish writers who had begun to outpace the middlebrow literary queens Fannie Hurst and Edna Ferber.

After that, Brody lay low for reasons unknown, surfacing only in 1947, when she reviewed some books for *The New York Times.* She died in May 1962 at the age of sixty-two.

Well into the 1930s, editors continued to take their cues from past experiences with women on the job, doubtlessly infused with long-held attitudes about women more generally. As always, the exceptions came at newspapers breathing their last. Two years before the New York *Evening Graphic* folded in 1932 it named a woman its city editor, as the *Los Angeles Herald* had done several decades before that. But that did not stop the straw man of women's presumed inadequacy from looming over the entire field like a gigantic scarecrow.

Ishbel Ross confirmed Brody's observation about the preference of editors for "fetching" girls, those who "fit smoothly into the social scene." At the same time, she cautioned any "girl reporter" against being "too beguiling," the kind who "dazzles the cubs and starts the copy boys writing poems." That type of woman's stock goes down, Ross said. "Trouble, beauty and sex are threats in any city room, and the three can telescope remarkably quickly into one."

Legendary figures like Stanley Walker, Ishbel Ross's city editor at the *New York Herald Tribune,* scowled at some of the newsroom behavior of women he witnessed in the 1920s and early 1930s. He wrote of those who brought attention to themselves in distracting ways, like sitting cross-legged on the corners of desks or on tables and railings. Walker did not say so, but men could and did do likewise with impunity. He acknowledged how important "pull" remained for the young woman who wanted a newspaper job, how often those who found a place had been a schoolmate of the publisher's daughter or the like. Curiously, he said, somehow the system still brought competent women into the field.

Others succeeded on merit alone. Ishbel Ross was one, a Canadian by way of the Scottish village of Bonar Bridge whose Toronto clippings were her only calling card. Catharine Brody, the Yiddish-

speaking peddler's daughter, was another. Neither, however, had the longevity in daily newspaper work of one of the greatest success stories of the era, the "Lady Bishop," Rachel Kollock McDowell. She demonstrated not just what a woman could do but how well she could do it.

McDowell could thank her upbringing for her edge, much in the way of Midy Morgan and her livestock a generation earlier, but with a far different expertise. McDowell had two forebears who were moderators of the General Assembly of the Presbyterian Church. This background was an enormous asset

Rachel Kollock McDowell
(Courtesy of The New York Times/*Redux)*

for a career in religion news. She started out in journalism in 1902 at her hometown paper, the *Newark Evening News*. By 1908, she had developed the religion beat for *The New York Herald* and remained on its staff until *The New York Times* hired her away in 1920. Women averse though the *Times* continued to be, it wanted McDowell enough to stave off a counteroffer she received from *The Sun*. Religion was a specialty side beat, but an important one.

McDowell achieved preeminence. In 1935, a *Time* magazine profile described her, in mid-career, as a "plump, energetic spinster in her 50's" who was "probably the ablest religious editor of any U.S. newspaper." She sustained that level of professional recognition and respect until her retirement in January 1949. She planned to write a memoir but died seven months later, at sixty-nine. Sweetly, her obituary in the *Times* made note of the pride she felt in having established what she called "The Pure Language League" at both the *Herald* and the *Times*. This was her one-woman crusade against the city room staples of blasphemy and profanity. She went so far as to bequeath $3,000 to the Newspaper Guild to perpetuate her mission. When the check arrived, a guild executive said he had no idea what they would do with the money.

Rachel Carson
(CBS Photo Archive, Getty Images)

Other women began to see their bylines appear off the women's pages, too. Rachel Carson, born in 1907, came into prominence in these years. She had graduated in 1929 from what was the Pennsylvania College for Women, now Chatham University, and went on to receive her master's in zoology from Johns Hopkins in 1932. As a writer of conservation pamphlets and radio scripts for the U.S. Bureau of Fisheries, she supplemented her income with features for *The Baltimore Sun.* By 1936, she had risen to editor in chief for the publications of the U.S. Fish and Wildlife Service while freelancing on the side. "Undersea," published in 1937, was her first major article for *The Atlantic.* In 1941, it became her well-reviewed first book, *Under the Sea-Wind,* the first of four, one of which, *Silent Spring,* in time, would bring the greatest, most lasting renown of all.

Ishbel Ross's move to New York from Toronto made her the second woman on the *New York Tribune*'s city reporting staff. Ross was the consummate cover-anything, cover-everything "front-page girl." Although as a rule she did not cover "women's news," she had the suffrage movement to thank for her first career break. In Toronto, an editor hired her to work in the paper's morgue, cutting clippings for the files, with the vague promise of a reporting assignment if the opportunity arose. It came five or six weeks later when no one else was available to cover the visiting British suffragist Emmeline Pankhurst. The editor sent Ross to Buffalo at three o'clock in the morning to board Pankhurst's train. Ross knocked on Pankhurst's stateroom door to ask for an interview and learned from an assistant that Pankhurst had laryngitis and needed to save her voice for her speech. Ross went back to her seat and drafted a brazen little note to let Pankhurst know what an interview with her would mean to Ross's career prospects. Pankhurst agreed to speak with her, laryngitis and all. Ross worked at the *Tribune* through its merger with the *Herald* and into the early 1930s, when she quit daily journalism to write a score of books; *Ladies of the Press,* published in 1936, was her first and still the best known.

Stanley Walker, in his 1934 memoir, *City Editor,* featured twelve of the most outstanding New York City reporters of his day, Ross the only woman among them. He lists a slew of her big-story bylines—the grisly murders and grueling trials, the royal visits, the celebrity and society divorces. There was nothing she couldn't cover, Walker said. To editors and colleagues, she was known as "a quiet, efficient, courageous and always dependable reporter," to which he added a backhanded accolade: "There is general agreement among newspaper men who worked with her that she was the best newspaper woman who ever worked in New York." Soon after, for a foreword to *Ladies of the Press,* he elaborated further on Ross's "unflustered competence," her "lack of giddiness, her clear forthright mind, her amazing and unfailing stamina on the toughest assignments, and her calm judgment." (Notice what the flip side of each of these compliments implied about the characteristics of other woman reporters.) Ross, he said, came closer than any other woman to "the man's idea of what a newspaper woman should be." The "man's idea," of course, was the only idea that mattered.

From firsthand experience, Walker devoted two pages to a biting enumeration of the long-standing accusations against woman journalists. He acknowledged that some reflected no more than outrageous prejudice. But he seemed to relish calling out the "slovenly habits of mind" he had witnessed, like the refusal to look up facts and names, and the screams for "service" from overworked underlings. Women, he said, were known to "sulk at reproof, disdain well-meant advice and, if rebuked sharply for a heinous offense, either burst into tears or lament that a monster office political cabal has been formed against them." They developed fixations on the men they worked with, even the married ones, he said, and "depend, even the good ones, too much upon their male colleagues to help them over the tough places in their assignments. They accept these courtesies as a matter of course, and then, without thanking the man, double-cross him as often as possible." He abhorred the way newswomen adopted the vernacular of poolroom sharks and what he said was their lack of a sense of honor or fair play. Women, he went on, are uniformly devoid of humor, not funny. They lack a sense of the comic or the grotesque, or any of the "high urbanity" that "distinguishes the conversation in a gentleman's club from the banter at a hen party." How often women claim commitment to the profession and then up and leave the job to marry "the first ape that comes along," he wrote. And those who stay, he charged, become "masters of dangerous office intrigue," even to the point of "carrying low tales about their own sisters in the profession and even about some poor lecherous copy-reader who bays at the moon."

Walker acknowledged that men could be guilty of many of the same charges and were known to exhibit such faults in "startling variations." For women, however, he said the range goes from "dishrags" to "queens," from "the sleazy, conniving little ignoramus to the straightforward, capable woman of education and character—with a thousand gradations in between." He believed, however, that the force of these indictments had begun to wane. His further reflection in some ways said the most about the root of the problem, about its primal origins: "Men are afraid of women, afraid and suspicious, for their dealings with this curious sex have taught them caution and skepticism."

Ishbel Ross, for Walker, was the grand exception. In the opening chapter of *Ladies of the Press,* Ross described her days as a front-page girl as missionary. She explained why she, and a few women like her, had so willingly sacrificed the public acclaim of regular columns under their bylines in the women's sections of the newspapers, steady hours that made it possible to "make dinner engagements and keep them," or gave them time "to buy their hats." "They have felt the bewitchment of a compelling profession," Ross wrote, and have "tasted its elixir." They could fathom doing nothing else. "Strange music sings in their ears," she wrote. "Visions haunt them as they walk the streets. They fall asleep with the sound of rumbling presses in their heads." No matter, she said, that they "have seen too much and it hasn't been good for their health." The base requirement for front-page work, she said, was not good writing, since they and plenty of other women had that skill. It was the ability to marshal and assemble the facts of a big story fast, under pressure, in perfect proportion. "This calls for lucid thinking, good judgment, and absolute clarity of style," she wrote. Unlike feature work and enterprise projects, "the pace is like lightning. The most experienced men sometimes fumble among the countless intricate threads when hell is let loose too close to the deadline."

She knew herself to be among the luckiest of women in the profession. For most of her woman colleagues, the chance to succeed at work that elicits such passion never came. "City editors rarely take chances," she wrote. "They want complete reliability. They can't depend on the variable feminine mechanism. They might get a superb job. They might get a dud. No allowances are made for the failure of the woman reporter. She must stand on her own feet and prove her worth every day." Failure at accuracy, the oldest of the charges against woman journalists as a group, still held, Ross wrote. She called it "the one chink in her armor." No amount of careful work by no matter how many women had managed to squelch the perception that women's work was sloppy. As late as 1936, in Ross's words, editors still had not managed to "accept the species without reservation."

Not inaccuracy but an accusation of bias ended the long career of Genevieve Forbes Herrick at the *Chicago Tribune*. Three years after she started, then Genevieve Forbes, she had escaped the shears and paste pots and in October 1921 reported a front-page immigration series that gave her national recognition. It ran every day for two weeks. For the reporting, with a fabricated British passport she assumed the identity of a young Irish immigrant who traveled steerage across the Atlantic to a surly, intolerant reception at Ellis Island, the New York port of entry. This was the same steerage idea that Nellie Bly proposed when she first approached *The World* for a job back in 1887. The impact of Herrick's series was enormous. Days after it concluded in the *Tribune*, the U.S. labor secretary formed a special committee to consider immigrant welfare at the principal ports and convened it in New

Yankee Disguised as a Colleen

Genevieve Forbes of The Tribune staff, as "Immigrant Forbes," trying to keep warm in her Irish smock and characteristic shawl head-dress. The Sinn Fein flag of orange, white, and green is all that she has to remind her of Wexford, Ireland, as the Statue of Liberty comes into sight.

Genevieve Forbes, later Genevieve Forbes Herrick, in the undercover guise she assumed as an Irish immigrant to report on the steerage experience

(Chicago Tribune, Oct. 17, 1921)

York the day after he announced it, saying conditions were "bad, even if not quite as bad" as she had reported. The day after that, President Warren G. Harding ordered "not only a shakeup in the force of inspectors but a revision of the rules and regulations." On December 20, she testified at length during extensive hearings before the immigration and naturalization committee of the U.S. House of Representatives. Like Bly two generations earlier, Herrick had executed a reporter trifecta: excellent series, excellent placement in the paper, significant impact. She moved on to the crime beat, but over the decades repeated references to her in print, including the subhead of her obituary in 1962, cited this early career triumph as her most important credit.

In the early 1930s, the *Tribune* posted Herrick in its Washington, D.C., bureau. The McCormicks, the *Tribune*'s conservative owners, objected to how cozy Herrick became with Franklin D. Roosevelt's administration—Herrick was in Eleanor Roosevelt's clique of favored woman reporters—and how favorably she was filtering advocacy for the president's New Deal into her stories. She was fired in 1934, but found work for NANA, the North American Newspaper Alliance syndicate. Despite her years of reporting crime and politics and the impact of her early enterprise, NANA engaged her to write about women.

In these years, several women assumed top management roles. The best of the success stories give testament to the potential value of women in power positions to the careers of women and other underrepresented groups further down the ranks. In Los Angeles, Charlotta Spears Bass published the *California Eagle* from 1912 to 1951. It was the first and largest newspaper serving the African American and other communities of color in the West. During much of Bass's tenure, she copublished with her husband, Joseph Bass, and together they increased the paper's circulation to sixty thousand. Before she took control, she ran the paper's subscription department and contributed as needed to the church and society news items, usually unsigned.

She bought the paper, on the block for back taxes, for $50. Bass was noted for her effective civil rights activism, her denunciation of

Charlotta Spears Bass

(Shades of L.A. Collection,
Los Angeles Public Library)

the Ku Klux Klan and unfair housing practices, and her protests against police brutality. She was active in the Republican Party until 1940 but dropped the affiliation as her politics radicalized. Her sustained flirtation with Russia and communism put her in the sights of the FBI and the House Un-American Activities Committee, alongside W. E. B. Du Bois, Paul Robeson, and other prominent African Americans. She ran for vice president of the United States with Vincent Hallinan on the Progressive Party ticket in 1952, which prompted *Time* magazine to describe her as the "dumpy, domineering Mrs. Charlotta Bass, Negro, former Los Angeles publisher, and, until 1940, a power in California Republican ranks."

Eleanor "Cissy" Patterson was a granddaughter of Joseph Medill, the owner of the *Chicago Tribune* and *New York Daily News,* where Patterson got her start as a reporter, after which she went to work for Arthur Brisbane at the *New York Evening Journal.* In 1930, Brisbane persuaded William Randolph Hearst to make her the editor of his financially strapped papers, *The Washington Times* and *The Washington Herald.* Hearst had refused to sell her the newspapers but finally relented in 1939. At that point Patterson merged the two properties into *The Washington Times-Herald.* From her power perch, she got behind favored woman reporters like Adela Rogers St. Johns, also a favorite of Hearst's, and boosted their careers.

In 1931, Patterson devoted one of her columns to a surreptitious encounter she had in Palm Springs, California. She had trespassed an estate in hopes of getting to interview the visiting Albert Einstein. Peeking from behind some bushes, she found him dressed in only a small white handkerchief knotted at each corner to shield his wild gray locks. Patterson fled. The day after her column ran, Brisbane playfully responded in his *New York American* column. Under such circumstances, he chided, Nellie Bly would have put a blanket over

Einstein and gotten the interview by sitting on the blanket and Einstein, if necessary, to keep him from getting away. As testament to the regard in which at least Brisbane still held Bly, she, at that point, had been dead for a decade.

Helen Rogers Reid did not follow Cissy Patterson's path. She started as social secretary to the wife of the publisher of the *New York Herald Tribune,* then married the couple's son who succeeded his father in the paper's top post. Helen Reid became the paper's advertising manager, then vice president, then publisher, an influential presence on the paper all along. As a committed feminist and suffragist, she was known for encouraging the paper's coverage of women and women's issues. At key points to come her personal intervention propelled two woman reporters a generation apart into having two of the most remarkable careers of the twentieth century. She divined that they could do the unexpected and then enabled them to do it.

PART THREE

GLOBAL CRISES

1930s–1940s

CHAPTER 7

Practice War

In January 1926, around the time that Catharine Brody unleashed her career frustrations and a colleague despaired over all the self-sabotage she had witnessed, Dorothy Thompson weighed in on these topics from her European roost. Six months earlier, Philadelphia's *Public Ledger* named her its Berlin correspondent and director of European services. As "the only American woman in such a position," *The Nation* asked Thompson to share with its readers the difficulties she had experienced as a woman who had advanced so quickly "to a post of great importance and influence."

To call Thompson "the only" was a stretch. Anne O'Hare McCormick would not be on staff at *The New York Times* for another decade, but her bylines from Europe had appeared in the paper frequently since 1921, attracting wide and serious attention. Alice Rohe no longer ran the United Press bureau in Rome as she had during World War I, but she remained in Italy on and off, never a star but well established, writing for magazines and syndicates. Sigrid Schultz, the French-educated American daughter of a well-known Norwegian painter, matched Thompson credit for credit, if not in public acclaim or collegial affection. Since the war's end, Schultz had been piling up *Chicago Tribune* bylines, datelined Berlin. In 1921, when covering a communist-led street demonstration, she narrowly escaped injury. George Seldes, the bureau chief, identified her in the story as the office secretary, although her byline was appearing regularly. It took sixty-four years and some prompting for him to correct her title and the record, to say that he trained her as a reporter in that period and

Sigrid Schultz
*(Wisconsin Historical Society,
WHI-105049)*

that she deserved more credit than he did for a number of his greatest "world scoops." The *Tribune* named Schultz its Berlin bureau chief late in 1925 and its chief correspondent for Central Europe the following year.

In an oral history interview, Schultz spoke warmly of Thompson, pointing out that they avoided bitter competition because Schultz worked for a morning paper and the *Public Ledger* published in the afternoon. Thompson, for her part, once recalled in a radio interview how Schultz had schooled her in the art of cultivating sources by inviting them home. The apartment Schultz shared with her mother was a high-value entertainment stop in Berlin for stage stars, diplomats, and Nazis "long before they came to power or anyone thought they ever would."

Thompson's essay in *The Nation* might well have acknowledged McCormick, who, with Thompson, was the other star in the making of the 1920s, two women whose astute journalistic acumen far surpassed the considerable charm and femininity they also possessed as key identifying characteristics. By 1926, McCormick, then forty-six, had been writing regularly and featured prominently for five years in *The New York Times,* covering everything from the rise of fascism in Italy to the bored American tourists flooding the Continent. She did this with no more than freelance contributor status under a standing edict from the newspaper's publisher, Adolph Ochs, who opposed the very notion of woman staff correspondents. Even during World War I, when men who left to serve vacated so many newspaper jobs, Ochs did not budge. Jane Grant, however, joined the staff in 1912, first as a stenographer. She took leave from the *Times* in 1914 to help the war effort in France, which is where she met her first husband, Harold Ross, with whom she cofounded *The New Yorker* in 1925. Their nine-year marriage ended four years later. During those years back in New York, Grant continued to work for the *Times,* having graduated to covering hotel news, became a regular at the Algonquin

Jane Grant and Harold Ross
*(Courtesy of the George Eastman Museum,
photo by Nickolas Muray)*

Round Table, and was promoted again. Ralph Graves, the *Times*'s city editor, assured her that the distinction of being "the first woman reporter to serve on the general staff" was hers.

In *The Nation*, Thompson denounced any talk of women's "firsts" as a "disservice," an "anachronism," and nothing more than "the specious feminism of women's magazines." In her view, the question of women's intelligence and ability had been settled far too long for any of that. She found ridiculous the press's propensity to jubilate every time a woman took a job in an unexpected field or rose high in rank. She bristled at the peculiar habit of U.S. editors to make so much of coifs and waistlines. Women's pages, she acknowledged, were practically the only point of entry for women who aspired to careers in journalism, but she dismayed at how the work these sections demanded consumed the talents of women with broader abilities and never let go. She suggested that publications follow the lead of the Paris-based U.S. editor who hired a "bright boy" to cover fashion. Her point, she said, was not that men can do women's jobs better than women but that men and women have interest in each other's lives.

The *Chicago Tribune* was among the many who were not listening. That same January 1926, a full-page house ad under the headline "Why Women Read the Chicago Tribune" showcased the paper's 369 woman employees. It listed all 24 of its woman writers and editors, among whom it classified only 3 as reporters: Genevieve Forbes Herrick of the Ellis Island immigration ruse; her partner on the city crime beat, Kathleen McLaughlin; and Schultz in Berlin. The rest of the women worked on the women's pages or on other aspects of the soft-news report.

In Europe, Thompson found that being a woman did not factor into the difficulties she experienced as someone new to the demands of work abroad. European men accepted worthy women as their intellectual peers. In fact, her only impediment to date had been her lack of an accurate sense of history or a clear idea of economics, not to mention her inability to speak any language but English. As a student, Thompson transferred to Syracuse University from the Lewis Institute in Chicago, where she lived with an aunt for several years after her mother's death and her father's remarriage. She graduated with degrees in politics and economics in 1914, helped by scholarships and the deep discounts that made the choice tuition free for a Methodist minister's daughter. Europe, however, was where she learned to "discipline my memory, and rid myself as far as possible of a sentimental way of looking at things."

Before that, after college, and during the New York suffrage campaign, she became an important movement organizer, speaker, and publicist in the area around Syracuse. Newspapers of the time give ample evidence of her prominence during the crusade's last laps. "We were radicals, liberals, and reactionaries," she would write years later, "raving beauties and plain as pikestaffs; demanding the vote or sweetly pleading for it." The struggle provided a full education in "politics, publicity, public speaking, organization and an insight into every variety of the human condition," she later wrote. It provided superb training in the inner workings of an effective social movement, and, more subtly, in how a smart, charismatic preacher's kid from not much of anywhere could learn to move through the world with sophistication, cultivating those in the best position to advance her career along the way. The battle for suffrage gave Thompson the opportunity to learn not only from the campaign's national leaders but also from the wealthy, worldly society women who embraced the cause in these years, among them Helen Rogers Reid.

By the summer of 1918, after the women of New York state won the vote—the federal fight took longer—Thompson took a job at a social service agency in Cincinnati just long enough to save the $150 that got her to Europe. Shortly before her twenty-seventh birthday, on June 19, 1920, she boarded the SS *Finland* for England with her friend Barbara De Porte, a Cornell grad whose Russian-Jewish descent would prove to be auspicious.

Also on the slow boat was a group of U.S.-based Zionists headed to London for a major conference on the future of Palestine. "To an anti-Semite the trip would be a torture probably," Thompson wrote to a friend, but she turned the time with De Porte and the Zionists into a twelve-day short course in modern Jewish history. The "alien temperament" stimulated her, so she immersed herself in conversation with these "extraordinary people." "If I keep on, I think I shall perhaps become the leading Gentile authority on Judaism," she wrote to a friend. The voyage gave her time to steep herself in the Zionist movement's background, the Jewish quest for a homeland, and what the upcoming conference might yield. By the time she reached London, Thompson, quick study that she was, felt confident enough of her sources and her grasp of the subject to persuade INS, International News Service, to carry her articles on the conference. Sometimes at only a few paragraphs, her stories ran in many of the agency's client newspapers back home, with her byline on front pages as often as not, and for a short time with the words "(An American Girl)" just beneath it.

Within a month, Thompson followed the news trail to Ireland, where she managed two exclusive interviews, one with Terence MacSwiney, the "martyr mayor" of Cork, only two hours before the British military raided city hall. ("Dead or alive, I shall be free in a month!") INS promoted the interview as MacSwiney's last conversation with an American reporter before his arrest. The next day, by chance, she encountered Eamon de Valera on a street in the Irish village of Greystones. When she asked him if the political party, Sinn Féin, would compromise on its demand for self-government, he "dug the toe of his tennis shoe into a crack in the sidewalk." This Eamon de Valera was not the veteran of the Easter Rising of 1916, the political leader during Ireland's War for Independence, and the president of the revolutionary republic's parliament. He was Eamon de Valera Jr., aged six. Thompson followed up with a series of serious pieces about Cork under military rule.

While her Zionist conference and Ireland reporting demonstrated how fast and tightly she could write, she showed her range with a longer, reflective piece on the conference for *The Outlook*. She accumulated many more bylines in print for her reporting from Italy and France and could document a blazing first six months in action as a foreign correspondent.

In the *Nation* essay, Thompson did not mention the role INS played in her European debut but made a point of praising the *Ledger* for never making her self-conscious about being a woman, for treating her impersonally from her earliest freelance days with the paper. Her education as a journalist, she said, she owed to "my colleagues whom I met on the ground of common enthusiasms, interests and difficulties." Thompson's ability to enlist and absorb the wisdom of the better informed became one of her unmistakable strengths. She was close to the men of the European press corps but never blind to the prejudice some of them harbored against women. "A member of the Associated Press recently said to me, frankly, 'Women can never see news. They see either "good" news or "bad" news.'" From this, Thompson surmised, "one must infer that a woman was responsible for the motto of the New York Times!" By that she meant "All the News That's Fit to Print."

She took the advice of Paul Mowrer, the veteran *Chicago Daily News* correspondent, who found her "more attractive, quicker-witted, stronger-willed than the normal run" of young woman hopefuls trying to anchor themselves in Paris, where he was based. He advised her to pick a lesser news capital to work from, a city where competition was thinner. By December 1920, Thompson's Vienna datelines started to appear, first for INS and then in a staff position for the *Ledger,* which set her up for the better assignment of Berlin. Colleagues who watched her in action throughout the 1920s described her as "Richard Harding Davis in an evening gown," summoning the dashing correspondent of Cuba and elsewhere, who died in 1916. The reference emerged from the time Thompson, in soiree dress, borrowed $500 from Sigmund Freud and sped off in 1926 to "cover a revolution," as the legend went; actually it was a possible coup in Warsaw. She earned the sobriquet "amiable, blue-eyed tornado" for the way she tore through Central Europe, winning the hearts of prime ministers and rival correspondents as she went. In the summer of 1921, she "scooped the world" by slipping into Esterházy Castle to interview the emperor Karl and the empress Zita of Austria, the deposed Hapsburg monarchs. The royal couple was being held at the medieval fortress after the first of their two failed attempts to remount the throne. At the time, Thompson could not disclose how she managed to "traverse the 8 kilometers, from Budapest to Tata castle, which was barricaded at every village, and to pass soldiers occupying the town, and to enter the castle's great iron gate, guarded by officers and soldiers." She learned that the emperor did not intend to take back his throne by force. Only later did she disclose that she made the trek posed as a Red Cross nurse.

The American correspondents in Europe were competitors who together functioned like a fraternity with Thompson as its sweetheart. She was never considered the "hellish nuisance" other woman reporters were, in George Seldes's recollection. He remembered her as "the only woman newspaper man," forgetting or unaware that Roy Howard of United Press had already dubbed Alice Rohe "the best newspaperman in America who never wore pants" and Arthur Brisbane had declared Nellie Bly at her death "the best reporter in America." Of Thompson, Seldes would gush years later to one of her biographers, "What a woman!" He also said she "never used sex-attraction to get her story." Did he mean to imply that was how the usual run of woman reporters functioned? Imagine how such a comment would have rankled his successor as the *Chicago Tribune*'s Berlin bureau chief, Sigrid Schultz, or Anne O'Hare McCormick, writing for *The New York Times.*

In 1928, Thompson's marriage to Sinclair Lewis, a second for both, brought her back to the United States. His Nobel Prize in Literature was still two years off, but his ten novels to date already included *Main Street, Babbitt,* and *Elmer Gantry.* Soon after the marriage, Thompson's own book, *The New Russia,* came out some months ahead of one by Theodore Dreiser on the same subject. At the time, Dreiser and Sinclair Lewis were among the best known, if not *the* best known, of all the contemporary novelists in the United States. Thompson cried plagiarism; too many of Dreiser's passages were too much like hers. "Bunk," Dreiser responded. He told the *New York Evening Post* the similarities grew out of the overlapping of their time in the country; he stayed for three months and she for one. He added the fact that they billeted in the same hotel, spoke often, shared material, and relied on many of the same Moscow sources, especially the weekly news bulletin of Russia's Society for Cultural Relations with Foreign Countries.

The enmity festered. In 1931, Lewis, by then a Nobel laureate, met up with Dreiser at an exclusive dinner in honor of the Russian writer Boris Pilnyak at New York's Metropolitan Club. Lewis was asked to offer a few words but said he felt "disinclined to speak in the presence of a man who has stolen 3,000 words from my wife's book on Russia and before two sage critics who have lamented the action of the Nobel committee in selecting me as America's representative writer." A strained silence followed until the twenty-five men gathered changed rooms for coffee and cigars. Dreiser and Lewis stood talking until Dreiser hauled off and slapped Lewis across the face. Twice. Another guest standing just behind Lewis restrained him from striking back.

Dorothy Thompson took a break from reporting and writing for her new role as wife and mother but soon resumed work full force. The celebrated couple inspired the characters played by Katharine Hepburn and Spencer Tracy in the 1942 comedy *Woman of the Year*. The family returned often to Europe, and by August 1934, a year and a half after Adolf Hitler became Germany's chancellor, her warnings about the Nazis angered the Germans enough to expel her, or, in the Nazi propaganda ministry's euphemism, to advise her to leave the country. Thompson provided her own version of the ouster, saying her offense was "to think that Hitler is just an ordinary man, after all," not the Messiah. "To question this mystic mission is so heinous that, if you are a German, you can be sent to jail," she wrote. "I, fortunately, am an American, so I merely was sent to Paris. Worse things can happen to one." To see her off, the English-speaking press corps crowded the Nord-Express station as she boarded the train and presented her with a bouquet of long-stemmed red roses.

A t about the same time, Anne O'Hare McCormick was thriving in Europe. McCormick was the class of 1898 valedictorian of her private Catholic high school, St. Mary's of the Springs Academy in Columbus, Ohio. Her father had deserted the family a year earlier. She traveled often to Europe with her mother, who was a writer and professional tour guide. After high school, she worked for a decade for the *Catholic Universe Bulletin,* rising to assistant editor of the Cleveland-based publication. At the age of thirty, in 1910, she quit to marry Francis J. McCormick, a wealthy Dayton plumbing importer-exporter whose work took him to Europe on frequent extended trips. She went too, and did a little freelancing when she could, helped along by her good training in French and Latin. In the St. Mary's yearbook of 1917, she offered advice to the girls who dreamed of journalism careers, writing, "Only the hardiest and most adventurous spirits have been able to force their way beyond that invisible but firmly established barrier which hedges in the masculine monopoly of the Fourth Estate."

She was already forty when she reached for opportunity beyond her Ohio roots. In 1921, she wrote to Carr Van Anda, the managing editor of *The New York Times,* with an offer to do articles for the paper during her frequent stays on the Continent. He told her to try. It wasn't long before she was so firmly established as a valuable *Times* contributor that the couple moved to New York City and took rooms at the Hotel Carlyle when not traveling abroad.

The story is often told of how in Rome in July 1921, McCormick, covering the opening address to parliament of Italy's king, Victor Emmanuel III, singled out the otherwise little noticed "parliamentary debutant" Benito Mussolini, the founder and leader of the new Fascist Party. McCormick wrote that he made "one of the best political speeches I have heard, a little swaggering, but caustic, powerful and telling." Eighteen months later, Mussolini had control of the country. At that point McCormick prophesied in print that Mussolini would come to leadership in Europe as a man "fired by the Napoleonic ambition to sweep the world off its feet. Sick of socialism, he is frankly a dictator. He proclaims violently that this is not time for democracy. A good-looking man, he glares through the camera into the eyes of the world to impress it that here at last are power and authority."

McCormick sat down with Mussolini more than once and with Hitler, Joseph Stalin, and the older de Valera, too. It's easy to imagine how embarrassing and infuriating this lowly stringer's accumulation of "gets" must have been for the better-supported chief American correspondents based on the Continent. As a rule, these

were men full of self-importance and swagger pitted against a charming, sparkly, matronly freelancer who, working for pin money, big-
footed them with dainty toes. No wonder they took to calling her
"Mistress McCormick" in cable traffic and "bitch" under one colleague's breath. She was, however, largely beloved.

Nan Robertson, in her 1992 book, *The Girls in the Balcony: Women,
Men, and "The New York Times,"* described how eager a listener Mc-
Cormick was said to be, how she never sought to "dazzle" with her
own banter, and how deeply religious she was—"a rarity in an irrev-
erent, blasphemous, frantic profession." Arthur Gelb, in his days as
a copyboy at the *Times,* recalled hearing so many stories about her
exploits before he joined the staff that he expected to find at her desk
a "wisecracking, flirtatious star reporter" like the one Rosalind Russell played in the 1940 comedy *His Girl Friday,* not a poised lady in
her sixties in a lacy hat. Clifton Daniel, who would become managing editor of the *Times,* was Bonn bureau chief during McCormick's
heyday. He confirmed to Robertson that in those years McCormick
never asked for or accepted the usual bureau courtesies when she
came to town, and yet in no time she would have lined up interviews
with everyone who mattered from the German chancellor Konrad
Adenauer on down. James "Scotty" Reston, who knew her from her
assignments for the *Times* in London and Washington, D.C., spoke
warmly of her "sheer gift" of personality, her intelligence, her confidence, and the "glow" she put on whatever she wrote. And yet Mc-
Cormick's name finds no place in the published memoirs of most of
her peers, the men whose careers were distinguished enough to rate
a front-page obituary in their newspaper homes, as she would.

Thompson and McCormick were savvy networkers, like so many
of the standout woman journalists who preceded them. Thompson
not only hosted the literati at home, but over the years added invita-
tions, as *Time* would report, to "more and more experts on foreign
and domestic politics, economists, historians and educators, whose
minds she assiduously plumbed." McCormick, in her freelance days,
befriended Adolph Ochs's daughter, Iphigene, and her husband,
Arthur Hays Sulzberger. This was before Sulzberger became publisher of *The New York Times* after his father-in-law's death in 1935.
"Anne had the map of Ireland on her face," Iphigene Sulzberger
recalled in her memoir, "but what stood out was her innate charm, her

Anne O'Hare McCormick and *The New York Times*'s Editorial Board
(Courtesy of The New York Times/*Redux)*

femininity, her dynamic personality. Her intelligence was a byword."
One of Sulzberger's first acts as publisher was to put McCormick on
the full-time payroll with her own regular op-ed column, alternating
with Arthur Krock's from Washington. Sulzberger also gave her the
first seat ever held by a woman on the *Times*'s editorial board and a
salary, ultimately, among the five highest on the news staff.

McCormick's fourteen prior years with reduced status at the
Times had no impact whatsoever on her standing in the profession at
large or in the wider world. Soon after 1926 and for years to come, she
and Thompson traded major awards and honors. In 1939, *Independent
Woman* featured Thompson in January; McCormick was its "Woman
of the Month" in July. There were honorary degrees, special prizes,
national radio broadcasts, and world-class symposia. The two were
forever being featured on panels, often together. They were peers,
not adversaries. Said Thompson of McCormick, "She is extraordi-
narily objective and completely refutes the often-uttered criticism
that women are always 'personal.' No American journalist is more
impersonal than Mrs. McCormick." Later, Thompson would say that
she and McCormick "often had a good laugh over friends, who, in
the hope of flattering us, had praised one of us to the disadvantage

of the other. I thought she was tops and always said so. She honored me by her esteem."

In 1937, McCormick became the first working woman journalist to receive the Pulitzer Prize since the founding of the awards in 1917. The announcement story on the *Times*'s front page is subdued to a fault. In the stories announcing previous and subsequent wins by *Times* reporters, their names appear in the subhead of the story announcing all the year's winners. The article that included McCormick's award does not mention her in either line of the headline, nor is her prize reported until the fifth of the six paragraphs of the story that appeared on the front page. It does note the $500 prize won for her dispatches from Europe in 1936 and then, oddly, it began to offer up the criteria for her prize category—correspondence, either foreign or from Washington—which had not changed from previous years. The story jumped to page 20 where the explanation of her award's parameters continued for four more lines. No criteria for any of the other Pulitzers were offered. Following the rest of the criteria explanation came one declarative sentence: "It was the first time that a woman received a major Pulitzer Prize in journalism." A brief biography of McCormick appears among the sidebars about the winners. Hers mentioned that she was the first woman to join the *Times*'s editorial page staff, but without use of the more august term "editorial board." It misidentified her high school as a college and said she had earned a doctorate in law from Dayton University. The degree conferred was honorary. It did not share the most telling human interest detail: that it took the *Times* fourteen years to decide to hire her full time.

What a lackluster rendering. Wouldn't the first woman to win journalism's highest honor for the *Times* or for any other newspaper warrant a headline and a fuller treatment? Dorothy Thompson's admonition about women "firsts" notwithstanding, wasn't this news? Did the slight stem from a desire, conscious or not, to avoid attacks from the green-eyed monsters who might have considered themselves worthier nominees? For this, there is some circumstantial evidence. Two days after the announcement of the prizes, Arthur Krock wrote to his bosses to tell them he had learned from a Pulitzer board member that McCormick's prize would have been his had the board not decided to favor a winner from among the foreign entries for 1937, rather than the Washington ones. Krock said he was sharing this information so that his bosses could counter any gossip about his being depressed not to have won again as he had in 1935. The next year, Krock raised the subject again. He now wrote that he had learned from two different sources that he was denied the 1937 prize because the *Times* nominated McCormick and not him. The point of his letter was to put himself forward for a 1938 nomination for his exclusive interview with President Franklin D. Roosevelt. The *Times* indeed nominated him and Krock won. His name appeared in the subhead of the *Times*'s Pulitzer announcement story.

The archives of *The New York Times* and those of the Pulitzer Prizes include actual or carbon copies of nomination letters sent and received. There is no letter on file from the *Times* in either repository sent on behalf of Anne O'Hare McCormick in 1937, or on behalf of Arthur Krock. McCormick's nomination came by acclamation from the Columbia journalism faculty members who made up that year's awards jury, which the board of trustees, all men, affirmed. To put McCormick's name forward, the jury of professors drew from the bound volumes of the *Times* housed in the school library.

Around the same time McCormick won her Pulitzer, Helen Rogers Reid brought Dorothy Thompson onto the staff of the *New York Herald Tribune* to write a thrice-weekly column called "On the Record." It changed Thompson's life. Reid was gambling that Thompson, dogged reporter that she was, could carry off the role of opinion writer. She managed to combine her talent for deep and quick reporting with "an astonishing capacity to read and absorb vast quantities of printed matter." A full-color portrait of Thompson, text in hand, speaking into a bulbous black microphone in the radio studios of NBC was the cover of *Time* magazine on June 12, 1939, with a five-page profile of her inside. "She rides in the smoking car," read the legend under her name.

The writer's lead clumsily backed into his main subject with an anecdote about McCormick, who had just been introduced at the New York World's Fair as "The Woman of 1939." From hundreds of nominations from the public, a jury of women chose her for the honor over such luminaries as Eleanor Roosevelt; the suffragists Carrie Chapman Catt and Alva Belmont; the artist Georgia O'Keeffe; and from the journalism world, Ida Tarbell and Helen Rogers Reid.

Thompson, the writer argued, could just as easily have been the winner, given her 7.5 million readers at more than 190 newspapers—McCormick's column was not syndicated—Thompson's 5.5 million radio listeners, her monthly column in *Ladies' Home Journal*, her six books, her six honorary degrees, and her more than a $100,000 in annual earnings (about $2 million in today's terms). His *Time* profile ran while Thompson was vacationing in California, showing "a plump pair of legs to the millions of women who think of her as something between a Cassandra and a Joan of Arc."

From a latter-day vantage point, the superfluous fixation on Thompson's legs is telling, as are the writer's descriptions of her as once a "chubby, grave-faced maiden," as "husky and exuberant," as "a buxom brunette," and as a "plump, pretty woman of 45, bursting with health, energy and sex appeal." He worked "plump" into the story twice. Even more galling is the insult folded into what seems to be his idea of a compliment: "She appealed to women because she wrote like a woman. She appealed to men because for a woman, she seemed surprisingly intelligent. She thinks, talks and sleeps world problems and scares strange men half to death."

The extraordinary success of McCormick and Thompson should have occasioned a sea change in the prospects for the most able woman journalists who toiled in the United States or in venues abroad. But in March 1937, with nearly twelve thousand women working as editors, feature writers, and reporters at newspapers, magazines, the wire services, and syndicates, prospects did not change. For most, the big leadership jobs, the front page, and the cover story all remained out of range. "There are just as few on the general staff as there were at the turn of the century," said the wife of the publisher of Minnesota's *St. Cloud Times* in a speech to a local reading society. She singled out a number of Minnesota women who owned or ran smaller papers or had solid local careers. She also shared a personal list of all-stars past and present, which included Anne Royall, Margaret Fuller, Midy Morgan, Grace Greenwood, and Gail Hamilton. Aside from Thompson and McCormick, she said, the woman journalists of 1937 "still have a long way to go to establish themselves as first-string news reporters."

CHAPTER 8

Depressionistas

Martha Gellhorn's legacy has endured well beyond those of Anne O'Hare McCormick and Dorothy Thompson. The storyteller has outlasted the pundits. And late in the 1920s, Europe would prove as fertile a professional proving ground for Gellhorn as it had been for her two predecessors.

In 1926, as Thompson and McCormick cemented their stature among the most incisive and knowledgeable American writers on world events, Gellhorn led the front page of the society section of the *St. Louis Star,* with portrait, to announce that she was off to college at Bryn Mawr. In St. Louis, the Gellhorns mattered, their comings and goings eagerly tracked in the local press. Bryn Mawr, just west of Philadelphia, was the alma mater of Martha's mother, Edna Fischel Gellhorn, "the most prominent woman in St. Louis," who, in 1916, "put over the greatest suffrage convention in the annals of America."

Dorothy Thompson
(Bettmann Archive, Getty Images)

The suffrage movement was as formative for Martha Gellhorn as it had been for Dorothy Thompson. The event Edna Gellhorn organized was staged on the opening day of the Democratic National Convention of 1916. Thousands of women dressed in white and sashed in yellow formed a "golden lane" on both sides of the avenue in front of the St. Louis Coliseum. Their aim was to press the Democrats to include a pro-suffrage plank in their party platform as the Republicans had done in Chicago. Martha, seven years old, was in line with her mother. By the time Martha turned eleven, she had organized and become president of the Junior Suffrage League at the Mary Institute, the private school she attended.

During Martha's college years, there were family summer trips to Europe, as there had been while she was in high school. She left Bryn Mawr after her junior year to work briefly in New York for *The New Republic*. Bylines in the magazine were rare for neophytes, but hers appeared three times in that summer of 1929: over her review of a book about "three girls who go wrong, trying to go right"; a mash note to the movie heartthrob Rudy Vallée after he appeared live at the Brooklyn Paramount; and her response to the magazine's review of D. H. Lawrence's *Lady Chatterley's Lover*. Lawrence, she contended, had not fulfilled his aim of wanting people to be able to "think sex, fully, completely, honestly and cleanly." By the fall, she was working at the *Times Union* in Albany, hired on the recommendation of the newspaper's music critic.

Gellhorn's beat was the ladies' clubs—imagine her disappointment—and sometimes the city morgue. The managing editor remembered denying her request to cover crime. Gellhorn remembered a boss who was always drunk and making passes at her. "The blonde peril" was what some people called her behind her back, but most of her Albany colleagues found her pretty and witty and liked being in her company. Her mother in these years would describe her as bold and too incautious, "a knight without armor." Her work in Albany left no impression beyond one unnamed copy editor's recollection of it as "lousy."

Three days before Christmas, Gellhorn had left the paper and was back in St. Louis. She soon traveled to Paris, where United Press hired her as a staff correspondent, which meant she transcribed copy telephoned in by stringers she thought of as "provincial ragpickers."

She remembered getting sent out to interview half of a popular song-and-dance act of Hungarian twins and a well-known French writer. Her name does appear over a couple of other features—one about Marie Chaptal, the French architect of the nursing profession whose softened criticism of American morals she included in a report to the League of Nations, and another about the marriage of a French actress to an Egyptian cotton king.

She traveled to North Africa on holiday with an American friend. On return to Paris, UP fired her. She attributed the sacking to both her poor skills at transcription and the outrage she expressed to her boss after his associate, a South American magnate, became far too "terrifyingly, middle-agedly ardent" in a taxi ride home from dinner. Her boss cited her unprofessionalism as the reason for her dismissal.

Freed from the daily grind, she produced for the *St. Louis Post-Dispatch* a series from Geneva on the woman delegates to the League of Nations conference and hornswoggled the paper into an assignment on spec that took her around the Southwest of the United States and into Mexico. The *Los Angeles Times* ran an item about the "chic youthful blond" who "blew into town" at the end of April 1931: "Martha can't be more than 23 or so, but she has been a correspondent in Paris for the United Press, done North Africa and is generally one of those bright modern girls who are going to make future city editors much more respectful to female writers."

By 1932, back in Europe, it was said that she had secretly married the French writer and politician "the Marquis Bertrand de Jouvenel of Paris," as the *Post-Dispatch* described him. Edna Gellhorn got the paper to stop using his title but remained silent on the actuality of the union. Jouvenel was the son of Henri de Jouvenel, also a writer and politician whose wife hosted an important Paris salon frequented by everyone who mattered in literary and political Paris. Gellhorn had known the younger Jouvenel for two years at that point; in fact, he was why she went to Geneva during the League of Nations conference. Their relationship was tense and intense, complicated by his being married, the disapproval of Martha's parents, and two pregnancies not carried to term. She was in Paris working for French *Vogue* when news of her ostensible marriage broke stateside.

In 1934, Gellhorn published her first novel, *What Mad Pursuit*, which did not break through, and that same year, with Jouvenel, she set out across the United States to do an eight-week survey of Depression-era living conditions in the mill sections of New England and the South. This was under the direction of Harry Hopkins of FERA, the U.S. Federal Emergency Relief Administration. Hopkins also sponsored the photographic documentation of the crisis by two woman photographers, Margaret Bourke-White, who became a staff reporter for *Fortune* in 1935 and for *Life* in 1936, and Dorothea Lange, who produced some of the Great Depression's most enduring and affecting portraits of the down-and-out. Gellhorn's reports for FERA, submitted in November and December of that year, are long, detailed, and poignant and always start with an apology from her for having produced them in haste. FERA dismissed her over an incident in Coeur d'Alene, Idaho, where she had urged a group of men to demonstrate their fury over how a crooked contractor exploited them. They smashed the windows of FERA's local office. The Roosevelts seem not to have been very upset about Gellhorn's role in the incident, for it was after this that the First Lady invited Gellhorn to move into the White House to help her with correspondence and her newspaper column, "My Day." Over the years, when Gellhorn needed favors, say, a letter of introduction from the First Lady to Helen Rogers Reid, or a presidential introduction to the U.S. ambassadors and embassy staffs in Europe, Gellhorn never hesitated to ask and always received.

Martha Gellhorn, May 1, 1946
(Freelance Photographers Guild, Getty Images)

H. G. Wells wrote the preface to *The Trouble I've Seen,* Gellhorn's book about her experience with FERA, published in 1936. To her editor's surprise, it sold well. *The Saturday Review* response was effusive enough to place a portrait of Gellhorn on the magazine's cover. Books woven out of "the very tissue of human beings" are almost impossible to evaluate as literature, the reviewer wrote, but Gell-horn's four stories, which "ring as true as a report from a relief worker's notebook," made her think of "the art inherent in their telling."

For Gellhorn, there was more freelancing, more time in Europe, and a parting of ways with Jouvenel. She memorialized her return to St. Louis in "Going Home," a *New Yorker* piece at the end of 1936. "Too bad we couldn't get to Spain this year," she wrote. "Do you want a ticket for the slaughter at Badajoz, do you want a conducted tour to watch Madrid burning?" This was just before the three hun-dred American volunteers of the Abraham Lincoln Brigade left the United States to join the fight on the side of the republican loyalists allied against the militarists, monarchists, and conservatives led by General Francisco Franco. Gellhorn soon followed with a group of writers led by Ernest Hemingway, whom she had met on a recent trip to Key West.

Neither Anne O'Hare McCormick nor Dorothy Thompson went to Spain during the war, although both devoted columns to it. Gell-horn was on the ground. Gellhorn told stories of the conflict's impact on ordinary people's lives, as she had done so well in *The Trouble I've Seen.* The Depression years, in large part thanks to the expansive FERA project, had given human misery great literary currency. For *Collier's,* Gellhorn wrote about the young volunteers, and for *The New Yorker* she wrote about her trip over country roads with medical personnel who were transporting bottles of blood to the hospitals at the front lines. ("You could hear the artillery distantly; it sounded as if a mountain were caving in.") She reported from the sector held by the Americans, who, that morning, with the English, French, and Belgians, had joined the loyalist Spanish troops in an attack. Every-one, she said, was "in the business of making death, planning it or getting it or keeping it off."

By the scholar Bernardo Díaz Nosty's count, more than 180 of Gellhorn's woman contemporaries from around the world also reported from Spain. The number included thirty-five women writ-ers with U.S. passports, among them Virginia Cowles, Gellhorn's soon-to-be travel-and-reporting buddy, who wrote with distinction for the Hearst papers.

Frances Davis, later Frances Davis Cohen, arrived in Spain with the first group of foreign reporters. She had left Boston and the utopian community in which she grew up for the "glittering prize" of a foreign correspondent's life from a base in Paris. She was the same age as Gellhorn. Her credentials included little more than a degree from Boston University and a couple of years engaged in the deadening work asked of women at small Massachusetts newspapers. None of the outlets she applied to offered to send her abroad or take her on once she got there. So, Davis took Dorothy Thompson's advice and set up her own little syndicate. In Paris, in the spring of 1936, at age twenty-eight, she joined the many "young escapees from Main Street," other women just as "hungry for adventure" as she was. A quick study in the customs, taboos, and rituals of the fraternity of scribes who gathered at the Café de Flore, she soon became a regular presence among them. As she would later explain, whenever two or more foreign correspondents are together, they solve their problems in concert. They share news leads and funds and their recommendations about where to eat, drink, or sleep. They pool transport and figure out how to get their stories across sealed borders and how to extract information when it is being denied. By summer, when word came that the Spanish borders had closed, Davis followed the men out the café door. "Blown by the wind, comprehending nothing," she raced down the rue Saint-Benoît to her pension, grabbed her passport and money, and took the next train to Hendaye at the border with Spain. She said she never bothered to ask who was at war or why.

Once in Hendaye, the men arrived in their chauffeured vehicle, intent on heading to Pamplona through the Dancharinea Pass. They had counterfeit safe-conduct passes to show the guards. They had one made for Davis, too, and offered her a seat in their car as they headed into rebel territory. She licked stamps onto twelve separate envelopes to mail her features to her clients back home. How she envied the men their urgency, their deadlines, the kinds of stories they would bang out on their typewriters for immediate release.

Davis figured out a way to make herself indispensable. She got money from each of the correspondents to cover hotel telephone charges, then collected their copy and hid it in her girdle to evade the military censors as she crossed the border into France. Once she reached Hendaye, she called each man's newspaper and dictated his story. This generous gesture on her part turned out to be her break. Her ingenuity so impressed the *Daily Mail* in London that the editor took her on as an accredited correspondent, as in "The Daily Mail's Only Woman Correspondent with Patriot Armies at the Front!" Note the use of the word "patriot" and not "rebel," the less loaded word choice favored by most correspondents. Of the *Daily Mail*'s bias, she would later say, "I was too full of the privilege of sharing the mechanics of reporting a war to worry too much over what the war was about."

In time, Davis could no longer bear being cast as a "patriot" mouthpiece. She got the *Chicago Daily News* to hire her, too, but held on to her rebel-friendly *Daily Mail* credentials to give her wider cover in the field. Davis's bylines soon began to appear more often. From the *Rochester Democrat and Chronicle:* "Calm, Horror Found in War . . . from the Only Woman Correspondent in the Rebel Area." In *The Hartford Courant,* about the autonomous province of Navarre in northern Spain siding with the rebels: "Woman Correspondent Describes Scenes in Spain." Davis was on her way. Soon afterward, she and her colleagues clambered and scrambled among the rocks to escape a bombardment at the Guardarrama Pass, also known as Alto del León. It left her with a nasty scratch on her leg that she neglected long enough to bring on septicemia, blood poisoning. She entered the hospital, deathly ill. During her confinement a dozen long-stemmed red roses arrived with this note:

FROM ONE NEWSPAPER WOMAN TO ANOTHER WHO ENORMOUSLY ADMIRES YOUR COURAGE AND GALLANTRY. DOROTHY THOMPSON.

Davis's condition forced her back to Boston for further treatment. Thereafter, she spoke through a hole in her throat—her vocal cords had been removed—which she elegantly concealed with bold statement necklaces and her hand placed gracefully in front of her neck. With such aids, she still was able to talk in a high, clear voice. She married, had a daughter, and published books about journalism, utopian communities, and her experiences in Spain.

Since the marriage of Eleanor Newell to Reynolds Packard, the two United Press reporters were always teamed, beginning with the Italian invasion of Ethiopia in 1935. They functioned much like Helen Johns Kirtland and Lucian Swift Kirtland had in their reporting for *Leslie's* during World War I. Eleanor, like Reynolds, was a staff correspondent, not a "special correspondent" or one of the helper-wives that James Creelman had described from the nineteenth-century conflicts he covered. In Spain, the Packards reported from the insurgent capital of Burgos, with frequent trips to the French border to file. " 'Parade of Dead' Sickens Reporter," read a headline over one of Eleanor's stories in April 1937. During a brief truce, she had seen Franco's forces gather three thousand bodies for burial. Note the headline did not say, "Sickens *Woman* Reporter."

Gellhorn's great friend Virginia Cowles covered the war from both sides. She was a terrific reporter, yet editors seemed to find the Boston blue book in her background as interesting as whatever she wrote. In July 1937, for example, she was one of only six of the hundreds of foreign correspondents then in Spain who was permitted to accompany the Spanish loyalist high command as it inspected the government's trenches at the Morata front. The headline over her detailed military report read, "Half of 300 U.S. Youths Fighting at Front in Spain Killed, N.Y. Socialite Discovers."

Virginia Cowles,
December 4, 1941
(CBS Photo Archives, Getty Images)

Gellhorn stayed in Spain six weeks, from March into May, and then traveled to Czechoslovakia. "Come Ahead, Adolf!" was the headline over a story of hers for *Collier's.* Once she was back in St. Louis again, the *Post-Dispatch* ran a blind item about her return, the kind of comment that would dog and irritate her all the rest of her days. It noted the "rising name" this "attractive blonde" was making for herself with her international broadcasts and her articles in *Collier's*. "She's got plenty of talent of her own," the item read, "but it hasn't hurt Martha Gellhorn any to have been a protégé of Ernest Hemingway."

Throughout the 1930s, a good number of women in Gellhorn's age-group fashioned estimable careers at home in the city desk mold of Ishbel Ross. They escaped the typecast of the women's pages and rose as professionals, despite how the Depression had impeded their career aspirations for a decade or more. As the war years ended, as the women neared and then moved into middle age, opportunity still came.

Consider the early working lives of Agness Underwood, Marvel Cooke, Pauline Frederick, and Edith Evans Asbury. Like Gellhorn, these were women born in the first decade of the twentieth century, between 1902 and 1910. Their careers shone less brightly, although a strong case can be made for the luminosity of Pauline Frederick. However, all of these women enjoyed unqualified contemporaneous success, repeated peer recognition, and popular standing with

Agness Underwood
(Herald Examiner Collection/ Los Angeles Public Library, photo by Perry Fowler)

the public and their peers in their respective news domains. Among them, though, only Pauline Frederick had a huge national profile.

Agness Underwood, orphaned at five, was a tenth-grade dropout and a mother of two in 1926 when she started on the switchboard at the Los Angeles *Record*. Within five years, she became the newspaper's "tough, rough, loud and vulgar" crime reporter. In 1935, as the *Record* went under, she joined the staff of the *Los Angeles Herald-Express*. Along with her interviews of major figures like Amelia Earhart and a series on the lives of women in California prisons, Underwood took the lead on just about every major murder in the city.

Marvel Jackson, later Marvel Cooke, grew up in a house her father had built near the University of Minnesota in Minneapolis, the only Black family living in the riverside neighborhood of Prospect Park. Cooke's father, Madison Jackson, equipped their backyard with swings, dollhouses, and a seesaw, the best toys on the block. "We didn't have parks like we have now," Cooke later recalled for the oral historian Kathleen Currie. "We were the most popular children in the area, and the parents couldn't keep their children away from our back yard. The women would then start talking with my mother and my father, and they became very popular. There was no way to get us out of that community." Early on, though, her mother, in frustration, once turned a garden hose on white neighbors who aggressively sought to force the family out.

Her father grew up on a farm in Ohio and completed several terms at Ohio State University between 1898 and 1890, both in the preparatory division and in the college, but did not graduate. He was the first Black person to be admitted to the bar in South Dakota. Unable to make a living as a lawyer, he remained a Pullman porter. Education

Marvel Cooke testifying before the U.S. House Un-American Activities Committee

(Bettmann Archive, Getty Images)

was a high family priority. Cooke graduated from the University of Minnesota in 1925, where she and her sister befriended Roy Wilkins, from Kansas City, "one of the most articulate Black students at the university" in Cooke's view, and an eventual editor, first of the *Kansas City Call* and then of the NAACP's *Crisis,* succeeding W. E. B. Du Bois. Wilkins, like Du Bois, became a nationally recognized civil rights leader and headed the NAACP. For a time, Cooke was engaged to Wilkins, but she broke off the relationship because she found his politics too conservative. Ultimately, she married Cecil Cooke, a Syracuse graduate and world-class sprinter.

After graduation and a job with the U.S. senator Henrick Shipstead, she moved to Harlem, where her introduction to Du Bois came through the place in his heart he kept for her beautiful mother. Years earlier, Amy Jackson, then Amy Wood, dated Du Bois the summer she kept house for a family in his hometown of Great Barrington, Massachusetts. In 1926, Cooke went to work for Du Bois at *The Crisis* as his editorial assistant and got to know the major figures of the Harlem Renaissance. Du Bois taught her magazine makeup and put her in charge of "The Browsing Reader," a bylined column of items from the Black magazines and newspapers. She moved on to become secretary to the women's editor of the *New York Amsterdam News* and wrote on the side.

At around the same time, Pauline Frederick, a 1908 baby like Martha Gellhorn, both five years younger than Cooke, finished high school as valedictorian of her class in Harrisburg, Pennsylvania. She went on to graduate from American University in 1930 with the highest honors for academics and student leadership from the

Pauline Frederick
(Pauline Frederick Papers, Sophia Smith Collection, Smith College)

university's College of Liberal Arts. That same year, Martha Gellhorn left Bryn Mawr, and another contemporary, Edward R. Murrow,
graduated from Washington State University with a major in speech.

Murrow spent his first five years out of school at two different
nongovernmental organizations. He started in journalism as a program booker for news makers at CBS Radio in New York in 1935.
Two years later, CBS sent him to London to direct its wartime operations from Europe. Frederick was no less active during the Depression years, but with nowhere near the ease of Murrow's or Gellhorn's
professional rise.

Frederick broke into journalism well before Murrow did by producing a score of interviews with the wives of diplomats and capital hostesses that she freelanced to Washington's *Evening Star*. The
articles ran almost weekly in the paper's Sunday society pages from
November 1931 to May 1932.

For years to come, Frederick continued to draw her stories from
the wives of officials and diplomats, who became key sources. Later,
she would turn her interviews with the wives and their husbands into
radio pieces for NBC. In Washington throughout the Depression,
she cobbled together a living teaching at a junior college and freelancing for the *Star* and for lower-tier outlets. These included *Uncle
Sam's Diary*, a publication aimed at the college set; NANA, the North
American News Alliance; and *United States News*, the forerunner of
U.S. News & World Report, for which she covered the federal government, including the State Department. As much as Frederick insisted
on recognition as "a regular reporter" not a "woman reporter," every
so often her clippings reveal the pressures and compromises required
of a woman freelancer who needed to make a living. Along with her
stories about official Washington, her byline appears over articles
with headlines such as "Do You Have Achromaticitis?" and "Autumn
Plans the Bedroom."

Edith F. Snyder was variously known in print over her five decades
in the profession as Edith F. Snyder, Edith Snyder Evans, Edith
Evans, and Edith Evans Asbury. She was eight years younger than
Agness Underwood, seven years younger than Marvel Cooke, and
two years younger than Martha Gellhorn and Pauline Frederick. A
brilliant woman, she, like Underwood and Frederick, came to journalism with no advantages of connections or background. Asbury

was the oldest of sixteen children from an impoverished Ohio home near the Indiana border, in "Ku Klux Klan country," as she put it, a place she could not wait to escape. A teacher recognized her promise and guided her to admission to Cincinnati's elite public high school, Walnut Hills, with its curriculum—Latin, Greek—modeled after the top East Coast prep schools. At Walnut Hills, another teacher led her to Western College for Women in Oxford, Ohio, which a scholarship and part-time hours in a fudge factory enabled her to finance. In 1929, after her sophomore year, she left school on learning from a career counselor that a woman could make a living as a newspaper writer.

Every Monday for a year, she took the fifty-mile bus ride to Cincinnati to beg the editor of the *Times-Star* to hire her. He kept telling her she lacked experience. In exasperation, she blurted back, how was she supposed to get experience if he wouldn't give her a job? At that, he hired her to assist on the women's page. She stayed until her marriage at twenty to an army captain and their move to Knoxville, Tennessee, where she finished her bachelor's and master's degrees in American history. She connected with the local intelligentsia, and by 1933 became a star reporter for *The Knoxville News-Sentinel.* "Front-page girl" would have been the applicable description had the term not long since gone out of use. Many years later, asked by Currie, the oral historian, if that was how she would describe herself, she said she was not familiar with the term. Did it mean "somebody out of the play *Front Page,*" she asked, "where people are absolutely eccentric and wild"? Or did it mean someone "who writes so well she's always on the front page"? Asbury was the latter.

By 1937, Edith Snyder Evans had outgrown Knoxville and the marriage. Alone, she went on vacation to New York and, without a new job, resigned from the *News-Sentinel* by telegram and did not return to Tennessee. For fourteen months, to make ends meet, she did a couple of stories for the Brooklyn *Times-Union* and took jobs as a publicist for a Poconos resort and then a Brooklyn hotel. She answered letters to the editor for *Life* magazine, giving up the prospect of an assistant editorship at Fawcett Publications to stay on at *Life.* A week later, her entire department went out of being. At last, in February 1938, she landed her dream job, at $25 a week, as a city reporter for the *New York Post.* It took no time to turn down an offer twice as large to be a researcher for *Fortune*. Another woman on the *Post*'s staff took Asbury under her wing, giving her advice she never forgot, like never ask the assigning editor for directions. Things were going well until the day the city editor sent her to the Gotham Hotel, where a man on the roof was threatening to jump. She stayed all day. At 5:00 p.m., she checked in by telephone to report that nothing had changed. The editor summoned her back to the office at once. She thought he was about to give her a plum out-of-town assignment, but it turned out that she had not survived a round of demanded staff cutbacks. Last in, first to go, she led fifty staffers out the door four days short of her six-month work anniversary. That meant under union rules she did not qualify for one week's vacation pay or any severance. The crying jag the firing set off lasted a full day; the bout with depression it brought on, much longer.

CHAPTER 9

Home Front

During World War II, the number of American woman journalists increased dramatically, yet those with stature below the stratospheric heights, which is to say everyone except Anne O'Hare McCormick and Dorothy Thompson, still had to fight for acceptance, opportunity, and stability in the profession. This was as true at the war fronts of Africa, Europe, and Asia as it was for the women of the Washington press corps and for the expanding group of women on staff in U.S. newsrooms.

Through the recommendation of a colleague, Edith Evans Asbury found a little work covering a murder trial for London's *Daily Telegraph* at $5 a day but had to take up publicity work yet again to make ends meet. Crossing the street one day, she ran into a colleague who had been a cub reporter in Knoxville when she was the paper's star. He offered to recommend her to his boss at the Associated Press. The military's claim on men had made hiring women a necessity again, so she got the job. "We didn't have the same esprit de corps or office friendships because we were all too busy," she told her oral historian. "If you work for a wire service, you work your tail off."

She again joined the working woman journalists, who, over the decade, would come to constitute nearly a third of all reporters and editors. The War Department provided one big boost with the post–Pearl Harbor priority it placed on reporting about wartime conditions for soldiers. In August 1941, the U.S. Army's Bureau of Public Relations organized a women's division expressly to encourage coverage of the health, discipline, food, clothing, and entertainment of its 1.5 million men. Each son, husband, sweetheart, brother, or father in uniform was said to engage the interest of at least four woman readers.

Editors looked to their woman reporters to provide a wartime iteration of the tried-and-true "as a woman sees it" angle and the "Four *Fs*" of food, fashion, furnishings, and family. News organizations had also grasped the importance to their readers and listeners, and thus to their revenue, of putting a war lens on the usual run of soft topics. To whom these assignments would fall was never in doubt.

Fannie Hurst was still waxing prophetic in 1942, her every utterance, it seems, carried by *The New York Times.* "We women are no longer the waiting Penelopes of war," she told a convention of two thousand women at the Hotel Astor. She urged them to see how valuable they were to the war effort and how it would expand their options later. She encouraged the all-women graduating class of Hunter College to envision themselves as "a new species of frontierswomen," ready to capitalize on the opportunities the war would mean and then hold them close, unlike their predecessors, the women who "managed to get inside the door" during World War I but then retreated when it was over. She could not wait for the woman bacteriologists and pilots and taxi drivers to stop being "cute news." She worried that the desire for "four walls and a man coming home with a pay envelope" would overtake the ambitions of the women in uniform and the daughters reared by the career women of the day. The home fires, she predicted, would roar for a short time, and after that women would reclaim their wartime gains. She predicted new status for women but only if, and when, they really wanted it.

In Washington, in 1944, the ninety-eight women among the four hundred correspondents accredited to cover Congress mounted an attention-getting outcry when the White House Correspondents' Association once again excluded them from its annual dinner. "None could dispute that Washington editors need women reporters," the press columnist for *Time* magazine remarked, referring to the protest's leader as the "pert president of the Women's National Press Club." With the magazine's customary stab of disparagement, he noted how the war's decimation of newsroom staffs had brought so many women on board. United Press, for example, had eleven

Flora Lewis
*(Courtesy of Lindsey Gruson,
photo by Bachrach Studios)*

women out reporting on Washington beats and eight more in the office. Before the war, there had been only one woman covering breaking news anywhere in town.

Time conceded that several of these women, scraped as they were from "the bottom of the manpower barrel," outperformed their competitors. Its columnist singled out twenty-two-year-old Flora Lewis of the Associated Press, a recent transfer to the capital from New York City. Only two years earlier, Lewis completed her master's degree at Columbia's graduate journalism school in the same class as another ambitious star in the making, Marguerite Higgins, who was working in New York City for the *Herald Tribune*. The article was about the woman correspondents in D.C., so of the two it only showcased Lewis. As the AP's junior reporter at the State Department, she had recently managed a twenty-four-hour beat with news of a U.S. embargo on oil shipments to Spain. Lewis's story, published January 28, 1944, made front pages across the United States and Canada, including the supreme prize of front-page pickup in *The New York Times*. No matter to Lewis that the paper credited only the AP. "I was very proud of that," Lewis said years later, "because the New York Times hated to use agencies."

Not long before, Eleanor Darnton joined a mass resignation from the Office of War Information to protest its sugarcoating of news about the war. She had recently become the widow of Byron Darnton, known as Barney, a revered *Times* correspondent who had been killed in New Guinea in 1942. Jobless at thirty-six with two sons to support, she appealed to the publisher to give her a job and he obliged, putting her on the general assignment staff in the Washington bureau. Soon the paper appointed her its new women's editor and moved her and her boys to New York. Her son John, a *Times*-man-to-be, would later write about his mother's "broad view of women's interests," her visionary idea of what women's pages could become if not so smothered in spun sugar. She wanted her reporters to produce stories about shortages; textile goods; the health, education, and well-being of children; and plans for related legislation, stories that could run in her section or just as easily in any other section of the paper. It was a vision the other editors did not share. "The news value of these stories is not obvious to men or to desks which for years have ignored the interests of women," she wrote in a five-page letter to the publisher that ended with her plans to resign. The stories, she argued, deserved placement throughout the paper, not confinement on the women's pages. The publisher persuaded her to remain at the *Times* and she did, but only for another three months.

In 1946, she started Women's National News Service, her own agency, with twenty-two subscribing papers at the outset. She partly financed the venture with the insurance settlement from her husband's death and her severance money from the *Times*. The service over the years served up a mix of substantive stories, including some on education, legislative efforts, and relevant stories from the UN and abroad. But alongside these was a steady diet of stories like the one about how thin one's arms should be to wear a sleeveless dress or face-lifts for men or warnings about the perils of spending too much time in the sun. For nearly a decade, the service "limped along," in John Darnton's phrase.

Off the women's pages, the talented, versatile Aline Mosby, a contemporary of Flora Lewis's and Marguerite Higgins's, rose as quickly as they did, but without their facility in languages or a prestige graduate degree or as prestigious a workplace. Her opportunity came in 1943, straight out of the undergraduate journalism school at the University of Montana as she joined the staff of United Press. Ability carried her through a career on three continents that lasted four decades. In the space of two years, she had postings in New York, Seattle, and Phoenix, and at her request she helped cover the foundational San Francisco Conference of the United Nations in the spring of 1945. Comparing the May and June clips with San Francisco datelines by Mosby for UP and by Flora Lewis for the AP, the two were in direct competition. Pauline Frederick covered the conference, too. She was freelancing for NANA but had been sent by her boss of six years, the NBC radio commentator H. R. Baukhage. From

1938 until 1944, between the ages of thirty and thirty-six, Frederick served as his editorial and radio assistant, earning her first regular paycheck since graduation as the American University wunderkind of 1930. For one with such promise, she spent an awfully long time in subservience. Of the three women at the San Francisco conference, Flora Lewis had the highest conference byline count.

After San Francisco, UP sent Mosby to Los Angeles into a dull but customary entry-level job rewriting stories into briefs for local client radio stations to "rip and read" over the air, but she soon landed the coveted Hollywood celebrity beat, where one of her early exclusives kick-started the career of Marilyn Monroe. Mosby identified the starlet as the nude featured on a calendar tacked to the walls of machine shops across the country. Mosby, on two assignments, had well-played nude moments of her own. She covered both a nudist convention and then a nudist charity event in the buff, which gave her stories maximum exposure. Photographic evidence survives. In one photo, which appeared in *Newsweek*, Mosby, fingers poised on her typewriter keys, taunted the camera with a peek into the lens over her bare right shoulder. In the second, she appeared limbs out in UP client papers, hiding her unclad torso behind a barrel. The photos were aberrations. Mosby built her Hollywood reputation on interviews with the likes of Errol Flynn, Charlie Chaplin, Howard Hughes, and James Dean, helped by advice Humphrey Bogart gave her. "Listen, kid," he told her. "Actors are just like people. Look 'em in the eye and bark back."

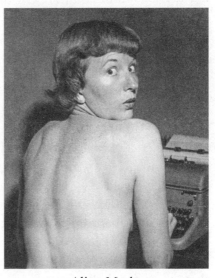

Aline Mosby
(United Press photo, August 1953, courtesy of Denise Dowling, University of Montana School of Journalism, and Anne Sunderg Siess)

For the woman reporters based in the United States during the war, their greater representation in newsrooms did little to counter the long-entrenched preconceptions and prejudices against them. Despite all the new woman exemplars the war years elevated, editors still considered any exceptional performance by a woman to be, well, an exception. *Time*'s press columnist sounded almost gleeful in 1942, writing about the chagrin of the "fat-faced, bullnecked, roughshod" managing editor of the *Chicago Journal of Commerce*. The dearth of available men had forced him to hire six woman copyreaders. Two dropped out during their two weeks of intensive training, and the remaining four caused the "cigar-chewing" night editor to explode over their unworldliness and woeful skills. The managing editor gave them another chance. He handed each of them the same wire story to copyread and headline but did not reveal that he had infused the page with fake information. Not one of them questioned the facts as provided and one left the *s* out of Chrysler in her headline. Resignations came at once from two more of the women, and the last two soon followed. "The Journal copy desk, though depleted," *Time* said, "is once more staffed by men."

A writer for *The Christian Science Monitor* seemed amazed by the "virtual revolution in the newspaper world" that women were creating. By the fall of 1943, they occupied upward of 60 percent of the country's newsroom staffs. The competence of this "group of green girls" he attributed not to their ability but to the oversight of veterans on the copy and rewrite desks. He acknowledged that "womanly wiles" had proved to be as effective a reporting strategy as "the brash, barge-in tactics" favored by men. Nonetheless, he wrote, despite the ability women demonstrated, they continued to labor in an atmosphere of "faint doubt and ridicule." A new survey of Chicago editors at the time could have been written half a century earlier. Women made good feature writers and worked harder than men, the editors allowed, but said they were limited in the beats they could handle well and were less skilled than the men they replaced. For once, there was no mention of inaccuracy as a congenital defect. More time would be needed, the columnist wrote, to find out if the issue was lack of experience or if the temperament of women simply made them ill-suited to the work. He did point out the one clear advantage women had over men: they were cheaper to employ.

At around the same time, in 1943, Genevieve Forbes Herrick offered thoughts about what would happen at war's end to this womanly swell. Her essay appeared in a published symposium put together by the admired journalism historian Frank Luther Mott, then dean of the journalism school at Missouri. Major reporters and writers contributed to the monograph, among them Raymond Clapper, H. V. Kaltenborn, and Joe Alex Morris. Herrick's essay was the token piece by a woman, a choice reflective of the minuscule value even this top journalism historian placed on what the woman journalists had meant to the coverage of the war.

Herrick looked back over her twenty-five years in the business to predict that the professional future of the women whom World War II brought into the field was likely to resemble what she saw as a cub at the *Chicago Tribune* in 1918. Returning World War I soldiers did not replace the women, she said, but many of the women left of their own volition, either returning to their homes and husbands back from battle or finding men to marry. Still others, aware of their inadequacy, "left for quieter pursuits in which they were better qualified." Still others like herself, who entered journalism in wartime, stayed on.

Even though Herrick escaped ever having to do time on the women's pages, she was careful to speak respectfully of the soft wartime reporting most woman correspondents had been engaged to produce. For the symposium, she put a positive spin on what she observed, no doubt mindful of her new post-*Tribune* employer, the War Department Public Relations Bureau. The contributions of journalism's women during the war, she said, showed "new and solid significance"; they turned the "woman's angle" into "a definite part of the national geometry." By writing about food, for example, the women's pages addressed the civilian economy. Despite all the "polite puff" in her Washington circles, all the condescension about how well the woman reporters were doing, Herrick offered her profoundly faulty prediction that women would never return to producing "froth and fluff." "Women journalists will not write *the* war stories," she wrote. "To say so would be foolishly feministic. However, the war story could never have been adequately written without women journalists. To deny this would be stupidly anti-feminine. This is the woman journalist's opportunity. I think she is making the most of it."

Despite the many high-achieving women of the 1930s and 1940s, categorization by gender still clouded the profession's thinking. The women who broke through the prejudices with talent and skill by then were many, but they had neither the power nor, it seemed, the inclination to pull up all the other women with them. Even after the war, the women who excelled were seen as novelties. Agness Underwood, the Los Angeles crime reporter, epitomized that description. By early in 1947, while still reporting on the "Black Dahlia," a woman whose bisected body had been found dumped in Leimert Park, the *Los Angeles Herald* took the unusual but not unheard-of step of naming Underwood its city editor. The career detail about her that no one ever omits is how she would assert her authority in mock anger by wielding the baseball bat or cap pistol she kept at hand.

Near the war's end, the Associated Press sent Edith Evans to federal court in New York City to help an overloaded colleague. She did so well on the beat that the AP made it hers, the only woman reporter in a cache of men who represented the city's various outlets. Annually, the group put on a gala dinner at which they honored a distinguished court personality. Edith Evans felt her colleagues spent more time with their mailing lists, ticket sales, and organizing chores for this event than they did covering the news. After the banquet, one of them handed her a check for $50, which he said was her share of the dinner's profits, worth about $700 today. Slowly, it dawned on her that the men were running a little racket in which she wanted no part. Given her options, especially as the only woman in the group, quitting, she felt, was her only choice.

At around the same time, she had married Herbert Asbury, an associate editor at *Collier's* and a novelist best known now for his 1927 book, *The Gangs of New York*. Jobless again, but with her husband's financial support, Edith enrolled in a PhD program at Columbia and went to work on a novel. In 1946, her old Knoxville paper reported that she was eighty-five thousand words into her story of a girl reporter who used to work in Knoxville. Asbury had only one more book in him, an informal history of prohibition. After *Collier's*, he wrote a handful of magazine pieces but soon stopped producing altogether.

As a result, by 1949, money was tight in the Asbury household. Edith Evans Asbury, at thirty-nine, gave up her novel and her doctoral pursuit on the verge of its completion. She began to hunt for work again, tided over by three résumé-enhancing magazine assignments from *Collier's* that came thanks to new friendships brought into her life through her marriage to Asbury. From those articles, she was proudest of her profile of Bess Truman, the elusive, publicity-deflecting First Lady who consistently declined to submit to interviews with members of the national press. Asbury got the assignment on the rebound from a far more prominent woman writer who could not manage to nail it down.

The same month that Asbury's profile appeared, *Cosmopolitan* published one by Inez Robb, who, unlike the unknown Asbury, had star appeal as a popular globe-trotting Washington-based "lighter side" columnist five days a week for INS, International News Service.

Robb's piece challenged the opinion of all the Washington gossips who had dismissed Bess Truman as a provincial hausfrau, "uncomfortable amid the splendors of the White House," "the most negative, colorless First Lady in our extrovert time." She wrote of the asset Bess Truman was to her husband on his cross-country whistle-stop train tour in the summer and fall of 1948, just ahead of his November presidential election victory. Robb applauded how ably Bess had been handling her duties as First Lady since President Roosevelt's death in 1945 had elevated her husband to the presidency. In *The Washington Post*'s "Magazine Rack" column, Katharine Graham characterized Robb's gushy take on the First Lady as a "superenthusiastic rave." Graham did not mention the competing piece in *Collier's*. A side-by-side comparison of the two articles showed Asbury's superior skill. Both reporters were excellent writers, Robb applying her general knowledge and good sense of the Washington scene. Asbury mined every newspaper morgue she could access and interviewed all her likely sources in Washington, who turned out to know next to nothing about the woman who had been in town since her husband became a senator in 1935. With no chance of a personal interview, Asbury got *Collier's* to arrange an invitation for her to a White House reception so she could at least observe the First Lady at close range, right up to their handshake. Asbury traveled to Kansas City for more sources and then on to nearby Independence, the Trumans' beloved hometown. She connected with their close childhood friends; their wedding guests; the town historians; and a brother and cousins who had photographs they happily shared. She interviewed Sue Gentry, who, in 1943, had moved into the city editor chair of *The Examiner*, the local paper, as its men left for war—that was the only reason she got the job, she never hesitated to say—and yet she kept the position for a decade of her seventy years on the staff. Bess Truman's bridge partners were talking, along with just about every other local with Bess-and-Harry lore to share. Judge Henry Bundschu, a Missouri Republican committeeman and a close friend of the president's, arranged for many of the Truman devotees to stop by to meet Asbury the night he invited her to his home for dinner.

That Bess Truman went to Barstow, an elite private girls' school in Kansas City, was easily known from the First Lady's terse bio in *Who's Who*. Inez Robb used the fact to explain why this midwestern small-towner was "not apt to be thrown off stride by finger bowls or foreign delegations." In Asbury's hands, the Barstow detail segued into a more complete picture of the background of one who had managed to remain so opaque over so many years. Bess Truman, Asbury revealed, was a superb athlete. She could fish, ride horses, and play excellent tennis. She had a pair of sleek greyhounds as girlhood pets. She could whistle through her teeth.

Robb steered clear of mentioning the one controversy the First Lady embroiled herself in. The incident occurred nearly four years earlier, in 1945, shortly after Truman was thrust into the presidency. The Daughters of the American Revolution refused to allow a Black pianist, Hazel Scott, to perform in Constitution Hall, which the private organization owns and runs. Six years earlier, the DAR acted similarly when it barred Marian Anderson from performing in its space for the same reason.

In the earlier instance, Eleanor Roosevelt as First Lady resigned her DAR membership in protest and enabled the event to move to the Lincoln Memorial. (Marvel Cooke covered the performance for the *Amsterdam News*, reporting how Anderson "stood in quiet, majestic dignity on the steps of the white marble memorial to the emancipator in beautiful Potomac Park" and "raised her glorious voice in stirring protest to the un-American attitude of the D.A.R.") In Bess Truman's case, she issued a statement decrying skin color as a reason for standing in the way of an artistic performance but did not rescind her prior acceptance of a DAR invitation to tea. Congressman Adam Clayton Powell, Hazel Scott's husband, protested. Bess Truman told him in a letter that her decision to attend the tea had nothing to do with the "unfortunate controversy." This infuriated Powell, who condemned her in public as "the Last Lady of the Land." That enraged

President Truman, who never again invited Powell to the White House. Asbury's article addressed the episode head-on, telling readers to bear in mind the First Lady's southern background. Asbury used the incident as one indication of how different Mrs. Truman was from Mrs. Roosevelt. The second sign was Bess's discontinuation of Eleanor Roosevelt's weekly select-women-only press conferences and how this new decision infuriated the woman reporters who lost their "run of the White House." Edith Evans Asbury was especially proud of how she had succeeded where others failed in profiling the First Lady without her participation. "Because I'm thorough," Asbury said years later. "I'm more persistent, and I didn't give up." That was a perfect summary of Asbury's entire professional life. Yet, at the time, the only job she could find led to three tedious years at the *New York World-Telegram* as assistant to the editor of the women's pages.

CHAPTER 10

Sidebars

Anne O'Hare McCormick responded with customary humility to her "Woman of the Year" honor at the New York World's Fair. "I have been moving around amid thunderous events," she said, "and I have stolen some of the thunder." In the first five months of 1939, she reported from thirteen countries where, in one magazine's description, "the air was crackling with the intensity and uncertainty of international impacts, and one sensation after another exploded in her ears." In January, in Palestine, she chatted after tea with the district commissioner of Jerusalem on the low stone wall around his garden while her taxi idled nearby. Twenty minutes later, two time bombs exploded under where they had stood. The following week she was in Rome as the British prime minister, Neville Chamberlain, failed to bring Benito Mussolini's Italy into the Allied fold. In March, she watched in Huszt, then the capital of Carpatho-Ukraine, where the flag changed three times in twenty-seven hours as the Hungarians replaced the Czechs. In April, as German aggression mounted in Poland, she was in London as Chamberlain told Parliament he had abandoned his policy of appeasement.

That August, Martha Gellhorn was with Hemingway in San Francisco de Paula, Cuba, finishing the novel she gathered material for in Czechoslovakia. She wrote to Eleanor Roosevelt to tell her that *Collier's* was sending her to Finland, where the Russians were expected to invade. From her vantage point in the Caribbean, what was happening five thousand miles away seemed "too fantastic to be true, like the horror plays they put on at the Grand Guignol in Paris." Yet the crowds of anxious faces in the U.S. consular office in Havana seared her with awareness, with fear and hatred, and with little doubt about the human toll to come. To fulfill her assignment, she told the First Lady, she would need to put aside the urge to think or judge. She would need to become "a walking tape-recorder with eyes." Her arrival in Europe came two months after World War II's official start. This time, she went armed with a letter of introduction from President Franklin D. Roosevelt asking all U.S. foreign service officers to extend "every assistance" to Martha Gellhorn during her anticipated five months abroad.

The articles for *Collier's* commanded good money, $1,000 apiece. They appeared in the magazine in the first four weeks of 1940 under headlines that traced Gellhorn's reportorial trek: "Slow Boat to War," "Blood on the Snow," "Bombs from a Low Sky," "Fear Comes to Sweden." By March, she was back in Cuba as the novel launched. *A Stricken Field* explored the lives of Germans who fled the Sudetenland for Prague as the Nazis overtook their homeland in 1938.

Prague teemed with refugees, people dislocated without recourse, caught in a predicament that her reporter-protagonist's high-level interventions could not fix. More than half a century later, Gellhorn disclosed that while in Prague in 1938 she had made fruitless appeals to the chief U.S. diplomat and the former head of the French military mission. The high commissioner for refugees of the League of Nations spent two days in Prague, she later wrote, and never saw a refugee. In 2017, when yet another world migrant crisis choked the ability or the willingness of receiving countries to provide refuge, a critic writing in *The New York Times* declared *A Stricken Field* to be not only Gellhorn's greatest novel but "essential reading for the political moment we're living through today."

In 1940, Dorothy Thompson still enjoyed preeminence. In April and May, following her *Time* cover the year before, profiles of her consumed pages and pages of two consecutive issues of both *The New Yorker* and *The Saturday Evening Post. The New Yorker* made much of Thompson's "double talent for brooding in print over the welfare of mankind and at the same time inflaming it to further disasters." The *Post* said how exhilarating and exhausting it was to be in her company, how she had no equal, man or woman, in "combined intellectual, physical and emotional energy."

Flora Lewis's astute grasp of international affairs, her successes covering the State Department, and her command of a couple of languages earned her a transfer from the AP bureau in Washington to its London office. She was twenty-three when she arrived in Great Britain on September 1, 1945, the day before Japan's formal surrender. That meant she never really engaged in any full-on war coverage. Her assignment was diplomatic, to cover the British Foreign Office and "the creation of the post-war international order."

To get accreditation was hellish, she told Kathleen Currie for her oral history, because of some problems "with the AP woman." She meant Ruth Cowan, who was the first woman reporter to be accredited to go overseas alongside Inez Robb of INS, both sent to cover the WAACs as they arrived in Algiers. Cowan clashed with the bureau chief, Wes Gallagher, and protested her treatment.

While the fighting was still under way, Ann Stringer of United Press, another serious reporter of the period as driven as Lewis, encountered the same issues Lewis had in seeking military accreditation to get overseas. "They let you know that because you were a woman, you were suspect," Stringer recalled for her memoirs. The bureaucrats kept emphasizing the problems that woman correspondents on-site were creating—the need for separate latrines, separate living quarters, and such. Nevertheless, despite the prevailing negativity and sense that war reporting should be "a man's job and a man's privilege," both Stringer and UP saw her as "a United Press newspaperman—not a newspaper woman"—who, in her widely shared view, "could write the pants off any man."

Flora Lewis grew up in Los Angeles, where she skipped a couple of elementary school grades to graduate from a public high school at fifteen. The Depression had hit her father's law practice hard, so there was no chance of her being able to go away to college for four years, yet her mother did arrange for a gap year for Lewis at a Swiss boarding school in Lausanne in 1938. The experience could not have been more formative or profound. Not only did Lewis gain fluency in French, but her classmates widened her worldview. She listened to Hitler's speeches with a girl from Austria. An Italian friend raised her awareness of Mussolini. She learned about Spain's Civil War from a girl whose family had been forced to flee. During the Munich Conference, on the Dutch freighter that carried Lewis back to the United States, there were blackouts every night "for fear of submarine warfare that didn't come." The entire experience "really changed me," she said. Her facility in French brought opportunities she never would have had otherwise, she told Currie, and the entire experience gave her "a certain capacity." It taught her how to get on with people from varied backgrounds.

In 1941, Lewis graduated from UCLA summa cum laude in political science, with a Phi Beta Kappa key, and she learned Spanish. She was not quite nineteen. Not long after the AP sent her to London, she married—during her lunch hour—the dapper Sydney Gruson of *The New York Times,* whom she knew from New York when he worked for the news agency the Canadian Press. Lewis kept her nuptials secret, because she did not want the AP to think that Gruson was why she sought the transfer. The other looming issue was what she had heard from other woman correspondents about their work life after marriage, how their bureau chiefs insisted they reveal their new particulars and forced them to quit as soon as they became pregnant.

Another driven woman reporter, Lewis's schoolmate Marguerite Higgins, obtained her credentials and arrived in Paris a full six months before Lewis got to London. Higgins was twenty-four and rising fast. She had been the *Herald Tribune*'s stringer on the Columbia campus the year she and Lewis were in the graduate journalism program. They were friendly enough to have almost become roommates, except that Lewis favored an uptown apartment and Higgins wanted to live in Greenwich Village. Lewis, years later, recalled a class assignment that required everyone to write an editorial on the same subject. Higgins got to the library first and checked out every relevant book. One of her professors recalled for a reporter that classmates found her arrogant and would quote her own prediction that she would someday be as well known in the newspaper world as Dorothy Thompson. The anecdotes were portents.

Higgins was from Oakland, the French-speaking child of a French mother and an American father whose career took the family to live in Asia and Europe during Marguerite's formative years. She graduated cum laude from Berkeley with a degree in French the same year Lewis graduated from UCLA. Higgins landed her overseas assignment as a war correspondent after a mere two and a half years on the *Herald Tribune*'s full-time staff. It was she, like Dorothy

Helen Rogers Reid at a dinner
in her honor at the Lotos Club, 1954
(United Press International)

Thompson a decade earlier, who also won the career-catapulting favor of Helen Rogers Reid. Higgins said she harassed every executive she could get to listen to her appeal for an overseas assignment, then outraged her colleagues, not to mention the foreign editor, by going straight to the big boss to win the approval to go. This she felt was justified because an avowed feminist like Reid would understand in the ways men would not "some of the pressures on women in the competitive newspaper world." Higgins also got unsolicited aid from the editor of the women's pages, who had Reid's ear. Beyond that, there was logic in the decision. Higgins spoke French like a native and had maternal aunts, uncles, and cousins in France; her husband was stationed in Russia at the Allied shuttle bombing base. It's hard not to be struck by how many opportunities ambitious women lost to the lack of empathetic people in the power structures of their newsrooms, those women, or men, in a position to pull for them, but also by how many opportunities their backgrounds and special skill sets helped them win. Skills mattered, but so did pull.

The two precocious Californians, Flora Lewis and Marguerite Higgins, had striking similarities in age, background, ambition, talent, drive, and interests. Both figure in the most authoritative count of 180 women who served as international correspondents between 1939 and 1945. The total is just over 10 percent of the estimated 1,600 correspondents on staff or otherwise tied to U.S. newspapers, magazines, feature syndicates, wire services, and radio networks. British and other international outlets engaged a few American woman reporters and vice versa. To put the figure in more perspective, it is more than three times the estimated forty-plus American women who reported under far-flung datelines during World War I, yet it amounts to about the same 10 percent of all woman journalists so engaged at the time.

During World War II, as in conflicts past, military censorship complicated the acts of reporting and writing for everyone. Women, as before, were subjected to an additional layer of restrictions meant to control where they could go and what they could do. Penalties for disobedience ranged from house arrest to loss of accreditation to court martial. The military forbade women to enter battle zones, to attend press conferences, or to access basic facilities like latrines and makeshift pressrooms. This never stopped the best of them. They ignored the restrictions or found ways around them, which frequently put them in the position of having to fawn, wheedle, barter, connive, push, flirt, or make themselves a nuisance until they prevailed. One reporter told Nancy Caldwell Sorel, author of *The Women Who Wrote the War,* of how in Honolulu she singled out the men who would help her with logistics, like the one who was willing to pick her up at her hotel at two o'clock in the morning and drive her to the censor's office in Pearl Harbor when she needed to get copy to New York. She knew that if she went at three in the afternoon, when the men usually filed, there was little chance the telegraphers would send out her story.

There was a side benefit to the thwarted desire of most of the women to chase World War II's biggest stories. The ban encouraged them to rechannel their attention away from the battlegrounds and onto the impact of the pain and disruption of war on everyday lives. The impulse to write about the human toll of war was not new, of course. Kate Masterson comes to mind for her story on the plight and activism of local Cuban women during the country's rebellion against Spanish rule in 1896, Nellie Bly for her reporting from the Pullman strike, a drought in Nebraska around the same time, or even her appeals on behalf of Austrian orphans and war widows during World War I, and Martha Gellhorn for her Depression-era reporting from Spain and from around the United States. By World War II, with so many more women mining this reportorial vein, it would become as major—and valued—an element of conflict reporting as any other.

Despite all the impediments woman reporters faced abroad, both the deeply ingrained attitudinal ones and those inscribed in regulations, there is ample evidence of discrimination overcome, of acts of bravery performed, of excellence under pressure, and of respect

The 1946 London playbill for *Love Goes to Press,*
and for the play's much later run at the Mint
Theater in New York, May 26–July 29, 2012

(Play program, Embassy Theatre, London, author's col-
lection; poster, Mint Theater, courtesy of David Gersten)

well earned. Sheer luck was sometimes the best enabler; breaking the
rules was another. To get around the impediments, women forged
alliances and overcame collegial dirty tricks, insults, shenanigans,
stereotyping, and the shortcuts and dubious practices of men with
bigger reputations and more powerful reach. Gellhorn and Virginia
Cowles spoofed it all in *Love Goes to Press,* their 1946 play, which had a
good run in London but flopped on Broadway. Gellhorn would claim
years later that she and Cowles made the play up whole cloth, but
for women of later generations who have been in similar situations,
much of the send-up rings strikingly familiar:

> TEX: You ought to pay that cook. He's been authoritative
> sources, reliable government circles, and last week, by God,
> you quoted him as a high-ranking Allied officer.
> HANK: I did not. That was my jeep driver.

Friendship and gallantry from better-resourced reporters and
military men always helped. Such offers came as goodwill gestures
or, just as often, as valentines from the lovestruck. The women saw

no basis for the discrimination they faced. They were capable. They had accreditation. They met their deadlines. Like the men, they carried the rank of captain, and the best of them dug their own trenches.

Yet in fairness to the military and to the assigning editors back home, most of the woman reporters arrived in the war zones without anything close to the background or experience that the Spanish Civil War gave women like Martha Gellhorn and Virginia Cowles. Most lacked deadline and hard-news training and the grit of Marguerite Higgins for the *Herald Tribune* or Ann Stringer and Eleanor Packard, who worked for United Press. The others mostly came as feature writers without even "front-page girl" experience or languages or the accrued continental exposure and wisdom that years in the field had given women like Anne O'Hare McCormick, Dorothy Thompson, and Sigrid Schultz. Homer Bigart, then of the *Herald Tribune,* despite an inauspicious start, would become one of the most admired war reporters of the period. The *Herald Tribune* left him in the role of copyboy for five years, an apprenticeship beyond endurance, his colleague Betsy Wade would later write. In 1940, the paper sent him to the Canadian border to cover army maneuvers and, in 1943, to London to cover the war. This was at his request, he told Wade, so he could avoid the draft. Women, by and large, left home without similar preparation or the backing that a full-time position at a newspaper or magazine back home would mean. Most were freelance "special correspondents," hired cheaply as contract stringers or paid by the piece. Others were local hires, often polyglots, who assisted with office administration and backstopped the men in their bureaus. The common expectation of women who wrote for publication was soft news and sidebars, not coverage of the major diplomatic and military moves. Their work was often mailed, not cabled. It mattered less.

Genevieve Forbes Herrick, in her postwar symposium essay, praised the dozen woman correspondents who had done "sustained, careful and sometimes brilliant work" covering the Blitz, the German bombing campaign on London between September 1940 and May 1941. At the fifth annual Front Page Ball of the New York Newspaper Women's Club, the president, Kathleen McLaughlin, late of the *Chicago Tribune* and by then with *The New York Times,* paid tribute by name to a dozen American woman reporters who had been under fire since Spain. "Surely," said Eleanor Roosevelt, the evening's celebrity draw, these women were "making or helping to make newspaper history in this critical period of civilization. Some of them are my personal friends, and all of them deserve the accolade conferred here tonight."

But beyond the celebration of woman reporters by other woman reporters, and of Helen Kirkpatrick, the one woman correspondent on whom the French and American governments bestowed medals of valor, the meaningful accolades were few. To have been present as a reporter at a major historical site or event of World War II—the Battle of the Bulge, Omaha Beach, Torgau, Buchenwald, Dachau, the Nuremberg trials—has proved a worthy biographical note in and of itself. Given the additional hurdles most of the woman correspondents had to clear to gain access to the war's most pivotal moments, they indeed deserve this notice for having been present. In a two-page spread, *Life* magazine ballyhooed Shelley Smith Mydans and Carl Mydans as its "first and most brilliant photographer-reporter team," who, between 1940 and 1942, "covered 45,000 miles and four wars," from the Russo-Finnish conflict through the battle for the Philippines, until Japan interned them in Manila for twenty-one months after its victories late in 1941. In an interview with Nancy Caldwell Sorel, Shelley Mydans was frank about her actual role: In New York, her title was researcher, not reporter. Overseas, she was a correspondent, and during the war, a war correspondent. And yet in every case, she said, her duties were the same.

After the UN conference in San Francisco in 1945, Pauline Frederick finally fulfilled her ambition to report from abroad. She caught the war's tail end with a reporting trip that took her to Morocco, Egypt, Burma, and China. She wrote stories for NANA and did a special series for the Buffalo radio station WNY from November 1945 to June 1946 about the war's impact on Europe's "Little People." She got considerable attention for at least one story from the Nuremberg trials, about how the Germans, spurred by the aviator Hanna Reitsch, "toyed with the idea of developing suicide planes to repel an invasion fleet." She did an exclusive report from Krakow on the return from Nazi looters of one of Poland's greatest art treasures, an altarpiece carved in the late sixteenth century by the German sculptor Veit Stoss, retrieved from a basement of the heavily bombed Nuremberg Castle.

By 1946, Edward R. Murrow was back in New York and a CBS vice president, putting together his postwar team. CBS showed almost no enthusiasm for the woman stringers the network leaned on overseas. Once back home, none got full-time jobs. Frederick, given her time and training with Baukhage, felt ready for a position on a national network after the war and sent Murrow an audition recording. He judged it "pleasing," but "not particularly distinguished." CBS forwarded Murrow's evaluation to Frederick, who reflected on it often with amusement in the more celebrated days of her career that followed.

For reporters, the shiniest gold stars, in wartime or peace, always go to those who create a universally recognized record of outstanding performance. The acknowledgment comes by way of excellence ethically achieved with reporting rigor, or brilliant writing, or by breaking news, or by producing exclusive coverage or major competitive scoops or all of the above.

Sometimes there is politics and bias in the decisions. Sometimes women simply did not get the credit they deserved. Among the forgotten women who qualify from this period is UP's Eleanor Packard. In Spain, in April 1937, recall that she bore witness to the gruesome spectacle of three thousand of Franco's dead in transit. In September 1938, Packard "scooped the world" from the German border near Eger in Czechoslovakia as fighting broke out between the Sudeten Germans and Czech soldiers and gendarmes. The headline in the *Nashville Banner* read, "Woman Reporter Scores Smash News Beat on Czech Fighting." Margaret Bourke-White photographed for *Life* the hostilities in the Soviet Union in 1941 after the Germans broke their nonaggression pact. By then, under the publisher Henry Luce, *Life* was a photo-saturated sensation of a magazine with a circulation of millions of copies each week. This made the daring Bourke-White famous, as did her extraordinary images, many taken under fire, from subsequent campaigns in North Africa, Italy, and Germany.

Collier's, like every other publication, went full bore in its coverage of the D-day invasion of June 6, 1944. In March, the magazine had published Sigrid Schultz's prescient commentary on how the Nazis would go about undermining the Allied invasion plans. Clearly, Schultz's more than two decades in Germany had paid off again. She predicted a second deluge of stories about a German "death ray" that did not exist and expert propaganda coupled with "political and economic trickery" to oppose the landing. She named those who would be involved in disseminating the falsehoods, including several reporters involved in promoting discord and disbelief of Allied claims. When the German defeat seemed imminent, she said to expect false reports of Hitler's death and the names of Nazis who were disloyal to him.

On July 22, *Collier's* crowed that "the Schultz predictions began to come true almost as soon as that issue of *Collier's* made its appearance on newsstands." Her piece pointed out the phantasmagoric pre-invasion stories Joseph Goebbels had been circulating about German weapons that could decimate entire Allied battalions and inventions that could make icebergs spring up like sea monsters in the English Channel. Schultz had also divined correctly that the Germans would try to undermine inter-Allied trust and signal which Germans would make the "right" eventual negotiating partners.

The cover line of *Collier's* D-day issue went not to Martha Gellhorn, its frequent and faithful correspondent since 1937, but to Ernest Hemingway, by then her husband of four years. The magazine gave him, not her, its only accredited slot with the invasion forces. The surge in circulation that a Hemingway byline would virtually guarantee must have buried any impetus on the part of editors to show loyalty to Gellhorn, not to mention how the military's restrictions on the movement of woman correspondents might limit her ability to report. Despite her fury at the decision, it did not end her affiliation with the magazine. She was wise to keep a major publishing platform and hold on to steady work despite the favoritism the magazine showed toward the man she was about to divorce.

Hemingway's D-day story, "Voyage to Victory," got the giant *Collier's* cover line. Inside, a half-page photograph shows him in a cluster of adoring GIs. Gellhorn, in the same issue, got only a single page for her sidebar about the "commuter war" that followed D-day, with the frequent movement of personnel between Britain and France. The table of contents identified them both with the word "Invasion" next to their names. In Gellhorn's case, this was the only hint that she too had crossed the channel on D-day. In fact, Gellhorn's coup was her arrival on Omaha Beach well ahead of Hemingway and every other correspondent. She snuck onto a hospital ship and hid in a bathroom until after the vessel sailed. On board were six American nurses preparing to receive the wounded. At dawn, "the greatest naval traffic jam in history" came into view. Gellhorn's daring and courage—bucked up with the contents of a flask—produced one of the most memorable stories of the war. On August 5, *Collier's* let it run for five pages two weeks after its main D-day issue and five weeks after the invasion itself. There was no cover line for Gellhorn, even though her story was better than Hemingway's.

As punishment for breaking the rules, the military withdrew Gellhorn's accreditation after D-day. For the rest of the war, she reported without her travel papers or authorization for rations. Although this did not stop her, it did oblige her to resort to an all-out charm offensive to keep in step. Yet she produced more distinctive coverage, work still in print, still read, still admired. As her biographer Caroline Moorehead quipped, "Her looks, her obvious courage, and her utter disregard for authority came in very handy."

Ann Stringer, born in 1918, was a full decade younger than Gellhorn and Pauline Frederick and two years older than Marguerite Higgins. Her generation came of age after passage of the Nineteenth Amendment, which enshrined in law, if not entirely in practice, the right of all woman citizens to vote. By 1922, the radical suffragist Alice Paul had put her proposed Equal Rights Amendment into the cultural conversation. This was before Stringer, Higgins, or Flora Lewis had even started school.

Stringer reported for UP from its bureaus in Dallas, Columbus, and New York and on foreign assignment in Buenos Aires during the military coup that brought Juan Perón to power. Stringer, like Eleanor Packard and Shelley Mydans, was a twofer. In college at the University of Texas in Austin, as Ann Harrell of Eastland, she married her schoolmate William J. Stringer Jr. in their senior year. UP hired him first and then Ann, after the agency sent him to Dallas. United Press, perennially cash strapped and understaffed, never had enough economic latitude to let its own flagrant bias against women get entirely in the way. She described their working relationship as separate, but in fact they were very much a team. In 1944, unhappy in Argentina, both were desperate to get reassigned to Europe. UP moved too slowly for Bill, so he struck a deal with Reuters with the understanding that Ann would join him and work for Reuters, too, as soon as her accreditation came through.

On a Thursday in September 1944, the day Ann was scheduled to leave for Europe, she took a call from a colleague in London who had terrible news. On August 17, Bill, traveling with an Acme News photographer named Andy Lopez and their army driver, Private Lawrence Sabin, advanced with the First Army. They stopped near Dreux, about sixty miles from Paris, to investigate a burned-out jeep. In Lopez's later account, as they slowed down to get a closer look, he heard a huge explosion. "We hadn't even heard a gun fired," Lopez said. "I looked around and saw that Bill was hit. He never knew what had hit him." The Germans had pointed an anti-aircraft gun at the jeep. The shell did not explode but hit Bill over the heart. "He was not mangled," Stringer said. "It was over in an instant."

It took the young widow about a month until grief reinforced her determination to get to the war front. UP's president encouraged her to come back to the agency and promised to send her abroad. She wrestled accreditation from the military and sailed for England. Before Walter Cronkite moved on to CBS and Harrison Salisbury to *The New York Times,* they were both her UP colleagues. Salisbury, as London bureau chief and later, with the wider view of foreign editor, saw how superb a "two-fisted competitor" she was, "the best *man* (I'll say that even if it sounds chauvinistic) on the staff," he wrote. "Annie illuminated every one of the assignments. She was all reporter—not 'girl reporter'—straight reporter."

Woman reporters had ample presence at the Nuremberg trials. Among them were Martha Gellhorn for *Collier's* and Tania Long with her husband, Ray Daniell, for *The New York Times.* Janet Flanner and Rebecca West both wrote from Nuremberg for *The New Yorker.* Flanner's five-part "Letter from Nuremberg" ran from January to March 1946. West's two-part account ran in October and November of the same year and became the basis for her best-selling book *A Train of Powder,* not published until 1955. At Nuremberg, Ann Stringer teamed up with Cronkite for the first time, but he had already "heard a lot about her," he would later write. He said she was tough, one of the best reporters he had ever known, someone who knew what she wanted and how to get it. "And yes," he added, "she was beautiful." Her fame, "as a beauty, a personality, and a ruthlessly competitive correspondent" had spread among the press corps. Her determination to be first with the big story not infrequently brought her into conflict with her UP colleagues, he wrote, and "created thorny jurisdictional problems for her immediate bosses," which included Cronkite.

He explained that a wire service's main task was to cover the trial's daily proceedings, "but the most sensational material was that still locked in the files of the Third Reich, the Wehrmacht, the Luftwaffe and the Navy. The Allies had seized them all and most of them were under heavy guard right there in the courthouse." That was where the untold stories of the war were buried, Cronkite wrote, the records of how the pogroms against the Jews, the concentration camps, and the gas chambers came to be, of Hitler's decision to call off the Luftwaffe's offensive against Britain on the eve of possible victory, of the German navy's U-boat campaign in the North Atlantic and machine-gunning of lifeboats crowded with civilians. The key was to know what documents to request. That required many contacts among the prosecution and defense teams "and then hours of discreet, diplomatic, clever probing—in the halls of the courthouse, at cocktails or dinner." This, he wrote, was Stringer's forte. Day after day, she scooped the competition. For a bureau chief like Cronkite, the way she confounded the opposition was sheer delight. He and Stringer did, however, quarrel. As the shock value of the Nazi atrocities wore off, and the stories moved from the front to inside pages of client papers, Stringer sought reassignment to a more active scene. Cronkite wanted her to stay. "That," he wrote, "was a fight I was bound to lose."

Stringer had crossed the ocean two years earlier to cover the major stories of the war, which was exactly what United Press had in mind. She, too, was not going to let restrictions get in her way. She told her own story best in two slim, limited-circulation paperbacks published in 1988 and 2000. In February and March 1944 she reported from Jülich Castle as Ninth Army soldiers crossed the Roer River and its dams in the first Allied offensive in the month since the Battle of the Bulge. From there she went on to witness the capture of Cologne and reported from the east bank of the Rhine at the Remagen bridgehead.

Ann Stringer at Torgau
(UPI / Getty Images)

Two other woman correspondents did likewise, *The Boston Globe*'s
Iris Carpenter and Lee Carson for INS. *Newsweek*'s press columnist
dubbed them "the Rhine Maidens," "a redhead, a blonde, and a brunette," and told of their brazen decision to ignore the restrictions on
women's movements ordered by SHAEF, the Supreme Headquarters
Allied Expeditionary Force. Military policy forbade woman reporters to go farther forward than the women's services, the WAACs, and
the nurses were allowed to go, which was far behind the front lines.

The *Newsweek* writer made a point of Carson's having been rated
one of Washington's best-looking woman correspondents. She got
to Normandy two weeks after D-day, joined up with the Ninth Air
Force, then the Third Army in time to enter Paris, and after that, the
First. He tipped his hat to Stringer's reporting at Jülich Castle and
wrote of how the three women had disproved the view that women
at the front distracted soldiers. They "asked no favors and gave
none," he wrote. "They dug their own foxholes and took front-line
life without complaint." SHAEF was unamused by the attention the
women had attracted because it fueled demands for the same privileges from the other American woman reporters on the Continent.

In response, SHAEF reiterated its rules, this time as an ultimatum with Ann Stringer's name evoked for emphasis.

Years later, Stringer would confirm that the three women were tenacious competitors but at the same time friends who "helped each other if we could without giving anything away." With the military, they acted as one. "If the Army was taking out after just one of us, we stuck together," Stringer wrote. "We had to."

By April 11, Stringer was with American troops in Leipzig and then at the Nordhausen concentration camp, where, in a dozen bombed-out buildings, the Third Army encountered some ten thousand German political prisoners, "about half of them dead and the rest dying," in Stringer's words. From Buchenwald, ten days after its liberation, scores of newspapers carried her story with its eleven-word lead: "The lampshade was made from the skin from a man's chest."

She headed toward the Elbe, toward Torgau, where the linkup between the American and the Russian forces was set to take place. She was mindful that her actions contravened SHAEF's direct orders. Verboten or not, she was determined that her report of the linkup would carry a dateline from the site and that she would have the story first.

Jack Thompson of the *Chicago Tribune,* as chairman of the First Army's war correspondent group, was the only reporter officially designated to be in Torgau for the event. He traveled by jeep over miserable roads to arrive in time for the linkup on April 26, 1945. He knew he had lost his exclusive as Stringer came into view, accompanied by Allan Jackson, a photographer for INS. From the Second Division, Stringer and Jackson had arranged to get to Torgau in separate two-seater L-5 spotter planes.

As Stringer recounted, she and Jackson got out of their planes and climbed over roadblocks to enter the village, where she spotted her first Russian, "a young man clad only in a pair of blue shorts and a cap with a red hammer-and-sickle pin. The Elbe River was swarming with Russian soldiers stripped to their shorts, swimming across to greet us."

The Germans had demolished all the bridges, so Stringer and Jackson found a couple of beat-up racing shells and rowed across the river. As soon as the Russians saw them, "they rushed down to the river through the tall, wet grass, and began yelling greetings. Amid shouts of joy and the ebullient shooting of machine guns pointed to the sky, we were met with cries of 'Vive Roosevelt!' and 'Vive Stalin!' " The Russians, she said, had not been told that Roosevelt was dead. The Russians and the GIs exchanged autographs. The commander invited the journalists to join them all for lunch and told Stringer that she was the first American woman he and his troops had ever seen. He seated her to his right in the place of honor for a feast of creamed sardines and eggs, both hard-boiled and raw; the Russians sucked the latter out of their shells. There were many toasts, first with cognac, then wine, then schnapps, then vodka, then what Stringer thought might be grain alcohol.

She knew she had a great story, "perhaps the greatest since the D-Day landings," she later wrote, but that would only matter if she could file first. After about an hour, she left the scene with her type-writer and Jackson's film.

Jack Thompson remained unconcerned about the possibility of being scooped by Stringer. Even though she was traveling by plane, he assumed that she would need to file through First Army censors, just as he had to do, since the military was tightly controlling any release of information. Stringer, though, asked her pilot to fly her straight to Paris. Since the L-5 could not go the distance, the pilot offered to take her as far as he could. In flight, they were heading west when a C-47 came into view. Stringer's pilot followed the U.S. transport plane until it landed in a field. He did the same. Stringer got out and rushed over to the two airmen in the C-47. Would they fly her to Paris so she could file her story about the Russians? "Oh, yes," one replied. "And I'm Stalin and he's Roosevelt."

Rather than try to convince them, she sat down on the grass under the plane's wing, opened her typewriter case, and started typing. The airmen came nearer and read over her shoulder. "When I looked up to ask their names and hometowns and typed that information into my story," Stringer said, "their attitude swiftly changed." The three of them climbed aboard the plane. Stringer kept typing until they landed at the airfield nearest Paris. She hitchhiked to the Hotel Scribe, where she and the other Allied correspondents were based, and headed straight to the censor's window to file her story and give over Jackson's film. UP arranged for her to broadcast the news, too, which turned out to be a total thrill for her mother in Kilgore, Texas, who caught her daughter's voice on the air by chance as she fiddled with the radio dial.

Thompson said it never occurred to him that Stringer would file through the SHAEF censors, avoiding the First Army entirely. "Perhaps I should have known better," he would say years later, "for not only was Ann a bright, attractive woman, she was a damned fine newspaper man and a fierce competitor. She was a pistol! And a pretty pistol, too." Iris Carpenter also provided her recollection of the episode for Stringer's memoir. In this version of her account, she called Stringer's achievement "magnificent" and "historic" as she acknowledged that Stringer had scooped her "flat out" for having made the same mistake as Jack Thompson. Carpenter decoded Thompson's gracious concession of defeat as an expression of his desire to slit Stringer's throat. The scoop, in fact, was just that huge. Interestingly, in Carpenter's account of the linkup for her 1946 memoir, she does not mention Ann Stringer at Torgau.

Back at the Scribe, colleagues had a range of responses to Stringer's sudden appearance in the hotel lobby. Drew Middleton of *The New York Times* said she should have stayed where she was because everyone was about to go and meet the Russians. Others felt badly for her because they thought she was about to miss an important story. Stringer found it hard to conceal her glee at the AP's anger once word of her scoop filtered back to Paris from headquarters in New York. UP's night manager told her that of all the Torgau copy he saw or heard in the days that followed—wire service, newspapers, broadcasts—hers was the best. Typically, it invited this headline in one California paper: "Russians Happy at Union of Armies: U.S. Girl Is Impressed."

Lee Miller, from Poughkeepsie, New York, was working for British *Vogue* when she transformed herself into a wartime photojournalist. She was about Gellhorn's age. A rare and alluring beauty, a model since childhood, often for her father, in a style presaging the familial work of Sally Mann. Miller trained in surrealism and surrealistic photography in Paris as muse, lover, and collaborator of Man Ray. She learned war photography on the job from the superb *Life* magazine photographer David E. Scherman, who later became an editor at the magazine. In August 1944, army public relations assigned her to photograph the efforts of a civic affairs team in Saint-Malo, a town at the French seaside in Normandy, thought to be quiet after the forces of General George Patton retook the northern Brittany coast. But when Miller arrived, snipers, marauders, and soldiers holed up in the town citadel were still on-site. "I owned a private war," Miller later wrote. *Vogue* published her spread. The army punished her with house arrest.

Lee Miller and David Scherman functioned as a team. They were with other reporters, several women, at the liberation of the Dachau concentration camp on April 29, 1945, and they, like so many others, left the scene imprinted with images that never ceased to haunt. Miller's photographs, for both the British and the U.S. editions of *Vogue* ("'Believe It' Lee Miller Cables from Germany"), remain among those from the liberation most often reproduced. Dachau would also provide Marguerite Higgins with her greatest World War II moment. Her story made the *Herald Tribune*'s front page on May 1, 1945. The giant banner across the top read, "Russians Raise Victory Flag over Reichstag; 7th Takes Munich, 'Free Germans' Cheer; Italy Is Proclaimed Won, Partisans in Trieste." Below, in a single column, were the opening paragraphs of Higgins's account. She and Peter Furst of *Stars and Stripes* were the first American correspondents through the gates to the sounds of German artillery in the northern part of the camp, where some of the prisoners "died trying to pass through electrically charged barbed wire. Some who got out after the wires were de-charged joined in the battle, while six ill-advised S.S. men, holding out in a tower, fired at them. The prisoners charged the tower and threw all six S.S. men out the window." The story earned Higgins a "campaign ribbon for outstanding service with the armed forces under difficult conditions" and a prize from the New York Newspaper Women's Club for the best foreign correspondence of 1945.

Later that same day, just twenty miles away in Munich, at 16 Prinzregentenplatz, Miller and Scherman had Hitler's luxurious but now abandoned eight-room apartment all to themselves, save the members of the command post of the 179th Regiment of the Forty-Fifth Division, which had commandeered it. Miller spotted hot water, soap, and clean towels and decided to take a bath. She set the scene with a framed image of Hitler and a statuette she moved into the bathroom. With her camera, she had Scherman photograph the scene for the British edition of *Vogue*. Separately, there are some photos of Scherman in the tub, too. In the picture of Miller, her head was turned toward the camera, revealing only one elegant unclad shoulder. Placed toes first against the tiled side of Hitler's white porcelain tub are her black combat boots, on a light-colored bath mat smeared with Dachau's mud.

Lee Miller

PART FOUR

ADVANCES AND SETBACKS

1950s–1970s

CHAPTER 11

Bridges

In the 1950s, woman journalists inched across a swinging rope bridge toward fuller acceptance but still in single file. Achievements in local, national, and international settings burnished top careers to a high gleam, but for everyone else, prospects beyond the women's pages remained as dim as ever. It took until 1951 for a second woman correspondent to win a Pulitzer; three more Pulitzers went to women before the decade was out. Edward R. Murrow's reject, Pauline Frederick, won broadcast journalism's top prizes, an Alfred I. duPont in 1953 and a George Foster Peabody in 1954, the year a college senior named Anne Morrissy caused a national sensation by becoming the sports editor of *The Cornell Daily Sun* and the first woman to cover a game from a seat in the press box of the Yale Bowl. Red Smith in the *New York Herald Tribune* described her in the manner no one seemed to challenge for far too long. He called her a "slick little chick whose name probably will be linked in history with those other crusading cupcakes such as Lady Godiva, Susan B. Anthony, Lydia Pinkham and Mrs. Amelia Bloomer." Smith did note the longer history of women who reported on sports but did not seem to know that it went back more than half a century.

There were a few forward-looking signs. Women like Aggie Underwood in Los Angeles who warmed city editor chairs during the war years kept their seats, and Black woman journalists gained long-denied accreditation in the Washington, D.C., press corps. A woman reporter on the staff of the *New York Herald Tribune* went to jail for ten days for refusing in court to reveal a source. The case itself was trivial, involving an item about Judy Garland, but the principles of press freedom it represented, the defense argued, were gigantic.

It was clear that neither gender nor race governed capability, talent, or guts. Yet what we now call "implicit" or "legacy" bias prevented consensus from firming up around this obvious conclusion, as did the attitudes that women themselves had formed and internalized over centuries. No one seemed to protest the thousands of put-downs ascribed to women in print, by women as well as by men. This is not a trivial point. Conditioning that turned Neanderthal thinking into supposed fact continued to severely limit the choices available to women. That helped lead to their willingness to accept the unacceptable. Powerlessness perpetuated the practice. Without meaningful protest or support from the top, the indignities continued, too often unremarked upon if not unnoticed. In the journalism industry, there was still the need to brush off inequity and unfairness, to seethe and shrug at overt bias, to submit to unwanted advances, and sometimes to swallow everything from embarrassment to humiliation to assault as part of the compact.

Take, for example, a minor case in point. "A Couple of News Gals Talk About Their Work" was the headline in 1958 over a column in the *New York Daily News* about two of the decade's mature, undisputed no-nonsense exemplars in international reporting and analysis, man or woman. The columnist, a woman in this case, began with busy Pauline Frederick without a minute to get her hair or nails done and "pert" Flora Lewis on leave from Warsaw going wild on a New York shopping spree. To appreciate the inanity, substitute the names of journalists doing similar work at the time, like Edward R. Murrow and Walter Cronkite. By 1958, a century's worth of women's achievements had made no discernible dent in the cultural frame. Nor did the example set by the Truman administration in its move to end entrenched discriminatory and segregationist policies in the military and federal civil service.

In the country at large, the kitchen-bound, high-heeled white housewife of the magazine ads, the one with an apron over her starched tea-length cotton shirtwaist, did not match the reality for a quarter to a third of the country's women. From 1930 to 1948, the overall percentage of American women employed outside the home creeped toward a third, rising from 22 percent to 28.6 percent; by

1960 the percentage was 33.34. In the field of journalism, the number of woman editorial staffers, buoyed by wartime gains, exceeded the national percentages.

The danger of losing whatever ground women had won since 1920 remained a recurrent theme in the writing and frequent public appearances of Fannie Hurst, the novelist and short-story writer, author of *Back Street* and *Imitation of Life*. Murrow featured her in a 1954 episode of *Person to Person,* his must-watch prime-time television interview program on CBS. From his desk in a network studio, Murrow's disembodied voice seemed to translocate into the salon of Hurst's grand triplex in the Hotel des Artistes on West Sixty-Seventh Street in Manhattan. In a pre-scripted question, he asked why she wrote about women, why her novels and short stories so often had an underlying theme of social injustice. "I think it's because I'm interested in minorities, Mr. Murrow," she replied in her faux for-the-movies, mid-Atlantic accent. Hurst grew up in the boardinghouses of St. Louis. "I'm interested in the people who have to contend with the pressure of larger groups," she said, "and I'm interested in women also because a great deal of what's happened to us makes us more interesting in our evolving processes than you mere men. Don't forget that in the last hundred years or so, nothing so much has happened to you in the way of change of your social status."

Hurst was nearly seventy when she appeared on Murrow's program. By then, she had been a household name on the national scene for more than forty years. Among woman journalists in the years when Hurst was at her apex, some striking role models for women in journalism emerged. First in line among those who came of age after the Great Depression was Marguerite Higgins, who left a trail of exclusives and nasty scuttlebutt everywhere she went; then Flora Lewis, her more subdued but no less dauntless Columbia classmate; and from the wire service world, Lewis's good friend the "young, blond, and good-looking" Montanan Aline Mosby, as *Collier's* described her in a 1956 credit line. Mosby's Hollywood run for United Press came to an abrupt halt in 1957 when her name came up in court during the pornography trial of a sleazy celebrity magazine called *Confidential* that Mosby was reporting on for the wire service. First, innocuously enough, Mosby, Agness Underwood, and other established Los Angeles reporters were named from the stand as those who declined to provide the magazine with damaging information about the stars. But then, the witness, seeking to confirm the magazine's legitimacy, spoke of its numerous mainstream contributors but named only Mosby because there was evidence for that. She accepted payment in checks made out to her personally rather than cash like everyone else. UP fired her. Mosby soon resurfaced in Brussels, helped by the company to get a job at the World's Fair of 1958. By year's end, she was at work in UP's bureau in London, where she took an immersive course in Russian in preparation for her transfer to the Soviet Union.

In this period, other American woman journalists reported from Russia as freelancers or local hires, and Marguerite Higgins came through earlier for several weeks on a Guggenheim Fellowship for her book about the country, published in 1955. *Newsweek*'s Whitman Bassow, whose Moscow tour overlapped with Mosby's, wrote that she was "the first truly professional female reporter" assigned full time to the country during those years. Her biggest scoop, not long after she arrived, eventually put her name in the files of the Warren Commission. On October 31, 1959, on tips from U.S. embassy sources, both AP and UPI, now merged with International News Service, reported that a twenty-year-old former U.S. marine from Texas, Lee Harvey Oswald, had applied to renounce his U.S. citizenship for "purely political reasons" to become a citizen of the Soviet Union. Two weeks later, Mosby telephoned Oswald at the Hotel Metropol and asked for an interview. He told her no at first, but then relented.

As she later told Kathleen Currie, the oral historian, although Oswald felt sure the Soviet elite would welcome him, he struck her as "a rather mixed-up young man of not great intellectual capacity or training, and somebody that the Soviet Union certainly wouldn't be much interested in." In her story, she described him as a "button-down collar type." He told her his defection felt "like getting out of prison." She further reported that although the Russians would give Oswald resident alien status, they would not grant him citizenship.

Soon after, he called her to express his anger at being hounded by the press. He said he had let her come meet him because she was a woman, because he thought she would show understanding. That almost made her feel sorry for him. Nonetheless, proud though she was of her big scoop, its greater significance would not come for four more years, when Oswald assassinated John F. Kennedy.

Marguerite Higgins generated endless rounds of gossip, around her questionable hygiene, her recklessness, her promiscuity, her ethics, her exploitation of other reporters, and some unforgivable un-collegiality. She was said to be "ruthless," "treacherous," "uncooperative," "unwilling to pool," to have "used her womanly wiles," "slept her way," and advanced "women's lib." One kinder response came from the entertainment critic Judith Crist, Higgins's colleague at the *Herald Tribune*. In an interview with Richard Kluger for his book about that paper, Crist attributed the vicious collegial enmity toward Higgins to her "movie star prettiness, almost like a cross between Betty Grable's and Marilyn Monroe's," her slender five feet, eight inches, her "super figure and those absolutely blue eyes." Flora Lewis, who, in Europe, often crossed paths once again with her graduate school mate, said Higgins was "very hard-working, very determined, not liked, partly because of jealousy, partly because she didn't always play fair. She would cut people out." The *New Yorker* writer Janet Flanner crossed the Atlantic on the same ship with Higgins in 1944. Initially she thought of her as a Goldilocks in need of protection. "If I'd known then what I know now," she told one of Higgins's biographers, "I'd have thrown her overboard."

After the war, in 1947, the *Herald Tribune* appointed Higgins its Berlin bureau chief and assigned her to cover the growing tensions between East and West at the start of the Cold War. She was only twenty-six at the time yet had amassed "more front-page stories than any other reporter in the last six months of the war," if a gossip columnist was correct. In barely five years on the newspaper's staff, she had spent three of them as a correspondent in Europe while the Continent was on fire. Higgins had no family in tow, which made the choice economical, and she had proven ability as a reporter who could break news. The paper had a boutique-sized foreign staff, so there was more ease of movement into coveted overseas posts than at larger, more seniority-bound outlets. She spoke German and French and had conveniently produced a series of editor-pleasing exclusives.

In typical Higgins style, they came while she did vacation-relief duty in Berlin for the man she angled herself into position to replace. In her 1955 memoir, she disparaged what she saw as a tendency of those from underrepresented groups to blame their lack of advancement on being Jewish, a woman, or Black. "This attitude offers great and comforting opportunities of fooling yourself," Higgins wrote, "because it prevents your facing up to the fact that just possibly the reason you aren't going to receive a certain promotion is that your talents aren't up to it."

Flora Lewis was up to it. The move of her husband, Sydney Gruson, to *The New York Times* started an affiliation that, between 1947 and 1955, would station their family in Germany, Poland twice, Palestine/Israel, Holland, Mexico, Guatemala, London, and New York. With Gruson's first transfer, to Warsaw, Lewis left the AP to freelance, having turned down the wire service's offer of placement in Paris, which she would have loved. "If I was going to be married," she told Currie years later, "I was going to be in the same city." By that time, the *Times* had established a firm no-couples policy. In Lewis's case, the edict meant no full-time opportunity with the newspaper, even though the company was uprooting Gruson at a rate of almost once a year. It was also well known that Lewis and Gruson sometimes tag-teamed, although they always kept a Chinese wall around their respective exclusives. Once, in Israel, when two stories developed north and south on the same day, Lewis covered one of them for Gruson and sent it to the *Times* under his byline. The London editor who fielded Gruson's copy, a great friend of them both, messaged back to say he could tell the difference between their writing styles and they should stop trying to fool him.

Before Lewis left London for Warsaw, she arranged to string with *The Economist,* the *Financial Times, The Observer,* the *Daily Express, Time,* and *France-Soir.* All paid "very little," she told Currie, so her aggregated income was only "supplementary" and remained so for more than a couple of decades. By November 1948, she added *The New York Times Magazine* to her frequent publications list with a profile of Chaim Weizmann, Israel's first president. That was in the year between the births of children one and two; the third child came in 1951. Permanent placement on the *Times*'s staff remained out of reach or, as Lewis would say years later, "impossible." Not only was she barred from a full-time job at the *Times*, but she was forbidden to work for any paper or organization that the *Times* considered a competitor.

Lewis's languages and deep grasp of world affairs enabled her to report and write from wherever the family ended up. With each move, she added or subtracted freelance arrangements to conform to the wishes and needs of editors. Lewis had a matter-of-fact attitude about her management of the family's globe-hopping lives, their children—hired minders helped—her marriage, and the impact of it all on her promising career. "His job was more important than mine," she said, "so I was prepared to be helpful." Through the second half of the decade, she had a regular London-based position with *The Washington Post*, which, she noted, was not then considered a competitor to the *Times*. She also wrote more frequently for national magazines and published the first of four books in 1958. She figured that having books on her résumé enhanced her status with prospective editors.

Of Marguerite Higgins in postwar Europe, Lewis recalled an episode reminiscent of that time in their Columbia days when Higgins hoarded all the relevant books everyone needed for a class-wide assignment. In Warsaw, Higgins gained advantage over her competitors by monopolizing for hours the only unmonitored telephone line to Prague, the one that all the correspondents used to sidestep the censors. "She was considered a very, very aggressive correspondent," Lewis said without apparent rancor, "but she was effective."

There were other such stories about Higgins. She upset a *Herald Tribune* colleague for maneuvering him into sharing with her his exclusive interview with the interim president of France, arguing that her command of French was superior, which was true. Then, he said, she commandeered the main story and relegated his to a sidebar. "Men didn't do that to other men," he told Richard Kluger. On personal authority, I can tell you men have done such things to women. Gellhorn and Cowles in their play, *Love Goes to Press*, suggest such antics. Another one of Higgins's *Herald Tribune* colleagues in Europe summoned his decades-old rage as he gave Kluger his version of why the paper pulled Higgins out of Europe in the middle of 1950. He acknowledged how hard and aggressively she worked, but he bristled at the way she extracted information from colleagues and never reciprocated; how she exaggerated the news value of her stories in a bid for better placement in the paper; and how she tried to hide her ignorance in ways that "antagonized sources, associates, and rivals." Higgins, in her 1955 memoir, showed self-awareness with an acknowledgment of just how "very wearing and in many ways unattractive" her "one-track preoccupied personality" could be.

The accusations were not purely professional. There was slut shaming, too. Kluger indulged in it at length without naming the men who told the tales. Could it be that those men were married and needed Kluger's protection while the reputation and fidelity of the also-married Higgins were fair game? Higgins was widely believed to have been the model for *Shriek with Pleasure*, a racy 1950 novel set in postwar American-occupied Germany. It featured a Berlin-based reporter who had "wit and intelligence but no moral scruples" and who, in the words of one reviewer, "used her body as a passport to many 'scoops.' " Flora Lewis considered the attacks on Higgins's aggressiveness "somewhat fair" but had a different, more evolved response to the accusations of promiscuity. To Currie, Lewis added a caveat inspired not by Higgins but by another colleague who faced similar accusations many years later. Initially, Lewis said she resented the few women who operated this way, buying into the cliché that their behavior was detrimental to other woman journalists because it forced all of them to have to defend themselves against the "bad reputation" smear. "I decided, what the hell—men do it," Lewis said. "Why shouldn't the women: They have just as much right to sleep around as men do if that's how they choose to live."

In May 1950, the *Herald Tribune* transferred Higgins to Tokyo, an order that took her unhappily out of the center of the action in Europe to a news backwater. As Higgins made her way to Japan, she put a good face on the reassignment, telling a society page reporter for the *Honolulu Star-Bulletin* that she was going at her own request because she wanted to be able to compare the impact of Russia in Europe, where Russia had "done distressingly well," with Russia's impact in the Far East. "Herald Tribune Tokyo Bureau Chief Is Attractive Woman" was the headline.

In Tokyo, she shared an office with Keyes Beech, the *Chicago Daily News* correspondent. Not two months later, a flash came over the wires: North Korea had invaded the South. Higgins, Beech, Burton

Crane of *The New York Times,* and Frank Gibney of *Time* caught the last plane to Seoul. They barely got out of the capital as the North Koreans were dynamiting the city's bridges. At one point, Higgins had to lug her typewriter fourteen miles on foot until Beech could rescue her in the abandoned Dodge he commandeered. Beech, Crane, and Higgins all wrote accounts of their dramatic arrival for their respective papers. Beech wrote just as personally as Higgins. Crane also included personal details but in flatter, more muted prose. The headline over Beech's front-page story read, " 'I Have a Feeling It's the Start of World War III,' Says Keyes Beech, Under Fire." He wrote of Crane's and Gibney's injuries, miraculously not serious, as a bridge blew up in their faces. He described the impact that lifted their jeep off the ground and shattered its windshield. Crane said a truckload of soldiers just ahead of them on the road, all of whom were killed, shielded the reporters' jeep from the worst. In their stories, neither Crane nor Beech mentioned Higgins as a member of their arrival foursome. "The war got off to a bad start for Higgins," Beech later wrote, "because she was not blown up on the Han River Bridge with Frank Gibney, Burton Crane, and me. Any story-making disaster that befalls other correspondents and inconsiderately omits Higgins will have to reckon with her ire." For her front-page story, the *Herald Tribune* turned Higgins's text into a frame of words around a delicate portrait of her, eyes downcast. The headline: "Seoul's Fall: By a Reporter Who Escaped."

The *Herald Tribune* rushed to get its senior military correspondent, Homer Bigart, into Korea. From the Pacific theater in 1945, Bigart's dispatches had already earned him the 1946 Pulitzer in "telegraphic reporting," especially for his work in the aftermath of the atomic bomb the United States dropped on Hiroshima. The biggest prize Higgins had managed from her World War II reporting was the aforementioned award from colleagues of the New York Newspaper Women's Club for her coverage of Berchtesgaden and the liberation of Dachau. Only in retrospect did she grasp the inadequacy of what she had produced in those instances, saying awards should reflect more than hers did for having turned up first on the scene.

One of Bigart's first acts on arrival in Seoul was to tell Higgins to go back to Tokyo. She refused. He cabled their editors back in New York to order her out. She sent her own cable in protest. A

Marguerite Higgins and General Douglas MacArthur, Korea, 1950
(Life *Collection, Getty Images, photo by Carl Mydans*)

compromise of sorts was reached. Bigart was made chief correspondent; Higgins could provide sidebars and color. She paid no
heed. When Lieutenant General Walton H. Walker sent her back to
Japan, insisting that war was no place for a woman, General Douglas
MacArthur himself interceded. He gave her a ride on his plane, an
exclusive interview, and full reinstatement.

Bigart ignored Higgins, froze her out. Beech got possession of a
jeep and invited Higgins to be his reporting partner, which gave her
greater mobility than Bigart had. Beech, in his memoir, reflected
on the attitude he and Higgins adopted as they "took chances that
many correspondents were either unwilling or too intelligent to take.
This was fine, so long as our luck held, for in covering a war, there
is no substitute for an eyewitness report." That very recklessness
made Bigart despise her even more since his own compulsion to
compete forced him to take life-threatening chances he otherwise
would never have taken.

Bigart was by far the greater talent. Even Higgins's friend Carl

Mydans acknowledged this in his four-page, photo-strewn spread for *Life* that showcased "Girl War Correspondent" Marguerite Higgins, the only woman among the three hundred reporters who covered the war in Korea. The profile and photos ran in October 1950. Mydans's text detailed her bravery and the adoring reaction she elicited from the troops. "Maggie Wears Mud Like Other Women Wear Makeup" was the tagline over *The Boston Globe*'s reprint of the story. The rivalry with Bigart, Mydans wrote, was "personal (and bitter)." The other correspondents ribbed them both about it mercilessly.

Both Higgins and Bigart won the 1951 Pulitzer Prize in international reporting, not as a joint award, but separately, along with Keyes Beech and another *Chicago Daily News* reporter and two reporters for the Associated Press. The citation in all six cases was for "their reporting on the Korean War," but the individual recommendations for each correspondent read differently. Bigart, for example, was honored for "his outstanding reports from Korea. Rather than take the easy way by writing far behind the lines, he wrote his vivid reports from the front. He went to extraordinary risks in gathering his facts." For Higgins, who had done the same and more, the explanation gave off a diminishing gender twist. It reads like an apologia, as if to deflect the eye rolls of men who might have thought themselves more deserving of the honor. Her award was for "fine front line reporting showing enterprise and courage. She is entitled to special consideration by reason of being a woman, since she had to work under unusual dangers."

Beech had the clearest vantage point for assessing Maggie Higgins at war. "Any one of her dispatches might have been written by a man," he wrote five years later. "Despite her success, Higgins never gave her readers what they really wanted," meaning the traditional women's angle. "Higgins never stooped to that," he wrote. She was "appallingly single-minded" in her quest for fame and "almost frightening in her determination to overcome all obstacles" with "more guts, more staying power, and more resourcefulness than 90 percent of her detractors. She was a good newspaperman."

Bigart would later express regret about the way he treated Higgins in Korea. "No way I can make my behavior toward her appear in a favorable light," he confessed to Harrison Salisbury, who shared those words in the foreword he provided for a collection of Bigart's war reporting not published until 1992. The book was curated by Betsy Wade, Bigart's colleague at the *Times,* where he moved after the *Herald Tribune,* where she also worked. Whenever the two of them spoke, Wade made a point of taking notes. At one point, Wade asked him directly about his legendary feud with Higgins. She wanted to know which was true of two circulating versions of what he said when he learned that Higgins had remarried and given birth. Did he say, "Wonderful, who's the mother?" Wade asked, or was it, "Well, did she eat it?"

"Yes," Bigart replied.

Some of the most successful woman journalists of the 1950s were late bloomers. In a profession that favors its youth, talented women not only got belated big chances but achieved their first major successes well into their years. All of them were women of Martha Gellhorn's generation, born between 1903 and 1911, and all encountered obstacles during the Depression and war years that Gellhorn's social status and connections helped her circumvent. But once established, they grew in importance as if age were not a factor. There is a suggestion that maturity and their un-girlish, less sexually charged presence might have been an unspoken advantage, an inverse asset to the power of pulchritude. Or perhaps their successes reflected the propensity of editors, extant right up to the present, to hire men for potential and women for experience. They might have lacked Gellhorn's cosmopolitan allure and flair, but they built enviable careers all the same, on their own terms, in their own milieu, and in their second acts.

Pauline Frederick's splash was different from Gellhorn's but no less significant. It came in the early 1950s, when she had been a reporter for the better part of two decades. Not until 1946, when she was thirty-eight, did she get an offer from ABC Radio in New York. At the start, the terms were only as a freelancer, but the network soon took her on full time. Her assignment was not to cover "so-called women's news" but something perhaps even less appealing, that is, "general news that would be 'particularly cute, under a woman's treatment,'" as *The New York Times* described her original brief. *Newsweek* featured Frederick in a press column a year later. In the headline, the magazine called her "The Spinster at the News Mike," borrowing one of Frederick's self-deprecating descriptions. Her profile in the *Times* carried the headline "Only One of Her Kind," describing her without mentioning her age as "a tall, lissome brunette of mellifluous voice and photogenic figure" who was doing six morning radio shows and three telecasts every week while on call for twenty-one hours more.

The UN would quickly become a substantive, serious beat where woman journalists found places alongside men in head-on competition, enabling women to show elevated analytical skill and intellect in the way a Washington or foreign posting had the potential to do. Frederick as a television reporter for ABC on a serious beat was by far the most visible among the UN correspondents. Men like Abe Rosenthal were assigned to the world body for a couple of years for the *Times,* as was Drew Middleton. And yet for men, the UN beat was a weigh station soon passed along the road to bigger and better assignments, while for women it was a parking garage.

In 1953, Frederick moved on to NBC, still covering the United Nations and other related major stories with an international angle. At the age of forty-five, she had arrived at the assignment that would make her a star. There were honorary degrees and the lecture circuit, much in the tradition of Dorothy Thompson and Anne O'Hare McCormick.

There were no similar honors for Marvel Cooke, who also had her biggest moments relatively late, but unlike Frederick she did not get her start in journalism until she was thirty. After her stint as assistant to W. E. B. Du Bois at *The Crisis* and as assistant to the women's editor of the *Amsterdam News,* she moved up in editorial rank to become the assistant managing editor of *The People's Voice,* a position she held until the Harlem-based weekly folded in 1948. The paper's publisher was Adam Clayton Powell, the New York congressman and pastor of the Abyssinian Baptist Church, whom Cooke knew through her husband, Cecil, because they attended university nearby; Powell at Cornell and Cooke at Syracuse. "There were so few black students in these colleges upstate," she told Currie, her oral historian, "they all knew each other." Late in 1949, Cooke broke a color barrier for all the major New York metropolitan newspapers with her hire by *The Daily Compass,* formerly *PM* and before that *The New York Star.*

As the *Alabama Tribune* pointed out, she was a full-fledged reporter and editor, "not confined to 'Negro' news." Cooke told Currie that she had come to the paper's attention over other worthy candidates because of the friends she had made through her active role in the Newspaper Guild. She already knew most everyone on the *Compass*'s small staff, including the city editor, Sol Abraham, a Guild colleague, who had helped with the design of *The People's Voice*. Abraham made the hire. She hoped for a salary of $100 a week, up from the $85 that Powell had paid. Abraham offered $125.

Almost immediately, Cooke, by then forty-seven, attracted wide attention for her searing investigation of the Bronx location of one of the "slave markets" operating at various locations around the city. She went undercover to experience firsthand the day jobs of the "paper bag brigade"—the women carried their work clothes this way—to gain their confidence. For a week she stood with the regulars in front of the Woolworth's at 170th Street between Jerome and Walton Avenues. "Negro women wait, in rain or shine, in bitter cold or under broiling sun," she wrote, "to be hired by local housewives looking for bargains in human labor." Cooke, in fact, had been reporting on the subject for fifteen years. The stark separation of the Black and white worlds meant the practice, born of the Depression when so many full-time housekeepers lost their jobs, was still a revelation for white readers of the mainstream press, at least those not engaged in the hiring practice. Colleagues bet Cooke a quart of scotch that she would be unconvincing as a housekeeper, but she managed to get a job on her last day on the corner. For the paper, she detailed the assaults on dignity the practice invited: the fear and physical risk from men who presumed the women were awaiting work as prostitutes; the insulting treatment from employers; the paltry pay rate; and the tricks employers used to pay the workers even less, like hiring by the hour instead of by the day and then surprising the women by releasing them after only sixty minutes. She ended with proposals for how to eliminate the exploitative practices. She did the same for her other two major multipart series for the *Compass:* the second, in twelve parts, headlined "Occupation: Streetwalker," offered a close look at the state of prostitution in the city, and the third, an exploration of teenage narcotics addiction.

The *Compass* folded in 1952. With its failure, Cooke opted for deeper political engagement. Her involvements before she joined the staff of the *Compass* triggered an appearance before Joseph McCarthy's U.S. Senate Subcommittee on Investigations in 1953. Cooke repeatedly pleaded the Fifth Amendment as committee members asked if she or other people she knew were members of the Communist Party. She dismissed the suggestion that anyone on *The People's Voice* had ever referred to her as "Madame Commissar." Long after 1956, when the Communist Party in the United States lost favor with its one million U.S. members over Stalin's excesses, Cooke kept her membership.

Unlike Cooke's more direct path to journalism, Alice Dunnigan's took her through eighteen years of teaching, a brief, unhappy marriage to a dirt farmer, and a second failed marriage to an abuser. While teaching, she wrote part time for the *Louisville Defender* and *The Louisville Leader,* where she became society editor in 1935. At the start of World War II, she passed the federal service exam and moved to Washington as a clerk-typist for the War Labor Board and started writing on the side for the Associated Negro Press, which provided copy to a hundred Black newspapers in the United States and Africa. When the association's founder, Claude A. Barnett, decided he needed a full-time reporter in D.C., Dunnigan took the job for $100 a week after a man offered twice as much declined. Accepting low bids was and has remained a common way for women of any description to wrest opportunity. By June 1947, Dunnigan was breaking ground for Black women. She was forty-one when she became the first Black woman with accreditation to cover Congress. That accreditation led to press passes for the State Department and the Supreme Court. She covered Truman's whistle-stop campaign trip, despite Barnett's refusal to pay the $1,000 fee required of all the reporters. She took a loan and covered it herself, taking a year to repay her lender. Writing was not her strength—copy

Ethel Payne
(From the Women in Journalism series [2002], © 2002 USPS®)

editors did cleanup—but she was one of only two or three Black reporters covering for a national audience the death of Jim Crow, the breakthroughs in integration, and the significant hiring of Blacks at wholly white institutions, like *The Washington Post*. She joined the Women's National Press Club in 1955.

Dunnigan might have had her tussles with writing, but not Ethel Payne. For *The Chicago Defender*, Payne reported and wrote about everything from *Brown v. Board of Education* to the Montgomery bus boycott to the desegregation of Little Rock's schools. She was insistent during White House press conferences on bringing the country's attention to the lack of action on integration, much to the irritation of President Eisenhower's team. In fact, she pursued confrontation. "If you have lived through the black experience in this country, you feel that every day you're assaulted by the system," she told her oral historian. "You are either acquiescent, which I think is wrong, or else you just rebel, and you kick against it. I wanted to constantly, constantly, constantly hammer away, raise the questions that needed to be raised."

Payne, too, came to journalism late. In 1948, when she was thirty-seven, she moved to Japan to work as a hostess for a U.S. Army Special Services club, primarily to organize recreational activities and entertainment for African American troops. In 1950, Payne showed Alex Wilson, a reporter for *The Chicago Defender* on his way to cover the war in Korea, the diary she had been keeping of her experiences in Japan. She had watched at close range the segregation of Black soldiers, who, under Truman's executive order, were not supposed to be segregated any longer, and observed the fate of the mixed-race children who remained in a society that gave them cold welcome. Wilson took the diary back to Chicago, where the *Defender* turned Payne's entries into blockbuster stories and then offered her a full-time position. She soon became the paper's Washington bureau chief, after which she became known as "The First Lady of the Black Press."

Edith Evans Asbury, as an assistant women's page editor on the *World-Telegram*, could not bring herself to cross the picket line when the guild went on strike in the summer of 1950. Instead, she carried a sign outside the building for all eighty-one days. She asked to be made a reporter on the city desk, but the women's editor would not release her. She asked the city editor to request her; he said he could not. Asbury made a list of all the city's papers and decided to start at the top. From her reporting days at the *Post* and the AP, she got to know a *New York Times* reporter who respected her work. She had not seen him in three years, but she called him just the same to see if the paper might have an opening. He checked with the city editor, who said he would see Asbury that day. As she rode the subway to the *Times,* she pulled an index card out of her purse and jotted down all her relevant dates: the *Cincinnati Times-Star,* 1929; *The Knoxville News-Sentinel,* 1931–36; *New York Post,* 1937; AP, 1938–45; *World-Telegram,* 1949–.

With more than two decades of experience at forty-two, Asbury was overqualified for the position available, to replace one of the four women on the city desk who was about to take maternity leave. The *Times* wanted to retain that number, so Asbury got the offer. The news that day, October 29, 1952, made her feel as if she were "tripping on air," she told Kathleen Currie, as if she were "about to enter paradise." By January, the reporter who had vouched for her became city editor and her direct report. "For the first time in my life, I had walked into the right place at the right time and called the right person," not only because she was working for someone who already respected her work, a man with two beloved daughters, but because it was a moment when the paper was receptive to a less stodgy writing style, like Asbury's.

The city editor remained in place until 1963, during which time Asbury's assignments kept improving. She did a major five-part series on aging in 1955. She was the only woman on a team of ten top reporters sent for weeks to assess the state of integration in seventeen southern states. The team's combined efforts consumed seven pages of the newspaper on March 13, 1956. Asbury's assigned territory matched her background: Kentucky and Tennessee. In 1958, she took on birth control. Numerous local awards came her way.

Yet as things tend to go in leadership transitions, she fared less well under the next city editor, Abe Rosenthal, although his successor, Arthur Gelb, admired her greatly. Gelb, in fact, felt a deep debt to Asbury, as he later wrote. Her "stubborn curiosity" helped get him started in his new post. "She understood *The Times*'s Ochsian

Edith Evans Asbury, 1956, featured in this full-page
New York Times ad in *The New Yorker*

(*Courtesy of* The New York Times, *published in*
The New Yorker, *March 23, 1957, photo by* © *Arnold Newman*)

standards of fairness, integrity and good taste—traditions she absorbed into her bones. She also knew the importance of passing them on to younger reporters who, in turn, passed them on to younger reporters. In my view, that was at the heart of the paper's vigorous survival."

Gelb especially favored Asbury for major trial coverage where, he reported, she would "always probe far beyond the testimony." On his watch, she covered the Black Panthers trial in 1967 and the Bobby Seale case in 1971. "I never considered Edith's gender when drawing up the assignment sheet, and I once confronted a young assistant editor who had handed her a story with a domestic angle." The journalist and author Anthony Lukas, at a party Gelb once hosted, recited his list of the *Times*'s greatest treasures. There was the "pure gold of Homer Bigart and the solid silver of Peter Kihss," Gelb quoted him as saying, "Joe Lelyveld, the imperial purple of future greatness . . . and Edith Evans Asbury, the dazzling white of dignity and style." Interestingly, however, there is no mention of any attempt to promote her or to put her on a management track, even given her prior experience as an assistant section editor.

In late March 1957, *Newsweek* brought attention to "The Girls on the Tribune." Sixty of the 445 people on the Chicago paper's news staff were women by then, a sizable increase over the 24 women the newspaper touted in its 1926 house ad, all but 3, at the time, assigned to women's work. The *Newsweek* writer seemed amazed that some of the year's biggest stories in the *Tribune* carried women's bylines, including a "brilliant, sharply written" jailhouse interview with the "thrill-killer" Nathan Leopold by Marcia Winn, "46, a slender brunette," and a major ten-part series on the migration of the 260,000 job seekers arriving in Chicago from the South by Norma Lee Browning, described as "the Trib's attractive, most publicized woman reporter." Women at the paper also covered police and finance, *Newsweek* noted. "Women have sharper perception on some things," the paper's city editor explained. "They don't get soured or cynical. By the time most men are 40 or 45, they're apt to throw a story down if it doesn't look big right off the bat. . . . Women keep the spark."

In the late 1950s, the spark had not yet ignited for Joan Didion, Janet Malcolm, and Gloria Steinem, all born in 1934, all young and just starting out. Malcolm, after succeeding her first husband, Donald

Malcolm, as editor of the student daily at the University of Michigan, wrote book reviews for *The New Republic,* where her husband had gone to work as an essayist and book critic. Didion, after graduating from Berkeley in 1956, won an assistantship at *Vogue* and stayed seven years, working her way up to associate features editor. Steinem, after college at Smith, spent the rest of the 1950s engaged in other kinds of work abroad and then back at home. As writers, outsized recognition for all three was in the offing, but not soon.

CHAPTER 12

Foment

The 1960s: a decade of change, liberation, exuberance, rage, rebellion, and grief. The Pill. The women's movement. The Beatles. The Cuban missile crisis. LSD. The Equal Pay Act. The Civil Rights Act. Vietnam escalation. "I Have a Dream." The assassination of President John F. Kennedy. LBJ. The Warren Commission. The assassination of Malcolm X. The assassinations of Martin Luther King Jr. and Robert F. Kennedy. Riots in Watts and Chicago. Black Panthers. Yippies. United Farm Workers. The Kerner Commission. *Hair.* The moon landing. The Manson murders. Woodstock. Marchers, protesters, consciousness raisers, and mobilizers, all on call to challenge discrimination, injustice, police brutality, apartheid, and the war in Southeast Asia. The decade convulsed in agitation for peace, equal rights, and equal opportunity, realizing none.

A book published in 1963 infused the national discourse once again with the question of women's place, spurring a broad swath of the country's women to press for change and others to react against it, both as they had a century earlier. The author of *The Feminine Mystique* was a "writer who keeps house" named Betty Friedan, a white, Smith-educated, suburban mom in her early forties with some background in labor reporting and a short stack of clippings in the women's magazines. To those of us who came of age during feminism's second coming, Friedan's exploration of "the problem that has no name" felt altogether new. Her book brought fresh awareness to age-old issues in much the way the suffrage movement awakened a critical mass of women and empathetic men to the impact of ingrained inequality and the subjugation it visited on women's lives.

That same year, Lynn Sherr, a recent Wellesley graduate with the résumé plumage of a guest editorship at *Mademoiselle* magazine, à la Sylvia Plath, came up against "the kings of New York journalism of the early 1960s" who could not have cared less about her early achievements. "What they said to me was 'We don't hire girls,'" Sherr said years later, "over and over." It was not any different at the general interest magazines, and television, she said, was "another exclusive men's club—invented by men, run by men, aimed at men. Extraordinary as it may seem, it never occurred to us to question that attitude. It's simply the way things were."

Realization dawned slowly that the civil rights legislation of the 1960s provided legal instruments that could address the entrenched discriminatory practices, both subtle and overt, that ruled the professional lives of so many women. The Equal Pay Act of 1963 made it illegal to pay men and women different wages for doing the same work in the same place, and the Civil Rights Act of 1964 banned employment discrimination based on race, color, religion, sex, or national origin.

The enactment of these laws coincided with the advancing strength of the women's liberation movement and the greater and ever-growing number of woman journalists in the field. Young women at that point were benefiting from the openings that the draft created as men were called up to serve during the war in Vietnam. By 1972, the percentage of journalists closed in on gender parity, yet for most women the chances for advancement looked much as they had seventy years earlier, in Nellie Bly's heyday, when women were only a tenth of all reporters and editors.

The situation for women at the weekly magazines in the 1960s symbolizes most graphically the range of conditions in the wider industry. The contrast between office culture at *Time, Life,* and *Newsweek* and at *The New Yorker,* for example, could not have been starker. As far back as 1940, Time Life Inc.'s owner, Henry Luce, speaking at *Time*'s twentieth anniversary celebration, described his newsmagazine's research department as "a modern female priesthood, the veritable vestal virgins whom levitous writers cajole in vain and managing editors learn humbly to appease."

Lynn Povich's book, *The Good Girls Revolt: How the Women of "Newsweek" Sued Their Bosses and Changed the Workplace,* traced her twenty-five years with the magazine, starting in 1965. With precious few exceptions, the women who worked at *Newsweek, Time, Life,* or *Look* almost inevitably started out in lesser positions than did men with like résumés. Povich joined the *Newsweek* staff as a secretary in the Paris bureau with an undergraduate degree in history and French from Vassar and no journalism experience. As was the custom, useful connections eased her way in. Her father, Shirley Povich, was a celebrated sports columnist at *The Washington Post,* which at the time was under the same ownership as *Newsweek.* Povich stayed in the Paris post for sixteen months, inspired by the bureau's lone woman reporter, Liz Peer, *Newsweek*'s "Brenda Starr." At twenty-nine, Peer was one of the very few women at the company with a reporter/correspondent title. Povich, on word of a possible opening in New York, traveled home steerage on the *Queen Elizabeth* at her own expense in a room so small she could touch the walls on either side of her bed if she stretched her arms out widely enough. She took Peer's advice and asked to work on one of the soft feature sections of the magazine, known as "the back of the book," where researchers had the best chance of being able to report. The inequities in the New York office could not have been more blatant. Povich recalled the summer that two equally qualified recent Columbia journalism school graduates joined the staff, he as a reporter, she as a researcher.

For the women on these staffs, the few promotions granted were often largely in name only. A researcher at *Life,* writing under a pseudonym in *Mademoiselle,* said that in 1970 only four women at the magazine ranked above assistant editor and those with more elevated titles often performed the same duties they had as researchers. Editors never nurtured or encouraged women to report or write, she argued, which undermined initiative and self-confidence.

Thirty years after Luce's speech, the pattern at *Time* and *Life* remained unchanged. Given how rankling this must have been, it is hard to understand why the women reacted so slowly in their own interest, especially given the period's loud and insistent drumbeats for change. Povich, in describing the women at *Newsweek,* alluded to the way they undercut their own interests by letting discriminatory practices persist unchallenged, just as women had been doing all along. She described herself and her colleagues in the mid-1960s as mostly middle-class girls of the postwar generation inculcated to become "good wives and mothers and maybe educated, but that's about it. Certainly not to have careers."

A woman journalist on the staff of a mainstream outlet at least had the occasional opportunity to help cover the decade's biggest stories, which felt heady, vital, and supremely relevant. That was the trade-off. "The wires were clacking, the phones were ringing, and we were engaged in lively conversations about things that mattered," Franny Heller Zorn recalled in an interview with Povich that she elaborated on years later. As Frances Heller, from 1964 to 1969, she rose at *Newsweek* from copygirl to clipping articles from other publications for the files to researcher to junior reporter. "It was thrilling to feel the pulse of the news and to have that special pipeline to the truth that civilians couldn't possibly have," she said, "even with all the crap we had to do." In 1968, Heller was assigned to shadow Catherine Deneuve in New York as *The April Fools*, her film with Jack Lemmon, was about to premiere. It fell to Heller to do much of the reporting for what would become the magazine's five-page, photo-rich profile of this new "French Star over Hollywood." Heller's contributions to the piece were substantial enough for the section editor to credit her by name with her photo on the story's page 3 cover note. She pressed to write the planned boxed sidebar about shadowing Deneuve, but the editor in charge refused. Women at the magazine were "pieces of fluff," he told her, as he gave the assignment to one of the men on staff who had spent almost no time with the star. A year later, another editor began stalking Heller obsessively, deluded enough about where he stood in her affections to shock her with his presentation of an engagement ring. Her gentle rejection triggered his anger and a threat to wreck her career. She moved on to another publication. As Lynn Povich put it, "Our 'problem that had no name' in the mid-1960s was sexism, pure and simple."

Obviously, Povich said, there were women who understood all along that what they were experiencing in the workplace was wrong, but it took "this huge social movement behind us questioning women's roles" to get most women "to rethink what our roles should be and what we were doing."

The situation at *The New Yorker* was nothing like this, even though it took the founding editor, Harold Ross, many years to accept the idea of women as reporters, or even as secretaries, according to his biographer Thomas Kunkel. Indeed, Jane Grant's close involvement during the magazine's earliest years, alongside her husband, surely figured in its relatively more egalitarian approach. Kunkel wrote that Ross "simply could never have pulled off *The New Yorker* as we know it without the likes of Jane Grant, Katherine [White] Angell, Lois Long, Dorothy Parker, Helen Hokinson, and Janet Flanner aka Genêt." Jane Grant's memoir added Elsie Dick and Muriel Draper and offered the greatest credit to Katherine White, the Boston Brahmin through whose hands every manuscript passed, because she "was able to impart to the magazine a finesse which Ross called 'taste.'"

As a staff member in the 1960s, Calvin Trillin had no idea of how the compensation system worked or if it was equitable. He found it mysterious, as if it emerged "from a room full of ancient female Jesuits with quill pens." Only William Shawn, who succeeded Ross, made the essential decisions in those days, "whether to encourage someone to do a piece, whether to buy it, if or when to run it, etc.," Trillin said. Among the other editors whose job it was to shepherd a piece through the closing process, he does not recall any women involved but allowed that he might be mistaken. He did remember that the celebrated fact-checkers included women, either by the time he arrived or soon after, and that all the copy editors were women, including "the fearsome Eleanor Gould, the czar of grammar and construction."

In 1963, *The New Yorker* hired twenty-five-year-old Jane Kramer from *The Village Voice* as the first of her ten books, *Off Washington Square: A Reporter Looks at Greenwich Village, N.Y.*, was being published. At around the same time, *Mademoiselle* featured Kramer in a piece that advised any reader who wanted to break into print to seek work at a weekly newspaper as Kramer had. At *The New Yorker*, Kramer joined Susan Sheehan, who had been on staff since 1961, and Renata Adler, since 1962. Janet Malcolm moved on from book reviewing at *The New Republic* after the birth of her daughter in 1962, and the following year *The New Yorker* published her poem "Thoughts on Living in a Shaker House." More pieces followed, but that took several years. Closer to the end of the decade came the critics Pauline Kael for film and Ellen Willis for rock music.

In 1963, the year Trillin joined the *New Yorker* staff, he said it was understood, even "taken for granted," that women, at least the woman writers, were full peers. "I suspect that the culture was set early on," he said in an email, adding that "any proactive attempt at gender balancing" would have been unnecessary. He did know about a targeted recruitment effort at the time to bring more Black voices into the magazine, which, by serendipitous extension, helped change his future.

At twenty-five, working in *Time* magazine's Atlanta bureau, Trillin was among the reporters who covered the University of Georgia's desegregation during the 1960–61 academic year. While reporting at the university, he befriended Charlayne Hunter, later Charlayne Hunter-Gault, who was at the center of the story. She and Hamilton Holmes integrated the university as its first two Black students, a rock-through-her-window, riot-provoking decision of such historic proportions that the two college sophomores would become national symbols of the desegregation movement with major attendant publicity, including her profile in *The New York Times*. Hunter had been building her way to a journalism career since a childhood fascination with the *Brenda Starr* comic strip. She was editor of the student newspaper at her all-Black high school in Atlanta and then tried to work for Georgia's college newspaper, *The Red & Black*, "but never got any assignments." So, she headed home on weekends to help Julian Bond and Carl Holman edit *The Atlanta Inquirer*, which she described as "the upstart newspaper they started when not even the Black press was covering the student movement in Atlanta." While still in

Charlayne Hunter-Gault
with Joe Lelyveld
(Courtesy of The New York Times/*Redux)*

school, she placed emotive personal pieces in *Jet* and interned as a sophomore under Norman Isaacs at *The Louisville Times,* that paper's first Black reporter. Trillin soon left Atlanta for *Time*'s headquarters in New York, promoted to join the magazine's staff of writers. He and Hunter stayed in touch by telephone.

Some months before her graduation in 1963, Hunter received a call from Leo Hofeller, the executive editor of *The New Yorker* under Shawn, who invited her to New York to interview for one of the magazine's editorial assistant positions, jobs mostly filled by graduates of Ivy League schools. Trillin said that at the time Shawn was in search of Black graduates from good colleges whom he could hire to improve the magazine's diversity and widen the scope of its coverage of the nation's racial struggle. At the time, Trillin said, it often happened that the most sought-after African American graduates favored higher-paying fields. Shawn understood that to attract top Black talent to the magazine, he needed to go beyond the usual system of word-of-mouth referrals, which effectively meant white candidates.

Hunter called Trillin to let him know she was coming to town for the interview with Hofeller. Trillin in turn arranged a dinner the night before with Hunter, Gerry Jonas, who was on *The New Yorker*'s staff, and his wife, the performance artist Joan Jonas. At the interview the next day, when Hofeller asked Hunter if she knew anyone at the magazine, she was able to say that Trillin had introduced her to Jonas and that she had known Trillin since he covered desegregation in Georgia for *Time.* At that moment, Jonas just happened to pass by Hofeller's office. Hofeller stopped him and asked him to find out if Trillin would like to come in for an interview. Trillin's name had surfaced only a few weeks earlier after Shawn admired *Time*'s unsigned mid-December cover story on Adlai Stevenson and learned that Trillin had written it.

Trillin's job at *Time* by then had lost its appeal. He grew tired of writing to a line count from the files of faraway reporters and then having the stories go through several more editing rounds to have the life "sucked out of them" by someone at the end of the chain not likely to have read the reporter's original effort. He joined *The New Yorker* staff in mid-March. Hunter came on board in June. "An Education in Georgia," Trillin's first and only multipart series for the magazine, ran in three installments, starting in July 1963. Hunter was a valuable in-house resource for the fact-checkers as Trillin's pieces went through the paces to publication. His book of the same title, his first, came out six months later.

Hunter was so much in the national conversation by then that her entry-level hire at *The New Yorker* and her first marriage soon after were news. A spokesman for the magazine told the AP that she, like the other editorial assistants, would be doing "no news or editorial work." Yet barely a year later, in the summer of 1964, still in the assistant pool and back from a six-month maternity leave, one long unsigned paragraph she wrote about the aftermath of a recent spate of riots in the Brooklyn neighborhood of Bedford-Stuyvesant led the magazine's "Notes and Comments" section. Within a year, two more of her pieces appeared, both memoirs. The magazine promoted Hunter to its "Talk of the Town" staff, and over the next two years she wrote at least seven more signed pieces. In 1968, she left to accept a Russell Sage Fellowship at Washington University in St. Louis to better her grasp of the social sciences and apply their methods to her work. During that time, her reporting for the magazine *Trans-Action* on the Poor People's Campaign of 1968 and the tent city the movement erected near the Washington Mall spurred a desire to get her "feet back in the street," as she put it in an interview. She accepted a job in Washington, D.C., as a local anchor and investigative reporter on the *News Four Probe* team of WRC-TV, the local NBC affiliate. Her charge, as newspaper ads for the show said, was to delve "into attitudes and issues of social significance." That remained her focus wherever she worked thereafter.

By 1968, the reverberations of *The Feminine Mystique* had fractured all the old assumptions, but internal battles, competing, contradictory objectives, and conflicting interests among ardent supporters confounded the work of the movement it spawned. The mission lacked the simplicity of the suffrage movement with its singular, ultimately inarguable goal of giving the right to vote to the denied half of the population who already should have had it. By comparison, second wave feminism was confusing. "What Do These Women Want?" asked a headline in *The New York Times Magazine*. Activist demands ranged from a nationwide network of child-care centers to tax code revisions with deductions for housekeeping and raising families, guaranteed paid maternity leave, revision in divorce and alimony laws, gay rights, abortion rights, and equal pay and equal treatment for equal work. The magazine's writer expressed surprise at having encountered "the only civil rights movement in history which has been put down, consistently, by the cruelest weapon of them all—ridicule." In fact, opponents spoofed and bullied and laughed at the suffragists just as relentlessly over the seventy years it took the movement to achieve its one clear aim. Would this second, far more diffuse push to change the status of women, so embroiled in internal squabbles, take as long or longer to reach its even more contested objectives? Would equality ever come?

In the 1960s, in a field of fifty thousand woman journalists nationwide, the publicity generated by the promotions, choice assignments, star billing, and stunning achievements of the few masked the situation of the many. Those who got stuck in women's and soft-news departments or in grunt jobs had little to no chance to be groomed, channeled, or mentored into the profession's most substantive, most highly valued work.

CHAPTER 13

Supernovas

Throughout the 1960s, the achievements of exceptional women brought glimmers of hope and change to those coming up behind them. More women than ever before won top prizes, amassed newsroom power, and gained singular recognition for their reporting at home and abroad, in some cases recognition that lasted. Their ability to achieve in the most competitive ranks was exceptional; they were exceptions that proved the enervating rule.

Judges for several top national prizes honored women over men for reporting and writing from the world's most challenging, competitive news sites, including Vietnam. From 1960 to 1969, however, the Pulitzer Prize board honored only three women aside the publications they represented; the other sixty-four named recipients of the prize in that period were men. In 1960, Miriam Ottenberg of the Washington *Evening Star* won for local reporting for her seven-part investigation of a local used-car racket. A week after Ottenberg received the news, a policeman jerked her back from a curb before a car she thought was half a block away almost killed her. As she later wrote, it would be years before she knew "that the two-layered look of the cars was a mirage created by double vision, and that the cause was multiple sclerosis."

Ottenberg, forty-six at the time, had been a hard-charging reporter since the late 1930s. She broke news repeatedly for the *Star* with her interviews and investigations. For years after the policeman's rescue, unaware of what was wrong, she "trusted my legs to take me into

Miriam Ottenberg on the popular television
game show *I've Got a Secret* with host Garry Moore
(Courtesy Everett Collection)

danger and out again." She ventured into Mau Mau country and into
Malaya "when guerrillas were shooting up the countryside," or posed
"as the willing dupe of con men." Her stories commanded national
attention through the further distribution provided by the NANA
syndicate. Other journalists often credited her reporting by name in
their own stories.

In 1963, the *Chicago Daily News* won the Pulitzer for public
service for Lois Wille's five-part, policy-changing series on the lack
of birth control availability
in the city. Wille was revered as a figure in Chicago
journalism, often report-
ing undercover to produce
reform-generating local investigations. Before she retired at sixty in 1991, she
had run the editorial pages
of the *Chicago Sun-Times*
and the *Chicago Tribune* and
won a second Pulitzer for
editorial writing in 1989. An
epitaph described her as a

Lois Wille
(Chicago Tribune)

reporter and editor whose influence on Chicago was "as deep and profound as that of any elected official," a woman of "immense talent, fortitude and considerable charm" with "admirers too numerous to count."

As the decade got under way, Aline Mosby was still thriving under a Moscow dateline, still with United Press International. At an embassy reception in March 1961, a verbal altercation erupted between Mosby, whom colleagues described as "a terrier of an American reporter," and the editor of *Izvestia*, Alexei Adzhubei, a known "bully and a prodigious drinker" who "cut up nasty." Suddenly Adzhubei smeared off Mosby's lipstick and eyeshadow. In Mosby's version, Adzhubei used his handkerchief; a colleague said he fished a napkin off the table, called Mosby a *prostitutka*, and told her to get out of his sight. She responded by reapplying her makeup.

It is hard to imagine there was no connection between the public face wipe and what happened soon after. Two young Soviets took the highly unusual step of approaching Mosby at a public event. She chatted them up all the same but found it staggering when they invited her to lunch the following day. This was not the sort of thing involving foreigners that ordinary Russians would do without risk in 1961. Nonetheless, she accepted the invitation and agreed to meet them at the Café Ararat, next to the Hotel Metropol.

She discussed the overture with her bureau chief and another colleague. They could not decide if the men were dangerous or if it might be worthwhile for her to meet them, perhaps to learn something useful. As Mosby recalled in her interview with Currie, the possibilities worried her enough to decline the invitation. The men persisted and she agreed to meet them in full daylight in a very public place. They called her at the bureau, which doubled as her apartment, and got her to agree to a new date at the Ararat. Still, she told her colleagues if she did not return within a few hours, they should call the police.

At lunch, the men downed cognac as they awaited their meals. They kept encouraging her to join them in a drink, and finally she agreed to a glass of champagne. Mosby had been collecting Russian icons, which the men seemed to know, and they brought a few with them for her to see. She turned away from the table at one point for a better look. As she turned back, she noticed that the champagne in her glass had taken on an amber tint, likely from a splash of cognac. The men urged her to try it, so, to be polite, she took a few sips. Within minutes, her head spun. She felt herself falling unconscious "instantly," and, she said, "I grabbed my handbag and went running out of the restaurant, weaving as I went." Outside on the sidewalk, a photographer and a policeman stood poised in wait.

Mosby swooned and passed out on the street. The officer hauled her off to a drunk tank, where she slept off the Mickey until a friend from the U.S. embassy collected her. As the story circulated, other journalists expressed sympathy and a little shock. "I had been very naive about that," she said. UPI decided against a protest or a news story, hoping the embarrassment would just fade away.

At UPI's request, colleagues in the foreign press also kept the incident quiet—until they wrote their memoirs—but a few days later an article about the lunch appeared in *Izvestia*, two humiliating photos flanking the text. In one, Mosby appeared disoriented as she exited the restaurant; in the other, she was passed out on a cot next to another woman in the same state. The photo showed Mosby prone, under a sheet, her décolletage exposed down to its lowest possible decent point. The story accused her of being publicly drunk to the point of oblivion, of haggling over the price of icons being offered by a "dandy," and of having consorted at other points with a convicted felon, a "so-called painter," and a "social parasite," in her pursuit of banned abstract Russian art from the 1930s. The article said Mosby offered the cognac in an attempt to negotiate a lower price and then

Aline Mosby in *Izvestia,* June 6, 1961

("Drugged, in the Moscow Drunk Tank," Izvestia, *June 6, 1961)*

slipped out of the restaurant, leaving the waiter with an unpaid check for 17 rubles and 14 kopeks. The article, full of falsehoods, read credibly. It went on to say that even if she were no more than a drunken speculator with an American passport, her behavior would have been hideous, but how much worse it was for an accredited correspondent in Moscow using her "slight command" of the Russian language not for reporting but for "dirty deeds, for drinking and debauching." What right did such a person have to report on the Soviet Union? "Where and how does she get her scoops? In a drunken stupor under the fence?"

The newspaper shared with its readers the blemishes in Mosby's background. "Nepotism and her daddy's fat wallet" had led to her hire at UPI, it said, and told the story of her pseudonymous work in Hollywood for *Confidential* magazine, how UPI had to fire her because of it, but how she somehow turned up thereafter as one of its correspondents in the Soviet Union.

Her bureau chief, Henry Shapiro, offered her the option of immediate reassignment, but a resolute Mosby opted to stay in Moscow. Her transfer to Paris came as planned, seven months later, at the start of 1962. That same year, Random House published her book about everyday Russians to favorable reviews. The cover tagline called her "the only woman correspondent in Moscow," but more accurately, she was the only woman reporting from Moscow sent by her company as a full-time staff correspondent at the time. In the fall of 1963, from her next post in Paris, Mosby was first on the scene at the border between Algeria and Morocco to cover the hostilities that became known as the Sand War.

At around the same time, *The New York Times* named Ada Louise Huxtable its first architecture critic. Huxtable was forty-two, an established, distinguished, award-winning author and architectural historian about to complete her six-volume series about the city's construction. She had graduated magna cum laude in art history from Hunter College and attended graduate school in art and architecture history at New York University's Institute of Fine Arts. She worked in the modern furniture department at Bloomingdale's until the Museum of Modern Art hired her in 1946 as an assistant curator in its department of architecture and design. She studied in Italy on a

Fulbright, had a Guggenheim Fellowship in 1958, wrote a published study of the Italian engineer Pier Luigi Nervi, and contributed articles to art and architecture periodicals and to *The New York Times Magazine.* Clifton Daniel, the *Times*'s managing editor, played the key role in bringing her to the newspaper full time, recruiting her twice, as it happened, because she at first declined. Many years later, in a tribute

Ada Louise Huxtable
*(Gene Maggio/*New York Times*/Redux)*

staged at the Museum of the City of New York, her successor would praise her as "the most important pioneer of architectural criticism in newspapers in our time," a critic who made people pay attention to the built city and care about it. When she died at ninety-one in 2013, the *Times* noted her obituary on the front page with a longer tribute inside and a follow-up appreciation the following day. *The Washington Post* proclaimed her "one of the most trenchant, biting and influential voices in her profession for more than half a century."

By 1963, in Pauline Frederick's tenth year at NBC, she had become another influencer. At fifty-six, she was "America's highest-paid, best-known female commentator on television or radio," as Gay Talese described her in his profile of her for *The Saturday Evening Post.* Her days and nights were so packed, he wrote, that they likely accounted for why she had not yet married. "The Perils of Pauline" was the title of his exploration of her aloneness, of her low opinion of her own appearance, which, she had told him, was the residue of a childhood spent as an "ugly duckling." He offered that he found her "quite handsome," an "erect, five-foot-nine-inch graying blond" with a "curvesome figure (always concealed in conservative clothing)," who "could pass as the headmistress of a school for girls." He thought she outshone the other women on television, who "often seem no more profound than the Weather Girl." Talese's profile paid considerable attention to Frederick's looks.

He also delved into her resentment of television's "glamour laws." "You can't look like an old crow on television," she told him. The extra hours the visual medium obliged her to spend on hair and makeup irritated her as much as the gender bias she experienced, although she did not call it that. These complaints became a recurrent theme in the many speeches she gave around the country. "When a man stands up to speak, people listen, then look," she would say. "When a woman gets up, people look; then, if they like what they see, they listen." Talese did not mention the major awards she had won, but he did cite her place in the top ten of a recent Gallup poll of the most admired women in the world alongside Jacqueline Kennedy, Queen Elizabeth II, Senator Margaret Chase Smith, and Eleanor Roosevelt. He also brought up the younger, "prettier" woman correspondents then "gaining great attention on rival networks."

In 1964, in *The New York Times Magazine,* a reporter singled out Frederick, Nancy Dickerson, and Lisa Howard as the only three women doing serious work on television at the time, the only three who made regular appearances on network news and public-affairs programs. And yet they too were being subjected to "a subtle but certain condescension." The writer based her assessment on interviews with news and advertising executives, who regurgitated the tired old arguments against women in journalism, retrofitted to the small screen: Women at home who controlled the channel tuning did not like to see other women on television. Women on television were not authoritative enough. Too few women on television were qualified for the work.

The next year, *Good Housekeeping* added four more names to "TV's Female Brain Trust": Barbara Walters, Marlene Sanders, Aline Saarinen, and Judith Crist. Walters joined the on-air team at NBC's *Today Show* in 1965 and became its cohost nine years later. This followed an inauspicious climb from a secretarial school to a small ad agency to assistant publicity director at a local NBC affiliate to producer at the same affiliate to writer for CBS News. Sanders, of ABC, was "anything but a frothy woman's page reporter," the magazine said. Long before Saarinen appeared on television, she had distinguished herself as an authority, critic, and lecturer, and Crist, once Marguerite Higgins's colleague at the *New York Herald Tribune,* had gained a following as the entertainment critic for *The Today Show.*

Gloria Steinem was more than telegenic but made her way by writing for magazines and newspapers. Her undercover pose as a Playboy Bunny for *Show* magazine in 1963 brought her enormous attention, much of it unwelcome. For years, she later wrote, she considered her eleven days as Bunny "Marie Ochs" (her grandmother's name; she used her grandmother's Social Security number, too) a career blunder, because it generated no desirable new assignments. Only later did she realize how effective it had been. She exposed Playboy's exploitative policies and stopped Hugh Hefner's staff from physically examining its Bunny applicants. She found it satisfying that her story "outlived all the Playboy Clubs, both here and abroad."

Late in 1965, Steinem wrote for *Harper's* about why she chose to freelance. She liked the freedom it gave her to learn new things doing work she cared about. In another piece for the *Times,* she wrote about the smart women the television networks had begun to employ. Yet even by including every woman above the level of secretary, she could count only twelve who were involved in show production, and that included "girls who are employed only for their skin tones, production assistants who spend a lot of time running out for light coffees, and assistant directors who have much less chance than their male counterparts of ever getting to be directors." Of the women associated with hard news, Steinem cited Frederick, Saarinen, Dickerson, and Walters, calling Walters the "woman now receiving more network exposure than any other." Four techniques could land a woman a job in television, Steinem wrote: the "foot-in-the-door," which was the route of Frederick, Walters, and Sanders; "get a scoop," as Lisa Howard did by interviewing Fidel Castro; "visiting expert," which Saarinen was before the network hired her full time; and the rarest of all, "newspaper experience" or a wire service background of the kind Lynn Sherr brought to ABC after seven and a half years at the AP.

On the print side, Agness Underwood, the onetime Los Angeles crime reporter, still with that cap pistol in the drawer of her desk and her baseball bat on top, moved up from city editor to assistant managing editor at the *Herald Examiner* in Los Angeles. She held the post from 1964 until her retirement in 1968. Jim Bellows, as editor of the *New York Herald Tribune* until its demise, hired Gail Sheehy for the paper's women's section staff in 1964, around when Tom Wolfe, Jimmy Breslin, and Richard Reeves also got their starts. In a reminiscence Sheehy provided for Bellows's memoir, she wrote of her coverage of "poor women, pregnant women, addicts in the prison system, and Harlem women on rent strike." It won her no favor with the section's editor, Eugenia Sheppard, but brought keen support from Bellows, who urged her to keep producing "the gritty stuff in the middle of all that fluff."

Charlotte Curtis crashed the boundaries of women's desk expectations in a different way and to even greater effect. In 1965, her fifth year on the *Times*'s staff, she became editor of its women's section, at this point redubbed family/style. She amassed power at the paper well beyond her section. It did not emanate from investigative triumphs or reporting on the Vietnam War or the civil rights movement, although her coverage of a fundraiser for the Black Panthers at the home of the composer Leonard Bernstein is legendary. Under the bland headline "Black Panther Philosophy Is Debated at the Bernsteins," she described the question-and-answer portion of the evening led by Bernstein with sentences like this: "Donald Cox, the Panther field marshal and a member of the party's central committee, did most of the answering, and there were even moments when both men were not talking at the same time." What set Curtis apart was the way she reimagined aspects of the often banal fare the women's pages customarily offered. She served it up as subtle, ongoing, ever-so-biting cultural critique. It was an approach hungrily embraced by the *Times*'s upscale readers and by her bosses. At the same time, it gained her the kind of respect that had always been reserved for women in the profession such as Ishbel Ross,

Charlotte Curtis

(New York Public Library, digitalcollections.nypl.org/items/ e73263c0-b5c1-0135-bfc2-03705d7f6e8e)

Anne O'Hare McCormick, and Flora Lewis, woman journalists who functioned professionally in the style of the men.

Curtis was thirty-three when the *Times* hired her, armed with eleven years of experience as a reporter and editor of women's news at her hometown paper *The Columbus Citizen*. Before that, she had enough presence and drive to win assignments from the *Citizen*'s editors while on summer vacation from Vassar. "She had the disposition of a thoroughbred," a former colleague told a reporter for *Time*. "Overtrained, overbred and tense. She had a pride in being able to cope. She was against copelessness." Years later, at a dinner party, Diane Sawyer asked Curtis when she first knew she was interesting. "The day after I was born, dear," she was said to have replied.

At the *Times*, Clifton Daniel championed Curtis as he had Ada Louise Huxtable. He brought Curtis into the circle of influence among the top editors and eased her into favored friend status with the then publisher, Arthur Hays Sulzberger, and his wife, Iphigene Ochs Sulzberger. With Daniel's backing, Curtis became a power nexus, rising in esteem and importance in ways unimaginable to her predecessors among the paper's women. Daniel "created me," she would say. Think back to Eleanor Darnton, the *Times*'s women's editor from 1943 to 1945, incensed by the buttery confections her staff was obliged to churn out but powerless to effect change. Turner Catledge, who moved from the *Times*'s managing editor to executive editor in 1964, reserved some credit for Curtis's rise; he wrote that it "also reflected a desire that many of us came to have for a fresh look at women's news."

Even after Clifton Daniel was replaced as managing editor in 1968, the year Turner Catledge retired from the top post, Curtis retained her position and power. Inside the *Times*, woman colleagues like Nan Robertson saw Curtis and Huxtable as *Times* women in the tradition of Anne O'Hare McCormick—that is, too good at what they did and too personally assertive for the men in charge to ignore. Outstanding talent, style, bearing, and determination distinguished them, to be sure, but it is likely not incidental that all three had strong support from those of higher rank and they had cultivated the friendships and the ears of the publisher and the publisher's influential wife.

The women's sections of the country's other newspapers were

also getting face-lifts in this period. The Associated Press formed and promoted a youthful, feminist-forward group of reporters for its "Living Today" features. Before Lynn Sherr moved on to television, she led what became known as the AP's "mod squad," after a popular television crime drama about a counterculture police squad. On staff with her was Jurate Kazickas, just back from a year and a half of freelancing in Vietnam and a shrapnel wound from a barrage of incoming artillery fire at Khe Sanh. Most women's jobs in the profession, though, remained unaffected.

Charlayne Hunter was well ensconced at *The New Yorker* when ABC hired Melba Tolliver as a secretary to its news division operations chief in 1966. Before ABC, Tolliver had worked as a registered OR and ER nurse; finished among the seven finalists in a New York City–wide beauty contest; modeled for *Jet* and *Ebony;* appeared in commercials for Feen-A-Mint gum, Lark cigarettes, and Singer sewing machines; and had a cameo in the 1966 Sammy Davis Jr. movie *A Man Called Adam.* Decades later, she would point to 1963 as the year she found her voice, the year "George Wallace declared 'segregation forever,' Lyndon Johnson was sworn in. Little girls killed in the bombing of the 16th Street Church in Birmingham. The murder of Medgar Evers. Thousands marching on Washington." That spring, she responded to a series in the *New York Herald Tribune* titled "Ten Negroes," a respected white reporter's attempt to provide readers with in-depth profiles meant to highlight the wide diversity within the country's Black community. Several newspapers reprinted the series, as did the *Congressional Record,* where it included the reporter's summary of what he learned over five months of reporting and the mixed, often hostile response his efforts brought, especially from African Americans. His account included in full, with

Melba Tolliver

(Photo by Susan Wood,
© *Susan Wood)*

permission, "one of the bitterest, angriest, and most contemptuous letters—and one of the most literate." It came from Tolliver. A key passage:

> Yet in all this time, no one has wanted or tried to know any-thing about us. No one cares when they run those beautiful shampoo commercials that we have kinky hair, most of it black with no hopes of finding out whether blondes have more fun. No one cares if our hands become "soft and white" no matter how many jars and bottles of Brand X we use.

During two broadcasting strikes in the spring and fall of 1967, Tolliver got her chance. Purex, the sponsor of Marlene Sanders's five-minute daily afternoon newscast, objected to the man ABC picked as her stand-in. The show, of course, was called *News with the Woman's Touch.* With no other woman reporter on staff, Tolliver's boss remembered that his twenty-eight-year-old secretary had on-camera experience, and he tapped her to fill in for Sand-ers. With no news background and almost no advance notice, Tolliver broke ranks with the strikers as Sanders's stand-in, credibly, as it turned out, save a minor stumble over the phrase "rain-swollen river." Tolliver's "big chance" became a story in itself, even though she returned to her secretarial duties after the strike until ABC could cre-ate a reporter training program with her future in mind. That launched her into a career as a major personality in New York City local television news.

Molly Ivins, as a reporter at the
Minneapolis Tribune, 1969
(Star-Tribune *via Getty Images,*
photo by Powell Krueger)

From Minnesota in this pe-riod, young Molly Ivins of *The*

Minneapolis Tribune was radiating heat. She had graduated from Smith in 1966 and finished graduate journalism school at Columbia in 1967. Just a year into this first full-time job, the paper was running boxed promotions to draw attention to her stories, incongruously wedged into a section of the paper where they seemed to be far off topic. One ran with her headshot on June 1, 1968. The promo read,

> What happens when four of Minnesota's top political bosses shut themselves up in a smoke-filled room? They play, the "Mr. President" game, that's what. Molly Ivins, a staff writer for the Tribune, will tell all about it this Sunday in the Homes and Recreation section.

At around the same time, Ellen Willis, with a single essay about Bob Dylan in the pop music magazine *Cheetah,* began her tenure as a rock music critic for *The New Yorker,* a position she held from 1968 to 1977. "No other pop critic has ever seemed so unbiddable," wrote a later rock critic five years after Willis's death in 2006, Sasha Frere-Jones. "There was no 'liking' a performer or an album—everything on the table was an idea or a feeling or a project that Willis wanted to measure, to assess which bits worked and which didn't. The variables were of more interest to her than the people or the recordings." As for Pauline Kael, competitors regarded her as the pioneer of an entirely new writing aesthetic, someone with more positive influence over film in the United States than anyone else in the preceding thirty years. To *The New York Times*'s critic A. O. Scott her work was both "enthralling and infuriating," often read "for the pleasure of disagreement, and the resentment she was able to provoke—in critical targets and rival critics." Roger Ebert called her "the most powerful, loved, and hated critic of her time."

Meg Greenfield, 1978
(AP photo by Barry Thumma)

In Washington in 1968, Meg Greenfield joined the staff of *The Washington Post.* She had trained in New York at *The Reporter* under Max Ascoli, "an equal

opportunity oppressor" who "embodied pre-regulation America."
In her memoir, she described him as a man who evolved from the
use of "big bitch" and "little bitch" to "darling" as pet names for the
two women on his staff. "But for all his faults," she wrote, "he had a
genius in editing. He put women in jobs as no one else did without
self-consciousness or contrived good purpose. He didn't see why he
should not." By twenty-first-century standards, "Ascoli was a walking human rights violation," she wrote. "I never wish I'd sued him.
I even miss him."

At the *Post*, Greenfield, who won her Pulitzer for commentary
in 1978, became a member of the rarefied group of woman reporters "who had been granted passes to function outside the female
compound," which in no way implied full equality. Washington, she
said, was a place where at dinner parties wives and woman reporters
alike were still expected to repair to a separate room after the meal.
On assignment, Greenfield and others in her position "intuitively
adopted a kind of Vietcong mentality: complicity to at least passive
exploitation of what we could fairly assume they assumed about
us." She said she never pretended to be a "dumb broad," but she also
never went out of her way to "disabuse them of the conclusion to
which so many had freely leapt on their own the minute you entered
the room." Hired as an editorial writer, she advanced to become
deputy editor of the editorial page the following year, then editor of
the page, a position she held for two decades.

The accumulation of more than a century's worth of examples
from the 1840s to the 1960s demonstrates that in terms of hiring, promotion, and choice assignments, the most ultra-ambitious,
ultra-talented, ultra-driven women encountered fewer obstacles
than others, especially when they also had vast knowledge or sophisticated prior training, or niche expertise. Or, they were exceptionally gifted thinkers and writers with a singular style. Those most
successful women had excellent prospects in journalism, even in the
earliest days, especially when their talents included deft newsroom
maneuvering. It is a generalization, but a true one, to say that men
by and large needed "just enough" apparent talent and capability to
get ahead, which worked even better when enhanced by the right

schools, clubs, and connections. Men on the rise never seemed to require the years of experience demanded of women with like ambition.

In fairness, women who became mired in jobs they found unsatisfying might have had the talent but lacked the overdrive that women needed, or the will or disposition to position themselves politically for more. Others might have lacked the background or ambition to reach higher. Some could not or did not want to go abroad as correspondents or undertake what was required in such a competitive field to get their names out front and kept out front. Knowing the odds against them, they might have considered it pointless to pursue a leadership path outside the women's sphere. Perhaps unspoken aspects of their personalities or personal lives precluded such ambition. Perhaps in their minds, journalism was no more than a great place to wait until the train to marriage and family pulled up. Or perhaps—and this was a major contention of the women's caucuses that would soon form—having never been nurtured or groomed or conditioned to consider themselves worthy of advancement in such an exciting, competitive, hardscrabble field, they lacked a sense of their own potential and never formed the expectations.

Of all the measures of how well women were doing in the 1960s, the best is enduring value, the rare pieces or bodies of work that have defied journalism's disposable nature. Women in the 1960s produced at least four seminal works. Atop the list is Rachel Carson's *Silent Spring,* which *The New Yorker* excerpted in three issues in 1962. In 2012, upon the book's fiftieth anniversary, Carson posthumously drew moving commemorative appreciations in the press and a declaration from *E: The Environmental Magazine* that she had ushered in the modern environmental movement and "changed the world." In her own day, the alarm she sounded against the pesticide DDT and its deleterious impact on the bald eagle and other birds garnered eight prestigious awards plus finalist status for the National Book Award.

Hannah Arendt's "Eichmann in Jerusalem" consumed the better part of two issues of *The New Yorker* and received similar attention in its half-centennial year in 2013, including academic conferences and panels in its honor at Yale, Wesleyan, and Harvard. That same year, the Schlesinger Library at Radcliffe built an exhibit around a look back at the feminist revolution unleashed by Betty Friedan's

Joan Didion
(Corbis, Getty Images, photo by © Ted Streshinsky)

Feminine Mystique fifty years earlier. Janet Maslin, the critic for *The New York Times,* expressed regret that she had not read the book closer to its publication date, even though she would have been only thirteen then. "I have a photograph of myself with Betty Friedan," she wrote in a retrospective musing. "We were together on a radio show. I was there because I was a critic for The New York Times and I arrived at the Times because of opportunities her book created. I wish I had known how much I owed her." Michelle Bernard in *The Washington Post* acknowledged the book's significance but objected to Friedan's exclusion of the issues specific to the lives of Black women. Bernard pointed out how that neglect made the work unimportant to the women of her community and "unintentionally set us down a path that divided us as sisters." On that score, the suffrage movement and first wave feminism had done even worse and, at times, with deliberate rather than unconscious intent. Other commentary took note of these omissions and others, as well as how dated the book had become.

There was no such caveat attached to the canonization of Joan Didion. Neither her star in the firmament nor that of her book *Slouching Towards Bethlehem* has ever dimmed. The essays the book contains, first published in *The Saturday Evening Post, Vogue, Holiday,* and *The American Scholar,* have invited reverence since the book first appeared in 1968. As recently as January 2021, Nathan Heller would tell *New Yorker* readers that it "has claims to being the most influential essay collection of the past sixty years." A year before she died, Hilton Als wrote in *The New York Review of Books* of "the metaphorical power of great fiction" present in her nonfiction, and how her work from the 1960s to the 1990s "anticipated the deeply troubling politics of today." At her death at eighty-seven in December 2021, the outpouring was inestimable. In *The New York Times,* the cultural critic Katie Roiphe said Didion created "a perfect conjunction of the writer with the moment." The book reviewer Parul Sehgal added that what Didion elicited was not mere admiration. "It is love."

CHAPTER 14

Vietnam

In 1965, Aline Mosby, from Paris, bemoaned how few American woman journalists still held staff correspondent positions in bureaus abroad. She wondered what had happened to the Nellie Blys, the Dorothy Thompsons, the Anne O'Hare McCormicks. In a story for *Dateline,* the magazine of the Overseas Press Club, she mused about the sizable "batch of women" who had been posted overseas during World War II and in its aftermath. Marriage had even led Marguerite Higgins to move her home base to Washington, D.C., limiting her international travel to "sporadic trips to check up on Saigon, Moscow, and other points."

Mosby said that several major media outlets had started to oppose the notion of women as staff correspondents in their bureaus abroad, although she did not say which ones had done so or why. As always, freelance, contract, and stringer arrangements with women remained as common as they were cost saving. Mosby said the only exception was Paris, where editors relied on women to cover the year-round fashion beat, which kept them busy enough to warrant a full-time hire. That could well have animated *Newsweek*'s decision to send Liz Peer to Paris in 1964. She had started on the magazine's New York mail desk six years earlier. Lynn Povich remembered Peer as a "gifted writer and versatile reporter" who "could match the toughest foreign correspondent with her cigarettes, her swagger, and her fluent French." Peer indeed covered fashion and food but also student protests, the speeches of the French president, Charles de Gaulle, art shows in Holland, holding companies in Lichtenstein, and more.

Other women at *Newsweek* who managed to advance were likely to be posted to a bureau like Boston's, where coverage centered on education, or to the United Nations. Lynn Povich, in an email exchange, gave her theory of why the UN became a relatively common assignment for woman reporters. Aside from the annual meeting of the UN General Assembly, where all the world's leaders convened, the reporting mostly involved soliciting reaction from emissaries to major international events and crises. "Not heavy lifting," she said, "just good relationships and source work, which women did well, although most of these women could be great foreign correspondents if given the chance and some were—either before or after."

Aline Mosby's *Dateline* piece also mentioned her good friend Flora Lewis, then reporting from London for *The Washington Post,* but not as full-time staff. Lewis, Mosby said, was one of the women who had been able to remain abroad "a good many years because their husbands did." That changed in 1965 when Sydney Gruson relocated to New York to become *The New York Times*'s foreign editor. Of the women reporting from Vietnam by that point, Mosby named only Beverly Deepe, who arrived in the country without a plan in 1962 but started stringing and would stay seven years. As Mosby's piece appeared, Deepe had joined the *Herald Tribune* as a "permanent correspondent." The newspaper shut down the following year.

Later in 1965, Mosby, too, left Europe for the United States to accept a Ford Foundation Fellowship to study Chinese at Columbia University in New York. This was in preparation for the hoped-for opening of a UPI bureau in Beijing that, in the end, took more than another decade to materialize. When it did, Mosby went, and for her reporting earned the French journalism prize La Plume d'Or. By way of China and postings at the UN and in Europe, she returned to Paris in 1970, where she remained until her retirement fourteen years later. Mosby could cover anything.

In 1968, *Mademoiselle* attempted to explain to its readers what it took for a woman to have a career like hers. The writer described "today's real life girl reporter" as a "charming, intelligent and often very attractive young woman," and asserted, erroneously, as we have already seen, that she was a "far cry from the popular image of the early woman reporter—the pushy battle-ax type, always trying to be 'one of the boys.'" The article quoted UPI's city editor saying that the four women on his staff had "brought sex into the newsroom . . . and it's getting damned hard for the men to concentrate and get any work done." He must not have read Catharine Brody's screed in 1926 or Stanley Walker's in *City Editor* in 1934 or Ishbel Ross on newsroom sexology, vintage 1936. Of the woman reporters in "real" positions in 1968, *Mademoiselle* named Mosby and the far more universally known and admired Nora Ephron, who, after a very abbreviated stint at little-chance-to-advance *Newsweek*, had moved on to the *New York Post*, where her decades of reporting and writing for the page, the screen, and the stage began before she moved on to *Esquire*. Ellen Goodman followed the man she would marry to Ann Arbor, Michigan, and then joined the staff of the *Detroit Free Press* before moving on to *The Boston Globe*. Susan Brownmiller saw the hopelessness of the *Newsweek* women's corral and also left. "Oh, hell," her memoir quoted one of her colleagues as saying, "Simone de Beauvoir could walk in here and they'd put her in research."

Almost on cue after Mosby's lament, the presence of women in overseas bureaus resurged. In 1969, *Cosmopolitan* surveyed the prospects and the lived reality of men and women from the United States as foreign correspondents. The illustration for the story was a suggestive full-page pop art drawing of a couple, both in dark glasses, she in a mini-length trench coat, he, in black bell-bottoms. Hands entwined, they both sit on the same Eero Saarinen tulip chair against a backdrop of stripes that swirl in a psychedelic profusion of black, white, lavender, coral, fuchsia, and orange, fanning out in three directions. Above the couple's heads, a horseshoe-shaped sign in stenciled letters announces, "ROMANCE. TRAVEL. ADVENTURE."

Of the full-time woman journalists overseas, the writer included both Paris-based correspondents, Mosby for UPI and "the pretty girl" Liz Peer for *Newsweek,* whom he interviewed at length. Gloria Emerson in London for *The New York Times* was the third. Emerson originally had joined the newspaper's staff in New York, on the women's page, in 1957. As she once explained, "Getting a job on the women's page was a gift from heaven, although I hated writing about shoes and clothes, all under the eyes of the advertising department, who measured editorial mention of retailers. You cannot imagine what it was like in those days." She left the newspaper in 1960, moved to Brussels to marry, then divorced, then returned to the *Times* in

Liz Trotta

*(Getty Images, photo
by Yvonne Hemsey)*

1964 in the Paris bureau, with fashion coverage a large part of her brief. In 1968, she engineered the London move, endeavoring to change her professional image with coverage of the conflict in Northern Ireland.

Other than Liz Trotta of NBC, the *Cosmo* story left out the rest of the growing contingent of woman reporters in Vietnam, presumably, again, because most of them were stringers. But the writer did quote advice to all comers from *The Montreal Star*'s Bernard Kaplan: "The fastest way I know of for a girl—or a man, too, for that matter—to become a correspondent is to find a war."

The woman reporters who found their war in Vietnam in the 1960s and 1970s attracted attention in the way woman journalists in every previous war attracted attention, with those same badly aging gee-whiz tropes about fearless good-looking young women who liked to court danger. In October 1968, a reporter for *Women's Wear Daily* contended that the women reporting from Vietnam represented "a new breed of newspaper woman," "a long way from the highly personalized, dramatic female of World War II and Korea as personified by the late Maggie Higgins." "They write and think like men, and the last thing they want to do is write the 'woman's angle.'" Of course, a number of woman journalists had been writing "like men" from war zones for decades and decades before Vietnam, despite the women's angle onus most were obliged to labor under and the other overt and tacit gender limits the military and their editors imposed on them. Writing like men was the hallmark of Higgins and Flora Lewis, of Ann Stringer, Eleanor Packard, Anne O'Hare McCormick, Martha Gellhorn, and Virginia Cowles; and at the nineteenth century's turn to the twentieth, of the globe-girdling Eleanor Franklin Egan and Anna Northend Benjamin and before them, Margaret Fuller in Italy. Domestically, in battles of a cultural or economic nature, Ida B. Wells and Ida Tarbell would be on that list. Imagine the reaction of Marguerite Higgins to such a statement had she not died two years earlier from leishmaniasis, a disease she contracted while reporting and writing like a man from Vietnam, as she had done in Korea, as she had done in Europe during World War II. And we've also seen how the most exceptional of the woman reporters of World War II risked censure, house arrest, or expulsion to report like men from the front, and how a few of them earned the military's blind-eye pass for their professionalism and skill.

By 1968, Anne Morrissy, the "slick chick" Cornell sports editor who penetrated the press box at the Yale Bowl in 1954, was in Saigon as an associate field producer for ABC News. She and the editor of *The Overseas Weekly,* also a woman, led a quiet but successful charge to reverse a military order from General William Westmoreland that would have effectively ended the ability of the woman correspondents to cover combat. Their effort was the only time during the war in Southeast Asia that the women took a collective stance against the discrimination they faced and managed to get the order rescinded. Ten women signed a letter promising not to ask for any special treatment or protections. Their World War II predecessors traveling along the Rhine never requested concessions, an example that should have provided ample precedent but by the time of Vietnam went unacknowledged or just forgotten.

Over the years of the Vietnam War, more than four hundred women had credentials, although Elizabeth Becker, author of *You Don't Belong Here: How Three Women Rewrote the Story of War,* told me that a sizable portion of these were wives of correspondents who served as office managers or helped out with bureau administration and wrote only on occasion if at all. About seventy-five of them were journalists, but even some of those spent only a few weeks in the country. Aside from the few woman staffers with full-time positions, most of the women reporting from the region wrote as freelancers under arrangements that excluded health insurance and other company benefits.

For six months, from August 1968 to February 1969, Liz Trotta was NBC's first full-time woman correspondent in Vietnam. On her return to New York, she became a weekday local news presenter in the 7:25 a.m. time slot. NBC soon showcased her with Pauline Frederick on an eight-city tour to talk about President Richard Nixon's first hundred days in office. From local reporters along the way came the inevitable woman-makes-good questions as well, causing Frederick, with her radio background, to say, "Most women listeners would prefer to hear the voice symbol of the husband and lover, rather than the sister or mother." She volunteered that her bosses knew better than to ask her to do a "woman's story. . . . I don't run a campaign. I cover the news." Trotta was asked if woman journalists were making a significant contribution. "No," she replied, "because most are still being put on the soft stuff. If there is a woman in this field who can make it, she's got to be twice as good as the next guy. She's *got* to be. She's open to criticism. But if she criticizes, she's labeled a prima donna or a bitch. If a man loses his temper, he is described as someone [fighting] for a cause, doing the manly thing."

By 1970, Gloria Emerson had worked her way via Northern Ireland to Vietnam. Years later, in her introduction to a book by a group of her fellow reporters, *War Torn: Stories of War from the Women*

Gloria Emerson with photojournalist Denis Cameron and interpreter
Nguyen Ngoc Luong, Saigon, South Vietnam, April 19, 1971

(© Richard Avedon Imagery, the Richard Avedon Foundation, photo by Richard Avedon)

Reporters Who Covered Vietnam, she wrote of the women over the years who had "flung themselves into a war for the adventure," usually young and unknown, "possessed of spirit and stamina, a passion for the story and the intent to be journalists" in a profession that was easy to infiltrate "if you wanted only to be a stringer." Emerson was not a stringer, nor, at forty-one, would she have been considered young. She arrived in Vietnam in 1968 as a full-time staff correspondent sent from London by her editors in New York City to the Saigon bureau of the *Times.* To get to Vietnam, Emerson "hammered" *Times* editors for the assignment to return to the country she had not visited since she joined the paper twelve years earlier. "No woman is fat in France, even when she is overweight," an early story of hers from Paris began. And yet in Vietnam she called out bogus body counts and medals pinned on officers who never went to battle. Emerson harbored no illusions about why her editors agreed to let her go. It was, she later wrote, "because the war was supposed to be over, so it didn't matter if a female was sent." More conflict reporting would follow—Nicaragua, Biafra, Guatemala, Gaza—so Emerson could fairly add "war reporter" to her résumé.

Frances FitzGerald

(Bettmann, Getty Images)

Frances FitzGerald was a freelance magazine writer who returned to Vietnam for her second stay, this time on assignment in 1971. The following year, *The New Yorker* carried a serial in five substantial parts, excerpted from the book FitzGerald was about to publish. In magazine form, *Fire in the Lake: The Vietnamese and the Americans in Vietnam* won a George Polk award. As a book, it was published in 1972 at around the same time as *The Best and the Brightest* by *The New York Times*'s reporter David Halberstam. Both books were admired, both critical of the U.S. role in Vietnam. FitzGerald was awarded the Pulitzer Prize for general nonfiction, the Bancroft Prize for history, and a National

Book Award. As the historian Arthur M. Schlesinger Jr. would offer, "If Americans read only one book to understand what we have done to the Vietnamese and to ourselves, let it be this one."

Among the woman stringers who "didn't matter" was twenty-five-year-old Sylvana Foa, who arrived in 1970, first connecting with *Newsweek* in Saigon, and then in the same role from Phnom Penh, Cambodia, where she added UPI to her client list. Foa persuaded her friend Elizabeth Becker to join her in Cambodia in 1973. Both women were Asia specialists who traded in their incomplete graduate studies to pursue journalism at war. They were hardly products of "enlightened decisions by newsrooms," Becker would later write. "We would have to find our own way to the battle zone." The lack of an official war declaration from President Lyndon B. Johnson made this pursuit less difficult. It meant no official censorship system was in place, nor were there any special restrictions on women's access to the battlefields, the rescinded Westmoreland edict notwithstanding. In Vietnam, to obtain local press credentials was enough.

Becker's arrival in Cambodia came a few months before April 20, 1973, when the Cambodians threw Foa out of the country. The only thing Foa remembered about that day is being hustled into a small room at Phnom Penh airport and waking up four days later in a hotel in Bangkok. The story she intended to "pigeon out" of Phnom Penh was still in her handbag, unsent. It was about the visit she received from two Indochina investigators for the U.S. Senate's Committee on Foreign Relations who sought confirmation of what she had been reporting for weeks off the transmissions she overheard on a $15 radio. They confirmed U.S. airplanes, under covert direction from inside their embassy, were bombing Khmer Rouge positions in areas the Cambodian government did not control, in contravention of the Cooper-Church Amendment of June 1970, which passed in revised form in 1971. Foa's reporting irritated the Americans enough for them to press the Cambodians to expel her. After meeting with Foa, the two Senate staff members appeared at the embassy for further confirmation, only to be ejected physically by marine guards. The report they produced about their trip confirmed Foa's details and prompted the Senate to order an immediate halt to the bombing. Their report also mentioned how badly the U.S. embassy staff in

Cambodia wanted Foa gone. On the front page of *The Washington Post,* David Greenway provided some context for Foa's ouster:

> Miss Foa's critics say that she exaggerates and distorts the news. Her supporters say that she has come closer to the bone of the American involvement here than any other reporter. Her supporters also say that high officials in the U.S. embassy have become personally involved in what amounts to a vendetta against Miss Foa.

On May 11, a related piece on the front page of *The New York Times* gave a perfect illustration of the dismissiveness that so often beset vulnerable war zone woman stringers like Foa, although the word "vulnerable" next to the name Sylvana Foa could not be more misplaced. Sydney Schanberg, the paper's staff correspondent in Phnom Penh at the time (and later, the author of *The Killing Fields*), reported on the embassy's role in the bombings. Schanberg experienced no fallout from the Americans or from the Cambodians and certainly no threat to expel him. His detailed story gave no credit to Foa, nor did it mention her or the price she had paid for her reporting. Yet thirty-two years later, at the end of a column of his in *The Village Voice,* Schanberg addressed his misdeed, writing that he had been aware of Foa's story as he was writing his own but told himself, "in a moment of rationalization and hubris," that his "was more comprehensive and better documented and therefore no reference to my colleague's UPI story was necessary." To this confession, he added, "It is always necessary." Years later, asked how she felt about Schanberg's tardy acknowledgment, Foa said, "I liked Sydney a lot and we worked well together on numerous stories." She added how much play her embassy stories attracted through UPI's distribution to its media subscribers. "But when you are a stringer," she said, "you rarely get a byline, much less credit."

Becker's book detailed the experiences of several woman journalists in Southeast Asia during the war with ample attention not only to the dismissiveness and insults but also to the sexual harassment and slut shaming they faced. To protest would have gotten them nowhere, Becker said, or might well have made things worse. What comes to mind is the treatment of so many woman reporters in prior conflicts, the experiences that Martha Gellhorn and Virginia Cowles spoofed as fiction in *Love Goes to Press,* the vicious running commentary Marguerite Higgins deflected throughout her working life, and the whispers and shouts of "she slept her way up" that Edith Evans Asbury remembered being leveled against some of her colleagues. Most women in Southeast Asia worked with no medical benefits, in fact, no safety net of any kind. At one point, after Becker covered an attack, her editor at *The Washington Post* cabled her to say, "No More Florence Nightingales. Will not repeat not pay hospital." Sylvana Foa told me the undercutting sometimes came from woman colleagues, too. A CIA agent once told her how amusing he found it when another woman reporter spread the word that Foa was making up stories for which he had been the prime undisclosed source.

Gloria Emerson's work from Vietnam preceded Frances FitzGerald's by two years. It earned Emerson a George Polk award, which recognized "intrepid, bold, and influential work" across all media. Eight more Polks would go to women during the 1970s. In fact, from the 1950s through the 1970s, women made an appreciable showing in the most competitive award competitions. During the 1970s, woman journalists won seven of the more than fifty Pulitzer Prizes with the names of reporters cited with their publications. Still few, but in the fifty-two years prior, since the founding of the prize, only five woman journalists had been so honored.

Gloria Emerson's book *Winners and Losers: Battles, Retreats, Gains, Losses, and Ruins from a Long War,* published in 1976, won a National Book Award. FitzGerald provided the foreword. The appearance of her towering six-foot-tall colleague interviewing the locals made FitzGerald think of a "Great Blue Heron looking into a pond." "Her safari jacket was crisp, and her dark hair shining but then apparently," FitzGerald wrote, "she always looked perfectly turned out, even after spending a night on some awful fire base."

Emerson's recollections of her Vietnam years for the introduction to *War Torn* appeared not long before her death in 2004. For years, she wrote, she would refuse to respond when anyone asked her, as they often did, what it had been like to be a woman in Vietnam. "I don't know," she once snapped at a radio reporter. "I've never been a man." In the essay, Emerson honored the woman reporters of earlier conflicts, Martha Gellhorn, in particular, who, in Vietnam at nearly sixty in 1967, "headed to a children's hospital and found everything." The reference was to Gellhorn's "Suffer the Little Children . . . ," published in *Ladies' Home Journal* in 1967, about her visit to the village of My Tho in the Mekong delta, where relatives brought their wounded children "however they can, walking for miles with the children in their arms, bumping in carts or on local buses," a place without patients over the age of maturity, which was twelve.

Beverly Deepe, in another instance, spoke to a reporter of the women who had been wounded, captured, and killed during the conflict. She did not name names, but one reference was surely to the photographer Dickey Chapelle, who, at forty-seven, after surviving assignments in Europe and Asia during World War II and the Hungarian Revolution of 1956, died instantly in 1965 after a lieutenant walking in front of her accidentally stepped on a booby-trapped grenade attached to the top of a mortar shell, from which shrapnel severed her carotid artery.

Did the women report differently from the men because that's what they were asked to do, what they wanted to do, or what they were best equipped to do? Asked this question years later by a reporter for *American Journalism Review,* the veteran AP correspondent Peter Arnett responded that he was not sure. He pointed to Emerson's potent exploration of the "hootch" maids of Vietnam, the local women whom GIs routinely hired for laundry, cleaning, and sex, and to reporters like Liz Trotta of NBC, who, he said, "wrote the bang-bang like everyone else." "In Vietnam," Arnett said, "you could count the number of women reporters on the fingers of one hand." Some, he said, took pride in their toughness, feeling they needed to seem masculine to succeed. "The women received sexist treatment from the men, including myself, who believed they shouldn't be there," he said. In Vietnam as in Korea, "they tended to be objects of ridicule or sexual desire."

Collective Action

By the time the 1970s arrived, woman journalists had been grumbling out loud for a hundred years about workplace discrimination, but until then the only widespread collective response had been to create a parallel universe of women-only clubs and awards. Three developments encouraged the adoption of more confrontational tactics: women apprehended that the fortuitous changes in American civil rights law of the mid-1960s applied to them; they embraced the light, heat, and oxygen of the women's liberation movement; and thanks to the Vietnam-induced increase in their numbers, they reached critical mass as full-time staff members throughout the media. Only then did the "good girls" at major news outlets, in Lynn Povich's apt characterization, group together, hire lawyers, gather evidence, and challenge their employers head-on.

In the vanguard of these efforts were the women at *Newsweek*, who, in the early months of 1970, planned in secret to file a discrimination complaint with the Equal Employment Opportunity Commission in Washington, D.C. A list they compiled to buttress their case symbolized their plight. On it were the names of nineteen young men with no prior journalism experience whom the magazine hired at the rank of reporter or writer. Women with similar or sometimes better credentials started and stayed on the bottom rungs of a company ladder with broken steps.

Across the country, women's liberation advocates in other occupations filed lawsuits and court briefs. Nonprofit centers opened for research and public advocacy, providing up-to-date statistics and relevant industry news, and universities established programs in women's studies that excavated long-buried history either decades out of print or never in books. At *Newsweek,* the timing of the women's job action could not have been more exquisite. It coincided with the publication of the magazine's March 23, 1970, cover story, a report on the country's "women in revolt," the words in red and blue against a bright yellow background, emblazoned with a solarized image of a nude woman with a raised fist. To explain the issue's focus, an inside cover note said that women across the country, convinced they had "little to lose but their domestic chains," had begun to challenge "the basic assumptions of what they consider a male-dominated society." They wanted redress in every area from wages to child rearing to sexual expression. When the issue appeared on newsstands, the two young women whom the editors assigned as researchers to that very story were downtown at the offices of the American Civil Liberties Union with forty-four of their colleagues. Together, they announced the gender discrimination suit they had just filed against their employer.

The irony of the timing of the announcement was not lost on reporters who covered the press conference. To write the cover story, *Newsweek*'s editors had assigned Helen Dudar of the *New York Post,* the wife of one of *Newsweek*'s top writers, Peter Goldman. The inside cover note did credit the two staff researchers who helped Dudar, Nancy Dooley and Judith Gingold. At no point during the month and a half that they all worked together did Dooley or Gingold reveal the planned women's action. Gingold, a Smith graduate and Marshall scholar, was one of the operation's leaders.

Some months earlier, Gingold had made the first call to the EEOC. At that point, none of the *Newsweek* women had yet understood how the landmark civil and equal opportunity legislation of the 1960s could help them personally. Lynn Povich, after five years on staff, including the Paris secretarial stint, was being promoted to the rank of junior writer. Yet neither the promotion nor her familial connection to the Washington Post Company stopped her from taking a leadership role in the job action. In New York, she was getting more opportunity than most of her peers, but attributed this to her luck in having worked for "one of the good guys." She had also seen firsthand how comfortable other editors were with taking woman staffers for granted. Povich not only helped organize the effort but was prominent in the repeated, often frustrating rounds of negotiations that followed over the next several years.

Women at other publications followed the *Newsweek* lead. Within two months, the women at Time Inc. filed a complaint of their own, with representation from the women at *Time, Life, Sports Illustrated,* and Time-Life Books. At *Time* in 1970, ninety-four of the magazine's two hundred woman employees signed charges filed with the New York State Division of Human Rights. They cited the late Henry Luce's "vestal virgins" affront from the 1940s and a more recent inter-office memo from *Time*'s managing editor, Henry Grunwald, which read,

> I don't intend to make a deliberate attempt to recruit or nurture female writers. There are no limits to careers for women at *Time,* up to and including senior editorships.... I must add in candor that I have not met many women who seem to have the physical and mental energies required for Time senior editing. (Of course, I have not met too many men who fill that bill either.)

Reader's Digest, Newsday, The Washington Post, The Washington Star, The Detroit News, The Baltimore Sun, the *New Haven Register,* the Associated Press, and *The New York Times* came next. At *The Washington Post,* all but three of the newspaper's forty woman editorial staff members signed a four-page statement that accused the newspaper of discrimination against women. Ben Bradlee, the *Post*'s top editor at the time, made this admission in his memoir: "I was not sensitive to racism or sexism, to understate the matter." The signatories to the statement objected to the "dumping ground" of the women's pages and the tendency those sections showed to diminish stories about women's rights. They called out the cringe-worthy terms so often used to describe women, saying that no one would call a man "Vivacious Robert Finch." "Stereotyping in the media," they pointed out, "means stereotyping in the public's mind."

Both at the *Post* and at the *Star,* the respective managing editors posted memos after meetings with delegations chosen by the woman editorial employees. The editors announced new policies to combat sex discrimination in the hiring of woman reporters and photographers, in assignments, and in the papers' news columns, where even the most unconscious infractions had the power to be destructive and to offend. Bradlee pledged all the paper's resources toward addressing the issues. "It is the policy of the Washington Post to make the equality and dignity of women completely and instinctively meaningful," he wrote at the time. As concrete acts, he banned the use in the paper of words such as "divorcée," "grandmother," "blond" (or "brunette"), or "housewife"—unthinkable if applied to a man. He identified "vivacious," "pert," "dimpled," and "cute" as clichés that had no place in the paper for that reason alone. Achievement stories about women were often "implicitly condescending" and "imply 'pretty good for a woman.'" The conditioning was embedded so deeply, the story templates so familiar, that the regrettable expressions showed up in the prose of woman writers too.

Bradlee's response to the women's action at *The Washington Post* surely felt like a victory at the time. But in April 1972, fifty-nine women who worked in the *Post*'s newsroom signed a six-page memo, calling out the editor, the publisher, Katharine Graham, and others for nearly two years of subsequent inaction. The number of women on staff at the paper was down slightly. The national and metropolitan staffs had doubled since 1956, but the number of women was up only from seven women to ten. Only two women were in assigning positions. There were other, more subtle signs of discrimination, too. The women pointed out how infrequently women were called upon to cover hard news or to write analysis, how often they were stuck in routine assignments or those with a clear women's angle, which meant less chance to win favored page placement in the paper or even to be published at all. The lack of visibility was its own Catch-22: it made the women appear to be less productive or even unproductive compared with the men and thus unworthy of top assignments or advancement. The women did not request a quota system—"women for too long have been the victims of quotas"—but they did make several affirmative action requests. They asked for a better men-women ratio, for active recruitment of experienced woman reporters, and for more women positioned to make real contributions, particularly as originating editors. They wanted equal standards for hiring, assigning, and promotion without reference to

marital or family status; the inclusion of women in specialized training for assignments that required it; the opening up of the national,
foreign, and sports staffs to women; and an examination of the company's pay policies to ensure fair treatment.

That same year, the women of *The New York Times* formed a caucus and began to prepare a case of their own. Gloria Emerson, still
abroad, still so grateful to have fought her way off the fashion beat,
was dubious about the plan. "Oh dear," Nan Robertson quoted Emerson as saying when she was asked to sign on, "they've let me ride my
water buffalo. Why should I get involved in this?" Ultimately, she
joined the job action. Charlotte Curtis and Ada Louise Huxtable,
however, the two women with by far the highest wattage, stood apart
from their less advantaged sisters. Edith Evans Asbury, by then over
sixty but still at full energy, was ready to do the same.

In fact, Asbury attended the initial meeting intent on ward-
ing off the younger "spitfires" from what she saw as a deeply ill-
advised course. At the meeting, the discrepancies in the treatment
of men and women on the staff could not have been made plainer.
For instance, Marilyn Bender, with a law degree, started—where
else?—on the fashion pages in 1959. Deposed for the suit, which she
did not join, she told of her promotion to Sunday business editor in
her seventeenth year on staff, a post that made her the one example
the paper had at the time of a woman in "a slightly elevated, managerial capacity." In that job, she told the lawyers, she earned less than
her deputy. Edith Asbury ultimately joined the suit, but only after
someone produced a list of the newsroom staff with salary figures
next to each name in descending order. Twenty-two reporters, all
men, earned more than Asbury. Only two men in the newsroom did
she consider her equals, Homer Bigart and Peter Kihss, the newspaper's respective "pure gold" and "solid silver" of Anthony Lukas's
toast to Asbury's "dazzling white of dignity and style." "Well, this
is what raised my consciousness," she told her oral historian. For
Asbury, just as stunning and embarrassing, really, was the realization
that her own misplaced sense of gratitude for having landed at *The
New York Times* after so many fits and starts had left her oblivious to
the way compensation reflects institutional value. She never paid
attention to raises nor earned more than a farthing above union scale,
she said; doing the work was too much fun. What she articulated

was the all-too-common response particular to women of not asking for acknowledgment when they deserved it, especially in the form of more money. The pervasive tendency was to expect that reward would materialize on merit but to say nothing when it did not.

Max Frankel, a onetime executive editor of the *Times,* confirmed in his memoir how the depositions and discovery for the *Times* case made the huge salary discrepancies plain and brought to light "a fair amount" of condescension from editors, all men, toward the women they employed. Sometimes, he said, these appraisals appeared in "coarse and insulting memos" that described women by their sex appeal and wardrobes.

The Gannett chain avoided many of the sexism pitfalls. As early as 1969, Al Neuharth, who built the company into the nation's largest newspaper chain, was pushing woman journalists to prepare themselves for management positions, even if they had to "scratch and claw a bit to get there." He seemed to intuit that more women in leadership positions would be good for business.

At the *Chicago Tribune,* Pamela Zekman, Anne Keegan, and several other woman reporters joined the staff in 1972, reflecting a new deliberateness at the *Tribune* and at many other outlets across the country about hiring woman reporters for general assignments, but not only in response to the wave of legal actions. Zekman and Keegan advanced rapidly. When Keegan died in 2011, the *Tribune* described her as "arguably the best female reporter/writer in the history of Chicago journalism." Zekman, peerless over decades in her investigative work, recalled how she, Keegan, and other woman reporters of the day chuckled over the helpful role their Vietnam draft exemptions played in their hires and their steadily upward career trajectories. Enormous talent was surely the larger factor.

Both Zekman and Keegan trained at Chicago's local wire service, City News Bureau. Keegan had moved from City News to UPI before the *Tribune* hired her, and Zekman advanced swiftly through the *Tribune*'s ranks because she had covered the criminal and federal courts for City News. That positioned her to become a driving force on the paper's new investigative task force, which in her day won two Pulitzer Prizes for local specialized investigative reporting, both involving undercover techniques. Zekman eventually moved on to the *Chicago Sun-Times,* where, in 1977–78, she conceived and

Pam Zekman with her Mirage tavern colleagues (*left to right*)
Bill Recktenwald of the Better Government Association, and
Zay Smith and Jeff Allen of the *Chicago Sun-Times*
(Chicago Sun-Times, *photo by Jim Frost*)

led an investigation into the city's unspoken, little-understood, but
long-suspected system of petty graft. The newspaper bought a tavern business it renamed the Mirage and staffed it with reporters and
photographers. There was collaboration with CBS for a nationally
televised segment on *60 Minutes* that cameramen filmed in secret. In
the paper, the series was twenty-five stories long, bringing a slew of
personnel and city government policy changes and other immediate
major reforms. It was an investigation that most Pulitzer watchers
presumed would win the 1979 Pulitzer for local specialized investigative reporting. It did not. The board decided that the surreptitious
methods it relied on "could send journalism on a wrong course," as
Ben Bradlee put it, even though the entry guidelines included no
such prohibition. Undercover tactics had been involved in numerous
previous winning probes over many years, including earlier prizes
the *Tribune* and other respected regional papers won in the local
special investigative category, especially when they resulted in the

kind of major impact Mirage brought, the kind that journalism in the public interest strives to create.

In 1972, dozens of women covered the national political conventions. Women were also well represented that year at the first annual "A. J. Liebling Counter-Convention" that *MORE* magazine staged. Two more would follow, each convened as a response from the much-maligned "liberal media" to the establishment press, as symbolized by the annual meeting of the American Newspaper Publishers Association taking place in the same city, where women were few. The "New Journalism" panel at the first *MORE* event in 1972 included Gay Talese and Calvin Trillin, *The New Yorker*'s Renata Adler and Pauline Kael, and Gail Sheehy, by then at *New York* magazine. Nora Ephron was one of the organizers and Gloria Steinem was also on hand. Charlotte Curtis moderated a panel of top celebrities of the day titled "How They Cover Me." A discussion of "racism, sexism, and elitism" consumed another time block. However, "Should There Be a Women's Page?" was the only dedicated women's topic that first year, which was telling about the distance yet to cover. Lynn Sherr as moderator told the attendees that she had once opposed the idea of "women's news," thinking it should be mixed in with the

"Should There Be a Women's Page?" A panel, April 24, 1972,
at the first *MORE* magazine counterconvention with author
Anne Roiphe, Enid Nemy of *The New York Times,* and
Lynn Sherr, still with the Associated Press
(Photographed by Jill Krementz)

rest of the paper, but her engagement with the women's movement had changed that. "I would like the women's page to say to women what I wish someone had said to me a long time ago," she told the crowd. What she envisioned was something "separatist and radical" that would eventually lead to the construct's complete demise. As usual, no consensus emerged. In *The Washington Post*, Sally Quinn described the session as "orderly if a bit dull." The reporter for *The Christian Science Monitor* called it a discussion without an upshot. "No one seemed to know what women want to read and where they want to read it," the reporter wrote, "or if it is even possible to generalize, since the audience varies from newspaper to newspaper."

At the next year's *MORE* event, Quinn, who *Newsday* described as the *Post*'s answer to Charlotte Curtis, protested the all-too-common assumption that Washington woman reporters slept with their sources. In her panel remarks, she told of a senator she did not name whose advance she resisted on a ride home he offered one rainy night. "What do you think?" he snapped, "I'm running a taxi service?" That same year, a panel devoted to "Covering the Canape Circuit" stirred up enough of a protest for being conceptually tone-deaf that at the third and last convention at New York City's Roosevelt Hotel, *MORE* included several substantive panels with women-specific themes: "Women in the Newsroom," "Is There a Female Sensibility?," and "Sugar and Spice: A Discussion of Women's Magazines." On top of that, in the Madison Suite on the convention's opening night, NOW, the National Organization for Women, mounted a multimedia presentation titled "Images of Women in the Media."

Common among the discrimination suit settlements, all out of court, came aggregate cash awards to be divvied up among the complainants, or funding plowed into new training efforts and pledges from management to recruit and promote women. At the *Times*, for instance, the settlement, which took effect in January 1979, awarded the complainants a total of $100,000 to offset their legal fees and created a $232,000 annuities fund "to compensate them for the historic costs of social discrimination." It offered no new or retroactive salary increases or promotions, an absence common in such cases, but the company did amend its equal opportunity initiatives with a new four-year goal of putting women into a quarter of all top editorial jobs. Even before the settlement, the moves toward rectification began. The *Times* promoted Le Anne Schreiber, at thirty-two, after only a few months in the number two position on the sports desk, to become the first woman sports editor at any major U.S. daily newspaper. And the paper hired Carolyn Lee, a woman with strong managerial experience for the period. She had risen to the number three position of news editor at *The Courier-Journal* in Louisville.

Schreiber, however, was miserable in the post and did not last. In her memoir, she recalled the isolation she felt from the lack of acceptance from her colleagues at the paper as well as those she interacted with in the sports world. "I was, depending on one's view," she wrote, "the bitch, the saint, the amazon, the token, the recipient of awards and death threats and ultimately, the ingrate, for insisting on my pre-agreed release after two excruciating years." She moved to the book review section. And Lee, despite the decade's worth of experience she brought, was put through the *Times*'s paces. She went straight to "the rim," where the pool of copy editors worked at five desks two deep, arranged in a rectangle. The traditional horseshoe-shaped table copy editors once sat around was long gone.

CHAPTER 16

Star Power

Throughout the industry in the 1970s, the impact of the new collective moves by woman journalists began to be measurable, in millimeters if not in miles. The lawsuits and EEOC complaints yielded earnest-sounding lip service, some prominent, billboard-worthy promotions, the nurturing of potential and promise, and some modest short-term victories for women in the rank and file. Decades of monitoring would follow as the various women's and minority caucuses persisted in efforts to effect lasting change. Editors and publishers put a few women in top positions and others into the "pipeline" with an eye toward their steady advancement.

The rise of Carol Sutton at *The Courier-Journal* from secretary in 1955 through the women's and the features sections to managing editor in 1974 created a burst of initial publicity and excitement that turned into a cautionary tale. The newspaper's announcement of what was "believed to be" the first woman to run a large U.S. newsroom was major enough to put Sutton on the cover of *Time* magazine in its 1975 gallery of "Women of the Year." Sutton lacked a hard-news background and had never attended a night news conference. During her brief tenure, colleagues accused her of spending too much time out of the newsroom in travel (for publicity appearances she made at the newspaper's behest); of filling the front page and the rest of the paper with too many features (after readers complained in surveys that the paper was dull); and of placing too much emphasis on far-off world events that did not engage the local housewife. Others criticized her indecisiveness and disorganization (long-known faults) and, overall, for being underprepared for the job. A few critics thought the paper fell short on the biggest story of the period, the court-ordered desegregation of the schools of Louisville's Jefferson County, even though it brought a Pulitzer Prize for photography.

To seem more serious, she adopted a curious, unsmiling, mono-tonic speaking style and never broke through to a comfortable one-to-one relationship with the publisher, Barry Bingham Jr. Neither he nor the executive editor, Robert P. Clark, nor her predecessor as managing editor, George Gill, stepped in to offer the training she lacked or the guidance she could have used. (Gill had recommended her for the job.) Both the paper's circulation and its revenue fell on her watch, which coincided with a dreadful national economic climate. Also, the managing editor of *The Courier-Journal's* sister paper, *The Louisville Times,* "lurked in the weeds to nail her every time he could," according to *The Patriarch: The Rise and Fall of the Bingham Dynasty.* Before Sutton reached the two-year mark as editor, Bingham and Clark shifted her out of the managing editor slot to assume a newly created executive position under the two of them. Within a week of the new appointment, Bob Schulman, the media critic of *The Louisville Times,* gave readers the humiliating backstory of her removal, attributed to Bingham himself. Sutton stayed on at the paper until lung cancer claimed her life at fifty-one in 1985. The major achievement of her editorship was a demonstrable increase in minority hiring.

Keith Runyon worked for Sutton on the women's pages as she transformed them, starting in 1972. She favored Runyon with some of the section's best assignments and travel opportunities. He adored her as a boss and remained her close friend and admiring colleague. In his view, she fell victim to the undercutting of jealous, change-averse managers, all men, who resisted her leadership and subjected her to "invidious backstabbing," as he later wrote. Her afternoon paper rival got her job.

Mary Anne Dolan had a résumé much like Sutton's—no city desk, no hard news—but fared far better in top management. She started in 1971 as a clerk in the women's department of *The Washington Star,* and five years later, the year Sutton shared the cover of *Time* with other notable women, Dolan became the *Star's* editor for arts and culture. This was a year after the afore-praised Jim Bellows took charge of the

Star after the demise of the *New York Herald Tribune*. On the strength of Dolan's superb orchestration of a dinner party for twelve at her home in Old Town Alexandria, Bellows tried out an idea on his wife: "Don't you think that someone who could pull that off without a ripple, with no serving or cooking help, could run a section of the *Star*?" he asked. He then named Dolan assistant managing editor for features. Later, Dolan told an AP reporter that Bellows had a "core understanding" of how well the little-recognized skills women had developed over eons could be an asset in newsroom leadership. What women have always done for their families, Dolan said, was what she did on the job.

In 1977, Dolan followed Bellows to Hearst's ailing *Herald Examiner* in Los Angeles with the same title she held at the *Star*. A year later, he promoted her to managing editor over the more logical choice, Frank Lalli, the paper's thirty-five-year-old city editor and an assistant managing editor. Unlike Dolan, who was thirty-one, Lalli had considerable experience with hard news, still the more customary background for moving into top newsroom positions. Privately, Lalli was told that had the times been different, with less pressure on management to promote women into executive slots, the higher post would have been his. Lalli soon moved on to a succession of better jobs in New York, but years later would say that Mary Anne Dolan was utterly worthy of the promotion she won and a highly talented editor who was great with people and great at her job, soft-news background notwithstanding. He also knew how close a working relationship she and Bellows had, an almost father-daughter bond that went back to their *Star* years.

The managerial prowess of Kay Fanning in these years was the stuff of legend. She and her second husband bought the *Anchorage Daily News* in 1967 and ran it together until he died in 1971. Then, on her solo watch, the paper's circulation grew from twelve thousand to fifty thousand and its extensive reportage on the Alaska Teamsters union won the 1976 Pulitzer Prize for public service. Fanning sold the paper to the McClatchy chain in 1979, and by 1983 had become the editor of her church's highly respected paper, *The Christian Science Monitor*.

Women, as emerging stars in the reportorial ranks, brought new sensibilities into the newsroom, along with new ideas about what got covered and how. In 1969, when Arthur Gelb was city editor of the *Times,* Charlayne Hunter left her television job to join the paper's metro staff. With a vow to report on the people, not the people as problems, she opened a bureau in Harlem, with office space the *Times* leased for her in a law firm on 125th Street and Seventh Avenue overlooking the Hotel Theresa. "We'd never had a bureau like that," she said. "I just felt that by being in the community on a daily basis, I would get a perspective that would be different from just dropping in." The concept was "hyperlocal" more than three decades before the *Times* would briefly experiment with posting lone live-in correspondents in a couple of specific neighborhood locales of its metropolitan coverage area. Gelb later told the *Washington Journalism Review* that Hunter's work in Harlem gave readers "a sense of being on the scene and explaining a complex story," especially given the level of racial tension in the country after the Malcolm X and King assassinations of 1965 and 1968. Hers, he said, was "one of the best jobs of reporting" he saw during his ten years as metro editor.

Gelb's memoir related the backdrop to a front-page story in the *Times* of January 12, 1970, reported by Charlayne Hunter and Joe Lelyveld. It told of Walter Vandermeer, a Harlem youth who had just turned twelve, the youngest person known to have died of a heroin overdose. The byline went to Lelyveld with an italicized credit "for assistance" to Hunter at the bottom of the story's continuation on page 18. Both reporters received a Publishers Award for the story, but two months later the wider recognition of a Byline Award from the Newspaper Reporters Association of New York City went to Lelyveld alone. Gelb knew how invaluable Hunter's research and guidance had been in the three weeks of reporting the story involved, as did Lelyveld, but the *Times* had a firm one-byline-only policy in those days. Gelb made a point of writing that he promised to make it up to Hunter. Years later, she told me she never gave as much as a second thought to her reduced credit in that instance. What mattered to her was that she and Lelyveld collaborated well to produce a good story, and from that experience she developed lasting relationships with the Vandermeers and others. She could not remember if Gelb had ever made a promise to make it up to her or fulfilled it. "It seems that being Black and a woman and a journalist—uh—it's an interesting challenge," one she said she feels she has managed "fairly well."

Hunter-Gault did not say more, nor would several established, accomplished Black woman journalists of the next generation and the one after that. This was in deference to Hunter-Gault—none of them deigned to speak for so respected a figure—but more, as one among them confided when pressed to explain the reticence, because the price to a career of speaking out about what it means to carry all three identities remains too high, even this far into the twenty-first century. Ava Thompson Greenwell's book, *Ladies Leading: The Black Women Who Control Television News,* presented interviews she conducted over several years with forty pioneering Black woman executive producers and news directors, not one with her name attached. Greenwell did this, she wrote, "to provide the most candor and to protect the women from retaliation. I wanted them to be honest without feeling their jobs were in jeopardy." The stories they shared document repeated instances of workplace bias and the different "levels and nuances" of microaggression and of racism and sexism, "many of which are covert or unconscious; and therefore difficult to name and address." They "demonstrate the harmful inequities that exist, even when you're the boss," Greenwell wrote, and told of the fear of making even the slightest mistake that Black women in decision-making roles continue to harbor. She also acknowledged that the experiences the women shared would ring just as familiar to white women, other women and men of color, and, by extension, other underrepresented groups.

Gelb was impressed by how many of the stories Hunter reported were born of her own ideas and how helpful she was in advising him on how to handle Black coverage. It was she who persuaded the *Times* to drop the word "Negro" in favor of the word "black," then lowercased. It followed the publication of a story she dictated over the telephone from Chicago about an important meeting of a large group of Black women. In those days, a dictated story would go through "eleven different editors." By the time her plane landed back in New York, the piece was already in print. Everywhere she had written "black," the editor had changed the word to "Negro." "I went ballistic," she said, "and I dictated to that phone, which then went to all eleven editors, my rationale for getting crazy about what had happened." Gelb said the change in policy at the *Times* led other major publications to do the same. If an anecdote about the value of a diverse staff is ever needed, this is a good one. Gelb also wrote that he found her work so impressive that he offered her the position of assistant metropolitan editor. In the 1960s or 1970s, even into the 1980s, such an appointment at the *Times* would have been industry news. "She turned me down," he wrote, "saying she was interested only in reporting." Many years later, she had no recollection of Gelb making this offer.

By 1978, after nearly a decade at the *Times,* Charlayne Hunter, by then Charlayne Hunter-Gault, left the paper. Between 1970 and 1977, her byline had appeared in the *Times* at least 363 times, an average of nearly once a week over the period. She won two Publishers Awards, evidence of high-level recognition within the *Times* organization. Her last *Times* story, about how the lack of bonding hurt the prospects of minority contractors, was among at least eighteen that played on page 1, although the front of the metro section in those years, where her byline appeared regularly, was considered fine display. She did not leave the paper out of grievance or in anger, she said, but from a desire to return to television, to confront new challenges, and to be part of the PBS team on *The MacNeil/Lehrer Report,* which in those days devoted its half-hour program to one subject reported in depth. She liked that the format gave her the opportunity to "break some new ground for an African American reporter," to "expand my own experience," and, in the process, to help diversify electronic media. By that point, Charlayne Hunter-Gault had been accumulating firsts for a very long time.

Shortly after her start at PBS, she spoke at a meeting of the committee on minorities of the American Society of Newspaper Editors. Figures released by Northwestern University at the time showed that two-thirds of the nation's newspapers had no minority employees, despite recent concerted efforts. In fact, over the course of ten years, the number of minority reporters and editors on daily papers had barely increased to 4 percent from its dismal starting point of 1 percent. At the conference, she criticized the nation's editors for not deploying the Black reporters on their staffs more broadly so they could bring a Black perspective to all the news. Why, for instance, were there no Black reporters at city hall?

In 1971, Melba Tolliver, the secretary thrust into the anchor chair at ABC, was assigned to cover the wedding of Tricia Nixon for New

York City's WABC-TV. Tolliver ignored her producer's demand to change the close-cropped natural hairstyle she had just adopted. Tolliver's producer called the look unfeminine and demanded she change it back or wear a scarf. "Unfeminine" was what the white station executives saw, she told a *Newsday* reporter years later, as if the only possible perspective on what constituted "feminine" was their own. These men, she said, had no idea of what it meant to her personally, as a Black woman, to wear her hair as it grew. Outrage over a hairstyle would never have erupted, she pointed out, had someone Black been in authority.

Tolliver held firm. The next day, the station canceled her studio appearances and her spot on the morning show and edited her out of all the film of the White House wedding. Someone leaked the story of what the station had done. The adverse publicity put the matter to rest. Tolliver got to keep her job and her hairdo. "But believe me," she told *Newsday,* "I was not unafraid during that time."

Eighteen months later, with that episode well behind her, a wide four-column headline over a lengthy profile in the Arts & Leisure section of the *Times* declared, "Melba? She's the Toast of the Town." Tolliver had become a "new kind of celebrity," a superstar reporter, "bred by television" and its "peculiar kind of intimacy," shared with nearly a million viewers every night on WABC's *Eyewitness News.*

The story described Tolliver as a woman with enough style to make a pair of white jeans and a plain blue T-shirt look like haute couture. Asked about the problems she encountered working in a field so dominated by men, Tolliver replied that they were fewer than the ones presented by being Black. She spoke of the women's movement as a thing apart, "a white family quarrel," but one that had been more successful in six years than Black people had been since Reconstruction.

During this period and long after, the *Times*'s efforts to increase racial diversity on its staff often proved ineffectual. Years later, Max Frankel, who, beginning in 1968, held several high-ranking jobs at the *Times,* including executive editor, wrote in his memoir of how desperately the *Times* needed a staff that matched its diverse ambitions. Too often, he said, the editorial leadership would find themselves "discussing an article about racial strife without a single black face in the room." "The more women and blacks, Asians and Catholics, immigrants and natives, midwesterners and southerners, the greater our reach," he wrote, "the better our grasp of the news." In the 1970s, the *Times* did make marquee-worthy moves for two of the most established women in the industry, Flora Lewis and Ada Louise Huxtable, and both the *Times* and *The Wall Street Journal* put a few of their promising woman baby boomers into the pipeline.

In July 1972, Flora Lewis, by then divorced from Sydney Gruson, became the *Times*'s bureau chief in Paris without ever having been a member of the staff. When Turner Catledge was the paper's editor, he had established the no-couples rule after incidents arose with "transferring people around and so on," as Lewis explained her situation to her oral historian. The net effect for Lewis was that for twenty-five years she remained a busy freelance contributor to the *Times* and a willing, frequent, undeclared, and only tacitly acknowledged shadow stand-in for Gruson. In a meeting she remembered without pleasure, she quoted Catledge as having told her, "Over my dead body will you ever be hired on *The New York Times*. As far as I'm concerned, you married the wrong man." *Time* magazine's press columnist pointed out how "curious" the new Paris arrangement was, especially since Lewis, who *Time* acknowledged was "a skilled journalist of wide experience," was writing a regular column for *Newsday* at the time. Gruson was by then an executive at the *Times* and very close to the publisher. It was surely a huge help to him personally for the *Times* to put his former wife on the regular payroll with full benefits as he married a new one. But, as John Darnton would later say, "I would be wary of these people who would say that Flora got to where she got because of Sydney, because the *Times*, you know, to me, it's a place of egos and rumors," a place, he said, where women far too often were accused of sleeping around to get ahead or otherwise not having succeeded on their own.

When the Paris offer came, Lewis at first said no because she wanted to stay in Washington, where she had just moved. The Los Angeles Times Company had just bought *Newsday*, and the new leadership was less receptive to Lewis's column than those with whom she had contracted. Besides that, it did not pay enough to provide a good living. So Lewis accepted the Paris offer. "A number of jaws went slack at the news that an 'outsider' was moving into one of the paper's choicest overseas jobs," *Time* magazine reported. The trouble started with John Hess, a senior reporter in the Paris bureau, who told unflattering stories about Lewis's years in Paris as Gruson's wife, the entitlement he said she exhibited, and the liberties with *Times* resources he accused her of feeling free to take. Lewis maintained that none of the things Hess said about her were true. "They were about Sydney," she contended in the oral history, adding that Hess had either mixed up the stories in his own mind or had done so deliberately. Hess told his editors he would only stay in Paris if he could bypass her authority and report directly to the foreign desk. He was angry to be cut out of a job he thought was his for the taking, Lewis said. His burst of ill-timed fury worked in Lewis's favor. The editors in New York told Hess he would have to report to Lewis or come home.

Without question, Flora Lewis was talented, capable, and prepared, but she also understood how much she owed to the luck of good timing. Two years in as bureau chief, she told an interviewer that had it not been for World War II, when opportunity for women opened up by default, she would not have gotten her first job at the AP. The *Times* offered her the Paris post not only because she was qualified but because of the "social climate." Five years earlier, she said, it would not have occurred to anyone to make her the *Times*'s bureau chief in Paris.

The arrangement she had with Abe Rosenthal, the *Times*'s executive editor at the time, was a four-year term in Paris after which she could return to Washington. But when 1976 rolled around, Rosenthal wanted her to stay abroad a little longer. She never left.

On September 26, 1973, the *Times* announced Ada Louise Huxtable's elevation to its editorial board, the second woman to hold the position since Anne O'Hare McCormick, who served for nearly twenty years, from 1936 until her death in 1954. Huxtable, in her new role, was to divide her time between her new post and "expanded duties" as architecture columnist for the paper's Sunday edition. Over five paragraphs, the appointment story highlighted Huxtable's long scroll of achievements to which her *Times* years had added honorary doctorates, including from Yale, Smith, and Williams; a Municipal Art Society award; the Architectural Critics Medal of the American Institute of Architects; and the first Pulitzer

Prize for distinguished criticism in 1970. Her successor, Paul Goldberger, had joined the staff of *The New York Times Magazine* fifteen months earlier in an entry-level position as he graduated from Yale. He was twenty-three. Goldberger would spend twenty-five years on staff until 1997, when he moved to *The New Yorker,* amassing honors and awards and distinctions along the way to match his predecessor's, including his own Pulitzer Prize for criticism in 1984. Given his knowledge of the newspaper and its culture, I asked what he thought might have happened if he had been a woman, a 1973 college graduate with a similar résumé. "It's difficult to know the absolute answer to your question," Goldberger replied. "But it's impossible not to believe . . . that a woman as an undergraduate would have had a more difficult time getting *The New York Times* to pay attention, especially those many years ago." This is such a good example of the truism, still extant: men get opportunity on the strength of their potential; women, for their experience.

In 1974, the *Times* promoted Charlotte Curtis to op-ed page editor, succeeding Harrison Salisbury. This made her the first woman among the paper's senior editors to join the *Times*'s masthead. A reporter asked Salisbury what prompted the choice. "Because there is no better reporter on the paper and reporting is the name of the game whether you are out on the street chasing or behind your desk figuring out what to chase," he said. "How many times do we have to learn and learn over again that all it takes to make a Dickens, a Balzac, a Talese, or a Curtis is a pair of sharp eyes, quick ears, strong legs and a knack of beating the hell out of a typewriter?"

Executives in the broadcast world were under the same diversity onus as their print counterparts. Pauline Frederick stayed a force in broadcasting throughout the 1970s. The UN would remain her beat at NBC until 1975, when, at sixty-seven, she moved on to National Public Radio as a foreign news analyst, a job she held for the next five years. Linda Wertheimer, employed in the first wave of hires as NPR came into being in 1971, was already on staff, just ahead of the network's other "founding mothers," Susan Stamberg, Nina Totenberg, and Cokie Roberts, all four in part because of the chance to build superb political reporting careers undeterred by the modest compensation NPR offered. "This is what I was meant to do," Wertheimer

told an interviewer as her twentieth anniversary with the radio network neared. She would still be on the air, as would Totenberg, to
celebrate the network's fiftieth. Cokie Roberts remained active in the
profession until her death at seventy-five in 2019. As if in testament
to the power of role models, Wertheimer once told an interviewer
that she had wanted to be a radio broadcaster since she first heard
Pauline Frederick over the air.

In these years, Barbara Walters emerged as an even more commanding presence and power on television than Frederick had been,
almost magically able to overcome bad calls, flagrant gaffes, and flops
of proportions monumental enough to fell a lesser force of any pro-
noun. ABC once published a list of her thirty worst bloopers, which
included her agreement with an interview subject not to air news-
making portions of her interview, information that immediately
appeared elsewhere; her calling a star with household recognition
by another celebrity's name; and some truly terrible interviews with
cartoon characters. In 1975, a decade into her time at *Today,* she had
become so valued that she reported top salary earnings of between
$200,000 and $400,000 a year, which would be between $1 million
and $2 million today. She offered up the figures for a vignette in a
series in *Cosmopolitan* that year titled "36 WOMEN with Real Power
Who Can Help You." The thumbnail sketch of Walters came first,
ahead of the financiers, company presidents and vice presidents, a
surgeon, a cancer researcher, a law school dean, a judge on the U.S.
Court of Appeals, and a top college officer. The justification for her
positioning would become even more evident the following year,
when ABC hired her away from NBC on a five-year, $1 million-a-
year contract that made her the first woman coanchor of the premier
nightly news program on a national network. She had the added
brief of producing interview specials each year with news makers
and celebrities. For the nightly news, she joined Harry Reasoner,
whose reaction to her presence in an anchor chair beside him was so
visceral, she recalled in her memoir, that he once recoiled physically
on the air "in front of millions of people" when she offered a collegial
touch to his forearm.

Walters's early days at ABC could not have gone worse. Yet as
Roone Arledge would later remark to a reporter, "She was expected

to deliver a miracle. Nobody could have." Not even her interview specials escaped demoralizing scrutiny, she wrote, even though they were considered her greatest strength and draw. Television critics accused her of everything from asking stupid questions to melding entertainment with news. Just about anything she said or did could generate a snide attack from somewhere. With grace and a clenched jaw, she endured Gilda Radner's running caricature of her on *Saturday Night Live,* with its comic exaggeration of her uniquely pronounced *r*'s. Radner aggrandized the flaw into a full-blown speech impediment. When Radner died, Walters signed her condolence note to the comedian's husband, Gene Wilder, "Baba Wawa."

Walters's memoir credited her support from Arledge once he became network president in 1977. That is also the year of her joint interview with the Egyptian president Anwar Sadat and the Israeli prime minister Menachem Begin, her own most prized, at the start of the historic peace process between the two countries.

As the 1970s progressed, television networks scrambled to showcase more women in substantive reporting roles and anchor positions. The women of television were at last in motion, well served by the law. In 1972, the Federal Communications Commission included women in its affirmative action mandate. Connie Chung got her start at CBS in 1971 as the network sought women of every description to put in front of the camera, as Chung told an NPR host. "Me, a nice Chinese girl; Michele Clark, a black; Lesley Stahl, a nice Jewish girl with blond hair; and Sylvia Chase, a blond shiksa." Carole Simpson came to NBC News in New York from WMAQ in Chicago, bringing Black star power to the network in 1975. That same year, NBC hired Judy Woodruff at the start of another enduring career, like that of Jane Pauley, whom NBC brought in from its Chicago affiliate in 1976 to replace Barbara Walters on *The Today Show.* At about the same time, Andrea Mitchell moved from radio reporting to CBS-TV's Washington affiliate.

In the magazine world, Janet Malcolm made a brief return to *The New Republic* in 1970 with an essay under her misspelled byline that explored the ambivalence of the modern liberated woman as she faced the dilemma over whether to work outside the home or in it. She addressed the issues inherent in the "mistress-servant" relationship.

Janet Malcolm
(Photo by © Nancy Crampton)

It was, she said, unlike hiring an electrician or psychiatrist. Hiring "help," she said, using the now unacceptable euphemism of the moment, amounted to "paying someone to do for you what you are capable of doing yourself." In the same period, her relationship with *The New Yorker* solidified. From 1970 to 1973, she was the columnist for "About the House," an interiors and design column that had been running since the magazine's earliest days, and then produced "On Photography," a column she continued to write for years. Her work attracted attention from peer critics at other publications, who quoted her insights in essays of their own. In the meantime, not long after the death of her first husband she married Gardner Botsford, her editor at *The New Yorker,* with whom she worked closely. Psychoanalysis, the profession of Malcolm's father, became her next recurrent theme. Her first such piece, about family therapy, appeared in *The New Yorker* in May 1978, attracting little notice beyond the magazine's readership, unlike the controversy her later reporting would incite.

At the newspapers, young women with evident talent got the attention of their editors who enabled their rapid rise. In 1976, Molly Ivins, at thirty-two, became the second woman to serve as Rocky Mountain bureau chief of the *Times* after Grace Lichtenstein, the first woman the paper made a national correspondent in 1974. Ivins had caught the paper's attention through her work for *The Texas Observer,* which she coedited with Kaye Northcott for five years after her time at the Minneapolis paper. Maureen Dowd started at *The Washington Star* as a "vastly overqualified dictationist," in Jim Bellows's phrase, after her graduation from Catholic University in 1973. She wrote about tennis while still in the dictation pool, then became a metro reporter, and then a feature writer. As an editor, Dowd said, Bellows was "very exciting, charismatic. He just gave off a vibe of someone looking for great stories" and seemed to love strong women. "He always had a sparkle and you felt that you could do anything with him at the helm." Hers was another career that Bellows nurtured, as he had those of Mary Anne Dolan and Gail Sheehy.

Anna Quindlen got her start at the *New York Post* in the summer of 1973 and became a full-time staffer a year later, once she graduated from Barnard. Three years later, the *Times* hired her as a general assignment reporter and to cover city hall. Jill Abramson and Jane Mayer connected as campus stringers for *Time* during their college years, but they already knew each other as schoolmates at Fieldston, the New York prep school that readied Abramson for Harvard and Mayer for Yale. They graduated from college a year apart, Abramson first, magna cum laude, in 1976. Abramson then worked for *Time* in its Boston bureau and had a stint at NBC News. Mayer, who graduated Phi Beta Kappa in 1977, worked at two small Vermont weeklies, then the larger *Rutland Herald* before she went to *The Washington Star* in 1980. Like Maureen Dowd—they became friends in those years— Mayer stayed at the paper until it was gone, and as for so many other *Star* alumni, greater things were in store.

The same would prove true for Lesley Visser, who, at twenty-one, under provisions of a Carnegie Foundation grant, joined the staff of *The Boston Globe* to cover a range of college and professional sports for fourteen years, starting in 1974. Two years in, she was covering the New England Patriots, the only woman at the time with a National Football League team as her beat.

Feminism, *Time* said, as if it were fact, had transcended the feminist movement. True, there were positive signs, but plenty of ground still to make up. New issues emerged. Companies instituted (short) maternity leave policies, for example, a belated acknowledgment of the permanent presence of women in the working world, but they paid no heed to the needs of families with two working parents, sometimes two working journalists, and what children might mean for the ambitious women involved who bore their offspring and the heavier load at home. Everywhere were signs of an impending shift in how women in the profession were viewed and treated, as was the case in the culture at large. What earned the most attention was how hard it all was and how little was being done to make it easier. As the *Time* cover story headline read at the start of 1976, "Women of the Year: Great Changes, New Chances, Tough Choices."

PART FIVE

REALIGNMENT

1980s–1990s

CHAPTER 17

Not Quite

Media companies beset by the discontent within, the legal onus from without, and the need to reflect the country's latest demographics kept trying to change in the 1980s, some with more fervency and better results than others. None did well enough. Progress brought plenty of success stories for woman journalists working in print and in television and radio, but the disappointments were no less stunning than they had been in the past.

Although women had long served on juries for the Pulitzer Prizes, a woman joined the nonprofit's board for the first time in 1980—not a journalist, but the president of the University of Chicago. A woman journalist, the chief editorial writer for *The Christian Science Monitor,* was added in 1981, the same year Mary Anne Dolan, at thirty-four, advanced in Los Angeles to succeed her mentor Jim Bellows as chief editor of the *Herald Examiner.* Bellows left her a livelier paper in far better shape than the one he found. In 1984, Dolan's third year in charge, *Ladies' Home Journal* put her on its list of "36 Women to Watch" as "the first woman to run the show at a major metropolitan daily without owning it." Her rank was higher than Carol Sutton's had been in Louisville seven years earlier, a significant time lapse. When an AP reporter asked how Dolan felt about her promotion, she shared how she reacted in 1980 when Sherry Lansing took charge of Twentieth Century–Fox. At the time, Dolan said, she could not imagine *The New York Times* ever putting a woman in charge. Suddenly that seemed less impossible.

Dolan told *Ladies' Home Journal* that her major achievement up to

Mary Anne Dolan and Jim Bellows in the *Los Angeles Herald Examiner* newsroom, December 1, 1981, the day he announced his resignation as editor and her promotion to the post

(Photo by Chris Gulker, gulker.wordpress.com)

that point was the paper's ambitious, innovative investigation of the city's garment industry. It appeared, novella-style, in seventeen parts in January 1979 while Dolan was still deputy to Bellows, or, as the *Los Angeles Times* called her, "the only female managing editor of a major metropolitan daily in the United States."

The series was the work and brainchild of Merle Linda Wolin, a reporter on the staff of the paper's then city editor, Frank Lalli. Wolin at the time was the only major media reporter in Los Angeles who covered the Spanish-speaking community as a regular beat. The proposal to go undercover in the city's sweatshops as an undocumented sewing machine operator was hers. Lalli loved the idea and took it to Bellows—Lalli was sure Dolan had been involved—along with his fears for Wolin's safety. Bellows gave the green light, but only on assurance from Lalli that he would spell out all the risks and reconfirm with Wolin that she still wanted to do it.

To blend in with California's 175,000 garment workers, 90 percent of whom were not American citizens, Wolin transformed herself into "Merlina de Novais," an undocumented garment worker from Portuguese-speaking Brazil. She perfected the guise thanks to her own theatrical training and coaching from two colleagues, Alberto

Aguilar, a well-known Spanish-language broadcaster for KALI, and J. Gerardo López, the associate editor of *La Opinión*. "Merlina" took jobs in three different sweatshops, meeting with Lalli daily after her shifts to discuss her reporting and how safe she felt. After five weeks, they decided to end the ruse. A fellow worker who wanted to date her had asked too many questions about her Spanish accent and background. Wolin's Spanish was fluent, but not native, hence the Brazilian pose. Lalli recalled that Wolin liked to underplay her considerable linguistic skill by saying it was "not bad for a Jewish kid from Cheyenne, Wyoming."

Lalli guided the project until he left the *Herald Examiner* in the summer of 1980 to become associate business editor of the *New York Daily News*. Wolin kept reporting and writing with Dolan in Lalli's role as "editor, sounding board, confidante, and nurturer." The work took eight months in all, including court proceedings that Wolin initiated against one employer who refused to pay her. Once published, the series showed the hold unscrupulous employers had over most of their workers as they labored under appalling conditions for terrible pay, ever fearful of deportation. López of *La Opinión* had the idea to translate and republish the series in Spanish, and Jaime Jarrín of KWKW proposed reading the Spanish version of the series over the air. KALI asked to do the same. Wolin brought these proposals to Dolan, who embraced them without a blink. The radio versions, read over the air each day, riveted Spanish-speaking Los Angeles, with the broadcasts often heard by the workers inside the fetid garment factories.

Because of all the project's elements, its print and broadcast interplay, and the English and Spanish translation, the team at the *Herald Examiner* correctly predicted a huge social and political impact for the series. The paper sold out the first day and doubled its press run for the remaining days of the series. *La Opinión* had similar success, as did the broadcasters. The series not only brought national press attention to the struggling *Herald Examiner* but earned Dolan and Wolin an invitation to appear in front of a congressional subcommittee charged with investigating the abuses of sweatshop labor, an initiative undertaken in direct response to Wolin's findings.

The Pulitzer Prize *jury* for 1982 chose "Sweatshop: Undercover in the Garment Industry" to win the gold medal for public service, the most prestigious of all the journalism award categories, but without consulting the jurors, the Pulitzer *board* that year, "at the midnight hour," Wolin said, overturned the unanimous recommendation in favor of the jury's third choice, a nomination from *The Detroit News.* This was pretty much what had happened in 1979 when the board declined to award the local specialized reporting prize to the *Chicago Sun-Times* for Pamela Zekman's Mirage tavern project because its undercover aspect bothered some members of the board.

Dolan responded much the way James Hoge as the editor of the *Chicago Sun-Times* reacted when Mirage was passed over. If the board was going to disqualify undercover entries, she said, they should have said so beforehand. In surveys, readers expressed appreciation for the results these investigations often brought and never cited undercover work as a reason for the public's rapidly diminishing trust in the press, which readers attributed to other deficiencies, like the frequency of errors and pandering to the powerful. *Newsday*'s publisher at the time, David Laventhol, acknowledged to a reporter that he and his board colleagues discussed the undercover question and that some members had expressed concern about its use, but said there was no stated policy against it. The board, he said, simply found the Detroit entry to be "clearly superior."

In the end, Wolin did receive several awards. A generation later, Tony Horwitz of *The Wall Street Journal* won his Pulitzer in 1995 for a series most remembered for his undercover stints as a line worker at two poultry processing plants, and in 2001, Charlie LeDuff was among the winners for the *Times*'s series "How Race Is Lived in America," for which he worked undercover in a slaughterhouse. In neither case was the use of subterfuge any less tainted a reportorial approach than it had been at the time of the *Sun-Times* and the *Herald Examiner* investigations, both led by women at lesser outlets whose work achieved far greater demonstrable external impact than did the latter-day winners.

Zekman, after Mirage, lost no traction. She left the *Chicago Sun-Times* for WBBM, the local CBS-TV affiliate, and over the next thirty-nine years produced investigations as effective on television as hers had been in print. The *Chicago Tribune* profiled her at length in 1985, citing the two Pulitzers she had helped win during her days on its own investigative task force and the first of the two duPonts she eventually won for her television work, along with two Peabodys and twenty-four Emmys by that point. Zekman, the writer said, was "arguably the toughest, most tenacious, most effective investigative television journalist in America; some would drop the caveat 'television' and simply say she's the best."

More broadly, the women's discrimination suits of the 1970s at last wound down, although it took until 1983 for a U.S. district court to resolve the case against the Associated Press. It ended in a consent decree, orders for the wire service to establish an affirmative action program, and a demand that the cooperative give $2 million in back pay to its woman, Black, and Latino employees. Responding to the settlement, Al Neuharth, the CEO of Gannett, admonished woman journalists to leave, threaten, or sue any news organization whose top leadership failed to honor its commitment to their advancement.

Among women, the hunger for collective action subsided even though their issues were far from gone. New Jersey provided a microcosm of conditions for women throughout the industry in 1981. *The New York Times* cited a survey of twenty-six daily newspapers that found women well represented among fifteen hundred full-time journalists, an average of about 36 percent of the reporters and editors working in the state. The number of women at individual papers ranged from a low of 14 percent of the staff to a high of 55 percent. All but three newspapers had women in supervisory positions, including Linda Grist Cunningham, at thirty-one, the executive editor of both the *Hudson Dispatch* in Union City and the Paterson *News*.

By 1987, three more women carried the top title at U.S. daily newspapers with circulations over 100,000. Others, like Cunningham, led at smaller, less prominent outlets. In 1987, four years after the much-beloved Kay Fanning began ably editing the 188,000-circulation *Christian Science Monitor,* she became the first woman to preside over the American Society of Newspaper Editors, known by its acronym, ASNE. In 1984, Sandy Mims Rowe, at thirty-six, took over as executive editor of Norfolk's combined *Virginian-Pilot* and *Ledger-Star,* the largest paper in Virginia, circulation 222,136. Starting in her twenties, her editors propelled her through the newsroom's pipeline from reporter to section editor (as a woman, she said, that section was features) to city editor to assistant managing editor to managing editor, through the merger, to the top job of executive editor for both papers in 1982. She held the position until *The Oregonian* recruited her in 1993 to lead the Portland newspaper, which she did until her retirement in 2010. On her watch, the Virginia paper won its first Pulitzer in twenty-five years, and of the five *The Oregonian* amassed during her years in charge, the earliest was the paper's first since 1957.

In 1987, Janet Chusmir, at fifty-seven, got the top job at *The Miami Herald*, with its circulation of just under 500,000. "Journalism History Made: A Woman Lands the Top Newsroom Job at Major Daily," the headline read over a story about it by the *Los Angeles Times* media reporter Tom Rosenstiel. He saw the Chusmir appointment as a "major breakthrough," largely because of the Miami paper's size and standing. A "landmark event," Kay Fanning called it. The *Los Angeles Herald Examiner* had a circulation of nearly 300,000 when Mary Anne Dolan took charge, but Rosenstiel diminished that significance by pointing out that unlike the more prestigious Miami paper, the *Herald Examiner* was in financial distress and trailed in influence when compared with its main competitor, his L.A. newspaper home.

It is hardly surprising that surveys at the time showed women to be 90 percent of all of the country's lifestyle editors and that the paltry 12 percent of all top woman editors were concentrated at smaller papers. Interestingly, of the four women who joined the more elite ranks in the 1980s, all but Kay Fanning rose to power through the features and lifestyle sections, the way Carol Sutton in Louisville, Mary Anne Dolan in Los Angeles, and Sandy Rowe in Virginia had, along with a number of the women who came up behind them. It was not a customary route to executive positions, but "features," by default, forged the pipeline for women with the widest circumference. Rowe, once questioned as to whether a woman from such a background could handle the top job, answered, "Just watch." As she explained years later, newspapermen were slow to awaken to their own self-interest and recognize the leadership potential of women. They were slow to grasp the disadvantage they put themselves in by ignoring the interests of half their potential readership, nearly half of their staffs, and half of the people on earth.

Academicians now started to address the subtler acts of discrimination, taking a closer look at gender bias as it appeared on the published page. In 1980, the *Columbia Journalism Review* carried a "Check Out Your Sexism" quiz that provided a guide to deleterious presumptions, such as "homemaking and parenting are not work." It called out the bias the researcher identified in pieces culled from several publications. From an examination of articles in *Time*, the researcher extrapolated that anyone could write a sexist sentence and often did. Of twenty copy editors listed on the magazine's masthead, eighteen of them had women's names.

There were anecdotal signs of progress. By 1980, the appositive for Flora Lewis, that "pert news gal" of 1958, had become that "once in a generation" reporter. Soon after, as *The Washington Post* settled its women's suit out of court, Ben Bradlee named Karen DeYoung the *Post*'s foreign editor. This was a major appointment for a woman at an elite paper, especially given that DeYoung had been on the staff for only six years. She continued to rise thereafter. Nevertheless, at the *Post* and at all the other large, high-prestige daily and Sunday papers, men held almost all the other top positions.

The EEOC and FCC regulations lost much of their bite under the conservatism of President Ronald Reagan's administration, but executives continued to push the white men in charge of various departments to hire outside their "comfort factor," in the phrase of Arthur Sulzberger Jr., who would become publisher of *The New York Times* as was his father before him. In junior executive roles before he became publisher, he championed the hiring and promotion of women and of gay, lesbian, Black, and Latino reporters and editors, to better reflect both the newspaper's mission and the country's rapidly changing demographics. It was not only the right thing to do but good for business, a case he made again and again. In 1984, six years after the suit was settled at the *Times*, Abe Rosenthal did send Sheila Rule to Nairobi for four years in her seventh year on the staff—a rarity for a Black staff member—and Susan Chira to Tokyo, not quite three years out of Harvard with a background in East Asian studies and fluent in Japanese. Chira considered her appointment an "accelerated opportunity" for a *Times* woman. Rule viewed her experiences at the *Times* "not through a women's lens but through a Black person's lens in that the newspaper discriminated against both Black men and Black women." In her recollection, almost no Black women had participated in the women's suit against the paper, but they did join the discrimination suit filed by people of color.

Still, even with such responses from the country's leading paper,

change at the *Times* and everywhere
else came slowly for the most part.
Sandy Rowe said the number of
women on ASNE's membership roster from the early 1980s into the 1990s,
when she was running papers in Virginia and Oregon, could have fit in a
shower stall. She saw the paucity of
great role models as a major deficit.
Her own rise with so few women to
look up to conditioned her to assume
that mantle for the women coming up
behind her, several of whom would
similarly succeed. From memory she
summoned the names of Amanda
Bennett, who would go on to lead *The*
Philadelphia Inquirer, Julia Wallace at

Sandy Mims Rowe
(Photo by Pete Perry)

The Atlanta Constitution, and Janet (Weaver) Coats at *The Tampa*
Tribune.

Nationally, by 1983, the number of woman journalists had grown
14 percent higher than the 1971 figure, but in the decade that followed, analysis by the same researchers showed no significant growth
despite the continued push to diversify from organizations like
ASNE and dramatic increases in woman journalism majors at colleges and universities. The researchers blamed the lackluster progress on stagnation in an industry hit by the two economic recessions
of the 1980s, the most severe in the first two years of the Reagan
administration, followed by the boom economy of 1984, and the second, the more gradual recession after the stock market crash of October 1987. Gene Roberts, editor of *The Philadelphia Inquirer* from 1972
to 1990, recalled that after "Black Monday," Knight-Ridder imposed
three full years of continual hiring freezes, with maybe a month's
respite somewhere in between. "We may have been worse than most
papers," he said, "but generally, there was an industry slowdown." A
drop-off in growth in the number of full-time journalism jobs left
little room for younger hires since the cohort who had entered the
profession in the 1970s was still far from retirement age and, in such
an uncertain climate, mostly stayed put where they were. When

Roberts took charge in Philadelphia, he was "in search of stability" in the leadership team he assembled, which made solid experience a major determinant. The top positions thus went to men. The staff he inherited was only about 10 percent women, but that figure grew steadily over the next four to five years. By the time he moved on, despite the periodic freezes and hiring slowdowns, the gender split at the *Inquirer* became nearly even, but not in the editor positions; the leadership team he installed in the beginning, he said, remained in those same posts for fifteen to twenty years. Nevertheless, "society was changing and newspapers were changing along with it," he said. In 1990, as he left the *Inquirer* to travel the world for a year and then join the faculty at the University of Maryland, the leadership team at the *Inquirer* began to reflect the new reality. Both the paper's managing editor and its news editor were women.

The 1980s was also the decade when the term "sexual harassment" took its permanent place in the workplace vocabulary. The experiences of Linda Cunningham over nine years at the two small papers in New Jersey and before that in Virginia were emblematic of what woman journalists all across the country were experiencing. She spoke to *The New York Times* about harassment's subtleties, the sly wink, the pat on the shoulder, the too-friendly policeman on the beat, the "Hi, sweetie, how are you?" Earlier in Cunningham's career, a sports editor she outranked became so enraged at having to report to her that he stood up in the middle of the newsroom and shouted for her to go home and bake cookies with her son. Throughout the industry, such stories are legion; the indignities experienced never cease to infuriate. In the late 1970s, a young federal budget reporter in UPI's Washington bureau recalled the desk editor who jovially insisted every day she come sit on his lap. Another UPI staff member, a young woman based in London, told of her visit to the company's headquarters in New York City. A top editor invited her for a drink after work, a courtesy often extended to visiting staff members based elsewhere and almost always accepted. They ordered drinks. He had already hinted at wanting to take her somewhere quiet and more private for dinner, but when she demurred, out of nowhere he asked, "If there weren't so many people in this bar, would you fuck me then?" The question left her so shaken she fled to her godparents on Long Island. Once back in London, she told her division chief what had transpired, not with the intention of reporting on the married man nearly twice her age, nor to get him fired. That would not have come to her mind in the late 1970s, nor to her London boss's. She shared what happened out of a different concern, one more typical of the period: that having spurned the overture, she worried that she had jeopardized her not-yet-approved bid to fill an opening in another overseas bureau for which she was abundantly qualified. After she confided in her editor in London, the transfer instantly came through. Clearly, no one in charge wanted to invite trouble. "God," she would say decades later. "I was naive."

Salary disparity persisted. At the Louisville *Courier-Journal,* Keith Runyon, the lone man on the women's pages under Carol Sutton in 1972, found it symbolic when he got a large, unexpected salary increase in 1978, well after he had moved on to the editorial page. It turned out, he told a Louisville public radio station, that he was one of the beneficiaries of the company's settlement of its women's lawsuit. Because of what he was initially hired to do, his starting pay had been set at the old "female rate."

Sylvana Foa stayed with UPI after reporting from Cambodia, rising to Bangkok bureau chief in 1979, then Asia division chief, then foreign editor before taking even bigger jobs at other outlets. Her UPI files contain a plea she made to her division chief from Bangkok, dated October 31, 1981. She asked for a salary increase and a living allowance adjustment, arguing that she had produced a competitive news report, brought the bureau in under budget, increased its client list, cleared up an inherited administrative mess, and did all of this for less than what her predecessor, who created the mess, earned when she replaced him two years earlier.

Even though by the 1980s women occupied up to 40 percent of hard-news and other desired positions, surveys showed the pipeline to upper management remained clogged. Only 120 of the country's 1,700 newspapers, 7 percent, had women as managing editors, and more than half of those were at papers with circulations under twenty-five thousand.

At *The New York Times* in 1983, four years after the company's settlement pledge to bring 25 percent of the paper's women into top editorial positions, the count stood at 16 percent. From 1982 to 1987, the annual salaries of woman staffers remained on average $13,000 lower than those of men. All the while, the positive impact of the larger number of women on staff was tangible. Anna Quindlen once spoke of how the presence of more women at the *Times* helped the paper right its coverage of Geraldine Ferraro, the Democratic vice presidential nominee during the 1984 presidential campaign. Why describe her suit and not his? the women would ask until, Quindlen said, the questions revealed how silly it was to describe what candidates wore.

For the leaders of the gender bias suit at the *Times,* career advancement stalled. Eileen Shanahan, one of the suit's seven complainants, took the number three position at the *Pittsburgh Post-Gazette* as senior assistant managing editor. Carolyn Lee said that many around the paper, particularly those who had worked with Betsy Wade on the foreign desk, believed that had she not sued the paper, had she not been such a union activist during Abe Rosenthal's executive editorship, she could have advanced much further, perhaps even rising to a masthead post. Asked about Wade, Rosenthal's successor, Max Frankel, said, "I don't doubt that Betsy Wade's union activities and discrimination suit aroused resentments on the business side of the *Times,* but that would not have affected my view of her talents or any assignment that seemed right."

Promotion to top management for women was far easier and far more common at companies with more severe financial constraints, fewer resources, and less prestige, which encouraged many women to stay at such places. At UPI in this period, the presence of women was so pervasive in the sought-after bureau jobs in European capitals that Eugene Blabey, the vice president of the Europe, Middle East, Africa Division, thought of himself and the staff as "Phil Spitalny and His All-Girl Orchestra," after a popular American dance band of the 1930s and 1940s. "It made economic sense," he said years later. "At UPI, we were always constrained by an inability to pay a lot because we didn't have a lot. By hiring women, you could get a lot better talent for the money by taking advantage of the fact that women are discriminated against." Blabey offered the comment for an article about the growing presence of women in fields including publishing, law, accounting, and psychology, all once top occupation choices of white "alpha males." Journalism could easily have been added to that list. As these fields diminished in prestige, the loss of interest from top candidates who were men opened space for women at the front of the job queue and then for Blacks and other underrepresented groups in line behind them.

The situation was different in the elite newsrooms where Janny Scott worked in these years, from 1985 to 1994 at the *Los Angeles Times* and from 1994 to 2008 for *The New York Times*. Her earlier experience was at *The Record* in Bergen County, New Jersey, and before that at *The Real Paper* in Cambridge, Massachusetts, after her graduation from Harvard. She mused informally about why elite outlets tend to evolve more slowly than smaller ones with less prestige. "My guess is the *Times'* absolute and somewhat justifiable faith in the rare quality of its report operated as a brake on change," she said. "Change there came through erosion, not excavation." By the time women began to gain more equitable opportunity, she said, "there had been enough erosion of the old ways, for many reasons, that women were finally seen as capable." Carolyn Lee, whom Abe Rosenthal elevated to become the *Times*'s photo editor in 1984, observed how even without much power the growing number of women on staff in and of itself made their presence and potential, their protests and their needs, harder to ignore.

In addition, more men with fresher outlooks were moving into decision-making positions, some actively seeking women and people of color to bring under their purview. David Jones, as Gene Roberts's successor as national editor at the *Times*, starting in 1972, was one of them. He was accustomed to women in professional roles. His mother was a rural schoolteacher; his wife, who also became a journalist, was his colleague on the student newspaper at Penn State, where women made up much of an excellent staff. Jones was the paper's editor in his senior year, and his chosen successor was a woman—in 1955. All of this was formative, he said, so when he got to the *Times* in 1963, he found it strange that the staff had so few women. When he became national editor, other influencing forces of the early 1970s were in play. "I have to confess that the women's caucus had formed and there was turmoil going on with Abe about hiring women," he said, but he experienced no exerted pressure from above to hire women. The notion came to him naturally, especially after the birth of his daughter in 1974. "It just made sense," he said. In the first ten of his fifteen years as national editor, Jones brought twenty-six women onto the *Times*'s staff, among them Carolyn Lee and Betsy Wade as editors and the reporters Grace Lichtenstein and Molly Ivins, his two Rocky Mountain bureau chiefs.

The picture for women in broadcasting was no less mixed. In 1982, the *Columbia Journalism Review* reported that 97 percent of all local television newsrooms had at least one woman on staff, a growth of 40 percent over the previous decade. And yet only 8 percent of television newsrooms and 18 percent of radio newsrooms had women in charge. More than a third of all the news anchors were women at that point, but only about 3 percent of them survived in that position beyond the age of forty. By 1984, only three women who had occupied anchor chairs for various programs still held sway: Marlene Sanders at fifty-three, Barbara Walters at fifty-five, and Betty Furness, an actress and consumer affairs advocate, at sixty-eight.

For the successful women of the medium, what happened to Christine Craft in Kansas City was deeply worrisome. She sounded the ageism alarm in 1981 with her lawsuit against the local ABC affiliate, KMBC. The station demoted her from anchor to reporter at age thirty-eight because after eight months in the featured chair, a focus group found her "too old, too ugly, and not deferential to men," which she made the title of her memoir, adding the subtitle *An Anchorwoman's Courageous Battle Against Sex Discrimination.* Craft initially won two discrimination suits against her employer, awards that higher courts overturned. Quietly, in New York, a group of fifty women in television created a fund to help defray Craft's legal costs and those of others in her predicament. In this group were women in the next wave of hires, women then in their twenties and early thirties.

In 1984, ABC had no woman correspondents abroad, no women in top management, no woman vice presidents, and no woman senior producers. The company's women in New York discussed their grievances but backed off from formalizing their complaints. At the time, rumors of budget cuts and women targeted for dismissal were already rampant in the ABC and NBC news departments, according to a writer for *Cosmopolitan* who interviewed thirty-six men and women in and outside the networks, finding evidence of "caution, submission, hurt, bravado, courage, anger and fear." The writer focused on the "aging" woman journalists who had begun appearing regularly as star television news reporters in the 1970s and who had not yet aged out. Among them was Connie Chung, not quite thirty-nine at the time and a fourteen-year TV veteran, and Lesley Stahl, already forty-three, who predicted—correctly as it turned out—that she would be around for years to come. "I'm just hitting my stride," she told *Cosmopolitan,* "I'm on the crest."

Carole Simpson was forty-seven in 1988 when she became the first Black woman to anchor a major network newscast, on weekends, at ABC. With help from her husband, the vice president of a computer company, she led a group of twelve ABC woman reporters who gathered data to present on a graph at a company event honoring Barbara Walters on May 9, 1985. They waited until after the presentation, and then Simpson stood up to call out the company's inadvertent pattern of "institutional sex discrimination." Over the next three hours, the women took the floor to make their case to the boss, Roone Arledge, who listened, Simpson recalled in interviews she gave to two authors. She said he acknowledged they were right, heard their call to hire a talent scout, and brought one on board. More woman hires soon followed.

"Dazzling, Dynamic" Diane Sawyer, as *Cosmopolitan* dubbed her in 1986, was a rising presence in network television, as was Christiane Amanpour on cable news at CNN, with her international daring and authoritative accent, polished during a convent school education in England after her family fled the fall of the shah and the rise of the ayatollahs in Iran. Sawyer worked for the Nixon administration White House before becoming a political correspondent at CBS in 1980, then coanchor of the *CBS Morning News* in 1981, then a correspondent for *60 Minutes* in 1984. In 1989, at forty-three, she began to coanchor ABC News's *Primetime* with Sam Donaldson, who was fifty-five. Amanpour started as a desk assistant at the Atlanta headquarters of CNN in 1983 soon after she graduated from the University of Rhode Island. She got her first major assignments three years later to cover the ongoing Iran-Iraq War. From there she went on to cover the democratic revolutions in Eastern Europe in 1989 and forged a consistently top-drawer career in international broadcast news in this period. This was well before women became so plentiful among the most visible foreign correspondents who specialize in conflict.

In the world of magazines, the wait-and-see news in 1984 was the

appointment of the British journalist Tina Brown as the third editor
in ten months of *Vanity Fair*. This followed the magazine's $10 mil-
lion reincarnation under the new ownership of Condé Nast after an
absence from newsstands of forty-seven years. Press columns in U.S.
publications focused not on Brown's appointment but on the exodus
of the editor Leo Lerman after less than a year. Not much more
was offered beyond her name, nationality, age (thirty), and degree
from Oxford. In a longer piece, the *Times* did note the "modern"
"satirical" edge she gave the British magazine *Tatler* during her four
years as editor in her mid-twenties, and the column she wrote for
the humor magazine *Punch* for four years before that. But the piece
devoted twice as much space to her marriage to Harold Evans, what
he would be doing "whenever I get to New York," plus a plug for his
new book about the falling-out with Rupert Murdoch that precipitated his resignation as editor of *The Times* of London. There was
no mention of Brown's collection of *Tatler* pieces, published around
that time as *Life as a Party*, the used paperback of which was selling
on Amazon in the late summer of 2022 for as much as $182.26. Not
long after her arrival in New York, Brown told a *Philadelphia Inquirer*
reporter about her plans for *Vanity Fair*, and why the woman who
transformed the "staid moribund" *Tatler* into one of the "snazziest,
jazziest social chronicles" in Europe had taken on the challenge of
salvaging the American magazine's revival. "I feel as though I'm on a
high wire," she said. "I just keep saying to myself, 'Don't look down,
don't look down.'"

In the universe of major awards, women certainly took an appreciable share of them but not in numbers proportionate to their growing presence in the field. For instance, 22 women were among the
decade's 128 journalists whose names appear as solo or team winners
of the Pulitzer Prize, but that figure represents only a hair less than
18 percent of the total.

In prestige, Janet Malcolm and Molly Ivins, two well-seasoned
professionals by this point, moved into the powerhouse ranks as
several of their younger counterparts queued up behind them as
women to watch. Of the old guard, Ada Louise Huxtable left the
Times at sixty, in 1981. She got a MacArthur "genius" award in the
first round of prize giving at the foundation, adding this to her many
prestigious appointments, and the high honor of induction into the

American Academy of Arts and Letters. But Charlotte Curtis's long and impressive run had a less spectacular finish. She held on to her *Times* op-ed post until 1982, when her name lost its masthead title of associate editor. At that point, Curtis began writing a social commentary column not for the op-ed page but for metro. That continued until 1986, the year before she died of breast cancer. All the same, considering the climate for women during the years Curtis worked as a journalist and the "women's work" she did, that she held on to her high standing for twenty of her twenty-five years at the *Times*, through several leadership successions, was impressive. At her death in 1987, the *Times* obituary said her 1960s chronicles of the lifestyles of the rich and powerful made her one of the nation's best-known journalists and "set a pattern followed by other writers." That same year, on June 20, the *Times* relented on its opposition to the use of the honorific "Ms." and began to allow it to identify women who chose to be called by it or whose marital status was not known. "The Times now believes that 'Ms.' has become a part of the language," an editor's note that day read, "and is changing its policy." A similar step came thirty years later, when "Mx." joined the list for individuals who preferred no gender designation at all.

Janet Malcolm was in her late forties when she trained her reportorial lens on psychoanalysis. For her second effort on the subject, a two-part series titled "The Impossible Profession," published at the end of 1980, she interviewed a number of psychoanalysts and spent the better part of a year in weekly visits with one in particular, without paying him, from the winter of 1978 to the summer of 1979. "For people who rarely talk in their work," she told the media columnist for *The Washington Post*, "they're very verbal when there's an opportunity to talk about their work." He called her piece "extraordinary." Three years later came "Trouble in the Archives," about Jeffrey Masson, the unorthodox program director of the archives of Sigmund Freud whom she interviewed a number of times over the course of a year. The libel suit he filed against her played out in the 1990s against the work for which she is best known, her two-part series "The Journalist and the Murderer," published in *The New Yorker* in March 1989. It is Malcolm's account of the collaboration of the author Joe McGinnis with the convicted murderer Jeffrey MacDonald, which McGinnis pursued for the sake of his book *Fatal*

Vision, which became a best seller. As her opening salvo, Malcolm hurled the line of lines:

> Every journalist who is not too stupid or too full of himself to notice what is going on knows that what he does is morally indefensible.

Reaction from journalists across the country was instantaneous. The controversy she triggered mounted for weeks and has lasted years. "The literary set is wondering if there isn't a grudge match taking place," *The Philadelphia Inquirer* mused. The headline over an Eleanor Randolph column in *The Washington Post* was typical: "The Critic and the Criticized: Outraged Journalists Dispute Cynical Portrayal of Their Craft."

In 1982, Jon Katz, then the new managing editor of the *Dallas Times Herald,* told his publisher that the thing he most wanted to do for the paper was hire Molly Ivins. He took the lead in luring her back to Texas and away from *The New York Times.* By then, she had left the Rockies for the paper's metro staff in New York City. Katz offered her a regular column "about anything and everything from anywhere in the state." As recompense, he offered "the moon." Her days with *The Texas Observer* had made her Katz's "favorite journalist in the world." She had courage and point of view; a truth teller with a sense of humor, he said. She captured the spirit of Texas but was unsparing. "She just told the truth."

Katz said the two of them clicked right away. He could tell he might prevail because he knew that "her soul was really in Texas." What he loved about her work was the way she "could stick it to people and then have a beer with them in the next minute." She was controversial, he said, but never personal or mean-spirited, and she had a genius for finding characters who were as amusing as they were revealing. He loved the way she could make a reader laugh in one paragraph and cry in the next. "Now, when you read columns," he said, "you just want to cry. She was so much of what journalism should still be." Her *Times Herald* columns were a great success until the paper folded in 1991 and she moved on to *The Houston Chronicle.*

After the collapse of *The Washington Star,* Maureen Dowd did a turn at *Time* magazine before the *Times* hired her for its metro section in

Anna Quindlen	Maureen Dowd
(The New York Times/*Redux*,	(The New York Times/
photo by Sara Krulwich)	*Redux, photo by Fred R. Conrad*)

1983, then transferred her to Washington in 1986. Dowd originally came to the *Times* on the recommendation of Anna Quindlen, then the paper's deputy metropolitan editor, who declared Dowd to be a better writer than anyone else on the *Times*'s staff. At the time, Charlotte Curtis had warned Quindlen not to read too much into her promotion to second-in-command on the metro desk, because the men would make sure she only ever had as much power as they wished her to have. She spent two years in the position, a period that included two pregnancies. "Do the best you can do for yourself and other women," Curtis told her, but said not to blame herself if that turned out to be inadequate. Quindlen also wrote the metro section's twice-weekly "About New York" column and, from 1986 to 1988, her highly successful column "Life in the Thirties," which was syndicated in sixty other newspapers. Max Frankel, in his memoir, said Quindlen was one of several promising woman candidates for the masthead and "only the first of many who chose to combine family obligations with writing rather than more arduous executive duties."

Gail Collins spent the 1970s assembling the building blocks of what would become a towering career in the decades to come. With an undergraduate journalism degree from Marquette, awarded in 1967, and a master's in government from the University of Massachusetts at Amherst in 1971, Collins founded a news service in Hartford the next year to provide Connecticut statehouse and political news, a venture she sold five years later when it had become the largest news

Gail Collins
(The New York Times/
Redux)

service of its kind in the United States. For the rest of the 1970s, she freelanced, wrote columns for a business journal in the state, and cohosted a public affairs program on Connecticut Public Television. After that, she spent four years as a finance reporter in New York for UPI, completed a Bagehot Fellowship at Columbia, and spent six years as a columnist for the *New York Daily News* starting in 1985. Then she wrote an op-ed column for the fledgling, upstart *New York Newsday,* the "tabloid in a tutu," as it was known for its tabloid page size and its high-end broadsheet style.

In 1988, Jill Abramson became Jane Mayer's colleague in *The Wall Street Journal*'s Washington bureau, first as a senior reporter and later as deputy bureau chief. Abramson came well equipped for leadership after two years as chief editor of Steven Brill's *Legal Times* and a decade before that learning from him as a member of his staff at *The American Lawyer.* It was there she first became known for the strength of her investigative work, which was also Mayer's strong suit.

Abroad, Marie Colvin benefited from the friendships she formed,

Jill Abramson and Jane Mayer as finalists,
1995 National Book Awards ceremony
(National Book Foundation, photo by Sonia Moskowitz)

especially those with her woman journalist elders who served as role
models and mentors. In Paris, she connected with Flora Lewis, by
then a *Times* foreign affairs columnist on the op-ed page, and Aline
Mosby, still at UPI, both then sixty-three. They took Colvin under
their wing in her year as UPI's Paris bureau chief before *The Sunday
Times* of London hired her away. When Colvin first got to Paris, she
stayed with Mosby at her apartment overlooking the Seine with its
"peach satin drapes, heavy antique furnishings and Russian icons,"
the "spoils" of an enviable international career like the one Colvin hoped to have. One of Colvin's biographers told of how Lewis
schooled Colvin in how to stay compos mentis under the influence
of too many martinis until she could get to a place where she could
write down what she had learned from a source. The virtuous circle
Colvin formed also encompassed Martha Gellhorn, Colvin's adora-
tion of whom would come through strongly in a BBC documentary Colvin narrated about Gellhorn's life and work after her death
in 1998. In conflict after conflict, Colvin modeled her reportorial
approach on Gellhorn's, endeavoring always to bear witness to war's
human toll. In 2012, Colvin was killed in the shelling of the building

Marie Colvin, pictured on posters carried by Seetharams
Sivam and Varatharajah Su, at a demonstration to protest
her killing in Syria

(AFP Collection, Getty Images, photo by Stan Honda)

where she had sheltered in the besieged Syrian city of Homs. She was fifty-six.

At the helm of the *Herald Examiner* in Los Angeles, Mary Anne Dolan was deliberate about filling half the newspaper's leadership positions with women, calling the effort her "experiment in management by family." In a piece for *The New York Times Magazine,* published in 1988, she lamented the sorry results of her experiment under the headline "When Feminism Failed."

In the piece, Dolan shared her steps to the *Herald Examiner*'s door after ten years in executive jobs, always working with colleagues to promote the role of women in journalism. Before she left Washington, she was in the group of women who met in Nora Ephron's apartment and worked to change the concept of "society pages." She marched on the Gridiron Club and annual White House Correspondents' Dinner during the push for women to be included. She and her friends had success getting women like herself into newspaper training programs and others onto the national and foreign news desks of their newspapers. At the *Herald Examiner,* she felt compelled to bring other women up with her, imagining that between men and women there would be "respect and generosity and adaptability and warmth and comity and nurturing," along with "honest conflict and competition, but also compromise and consensus, and, therefore, success." Her goal was to supplant the old "male business model" with something altogether new, and better.

Instead, she wrote, the women she appointed, in their quest for masthead status, took on the worst, sometimes the most hilarious, aspects of "stereotypical corporate ladder-climbing." Formal meetings with the "boss" quadrupled, and words like "facilitate" and "strategize" came into vogue. Memos abounded. "Everyone was suddenly afraid that somebody else knew something she didn't. Or had a more impressive title." During visits from Hearst Corporation executives, Dolan wrote, the women whom she had placed in power positions courted the men like coquettes in worship of some ancient pagan king. Women she had perceived to be wise, funny, and mature came off to the staff as "brittle, conniving, power-hungry and unyielding."

In the end, Dolan divined that women were stymied by having had so few woman role models in upper management, and how little confidence they had to strike out and do things in new ways. No one, she said, "wakes up one morning and naturally knows what to do, or what not to do with power—how to avoid addiction to it, how to protect it, how to give it away." In 1985, Dolan, exhausted and disappointed after four years in the job, stepped down to become one of the paper's weekly columnists and a commentator and consultant for ABC News. In the four years that remained until the paper shut down, not one of the women she promoted was even considered as her possible successor.

CHAPTER 18

Power Coupling

Abe Rosenthal, as executive editor of *The New York Times,* did put some women in marquee positions but evinced no appetite for accommodating the needs of the men on his staff whose wives had impressive journalism careers of their own. By the mid-1980s, despite the changing position of women in the profession, the restrictive model for overseas deployment to which Turner Catledge subjected Flora Lewis remained in effect. As we've seen, Lewis became the *Times*'s Paris bureau chief under Rosenthal in 1972 only after her divorce from Sydney Gruson.

In the nomadic world of the foreign correspondent, John Darnton's 1982 Pulitzer Prize for his reporting from Poland on Lech Walesa and the Solidarity movement provided one of several painful sidebars. Darnton, remember, learned his feminism at the knee of his mother, Eleanor Darnton, the short-lived women's editor of the *Times* in the mid-1940s. The newspaper sent him to Warsaw in 1980, accompanied by his wife, Nina, just as Poland's workers challenged communist authority by going on strike and "the whole world began to get interested," Darnton recalled. Although Nina's background was in theater, she gained journalism experience as Darnton's aide-de-camp, freelancing during the prior four years while Africa was their base.

Rosenthal saw a Nina Darnton credit in *Newsweek* at the end of an exclusive report about the loyalties of the Polish military. The state of emergency in Poland left *Newsweek* unable to get its own correspondent into the country, and Nina provided a way for the magazine

John and Nina Darnton, 1982
(In Warsaw, personal collection of the Darntons)

to establish its own Warsaw dateline. NPR did the same. Through Craig Whitney, the *Times*'s foreign editor, Rosenthal expressed his marked displeasure with Nina's *Newsweek* arrangement. It would be "best for everyone," Whitney wrote to Darnton, if Nina stopped it. "Well," Darnton replied, "it wouldn't be 'best for everyone.' It wouldn't be best for Nina." For Nina to forfeit her *Newsweek* arrangement would mean a significant loss of income for the family as well as a loss of satisfaction in her work. Darnton argued further that *Newsweek*, as a weekly, presented no competitive threat to the daily *Times*.

The next letter came from Rosenthal. Darnton was wrong, he countered. Every other outlet should be seen as competition. Nina was able to work for *Newsweek* only because she had a visa provided to her as a *Times* spouse. Had she presented herself to the Polish authorities as a correspondent, they would never have let her cross the border. Rosenthal said he did not question the couple's loyalty to the *Times* but worried that Nina's actions would encourage other *Times* wives to write for competing publications. What if the Poles expelled Nina for something she wrote for *Newsweek*? What then? Craig Whitney made the point that if Nina held on to her *Newsweek* role, the Darntons would have to come home.

Nina dismissed as dishonorable *Newsweek*'s suggestion that she forgo a byline in a continuing role for the magazine. In the end, she said, she did not feel this was a battle she could win, especially because Rosenthal's argument was largely corporate, not sexist. Nina in fact came to Poland financed by the *Times* as John Darnton's wife, not to cover Solidarity for another outlet. So why should she, or, by extension, the *Times*, furnish *Newsweek* with a bargain-priced correspondent that the *Times*, in effect, underwrote? "It didn't seem to be that unreasonable," Nina said. "I hated it, but that was all true."

Soon after, in the basement of Warsaw's Victoria Hotel, Nina shared her story with Flora Lewis, who was in Poland on assignment as a foreign affairs columnist. Since 1980, this post had made Lewis the third journalist and second woman to hold the position following Anne O'Hare McCormick and her successor, C. L. Sulzberger. To Lewis, the exasperating outlines of Nina's saga rang all too familiar. She offered to back Nina if she wanted to mount a challenge, "but of course nothing came of it," John Darnton said years later. "What was Nina going to do?" Nina still did Poland-related work for NPR and for the Outlook section of the *Los Angeles Times*.

Early in 1982, as the situation in Poland calmed down, Rosenthal summoned all the *Times*'s foreign correspondents in the area to Paris to celebrate Darnton's Pulitzer. Rosenthal expressed some nervousness about seeing Nina given what he had cost her. He offered what he thought was a way to make things right. His idea, John Darnton recalled, was for Nina to become a full-fledged member of the Madrid bureau, where John was posted next. "A husband-and-wife team" was his phrase. Indeed, once the couple was in place, Darnton went frequently on reporting assignments to North Africa, leaving Nina to run the bureau alone. Spain had installed its first socialist government since the civil war, so there was plenty of work.

What Rosenthal had meant by "husband-and-wife team" soon became clear. Nina could write stories the *Times* would pay her for by the piece. She was not put on the *Times*'s payroll, nor was she offered a contract. Much to her retrospective shame, it had not even occurred to her to ask for one.

Even in the years after the *Times* settled the lawsuit its woman employees filed against it in the late 1970s, Rosenthal continued to hold fast to the position he took with the Darntons. As late as the mid-

1980s, despite the legal and societal pressure to address the women's professional concerns, the *Times* still had made little to no accommodation for the rising phenomenon of the power couple. At that point, in the paper's Washington bureau, David Shribman, Phil Taubman, and Steve Weisman all had wives at other outlets with careers as promising as their own. Shribman's wife, Cindy Skrzycki, was at *U.S. News & World Report;* Taubman's wife, Felicity Barringer, was at *The Washington Post* reporting for the national desk; and Elisabeth Bumiller, married to Weisman, was on the staff of the *Post*'s Style section, doing features and big society and political profiles.

On May 14, 1984, Shribman was covering the campaign of Gary Hart, the Democratic presidential hopeful. From a phone booth in a mall in downtown Omaha, he called in to the *Times*'s Washington bureau to get his messages. The clerk put him through to the bureau chief, Bill Kovach, who told him that Rosenthal wanted Shribman to become the paper's UN correspondent. It was a tremendous opportunity, Kovach said, one that could put Shribman's career on an entirely different and exciting new course.

Shribman paused. "Am I allowed to say no?" he asked. Kovach told him that would be a mistake. From notes, Shribman paraphrased what came next:

> "You know, I have a wife who works. I just can't pick up and move on." Bill says to "give it some thought, I want to be able to tell Abe your reaction after the 5:15 p.m. meeting." I explain to him that basically—I'm editing my notes here—that the job doesn't appeal to me, that it takes me away from what I wanted to do, that I'd gone to New York ten weeks earlier to speak with Seymour Topping, the managing editor, after having been offered and refused the Nairobi bureau. I took the time then to tell Topping that my interest was national reporting, plus Canada. (I later became a dual citizen, by the way [his mother was Canadian], and am now teaching at McGill and writing regularly for *The Globe and Mail.*) I was worried about having to choose between my wife and my job. Topping had said I wouldn't be pushed too hard to move, and that I was all too much worried about this. But now the issue was here again. I mentioned my conversation

with Topping to Bill, and he said the situation had changed
and that Abe was terribly excited about the prospect of me
at the UN, where he had served as a young reporter, and in
a few years it would make me eligible for any assignment I
wanted, including Canada. I told Bill that I thought the UN
was the biggest bore going—maybe not the smartest thing
to have said, but I did say it—and he told me that wasn't
wise and that he, Bill, was under pressure to give Abe an
immediate reply. I told him I didn't buy a suit that fast, but
that I would go to McDonald's and have a Coke and talk to
my wife.

Shribman then called his wife to share what Kovach said and to
get her reaction. She did not want to move. *U.S. News* was in the
midst of a complicated financial restructuring, and she had been at
the magazine only six months. Moreover, in that magazine's culture,
reporters who worked in the bureaus commanded less respect than
those at the D.C. headquarters; a move to New York would be seen
as a demotion. And more, Shribman said, "she particularly objected
to being bullied around by *The New York Times* after she had put up
with a lot," not the least of which were the weeks upon weeks left
alone while Shribman followed the campaign trail.

Shribman called Kovach back. He said the assignment held no
appeal, would take him in a direction he had no interest in going,
and that moving would create some personal headaches. He wanted
to continue covering the campaign and had already been assured he
would not have to move until after the election, when he would be
open to Boston, Chicago, Toronto, or Detroit. Kovach told him this
response was a big mistake, that Rosenthal would not understand
and would "object violently," and that Kovach could not predict the
consequences. Shribman said he was prepared to live with whatever
came. "I didn't want to go. My wife didn't want to go," he wrote in
his notes. "I said that she was willing to sacrifice for my career, but I
was unwilling to ask her to do so, especially for something I did not
want to do myself. Kovach said he would try to contain the damage."

The next day, from Denver, still with the campaign, Shribman
got a message from Kovach to call again. "Kovach: 'I'm taking you
off the campaign. Come home.'" Kovach told Shribman he had

been reassigned to the metropolitan staff in New York, "effective in sixty days." Shribman sought counsel from friends and mentors. Hart won the Nebraska primary, and Shribman flew home to D.C. Kovach called and asked again if Shribman was going to accept the assignment to New York. "I told him I had had no time to discuss this face-to-face with my wife, that this all had been conducted in a phone booth, and that I didn't want to answer. He said he was under pressure to give Abe an answer, yes or no. Would I go to New York or was I quitting?"

Shribman and Kovach chatted the next morning, not only about the campaign, but more so about the changing roles of men and women in the business. Kovach said for Shribman to turn down an assignment as choice as the UN shocked Rosenthal, who was coming to Washington the next day. However, Kovach said, Shribman should only meet with Rosenthal if he could see his way clear to taking the UN post.

Shribman promised Kovach an answer by noon, then asked for more time, which Kovach did not give him. Again, Shribman conferred with friends and mentors, among them Ralph N. Manuel, the dean of Dartmouth, where Shribman had gone to college, who told him, "No one in good conscience could work for a place that treated people that way." Ben Bradlee, the chief editor of *The Washington Post*, got wind of what was happening and called Shribman to ask if he would have lunch with another top *Post* executive, Len Downie. "I did go to that lunch," Shribman said. Then Shribman took a long, long walk to his wife's office "on Twenty-Fourth Street. Everyone thought I had disappeared," he said. "She thought I had killed myself."

Meanwhile, Rosenthal arrived in Washington and asked to see Shribman immediately, so Shribman took a cab back to the bureau, where Rosenthal was standing at the threshold of Kovach's office. He invited Shribman in, telling him he wasn't at the dentist, that he should relax. Shribman took off his suit coat and tie. He paced. Rosenthal paced. Then Rosenthal pitched the UN assignment as the great opportunity he considered it to be. He spoke of his own experience as a young man reporting from the world body, adding that the paper needed people who were willing to move when he ordered them to transfer, especially young people. *The New York*

Times, he said, was not the "Washington Times," meaning placement in D.C. was not permanent. He accused Shribman of being rigid, of having been given many opportunities and not accepted responsibilities, and thus of letting the paper down. "And this is the key exchange," Shribman read from his notes. " 'Were you married when you joined the paper?' he asked. I said I was. 'Then you should never have come.' "

The more Rosenthal talked, the more Shribman realized that he did not want to work for someone who bullied him, who called him a disappointment, and who said he would never have hired him had he known this would be his behavior. "He minimized my wife's situation. 'It's just a job,' he said, pointing out that there were plenty of reporting jobs in New York City." When Shribman declined to budge, Rosenthal told him, " 'You must leave.' That's a quote."

Once again, Shribman walked to his wife's office and from there put in a call to Kovach, who said he was sorry. He suggested Shribman wait until Saturday to come back to the office and clear out his things, so as not to cause disruption. Other than that, Kovach told him, he should not return.

Shribman landed on his feet. He went to work for *The Wall Street Journal,* where he spent a decade, then to *The Boston Globe* for another decade and a Pulitzer before he ascended to the top job at the *Pittsburgh Post-Gazette.* On his watch, the paper won a Pulitzer for its coverage of the 2018 massacre at the Tree of Life synagogue. Shribman remained devoted to Kovach. "I truly love the man," he said, and spoke of their "wonderful rapprochement." Shribman remains sorry about all that transpired. "No one," he said, "wants to quit *The New York Times* at age thirty."

Looking back, when Shribman became an editor himself, he saw things somewhat differently. He understood that Rosenthal was acting out of conviction that the three young men "on the upswing" in the paper's Washington bureau, the three with journalist wives at other outlets, had to be willing to accept a transfer. "I don't condone this by any means, it's horrifying in a way, but I did understand that it's difficult to deal with two premiers in a couple. I always went out of my way to make sure that I never pressured anybody. But I did see that it's not the easiest thing. I mean, this was not easy for Abe, but he didn't have to be a barbarian."

Felicity Barringer had been married to Phil Taubman for five years when she joined *The Washington Post*'s national staff in 1976 after three years at the Bergen *Record* in New Jersey. The couple married in 1971 as she was graduating from Stanford, where she edited *The Stanford Daily*. Before *The Record*, she spent a couple of years as a freelancer and in the Harvard News Office while Taubman worked for *Time* in its Boston bureau. Weisman and Elisabeth Bumiller married in 1983. She had been at the *Post* since the end of her graduate school year at Columbia journalism school in 1979. Before that, after graduating from Northwestern, she worked for *The Miami Herald*.

At the *Post*, Barringer covered various governmental departments and agencies, like OSHA and the EPA, for what the *Post* called its Federal Report. After Boston, *Time* sent Taubman to New York and then to Washington, and for about eighteen months he worked for *Esquire* until the *Times* hired him away in 1979. In 1984, he, like Weisman, "put up his hand" for an overseas assignment. Moscow was offered. Barringer was on board for such a move. She was sanguine about her professional prospects abroad, even if it meant giving up her full-time job at the *Post*, which, with no openings in Moscow, the *Post* told her she would have to do. She and Taubman had good connections throughout the industry, and with two sons under the age of four the prospect of freelancing without daily deadline pressure held subliminal appeal. Nevertheless, she said, "I never imagined going to Moscow would mean quitting my job, at least not when we first started talking about it." Not until Abe Rosenthal put up unexpected barriers did Barringer start to think her career was being taken away from her.

Initially, neither the *Post* nor the *Times* would—or could—credential Barringer in Moscow, where a governmental reciprocity arrangement limited the number of correspondents each country's outlets could employ. Both the *Post* and the *Times* had their full complement of reporters and others already in queue to follow them. She and Taubman sat down with Rosenthal to discuss Barringer's alternatives. At that meeting, Rosenthal not only forbade her to write for the *Post*, should the opportunity arise, but said that her doing so would concentrate too much power in one family. He rejected her suggestion that she contract with a regional paper or two. He said he would permit her to string for the *Times* if the Soviets would allow

Felicity Barringer, Phil Taubman, and their sons
(Taubman family personal collection)

it, knowing this was not an immediate option. When she asked him if the *Times* would hire her once she and Taubman returned to the United States, Rosenthal did not commit.

"The tone of that meeting for me turned very cold, very fast," Barringer recalled, adding that a subsequent attempt to smooth things over by the then managing editor, Arthur Gelb, made matters worse. She said he offered to help her "publish a book or whatever," recalling words that still offended decades later. "They didn't care what I wrote or what talent I had or what I could bring as a professional," she said. "It had nothing to do with me as a professional. It was like, if I did macramé, they would get me wool. It had to do with 'keeping the little woman happy.'"

Luckily for Barringer, within a year Mikhail Gorbachev ended the reciprocal visa restrictions, and Barringer was able to obtain accreditation and become a contract stringer for the *Times*. Her first Moscow-datelined story appeared above the fold in the center of page 1 on March 7, 1986. It was about an unmanned Soviet spacecraft that sent back the first pictures of the more-than-four-billion-year-old icy core of Halley's comet. "As I look back on it," Barringer said, "there were plenty of reasons to make it a front-page story. But I felt it was a little bit of a guilt front-page story."

Elisabeth Bumiller was in a parallel situation as the *Times*

transferred Weisman to New Delhi not long after the Taubmans
moved to Moscow. It was understood that after the 1984 election
Weisman would be reassigned, and Bumiller was ready to move. In
her case, the *Post*, too, already had a Delhi correspondent and thus
no permanent opening for her in India. Rosenthal initially opposed
Bumiller continuing to write for the *Post* at all, giving as his reason how few journalists for U.S. outlets had bases in the country.
Bumiller found this "ridiculous," "outrageous," even. She was a veteran reporter at that point, initially recruited out of Columbia by
Sally Quinn, who brought her to the *Post* to "write parties" for the
Style section. ("Parties" was certainly not Bumiller's assignment of
choice out of journalism school, she said, but getting a foot in the
door at the post-Watergate *Washington Post* of 1979 definitely was.) As
reporters, she and Weisman often found themselves in competitive
situations and managed them "like adults." So why, she wondered,
would their situation in Delhi be any different? More than that, Weisman said years later, her intention from the start was to stick to writing features, not to venture into hard-news coverage, which would
have put her at odds with the Delhi bureau chief and in competition
with her husband.

In this case, Ben Bradlee and Abe Rosenthal met to discuss Bumiller's prospects abroad. (It was Abe who "made the rules," John
Darnton said.) The *Los Angeles Times* wrote about it, describing the
discussions as "sensitive and complicated," involving "various editors
at both papers," and reporting that Bradlee managed to extract a concession. He challenged as "probably illegal" Rosenthal's contention
that husbands and wives should not compete with each other. In a
later recounting, *The Washington Post* quoted Rosenthal saying he did
not remember talking to Bradlee about the matter "except maybe,
when he yakked at me for a minute at a cocktail party." Bradlee,
however, told the *Post* that Rosenthal had been "petty" in discussing
the matter, and Len Downie described Rosenthal's attitude about it
as "awful." In the end, Bumiller continued to write for the *Post* from
abroad, limited under a $30,000 contract, which was less than her
salary had been, and to write no more than fifteen feature stories a
year. The arrangement pleased her, because the *Post*'s former foreign
editor Peter Osnos, by then an editor at Random House, had offered

Elisabeth Bumiller and Steve Weisman
in New Delhi, India, 1980

(Photo by Geraldine Baum)

her $5,000 for the right of first refusal on an eventual book she might write from India.

Weisman picked up the story nearly four decades later, recalling the deal Rosenthal, Bradlee, and Katharine Graham, the *Post*'s publisher, worked out during the Democratic convention in San Francisco in the summer of 1984. "Abe never denied that he agreed once he understood that she and I would not be competing with each other," Weisman said. "As it happens, everyone remembers her pieces more than any of mine, and her book *May You Be the Mother of a Hundred Sons* still sells in India." The book was her first of three. Bumiller struck a similar arrangement with the *Post* when the couple moved on to Japan.

As Bumiller and Weisman prepared to leave the United States, Sally Quinn and Bradlee hosted a farewell party at the Bradlee town house in Georgetown. More than three decades later, in 2019, when Columbia's graduate journalism school honored Bumiller at its annual alumni event, Geraldine Baum, her close friend since their undergraduate days at Northwestern, made the introductory remarks. Baum enumerated Bumiller's achievements, as an author and by then not only a member of the staff of the *Times* but its Washington bureau chief with a berth on the paper's masthead as an assistant managing editor. At the time of the farewell party, Baum was a reporter for *Newsday* and had flown to Washington to attend. She recalled a crowd so star-studded, she was the only person in the room she had never heard of. The toasts went on and then, as everyone was ready to get back to the bar, Bradlee realized he had neglected to ask the chair of the board of *The Washington Post* to speak. He looked over at Katharine Graham, seated alone on an ottoman. "Katharine," he said, "would you like to say something?" Baum said everyone leaned in and in what seemed like a whisper, Mrs. Graham deadpanned, "I want to thank Abe for allowing Elisabeth to write."

CHAPTER 19

Moving Up

The choice of Max Frankel to succeed Abe Rosenthal as executive editor of *The New York Times* in 1986 brought the conundrum over couples to an end. As Frankel told the story in his memoir, the paper's editors at last figured out how to accommodate journalists of equivalent talent who happened to be husbands and wives, even within the company, even in the same bureau. It might have helped that the widowed Frankel had been discreetly courting Joyce Purnick, a formidable *Times* metro reporter and columnist. Their marriage in 1988 did not oblige Purnick to find another job. In place of quitting or losing status, she accepted an offer to write on urban affairs for the *Times*'s editorial board, well outside her husband's newsroom purview. In February 1989, the magazine *Manhattan, Inc.* included their photographs in a Valentine's Day feature that identified Purnick as an editorial writer who was "half of the Times' leading media couple" and Frankel, as executive editor, in a position to "share sources and resources with his bride."

Frankel understood the complications that newsroom couples posed, but also knew that Abe Rosenthal's bull-in-a-china-shop approach to the Darntons and to David Shribman was not the best way to solve the problem, nor how Rosenthal suspended Felicity Barringer's career options and curtailed Elisabeth Bumiller's at *The Washington Post*. Even though Frankel and Purnick took pains to keep their relationship from interfering at work, the risks of "undesirable competition, collusion, or favoritism" remained. Purnick, he wrote, as a widely admired colleague with "a healthy disdain for executives," suddenly found herself sought out as a "conduit for complaints." In the cases of Barringer and Bumiller, the *Times* made a place for them full time, initially both in New York City, in the same newsroom as their husbands, but in different departments. It took fifty years, but by 1993, when Barringer joined the *Times*'s staff as deputy editor of the "Week in Review," and two years later as Bumiller signed on at metro, to be husband and wife in the *Times*'s newsroom had become a nonevent.

So had the presence of women, married or single, with children or without, who occupied upper management positions at other outlets across the country if not at the *Times*. In Frankel's memoir, he wrote of the "urgency" he felt to promote more women, and not only because the *Times* had yet to meet the 25 percent women-in-management goal set in the 1978 settlement of the women's legal action. On moral grounds, his own minority background as a German-Jewish immigrant had sensitized him deeply to the wrongs of exclusion. As he became executive editor, no woman had yet reached the news-side masthead. None had yet led the paper's all-important hard-news sections—metropolitan, national, foreign, and business. Even his initial masthead appointees had been white men, so the imperative he felt to broaden the scope involved social justice, the need he saw to strengthen the paper with a workforce as diverse as possible, and a desire to give the women already on staff a strong and clear signal of his commitment to them. Arthur O. Sulzberger Jr. also promoted these ideas while he was assistant publisher and then deputy publisher, until midway through Frankel's term, when Sulzberger succeeded his father. "Max felt this himself," Sulzberger said. "It was something we shared. So I can honestly say he and I were early on partners in beginning to push for this."

In fact, during Frankel's eight years as executive editor, ending midyear in 1994, the number of women who were *Times* news professionals more than doubled, from 15 percent to a third of the staff. During his tenure, he recalled in his memoir, those who applied to work at the newspaper and those the paper recruited were as likely to be men as women. Hiring reflected that effort. And yet despite the strong obligation he felt to advance women and other underserved groups into the top positions, in his view the pool of available talent remained too shallow to produce candidates who could head up the paper's prime sections.

This assertion is mystifying, given that since the 1970s, at other outlets around the country, at least a few women were thriving in upper management positions, on top domestic beats, and in the most desirable correspondent posts in Washington and abroad. By 1988, for example, the roster of ASNE included eighty women among its thousand members. True, most worked at small publications, but a handful were at newspapers ranked in the top tier. By Frankel's own estimate, by the end of his term, if women came to represent a third of his newsroom's staff, they would have numbered in the low hundreds. Even if no more than a talented tenth of them had the ambition or could be encouraged or persuaded into the pipeline to leadership, that would have made perhaps a dozen or two dozen available woman candidates to consider for the kinds of positions their counterparts elsewhere in the industry had begun to occupy. Remember, too, the *Times* prided itself on its ability to attract and hire the brightest and the best.

Frankel explained the impediments to bringing women into upper management in those years. Some prospects proved to be disappointing leaders. (Of course that was true of plenty of men who moved from desk to desk, eyed on the way up until they were not.) Other women seen as potential candidates declined to change tracks, citing how the erratic management work schedule and administrative burden conflicted with rearing their children. Still others, he wrote, put the career needs of their partners ahead of their own.

Yet by the time Frankel took charge, Sandy Mims Rowe was in her second year as editor of *The Virginian-Pilot* at the start of what would become twenty-three consecutive years in a top position at a large-circulation regional paper. She had a one-word reaction to Frankel's explanation of why, as executive editor, he found it so difficult to promote women into key posts: "Malarkey." Her own good fortune, she said, derived from having come up among decision makers unchoked by "the limits of their own experience," unlike most white men in power at the time. She had bosses who were open to the advancement of people whose careers did not mirror their own.

At the *Times,* in October and November 1986, shortly after Frankel took charge, he received confidential memos that he requested from five of his top deputies, all men, having asked for their thoughts on whom to promote into key positions and why. Most listed Carolyn Lee as an excellent prospect for promotion. Soma Golden's name also came up more than once. Lee had been picture editor for two years at that point, and Frankel quickly got to know her as a "lively presence" in the daily front-page meetings. Since then, she had become senior editor to Warren Hoge, the assistant managing editor for business and personnel affairs for the thousand-person newsroom. She was admired as an editor and had a high likability quotient in the newsroom. Nan Robertson, in *The Girls in the Balcony*, described as one of Lee's great strengths her ability to speak up and speak her mind with "such grace and good humor that almost nobody took offense." Frankel personally brought Soma Golden onto his team when he ran the editorial page from 1977 to 1986. He made her the Sunday business editor, a section she ran so well that Lee still speaks of it with admiration all these years later. Then, in 1987, Frankel, again "determined to give an encouraging signal to women," promoted Golden to the senior post of national editor, the first woman to edit a major news desk at the *Times*, not counting Le Anne Schreiber's short, reluctant run as the paper's sports editor. By the time of Golden's national desk appointment, she had twenty-five years of experience, fourteen as

Carolyn Lee
(The New York Times/
Redux, photo by Marilynn K. Yee)

an editor at the *Times* and eleven before that at *Business Week* as both a reporter and an editor.

On the last day of 1989 came the biggest management win to date for a woman at the *Times* when Frankel elevated Carolyn Lee to take Hoge's position, also at the rank of assistant managing editor, another first. The promotion came in her eleventh year at the paper with nine before that at top regional papers in the South. Under Rosenthal, her relegation to the copy desk on arrival was customary in 1978, she said, but she advanced quickly during his tenure to assistant national editor and then to assistant news editor before she took charge of the picture desk.

A woman as assistant managing editor at the start of 1990 was an enormous breakthrough at the *Times,* but hardly news elsewhere, given the number of women who had been occupying higher positions at other outlets around the country, a few at prestigious outlets as well. As noted, the legal agitation of the 1970s had some editors and publishers on alert to the need and importance of bringing more women and people of color onto their staffs and to the obvious value of keeping down disaffection among those already in their ranks. Before long, Carolyn Lee observed, the annoyance editors experienced from the most vocal agitators and the repeated entreaties for better conditions, greater opportunity, and more extensive and sensitive coverage wore down resistance to the new and different. Although Frankel had demonstrable success in bringing more women aboard, his memoir acknowledged that his desire to put more women and people of color in top newsroom positions continued to vex.

For several years already, the handful of outstanding women who had advanced at other prestigious newspapers drew attention as beacons of change. In 1988, Geneva Overholser rejoined *The Des Moines Register* as its chief editor. Before that she had spent two years on the *Times*'s editorial board after a three-year term as the *Register*'s deputy editorial page editor and two years before that on the storied regional paper's editorial staff. She was a Nieman fellow in 1985–86, the year Gannett bought the *Register* from the Cowles family but retained Charles Edwards as publisher. Edwards knew and respected Overholser from her earlier Iowa days and sought to make her editor. Her relatively modest city room experience did not readily suggest preparedness for such an important role, certainly not to the Gannett executive in New York who interviewed her before the offer. On paper, he told her, she would not even have made the short list, but he nevertheless considered Edwards "a good judge of horseflesh." "Horseflesh!" Overholser winced twice in recollection of the encounter, still incredulous more than three decades later at the executive's word choice, which, like any savvy woman of the period, she let pass.

The woman peers around the country whom Overholser remembered best are Sandy Rowe and Janet Chusmir, who was at the end of a successful three-year stint in editorial charge of *The Miami Herald,* a tenure cut short by a brain aneurysm that caused her death at sixty at the end of 1990. Chusmir, like Rowe, led her paper to a Pulitzer, as Overholser would, and Chusmir orchestrated the enlargement and redesign of the *Herald*'s Spanish-language sister paper, *El Nuevo Herald.* In 1993, the year Rowe left her editorship in Norfolk to take charge at *The Oregonian,* she also became the second woman to lead ASNE, as Kay Fanning had before her.

O n July 11, 1989, an op-ed calling for the naming of rape vic-tims in print appeared the same day in both the *Times* and *The Des Moines Register.* The byline belonged to Overholser, who argued that to refrain from naming rape victims negated the key journal-istic tenet of "printing the facts as we know them" and revictim-ized victims by perpetuating the stigma attached to the crime. She urged women who had been raped to come forward and identify themselves, much in the way that those who previously would not have gone public about being gay or suffering from AIDS or hav-ing undergone an abortion had begun to do. Or, more to the point, she wrote, they should be named in print in the way of victims of other crimes. As a woman and a top editor, Overholser was in an excellent position to make such an argument, providing yet another example of why wide diversity is essential in journalism. Overholser understood this and felt fortunate to be able "to turn a spotlight on such an issue."

Her essay prompted a telephone call from a reader named Nancy Ziegenmeyer, a rape victim who, responding to the essay, expressed her readiness to go public. Overholser assigned the story to one of the staff reporters, Jane Schorer, who, years later, described herself in an Iowa public television interview as someone "seen as a sensitive writer who could work with people, especially this woman." Over-holser used her power to organize the rest of the *Register* newsroom staff for a full-court press on "a critically important topic nobody wanted to focus on." The five-part series ran in late February and early March 1990, generating wide attention and follow-up over the next ten months. Schorer recalled how surprised the newsroom was at the receptivity of readers to such in-depth reporting on a subject so taboo, to having it "humanized." She made no pretense of remaining emotionally detached as she reported and wrote the story. "It drained me," she said.

The Des Moines Register won the Pulitzer Prize for public service in 1991 for Schorer's account of Ziegenmeyer's journey from the crime to the trial. The citation pointed out how the significance of the reporting went beyond the story itself because it encouraged a reconsideration of the long-standing stance of news outlets to protect an individual's privacy in such cases. Overholser said years later that the series generated meaningful conversations throughout the industry, but did not lead to lasting changes in policy. This unpopular topic, so important to women, "faced strong headwinds and showed little immediate effect," she said, reflecting in part the reluctance of the men who dominated the industry's top rank to take this step. The long-standing policy was anachronistic and paternalistic, she said, as in "'protect this poor woman.' Did that ever prove helpful?" Overholser asked. "Look at how much harder it is to believe a person whose name is not attached." And yet, even thirty years later, women themselves are not of one mind about having such information shared with the public, another likely contributor to the lack of change.

"Best Editor, Best Newspaper, Best of Gannett." That is how the legend reads next to Overholser's photograph on the full-page ad Gannett placed with pride on the cover of *Editor & Publisher*. Not only did Gannett promote the success of the series, but the company gave Overholser top honors at "Best of Gannett," the finale banquet of the company's year-end meetings. It was a night Ron Cohen remembered all too well.

Cohen at the time was executive director of the Gannett

Geneva Overholser
(*Courtesy of the* Washington Journalism Review, *cover, September 1990*)

News Service and had been since 1987. These were years when the company's corporate earnings set records every quarter, when the mood was upbeat and self-congratulatory, when, he recalled, "the liquor flowed and servers heaped shrimp the size of baseballs onto cocktail platters at endless rounds of lavish parties." But he also knew that among the elite of the profession, "the name 'Gannett' was too often a punchline."

Overholser went to the podium to accept her honor. She spoke for three minutes. "Here's my dream for the next risk-taking, history-making endeavor," she said in part,

> Let Gannett show how corporate journalism can serve all its constituencies in hard times. As we sweat to the end of the ever-increasing quarterly earnings, as we necessarily attend to the needs and wishes of our shareholders and our advertisers, are we worrying enough about the other three? About our employees, our readers, and our communities? I'll answer that: no way.

In the instant after she finished, Cohen leaped to his feet to offer vigorous applause and in the same moment became aware of a room that had suddenly gone dead. To Cohen, the time lapse of ten, maybe fifteen seconds felt like "an embarrassing eternity." A little faint applause did emanate from other parts of the room, but he saw no one else stand. After the dinner, several stunned executives asked Edwards, the *Register*'s publisher, why he had allowed his editor to make such a speech. He replied that he was not in the habit of telling her what she could or could not say. Nevertheless, Overholser, recognizing the difficult position she had put him in, obliged his sheepish request for her to write to his corporate boss to profess her loyalty to the company. Cohen said he "realized with some chagrin but no regret" that he and Overholser had suddenly become unlikely candidates for a Gannett hall of fame. Not long after, and for reasons never given, Gannett kept Cohen in the company but replaced him in the top news service job. Overholser with her galloping national stature, such a plus for the *Register* and for Gannett, remained in place.

The *Register*'s 1991 Pulitzer was among eight of eighteen to include the names of women alongside the names of the publications they represented, an unusually large proportion to date for a given year. Susan Faludi won for her reportage for *The Wall Street Journal* on the human cost of a leveraged buyout. That same year she won a National Book Critics Circle Award for her provocative best seller, *Backlash: The Undeclared War Against American Women. Backlash* set out to debunk the myth that women were fleeing the workplace and to counter the prevailing sense that women themselves were to blame for the slow pace of their advancement. Faludi argued that the anger and resentment women continued to exhibit stemmed from justice and fairness denied. She called out the media for its central role throughout the 1980s in "propagating the myths of the backlash" and for blaming women themselves for their lost or unrealized gains. She poked at women for their disinterest in forming caucuses like those of the 1970s and for not calling their employers to account when there was still so much accounting to do.

For the decade, the number of winners of the Pulitzer Prize who were women inched upward to a respectable 25 percent from 18 percent of all named solo or team prize recipients in the 1980s. They included Carol Guzy of *The Washington Post,* who in 1995 won her second of four Pulitzer prizes, this one for spot photography on the crisis in Haiti and its aftermath. It is also worth noting that five women of color were among the thirty-two women on the prize's annual lists between 1990 and 1999. The awards to Liz Balmaseda, Sheryl WuDunn, Michiko Kakutani, Margo Jeffer-son, and Isabel Wilkerson accounted for 15 percent of the total number of women honored, a number far greater than the still-too-meager numbers of women or even people of color in the field. Wilkerson's recruitment to *The New York Times* came by way of Anna Quindlen, who collected her own Pulitzer for commentary in 1992. She recruited Wilkerson right out of Howard University, where Wilkerson had accumulated a precocious pile of bylined articles in prestige publications, notably *The Washington Post.* Quindlen, remember, had also brought Maureen Dowd to the attention

Isabel Wilkerson
(Erik S. Lesser/The New York Times/*Redux)*

of the *Times*. Dowd, the lone woman to win a Pulitzer in 1999, was honored for her commentary on the Clinton/Lewinsky scandal. Four years earlier, in 1995, she had assumed the effective "women's slot" on *The New York Times*'s op-ed page. Her column called "Liberties" supplanted "Public & Private," which Quindlen started in 1990, her third and last column for the paper since 1981.

At last there were signs that the issues women had been facing as war correspondents for almost a century had begun to recede. It became unremarkable, even commonplace, for women to be sent overseas as full-fledged, full-time staff correspondents, with commensurate salaries, benefits, and risk and hardship protection, even in the most sought-after bureaus and conflict situations abroad.

Between 1970 and 1992, the number of women who served abroad as correspondents jumped from 6 percent to 33 percent, according to the Brookings Institution. The increase encouraged the *American Journalism Review* to take a look at the women "flocking to the world's war zones" to report. Had their conditions improved since Vietnam? Were they better equipped than men to cover a conflict's humanitarian crises? Opinion came back mixed. One respondent said men who report from conflict zones "sit around talking about 62mm mortars and AK-47s and Kalashnikovs," adding, "I've heard some of the guys say that war is a high—that it's even better than sex." Yet others pointed to the work of *Newsday*'s Roy Gutman, who won both a Pulitzer and a George Polk award for "courageous and persistent" reporting on the atrocities in the Balkans.

The woman war reporters interviewed for the story said that although sexism persisted, the situation for women in war zones had improved. Old stereotypes had started to break down. This they attributed to the greater prevalence of women "in the mix," meaning—this was key—not only more women in the field but more women back home in positions to set the news agenda. There was also a perceived new willingness on the part of the men who ran things to "give women equal consideration for topnotch, tough assignments." At the same time, some women still complained of being subjected to extra paces and often stringer status first to be able to land dangerous high-profile assignments, even when they had ample prior conflict experience.

Caryle Murphy had an excellent vantage point from Cairo, where *The Washington Post* sent her as its staff correspondent and bureau chief starting in 1989. By the time she went, Murphy had fourteen years with the paper, starting first in 1976 as a stringer in Angola, where she had gone to freelance after two years as a teacher in Kenya. Murphy watched Angola's transformation from Portugal's "tethered colony with a free-wheeling, capitalist economy to a proudly nationalist state 'on the road to socialism.' " She reported from Angola until August 4, 1976, when the authorities placed her under house arrest while they investigated her for ostensible activities against the state. Eleven days later, the government expelled her. She had run afoul of the country's director general of information for language in one of her articles that he found insulting. Although a friend had warned her that she was under investigation, it did not occur to her to leave the country. She had nothing to hide, she said. She even welcomed an honest investigation that would clear her of an attendant false charge that she worked for the CIA.

Her first-person piece about her expulsion, datelined Lisbon, appeared in the *Post* with her portrait on August 17, 1976. By Labor Day, she was in Washington writing metro stories—on staff, but with probationary status for the first six months. Fourteen months later, the *Post* sent her to South Africa for five years, then back to Washington again for eight, largely to report on the federal courts and immigration, then Cairo. During her five years in Egypt, Murphy watched woman correspondents become more of a norm. *The Philadelphia Inquirer,* the *Los Angeles Times,* VOA, CNN, *Newsday,* and *The Miami Herald* had also sent women to run their bureaus in the volatile region.

That first year in the Middle East, Murphy suffered from a still-undiagnosed condition that had her sleeping sixteen hours a day. Still unwell in late July, she was sent by her editors to Kuwait. She was back in Cairo a few days

Caryle Murphy
(Passport photo, courtesy of Caryle Murphy)

later but at her editors' insistence returned to Kuwait right away. She filed a story on July 30, 1990, about Iraq expanding its force near the Kuwaiti border. As negotiations between the two countries opened, Iraq took a hard line, she reported on August 1. One day later, Iraqi forces invaded their tiny neighbor to the southeast, declaring falsely that they had acted "in support of Kuwaiti revolutionaries who conducted a coup against the government of the ruling emir, Sheik Jabir Ahmed Sabah." A second story on page 1 the same day had more details of the invasion and its "vivid tableau of destruction." Her seventh-floor window a few blocks from the palace at the Kuwaiti International Hotel gave her "a front-row seat."

Murphy managed to keep filing for several days until the Iraqis imposed a news blackout. After that, with the U.S. embassy uncooperative, she managed to file sporadically by hurling copy over the wall of the Swedish embassy, hoping someone would find it and send it on to the *Post*. One day she shared an elevator with a Kuwaiti, to whom she found herself explaining her plight. She was an American correspondent, she told him, trying to get news out of the country. He told her to meet him at the same time the next day, same place. From there, he took her to safety, in hiding, with his family, and to a satellite phone to which he somehow had access. That enabled her to dictate copy to Washington with some regularity until Saddam Hussein threatened to hang any Kuwaiti who sheltered a foreigner. Murphy knew she could no longer imperil the strange angels who had taken her in. They arranged for her to be smuggled out in a caravan of nine cars headed for the Saudi border. "Everywhere we looked," she said,

> cars were trapped in the sand, their engines dead or wheels stuck. With their hoods and trunks stuck in the air, they were pitiful, out-of-place sign posts of the desperate flight from Kuwait. One could only look and hope that the people who once sat in them—hot, thirsty and near despair—had been picked up by friends.
>
> Three times, we had to stop to dig one of our cars out of the sand. Two of the nine vehicles had to be abandoned when their engines failed. We bounced along, holding our breath and scanning the horizon for Iraqi patrols.

Murphy's reports from hiding yielded one of the 1991 Pulitzer Prizes and a George Polk award as well. The *Post*'s assistant managing editor for foreign news said her Pulitzer was as much for her personal courage as for her outstanding reporting.

Neither during the war in the Persian Gulf nor during Murphy's entire time in the Middle East can she recall encountering any work-related problems because she was a woman. Sometimes, she said, it became an advantage, like the remarkable way the helpful stranger in an elevator in Kuwait came to her aid, or the camouflage a veil provided during her escape to the Saudi border. Other women over the decade made the same point about the potential and actual advantages their being women meant in such situations, adding that members of the military often welcomed the change a woman reporter's presence brought. Still others pointed up the drain on personal relationships that war reporting caused—for everyone, of course—and the added risk of rape that woman reporters were more likely to face alongside the ever-present threat of kidnapping and torture to reporters of any gender. And there was more: Sonni Efron, a *Los Angeles Times* reporter, accepted an assignment in Chechnya shortly after her marriage, not telling her editors that she was pregnant. *Quill,* the magazine of the Society of Professional Journalists, recounted how a sniper battle at a hospital forced Efron to take cover under a mattress in a nearby basement. To herself she wondered what could be happening to her unborn child, who indeed survived the ordeal. "You have a moral obligation to tell the story and do the best job you can," Efron said, "but you also have a moral obligation as a parent not to get killed." Efron is now the president of the National Press Foundation.

Awards, attention-getting promotions, and prominent global assignments were not the only means of assessing progress. In 1991, Max Frankel clearly laid out the *Times*'s position on sexual harassment: "We not only deplore it, we act against it vigorously and urgently. . . . Such behavior is intolerable even if we cannot anticipate or define every variant." His memo followed by only a couple of days the testimony of Anita Hill before the U.S. Senate Judiciary Committee as it considered the nomination of Clarence Thomas to the U.S.

Supreme Court. When word filtered out that Hill would testify to Thomas's misbehavior, Nina Totenberg, sensing a big story about to break, went to see the Democratic members of the Judiciary Committee, all men, to hear their thoughts, especially since Thomas had once been the head of the Equal Employment Opportunity Commission, responsible for enforcing the laws against sex discrimination. The senators brushed her notion aside. "No silver bullet," the senators told her. Totenberg broke the story. "If the behavior Hill described on the part of Thomas existed today," Totenberg said in a documentary years later, "it would blow the roof off places. Things really have changed—in part, because we've discussed it."

In testimony, Anita Hill detailed several humiliating instances, the worst of which was Thomas discussing "pornography involving women with large breasts and engaged in a variety of sex with different people and animals." Sandy Rowe led the usual news meeting at *The Virginian-Pilot* that day in a roomful of men. "There was a lot of mumbling," Rowe said. The men were attempting to indicate what had been said without repeating it. They tried to frame what transpired in the Senate hearing room as nothing beyond a woman making accusations. "No," Rowe told her colleagues. "This is a story about the workplace." What happened to Anita Hill was something she and other women recognized clearly from their own experiences. "When you broaden the scope of who is at the table, you broaden the definition of what is news," Rowe said. Narda Zacchino said the *Los Angeles Times* was late with its story because the paper's Washington editors at the time, all men, simply "didn't get it." Not so for the women in the bureau, or for any woman who identified with the proffered accusations. For them, Zacchino said, Hill's testimony set off "a 'click' that went off in their brains," which activists described in her paper as the realization of powerlessness and of "the fundamental differences in the ways men and women experience the world."

Two years later, on July 7, 1993, twenty-two women at *The New York Times* petitioned the publisher for clearer sexual harassment guidelines "in light of recent reports of sexual harassment at the company," not disclosed. Two months after that, a new set of guidelines went further in its definition than Frankel had in 1991. The new memo from the publisher, Arthur O. Sulzberger Jr., began,

While it is not always easy to define precisely what harassment is, it certainly includes unwelcome sexual advances, requests for sexual favors, and other verbal or physical conduct of a sexual nature, such as uninvited touching or sexually related comments.

A few months earlier, on May 24, 1993, *The New Yorker* published a documented, surgically precise refutation of *The Real Anita Hill: The Untold Story*, a book that purported to be an unvarnished tell-all by David Brock. Much later, Brock admitted that his book was no more than his attempt to demolish Hill's character and that of her witnesses, and that he had written it to integrate himself into the "extensive political machinery of the right." The joint bylines on *The New Yorker*'s refutation piece were those of Jill Abramson and Jane Mayer, still both at *The Wall Street Journal*. They were able to turn the piece out quickly because they had already spent months reporting on the Bush administration's orchestration of the Thomas nomination, which became the foundation of their book, *Strange Justice: The Selling of Clarence Thomas*. The months of reporting on Thomas bonded them as friends. A shared reaction to the prurient proceedings in the staid Senate caucus room sparked another deep friendship, between Abramson, who covered the hearing for the *Journal,* and Maureen Dowd, who reported it for the *Times.* Dowd and Mayer were already friends from their days at the *Star,* so one could say the nomination of Clarence Thomas to the Supreme Court inspired the warm, lasting friendship the three women share.

Activists and advocacy groups outside the newspapers themselves supplied new tactical weapons for assessing the progress of women in a media context. In 1978, ASNE's human resources committee began to publish statistics on minority hiring and, in 1990, joined forces with Betty Friedan's Media Watch to copublish an annual women's "bean-count," much to Max Frankel's annoyance. Their survey of ten newspapers large and small tracked how often these papers featured women as news subjects or news sources and how many women's bylines appeared on their respective front pages. The survey found that the number of women's photos on this group of front pages indeed increased over the previous year but the growth in the number of women's bylines and of women quoted as sources was negligible. The study did not include the magazine world, but there, too, subtler manifestations of the disparity prevailed. Betsy Carter, the editorial director at *Esquire* before she launched *New York Woman*, drew attention to the nomination for a national magazine award of Andrew Grove, the CEO of Intel, for writing for the business magazine *Fortune* about his personal bout with prostate cancer. "It was terrific, a breakthrough for Fortune," Carter told *The Washington Post*'s Paula Span. But it also reminded Carter of the many woman writers who had written "brilliantly" for women's magazines about their experiences with breast and ovarian cancer but with no wider peer recognition. And yet, she said, "when a guy did it, it got nominated."

Frankel denounced the "mischievous publicity" that the bean-counting exercise generated, calling the study's methodology "bizarre and unworthy." Why, he asked, had its architects demonstrated so little awareness of the differing missions and responsibilities of papers of different sizes? "As soon as Mr. Gorbachev lets Mrs. Gorbachev do his deciding or even speaking," he told Eleanor Randolph of *The Washington Post*, "we will be quoting or photographing more women on Page One.... [B]y that I mean that if you are covering local teas, you've got more women [on Page One] than if you're the Wall Street Journal." Despite the many demonstrable improvements in equity Frankel had instituted—the doubling of the number of women on staff, some rectification in salary discrepancies, special "senior correspondent" bonuses that included several women, a woman national editor, a first *Times* woman as assistant managing editor—the newspaper ranked last in the survey for the second year in a row, just below the *Chicago Tribune* and *Los Angeles Times*. These would be the earliest of the *Times*'s abysmal rankings in this survey for years to come.

In his memoir, Frankel described this episode as the first of his "self-inflicted crises." Claudia Payne, the paper's lifestyle editor, recalled that as soon as Frankel's tea party remark appeared in the *Post*, an "utterly predictable outrage" arose among the women in the newsroom, despite the prevailing sense that Frankel was trying his "very earnest best" to improve their lot. Still, she said, the women felt an imperative to display their displeasure. She suggested they have campaign buttons printed with encircled teapots slashed with a red diagonal, something easily accomplished in no time in nearby Times Square. A member of her staff volunteered to get the buttons made. Once she returned, the women of the Style section pinned them onto their blouses and jackets and women from other desks came to take the rest. "There must have been additional purchases because more women ended up wearing them than I could have supplied," Payne said. In Frankel's recollection, it seemed as if all the women on staff, "with the merciful exception of his wife," appeared the next day bejeweled in tea bags dangling from their ears. A few women thought there actually might have been some self-styled earrings, too, but the buttons predominated.

Frankel took the protest as a "good-humored reproach, itself a tribute to the relaxed atmosphere of our newsroom," he wrote. Suzanne Daley, then a metro reporter on her way up, called the demonstration "quasi-good-natured" since women were angry at the time over their still limited opportunity to move up. A petition followed, Frankel wrote, "repeating that I had 'undermined' my own achievements and begging for an explanation." He responded with an apology for causing offense and for obscuring his real point. But at the same time, he deeply resented the survey's implication that the *Times* discriminated in its coverage and was "last" in its treatment of women and news of special importance to them. "All of us," he said, "are owed an apology for that implication."

One month later, on May 28, 1990, Frankel was pleased that four of the paper's seven front-page articles had women's bylines. A year after that, almost to the day, women had generated five of the paper's six page 1 stories, all on substantive themes.

The ASNE–Media Watch survey also included an embarrassing statistic on minority hiring in the industry in 1990, up a minuscule one-third of 1 percent. "Tough Times Cut Opportunities for Minority Journalists" was the headline over a *Times* media column near the end of that year about that figure. At the same time, advertising revenue had diminished to such an extent across the journalism landscape that the kinds of hiring freezes Gene Roberts spoke of, the periodic response to economic downturns, were in effect again just about everywhere. These were among the counter-valences in play throughout the push for more equity for women as well as for people of color and gays and lesbians. In those years, Frankel said the

Times lost valued Black colleagues, several of whom were women, to other papers or other pursuits. "I left behind a staff that was about 85 percent white—only a few points less white than when I arrived," Frankel wrote. He was proud, however, of the three Pulitzers won by Black staff members during his tenure—the reporter Isabel Wilkerson and the critic Margo Jefferson were two of the three—as he acknowledged his failed effort to "reach that critical mass."

For a woman to write a regular column from Washington, D.C., on the op-ed page of the *Times* in 1995 was about as visible in power circles as a woman running for high public office. In *The New Yorker,* under the headline "Hear Me Purr," James Wolcott devoted six pages to his assessment of Maureen Dowd's place on the very short list of previous woman op-ed page columnists for the *Times.* He did not mention Anne O'Hare McCormick, but he said of Flora Lewis that "when she wrote about foreign affairs, she didn't write as a woman; she wrote as a foreign-affairs specialist." Anna Quindlen, by contrast, "was all woman," "a kind of Liv Ullmann of bountiful empathy" who "displaced" *The Boston Globe*'s Ellen Goodman as "the thinking person's favorite sensible feminist." "Where Quindlen presided like a mother hen in print," Wolcott wrote, "Dowd acts like a chick—pun intended." He explained that the term "chick" was making a comeback, but in 1990s style, as a "post-feminist in a party dress, a bachelorette too smart to be a bimbo, too refined to be a babe, too boojy to be a bohemian." He mused about the "butch sensibility" of so much writing by women in the 1970s and its failure to "moderate or modulate into maturity." Instead, he said, too much of the feminist and postfeminist writing of the 1990s reverted to "popularity-contest coquetry. I'm not sure there has ever been more sheer *girlishness* in journalistic writing than there is today."

Wolcott dismissed the "bonhomous attitude" Dowd's prose conjured, and its "trail of cigarette smoke," he wrote. "Chicks are so unthreatening to men." By way of contrast, he cited leftist writers like Ellen Willis, who had moved on from rock to wider cultural critiques; Barbara Ehrenreich and Katha Pollitt, who attacked issues "with the contentious spirit and idea-crunching machinery of the old *Partisan Review*"; and Florence King, on the right, who "is quite happy to let the world go its own damned way." Dowd, he said, came across as "the only dame dealt into the poker game."

For Christopher Hitchens, writing in *Vanity Fair,* Dowd was "Top Dowd" for her facility with telling details, her place at the center of the controversy over the use of opinion in reported journalism, and her promise to him "not to become the princess of the boringly evenhanded."

Four years later, Dowd's name appeared under the moniker "The Opinion Shaper," high on the *Ladies' Home Journal* list of "America's 100 Most Important Women," "the influencers" of 1999, topped by Hillary Clinton, Oprah Winfrey, and that "goddess of domesticity," Martha Stewart. Further down the list were Susan Faludi for her books; Nora Ephron for her movies; Katie Couric as the "$7 million-a-year co-anchor" of *The Today Show;* Karen Jurgensen, the new editor in chief at *USA Today;* Diane Sawyer, "the queen of the nighttime news magazine '20/20,'" who by then was also cohost of *Good Morning America;* the septuagenarian Barbara Walters, whom the magazine crowned "the first lady of journalism"; and Tina Brown, "the brash and brainy" "queen bee of buzz," for her fourteen years as editor first of *Vanity Fair,* from 1984 to 1992, followed by six years as *The New Yorker*'s fourth editor since 1925. In all, Brown would win four George Polks, five awards from the Overseas Press Club, and ten National Magazine Awards. Brown, in the opinion of the media columnist of *The Washington Post,* transformed *The New Yorker* "from a fading cultural institution to a fiercely topical, sometimes glitzy magazine that continued to hemorrhage money." She resigned, she told him, because Harvey Weinstein at Miramax offered her "something the New Yorker couldn't offer me: equity, a partnership, the ability to create a new media company."

Not on the *Journal* list was Janet Malcolm, who spent the early 1990s embroiled in the libel suit filed against her by Jeffrey Masson for her portrayal of him in her *New Yorker* story about his controversial directorship of the Freud Archives. In these years, she described herself as "the fallen woman of journalism." Malcolm had challenged the ethics and morality of the journalism profession itself.

"Who's Afraid of Janet Malcolm?" was the headline over Robert Boynton's profile of Malcolm in the women's magazine *Mirabella* in 1992. He coyly suggested readers never show Malcolm the interior of their apartments or cut a tomato in her presence, lest she describe them mercilessly in print. To make his case, Masson cited quotations Malcolm had fused from a year's worth of conversations and presented as if they happened on one occasion and not necessarily in the actual words he spoke. Boynton posited that the wide attention Malcolm commanded then, and the enduring controversy over what she said and wrote, stemmed from the "immensity of her thesis that every interview is but a deceptive prologue to a grand betrayal," and her contention that "the literally true may actually be a kind of falsification of reality." Deepening the controversy was her omission in "The Journalist and the Murderer" of any reference to her own interactions with Masson for "Trouble in the Archives." A reputation for coldness arose from her work, the critic Katie Roiphe later wrote, describing Malcolm as a master of "brutal precision."

Boynton covered the court proceedings for *The Village Voice*, calling what transpired a "signifier for some of our society's most bitterly fought cultural battles about the press." It forced journalists to face some uncomfortable truths they preferred to ignore. Malcolm's lead sentence alone—"Every journalist who is not too stupid or too full of himself"—had made her words a fixture on journalism school syllabi and throughout the profession. Her contention became, as the *Columbia Journalism Review* put it, "received wisdom." Malcolm prevailed in court in November 1994.

After Malcolm's death in 2021, Roiphe, who conducted the last interview with her, for *The Paris Review*, reflected on Malcolm once again. "Was she perceived as harsh because she looked very closely at people, observed on a superior plane, and could wring from ordinary happenings more refined and precise meanings than other practitioners of the craft?" Roiphe added the words of one of her undergraduates: "She's like a psychoanalyst freed from the need to heal people."

Joe Lelyveld succeeded Frankel as the *Times*'s executive editor and brought Gene Roberts back to the paper as his number two. Before Philadelphia and the seventeen Pulitzers the *Inquirer* won during Roberts's eighteen years in charge, he had been the *Times*'s national editor. On his return in 1994, he found a changed place. The promotion of women and minorities had become a clear priority, Roberts said, "something on everyone's mind," from the assistant managing editors on up.

Frankel's wife, Joyce Purnick, resumed her "Metro Matters" column when her husband retired. Early in 1997, with Lelyveld in charge, she became the deputy to the metropolitan editor, Michael Oreskes, and succeeded him later that year when he became Washington bureau chief. The announcement of her appointment noted that she was the first woman to hold this key *Times* post. When less than two years later she left it to return to writing her column, Lelyveld told the staff that Purnick had made "an indelible mark in one of our most demanding leadership roles." There had also been two instances during her tenure that put her in conflict with the women on her staff. In one case, she ended a four-day workweek and informal job-sharing arrangement that Oreskes had instituted on metro for mothers of young children. It replicated an arrangement Soma Golden, as national editor, had made with Tamar Lewin four years earlier when her first child ended up in neonatal intensive care. Lewin held on to the arrangement for the next twenty years. Purnick's decision still rankles those on metro who experienced the reversal's impact. It might have been coincidental to the sensitivity Oreskes exhibited in making this accommodation, but those four years, from 1993 to 1997, coincided with his own introduction to fatherhood and life in a home with one, and then two, children under four, and a working journalist wife, Geraldine Baum. Her own paper, by then the *Los Angeles Times,* had not moved to ease the lot of the working mothers on its staff. In retrospect, Oreskes said the births of his children surely factored into his empathic response, but what he remembered most was his own strong feeling that he wanted to retain the women directly affected, Esther Fein, Elisabeth Rosenthal, and Janny Scott, among the very best journalists on his staff.

Oreskes said that there was more than one objection to the four-day-week from top management. "It was not a pure financial net zero because benefits remained full even if pay went to part-time," he said, and some people thought it was harder to manage part-timers. Nonetheless, Oreskes, as other section editors had and would, believed the extra effort was best for the company in both the short and the longer run to keep some exceptional women on the staff. "I judged it highly unlikely that my refusal to grant flexibility would coerce them into working full-time when they needed time with their child," he said.

In Purnick's second year as metro editor, she gave the commencement address at Barnard College, her alma mater. In the speech, she offered up opinions that some pundits found outrageous, and others celebrated for her frank articulation of what they saw as a hard truth. "There is no way in an all-consuming profession like journalism that a woman with children can devote as much time and energy as a man can," she told the graduating class. Of herself, she said, "I am absolutely convinced I would not be the metro editor of The Times if I had had a family." Although a woman cannot have it all, she said, "you can have most of it, in ways that women could not just a few generations ago."

The Times's staff was "indignant," The Baltimore Sun reported. Editors of the magazines devoted to working women countered Purnick's assertions with examples of women in other industries whose children posed no barrier to their success. "Where do these people live?" the Sun columnist shot back, "Planet Parenthood?" In an interview with The Sun, Purnick acknowledged that she unintentionally had "touched a raw nerve." "If she had kids," the Sun columnist said, supporting Purnick's contention, "she'd know how right she was and she wouldn't have to backpedal and apologize, which is what she has been doing for the last week."

Fulfilling the needs of children and family has always created complications for working women, but it has never stopped the most ambitious. In August 1999, at forty-two, Margaret Sullivan, with an eleven-year-old and a six-year-old at home, became editor in chief of her hometown paper, The Buffalo News, having risen steadily through the ranks during her nineteen years on staff. She calculated that the promotion made her one of only twelve women in editorial charge of one of the country's hundred largest-circulation newspapers.

Sullivan started at the News as an intern in 1980, with a master's degree from Medill, the journalism school at Northwestern, and a BA from Georgetown. Her assignments involved business and government coverage, feature writing, and a regular column. Murray B. Light, the same editor who initially hired her, named her assistant city editor after seven years, and then assistant managing editor for features, and then managing editor, the second-highest post. When Light retired, the publisher, Stanford Lipsey, elevated her to the top job. Wow, she thought to herself at the time. That's the first line in my obit.

CHAPTER 20

Moving On

On July 1, 1995, *Quill* reported that many "pioneering" women had moved out of daily journalism and on to other pursuits. Jane Mayer left *The Wall Street Journal* for *The New Yorker* that year, and Anna Quindlen quit the *Times* again, this time to devote herself to writing novels. Joann Byrd finished a four-year term as ombudsman of *The Washington Post* and moved to Florida to teach ethics at the Poynter Institute for Media Studies. Before Byrd arrived at the *Post*, she had spent three years as executive editor of another *Post* property, the *Daily Herald* in Everett, Washington, population fifty-seven thousand. In other attention-generating moves, Connie Chung's two-year coanchor collaboration with Dan Rather ended at CBS, precipitating her move to ABC. And *Talk* magazine, Tina Brown's venture with Harvey Weinstein, launched at a boldfaced bash on Liberty Island on August 2, 1999, reached a circulation of a reported 670,000, and then abruptly shut down after only two and a half years.

Maggie Balough was out at the *Austin American-Statesman* by mid-February 1995; she had led the paper for six of her seventeen years on staff. Two months later, at the ASNE convention, she spoke of the climate of fear that pervaded the industry and the onus put on editors to boost the bottom line by agonized owners as their profit margins fell. Balough's departure brought scant attention beyond a bland announcement story in the paper's B section. Her publisher, Roger Kintzel, attributed her "parting" after "months of discussion" to a disagreement over "how best to build" on the "solid editorial foundation" she had laid for the paper. One day before Balough's exit, Geneva Overholser, who, at forty-six, had become a magnet for prestigious industry appointments, magazine covers, and honors, twice named the best editor in the country, shocked her staff and the wider journalism community by announcing her resignation as editor of *The Des Moines Register*. Her managing editor, David Westphal, resigned the same day.

The *Register* announced their decisions in a front-page story on Valentine's Day, with a headline that included the words "News Staff Expresses Shock." Both Overholser and Westphal emphasized that dissatisfaction with Gannett was not their reason for moving on, but Overholser did allow that having to defend "decision after decision after decision" had worn her down. Charles Edwards, still the publisher, praised their dynamic leadership and wise counsel, especially as the newspaper shifted from a statewide to a largely regional focus. Both Overholser and Westphal said they had feelers out for new jobs but had not yet found them.

The following day, a *Times* reporter weighed in on the two resignations, saying the decisions "reopened a bitter debate in American journalism about whether corporate pressure for profits is stripping the quality from many American newspapers." Throughout the industry, the reporter wrote, Overholser's colleagues knew how frustrated and disillusioned she had become over "the impact of business concerns on the newsroom." She had often spoken out about the way financial pressures can conflict with readers' needs. The story quoted Jim Squires, the former editor of the *Chicago Tribune*, saying that in the thirty years up to 1990, there had been as much as an 11 percent drop in the revenue that newspapers devoted to news gathering. The *Washington Post* media critic wrote of the "burnout syndrome" these two resignations symbolized and how short Overholser's tenure had been compared with, say, Ben Bradlee's twenty-seven years as editor of *The Washington Post* or Abe Rosenthal's seventeen at the *Times*. The *Tribune* likened Gannett to Walmart for its high standing on Wall Street if not in the news establishment. The *American Journalism Review* mostly agreed.

Five days after the announcement, Overholser, still at the *Register*, devoted a column to her decision. "If I'm so optimistic about the future of this newspaper, and I am, then why am I leaving?" she asked, and answered: "Because 6½ years at this job—this wonderful,

enlivening but demanding and time-consuming job—is enough."
She repeated that she was looking for a new position, likely not as
an editor. Within a month, Westphal joined the McClatchy chain as
deputy Washington bureau chief, and a month after that Overholser
succeeded Joann Byrd as ombudsman of *The Washington Post.*

In June 1995, only days after Overholser moved into her new job
in Washington, the *Register* reported that she and her husband of
twenty-one years had filed for divorce. When an *American Journalism
Review* interviewer asked her if she could explain why her resignation
commanded such outsized attention, Overholser said, "Because I'm a
loudmouth in an era when nobody in the editing ranks says anything,
and because I'm one of the few women, was one of the few women, in
a prominent editor's job." Pressed to say if there were other reasons,
she added, "It is also true that there were powerful personal reasons.
My personal life was in a real state of change that contributed to
my leaving. I'm getting a divorce and I've come out here to begin
a new chapter in my life in a number of ways, both personally and
professionally."

The *Register* republished these comments, adding information
obtained from District of Columbia real estate records that showed
Overholser and Westphal had purchased a house together. Although
the wide coverage of the resignations read like a "journalistic morality play" that pitted newsroom values against the zeal for corporate
profit, the *Register* said it now seemed that the readers in Des Moines
had been offered an incomplete account of events. It quoted Overholser saying there were ample, numerous, passionately held professional reasons for her departure, about which she was truthful, and
that she questioned why Iowa readers should have interest in her
personal life as a private citizen in Washington, D.C. She called the
inquiry "insulting."

Three days later, with a thumbnail line sketch of Overholser's face
embedded in the text, *The Wall Street Journal* carried a story about her
on its front page. It pointed up the irony in her indignation, given
her advocacy of publishing the "intimate details of private lives," and
not only in rape cases.

Gannett "burned inside" over the media criticism of the company
that Overholser's decision to depart generated, the *Journal* story said,
including the insinuations about "tight budgets and bottom-line

pressure"—especially after the more personal reasons for her decision came to light. The company's chairman, John Curley, asserted that despite a drop in profit while Overholser was in charge, the *Register*'s news budget and news space had grown. The article ended with the scene in the *Register* office the day Overholser and Westphal announced their plans. Several staffers asked if there was anything else they should know. Nothing was offered. "We all look like idiots," one of her colleagues was quoted as saying. "I think the rest of the state of Iowa is laughing at us."

Overholser then devoted one of her *Post* ombudsman columns to explaining herself yet again. She expressed regret over her "personal life" comment, acknowledging that indeed there was news value in reporting such information, given the context. She noted how the two Iowa resignations had become a symbol of the frustrations being felt throughout the industry, whether she and Westphal wanted to be symbols or not. She again explained that what seemed like deliberate omissions on her part reflected no more than the unsettled state of her personal life at the time. Nonetheless, she said, "none of that holds the kind of power for people that this one fact holds: Eight months later, the two of us are together here in Washington." Overholser offered her resignation to the *Post*'s editor, Len Downie, who, she said, saw no reason to accept it. He confirmed this years later. "What happened in Des Moines," he said, "did not involve journalistic integrity that would have a bearing on her work at *The Washington Post*."

The article in *Quill* reminded readers that the Society of Professional Journalists, founded in 1909, took sixty years to admit its first woman member; that barely a generation had passed since women in top jobs had ceased to be a curiosity; and that the goal of full diversity was still well out of reach. Reginald Stuart, the society's president, called for "a new approach and a new mindset in these jobs." "We still count noses in news meetings," he said "and wonder why males outnumber women 2-to-1."

The story named sixteen women in high-prestige positions if not the top jobs, led by the two women who carried the title of assistant managing editor at the *Times*, Carolyn Lee, since 1990, and Soma

Golden, whom Max Frankel had put on the masthead at the same rank in July 1993, a year before he stepped down as executive editor. To succeed Golden as national editor, he again named a woman, one with a deep and impressive résumé, but unusually, one with no prior experience at the *Times*. That brought Suzanne Daley, by then the deputy metro editor, into Frankel's office with a flip chart to present to him and his then managing editor, Joe Lelyveld. On it, she documented how few *Times* women to date had been sent to Washington or overseas. In the paper's culture, these were invariably understood to be the two key stepping-stones to major promotions. By 1995, with Lelyveld in charge, eight women had won overseas assignments by Daley's count. The figure included her own posting to Johannesburg soon after Nelson Mandela became South Africa's president. Better opportunities became more common for women at the *Times*, if not yet more penetration of the masthead. Daley's successor in Johannesburg was also a woman, Rachel Swarns, the *Times*'s first Black bureau chief in South Africa in 1999. She had joined the *Times*'s staff from *The Miami Herald* in 1995. Years later, Gene Roberts, while serving as Lelyveld's managing editor, remembered Swarns as "one of the strongest reporters on the staff, regardless of race or sex." Daley went on to serve as Paris bureau chief, education editor, national editor, and an associate managing editor; Swarns next went to Washington, during which time she covered Michelle Obama's first year as First Lady and wrote *American Tapestry: The Story of the Black, White, and Multiracial Ancestors of Michelle Obama*. After that, Swarns wrote a weekly column from New York and became one of the paper's senior writers.

And yet, significantly, so long after the women's lawsuit settlement at the *Times*, so long after women were holding higher rank elsewhere, neither Lee nor Golden as women on the masthead was seen to be a contender for the top spot. As superb as they were as editors and managers, they were understood to lack elements of the customary top leadership profile, the stepping-stones Suzanne Daley spoke about. They had not been groomed for higher positions, nor did anyone in a position to act think they should be. Neither had an expansive, distinguished reporting background or significant experience in Washington and/or as foreign correspondents. Lee, when asked long after her retirement if she ever aspired to be executive editor, said the thought never crossed her mind. She knew that as someone who had risen on a straight editing track, she lacked the right background. Golden, adjusting to the adult onset of type 1 diabetes while being "a wife, a mom, and a top editor of the *New York Times* all at once," felt during those years that she was at the limit of her capacity.

Quill did list a number of woman journalists around the country in upper management in 1995. Among them was Carolyn Phillips at *The Wall Street Journal,* who had been promoted to assistant managing editor from her post as one of the paper's three woman bureau chiefs, thus making her the newsroom's highest-ranking person of color at the time. Even though the *Journal* did not hire its first woman journalists until the 1960s, she said, by the 1990s, women had become "very much bone and muscle in the newsroom. We're not the exception anymore." Jill Abramson and Jane Mayer, bone and muscle by any reckoning, did not share this view. Abramson, recalling her days as an investigative reporter for the *Journal* and as its deputy Washington bureau chief, saw Phillips's comment as no more than management spin. Mayer, from her experiences during eleven years at the *Journal,* agreed. "My sense is like Jill's," she said years later. "It was better than in the early 1980s but still far from a place where women were equal." Mayer's 1980s assignments for the paper included Beirut during the bombing of the American military barracks in 1983 and 1984 and as its first woman on the White House beat. The period, she said, was the hardest of her professional life. Her editors forbade her to cover the international arms control summits of the Reagan years, operating out of the unspoken assumption that only men could understand the complexities of military and national security matters. "Girls don't do throw weight" was the saying at the time, she said years later, meaning the weight of the payload a given missile can carry. Her boss not only refused to send her to the Reykjavík summit in October 1986, but suggested instead that she do a feature on Adolfo, Nancy Reagan's favorite dress designer. "It was a comment he made off the cuff, not as a joke or as a deliberate insult," Mayer said, elaborating on something she told the magazine *InStyle.* "It was just a reflection of his thinking." She let the insult go and learned to bide her time, pick her fights, and find more effective ways of getting the powers that be to yield—chiefly, by outshining everyone else.

Phillips, fired in 2002, sued the *Journal* for racial discrimination. She charged that she had been passed over for assignments that went to less qualified colleagues and that she found her duties reduced on return from disability leave. The suit was settled out of court in 2010.

In 1995, Gail Collins, late of the *New York Daily News* and *Newsday,* joined *The New York Times*'s editorial staff. Four years later she began her twice-weekly op-ed column that would lead to much more. In 1997, at a book party, Maureen Dowd mentioned to Abramson that the incoming *Times* Washington bureau chief, Michael Oreskes, was on the lookout for excellent women to hire, women who could drive a story. Dowd had a "strong eye for talent," Oreskes said long after, so he always consulted with her. But beyond that, he felt that the company needed more women in leadership roles, women who could shape coverage, women who could assign and edit stories. That had also been his posture as metro editor, and, after Washington, as editor of the *International Herald Tribune* with Alison Smale in the number two position. "In all three jobs, I had a woman second in command who then succeeded me," he said. "That mattered." He could not recall any memos or oral directives from above to this effect at the time, nor could Joe Lelyveld or the publisher, Arthur Sulzberger. None of them remembered any concerted press to right the imbalance that Max Frankel had tried to fix, or anything like the understanding Flora Lewis alluded to when she commented on her luck to be named Paris bureau chief in the "social climate" of 1972, while the *Times* was putting a premium on the hiring and promotion of women and people of color.

Abramson responded to Dowd's appeal by suggesting herself, and Oreskes offered her a job. Two years later, he named her Washington editor. A *Village Voice* writer quoted an unidentified *Times* insider calling the decision one of the best things to happen to the bureau in years because Abramson knew how to exercise power "gently and intelligently," had a mind that "can contain multitudes," and knew how to get along well with the boss.

Among Washington news denizens, Abramson had built a reputation as an honest, superb, hardworking reporter with a temperament that inspired awe. "She's able to be smart without being arrogant," the *Voice* reporter wrote, quoting an unnamed colleague who offered, "She doesn't strut. She doesn't preen," and that unlike most reporters, "she is neither insecure nor an egomaniac." Colleagues and former colleagues saw her as brave with "balls like cast iron cantaloupes."

Much of Abramson's management experience over the years was as the second-in-command, as the deputy to a man. In that capacity, she said years later, she saw herself "somewhat cast in the role of 'Mom.'" Staffers felt free to walk into her office and share their worries and problems. They would ask her not to share with "Dad" what they had told her in private. In time she learned that they really did want their issues relayed and their problems fixed, but also preferred to believe the resolution came without her intercession, that "Dad" had recognized their worth and talent, and that the problems had "magically drifted away."

In December 2000, Abramson succeeded Oreskes as the *Times*'s Washington bureau chief. Her promotion received only passing notice—until June 2002, nine months into the stormy, short-lived executive editorship of Howell Raines, who succeeded Joe Lelyveld. In a lengthy look at Raines's imperious reign, Ken Auletta recounted for *New Yorker* readers how Abramson had clashed with Raines over what she experienced as heavy-handed disrespect, deliberate undercutting, and humiliation from the diktats he delivered during her phone-ins to the daily news meetings in New York. When the managing editor, Gerald Boyd, visited Washington, she told him she would quit if Raines did not stop it. Raines apologized the next day, but Abramson said what assuaged her was a call from Janet Robinson, then about to be named company president.

In this period, it could not have escaped the notice of women at the *Times* that across town, at a competing New York paper, a woman had become the top editor. In 1998, the publisher of the *New York Daily News*, Mort Zuckerman, put Debby Krenek in charge as the paper's fourth editor in five years. Its circulation was still higher than 500,000 copies, but like so many other newspapers of the day, the *News* was on a downhill plunge. Krenek's elevation underscored another reality for the women and others in underrepresented groups who were on the ascent in the 1990s and thereafter: their greatest opportunities in the news business came as advertising revenue evaporated and readers and viewers abandoned these traditional media as their major information source. *Daily News* staffers expressed doubt that Krenek, who had been holding down managerial positions since she was in her twenties at the *Dallas Times Herald,* had the "brassy journalistic courage or the big ideas" to keep the paper competitive. The *American Journalism Review* quoted the paper's former features editor saying Krenek's great value to the publisher lay elsewhere; if Zuckerman wanted something done, Krenek delivered.

At the century's close, the faculty of New York University's journalism department, joined by a large, distinguished group of reporters and editors, deliberated long and hard to create a list of the top hundred works of journalism in the United States during the twentieth century. Rachel Carson, at number two for *Silent Spring,* was the woman highest on the list. Ida Tarbell for "The History of Standard Oil" was number five; Hannah Arendt's "Eichmann in Jerusalem" was twentieth; Joan Didion's "Slouching Towards Bethlehem," twenty-third; Dorothy Thompson's reports on the rise of Hitler came in at number thirty; Martha Gellhorn placed thirty-fourth for her 1959 collection, *The Face of War;* and Betty Friedan's *Feminine Mystique* was thirty-seventh. Further down the list, Pauline Kael and Janet Flanner, as Genêt, appeared, as did two other *New Yorker* writers, Lillian Ross and Jane Kramer, each listed twice. Susan Sontag, Margaret Bourke-White, and Melissa Fay Greene also had berths. Given that for the greater part of the twentieth century, the profession's rule of thumb was to devalue, exclude, diminish, dismiss, or ignore its woman practitioners, how remarkable for this many of them to warrant such a fine retrospective distinction.

PART SIX

STATE OF PLAY

2000s–Early 2020s

CHAPTER 21

Assessment

At the start of the new millennium, a recession coupled with new forms of news and information delivery bludgeoned an already-battered legacy media. Google and Facebook digital ad earnings cut deeply into print advertising, the chief source of media revenue for a century and a half. Quality newspapers eliminated layers of long-standing subeditors and copy chiefs who enhanced quality, style, and accuracy. Reliance on freelancers grew, their pay rates frozen at 1980s levels. Moves to thinner, cheaper paper stock, shorter articles, and

Margaret Sullivan in the *Buffalo News* conference room
(Photo by Brendan Bannon)

fewer pages coupled with much smaller staffs did not stem the crisis, nor did any of the more innovative efforts to stay solvent. These included the counting of digital traffic, partial digital paywalls, events and guided tours, courses, ads on the front page, and the acquisitions of companies that were more digital and believed to be more profitable.

In the 2000s, the Pulitzer count for women and men began to reflect more closely their respective numbers in the industry. As newspaper editors, women accounted for 20 percent of the total, with most still situated at the smallest papers. In 2001, Gail Collins became the editorial page editor of the *Times,* a key masthead appointment and another woman first for the paper. On the news side, Carolyn Lee and Soma Golden held their positions. Kathleen Carroll became the executive editor of the Associated Press in 2002, the first woman in that post, but despite AP's wide and deep national and international reach through more than two hundred bureaus in ninety-nine countries, its appointments attracted little press beyond the industry. Carroll was succeeded in 2016 by Sally Buzbee, who would garner much wider notice, but not until *The Washington Post* named her its first woman executive editor in the spring of 2021. As Buzbee started her new position, she received a letter signed by a group of the *Post*'s woman alumnae over the past fifty years, those who had worked as the paper's writers, editors, researchers, photographers, foreign correspondents, news aides, and editorial writers. They had lived through the changes, some that required lawsuits, EEOC complaints, and negotiations over equal pay, maternity leave, and part-time status, they told her, asking to meet with her when she felt she had the time. "You are part of what we worked for," they wrote, "and we're thrilled."

Between 1970 and 2000, the number of women in television

Sally Buzbee, 2020
(Washington Post, *Getty Images*)

newsrooms tripled. By 2000, fifty times more women held slots as news director than they had thirty years earlier. Overall, throughout a media industry in tumult, more newswomen held decision-making positions than ever before, as Liane Hansen intoned for the 2001 documentary *She Says: Women in News*. Hansen's voice introduced this thoughtful look backward at what women in every medium had brought to journalism's reset, if rickety, table, relying on interviews with those who had succeeded and were succeeding still.

In the *Columbia Journalism Review*, the managing editor of *Sports Illustrated* credited the provisions of Title IX with the "dramatic increase in the talent pool" that had helped make women a fixture in major-league sports coverage. The 1972 measure forbade educational programs that receive federal funds to discriminate on the basis of sex. Melissa Ludtke's 1978 lawsuit, which opened the New York Yankees locker room to woman reporters, had been another huge step forward, although in 2000 the *Columbia Journalism Review* said woman sports reporters continued to find newsrooms less liberated than the locker rooms had become. To sports editors in the old-boy network, it still felt less risky to hire a man. Johnette Howard, a sports columnist for *Newsday*, considered it progress that the attacks in her hate mail had gotten shorter. "You're a dumb broad and you don't know anything about sports" now ended at the word "broad." Lesley Visser was not the first woman to cover pro football, but she broke ground in the coverage of televised sports when she joined the previously all-men team for *Monday Night Football*. "I wasn't at the dawn of women covering sports," Visser would say, "but I made the breakfast." Yet in 1991, *Sports Illustrated* pointed out that no woman had yet done any nationally televised play-by-play, although there had been a single regional instance in 1987. Rectification took another thirty years. In 2006, along with Jane Pauley and Lesley Stahl, the Museum of Television and Radio added Visser to its "She Made It" roster, noting her numerous awards and Hall of Fame honors. The International Olympic Committee even offered her its torch. Around the same time, men among the sportswriters began "tripping over themselves," the *Columbia Journalism Review* wrote, to cover the major events in women's sports like the 1999 Women's World Cup in soccer.

Lisa Olson, a sports columnist for the *New York Daily News*, brought attention to what seemed like a new level of acceptance for women on the beat by the year 2000. She attributed this in part to how common it had become for college women to cover sports for their school papers. This had the dual value of accustoming eventual professional athletes among the college players to the involvement of woman reporters as the women added a layer of experience and training to their preparation for eventual jobs. This is not to say that loud objections, ill-treatment, and unceremonious ejections entirely stopped. Nonetheless, as we've seen, for women at least, subject matter command, prior skills training, and experience beget opportunity and acceptance. It took a century, but the presence of woman sportswriters, the *Columbia Journalism Review* reported, had ceased to be "this unique bizarre thing."

Politics was another arena where woman reporters, after a century and a half, at last ceased to be a curiosity. In 2002, Beth Harpaz published *The Girls in the Van: A Reporter's Diary of the Campaign Trail*. Her title played on Timothy Crouse's classic, *The Boys on the Bus*, about the tribal rituals and social world created and inhabited by the men who covered the Nixon-McGovern presidential campaign of 1972. Harpaz, reporting for the AP, chronicled the woman reporters assigned to Hillary Clinton's victorious run in 2000 to become a senator from New York state. Reviews pointed up the contrast between the two groups, including the greater attention the women on such assignments paid to family and children back home.

The documentary *She Says*, which aired on PBS, was awarded the 2002 Emmy for Outstanding Long-Form Informational Programming. The ten women profiled shared recollections of how far they had come from the demeaning experiences of their early years at the hands of colleagues and bosses, incidents they felt at the time they had no choice but to let pass. Almost any woman journalist has stories as or more shocking than those recounted on camera, but theirs are representative. Rena Pederson, the editorial page editor of *The Dallas Morning News*, started out at bureaus of both AP and UPI. She spoke of one editor who found it amusing when she was on deadline to come up behind her and snap her bra strap. Judy Woodruff, then the prime anchor at CNN, recalled her excitement over her first great job offer from the news director of an ABC affiliate as she was about to receive her bachelor's degree in political science from Duke. As she turned to leave his office, he called out, "How

Carole Simpson
(ABC Photo Archives, Getty Images)

can I not hire someone with legs like yours?" In a later job, her boss expressed surprise that she should raise the issue of how much more her coanchor was earning than she was, especially since she earned so much for a woman. Carole Simpson was still ABC's weekend anchor when the documentary was filmed. She told of coworkers in her earliest days who would open the door to the announcer booth, drop their pants, and moon her while she was on the air. Being "put through the fire" made her stronger, she said. She meant that literally, because on one occasion a colleague set her script ablaze.

In the film, Simpson looked straight into the camera and gestured to the busy Sunday newsroom behind her with its two Asian Americans, two Black Americans, and plenty of women. The weekend staff, she said, was as diverse as America, including those in the editing suites out of view. On Monday, she said, for a regular viewership far greater than the weekend's, those same seats would project a very different array. There would be very few women, she said, and no one of color. When she started in network television in 1974, if someone had asked her if she thought there would still be three white men as the network's top weeknight anchors a quarter of a century later, she would have said "impossible." And yet that was still the case.

Several of the women interviewed spoke movingly about the turning point on sexual harassment that Anita Hill's 1991 testimony before the Senate Judiciary Committee became for woman journalists. Judy Crichton, a producer for the investigative program *CBS Reports,* spoke of how often men blamed menstruation or menopause when woman colleagues expressed their irritation. She also commented on how the unaddressed issues created by the work-and-home conflict were victimizing younger women. No one, she said, was grappling with the "human accommodations" that the profession so badly needed—day care, flextime—if it wanted women to be able to function fully in the mix. Paula Madison, the news director of WNBC-TV in Los Angeles, said she thought her uncommon background, having grown up on welfare on the streets of Harlem, slowed by at least two years her rise to news director. All the same, she said, it was simplistic to think that only people of color or women could "move the agenda." Every person who ever promoted her was a white man. Madison said her opportunities had always come because she was in the right place at the right time and ready to accept a new challenge. "But, I guarantee," she said, "there were hundreds if not thousands of African Americans before me that could have done these jobs."

Anna Quindlen prided herself on writing "conspicuously as a woman" for *The New York Times* in the "particularly female" way her columns brought the public and private together. When asked if she had ghettoized herself in the "girl group" by writing so often about child care, abortion, and sexual harassment, she said they were the cutting-edge issues of the end of the twentieth century, and none of her excellent colleagues on the op-ed page had shown any willingness to take them up. UPI's Helen Thomas reflected on a career during which she had reported from the White House on every American president from John F. Kennedy to Barack Obama. "There is acceptance now," she said, "but every door had to be broken down separately. The National Press Club. The White House Correspondents' Association. The Gridiron Club, all were exclusively male."

Dramatic gender imbalance on journalism's various playing fields was Geneva Overholser's theme in a piece she wrote for the *Columbia Journalism Review* in 2002. She tallied the number of women who had covered the major stories of the previous two years. For the Florida election fiasco of 2000 with its hanging chads, the byline count in five Florida papers and *The New York Times* was 135 stories by men and 22 by women. In the week after the attacks of September 11, 2001, the op-ed pages of the *Times, The Washington Post,* and the *Los Angeles Times* carried 88 signed pieces about the catastrophe, only 5 with women's bylines. Gender imbalance persisted in newsroom leadership: the number of women in these posts had stayed at 30 percent of the total for several years. Northwestern's Media Management Center found that among the women serving as president, publisher, or CEO of one of the 137 newspapers with circulations above eighty-five thousand, only 8 percent were women. The industry, Overholser wrote, seemed to be creating its own pink-collar ghetto in "a trade shunned by men, except for those who run it."

As she perused the Northwestern center's list of published research, a study about the expectations of the next generation, the Gen Xers, and their rejection of traditional newsroom culture stood out. "These folks don't want to work long and irregular hours, want to be well paid, and expect to get help with advancement," she cited the study as saying. For members of Overholser's generation to express such an attitude, she said, would have been unthinkable. And yet, the study went on, "They are part of a job-hopping generation, so their needs will have to be taken seriously because there is a shortage of good replacements coming up behind them."

Margaret Sullivan was prominent among the dozen or so woman executive editors of the first decade of the twenty-first century who rose to lead one of the country's one hundred largest newspapers. The women in this group were courteous and respectful of each other at industry meetings, she said, but did not bond as a sisterhood of elites. They were not bent on carrying the women's rights banner aloft, say, in the style of the Women's Caucus in Congress, formed in 1977, or even further back, when woman journalists and other editorial workers formed groups to address their grievances, emboldened by the equal opportunity legislation of the 1960s. Sandy Rowe, as one of the earliest of the 1980s woman executive editors, recalled their warm camaraderie at ASNE meetings, and that the organization funded special events for women during the conventions. But the focus of these gatherings, she said, was largely social. Rowe said it would be hard to categorize this rarefied group of women as anything other than highly self-motivated and self-directed individuals. Their inclination, she said, was to be seen first and foremost as editors worthy of respect and distinction, without any additional labeling that would set them apart as executives any more than their gender already did.

Sullivan's most pressing imperative in Buffalo was the need for greater racial diversity, so that became her prime hiring focus, and several of the people of color she hired were women. For woman role models, she looked to those of a generation or more before her, writers like Joan Didion and Nora Ephron. The woman editors she most admired included Overholser, Ann Marie Lipinski, and Charlotte Hall. Lipinski, at the *Chicago Tribune,* rose to metro editor in 1991, to managing editor in 1995, and to chief editor and senior vice president by 2001; Hall was the managing editor and vice president of *Newsday* before she took the top job at the *Orlando Sentinel* in 2004. Shortly before Hall's move south, she reflected on the unending challenges that newsroom culture imposed on women and called out women's underrepresentation at such a late date in sports, as photographers, in Washington bureaus, and in the upper newsroom echelons.

In 2003, Bill Keller, as executive editor of *The New York Times*, brought Jill Abramson to New York from Washington to become one of two managing editors, twinned with John Geddes, who had carried the deputy managing editor title since 1997. The *Washington Post* media columnist identified Abramson as "a rising star of the post–[Howell] Raines era." Keller told him that Abramson "sets the bar really high," that she had "lots of guts." He knew her as someone who would tell him when he was doing something stupid without reporting it to the press. He was especially admiring of her "reporter's DNA" and the tough-mindedness and patience her background in investigative work had given her. The *Post* columnist did not fail to mention that no woman at the *Times* had ever before reached so high a rank. To this Keller responded, "If you took gender out of the question and asked 50 people, she'd get the job by acclamation." Abramson's former boss in the Washington bureau of *The Wall Street Journal* remarked on her straightforwardness, how she never hesitated to walk up to someone who was screwing up and say so. It might be off-putting, he said, but no one ever missed the point. Keller said his need for a second managing editor reflected the *Times*'s global aspirations and the need for someone, meaning Geddes, to take specific charge of the paper's television, website, and *International Herald Tribune* divisions. Abramson's focus would be the news.

To those assembled for a Shorenstein Center conference at Harvard in November 2007, Ellen Goodman, by then a veteran *Boston Globe* columnist and 1980 Pulitzer Prize winner, said the time had come to expand the focus beyond basic discrimination and glass ceilings, "to see where progress for women has stalled and how we might jump start another period of change." True, she said, many more woman soldiers were fighting in the war in Iraq and more women than ever were reporting it. But at a third of the total, the percentage of women at daily newspapers and in other media had not changed in twenty-five years. Women in 2007 held 29 percent of top newspaper jobs, and another 18 percent were publishers. She called this no more than "a cup one-third full." The news itself remained segregated in her-and-his "pink and blue" culs-de-sac, she said. With few exceptions, the men who blogged and hosted television and radio talk shows focused on politics; women talked relationships. Workplaces had yet to adopt family-friendly policies, and the public nastiness toward woman writers was more vicious than ever. "The political has become stunningly personal," Goodman said. Women were not just stuck "but in some ways spinning our wheels."

Tina Brown resisted wheel spinning. *Politico* credited her with the transformation of the business of the American magazine and the creation of the "cult of celebrity" the world had come to take for granted. Her biography of Princess Diana reached the top of the best-seller list in 2007, after which she took charge of her friend Barry Diller's online start-up, *The Daily Beast.* It was indicative of the confidence Diller placed in her, *Politico* wrote, that the venture followed the estimated $50 million in losses she accumulated as editor of *Talk* between August 1999 and January 2002. At the *Beast,* she exhibited her trademark energy, drive, and imagination but, in *Politico*'s view, too slim a grasp of digital journalism's confounding new demands. Staffers said she clung to outmoded practices, like faxes and paper printouts, and that she hired no web natives. Her "slick sensibility" was apparent in the product, but it offered no real competition to, say, Arianna Huffington, who understood better than Brown that the internet was more "low-low than high-low," which helped grow the user base of *The Huffington Post* into the many millions. That in turn enabled its sale to AOL for $315 million off an initial $5 million investment as Brown struggled to demonstrate what she wanted the *Beast* to become.

Two women, the *Washington Post* reporters Dana Priest and Anne Hull, won the public service Pulitzer in 2008 for the stunning impact of their investigation into the abysmal conditions for returning soldiers at the Walter Reed National Military Medical Center. The series involved several undercover aspects that did not get in the way. True, *The Washington Post* had great prestige, and by 2008 woman journalists had reached far better standing in the profession than they had when Pamela Zekman's Mirage Tavern series for the *Sun-Times* came up for consideration in 1979 or Merle Linda Wolin's sweatshop probe for the *Herald Examiner* in 1982. But the composition of the Pulitzer board in each case is perhaps worth noting: In 2008, five of the board's sixteen members were women. In 1982, two women served, and in 1979, none.

In 2009, Jessica Bennett and two of her young colleagues at *Newsweek* had little to no awareness of their forty-six forebears at the same magazine as they passed around a worn copy of Susan Brownmiller's *In Our Time: Memoir of a Revolution.* From the book, they learned in detail about the women who had sued their magazine for gender discrimination forty years earlier. The information brought cognizance to how little had changed. Bennett, Jesse Ellison, and Sarah Ball shared their epiphany in an essay *Newsweek* published in March 2010. They wrote of their background as valedictorians and state-champion athletes; of the scholarships they won; of how they had cheered the appointment of a third woman Supreme Court justice; and of their excitement over the almost first woman president. They watched as women first became the majority of American workers and believed Maria Shriver when she declared in 2009 that the battle of the sexes was over.

And yet, as their generation entered the workforce, disillusionment had become their byword. True, *Newsweek* at this point had plenty of women on its writing and reporting staffs, but few managed to win the assignments considered most consequential. Bennett and her colleagues asserted that men still got promoted faster, too often on the strength of reputations aggrandized with the rejected pitches that women on the staff first proposed. Only six of the forty-nine *Newsweek* cover stories of 2009 carried the bylines of women, they pointed out. They cited studies that illuminated the "persistent disparities rooted in gender dynamics," the fear women continued to have of being labeled "bossy" or losing the chance to be regarded as "nice" by asking, for example, for a starting salary above the initial offer.

The young women gave space to explicit incidents in their own lives so like the workplace behavior women had been contesting out loud or under their breath for a century and a half. There was the unnamed manager who "winkingly" asked one of them to bake him cookies; the young colleague whose older boss, a man, kept hanging around her desk. They quoted Rachel Simmons, author of *The*

Curse of the Good Girl: Raising Authentic Girls with Courage and Confidence,
saying that their generation had been left to contend with what Simmons described as a "yes, but" framework. "Somewhere along the
road to equality, young women like us lost their voices," the essay
read. In the workforce, they encountered a baffling, alien "fog of
subtle gender discrimination" with no social movement behind it
and no language to describe it. They found themselves lacking the
confidence to give the unwelcome behavior a name.

At almost the same time, the National Archives sponsored a Wom-
en's History Month panel titled "Women in Leadership: Journalism."
The much-beloved Cokie Roberts moderated for the panelists Gwen
Ifill of PBS and Diane Rehm of NPR, both, like Roberts, honored
members of the most recent old guard. With them was Katharine
Graham's granddaughter Katharine Weymouth, an attorney, who, she
said with a note of self-deprecation, "came to journalism by way of
fraud by being born into the right family." At the time, she had been
publisher of *The Washington Post* and CEO of the company for a year.

Roberts set the context by providing a brief history of women
in the field, telling the audience about Anne Newport Royall and
the prosecution she faced down on the charge of being a "common
scold"; of the daring Nellie Bly and the bold Ida B. Wells; of the
woman correspondents of World War II abroad and the "Rosie the
Reporters" who lost their places back home when the men returned
from battle. She spoke of the lawsuits of the 1970s and what they
owed to the civil rights legislation of the 1960s; of Pauline Frederick
on television during the 1948 political conventions; of the men-only
doors that woman reporters broke down in Washington; and of what
Katharine Graham disclosed in her memoir about what she overcame to run *The Washington Post.* Roberts spoke of how little accommodation there had been for the needs of women as their numbers
in the field burgeoned. The way it had always been was the way it
remained, she said, because the men in charge liked the way it was.

Diane Rehm spoke of her late start in the business at thirty-seven
in 1973, after fourteen years at home rearing her children. Rehm
contended that women made better listeners than men and made the
point with an interview of hers with President Jimmy Carter in 1996.
Twice as they spoke, she committed the unpardonable broadcaster
sin of allowing ten seconds of dead airtime to pass while she waited

BLACK HERITAGE

usa forever

Gwen Ifill

2020

Gwen Ifill

*(Gwen Ifill from the
Black Heritage series,
© 2020 USPS®)*

for Carter to answer two different questions. Had he and the First Lady ever contemplated divorce? They had. What happened when they did? They got on their knees and prayed.

Gwen Ifill's career began with an internship in 1977 that turned into a job at the *Boston Herald American* after her graduation from Simmons College. She showed her bosses the note that appeared on her desk one day that began with the n-word and demanded she leave. She did not give in. In 1981, she moved on to the evening edition of *The Baltimore Sun*, then *The Washington Post*, then *The New York Times* until 1994. She then went to report from Capitol Hill for NBC before going to PBS to become the moderator of *Washington Week in Review* and a senior correspondent for *PBS NewsHour*. By 2013, she would join Judy Woodruff as the show's coanchor. Ifill said she had benefited repeatedly from being underestimated, "because when they write you off, you can come back for the kill." She emphasized, as others had so many times before her, the importance of diversity, of hiring women, Blacks, young, old, even diversity of background, as someone like herself who had lived in public housing. That way, she said, everyone then brings something distinct to the table. Ifill responded to a comment to the panel submitted by a student at Duke. The young woman said she and her classmates were being told to avoid reporting incidents of sexual harassment so as not to be seen as whiny or as troublemakers. "Depressing," Ifill said, "that our daughters are not walking through the doors we opened." As always, the power imbalance was still in play, the panelists agreed. Cokie Roberts offered a rejoinder: "White men. They still run everything," and then in a stage whisper, "into the ground."

The following month, the ombudsman of National Public Radio pointed out that since the inception of NPR in 1971, the radio network had been a leader in promoting equity for women. Women led three of the network's five biggest shows. The CEO and head of the news department were women at the time, as were many of the company's first-tier executives. But the ombudsman's research also showed a lack of woman news sources or women as regular on-air commentators. The figures for NPR, she wrote, reflected the situation everywhere and the odds were simply not in women's favor. For instance, of the twelve outside commentators who appeared on NPR at least twenty times over fifteen months, the only woman was Roberts, a former staff member, who appeared fifty-one times on *Morning Edition*. An examination of 104 shows over a nine-month period using a sampling technique showed that listeners heard from 2,502 men who were not staff members, but only 877 women. "For listeners," said Sheila Gibbons, the editor of the *Media Report to Women*, "it suggests that there aren't many women with something important to say about the key issues of the day. It follows that they don't have very big roles in shaping what those issues are, or making policy to deal with them. That's nonsense, of course."

In 2010, women claimed four spots on another expertly curated list, this time pinpointing the ten best works of American journalism for the years from 2000 to 2009. At 40 percent, this second such reckoning from NYU Journalism's faculty, joined again by a group of top reporters and editors, exceeded the percentage of women in the profession overall. It signaled parity—in terms of excellence at least.

CHAPTER 22

The More Things Change

In the 2010s, the feminist discourse infused the ether again. *The Guardian*, in April 2011, offered up a relatively exhaustive celebration of history's exceptional American and European woman journalists. A year before the piece appeared came several books that examined the question of women's place anew, including Lynn Povich's retelling of the *Newsweek* story in *The Good Girls Revolt*, which came out in 2012, followed by its televised serial version in 2015. As always, though, the good news and the grievances tripped over each other.

In the early part of the decade, the cultural imperative to hire, promote, and deepen coverage of underrepresented groups became impossible to ignore. Efforts to increase newsroom representation of the LGBTQ+ community and people of color often increased the number of women on various staffs since many of these targets of opportunity met more than one criterion and the women among them further distinguished themselves with the multiple perspectives they brought to the work. A sign of the times was the Associated Press's naming of Sonya Ross, a twenty-four-year veteran of the wire service, as its first editor for race, ethnicity, and demographics "at a time," the announcement said, "when sophisticated reporting by and about racial minority communities is not keeping up with the pace of their growth." The appointment received little attention at the time and even less six years later when Ross, still in the same role, sued the AP for harassment and racial discrimination. There was even less coverage three years after that when she settled her suit and retired from the company to form her own firm. In fact, the only news about a woman journalist to capture attention in this period—immense national attention, as it happened—was the decision of *The New York Times* to make Jill Abramson its executive editor after her eighth year as one of the paper's two managing editors. The Women's Media Center was exultant, trumpeting the news as a breakthrough, decades in the making.

In many ways, though, a woman in the top executive news job at a large-circulation, prestigious publication was not news. Thirteen years had passed since Debby Krenek became editor in chief of the *New York Daily News,* described in the *American Journalism Review* as that "perpetually turbulent newsroom with a macho culture, a mercurial owner, [and] major production problems." Kathleen Carroll was in her ninth year as executive editor of the vast and global Associated Press. In the heartland, Ann Marie Lipinski had been executive editor of the *Chicago Tribune* for a decade. In 2006, Abramson herself had mused in print about the absence of "first woman" mentions in the coverage of Katie Couric as she assumed the venerated Walter Cronkite role as the new solo anchor of the *CBS Evening News.* It would be a "pretty giant step for womankind," Abramson wrote, if omitting the "first woman" aspect of Couric's still fine achievement signaled the end of that tired, counterproductive angle.

And yet, for reasons that still held powerfully true in 2011, to reach the apex of the news-side hierarchy at the *Times* simply meant more. Remember Clifton Daniel saying a woman would never be *an* editor, let alone *the* editor, of *The New York Times?* Years later, Abramson would say, explaining the enormous attention her appointment received, "Anything that happens at *The New York Times* is a big deal."

With news of Abramson's appointment, friends of Harriet S. Rabb sent her congratulatory notes in recognition of the attorney's central role in the women's gender discrimination suits of the 1970s, including those of *Newsweek* and the *Times.* Betsy Wade, the first named plaintiff in the *Times* case, told a reporter that Abramson had come through a "very long, thin pipeline" in the best possible way, by "the long, steady course of working your way along." Susan Chira, the *Times*'s foreign editor, told *The New Yorker* there was no "tokenism" in the choice. "Jill studied for the job," she said, "and she earned it." Other women shed tears. Chira recalled the bitterness and anger of so many *Times* women throughout her thirty years on staff, since 1981, and how thwarted they felt, adding, "I can't believe how far we've come."

Ample time had passed for all the key people to observe and assess Abramson's management skills and style up close. Certainly, the publisher, Arthur O. Sulzberger Jr., had, as Abramson recounted with specifics in her 2019 book, *Merchants of Truth: The Business of News and the Fight for Facts.* Despite the newsroom excitement her appointment brought, she knew she was not universally popular and that several editors had implored Sulzberger not to select her. "I was seen as playing favorites and as being overconfident of my opinions," she wrote. "I had a bad habit of cutting people off and didn't listen enough. In short, I was seen as 'pushy.' " "Pushy," she added, was also a familiarly gendered refrain about women in powerful jobs.

In the months before the big news, *New York* magazine profiled the "heiress apparent," reporting that among the rank and file she was "both respected and feared" and considered "imperious" and "critical," especially when she thought the *Times* was losing ground to competitors. She had been successful working under Bill Keller. She had important support from Janet Robinson, the newspaper's president at the time of her appointment, who, Abramson said, "always had my back." Robinson's firing three months into Abramson's new job meant the loss of a key ally, which Robinson's successor, Mark Thompson, late of the BBC, did not become. At the private lunch with Abramson where Sulzberger made the offer, there was no flattery. He ticked off her faults, wanting to know if as executive editor she would be "the good Jill or the bad Jill." She told him she would work on her shortcomings.

At the time of Abramson's elevation, those who had been friends with Sulzberger for decades knew how much he hoped, as part of his own legacy, to see a Black executive editor lead the *Times*'s newsroom. As Abramson took charge, Dean Baquet was serving as one of six assistant managing editors. His experience was as long and deep as Abramson's, further enhanced by a Pulitzer for investigations his team won for the *Chicago Tribune* before he first joined the *Times* staff in 1990, his four years as managing editor of the *Los Angeles Times,* and the two years he spent as that paper's executive editor.

The publisher fired him over his opposition to newsroom job cuts. The next year, when he rejoined *The New York Times* as Washington bureau chief, Abramson had a hand in wooing him back. And, as she acknowledged, Baquet had the advantage of being extremely well liked among the staff, herself included. They shared interests, and he was the first editor to make her feel welcome when she joined the staff in the Washington bureau in 1997.

It was somewhat curious that Sulzberger, given his long-held goal, chose Abramson over Baquet. Asked why, years later, Sulzberger said he chose her because she had earned the title and because as managing editor at the time—Baquet, as an assistant managing editor, was two rungs down—she was next in line; it was her turn. Her journalistic acuity mattered most, he said, despite whatever management issues had surfaced. It's fair to point out that most of her predecessors had management deficits of one kind or another. As one insider asked in a *New Yorker* piece, " 'Tough and abrasive?' (a) Abe Rosenthal (1977–86); (b) Howell Raines (2001–03); (c) Max Frankel (1986–94); (d) Jill Abramson (2011–14); (e) all of the above." When Sulzberger asked Abramson to make Baquet her next in line, she readily agreed over her preferred choice. When John Geddes left the company in 2013, Baquet became the sole managing editor.

The commentariat made much of Abramson's ascension, encouraged by the paper's publicity department. Stories appeared almost immediately in *The Atlantic, The Washington Post, The New Yorker, The Nation,* CNN, *Politico, The New York Observer, The Guardian,* and *The Daily Beast.* For *The New Yorker,* Jane Mayer offered a reminiscent valentine to her friend about their *Wall Street Journal* reporting that became their book about Anita Hill and Clarence Thomas. "Jill has been a champion of old-fashioned, thorough, fact-based journalism—skillful and relentless in reporting, fearless in debunking lies," Mayer wrote. Ken Auletta, for the same magazine, shadowed Abramson on her first day in her new job, September 1, 2011. His piece ran six weeks later at eleven thousand words, illustrated with a stately full-page, black-and-white portrait of Abramson, posed with a golden retriever puppy who looked just like the subject of *The Puppy Diaries: Raising a Dog Named Scout,* her sweet if imperfectly timed book, published into the parallel news of her august new post. Auletta's story included unfavorable characterizations of Abramson provided by staffers he did not name: intimidating and brusque, remote, and "slightly similar to the talented but volcanic Howell Raines."

Abramson, on Baquet's suggestion, almost immediately promoted Susan Chira to become one of six assistant managing editors alongside four men and Michele McNally, who had overseen the photo operation at the paper since 2004. McNally was considered a "transformational figure in photojournalism." Over her fourteen years as a top newsroom manager, the *Times* was said to have won more Pulitzers, George Polks, Emmys, Overseas Press Club prizes, duPonts, and other awards for photography than most news organizations could show for their entire existence. Susan Edgerley, another one of the six since 2006, later came off the masthead and became dining editor.

In July 2012, not even a year into Abramson's tenure, she was included in the "Divine Sisterhood," a list compiled by the staff of the *Columbia Journalism Review* of "40 women who changed the media business in the past 40 years." It went in alphabetical order from Abramson straight through to Susan Zirinsky, known as Z, then a senior executive producer at CBS News and long a force in network television.

That fall, *The Buffalo News* announced that Margaret Sullivan, at fifty-five, in her thirty-second year with the paper and her thirteenth as the boss, was about to become the fifth public editor of *The New York Times*. Sullivan had already built a reputation for excellence beyond her region. By then, she had served four times as a juror for the Pulitzer Prizes and a year on the Pulitzer board, a post the *Times* obliged her to resign. Sullivan had little doubt that Abramson influenced the publisher's decision not to put a fifth white man in the role. "I think she made that case to Arthur Sulzberger; it was something she cared about," Sullivan said years later, an impression Abramson confirmed. The *Times*'s press release about the appointment quoted Abramson's appreciation for Sullivan's background, her adeptness with new platforms, and the way she interacted with readers. *The Buffalo News* story about her resignation included a cogent example. In the late summer of 2010, the paper's coverage of a fatal restaurant shooting spree provoked outrage in the city's already disaffected Black community by detailing the criminal past of seven of the tragedy's eight victims, four of whom died from the attack. Sullivan, as editor, stepped up to own the paper's ill-considered decision. In the piece about her new post, a Black district councilman and pastor extolled her editorial leadership. In that tense moment, he said, she showed up, took the heat, offered to make changes, and kept her promises.

Sullivan had hardly warmed her new seat at the *Times* when she showed her mettle again. A month into the new job, before Mark Thompson had arrived in New York, she used her new column to question his fitness to succeed Janet Robinson as company president. On his watch at the BBC, the network decided not to air an investigation it conducted into pedophilia charges against one of its major on-air personalities, who had died. Thompson maintained that the decision did not involve him. Numerous other instances brought Sullivan admiration from the severest of media critics. "Simple, really," said Jay Rosen, an NYU professor and media critic who blogs as *PressThink* and has a Twitter following of more than 300,000. "She was more capable of gaining critical distance on her profession than 99 percent of the people in that profession." One column that stood out particularly came midway through her four years at the *Times.* In 2014, as the Obama administration weighed the prospect of military action in Iraq once again, Sullivan resurrected the paper's "troubled history," expressly its flawed and damaging coverage of the run-up to the invasion of Iraq in 2002 and 2003. Sullivan did not name Judith Miller, whose star at the *Times* fell quickly when retrospective looks at her reporting deemed it too often inaccurate. The criticism eventually forced Miller's resignation.

In another look back for a *Slate* podcast, editors and colleagues on the same beat as Miller were quick to offer up what was not said at the time: that plenty of reporters—men—made the same mistakes Miller made. "There was this prurient and sexist fascination with her relationship to sources," Franklin Foer said, alluding to persistent rumors about the lines Miller ostensibly crossed and gossip that she used her sexuality to gain information. The attacks were reminiscent—even to the choice of words—of those leveled against Marguerite Higgins. "Pushy" and "sharp elbows" were descriptors Miller's colleagues applied to behavior Miller herself considered "ambitious." After she joined the *Times* in 1977, she occasionally quoted a congressman she was dating. Questions arose over how frequently top international news makers would grant her hard-to-land interviews when she reported from Egypt and Lebanon in the 1980s. In the case of King Hussein of Jordan, she would later say, he simply preferred a woman journalist's reportorial approach. At the time, the American women reporting from the region who served as full-time staff correspondents for major U.S. outlets could be counted on a few fingers. "On the other hand," Foer said, "it's pretty clear that her relationship to her sources was a constant problem in her career."

It bothered James Risen how the *Times* and other media isolated and blamed Miller. This was despite the more muted attention, or none, his own Iraq stories in the paper received in the early years of the twenty-first century. Stephen Engelberg was Miller's first editor on the Iraq story. He, too, said plenty of men on the beat were equally wrong about the invasion. "Judy was a very, very convenient scapegoat for everybody," he said, "to kick Judy and move on. I'm quite convinced of that."

In writing about that period, Margaret Sullivan won plaudits for reminding her colleagues how overreliance on leaks from anonymous sources and too-easy access to government leaders had led the *Times* astray. She also pointed to the lack of hard questioning from editors of what reporters were putting forth, and she warned the editorial page staff against amplifying the voices of neoconservatives and interventionists without the counterweight of opposing views.

Abramson had been forthright over the years about the *Times*'s credulity in that instance and addressed it again in a second interview with Ken Auletta during the New Yorker Festival of 2013. She spoke candidly about the paper's missteps in the Iraq War lead-up, which occurred during her Washington years. Amiably, Abramson fielded these questions and his softballs about the fortuitous changes she had been making on her watch as executive editor. She touted the enriched storytelling the paper had begun to produce on her watch with the enhancements of video and motion graphics, as its much-lauded "Snow Fall" package had shown, an arresting multimedia examination of a fatal avalanche. "I think it's not an exaggeration to say that we're creating a new way of reading," she said with evident pride.

Auletta did not ask about the buyouts she had been obliged to urge

At the New Yorker Festival on October 5, 2013,
Ken Auletta interviews Jill Abramson
(Getty Images, photo by Thos Robinson)

starting in January 2013 in hopes of avoiding the need to lay off anyone. Among the senior staff members who did leave were some of her
closest colleagues, which, she said years later, deprived her of some
of her strongest newsroom support. The masthead was more Baquet's
than hers, she said, because she had ceded much of the choosing and
the cultivation of the team to him. It took time for her to realize that
this and the senior staff departures she encouraged had been severe
tactical errors. Abramson found herself feeling isolated and alone.

About halfway into the conversation, Auletta summoned up a blis-
tering takedown of her leadership that *Politico* published six months
earlier. In the piece, unnamed colleagues, identified as "more than a
dozen current and former members of the editorial staff," let loose
on her for being stubborn, condescending, abrasive, hot-tempered,
and difficult to work with. The writer asserted that a year and a half
into her executive editorship, Abramson was "already on the verge
of losing the support of the newsroom."

Sources quoted in the piece commended her skills and her experience but questioned whether she had the temperament to continue
to lead, saying her attitude toward other editors and reporters left
"everyone feeling demoralized; on other occasions, she can seem
disengaged or uncaring." Much was made of a recent contretemps

with Dean Baquet that media reporters at various outlets had written about. After Abramson blamed Baquet for coverage she found lackluster while she was away, he burst out of her office, slammed his hand into a wall, and stormed out of the newsroom for the rest of the day. Abramson, in *Merchants of Truth,* acknowledged that for her to have caused such a reaction was "not exactly the image of a well-oiled journalism machine."

Sulzberger seemed unconcerned about the incident or about the *Politico* piece, she recalled. He reassured her that such attacks came with the territory. In the piece, Baquet gave Abramson a strong defense. He called unfair the "really easy caricature" of "the bitchy woman character and the guy who is sort of calmer" and countered another criticism, that she was absent too often. "She's the executive editor of one of the most important news organizations in the country," he said. "And the first woman. She's an important spokeswoman for the industry, which is part of the gig." He did not think people gave her the credit she deserved. Abramson considered his comments sheepish. The story did include a company spokesperson emphasizing that two weeks after Baquet's public outburst, the *Times* won four Pulitzer Prizes "for stories conceived and executed under her direction." Four more Pulitzers she could fairly claim were in the near offing.

Auletta, at the New Yorker Festival, asked Abramson to comment on the *Politico* piece. He asked if she agreed with the way the British journalist Emily Bell had attacked it as a "hatchet job" for its sexism and its atrociously weak sourcing. Bell had come to the United States from Britain in 2010 to head up the digital journalism center at Columbia's journalism school. Before that, she ran the websites and digital content of *The Guardian,* where she responded to the *Politico* attack. The only reason the piece deserved attention at all, she wrote, was for the way "it fuels an exasperating and wholly sexist narrative about women in power." Every anonymous source who trashed Abramson could have been balanced with how much more present she was in the newsroom than her predecessors. Bell suggested readers substitute every reference to "Jill" in the piece with "Jack" to see how truly sexist the critique had been. "When was the last time the approachability of a male editor made for copy?" she asked. *Politico* neglected to cover the "ingrained sexism in journalism, where a woman's character traits are central to a critique of [how] she does the job." Not so for men, who are judged more on their output and success. At no point was the reader asked to consider whether Abramson's abrasiveness had made the *Times* a better newspaper, Bell wrote, "even though the subjective view suggests it has."

Abramson told Auletta she agreed with Bell "somewhat." "Likability," she went on, "unfolds in a way for women that's different than for men." Is it inevitable, Auletta then wondered, for an editor to be perceived of as "not nice" because of the tough, unpleasant decisions editors must make? "No," Abramson said. "But I think in my case more attention would be paid to that issue."

Their conversation continued until the hour was up. When Auletta brought up the pitfalls of "horse race" coverage of politics, Abramson hastened to agree. It worried her to see politics covered "almost like sports," with a relentless focus on incremental wins and losses that favor fleeting "scooplets" over actual scoops. To that, Auletta asked her why she didn't just end the horse-race coverage. "You're the boss," he said.

Abramson retained her composure, as she had throughout the conversation, and calmly, even endearingly, said, "Can I go home now?" She reminded him that she had gotten up at 8:30 on a Saturday morning for an experience that was "starting to feel like root canal." That brought a burst of supportive laughter and applause from the audience. "See?" she said, feeding off the crowd's reaction. "I'm not abrasive. I'm humorous."

That appearance took place on October 5, 2013. Three months later, at the start of the New Year, Margaret Sullivan sat down with Abramson to discuss the editor's plans for 2014 and to review what had been accomplished to date. Abramson spoke of the "point of pride" she felt for having five women among ten masthead editors. She named three other women to other top newsroom positions during 2013. Abramson had encouraged Jodi Kantor to spend a year working on gender-related stories. With Rebecca Corbett as her key editor, Kantor's effort yielded significant stories about how unwelcome woman students at Harvard Business School felt in its "hyper-competitive culture" and how the adoption of automated scheduling at big chain stores had caused working mothers to suffer. A day after that story ran, Starbucks amended its policy. Five years earlier, while

Abramson was still managing editor, she put Kantor on the 2008 election campaign team, a move that its other members resisted. Kantor, Abramson said, turned out to be a "scoop machine."

Sullivan asked about some significant departures of high-profile talent that had happened with Abramson in charge. Abramson replied that the paper had enough depth and breadth to absorb the losses, reminding Sullivan that the staff had held steady at 1,250 people while so many other newsrooms across the country shriveled. She emphasized her commitment to "protecting on-the-ground reporting like a fierce lioness" and mentioned the recent hires of Pulitzer Prize winners, including Frances Robles, who is Latina, and Sheri Fink. When Sullivan asked what Abramson wanted her stamp on the *Times* to be, she replied, "Journalism of depth, creativity and purpose that is found only in The New York Times."

That year's annual personnel evaluation was brutal, the first of its kind Abramson received from Sulzberger, focused only on "my personality's supposed flaws." "In shockingly personal terms," she recounted in *Merchants of Truth,* "the letter described my moodiness and statements from my closest colleagues that I was a difficult manager. It said nothing about the substance or quality of my work. If I had to boil it down to one sentence it would be 'People think you're a bitch.'"

She read the letter in Sulzberger's presence and then asked him point-blank if he wanted to replace her. He said no, but that he did want her to take the letter seriously. Soon after, a new head of the video operation joined the staff. She told Abramson that she had been offered an executive coach, paid for by the paper, and had found the process enormously helpful. Abramson asked for and got the same coach. By April, when Abramson asked Sulzberger if all was well, he acknowledged the improvement.

Margaret Sullivan devoted her column of May 12, 2014, to the now customarily sorry findings of the Women's Media Center in its annual women-in-the-industry accounting. "Still Talking About It," Sullivan's headline read. " 'Where Are the Women?' " The report could have been written decades earlier. At the ten most widely circulated papers in the country, men had 63 percent of the bylines in the front sections, a figure that reached 70 percent at the *Times.* Women were still more likely to cover lifestyle issues over crime, justice, or world politics. Men as opinion writers at the major papers outnumbered women four to one. Sullivan sought comment from Janet Elder, then one of the paper's deputy managing editors. "Women are running things," Elder said. "That's an accepted part of the culture. It's not 'wow, there's a woman in the meeting,' anymore." Nonetheless, Elder did not have a good answer for why the gender gap persisted among those who gather and write major news, although she did bring up the difficulty women continued to face because they "still bear the lion's share of responsibility for children, family and households."

She spoke of how hard it is to balance demands at home with a frontline newsroom post, offering herself as an example. If her son had not already gone to college, she said, not only would she have been unable to take on the twelve-hour days her job now demanded, but she would not have wanted to work such long hours. It was almost as if she were offering belated confirmation of the contested arguments of Max Frankel as executive editor and Joyce Purnick as metro editor all those years ago. Her remark about women in a news meeting no longer precipitating a "wow" was eerily reminiscent of the women as the "bone and muscle" comment almost twenty years earlier from a woman assistant managing editor at *The Wall Street Journal,* the one both Abramson and Mayer later said they did not think rang true to their experience. Elder did acknowledge that many women had found a way to manage both parts of their lives effectively and pointed with admiration to Jodi Rudoren in Jerusalem and Anne Barnard in Beirut at the time, two mothers of younger children among the many at the *Times* who had managed to do it all.

Sullivan offered her own view of the importance of equity, much like those being widely shared as the ever-smoldering issues of race and gender converged at the forefront of newsroom consciousness. "A diversity of outlook with its range of voices" was critical, she said, because it better reflected the world. It mattered who was in charge, just as it mattered who was writing, reporting, and presenting the news. She hoped the day would come when it became completely unnecessary to discuss this stubborn absence of women in critical roles. "But," she said, "we're not there yet."

Times Ousts Jill Abramson as Executive Editor, Elevating Dean Baquet" was the front-page headline in the *Times* on May 14, 2014, two days after Sullivan's "Where Are the Women?" lament. Sulzberger had shared his decision with the hastily assembled staff, citing vaguely as his reason "an issue with management in the newsroom." Baquet then thanked Abramson, who was not present, for teaching him "the value of great ambition," and John Carroll, whom he served as managing editor at the *Los Angeles Times,* for teaching him that great editors could also be humane.

David Carr and Ravi Somaiya, who wrote the story under the headline, quoted unnamed "people briefed on the situation" who spoke further about the "serious tension" in Abramson's relationship with the publisher, of complaints that she was "polarizing and mercurial," and of criticism that some of her personnel choices had not worked out. There was talk of other clashes with Baquet, most recently over her plan, well discussed and confirmed with Sulzberger and Thompson but not with Baquet, to reinstall a second managing editor alongside him. Not only had Abramson excluded Baquet from these discussions, but she was not forthright in letting him know how far along they had gotten, nor that she had made an offer to Janine Gibson of *The Guardian.* The need for a strong digital presence on the masthead had become all too painfully clear in the conclusions of the major "Innovation Report," led by A. G. Sulzberger, Arthur's son, into how well the *Times* was doing against other outlets in this critical regard. In short, far from well enough. Also, as Abramson explained in *Merchants of Truth,* "the idea of having a true partner, another woman who had made brave journalism decisions and was forging her way into the future, appealed to me immensely."

Baquet contended that the plan for a second managing editor beside him again only became clear when he, Gibson, and Abramson lunched together and Gibson mentioned in passing that the offer had effectively been made. Baquet took his fury to Abramson first. She asked Sulzberger to take Baquet out to dinner and to reassure him of his primacy, that her job one day would be his. When she asked the next day how the conversation had gone, Sulzberger told her it had been very tough but said no more. According to Carr, the best media reporter of the era, Baquet made clear to Sulzberger "that an important insurance policy for the newspaper's future was going to leave the building." Friday morning, May 9, Sulzberger asked to see Abramson and told her he had decided to make a change. Baquet would be taking her job.

Over the coming days, speculation mounted about possible reasons other than the stated ones for the unceremonious ouster of the first woman to lead the newsroom of the *Times*. Charges of sexism were manifold and loud. "Editing While Female" was the title of a lengthy confessional from Susan Glasser, the editor of *Politico,* about her own painful experience of being similarly maligned. Plenty of other women weighed in. Rebecca Traister in *The New Republic* summoned the "glass cliff," a description "of what happens when people who've long been sidelined from power finally get a chance at prominent jobs." Were there more equity, she wrote, these comings and goings would warrant little more than passing gossip. A Poynter Institute blogger pointed out all the many positive things there were to say about Jill Abramson's tenure, quoting Margaret Sullivan, who lauded Abramson for "keeping the paper straight." *Slate* said how proud Abramson made other woman journalists feel; and *AllDigitocracy,* an online platform devoted to examining the impact of the digital revolution, expressed worry about the unfortunate interplay of sexism and racism as Baquet took over. "From now on," the writer prophesied, "despite all of Baquet's credentials including his Pulitzer Prize, people will quietly wonder whether a still sexist *New York Times* elevated an African American, at least in part, to give itself cover for firing an uppity woman."

It soon emerged that Abramson had earlier engaged an attorney to address what she saw as dramatic salary discrepancies between her pay and those of her predecessors, both when she was managing editor and when she was executive editor. This poured more fuel on the feminist fires, but in Carr's view it was no more than a sideshow. Sulzberger maintains that she was not paid any less, although the packages were constructed differently, reflecting different dates of hire and different experiences, assignments, promotions, and conditions along the way. This was an assertion Abramson continues to dispute. Sulzberger also said her decision to hire an attorney to renegotiate for her, unusual though it was, had not factored into his move.

Adding to the cacophony was a women's chorus loud enough for Sulzberger to respond to with an internal memo a few days after the newsroom announcement. He acknowledged the paper's strengths on Abramson's watch but at the same time accused her more specifically of "arbitrary decision-making, a failure to consult and bring colleagues with her, inadequate communication and the public mistreatment of colleagues." In the New York newsroom, Abramson habitually walked past a woman colleague with whom she had long been friendly as if they had never met. Ethan Bronner recalled that when he was deputy national editor, she scolded him in public, erroneously twice, and followed up on one of those occasions with the further embarrassment of a public apology.

Sulzberger's list went on. Abramson had "lost the support of her masthead colleagues and could not win it back." Carr pointed out how Abramson had managed to rise in a patriarchal business and a man-dominated organization "by displaying superlative journalistic instincts and never backing up for anyone." He mentioned the cover of the previous Sunday's *New York Post*, a photo pickup from Instagram, posted by Abramson's daughter, the physician and writer Cornelia Griggs. It showed her mother in boxing gloves and a sleeveless T-shirt, gloves up in front of a black punching bag with her right shoulder tattoo of a Metropolitan Transit Authority subway token on full display. "Mom's badass new hobby," the caption read. "#girls #pushy @jabramson64."

"How did our workplace suddenly become a particularly bloody episode of 'Game of Thrones'?" Carr asked in print. Of the fraught moments he had witnessed during his years at the *Times*, none rivaled this one. There were no remarks from Abramson to her staff as she departed. "It is one thing to gossip or complain about your boss," Carr wrote, "but quite another to watch her head get chopped off in the cold light of day. The lack of decorum was stunning."

In the following days, media reporters and critics aggregated the story's many elements. In Auletta's summation, Abramson, brilliant though she was, "had not always managed up, or down, with particular grace."

Abramson was conscious of how hard it had been from the start for her to connect with Sulzberger, that they had never developed the kind of rapport he had with Baquet. While she was managing editor, Sulzberger had entrusted her with recruiting to the *Times* his son, A.G., who would later succeed his father, and Arthur's nephew Sam

Dolnick. But their publisher-editor relationship, the most important one an editor must have, never got easy. Nor was Abramson as close to the rest of the masthead team as she needed to be. She had the same discomfort with Thompson, the CEO, with whom she would clash repeatedly over the business-side encroachment that consumed so much of her time, taking her away from the news, the part of the job she loved best.

In *Merchants of Truth,* Abramson concluded there was no simple reason for what happened. "I was a less than stellar manager," she wrote, "but I also had been judged by an unfair double standard applied to many women leaders. Most of all, I became the first woman editor at a very bad time in journalism, when a failed business model was bringing into question almost every principle of journalism that I had learned during more than 30 years in the profession."

Whether or how much gender factored into Abramson's dismissal can still be debated. Speaking on NPR, Baquet blamed Abramson's demise on her failed relationships and the "significant disagreement between Jill and the publisher and Jill and me." He added, "I never said to anyone 'It's me or Jill.' I think that's a simplistic calculation." He acknowledged, however, that he had made his unhappiness known, especially about the clumsily handled offer to Janine Gibson. NPR reported that Baquet had confided his frustration to other

Maureen Dowd, Jill Abramson, and Jane Mayer at
Abramson's sixty-fifth birthday party, 2019
(From Jill Abramson's personal collection, photo by Bill Cunningham)

editors as well as to Sulzberger, along with his concern that such a co-appointment could marginalize him. Abramson, asked by NPR to comment, refrained. Baquet made an additional point of expressing his "tremendous respect" for Abramson, adding, "I mean it when I say that three years from now nobody is going to remember this. What they'll remember is she was a great journalist and a landmark editor." Abramson remembers. With many more than three years gone, she has considered and reconsidered her own view of what transpired in 2014. "Dean," she said, "stabbed me in the back."

The shock of the Abramson firing did not end with her departure. The story reverberated for months, coupled in the wider world with the resignation in France the same day of the editor of *Le Monde*, Natalie Nougayrède, just as Barbara Walters retired from ABC— at eighty-five—to an outpouring of gratitude from newswomen, repeated at her death late in 2022, for all the ground she broke. The Pew Research Center reported that between 1998 and 2012, neither the total number of woman journalists nor those in leadership roles had substantially changed. Radio was the only place to record a notable increase in the number of women, but not as leaders. The pay disparity gap was as wide as ever, estimated at around 17 percent.

In September 2014, a Nieman Foundation study cited the persistent, pernicious effect of gender disparity in journalism leadership. It remade all the oft-heard arguments for why it was critical to do something about it: to broaden the array of voices, to create appeal across cultural groups, and to best serve the public as watchdogs and truth tellers. Content analyses and anecdotal evidence made clear that the gender of a newsroom leader could impact "everything from what stories get covered and how, to who gets promoted and why." In 2004, the number of women in charge at the twenty-five largest-circulation daily newspapers totaled seven; ten years later, the figure was three.

The study, which appeared in the foundation's publication *Nieman Reports*, looked to the new digital start-ups for signs of hope but did not find them. Old imbalances remained a constant. Where women (or any underrepresented group) do not have the same opportunities as (white) men, the report said, they have no chance of having the same level of influence. The writer did note the new set of expectations that millennials were bringing into newsrooms vintage and new. This was much of a piece with the insight about the previous generation, Gen X, that Geneva Overholser cited from an academic study in 2002. Of the millennials, the newer piece said, "They're far less wedded to the idea of staying at one organization, or to what title they have. They're far more aware of the need for a diverse set of voices and have fewer preconceived notions about what a leader looks like. They hear 'editor' and are just as likely to think Arianna Huffington as Ben Bradlee."

Of course, everything problematic that held women back in the business or in presence on the page was also true for people of color. Carr, in his summation of the Abramson firing, alluded to the swirl of issues that caused these two worthy, necessary pushes for change to crash into each other. He wrote of the pride Sulzberger felt in having created a dream team, "two talented journalists to lead the paper who were not white men," a dream that never really became a team. Carr celebrated the smart and courageous leadership Baquet had already demonstrated and the way he made the very endeavor of journalism seem grand. "But," he wrote, "the sense of pride that we should all feel at his ascension—as a great, decorated journalist and the first black executive editor of The New York Times—has been overwhelmed by the messiness surrounding it."

#MeToo, You, Too

Three years into Dean Baquet's tenure as editor of *The New York Times*, another public bout with the "messiness" emanated from the ill-chosen words of the eighty-four-year-old Gay Talese. The imbroglio erupted Saturday, April 2, 2016, as Talese finished his keynote address to a crowd of more than five hundred people, largely women, at an annual narrative nonfiction conference at Boston University. Talese mentioned his part in a new documentary about his friend Nora Ephron, who was also his cousin by way of her marriage to Nick Pileggi. In the question-and-answer session that followed, a woman in the audience asked him which other woman journalists inspired him when he started out. Talese searched his mind for a moment to think of what to say, then summoned the name of the novelist and critic Mary McCarthy. He paused in reflection again before saying, "None." None, he went on to explain, none wrote about the strangers and odd unsavory characters he often chose as subjects. "Joan Didion," a voice in the audience called out. Talese acknowledged his admiration for this "educated, beautiful writer," but said again that she did not write as he did about the likes of mobsters, voyeurs, and porn kings. He did not mention the profiles he had done of more savory characters, like, say, Frank Sinatra, with a terrible cold, that became a classic. Educated women, he said as if it were fact, like to write about educated people.

Women in the auditorium seats began tweeting before Talese left the stage. "This keynote just became a case study in the deep thread of chauvinism that still runs through journalism," wrote

Amy Littlefield, a freelancer associated with *The Nation*. Later, she explained that the moment Talese uttered the word "none," she felt "erased." The investigative reporter Nikole Hannah-Jones, who had given her keynote the night before, posted several times: "Gay Talese was all good until he started talking about how women don't like to hang around under-educated seedier types. Um, whut?" And, "It is inevitable. Your icons will always disappoint you." On a playful note, confessing her own love of fashion, she posted a photo of his dressy black-and-oxblood two-tones with the tweet, "Gay Talese partially redeemed for sexist remarks by wearing baddest shoes." Michelle García, a writer for *Guernica*, was among the women who walked out. "Listening," she later wrote, "had become unnecessary."

Among journalists, Hannah-Jones had been rising steadily in national prominence since she joined the staff of ProPublica at the tail end of 2011, recruited by Stephen Engelberg, who was the investigative nonprofit's managing editor at the time. Engelberg knew Hannah-Jones well from *The Oregonian*, where he was Sandy Rowe's managing editor until 2008. When *ProPublica* received a Ford Foundation grant to establish its race beat, Engelberg immediately thought of Hannah-Jones and the investigative edge she gave to coverage of fair housing laws.

Nikole Hannah-Jones at the Power of Narrative
Conference, Boston University, April 1, 2016
(Photo by Nikita Sampath)

Engelberg remembered calling her up as the offer was being made to say how excited he was about her coming to ProPublica. "We're going to have a great time," he told her. "You will be the only reporter at a national level covering civil rights and race. We'll have the whole field to ourselves, and we can do whatever we want." Her investigative experience was not as extensive as some other ProPublica hires, but Engelberg was sure about his choice, enough to tell the executive editor she was a hire whose success he felt confident he could guarantee. And indeed, over the next four years, Hannah-Jones produced award-winning investigations on segregation in housing and in schools.

By the time of BU's conference, Hannah-Jones had left ProPublica for *The New York Times Magazine*, where she had been on the staff for nearly a year. When the editor, Jake Silverstein, announced her hire in April 2015, he described her as "a reporter's reporter, a born skeptic with a knack for deep investigations," "a remarkable nose for stories, and a flawless bullshit detector." He called her work "profound and tenacious." That same year, the *Times* was contemplating the steps it would take to deepen its coverage of gender and of race. The Hannah-Jones hire was one of them. The MacArthur Foundation, in bestowing on her its "genius" award two years later, cited her for "chronicling the persistence of racial segregation in American society, particularly in education, and reshaping the national conversation around education reform."

Another decision at the *Times,* made early in January 2016, had media critics questioning its wisdom in light of the country's churning racial turmoil, not understanding that a broader new initiative was in the making. Tanzina Vega was taken off the race and ethnicity beat under the national desk, a position she had persuaded Jill Abramson to create for her early in 2014. Baquet and Susan Chira, who by then had risen to become one of Baquet's three deputy executive editors, explained that the subject was simply too large and too complex to be contained in a single reporter's beat; bigger ideas and new approaches to the paper's race coverage were in the works.

On the gender front, there were parallel moves. Jessica Bennett was freelancing regularly for the *Times,* mostly for the Style section. Her work still had the gender focus she carried with her from *Newsweek.* Every chance Bennett got, she urged her editors at the

Times to create a formal gender beat and to hire her to work it, but the entreaties of a freelancer carried little weight. In March 2015, Bennett produced a profile of Monica Lewinsky, the woman at the center of the Clinton impeachment scandal who had not been heard from publicly for a decade. "It prompted what we are now very frequently doing," Bennett said, "which is, having conversations about how women were treated in the media in the past." Through the grapevine, Bennett learned that Baquet liked the story. She seized that wedge to get a meeting with him, knowing that Chira had been lobbying internally for a dedicated gender position. Bennett got the meeting and pitched a position as gender correspondent, but nothing more came of it immediately.

Only when Gay Talese boarded the train to return to New York did he learn about the uproar he had caused in Boston. In an interview with the *New York Daily News*, where a story about the dustup ran the next day, one of the BU faculty members who had been onstage defended Talese, saying he was not getting a fair shake, that very few women wrote narrative nonfiction in the 1950s and 1960s, and that was Talese's context, "his world." Talese himself would reiterate this line of thought to *The New Republic*. "I'm talking about ancient history now," he said, "but it's the only history I came out of." That history, for Talese at least, seems not to have had a place for the woman reporters active in his era such as Martha Gellhorn, Gloria Emerson, Georgie Anne Geyer of the *Chicago Daily News*, or Edna Buchanan, a mystery writer and crime reporter for *The Miami Herald* since 1973. Her 1986 Pulitzer Prize honored her "versatile and consistently excellent police beat reporting."

On Monday, April 4, 2016, Talese told a *Boston Globe* columnist that he admired several contemporary woman writers, naming Susan Orlean, Larissa MacFarquhar, and Katie Roiphe, who had interviewed him for *The Paris Review* in 2009. He also mentioned Lillian Ross, who wrote for *The New Yorker*. Most of them were aware of his admiration, he said, because he had blurbed their books or sent them kudos. Orlean, whose own exceptional work included a good share of oddballs, also had Lillian Ross on her list of great woman journalists of Talese's generation or nearer it, along with Joan Didion, Janet Malcolm, and Jane Kramer. "I'm just getting started here, folks," she tweeted. The *Globe* column came down hard on Talese for his altogether false assertion that woman journalists avoid gritty subject matter.

On Tuesday, Amy Littlefield's report of the brouhaha for the website *Rewire* included new details that Nikole Hannah-Jones shared with her from a private reception BU hosted for the conference speakers. Once Talese learned that Hannah-Jones was a staff writer for *The New York Times Magazine,* he seemed to fixate on this narrow fact. "He asked again if I was actually a staff writer. And I said yes," Hannah-Jones told Littlefield. He asked how she had gotten hired. "I said they called and offered me a job." He asked who had hired her and why. For Hannah-Jones, as the only Black person in the room, her presumed subtext of his line of inquiry was miserably familiar. It was what the cultural critic Touré would explain as the "résumé check," designed to denigrate, consciously or not. As Hannah-Jones told Littlefield, "I feel like I've been explaining why I'm in a room where apparently people think I'm not supposed to be most of my life. So I know when someone is asking me that question."

As the reception ended, Hannah-Jones and another woman were trying to decide which conference session to attend next. Talese walked over to them, ever the keen observer of detail and clearly taken with Hannah-Jones's glittered and polished nails. Perhaps what came next was no more than a clumsy stab at banter, blundering and tone-deaf though it was. Talese asked Hannah-Jones if she was going to get her nails done. The comment left her speechless. "Part of it was, I mean, I just come from a family where respect for your elders is very ingrained," she told Littlefield. "But part of it is feeling like, honestly, as a Black woman, that it would be very hard for me to say something without coming off looking like all the stereotypes that women and Black women get. It was a hard moment for me to realize that even at this point in my career I could still be silenced."

García, as a conference speaker, also attended the event. She approached Talese as he reached for his fedora, touching his arm to get his attention so that she could introduce herself. She wanted to tell him what had been on her mind since she walked out on the question-and-answer portion of his talk. "I did this to show that a woman had covered the 'underbelly' that Talese had stated women were reluctant to report on," she said several years later. She started by listing her bona fides: she told him she had reported on the aftermath of the Mexican president Felipe Calderón's drug war with its tens of thousands of dead and disappeared and reeled off her other experiences "with misfits, criminals, and the outcast, on both sides of the border." Talese wanted to know if she had interviewed a voyeur. Not yet, she told him, but offered that she once tagged along with a film crew looking for prostitutes in the early morning. Then she suggested to Talese that they pose together for a photograph so that he could remember he had met her. "Well yes," he replied, she wrote, "you're a sexy woman." A shot was snapped. Later, García, Adriana Gallardo of ProPublica, and Hannah-Jones compared race and gender notes on their Talese encounters. All of this García reported in *Guernica* under the headline "Me and Gay Talese in the Middle." In her piece, she reproved herself for not having opened her encounter with him by attempting to disprove Talese's assumptions. She wished she had talked about her work on the fight, largely waged by women, against the impunity of the disappeared. Only later, she said, did she realize that by citing the same types of stories Talese and the wider industry prized most, she was "reinforcing a genre that centered on a white male experience and perspective on the world." This happened even though she knew better, even though she knew that Talese's work had come to represent only one of many possible perspectives, work now considered "just another genre," as her own work was just another genre, his no longer regarded as an absolute.

The tweets, the stories, the blog posts pilloried Talese for days, an experience not unlike the Twitter onslaught directed at Jeffrey Goldberg, the editor of *The Atlantic*, three years later. To a journalist reporting on his magazine's industry-leading staff diversity profile—75 percent women at the time, led by Adrienne LaFrance as executive editor—he volunteered that a diversity arena where the magazine lagged was in who could do the "really, really hard work" of writing the ten-thousand-word cover stories for *The Atlantic*'s print editions. Goldberg said those who currently had this ability were still "almost exclusively white males." His point, he tweeted later, was to say he wanted the magazine to start providing the step-by-step training that could help bring a more diverse array of writers along, but that did not help. As Andi Zeisler, the cofounder of Bitch

Media, tweeted, "Has anyone told Jeffrey Goldberg about women who write books?"

In Talese's case, on the Wednesday after the conference weekend, the Style section of *The New York Times* weighed in with an account derived primarily from a reporter's visit to Talese at his Upper East Side town house. Talese said his now infamous "none" reflected his having misunderstood the question, that his earliest inspiration had been from sportswriters like Red Smith of the *New York Herald Tribune*. Talese said that he indeed tried to emulate novelists like Carson McCullers—novelists—just not any of the woman journalists of his era, although he admired many. He echoed the list of women in Susan Orlean's tweet—Lillian Ross, Joan Didion, and Janet Malcolm—and added Nora Ephron and Susan Sontag. He admired them all, he said; they just hadn't shaped him. When he uttered "None," he said he wished someone onstage had followed up to ask him what he meant. Had that happened, he said, he would have explained that when he was starting out, very few women wrote on seamier themes. There again, he must have meant how few women who reported on seamier themes crossed his field of vision. Gail Sheehy was at the *Herald Tribune* then, consigned to the women's section ghetto, alas, but writing about the poor, the imprisoned, and the Harlem women on rent strike. Consider the superb women at the *Times* and elsewhere not on his scope when he wrote *The Kingdom and the Power: Behind the Scenes at "The New York Times": The Institution That Influences the World*, now a classic, published when Talese was thirty-seven with second wave feminism in full, raging swing.

On Thursday, Margaret Sullivan flayed the *Times*'s story. "Not ready for prime time," she called it, notable for its "rather one-sided sympathy for the celebrated writer." Dean Baquet had responded to the article with a statement on the *Times*'s corporate website. Sullivan quoted it in full. Had he been asked to comment for the piece, Baquet wrote, he would have extolled the gifts of Hannah-Jones as "one of the most accomplished and prominent journalists of her generation," one who has "made it her mission to write about some of the most pressing, intractable issues in American life." He called her "a unique combination of a reporter with investigative zeal, unfailing integrity and a writer's eye for telling, human detail." He said he considered her decision to join the staff of the *Times* one of his proudest moments as editor.

Baquet said that beyond the fact that the *Times*'s story was flawed and the treatment of Hannah-Jones unfair, the entire incident carried greater implications for the newspaper. "Too often," he wrote, "we are clumsy in handling issues of race and gender and this story was another unfortunate example. We have made strides in our coverage and culture, but the best solution is to continue building a more diverse, inclusive newsroom."

Likely by coincidence, the same month as the BU conference and Baquet's ringing defense of Hannah-Jones, the *Times* made more changes internally. It launched "Race/Related," a newsletter that soon attracted some fifty thousand subscribers, and in August 2016 a cross-desk team with the same "Race/Related" title was in place.

At around the same time, the search began for an editor to "help tell the story of how gender shapes lives." The opinion section, too, sought someone with similar expertise. New achievements by the paper's woman reporters brought fresh credit. In the spring of 2016, Alissa J. Rubin won the Pulitzer for international reporting for "giving voice to Afghan women who were forced to endure unspeakable cruelties." In May, Megan Twohey and Michael Barbaro reported and co-bylined a story with a very long tail about the Republican presidential hopeful, headlined, "Crossing the Line: How Donald Trump Behaved with Women in Private." For Twohey, Trump's counterattack turned into "the most bruising reporting stretch of her career." By July, Emily Steel, a business desk reporter with a focus on media, broke through with her reporting on the hard-to-confirm indications of rampant sexual harassment of the women at Fox News. Until then, information made available always seemed to boil down to allegations met by flat denials. To do the work properly, Jim Rutenberg, the *Times*'s media columnist at the time, explained, it was critical to find hard evidence, to get beyond the mutual hurling of accusations. After Roger Ailes resigned as the head of Fox News in July, Steel and Michael Schmidt began to pursue the sexual harassment accusations against Fox's popular host Bill O'Reilly, which yielded a substantial paper trail of negotiations and nondisclosure agreements.

In October 2016, Baquet made Joe Kahn sole managing editor. Susan Chira moved back into reporting for the first time in decades

and became the senior correspondent for gender issues. Susan Dominus, a staff writer at the magazine, applied a "gender perspective" to
her coverage of the Trump–Hillary Clinton presidential campaign.
Elsewhere, gender was continuing to rise in the cultural conversation.

"What's going on?" Dominus, the host, asked rhetorically to introduce her podcast of October 14, 2016, about all the changes happening inside the *Times*. Neither the editorial- nor the news-side
gender editors had yet been chosen, but Chira's new gender focus
had been announced. Dominus wanted to know if all the moves signaled admission of the paper's "insufficient attention to gender in the
past." No, Chira said. She explained that the gender category was not
"shorthand for women's issues," that it covered "all manner of identity formation and construct—LGBTQ, the nonbinary, the works."
The point, she said, was to step up the intensity of the coverage on
all these fronts. Audience research had shown that constituencies
the *Times* wanted to reach—women, younger readers, and readers
outside the United States—had keen interest in these topics.

Was the gender focus meant to match the race focus, which was
further along? "Well of course they intersect," Chira replied. "And
they'll be covered as they intersect." News was driving the focus on
race, meaning the repeated police shootings of Black men, the end
of the Obama presidency, and the racial legacy of Obama's eight
years in office. Editors, she said, understood well that issues of race
and gender are related, "but we also think each of them can bear
a separate focus." She did not mention the harassment and assault
investigations by then well under way. Chira was adamant that the
whole point was not to ghettoize either subject, and for the gender
focus to work much as the race focus was already working.

Jessica Bennett decided not to apply for the gender editor job. At
the time, in the fall of 2016, her days were packed with the publicity
blitz for her book, *Feminist Fight Club: An Office Survival Manual (for a
Sexist Workplace)*. The thought of having to compose another memo
annoyed her, and her preference in any event was to keep writing.
"Then the election happened," she said, and the unexpected defeat
of Hillary Clinton, and the energy and magnitude of the Women's
March in Washington and in cities and towns across the nation.
Donald Trump's first day in the White House "felt like this huge

galvanizing moment," she said. "For me personally, it was like, 'Oh, fuck. I messed up. I really want this job.'"

Chira told Bennett there was still time to apply. Another gigantic memo followed. The issues around gender questions kept swirling in the culture throughout the rest of 2016 and into the New Year.

So did the issues around race. In December, the new public editor, Liz Spayd, called the paper out for how few Black, Latino, or Asian reporters were involved in the paper's election coverage and how on the masthead only the executive editor was not white. Baquet responded, "We're not diverse enough, but I think they'd say I have a commitment to it and that it's gotten better in the past year. My effort to diversify has been intense and consistent."

More was happening beyond the election's aftermath. On January 10, 2017, Emily Steel and Michael Schmidt's first piece ran on the settlements that Fox News paid out to Bill O'Reilly's many accusers. More stories followed. The next target was the Hollywood producer Harvey Weinstein, an investigation led by Jodi Kantor and Megan Twohey, with Rebecca Corbett as the key editor. They all worked flat out on the probe for the better part of 2017. "Without O'Reilly, there is no Harvey," Rutenberg said. "There is no #MeToo."

In March, Spayd bemoaned what the headline over her column called "The Declining Fortunes of Women at the Times." She was

Megan Twohey and Jodi Kantor
(The New York Times/*Redux, photo by Earl Wilson*)

reacting to the gender composition of the top editors who presented the newsroom with "a bold new phase of digital innovation." All of them were men. Spayd laid out how women had "skidded down" the paper's power structure in the three years since Jill Abramson's firing. Fewer women were leading big news departments; fewer still were in the pipeline. That, she wrote, meant fewer women were deciding which big stories get assigned, what the broad coverage priorities should be, or what a reenvisioned *Times* should look like. She did note that the Washington bureau chief was still Elisabeth Bumiller, who put many woman editors into available slots. Three new women had joined the masthead in New York City in 2017; Bumiller went on the list in 2019. Women were leading the arts and culture, book, photo, and video desks. "There are probably more distinguished women in this newsroom than at most any newspaper in the country," Spayd wrote, but for the first time in fourteen years men were first and second in command of the national, international, metro, sports, and business desks. The next editing tier in every case looked like the one ahead of it. The reporter ratios were similarly questionable, she wrote, with men still claiming the largest share of bylines in the first section of the paper.

Women on staff, Spayd wrote, complained most about what they saw as a backslide from earlier gains. Baquet responded by telling her he was "forcefully working to get women into positions of authority." He cited the three promotions of women to the masthead and added, "There's no question that with women in positions of authority you will see stories covered in different ways."

As millennials entered their childbearing years, *Nieman Reports* asked in a 2017 survey, "Where are the mothers?" To attract and retain them, the report admonished, news organizations had better adapt. It cited studies that showed women as journalists at higher risk of burnout than their counterparts, largely because of the unsupportive policies of their companies. The proposals in the study were hardly revolutionary but still held: give paid maternity leave; give fathers and non-birth partners paid family leave; create official work-from-home and flextime policies; prioritize a good work-life balance for everyone.

Bennett got the gender editor job at the *Times,* considered a first in the United States, although there had been similar positions abroad since 2004. The next year *The Washington Post* followed by naming a gender columnist; other American outlets established such posts thereafter.

Bennett's start date at the *Times* was in September 2017, just as Kantor and Twohey were gearing up to break their bombshell Harvey Weinstein investigation exposing decades' worth of sexual harassment and abuse charges against him and the nondisclosure agreements and settlements that followed. The worldwide #MeToo movement exploded in its wake. This meant, Bennett said, that every plan that had been made for her new gender editor post got put on hold as focus shifted to covering the Weinstein developments.

The tagline "Me, Too" first appeared in 2006 when Tarana Burke formed a nonprofit to help underprivileged survivors of sexual harassment and abuse. Within a decade, #MeToo became, in many ways, the hashtag and rallying cry for a redux of feminist social movements past but refashioned for a new era, in the image of the Generation X and millennial women and the gender nonconforming people at its core. The early stories kick-started the major impact that followed, an avalanche of high-level suspensions, firings, and forced resignations of men across all industries. Journalism was not spared.

Woman journalists figured in the larger story, as reporters, accusers, and commentators. Those who did the reporting worked in teams or alone, as Jodi Kantor had been doing as far back as 2013, or Julie K. Brown at *The Miami Herald*, whose persistent investigations would eventually put Jeffrey Epstein behind bars a second time for his sexual abuse of the underaged. Brown identified eighty girls snared in Epstein's web, some as young as thirteen. Her work also put Alex Acosta under a cloud for the secret deal he struck with Epstein when Acosta was U.S. Attorney for the Southern District of Florida, a deal that eased Epstein's prison time for his 2008 conviction. This helped spur Acosta's resignation as Trump's secretary of labor.

Later, Julie Brown and Jane Mayer reflected in print on the difficulties they had encountered as women in their respective investigative pursuits of the powerful. "You know they are going to try to find a way to mess with you," Brown told *InStyle* of her efforts to expose high-level corruption. The writer reminded Mayer of her editor's comment that no one wanted to be on the receiving end of a call from Jane Mayer in reporter mode. "Oh, God, I feel like the grim reaper," she said. "I hope it doesn't interfere with my ability to keep getting people on the phone, that's all. It's funny, though. I guess this means they are finally taking us seriously. Which is progress."

Brown spoke of how especially hard investigative work was for women who undertake it. She mentioned the public attack Epstein's former attorney Alan Dershowitz waged against her to the board of the Pulitzer Prizes, and the difficulties she often encountered when she tried to get her editors to back investigations she wanted to pursue. "You have to fight for your own stories sometimes," Brown said. "That's frustrating because you feel passionately about what you do, but you don't want to alienate your editors. In reality," she said, "men don't see stories the same as women. They just don't." *She Said: Breaking the Sexual Harassment Story That Helped Ignite a Movement*, the book about the Weinstein investigation by Jodi Kantor and Megan Twohey, included the backstory of all the viciousness they faced from the pro-Weinstein forces as they did their reporting. Inside the *Times*, however, support was unwavering.

The Pulitzer Prize eluded Julie Brown, although her work won a George Polk award, a Hillman Prize, and, from the National Press Club, the Neil and Susan Sheehan award for investigative journalism. The 2018 Pulitzer for investigative reporting went to the staff of *The Washington Post* for its "purposeful and relentless" work in 2017 on the background of Roy Moore, which, the citation said, "changed the course of a Senate race in Alabama by revealing a candidate's alleged past sexual harassment of teenaged girls and subsequent efforts to undermine the journalism that exposed it." The gold medal for public service went to Kantor and Twohey for the *Times*, and to Ronan Farrow for *The New Yorker*, "for explosive, impactful journalism that exposed powerful and wealthy sexual predators, including allegations against one of Hollywood's most influential producers, bringing them to account for long-suppressed allegations of coercion, brutality and victim silencing, thus spurring a worldwide reckoning about sexual abuse of women."

At the *Times*, Jessica Bennett's new mandate was far broader than sexual harassment and assault. As Chira had already laid out, "gender" did not just signify "women." Bennett's job was "to drive coverage of how gender shapes the lives of people across the globe." But the cascade of developments across all industries put sexual harassment and assault in the forefront. "For the first time in history," Bennett wrote in announcing a new gender newsletter in early December 2017, "powerful men are falling like dominoes, and vulnerable women are being believed." At the *Times* and elsewhere, top woman writers expressed themselves in essays meant to deepen understanding of the stakeholders and the stakes. Women put aside abiding fears of censure and retribution as they hurled accusations against their bosses and colleagues for everything from discomfiting workplace innuendo and after-hours come-ons to rape and other forms of aggravated assault. Many of the accused men were well known or highly respected throughout the industry, among them those who had been supremely supportive of the women on their staffs. A private Excel warning sheet with a long list of "shitty men" in media accidentally went public, unvetted, with accusations from women that attached names to the full spectrum of misbehavior. Long-delayed investigations followed. Top figures lost their jobs. In August 2018, *Vox* named fifty-seven men in journalism accused and most acted against by that date. The impact has been profound and lasting. As I write, hardly any, if any, of the men have been able to find their way back into grace.

The willingness to name names in whispers or in flagrant public attacks brought on the brutal pummeling of and lethal threats against the accusers and essayists that social media so demonically incited and continues to incite, inviting legal action in some cases from both the accusers and the accused. Attention was also brought to the verbal and social media abuse and threats to personal safety that target women who report across the world from unwelcoming terrain or those who write on incendiary topics. In Ta-Nehisi Coates's view, the sometimes hostile reaction to the *Times*'s 1619 project, a "reframing" of America's founding with slavery and resistance at its center, made Nikole Hannah-Jones as project editor a target in the extreme. This was, he said, "in large part because of who she is"—a strident, proud, effective Black woman, he told *Vanity Fair,* who does not back down. Although Coates's own writing has attracted its share of hostility—especially for his published work on the case for Black reparations—he said he personally had never been subjected to racism and sexism at the level Hannah-Jones has had to endure. "Not even close," he said. Hannah-Jones expressed something similar

Nikole Hannah-Jones
(The New York Times/*Redux,*
photo by James Estrin)

when an expanded version of the 1619 enterprise came out in book form. To NBC, she said in 2021 that having to face constant attacks "not just on the work but on my credibility as a journalist" had made her a symbol. "And I think we would not be being honest if we didn't say me being a Black woman in particular, a Black woman who looks and presents the way that I do"—arrestingly colorful wardrobe, commanding bright red-orange hair—"that I didn't get a certain, extremely vicious type of pushback."

In the early fall of 2018 and again in the spring of 2019, before the COVID-19 shutdowns, Jessica Bennett staged the New Rules Summit, a gathering of a group of successful leaders across businesses to "explore some of the challenges faced by women in the workplace and how to bring about change." "The Old Rules of the Workplace Aren't Working. At Least Not for Women," a headline over one summary of the event's conclusions read. The number of woman chief executives of Fortune 500 companies was 5 percent, which was a quarter of a point lower than the count in the previous year. Census figures showed that white women needed to work four extra months each year to earn what white men earned and that women of color needed to work more hours than white women to meet that figure. Another study showed that 81 percent of women had experienced some form of sexual harassment.

Bennett and Chira staged a conversation the first year about how conditions had changed for woman journalists since Chira first went to work in 1981. They reflected on the testimony of Christine Blasey Ford during the U.S. Supreme Court nomination hearing of Brett Kavanaugh and how it echoed Anita Hill's more than a quarter of a century earlier. "It's important to remember how vilified women were for speaking out—how they were grilled, mocked, and dismissed,"

Chira said. "And I think many women drew the lesson that making accusations was futile, that much as in prosecutions of rape, women would be victimized twice over. We grew up not believing that we would be believed." Newsrooms, she said, were "notoriously raunchy and sexually charged places," so for her, given that history, it was simply remarkable that the #MeToo movement had brought so many men to account. Bennett spoke of how learning about what the women of *Newsweek* had endured in the 1960s helped her understand that the problem was more systemic than personal when she found herself passed over for promotions and interrupted in meetings, had her ideas stolen, or discovered how much less she earned than her colleagues who were men. Chira repeated what she had said when Jill Abramson became executive editor of the *Times* back in 2011, that she herself had been given opportunity, as were many women of her generation, but she had also watched the careers of others become "completely stymied."

Chira said that she and her peers underestimated how subtle the barriers were and had not thought systematically about finding ways to break through them. The focus for women of her generation always seemed to be on getting ahead personally, of putting their heads down, enduring whatever it took, and doing the work to get to the next rung but with no guarantee of advancement. This could be said of the generation of women before hers as well and the few woman executive editors of the 1980s and 1990s. "We wanted to be taken seriously," she said, "to have the chance to prove what we could do." Younger women still faced what her cohort faced, she said, for example, the danger of speaking out about errant men with the power to derail careers. "It still takes courage, and so many women still suffer the consequences," she said, "but now there are consequences for men." Chira said Bennett's generation—Bennett was born in 1982—had been inculcated with different cultural and educational signals; "1980s girl power" was Bennett's phrase. They were far more impatient and far less accepting than Chira's generation had been, and far better primed to recognize bias and to act more quickly to confront harassment or inequity when they encountered it. "What are the new rules for leadership?" Bennett asked Chira. Great leaders, Chira replied, see potential in people "who don't fit

the traditional mold and they actively question what they need to do
to create such a work force.... It means taking chances on women
just as we take chances on men."

Among the journalists present at the 2019 event was Susan Zirinsky, who had become the first woman president of CBS News.
Zirinsky expressed her commitment to taking the network "organi-
zationally and spiritually to a better place" after what at that point
had been three name-brand network firings for sexual misdeeds. In
the not quite two years before she stepped down, she put a much
more robust human resources team in place to listen, to make recommendations, and to act. Elisabeth Bumiller was especially proud that
her *Times* staff in Washington was 45 percent women and younger
and more diverse than ever before. Women, she said, held 70 percent of the bureau's editor slots. Maggie Haberman, the indefatigable
White House reporter, whose coverage of the Trump administration
had given her high visibility, said what kept her going was her belief
in the importance of what she was doing and the opportunity it gave
her to model possibility for her ten-year-old daughter. This was a
far cry from 1979 when, Stephen Engelberg recalled from his days in
the bureau, the total number of woman reporters was three. These
included the Supreme Court reporter, Linda Greenhouse, who was
"amazingly talented and really important in the industry and for
women in journalism," and Maggie Hunter, who covered Congress
and the White House while most other women in Washington journalism were assigned to report on the First Lady, as her obituary
pointed out. She died at seventy-eight in 2001.

In the first years of the 2020s, with the industry still in free fall, the
number of news workers of any gender or any ethnicity or race
employed anywhere across the industry was down 30 percent. Long-
established patterns suggested that the severity of the downturn had
allowed woman reporters and aspirants to leadership to shine more
brightly than they might have in better times. There was evidence in
the third of NYU's carefully selected "best" lists, this one the "Top
Ten Works of Journalism of the Decade," for the years from 2010
to 2019. It included reportage that interrogated aspects of the most
pressing, controversial issues of the period: race and the enduring

legacy of slavery; poverty and the global economy; the human toll of climate change; and the brutal impact of gender inequity, specifically the sexual abuse of women at the hands of more powerful men, a topic that in earlier days might have ended up buried on the women's pages if it made print at all. Women produced seven of the honored works, including those on these important themes. Three were the work of women who were also Black.

As expected, *The New York Times* named its managing editor, Joe Kahn, to succeed Dean Baquet, an appointment announced in the spring of 2022, supported by two new managing editors, Marc Lacey and Carolyn Ryan. The announcement story made a point of noting that Lacey was the third Black journalist to serve in the role and Ryan, a woman, was the first openly gay journalist in the newspaper's number two newsroom position.

And yet the larger societal issues for women did not recede. Four behavioral scientists writing in *Harvard Business Review* presented statistics showing that in all the world's media, news about women, half the population, appeared only a quarter of the time. Such gender imbalance reinforced and perpetuated harmful gender stereotypes, they wrote, adding, "It is clear that the media must change how it reflects the world—but who can change media?" Globally, online harassment of woman journalists grew dramatically worse. Some newsrooms added the position of "online safety editor."

At around the same time, the *Times* and other outlets began to de-emphasize their gender-specific initiatives. Bennett said the move represented the sense that gender issues had become sufficiently embedded in the work being produced by the various desks. Susan Chira left the *Times* to become editor in chief of the Marshall Project, a nonprofit focused on criminal justice. Bennett's job description at the *Times* changed from gender editor, to editor at large for gender issues, to opinion writer on gendered themes.

Since 2005, the Women's Media Center has served as the locus for status reports on the state of women in all U.S. media. Its most recent report available in 2022 offered a number of statistics worth celebrating in its more than one hundred snapshots of the state of play at various legacy, nonprofit, and digital for-profit media outlets.

At *The New York Times* in 2021, women as newsroom leaders outnumbered men in such positions, and the proportion of people of
color across departments was up 7 percent since 2015. At the same
time, however, a key finding in the company's own most recent report
showed the *Times* was "too often a difficult place to work for people
of all backgrounds—particularly colleagues of color and especially
Black and Latino colleagues. It calls for us to transform our culture." The percentages of women and people of color were often
up elsewhere, too, with women sometimes at parity or even in the
majority of the staff. Yet the center's more than 250-page report,
compiled from 109 studies, still showed women overall to be "sorely
lacking" in "all realms of media," from visibility to representation.
There were still too few women covering major stories, too few
women featured as experts and opinion leaders, and too few women
of diverse backgrounds involved in either way. "Media frames our
democratic debate and media interprets and amplifies our policies
and our politics," Julie Burton, the center's president and CEO, said
in a foreword. "Media tells us who has power and who matters."
Media, Burton said, was still sorely lacking.

In its "Toward Parity" conclusion, the center called for a redou-
bling of effort on the part of all media to be more inclusive, to do a
better job of covering those in underrepresented categories, to ensure the inclusion of persons of color and the gender nonconforming. It called for personnel audits, intentionality in staffing, regular
conversations to raise awareness of the need for gender and racial
parity, more mentorship, and more seriousness about work-life balance. To news organizations specifically, the center added the importance of diversifying the source lists for stories, avoiding biased
or coded language and imagery, establishing standards for defining
sexism, racism, and ageism, and ensuring that none of these creep
into the workplace. There was a call to pay more attention to comments from readers, viewers, and users. In short, the report sang the
now centuries-old women's refrain: progress, setback; push, pull.

The 19th*, an Austin-based "independent, nonprofit newsroom
reporting on gender, politics and policy," launched in the summer
of 2020 as the Nineteenth Amendment to the U.S. Constitution
turned one hundred. The site, 19thnews.org, initially announced as
its focus "the intersection of gender, politics and policy," with a deep

commitment to elevating the voices "of women who are underrepresented in and underserved by American media." These included women of color, women who do not live on the country's East or West Coast, and women of limited means. Margaret Sullivan pointed all of this out in a *Washington Post* column about the site a year after it launched.

The founders, Emily Ramshaw and Amanda Zamora, both late of *The Texas Tribune,* another Austin-based digital nonprofit and a very early online success story, quickly broadened the mission they initially announced. They acted in response to the global COVID-19 pandemic that descended just as they began, to the murders of Breonna Taylor and George Floyd, to the waves of racial protests that engulfed the country, to the violence triggered by the 2020 presidential election, and to the galvanizing of efforts in state legislatures across the country to restrict transgender rights.

In May 2022 during a "pretty seismic week" at the 19th*, word leaked out about the drafting by the justices of the U.S. Supreme Court of their decision soon after to overturn *Roe v. Wade,* the constitutional protection of the right to an abortion. Ramshaw pointed out that abortion is far more than a gender issue; the availability of such services "touches so many aspects of society—the economy, for one."

In our interview, she shared how the site was doing midway through its second year: beyond all expectations. There had been frequent placement of the site's reporting in dozens of other outlets as hoped, wide attendance at its events, a budget of $9 million in 2022, and fundraising to support it well in excess of the $5 million the leaders initially sought. The expected staff of twenty had become fifty, among them 65 percent women of color, 25 percent queer, and 19 percent living with disabilities, all encouraged "to bring their full-lived experience to the work," Ramshaw said, a counter to "this myth of objectivity that has been the white male gaze."

The 19th* is also well out front on staff benefits—six months fully paid family leave, four months of fully paid caregiving leave, full payment by the nonprofit of employee health-care premiums, additional mental health stipends, and seven weeks of annual paid time off from the moment an employee joins the staff. Other successful nonprofit newsrooms run by women, such as Carroll Bogert and Susan Chira at the Marshall Project and Elisabeth Rosenthal at Kaiser Health

News, also have staff compositions and benefit packages that exceed the industry standards, although none goes quite so far as the 19th*. "I hope," Ramshaw said, "that if nonprofit newsrooms like the three of ours can offer these types of benefits and these types of opportunities to their colleagues, the big dogs can play in that sandpit, too."

Ramshaw was adamant that the 19th*'s pivot to emphasize racial justice and the LGBTQ+ community as integral elements of its mission in no way had diluted the initial women-focused conception of its founders. "I feel in my bones that a rising tide lifts all boats," Ramshaw said, "and we at the 19th* want to avoid making the mistakes of so many exclusionary movements of the past. You can see it in our journey. We widened our mission in the first year to serve not just women but to serve the LGBTQ+ community. We reframed our mission statement from nonpartisan to independent," to make clear the site would not engage in "both-sides-ism." "We will always cover everyone without fear or favor," she explained, "but are not going to sit on the sidelines when it comes to gender equity or racial justice. I feel very strongly that we have an obligation in this moment to do a couple of things: to level the playing field for women of color and queer people in legacy media in a way that it simply has never happened before; to provide opportunities for people from all kinds of backgrounds to see themselves reflected in American media for the first time; and to create pathways to leadership for people who haven't had those opportunities by turning on its head the whole notion of what equitable pay looks like, what fair and generous benefits look like."

At the suggestion of Errin Haines, one of the site's "founding mothers," the team added an asterisk to the 19th*'s name as "a visible reminder of those who have been omitted from our democracy." She noted the offensive, marginalizing treatment of Black suffragists as the movement's white leaders tried vainly to curry favor for their movement with their steadfast political opponents in the South. The team also wanted to underscore the "unfinished business" of enforcing the Nineteenth Amendment's constitutional guarantee of the right of every citizen to vote without discrimination by sex.

The asterisk in the 19th* evoked another asterisk, the star that identified Margaret Fuller at the end of her columns in Horace Greeley's *New York Tribune*. The team at the 19th* was unaware of the perfect allusion they had created until it was pointed out. The unintended double meaning brought *Undaunted* full circle. It summoned the long unbroken line of remembered and forgotten American woman journalists of every description and the impact they have had over the past 180 years: their earliest efforts at righting the nation's wrongs; their formative investigative and immersion reporting with the power it demonstrated to induce response and reform; the development of the interview as a key journalistic method; the focus they put on the human toll in the world's internecine, binational, and global crises; and most of all, their significant, undisputable presence among the creators of the greatest, most affecting works of journalism of the late nineteenth, twentieth, and twenty-first centuries to date.

Women at the top of the field have influenced journalism's every aspect, including the widening of its topics, the more inclusive scope of coverage, and the modeling of employee benefits that come closer than ever before to meeting the needs of the people who do the work. Women of all descriptions have faced down and overcome all manner of impediment to become integral to this enterprise, including the barriers in thought and action they allowed to stand too long and those they created or perpetuated themselves. Through their example, their collective and personal effort, their performance, their breakthroughs, and the changes their presence and engagement have brought, women have proved to be essential to this vital, imperiled profession and to the never-finished effort to keep making it better.

ACKNOWLEDGMENTS

The idea for this book came from its editor, Jonathan Segal, a man I had never met. He cold-called me by email, writing that he was "keen to commission a history of women in American journalism" and wondered if I would be interested in discussing such a project. On the telephone, he explained more about what he had in mind; he had already thought it through. At lunch soon after, he told me that the idea was one of several he dreamed up and kept on Post-it notes until they lost their appeal. This one did not.

Since I began the work, his collaboration has been full and intense at every step. All the inadequacies in these pages are mine, but the effort he put into making this book better than it might otherwise have been was boundless, well beyond anything I have been fortunate enough to experience in five excellent prior outings. Jon's assistant, Sarah Perrin, did the crucial minutiae as the book made its way to publication. The skilled copy editor, Ingrid Sterner, and the Knopf production team of Nicole Pedersen and Peggy Samedi, left me in awe, as did the artistry of Emily Mahon, who created the book's striking jacket, and Betty Lew, who designed the book's beautiful interior. Kathryn Zuckerman and Ellen Whitaker ably brought the book to the public.

My debt to Nicholas Lemann is deep. He had a lot to do with why this project came my way and helped me get it going. I also need to single out my wonderful friend Alex Beam for his tough reading of the manuscript's way-way-too-long earliest draft. As always the sine qua non is Philippa Brophy and Jessica Friedman, too.

I have tapped many other minds for this project, not the least of whom are the hundreds of reporters, authors, and photographers cited in the text and notes. Among my journalism history and biography colleagues, special commendation goes to Maurine Beasley, Elizabeth Becker, David Blixt, Kathleen Brady, Diane Bragg, Jinx Broussard, Denise Dowling, Chris Dubbs, Carolyn Edy (deluxe), Michèle Midori Fillion, Teri Finneman, Jonathan Fitzgerald, Elisabeth Fondren, Kathy Roberts Forde, Allison Gilbert, Rachel Grant, Melissa Greene-Blye, Marilyn Greenwald, Donna Halper, Lori Harrison-Kahan, Nick Hirshon, Eliot King, Carolyn Kitch, Kevin Lerner, Tracy Lucht, Stephen Macek, Jane Marcellus, Megan Marshall, David Mindich, James McGrath Morris, Jennifer Moore, Ray Moseley, Bernardo Díaz Nosty, Candi Carter Olson, Ernest Perry, Erica Pribanic-Smith, Jane Rhodes, Lance Richardson, the late Keith Richwine, Ford Risley, Gene Roberts, Amber Roessner, Anne Sundberg Siess, Linda Steiner, Bob Stepno, Susan Swanberg, the late Mike Sweeney, Kim Todd, John Van Sickle, Kimberly Voss, Pamela E. Walck, Steve Weinberg, Rob Wells, and Ben Yagoda.

I drew just as indiscriminately on the incisiveness, wisdom, friendship, and support of my close NYU colleagues and friends: Mohamad Bazzi, Eliot Borenstein, Meredith Broussard, Rob Boynton, Ted Conover, David Dent, Frankie Edozien, Dan Fagin, Alexis Gelber, Meryl Gordon, Eliza Griswold, the late Pete Hamill, Perri Klass, Yvonne Latty, Tom Looser, Anne Lounsbery, James McBride, Pamela Newkirk, Adam Penenberg, Joe Peyronnin, Katie Roiphe, Jay Rosen, Andrea Rosenberg, Jason Samuels, Matthew Santirocco, Rose Sculley, Charles Seife, Stephen Solomon, Mitch Stephens, Rachel Swarns, Leslie Wayne, and Larry Wolff. As I moved toward retirement after twenty-two years at NYU, the sabbatical the university granted for the 2020–2021 academic year, my last one on the faculty, was crucial. I am also grateful to my classes of honors undergraduates and graduate students for filling my life with wonder and deepening my grasp of the shifts in cultural understandings and expressions their generation has championed. I miss you.

Others whom I have long counted as friends, or now would like to count as friends, gave of their memories, skills, resources, contacts, goodwill, and time, either as interviewees, as readers of passages, or as facilitators on the hunt for reliable information. The second half of the book would not exist without Jill Abramson, Dean Baquet, Felicity Barringer, Elizabeth Becker, Soma Golden Behr, Jessica Bennett, Ethan Bronner, Terri Brooks, Elisabeth Bumiller, Paula Butturini, Susan Chira, Ta-Nehisi

Coates, Ron Cohen, Gail Collins, Ann Cooper, Suzanne Daley, John Darnton, Nina Darnton, Mary Anne Dolan, Maureen Dowd, Claudia Dreifus, Susan Edgerley, Sonni Efron, Stephen Engelberg, Esther Fein, Sylvana Foa, Max Frankel, Michelle García, Gabrielle Glaser, Paul Goldberger, Ellen Goodman, Lindsey Gruson, Charlayne Hunter-Gault, David Jones, Charlie Kaiser, Jodi Kantor, Jon Katz, Frank Lalli, Carolyn Lee, Joe Lelyveld, Tamar Lewin, Grace Lichtenstein, Amy Littlefield, Jane Mayer, Marjorie Miller, Eileen Murphy, Nancy Newhouse, Michael Oreskes, Geneva Overholser, Claudia Payne, Jeff Perlman, Lynn Povich, Anna Quindlen, Emily Ramshaw, Gene Roberts, Elisabeth Rosenberg, Sandy Mims Rowe, Jim Rutenberg, Janny Scott, Lynn Sherr, David Shribman, Cindy Skrzycki, Margaret Sullivan, Arthur Sulzberger, Arthur Gregg Sulzberger, Phil Taubman, Cathy Booth Thomas, Calvin Trillin, and Steve Weisman. I also want to acknowledge John Burnham Schwartz, a passing acquaintance at a book party, who suggested I make relationships central to the book's structure.

The shutdown of libraries during the COVID pandemic put a particular burden on the research librarians whose resources I needed all the same. Special thanks go to the many libraries and collections named in the illustration credits. To those I add my deep gratitude to Jeff Roth, *The New York Times*'s archivist; Tony Dudek at the *Chicago Tribune;* Dana Canedy, when she was directing the Pulitzer Prizes; and Sean B. Murphy of the Pulitzer staff. At the New York Public Library, Meredith Mann in rare books and archives and Maurice Klapwald in reproductions were as wonderful to me as they have always been; as were Jane Parr at Boston University's Howard Gotlieb Archival Research Center; Robert Henning at the Rockpile Museum in Campbell County, Wyoming; Alison Mills at Bryn Mawr; David D'Onofrio at the U.S. Naval Academy; Gwendolyn Coddington at McDaniel College; Amy Rohmiller at the University of Dayton; Nicolás Cabrera at the Denver Public Library; Polly Cancro at the Morgan Library; Melanie Gilati at the United Nations; Carolyn Waters, director of the New York Society Library, and the librarian Barbara Bieck, who spent months with me combing twenty years of the library's pristine, full still-on-paper run of *Leslie's;* Jeanne Gutierrez at the New-York Historical Society; at the East Hampton Library, Andrea Meyer of the Long Island Collection, Deborah Donohue for Interlibrary Loan, and Dennis Fabiszak, director, who provided dozens of favors; Patricia Kranz of the Overseas Press Club; and at the New York Genealogical and Biographical

Society, Jen Davis and the director, Josh Taylor, who unraveled more than one genealogical mystery I could not crack. I am also especially grateful to the Martha Gellhorn Estate, which granted me access; to the Lee Miller Estate, which was generous with information; to Lucy A. Dalglish at the University of Maryland as publisher of the *Washington Journalism Review*; to Columbia University's Rare Book and Manuscript Library; and to the Washington Press Club Oral History Project and its oral historian Kathleen Currie, whose interviews proved invaluable.

Over these years, a number of research assistants did superb stints on this book's behalf: of my talented former students, chapeaux to Hannah Beckler and Holly Pickett over many months and to Stephen Groves, Cecilia Nowell, Emilia Otte, Aron Ouzilevski, and Ben Weiss. Andrea Rosenberg, NYU Journalism's finest asset, ably brought to the finish line the arduous permissions work on the images now in the book. I received additional assistance from Linda Hubbard and Randy Herschaft in tracking down photographers and high-resolution photos. While I work, I need totems. My daughter Brett Kroeger made and remade a giant chapter-by-chapter photo mural for me every time I replaced or added a picture, which was often. The mural supplanted the thirteen-foot-long timeline on which I plotted the lifespans of the hundreds of woman journalists I initially considered for inclusion against the most significant events of their respective eras. Ellen Collins stepped in for a whip-smart call-and-response marathon as we tamed the unruly endnotes. Special mention goes to three emerging researchers: my grandson Jacoby Weiner and Hampus Vanderberg, who put in a hard day's work at a critical early juncture, and Jocelyn Jarro, who, in the dust storm of a renovation, translocated the hundreds of books and files on paper I amassed for this project after the unexpected move from one house to another. It took place on a few weeks' notice midstream.

The support, insights, and challenges from my smart, knowledgeable, long-serving friends thread through these pages. Sweet care in these strange years came from Marilynn Abrams, Patricia and Alan Abramson, Susan and Ahmed Akkad, Anda Andrei, Geraldine Baum (deluxe), Alex Beam, Slava Bednarz, Marsha Bilzin, Flip Brophy, Sarah Challinor, Ellen and Chuck Collins, Ann Cooper, Sue and Rick Davies, Gioia Diliberto, Claudia Dreifus, Dennis Ferrando, Sylvana Foa, William Ghitis, Carolyn Logan Gluck, Susan Tarrance and Stephen Golden, Gail Gregg, Elizabeth Harlan, Jamie Meltzer and James Kayler, Kirsten Lundberg, Ilene

Mandell, James McBride, Malka Margolies, Nancy and John McGuirk, Bernadette Murray (deluxe), Patricia O'Toole, Gail and Roy Parker, Ricki Peltzman, Marsha Pinson, Rachel Pinson, Lynn Povich, Savine and Luke Pontifell, Lance Richardson (deluxe and deserving of the double listing), Sheila Rogers, Elisabeth Rosenthal, Amy Levin Schaeffer, Lauren Schwartz, Janny Scott, Lynn Sherr, Patti Silver, Alison Smale, Dinitia Smith, Paula Span (deluxe), Anne Thomas, Suzanne Thompson, Monica Torres, Adam Vine, David Vine (deluxe), Steve Wasserman, and Franny and Dick Zorn.

There are not enough appreciative things to say about my family, especially the love and support they have shown since Alex's unexpected death in his sleep on February 23, 2021. Alex made this book and every other book of mine possible, not only because he shopped and cooked in ways that enchanted, not only because he provided the enviable environments in which I've been privileged to be able to work, not only for a love supreme, but because he never balked at listening whenever I needed to read aloud, which was often, sometimes as much as ten thousand words at a time. My mother, gone now a decade, was always willing to do the same. That was luck. I've been fortunate to have had the solicitous and loving support of our children, Brett Kroeger and Josh Weiner, Bettina Bosé and Andrea Goren, and Selina and Ari Komeran; my brother Randy Weinstein; my sisters-in-law Ellen Walterscheid, Viviana Kasam, and Micaela Monti; and my brother- and sister-in-law James and Manuela Goren. Ellen, Vivi, and my niece Arielle Goren did double duty as editorially astute friends. There will never be the right words to honor the care that came in continuous flow from Anda Andrei and Billy Ghitis or to say how much it meant, especially in the hardest days. Add to them so many of my friends noted above whose names are showing up for the sixth time in thirty years in a group like this one. Had there been occasions for such compilations before I could put them in books, they would have been on those lists, too.

NOTES AND SOURCES

ABBREVIATIONS

AJR American Journalism Review

AP Associated Press

ASNE American Society of Newspaper Editors

CJR Columbia Journalism Review

KC Kansas City

LA Los Angeles

LAT Los Angeles Times

NANA North American Newspaper Alliance

NY New York

NYT New York Times

SF San Francisco

UP United Press

UPI United Press International

WP Washington Post

WSJ Wall Street Journal

Chapter 1. The Asterisk

3 Nursing became another: S. J. Kleinberg, *Women in the United States, 1830–1945* (New Brunswick, N.J.: Rutgers University Press, 1999), 105. See also U.S. Government, *Population Comparative Occupation Statistics, 1870–1940* (Washington, D.C.: U.S. Government Printing Office, 1943), 14; Claudia

Goldin and Kenneth Sokoloff, "Women, Children, and Industrialization in the Early Republic: Evidence from the Manufacturing Censuses," *Journal of Economic History* 42, no. 4 (Dec. 1982): 741–74; Nancy Folbre and Marjorie Abel, "Women's Work and Women's Households: Gender Bias in the U.S. Census," *Social Research* 56, no. 3 (Autumn 1989): 545–69.

4 Cornelia Walter's opportunity: Walter, before she turned thirty, quietly promoted herself from theater critic to editor in chief of the *Boston Transcript* to replace her brother, Lynde Walter, in 1842. As his secretary, she stood in for him during his long illness and then assumed his position when he died, matching his salary at $500 a year. See also *NY Tribune,* Sept. 2, 1842; *NY Herald,* Sept. 2, 1842; Ishbel Ross, *Ladies of the Press: The Story of Women in Journalism by an Insider* (New York: Harper & Brothers, 1936), 481–82; Edgar Allan Poe, *Broadway Journal,* Nov. 1, 1845; *Baltimore Sun,* Sept. 3, 1847; "Personal," *NY Tribune,* Feb. 4, 1898; "Poe Wrote of Her," *Burlington Free Press,* March 4, 1898; "Literary Notes," *Outlook,* Feb. 19, 1898.

5 "the most powerful of any American mind": Fuller to Elizabeth Palmer Peabody, Groton, Feb. 3, 1836, in Robert N. Hudspeth, ed., *Letters of Margaret Fuller* (Ithaca, N.Y.: Cornell University Press, 1983), 1:210, and Fuller to Peabody, Groton, Feb. 3, 1836, in Mary Van Wyck Church, "Biography of Elizabeth Palmer Peabody," MS, 298, Massachusetts Historical Society, as cited in Megan Marshall, *Margaret Fuller: A New American Life* (Boston: First Mariner Books, 2013), 85.

5 His death left: Fuller's formal education began at the Port School in Cambridgeport in 1819, then the Boston Lyceum for Young Ladies from 1821 to 1822, and in 1824 at the School for Young Ladies in Groton.

5 "bright and ugly": Margaret Fuller Journal, ca. early March 1834, box A, Margaret Fuller Manuscripts and Works, Houghton Library, Harvard, quoted in Charles Capper, *Margaret Fuller: An American Romantic Life: The Private Years* (New York: Oxford University Press, 1992), 1:61.

6 "mentally, the best": Horace Greeley, *Recollections of a Busy Life* (New York: J. B. Ford, 1868), 171.

6 "The men thought": Ralph Waldo Emerson, "Visits to Concord," in *Margaret Fuller Ossoli, Memoirs of Margaret Fuller Ossoli,* ed. Ralph Waldo Emerson, James Freeman Clark, and W. H. Channing (Amazon Digital, 2008), 1:199.

6 Nathaniel Hawthorne: See, generally, Thomas R. Mitchell, "Nathaniel Hawthorne and Margaret Fuller," in *Margaret Fuller's Cultural Critique: Her Age and Legacy,* ed. Fritz Fleischmann (New York: Peter Lang, 2000), 3:109–20.

6 "a little diplomatizing": Emerson, "Visits to Concord," 199.

6 "a soaring Transcendentalist": Julia Ward Howe, *Margaret Fuller (Marchesa Ossoli)* (Boston: Roberts Brothers, 1883), 186.

7 "trick of incessantly": Emerson, "Visits to Concord," 199.

7 "the life of thought": Fuller to [Sophia Ripley?], Aug. 27, 1839, in Hudspeth, *Letters of Margaret Fuller,* 2:87.

7 Child had been: Nancy Craig Simmons, "Margaret Fuller's Boston Conversations: The 1839–1840 Series," *Studies in the American Renaissance* (1994): 201.

7 "a new stimulus": Fuller to Susan Prescott, July 11, 1825, in Hudspeth, *Letters of Margaret Fuller,* 1:151, as cited in Carolyn L. Karcher, "Margaret Fuller and Lydia Maria Child: Intersecting Careers, Reciprocal Influences," in Fleischmann, *Margaret Fuller's Cultural Critique,* 3:75–88. See also Edgar A. Poe, "The Literati of New York—No. V, Some Honest Opinions at Random Respecting Their Authorial Merits, with Occasional Words of Personality," *Godey's Lady's Book,* Sept. 1846.

7 When Fuller was sixteen: Hudspeth, *Letters of Margaret Fuller,* 1:54, as cited in Karcher, "Margaret Fuller and Lydia Maria Child," 75–88. De Staël died in 1817 when Child was in her teens and Fuller, seven.

7 "first woman": Greeley, *Recollections,* 174; "Works of Mrs. Child," *North American Review,* July 1, 1833.

7 Child in time: Lydia Maria Child, *The Biographies of Madame de Staël and Madame Roland* (Boston: Carte and Hendee, 1832).

8 The wide distribution: Bill Daley, "Lydia Maria Child's 'Frugal Housewife' the Must-Read Book of Its Day," *Chicago Tribune,* July 14, 2015; "Foreign Literary Gossip," *New-Yorker,* Dec. 29, 1838. The thirty-second U.S. edition, published in New York in 1850, is marked "enlarged and corrected by the author."

8 *An Appeal in Favor:* Lydia Maria Child, preface to *An Appeal in Favor of That Class of Americans Called Africans* (Boston: Allen and Ticknor, 1833). See also Carolyn L. Karcher, *First Woman in the Republic: A Cultural Biography of Lydia Maria Child* (Durham, N.C.: Duke University Press, 1994), 182–93.

8 "I am fully aware": Child, preface to *Appeal in Favor.* For fuller treatment, see Karcher, *First Woman in the Republic,* 182–93.

8 Sales slowed: Karcher, *First Woman in the Republic,* 148.

8 A month before: "Works of Mrs. Child," *North American Review,* July 1833.

9 *An Appeal,* the magazine: "Art. VIII.—*Slavery. An Appeal in Favor of That Class of Americans Called Africans. By Mrs. Child, Author of the Mother's Book, &c., &c.,* Boston. 1831 [*sic*]," *North American Review,* July 1, 1835.

9 "cannot, ought not": "Candor," *Literary Journal, and Weekly Register of Science and the Arts,* Oct. 12, 1833.

9 As she became more deeply: See, for example, "Mrs. Child's New Work,"

Liberator, Sept. 7, 1833; *Abolitionist,* Sept. 1833; *Colonizationist and Journal of Freedom,* Oct. 1833.

9 "first woman": [William Lloyd Garrison], "Mrs. Child," *Genius of Universal Emancipation,* Nov. 20, 1829, cited in Karcher, *First Woman of the Republic,* 617n1.

9 When Fuller was compared: Charles Capper, *Margaret Fuller: An American Romantic Life: The Private Years* (New York: Oxford University Press, 1992), 1:319; Greeley, *Recollections,* 174.

9 "urgent assault": Emerson, "Visits to Concord," 199.

9 "We like her": Dolores Bird Carpenter, *Selected Letters of Lidian Jackson Emerson* (Columbia: Missouri University Press, 1987), 49.

9 "never confounded relations": Emerson, "Visits to Concord," 211; Emerson, A. W. Plumstead, and William Henry Gilman, *The Journals and Miscellaneous Notebooks of Ralph Waldo Emerson: 1848–1851* (Cambridge: Belknap Press of Harvard University Press, 1975), 2:495.

10 "literature, philosophy, and religion": Joel Porte and Saundra Morris, eds., *Emerson's Prose and Poetry* (New York: W. W. Norton, 2001), 549.

10 "vivacious friend": Emerson to Thomas Carlyle, March 18, 1840, cited in Ossoli, *Memoirs,* 1:151.

10 annual salary of $200: Greeley, *Recollections,* 169–70.

10 Neither Fuller nor Child: See, generally, Linda S. Hudson, *Mistress of Manifest Destiny: A Biography of Jane McManus Storm Cazneau, 1807–1878* (Austin: Texas State Historical Association, 2001). Jane Cazneau, born in upstate New York near Albany, was also a congressman's daughter. She was three years older than Fuller, studied at a women's college, married at eighteen, had a son at nineteen, and separated from the husband at twenty-four. She made the newspapers the following year as a named correspondent in Eliza Jumel's divorce proceedings against the former vice president Aaron Burr, a much older friend of the family who, in 1832, was involved in her failed Texas land dealings. Of her early published stories, see, for example, "Josephine" [Jane McManus Storms Cazneau], "Maria Christina of Spain," *New-Yorker,* Dec. 3, 1840; "The Book of Mormon," *New-Yorker,* Dec. 12, 1840; "Female Sovereigns," *New-Yorker,* Dec. 19, 1840, and Dec. 26, 1840; Horace Greeley, "To Our Friends," *New-Yorker,* March 13, 1841. Headlined "Letters from the Mediterranean by an American Lady," thirteen of the fifteen appeared on the following dates in 1841: April 17, April 24, May 1, May 8, May 15, May 22, May 29, June 5, July 17, July 24, July 3, Aug. 7, Sept. 11; Unsigned via the *Charleston Standard,* "[Cora] Montgomery," *Cleveland Plain Dealer,* April 6, 1954; [Cazneau], "Woman in the Nineteenth Century," *NY Sun,* July 29, 1845; Fuller to James Nathan, June 12, 1845, in Hudspeth, *Letters*

of Margaret Fuller, 4:116–19n, cited in Hudson, *Mistress of Manifest Destiny,* 69; Caroline Sawyer to Mirabeau B. Lamar, as cited in Philip Graham, *The Life and Poems of Mirabeau B. Lamar* (Chapel Hill: University of North Carolina Press, 1938), 71.

10 "manna in the wilderness": Greeley, *Recollections,* 170. For more mocking critiques of the publication, see, for example, "From the NY Evening Signal," *Buffalo Commercial Advertiser and Journal,* Aug. 7, 1840; "The Dial," *Boston Quarterly,* Jan. 1841, 131–32; "The Dial-Number Two for October," *Boston Post,* Oct. 12, 1840.

11 "these two rarest": Greeley, *Recollections,* 169.

11 He operated: Charles Capper, *Margaret Fuller: An American Romantic Life: The Public Years* (New York: Oxford University Press, 2010), 2:570n3–4.

11 The solo entrepreneurial: Royall's itinerant work included her 1826 "Sketches of History, Life, and Manners in the United States by a Traveler," her 1830 "Letters from Alabama," and "Mrs. Royall's Southern Tour" of 1830–31. See Maurine Beasley, "Anne Royall, Huntress with a Quill," *Quill* 78, no. 4 (May 1990); findagrave.com.

11 As editor, she preferred: Liz Watts, "Lydia Maria Child, Editor of the *National Anti-Slavery Standard,* 1841–1843," *Journalism History* 35, no. 1 (Spring 2009): 12–22.

12 *The Dial* published: Lydia Maria Child, *Letters from New York* (New York: Charles S. Francis, 1843). See also Edwin G. Burrows and Mike Wallace, *Gotham: A History of New York City to 1898* (Oxford: Oxford University Press, 2000), 678.

12 *The Dial* reviewed it: [Margaret Fuller], "Critical Notices: Letters from New York. By L. M. Child," *Dial,* Jan. 1844.

12 The book, which Child: Karcher, *First Woman of the Republic,* 309, 689n42.

12 "The Great Lawsuit": Margaret Fuller, "The Great Lawsuit: Man Versus Men. Woman Versus Women," *Dial,* July 1834; Paula Blanchard, *Margaret Fuller: From Transcendentalism to Revolution* (New York: Dell, 1978), 160–62, citing "Great Lawsuit."

12 "the only woman in America": "Woman—Her Sphere and Needs, from *The Dial* for July," *NY Tribune,* July 14, 1844.

13 Most of Fuller's friends: Quoted in Joan Von Mehren, *Minerva and the Muse: A Life of Margaret Fuller* (Amherst: University of Massachusetts Press, 1994), 215.

13 The salary: Capper, *Margaret Fuller,* 2:197, citing Ann W. Weston to Caroline and Debra Weston, [Jan.] 24 and 27, 1845, Weston Papers, Department of Rare Books and Manuscripts, Boston Public Library.

13 "produce something excellent": Letter, undated to unknown recipient [1845], in Hudspeth, *Letters of Margaret Fuller,* 4:39.

14 Fishkill was close: Fuller's friend was Georgina Bruce, Eliza Farnham's assistant.

14 Her observations: Margaret Fuller, *Woman in the Nineteenth Century* (New York: Greeley & McElrath, 1845), 132–33, 153.

14 "entirely charming": Fuller to Emerson, Nov. 17, 1844, in Hudspeth, *Letters of Margaret Fuller,* 3:243, 250.

14 Her first *Tribune* column: Fuller, *NY Tribune,* Dec. 1, 7, 11, 12, 16, 1844.

14 *Letters from New York: NY Tribune,* Dec. 20, 1844.

14 Two days later: L. Maria Child, "Kindness to Criminals: The Prison Association," *NY Tribune,* Dec. 20, 1844; L. Maria Child, "Letter XXIX: The Prison Association," *Boston Courier,* Dec. 8, 1844, in *Letters from New York* (New York: C. S. Francis, 1845), 2:258–71.

15 "Now is the time": Fuller to Channing, Dec. 31, 1843, in Hudspeth, *Letters of Margaret Fuller,* 3:258–59.

15 "I have always felt": Fuller to Mary Rotch, Jan. 1, 1845, in Hudspeth, *Letters of Margaret Fuller,* 4:45.

15 Despite all the things: Full version is in Ossoli, *Memoirs,* 2:154; shorter version without this in Greeley, *Recollections,* 177.

15 To Greeley, Fuller became: Ossoli, *Memoirs,* 2:158; Margaret Fuller to Eugene Fuller, March 8, 1845, in Hudspeth, *Letters of Margaret Fuller,* 4:56.

15 Fuller's first reporting: [Margaret Fuller], "Our City's Charities, Etc.," *NY Tribune,* March 19, 1845. See also Fuller to James Nathan, June 24, 1845, in Hudspeth, *Letters of Margaret Fuller,* 4:121; [Margaret Fuller], "Prevalent Idea That Politeness Is Too Great a Luxury to Be Given to the Poor," *NY Tribune,* March 31, 1845; "Asylum for Discharged Female Convicts," *NY Tribune,* June 19, 1845.

16 Both Child and Charles Dickens: See Charles Dickens, *Notes on America* (New York: Harper & Brothers, 1842), 37, where he mislocates the island, and Child, "Letter XXIX," Oct. 6, 1842, in *Letters from New York,* 1:210–224. This combines letters that appeared in the Oct. 6 and Oct. 13, 1842, issues of the *National Anti-Slavery Standard.* The city began developing the island with the penitentiary in 1832, adding the asylum in 1839 and the other facilities thereafter, so even their reports might not have been the earliest.

16 "I doubt": Greeley, *Recollections,* 180.

16 Child and Fuller: Fuller followed up the advance notice she had already given to the second volume of *Letters from New York* before it was released with another name-check for Child. Fuller put the re-release of Child's *Philothea: A Grecian Romance* at the top of the *Tribune*'s "New Publications" column of May 26, 1845. Three months earlier, Child preempted all other reviewers with enthusiastic critiques of *Woman in the Nineteenth*

Century. These ran in three influential outlets: Edgar Allan Poe's *Broadway Journal,* the *Boston Courier,* and Greeley's *Tribune,* where, as if in homage, Child signed herself not as Mrs. D. L. Child, or Lydia Maria Child or L. Maria Child, or Mrs. Child, as she variously appeared, but *Dial-,* not *Tribune-,* style, obscuring her identity with a lone initial "C." See Lydia Maria Child, "Reviews: *Woman in the Nineteenth Century,*" *Broadway Journal,* Feb. 15, 1845; unsigned, "New Publications," *NY Tribune,* May 26, 1845; "C." [Lydia Maria Child], "Woman in the Nineteenth Century," *NY Tribune,* Feb. 13, 1845.

16 Child reviewed: For fuller treatment of the Child and Grimké books, see Karcher, *First Woman in the Republic,* 225–26.

16 "Is love a mockery": Child, "Reviews: *Woman in the Nineteenth Century.*"

17 Edgar Allan Poe's: Charles Frederick Briggs, "Review: *Woman in the Nineteenth Century,*" *Broadway Journal,* March 1, 1845.

17 Other reviews: *Charleston Mercury,* March 11, 1845.

17 Poe himself weighed in: Edgar A. Poe, "The Literati of New York City—No. IV," *Godey's Lady's Book,* Aug. 1846.

17 Among those he included: See Poe, "The Literati," *Godey's Lady's Book,* May–Oct. 1846.

17 Poe was quick to disavow: Poe, "The Literati," "Sarah Margaret Fuller," *Godey's Lady's Book,* Aug. 1846.

17 Greeley, while aware: Greeley, *Recollections,* 175.

17 The book remains: S. M. Fuller, *Summer on the Lakes* (New York: Charles S. Francis, 1843); Margaret Fuller, *Papers on Literature and Art* (New York: Wiley and Putnam, 1846).

17 "This year, which declares": Fuller, "Fourth of July," *NY Tribune,* July 4, 1845, as cited in Leslie Elizabeth Eckel, *Atlantic Citizens: Nineteenth-Century American Writers at Work in the World* (Edinburgh: Edinburgh University Press, 2013), 55–56.

18 "magnetic sway": Greeley, *Recollections,* 179.

18 "modified": Ibid., 191.

18 an asterisk, a "star": Fuller to Caroline Sturgis, in Hudspeth, *Letters of Margaret Fuller,* 4:59.

18 One scholar: Larry J. Reynolds, *European Revolutions and the American Literary Renaissance* (New Haven, Conn.: Yale University Press, 1988), 57.

18 poetry of Walt Whitman: Walter Whitman, "Resurgemus," *NY Tribune,* June 21, 1850; Walt Whitman, "Poem of the Dead Young Men of Europe, the 72d and 73d Years of These States," in *Leaves of Grass* (Brooklyn: Fowler & Wells, 1856), 252–54. See also Reynolds, *European Revolutions and the American Literary Renaissance,* 62–78, 137–39.

19 Jane Cazneau has been relegated: From the published record, Jane

Cazneau's reporting from the Mexican-American War was an eyelash ahead of Fuller's from the revolution in Italy. See Cora Montgomery, *The Eagle Pass; or, Life on the Border* (New York: George P. Putnam, 1852). See also, via the *Charleston Standard,* "Cora Montgomery," *Cleveland Plain Dealer,* April 6, 1954. See also "Cora Montgomery," *Western Literary Messenger,* May 1854. See also Megan Jenison Griffin, "Partisan Rhetorics: American Women's Responses to the US-Mexico War, 1846–1848" (PhD diss., Texas Christian University, 2010); Tom Reilly, "Jane McManus Storms: Letters from the Mexican War, 1846–1848," *Southwestern Historical Quarterly* 85, no. 1 (July 1981): 21–44. Author cites Cora Montgomery bylines in the *NY Sun,* Dec. 12, 17, 18, 23, 24, 1845, and April 3, 4, June 4, 13, 1846. About Cuba: *NY Sun,* Jan. 12, 16, 25, 30, Feb. 8, and March 17, 25, 26, 1847. About Mexico: *NY Sun,* Feb. 12, April 15, 16, 19, 24, 28, 30, May 3, 6, 7, 14, 21, 22, 24, 1847. And for the *NY Tribune:* Jan. 14, 18, April 20, 30, 1847; *Public Ledger,* April 22, 1847.

19 "In fifty years": Rufus Wilmot Griswold, *The Prose Writers of America with Portraits from Original Pictures* (London: Richard Bentley, 1847), 44–45.

19 In January 1848: "Social Tendencies of the Press &tc," *Harbinger,* Jan. 14, 1848.

19 "the first woman in America": Capper, preface to *Margaret Fuller,* vol. 1.

20 As the ship approached: "The Wreck of the Elizabeth," *NY Tribune,* July 23, 1850. Greeley sent Bayard Taylor to the scene.

20 "lose no time": "Death of Margaret Fuller," *NY Tribune,* July 23, 1850.

20 "the loftiest, bravest": Greeley, *Recollections,* 191.

20 "No event has occurred": "Margaret Fuller Ossoli," *NY Tribune* via the *Southern Literary Messenger,* Sept. 4, 1850.

20 Fuller's last published piece: "Annexation," *United States Magazine and Democratic Review,* July–Aug. 1845. Sometimes the term "manifest destiny" is attributed to the editor John O'Sullivan.

20 Fuller's piece: [Margaret Fuller], "Recollections of the Vatican," *United States Magazine and Democratic Review,* July 1850; "Obituary," *United States Magazine and Democratic Review,* Aug. 1850.

20 When Child died: "Lydia Maria Child," *Boston Globe,* Oct. 21, 1880; *NYT,* Oct. 21, 1880.

21 Cazneau, by coincidence: "List of All on Board," *NY Tribune,* Dec. 28, 1878. Cazneau is listed among the passengers of the *Emily B. Souder,* which ran aground and sank after it sailed from Santo Domingo and Turks Island on Dec. 8, 1878. Although she met a fate similar to Fuller's twenty-eight years later, notice of her death was modest.

21 Cazneau had as her advocate: Robert E. May, "Cazneau, Jane Maria Eliza McManus," *Handbook of Texas Online,* Texas State Historical Association.

21 In Fuller's case: "Melancholy Shipwreck," *Newport Daily News,* July 24, 1850.

21 In February 1852: Marshall, *Margaret Fuller,* 379–90.

21 Reviews were mixed: "Reviews: Memoirs of Margaret Fuller Ossoli," *Athenaeum,* Feb. 7, 1852; "Review of Memoirs of Margaret Fuller Ossoli," *Prospective Review* 8 (1852): 199–218, and "Vanity Versus Philosophy: Margaret Fuller Ossoli," *United States Magazine and Democratic Review,* June 1852, both as cited in Thomas R. Mitchell, *Hawthorne's Fuller Mystery* (Amherst: University of Massachusetts Press, 1998), 5.

22 Nevertheless, the book sold: *NY Home Journal,* March 3, 1852, as cited in Joel Myerson, *Margaret Fuller: A Descriptive Bibliography* (Pittsburgh: University of Pittsburgh Press, 1978), 39.

22 "How can you": Ralph Waldo Emerson, *The Journals and Miscellaneous Notebooks,* ed. A. W. Plumstead, William H. Gilman, and Ruth H. Bennett (Cambridge, Mass.: Belknap Press of Harvard University Press, 1975), 11:488, as cited in Christina Zwarg, "Emerson as 'Mythologist' in *Memoirs of Margaret Fuller Ossoli,*" *Criticism* 31, no. 3 (Summer 1989): 216–17.

22 2014 Pulitzer Prize: "The 2014 Pulitzer Prize Winner in Biography," pulitzer.org.

Chapter 2. The She Lot

23 By 1879, Washington: Maurine Hoffman Beasley, *Women of the Washington Press: Politics, Prejudice, and Persistence* (Evanston, Ill.: Northwestern University Press, 2012), 13; Beasley, "Mary Clemmer Ames: A Victorian Woman Journalist," *Hayes Historical Journal* 2, no. 1 (Spring 1978).

23 Their bylines: Burrows and Wallace, *Gotham,* 678.

24 most read book: Joan D. Hedrick, *Harriet Beecher Stowe: A Life* (New York: Oxford University Press, 1994), 208, 222–23.

24 Greenwood likened Stowe: Greenwood to Bailey, Sept. 22, 1851, reprinted in *National Era,* Feb. 23, 1854, as cited in Eckel, *Atlantic Citizens,* 130.

24 *The Daily Telegraph:* "Alas!," *National Era,* Nov. 29, 1849.

24 Without having seen: "Godey's Lady's Book," *National Era,* Dec. 27, 1849.

24 Greenwood was soon: However, Greenwood's last piece for *Godey's* appeared amid the controversy: "Philip Hamilton and His Mother," *Godey's Lady's Book,* Jan. 1850.

24 Even the mainstream *Independent:* "A Man in the Market," *Independent,* Feb. 21, 1850. Greenwood thought she was on the February cover of *Godey's,* although she wasn't, and sent around word, in case anyone was in doubt, that she had severed all connections to the publication. See "Godey's Lady's Book," *National Era,* Feb. 7, 1850, and previously, "Godey's Lady's Book," Dec. 27, 1849.

25 The publicity: See Charles D. Cleveland, *A Compendium of American Literature, Chronologically Arranged with Biographical Sketches of the Authors and Selections of Their Works* (Philadelphia: Parry & McMillan, 1859), 427.

25 *The National Era* republished: "Godey's Lady's Book," *National Era,* Dec. 27, 1849.

25 Reviews might have been: For example, "Greenwood Leaves," *Home Journal,* Dec. 22, 1849; "Greenwood Leaves," *Pittsburgh Post,* June 5, 1850.

25 "a sincere, genial": "Literary Notices," *Harper's Magazine,* Jan. 1852.

25 Greenwood's signature style: In all, in book form, there were twelve collections of her articles. See, for example, "Letters from" Europe in 1852: "Grace Greenwood," *NYT,* Sept. 7, 1852; "Ireland," *NYT* via *National Era,* Oct. 12, 1852; "The Home of Burns," *NYT* via *National Era,* Nov. 6, 1852.

25 fifteen daily papers: "Journalism in New York," *American Whig Review,* Nov. 1851.

25 of the thousand talented writers: Greeley to H. Hubbard, April 12, 1844, and June 30, 1845, and Greeley to Worthington C. Ford, Sept. 1870, Horace Greeley Papers, NY Public Library, as cited in Andie Tucher, *Froth & Scum: Truth, Beauty, Goodness, and the Ax Murder in America's First Mass Medium* (Chapel Hill: University of North Carolina, 1994), 134, 228n9.

25 Throughout the 1850s: See, for example, William Cullen Bryant, "Reminiscences of the New York Evening Post," *Littell's Living Age,* Feb. 7, 1852; "The Press in the Nineteenth Century," *Eclectic Magazine of Foreign Literature,* March 1853; "Horace Greeley," *Putnam's,* July 1855; "An Interesting Book: Memoirs of James Gordon Bennett," *Home Journal,* July 28, 1855; "The Profession of Journalism," *Albion,* Jan. 29, 1859; Hon. F. P. Stanton, "The Press in the United States," *Continental Monthly,* Nov. 1862.

26 Like their most able predecessors: Charles Wingate, *Views and Interviews on Journalism* (New York: F. B. Patterson, 1875), 147.

26 Census figures for 1860: Stanton, "The Press in the United States."

26 the "She lot": "The Liberty of the Press," *Vanity Fair,* June 20, 1863.

26 "doom me to gossip": "M.C.A." [Mary Clemmer Ames], "Washington Through New Spectacles," *Springfield Republican,* Jan. 11, 1862, also cited in Mark Wahlgren Summers, *The Press Gang: Newspapers and Politics, 1865–1978* (Chapel Hill: University of North Carolina, 1994), 138.

27 "The rebel batteries": M.C.A., "The Battle of Harper's Ferry as a Woman Saw It," *NY Evening Post,* Oct. 15, 1862.

28 "The Battle of Harper's Ferry": See, for example, "The Battle of Harper's Ferry as a Woman Saw It," *Daily Alta* (Calif.), Oct. 27, 1862; *Sacramento Daily Union,* Oct. 21, 1862; *Times-Picayune,* Nov. 9, 1862. Scholars report no other Civil War battlefield accounts by woman writers, although recognition is due to "Sarah, Lizzie, and Lida," Sarah Steer and the Dutton

sisters, three twentysomething Quaker "maidens," who, in 1864 and 1865, published eight issues of their pro-Union underground *Waterford News* from well inside rebel territory, also in Loudon County, Virginia.

28 "Women's Right to Labor": M.C.A.,"Women's Right to Labor," *Independent*, March 24, 1864.

28 Clemmer spent some time: See Beasley, "Mary Clemmer Ames."

29 Bowen was paying her: "Personal," *Harper's Bazaar*, Feb. 25, 1871; Beasley, *Women of the Washington Press*, 13; Beasley, "Mary Clemmer Ames."

29 "Dear Sirs": Mary Abigail Dodge [Gail Hamilton] to editor, responding to request for terms, Jan. 14, 1887, in Gail Hamilton, *Gail Hamilton's Life in Letters*, ed. Hannah August Dodge (Boston: Lee and Shepard, 1901), 2:885; Mary Abigail Dodge to ?, letter fragment, Sept. 1895, in ibid., 1065.

29 Over the years, gossipy: For example, "Mary Clemmer Is Dead," *WP*, Aug. 24, 1884; "Grace Greenwood Dead," *NYT*, April 21, 1904; "Gail Hamilton Passes Away," *SF Chronicle*, Aug. 18, 1896.

30 "Quick read": Mary Clemmer, "The Journalist," in *Poems of Life and Nature* (Boston: James R. Osgood, 1883), 137–41.

30 "quick to take advantage": William Wells Brown, *The Rising Son; or, The Antecedents and Advancement of the Colored Race* (Boston: A. G. Brown, 1882), 539–40. See also Jane Rhodes, *Mary Ann Shadd Cary* (Bloomington: Indiana University Press, 1999).

30 Reprints of Swisshelm's: For example, *Charleston Mercury*, Nov. 20, 1849; *Boston Herald*, Oct. 24, 1849; "Fashion Plates," *Detroit Free Press*, Oct. 11, 1849; "On Bathing and Kissing," *New Orleans Picayune*, Sept. 6, 1849; "Letter to Country Girls," *Edgefield (S.C.) Advertiser*, May 13, 1849; "Plain Talk," *Baltimore Sun*, Aug. 8, 1849.

30 "Mrs. Swisshelm's Letter": Fuller's final column for the *Tribune*: "European Affairs Discussed by Our Correspondent," *NY Tribune*, Feb. 13, 1850.

30 Cary was an important: With thanks to two professors, the Civil War journalism historian Ford Risley and Cary's biographer, Jane Rhodes. Ford Risley, email exchange with author, Feb. 18, 2022; Jane Rhodes, email exchange with author, May 25, 2022.

30 "tart and spicy": *Pittsburg Post*, April 23, 1850.

30 "social distinction": Jane Grey Swisshelm, *Half a Century* (Chicago: Jansen, McClurg, 1880), 131.

30 That stopped abruptly: Jane Grey Swisshelm, "Mrs. Swisshelm's Estimate of Daniel Webster," *Liberator*, May 3, 1850, via her column in *Pittsburgh Saturday Visiter*. See also Swisshelm, *Half a Century*, 84–87, 133–35.

30 managed to persuade Vice President: *Pittsburg Post*, April 23, 1850; Swisshelm, *Half a Century*, 130–31.

31 Gail Hamilton not only: Maurine Beasley, "Mary Abigail Dodge," *Essex Institute Historical Collections,* April 1980, 82–100.

31 "is a large and brilliant": "Personal," *Harper's Bazaar,* Aug. 11, 1877.

31 "of being beset by deferential publishers": "The Contributors' Club: A Reverie over a Book," *Atlantic,* Nov. 1901.

32 This was especially irksome: "The Dickens Banquet," *NYT,* April 19, 1868; "The Dickens Dinner," *Hartford Courant,* April 14, 1868.

32 "a scholar and a talker": Jennie June, "Margaret Fuller's Life," *Winona Republican,* Dec. 15, 1883.

32 "Jane writes pretty good": *Pittsburgh Gazette,* April 18, 1868.

32 "new society": "Blue Stocking Club," *Detroit Free Press,* April 24, 1868.

32 "to remove in some degree": "The New York Sorosis," *Chicago Tribune,* Aug. 20, 1868.

33 "the best-known woman journalist": "Mrs. Jennie C. Croly Dead," *NYT,* Dec. 24, 1901.

33 a writer for *Galaxy:* Justin McCarthy, "American Women and English Women," *Galaxy,* July 1870.

33 Nelly Mackay Hutchinson began: "The Press," *Rochester Democrat and Chronicle,* Feb. 16, 1871; Karin L. Hooks, "Ellen Mackay Hutchinson," *Legacy* 30, no. 2 (2013): 369–81.

33 In Hutchinson's view: Nelly Mackay Hutchinson, "Woman and Journalism," *Galaxy,* April 1872.

34 "feminine literary lights": "New York," *Chicago Tribune,* Jan. 12, 1973. The writer named Hutchinson, Rebecca Harding Davis, Lucia Gilbert Runkle, Kate Field, and Louise Chandler Moulton.

34 "by the thousands": F. B. Sanborn, "Journalism and Journalists," *Atlantic,* July 1874.

34 "wholly impartial": Hutchinson, "Woman and Journalism."

34 "Aside from their ability": "Personal," *Harper's Bazaar,* Feb. 25, 1871.

35 "with pencils in her mouth": Mary Clemmer Ames, "Newspaper Letter-Writing," *Independent,* March 24, 1870.

35 Perhaps it derived: Special thanks to David Vine for this insight.

35 Hamilton lost the needle: "Ochram," "Literary Women," *SF Chronicle,* March 17, 1878. See also Hamilton's periodic *NY Tribune* series, 1877–78, starting with "Civil Service Reform: Letter from Gail Hamilton," April 21, 1877, and ending with "Gail Hamilton Sums Up: Final Words on Civil Service Reform," Nov. 16, 1878.

35 "suspicion of intrigue": *New Century for Woman,* Aug. 26, 1876.

35 "We have had more weighty": "Contributors' Club: A Reverie over a Book."

35 "a potent force": "Mary Clemmer Hudson from the *Boston Traveller*," *Literary News*, Sept. 1884.

36 "To serve thy generation": Clemmer, "Journalist," 137–41. Dewitt Gray of the *Utica Observer* read Clemmer's poem to the gathering. *Buffalo Commercial*, June 9, 1881.

36 Jane Croly counted sixty: Wingate, *Views and Interviews on Journalism*, 146–50.

36 "a large amount of work": Ibid.

37 Croly's own handprint: See, for example, ad for the *NY Dispatch*, "Gossip with and for Ladies," *NY Tribune*, Aug. 31, 1856; ad, "A Highly Interesting Number, the New-York Dispatch," *NYT*, Feb. 14, 1857; and "A Lady on Economy" (refers to Croly's "Parlor and Sidewalk Gossip" column by then in the *Sunday Times*, not the *NYT*), *Augusta (Ga.) Evening Dispatch*, April 26, 1858.

37 In 1875, Croly: Wingate, *Views and Interviews on Journalism*, 146–50.

37 "We shall now learn": "Femininities," *Saturday Evening Post*, April 30, 1881.

37 "The one thing to hope": "A Woman's Busy Life: Jennie June Tells About Her Professional Career," *Indianapolis Journal* via the *NY Mail and Express*, Feb. 20, 1887.

Chapter 3. The Breakout

41 "back with a whoop": Ida M. Tarbell, *All in the Day's Work: An Autobiography* (New York: Macmillan, 1939), 81–82.

41 In the newsrooms: In these years, at various papers in Chicago and later in New York City, Margaret Sullivan stood out as an able reporter and editorial writer of the highest caliber on political themes, although much of her work appeared unsigned. At her death at fifty-six in 1903, obituary headlines everywhere invariably include the word "brilliant." See Gillian O'Brien, "Patriotism, Professionalism, and the Press: The Chicago Press and Irish Journalists, 1875–1900," in *Irish Journalism Before Independence*, ed. Kevin Rafter (Manchester, U.K.: Manchester University Press, 2011), 126–28. Also, for example, "The Formal Ceremonies," *NYT*, May 7, 1889; "The World's Fair," *SF Chronicle*, May 7, 1889; Margaret F. Sullivan, "Progress of the World," *Detroit Free Press*, May 7, 1889. Also, "A Brilliant Woman Dead," *Baltimore Sun*, Dec. 29, 1903; "Margaret Sullivan, a Brilliant Writer, Dead," *Washington Times*, Dec. 29, 1903.

41 By then, Mary Ann Shadd Cary: Rhodes, *Mary Ann Shadd Cary*, 156.

42 After the conflict: "National Woman Suffrage Association," *National Citizens and Ballot Box*, March and Sept. 1878 and June 1879.

42 In February 1887: Wingate, *Views and Interviews on Journalism*, 147.

42 "exactness and accurate": "Woman's Busy Life."

42 "find it impossible": Nellie Bly, "Women Journalists," *Pittsburg Dispatch,* Aug. 21, 1887.

42 Dana's remarks appeared: Ibid.

42 *Pittsburg Dispatch:* Pittsburgh lost its *h* in 1891 and regained it in 1911.

43 In 1872, as a cub: Hutchinson, "Woman and Journalism."

43 At the time, she was one of seven: *Indianapolis News,* Dec. 24, 1872.

43 "as a pioneer": "Ellen Mackay Hutchinson," *NY Tribune,* Aug. 15, 1933.

43 "pug-nosed poetess": See, for example, "Personal," *Pittsburgh Commercial,* Oct. 23, 1965, and "Telegraphic Summary," *Baltimore Sun,* April 19, 1888. Before Hassard, the *Tribune*'s literary editor was George Ripley. See also "Gotham Gossip," *New Orleans Picayune,* Dec. 5, 1886.

43 "unsurpassed": Bly, "Women Journalists."

44 "large estates": "Buying Horses for a King," *NYT,* June 5, 1892.

44 In New York, Raymond died: Debby Applegate, *The Most Famous Man in America* (New York: Doubleday, 2006), 386.

44 He barely glanced: "Horace Greeley's No," *Nashville Union,* April 12, 1873.

44 "An Irish Lady's Opinion": "Saratoga: An Irish Lady's Opinion of an American Watering Place—What She Thinks of American Gentlemen— the Races," *NY World,* Aug. 11, 1869.

44 spotted in Central Park: "Middy Morgan on Horseback," *NY Sun,* Nov. 15, 1869.

45 "It cannot be otherwise": "The American Institute: Farmer's Club, June 28, 1870," *NY World,* July 1, 1870.

45 Other attention-getting: Throughout her career, Morgan also wrote for other publications, including the *Tribune.* She is reported to have had a number of well-paying side jobs similar to the oft-retold service she performed for the sporty Italian sovereign of selecting horses for him in Ireland and bringing them to him in Italy. This would have been before ethical or competitive guidelines forbade such conflicts of interest. She was much beloved and respected both by colleagues and by the agricultural community.

45 In 1886: "Woman as Journalists in America," *Pall Mall Gazette,* May 13, 1886.

45 "that cover the little hands": "Middy Morgan," *Arthur's Home Magazine,* Jan. 1881.

45 One sketch reported: "Middy Morgan: A New York Market Reporter," *Manitoba Daily Free Press* via *NY Letter,* June 12, 1880.

45 "a woman can do anything": "A Newspaper Woman," *Atlanta Constitution,* June 4, 1892.

46 Campbell: Hester M. Poole, "Sorosis," *Good Housekeeping,* April 12, 1890. The "Club of the True Brotherhood" she alludes to in one of her articles appears to be a transmogrification of Sorosis.

46 "conceived in sin": Helen Campbell, "What a Radical Found in Water Street," *Sunday Afternoon,* Dec. 1878. Also, Susan Henry, "Reporting Deeply and at First Hand," *Journalism History* 11, no. 1–2 (Spring–Summer 1984): 18–25; and Robert W. Dimand, "Nineteenth-Century American Feminist Economies: From Caroline Dall to Charlotte Perkins Gilman," *American Economic Review* 90, no. 2 (May 2000): 480–84.

46 She chronicled: Campbell, "What a Radical Found in Water Street," *Sunday Afternoon,* Dec. 1878; "An Experience Meeting in Water Street," Jan. 1879; "Sunday in Water Street II," Feb. 1879; "The Tenement House Question," April 1879; "Six Stories in One," May 1879; "An Experiment and What Came of It," June 1879; "Max," July 1879; Campbell, "Studies in the Slums," pts. 1–6, *Lippincott's,* May, June, July, Aug., Sept., and Oct. 1880; Campbell, "Prisoners of Poverty: Women Wage-Workers, Their Homes and Their Lives," pts. 1–21, *NY Tribune,* Oct. 24, 31, Nov. 7, 14, 21, 28, Dec. 5, 12, 19, 26, 1886, Jan. 2, 9, 16, 23, 30, Feb. 6, 13, 20, 27, March 6, 13, 1887; Helen Campbell, *Prisoners of Poverty: Women Wage-Workers, Their Trades and Their Lives* (Boston: Little, 1900).

46 "the condensed cry": Hester M. Poole, "Correspondence: Letter from New York," *Open Court,* May 12, 1887. See also, for example, "Current Literature," *WP,* April 17, 1887; Helen Campbell, *Prisoners of Poverty Abroad* (Boston: Roberts Brothers, 1889).

46 appointment as a lecturer: "Authors' Social Settlement: Good Work of Two Women Writers," *Chicago Tribune,* Feb. 2, 1895.

46 "with an iron clasp": "Talk About Books," *Chautauquan* 7, no. 9 (June 1887): 575.

46 "thrilling pictures": Ida Tarbell, "Women in Journalism," *Chautauquan* 7, no. 7 (April 1887): 393–95.

46 Tarbell countered the assertion: Mary Lowe Dickinson, "Clerical Pursuits," *Chautauquan* 7, no. 3 (Dec. 1886): 135–38; Ida Tarbell, "Women as Inventors," *Chautauquan* 7, no. 6 (March 1887): 355–57.

47 By 1890, women made up: Steiner et al., "Gender at Work," *Journalism History* 23, no. 1 (Spring 1997): 2–12.

47 The business side: See, for example, Lamar W. Bridges, "Eliza Jane Nicholson and the *Daily Picayune,* 1876–1896," *Louisiana History* 30, no. 3 (Summer 1989): 263–78; Editorial, *New Orleans Daily Picayune,* Sept. 12, 1895; Sidney Herbert, "Woman in Journalism: Woman as a Successful Editor, Publisher, and Business Manager," *Southern Cultivator,* May 1883; Also, "The House of Illustrated Literature," *Frank Leslie's Popular Monthly,* Aug.

1883; "Mrs. Frank Leslie Retires," *Atlanta Constitution*, Oct. 7, 1900; and "Leslie Million to Aid Suffrage," *NY Tribune*, Oct. 8, 1914.

47   top jobs: "Howard's Gossip," *Boston Globe*, Sept. 12, 1887; "Women Editors," *Journalist*, Sept. 24, 1887.

48   She readily accepted: Tarbell, *All in the Day's Work*, 64.

48   Ida B. Wells attended: Linda McMurry Edwards, *To Keep the Waters Troubled: The Life of Ida B. Wells* (New York: Oxford University Press, 1998), 12; Rust College, "Ida B. Wells Social Justice Weekend," rustcollege.edu.

48   dispute with the school's president: Edwards, *To Keep the Waters Troubled*, 13.

48   she moved to Memphis: Ibid., 25–31.

48   "Princess of the Press": [Lucy Wilmot Smith], "Some Female Writers of the Negro Race," *Journalist*, Jan. 26, 1889. See also Edwards, *To Keep the Waters Troubled*, 90–91.

49   the horrors of lynching: See Ida B. Wells-Barnett, *A Red Record: Tabulated Statistics and Alleged Causes of Lynching in the United States, 1892–1893–1894* (Chicago: Donohue and Henneberry, 1895); Ida B. Wells, *Crusade for Justice: The Autobiography of Ida B. Wells*, ed. Alfreda M. Duster (Chicago: University of Chicago Press, 1992); Edwards, *To Keep the Waters Troubled*.

49   The editorial announcement: "Miss Tarbell's History of the Standard Oil Company: Editorial Announcement," *McClure's*, Oct. 1902.

50   "such authority and eminence": "Ida M. Tarbell," *Austin Statesman*, Dec. 28, 1904.

50   Tarbell told an interviewer: Herbert Brewster, "The History of Standard Oil," *Atlanta Constitution*, Jan. 11, 1903.

50   Her work as a historian: See Steve Weinberg, *Taking on the Trust: The Epic Battle of Ida Tarbell and John D. Rockefeller* (New York: W. W. Norton, 2008).

50   waged a militant crusade: See Robin Hardin and Marcie Hinton, "The Squelching of Free Speech in Memphis: The Life of a Black Post-Reconstruction Newspaper," *Race, Gender & Class in Media* 8, no. 4 (2001): 78–95.

50   Nightingale ended up: *NY Age*, Feb. 6, 1892.

50   "Nobody in this section": Ida B. Wells, *Southern Horrors: Lynch Law in All Its Phases* (New York: New York Age Press, 1892); Ida B. Wells, "Southern Horrors," *NY Age*, June 25, 1892.

51   "sharp as a steel trap": "Some Female Writers of the Negro Race," *Journalist*, Jan. 26, 1889.

51   Fortune started: "A Fine Musical Recital; Relative to Journalism, a New Drama; Personal Notes," *Cleveland Gazette*, June 7, 1888.

51   "Southern Horrors": Wells, *Southern Horrors*.

51   "outstanding and courageous": Special citation for Ida B. Wells, pulitzer.org.

52 "There is, perhaps": Tarbell, "Women in Journalism," 393–95. In the article, Tarbell quoted woman journalists from around the country who told her success depended on "unflagging interest in a subject, general information, wide-awake interest in current events," and "patience, common sense, good judgment, quick perceptions, and action." One woman editor said success followed those who had brains and energy enough to make their own way when none was prepared for them. Tarbell's own conclusion seemed a little pat, but held out hope. For women with ability, opportunities would follow. "Any woman who can do as strong and finished work as a man," she said, "will find a position."

52 met with Joseph Howard Jr.: Joseph Howard Jr., "Howard's Letter," *America*, Aug. 15, 1888.

53 "Women are always anxious": Bly, "Women Journalists."

53 "Not unless the public taste": Ibid.

54 The idea went considerably: Nellie Bly, "Behind Asylum Bars," *NY World*, Oct. 9, 1887.

54 escapade pulled off by Julius Chambers: [Julius Chambers], "The Lunacy Law Tested," *NY Tribune*, Aug. 29, 1872; "Among the Maniacs," *NY Tribune*, Aug. 31, 1872; "Abuses of Lunatics," *NY Tribune*, Sept. 2, 1872. Also, for example, "New York," *Detroit Free Press*, Aug. 28, 1872. Thanks to Andie Tucher for pointing out this series.

54 "On the 22d": Nellie Bly, *Ten Days in a Mad-House* (New York: Munro, 1887).

54 Her first big exposé: Brooke Kroeger, *Nellie Bly: Daredevil, Reporter, Feminist* (New York: Times Books, 1994), 79–116.

55 "The great successes": Howard, "Howard's Letter."

56 In fact, the can-do: See, generally, Kim Todd, *Sensational: The Hidden History of America's "Girl Stunt Reporters"* (New York: Harper, 2021); Elizabeth Faue, *Writing the Wrongs: Eva Valesh and the Rise of Labor Journalism* (Ithaca, N.Y.: Cornell University Press, 2002), 68, 318n35; "The Plain Facts," *Minneapolis Tribune*, May 13, 1888, cited in Faue; Nell Nelson, "City Slave Girls," *Chicago Times*, July 30, 31, Aug. 1–4, 5, 6–11, 12, 13–18, 19, 1888; and "Thanks 'The Times,'" *Chicago Times*, Aug. 21, 1888; Nell Nelson, *The White Slave Girls of Chicago* (Chicago: Barkley, 1888); Annie Laurie [Winifred Bonfils Black], "A City's Disgrace," *SF Examiner*, Jan. 19, 1890.

56 Howard ended his column: Ellen Mackay Hutchinson, *Songs and Lyrics* (New York: James R. Osgood, 1881), 28–30. See Hooks, "Ellen Mackay Hutchinson." In the Stedman-Hutchinson correspondence, Hooks points out, Hutchinson often signs herself "Priscilla," the subject of one of the poems in *Songs and Lyrics*, who is "partly woman, partly saint."

56 "Girls, go in": Howard, "Howard's Letter."

57 "made the significant interesting": Bill Kovach and Tom Rosenstiel, *The Elements of Journalism* (New York: Random House, 2001).

57 She toured the country: Courtesy of the Bly novelist David Blixt, who found eleven Bly novels via the London edition of Norman Munro's *New York Family Story Paper,* called *The London Story Paper.* Most U.S. versions of Bly's stories in the publication, except the first, remain unlocated. "Eva the Adventuress," July 5–Nov. 1, 1890 (Dec. 22, 1889–April 20, 1890, in the United States); "New York by Night," April 4–June 27, 1891; "Alta Lynn, M.D.," July 4–Sept. 19, 1891; "Wayne's Faithful Sweetheart," Dec. 26, 1891–March 26, 1892; "Little Luckie," May 21–Aug. 13, 1892; "Dolly the Coquette," Nov. 5, 1891–Jan. 21, 1892; "In Love with a Stranger," Jan. 14–April 15, 1893; "The Love of Three Girls," June 3–Sept. 2, 1893; "Little Penny," Oct. 21, 1893–Jan. 13, 1894; "Pretty Merribelle," Aug. 25–Nov. 24, 1894; "Twins and Rivals," March 16–June 8, 1895.

58 "Nellie Bly Returns": "Nellie Bly Returns," *NY Evening World,* Sept. 13, 1893; "Nellie Bly Again: She Interviews Emma Goldman and Other Anarchists," *NY World,* Sept. 17, 1893.

58 Her success with the interview: Nellie Bly, "Eva Hamilton's Story," *NY World,* Oct. 9, 1889; "Champion of Her Sex," *NY World,* Feb. 2, 1896; "Are You an Anarchist?," *NY World,* July 17, 1894. Bly, "Nellie Bly in Pullman," *NY World,* July 11, 13, 15, 1894; Bly, "Cheers for Nellie Bly," *NY World,* July 15, 1894; "With the Female Suffragists," *NY World,* Jan. 26, 1896; "Nellie Bly and Two Women Contrasts," *NY World,* Feb. 26, 1896; "Nellie Bly on the Job," *NY Evening Journal,* March 3, 1913. See also Kroeger, *Nellie Bly,* 282–88 and 373–76, and "When the Suffrage Movement Got Its Makeover On," The Gotham Center for New York City History, Nov. 21, 2017, gothamcenter.org.

59 No longer did he think: See Foster Coates, "Women's Chances as Journalists," *Ladies' Home Journal,* Sept. 1890, and "Women in Journalism," *Ladies' Home Journal,* Sept. 1892.

59 "A man meets": [Charlotte O'Conor-Eccles], "The Experiences of a Woman Journalist," *Blackwood's Edinburgh Magazine,* June 1893. Identified as Eccles in "The Experiences of a Woman Journalist," *Maitland Mercury and Hunter River General Advertiser,* Oct. 2, 1893.

59 "the only Indian": Bright Eyes [Susette La Flesche], "Pleading for Her People," *Omaha World-Herald,* Jan. 3, 1891. Also see Bright Eyes, "Horrors of War," *Omaha World-Herald,* Jan. 2, 1891, cited in Kevin Abourezk, "From Red Fears to Red Power: The Story of the Newspaper Coverage of Wounded Knee 1890 and Wounded Knee 1973" (master's thesis, University of Nebraska–Lincoln, 2012). A month later, Teresa Howard

Dean arrived at the reservation alone for *The Chicago Herald.* Dean also wrote for *Town Topics* as The Widow (she was divorced). In 1893, Mary Hannah Krout, delayed by a broken foot, covered the aftermath of the Hawaiian revolution for *The Inter Ocean,* which played her stories prominently (Feb.–April 1893). They are not bylined, but see, for example, item on ship passenger arrivals, *Honolulu Advertiser,* Feb. 22, 1983; "Personal," *Hawaiian Star,* March 31, 1893; "The Hawaiian Question," *Wheeling Daily Intelligencer,* June 8, 1893. Special thanks to Carolyn Edy for her prodigious research and repeated consultations. Carolyn M. Edy, *The Woman War Correspondent, the U.S. Military, and the Press, 1846–1947* (Lanham, Md.: Lexington Books, 2017), 20–21.

59 Sadie Kneller Miller: Thanks to the late Keith Richwine of McDaniel for his research on Miller, which also pointed the way to other finds.

60 "bright, pretty, accomplished": "The Senators Slump," *WP,* Aug. 12, 1895. Five years earlier, for the 1890 baseball season, *Sporting Life* carried baseball stories under the byline Ella Black that were a subject of gender controversy never entirely resolved: "A Woman's View," March 5; "Feminine Fancies," April 2; "Only a Woman," April 12. Also, "Baseball Notes," *Wilkes-Barre (Pa.) Sunday Leader,* June 15, 1890. See Mike Sowell, "Is She or Isn't She? Exploring the Gender Identity Controversy over the First Female Byline in a National Sports Publication." *Journalism History* 37, no. 4 (Winter 2012): 228–37.

60 number of woman journalists: By 1890, the 888 woman journalists made up 4.1 percent of the total 21,849 number of journalists in the country. In 1900, when the total number of journalists increased to 30,038, the percentage of women nearly doubled to 7.3 percent, or 2,193 women. Ten years after that, in 1910, the number of women about doubled again to 4,181—12 percent—among a total of 34,382 journalists across the country. See Kleinberg, *Women in the United States,* and U.S. Government, *Population Comparative Occupation Statistics, 1870–1940,* and Department of Labor.

60 By an 1891 estimate: Foster Coates, "Side Talks with Boys," *Ladies' Home Journal,* Oct. 1891.

60 For women the following year: Coates, "Women in Journalism."

60 "There is, I know": Foster Coates, "Women's Chances in Journalism," *Ladies' Home Journal,* Sept. 1890.

60 Interest in journalism careers: For example, "A Woman's Experience of Newspaper Work," *Harper's Weekly,* Jan. 25, 1890; "A Trades College for Women," *Good Housekeeping,* March 1890; "Some Methods of Earning," *Good Housekeeping,* April 26, 1890; George J. Mansoy, "Reporters,"

Cosmopolitan, June 1890; Coates, "Women's Chances as Journalists"; "Journalism as a Profession for Women," *Review of Reviews,* April 1891; "Woman's Place in Journalism," *Yellowstone Journal,* July 25, 1891; Fannie Aymar Mathews, "The Woman's Press Club of New York City," *Cosmopolitan,* Aug. 1891; Coates, "Women in Journalism"; W. T. Stead, "Young Women and Journalism," *Independent,* Sept. 22, 1892; Emily Crawford, "Journalism as a Profession for Women," *Eclectic Magazine of Foreign Literature,* Dec. 1893; "Woman in Journalism," *Speaker,* Sept. 2, 1893; "The Experiences of a Woman Journalist," *Blackwood's,* June 1893; "Women in Newspaper Work," *NYT,* Sept. 6, 1894; Margaret Sangster, "Editorship as a Profession for Women," *Forum,* Dec. 1895; Florence J. Dyer, "Professions and Occupations for Women," *Zion's Herald,* April 3, 1895; "The Men's Corner in Journalism: The New Woman Turns the Tables," *Current Literature* 19, no. 3 (March 1896): 242; Helen M. Winslow, "Some Newspaper Women," *Arena,* Dec. 1896; Haryot Holt Cahoon, "Women in Gutter Journalism," *Arena,* March 1897; Hayden Carruth, "Stories by Reporters: A Girl Who Became a Reporter," *Youth's Companion,* April 22, 1897; Cynthia Westover Alden, "Women in Journalism," *Frank Leslie's Popular Monthly,* Dec. 1898; Elizabeth Jordan, "What It Means to Be a Newspaper Woman," *Ladies' Home Journal,* Jan. 1899.

61 "not very good": Coates, "Women in Journalism."

61 W. T. Stead distilled: Stead, "Young Women and Journalism."

61 "thorough study": [Ida Tarbell], "Women in Journalism," *Critic,* Aug. 9, 1890. See also Elizabeth G. Jordan, "The Newspaper Woman's Story," *Lippincott's,* March 1893. In *The Journalist,* May 13, 1893, Jordan writes, "There is a vast difference between what has been accomplished and what is claimed. It cannot be pointed out too soon for the benefit of the ambitious girls whose pathetic little letters are filling our editorial waste-baskets."

61 Margaret Welch: Margaret H. Welch, "Is Newspaper Work Healthful for Women?," Papers of the Silver Question, the Unemployed, Crime and Punishment, Education and Health, Saratoga Papers of 1894, *Journal of Social Science* 32 (Nov. 1894): 111–16. Also, "Women in Newspaper Work," *NYT,* Sept. 6, 1894. Of Welch, as the *NYT*'s Saratoga summer correspondent and "Her Point of View" columnist, see *Publishers Weekly,* Aug. 27, 1892. See also Cahoon, "Women in Gutter Journalism."

62 "premium on mediocrity": E. A. Bennett, *Journalism for Women: A Practical Guide* (London: John Lane, 1898). Also, "Journalism for Women," *Academy,* May 14, 1898, and "Journalism for Women," *Critic,* Sept. 1898. See also Edwin Shuman, *Steps into Journalism: Helps and Hints for Young Writers* (Evanston, Ill.: Correspondence School of Journalism, 1894), 150.

Chapter 4. From Cuba to the Far East

64 On March 8, Commander Bly: "Nellie Bly Proposes to Fight for Cuba," *NY World,* March 8, 1896.

64 Over the coming days and weeks: "More Trouble for Cuba," *Philadelphia Inquirer,* April 1, 1896, via *Toledo Blade; Oberlin Herald,* Dec. 10, 1896; *Galveston News,* March 13, 1896; *Arizona Republic,* March 21, 1896; *Salt Lake City Argus,* April 11, 1896.

65 The *Journal* had a good team: "Murat Halstead Sails," *NY Journal,* Jan. 26, 1896.

65 "WEYLER TALKS TO A WOMAN": "Weyler Talks to a Woman," *NY Journal,* March 14, 1896.

66 Kittie K: "Stories of the Day," *Mansfield (Ohio) News Journal,* June 6, 1900.

66 "special work": "Kate Masterson," *Writer* 13, no. 6 (June 1900): 90–91; "Mrs. Kate Masterson," *Life,* March 7, 1911.

66 "Her sex will hinder": Jordan, "Newspaper Woman's Story"; *Journalist,* May 13, 1893.

66 When Masterson joined: Kate Masterson, "Hundreds Starving and Freezing in the Bleak North," *NY Journal,* Jan. 26, 1896; "The Amazing Possibilities of Professor Roentgen's Great Discovery," *NY Journal,* Feb. 16, 1896.

66 its exclusive interview: "Weyler to the World," *NY World,* March 4, 1896.

66 Weyler also flirted: "World of Women," *Utica Herald-Dispatch,* Sept. 24, 1900.

67 Masterson broke more news: Kate Masterson, "The Massacre at Dolores," *NY Journal,* March 20, 1896; "A Journal Woman in a Spanish Dungeon in Cuba," March 29, 1896; "The Cuban Baby's Cabinet," April 2, 1896; "Brave Women and Young Girls Fighting in the Cuban Army," April 5, 1896.

67 "fully supplied with credentials": "Off for Cuba," *Cincinnati Commercial Gazette,* March 29, 1896.

68 This included the *Chicago Tribune:* "To Send Society Editor to Cuba," *Chicago Tribune,* March 19, 1896; "Off for Cuba," *Lawrence Journal,* April 4, 1896. Masterson stories: *Chicago Tribune,* March 16, 1896, and March 20, 1896.

68 "naturally quick sympathies": "Woman as a War Correspondent," *Columbus Dispatch,* April 7, 1896.

68 She attended the University of Kansas: *Graduate Magazine of the University of Kansas* 30, no. 9 (1932): 16; "Our History," journalism.ku.edu. KU offered its first journalism course in 1891 and established a journalism department within its College of Arts and Science in 1909 and its William Allen White School of Journalism in 1944.

68 John DeBras Miles: "Death of Col. Miles," *Lawrence Daily Journal*, March 21, 1925.

68 "OUR WAR CORRESPONDENT": "Our War Correspondent" and "Cuban Women," *Cincinnati Commercial Gazette*, April 5, 1896.

68 The *Journal's* two-column sketch: Josephine Woodward, "Cuban Woman," *Cincinnati Commercial Gazette*, April 5, 1896; "Castilian Life," April 13, 1896; "Weyler Talks," April 16, 1986; "False Reports," April 18, 1896; "Havana and Her People," April 26, 1897; "Among Cuban Women," May 3, 1896.

69 Butcher had not eaten her: *Marion Daily Star*, April 17, 1896.

69 "The question": *DeKalb (Ill.) Daily Chronicle*, May 13, 1896.

69 published a quickie book: Murat Halstead, *The Story of Cuba: Her Struggles for Liberty: The Cause, Crisis, and Destiny of the Pearl of the Antilles* (Akron: Werner, 1898).

69 All the same, to keep perspective: Up to this point, at the top of the profession, the inclusion of women in conflict situations mostly happened when it served an immediate commercial notion or when women already abroad at their own or someone else's expense offered freelance pieces. Fannie B. Ward, for example, had been traveling throughout Latin and South America since the 1880s by that point, placing stories as she went. On Aug. 7, a good five months after Kate Masterson and Josephine Woodward sang their soprano arias in Havana, the New York *World* carried a story by Cecil Charles, relegating it to page 7. She got very little ballyhoo.

69 "an entirely new avenue": "Woman as a War Correspondent," *Columbus Dispatch*, April 7, 1896.

69 women who ventured afar: Also, Mary Hannah Krout, for Chicago's *Inter Ocean*, who arrived in Hawaii in the immediate aftermath of the rebellion that led to its declaration as a republic.

70 "a pretty girl of erratic habits": "She Simply Obeyed Orders," *SF Call*, Aug. 2, 1891. Also, "Margherita Arlina Hamm," *Journalist*, May 7, 1892.

71 outbreak of the Sino-Japanese War: Special thanks to Dr. Tom Looser, NYU, for his help in deciphering the various Hamm claims. For Hamm's travel on the SS *China*: "List of Manifest of Alien Immigrants for the Commissioner of Immigration, from Yokohama, August 7, 1894, Arriving at the Port of San Francisco, 20 August 1894"; "Vessel Dates of Arrival, SS China, August 20, Page 123."

71 Once back in the United States: "From the East," *Brooklyn Standard Union*, Sept. 13, 1894.

71 Yet only the *Rocky Mountain News:* See "The Korean War," *Salt Lake Herald*, Sept. 1, 1894; "Russia Is Behind It," *Rocky Mountain News*, Sept. 5, 1894;

Margherita Arlina Hamm, "Poor Little Corea," *Inter Ocean,* Sept. 10, 1974; "Is Bright for Japan," *Chicago Tribune,* Sept. 10, 1894; "From the East," *Brooklyn Standard Union,* Sept. 13, 1894. See also on Hamm, Alice Fahs, *Out on Assignment: Newspaper Women and the Making of Modern Public Space* (Chapel Hill: University of North Carolina Press, 2014).

71 "She says she has been": "Is Bright for Japan."

71 Fales, as a diplomat: "From the East," *Brooklyn Standard Union,* Sept. 13, 1894.

71 "The Only Woman": J.C.C., "The Only Woman War Correspondent: Margherita Arlina Hamm," *Journalist,* Sept. 8, 1894.

72 "the first authentic news": Janey Mulhern Coard, "For Women," *Pittsburg Press,* Aug. 11, 1895. Also, Margherita Arlina Hamm, "Work of the W.C.T.U.: Observations of a Delegate," *Brooklyn Eagle,* July 7, 1895.

72 Newspaper archives make clear: Associated Press, "Has Fighting Begun?," *NY World,* July 24, 1894. Datelined Shanghai, the cable may well have come from Hamm, but she does not mention this in her recounting of what transpired in Maude Andrews, "A Chat with Miss Hamm," *Atlanta Constitution,* Jan. 31, 1895. Also, "Naval Fight Off Corea," *NY World,* July 28, 1894. "The first overt act of war was committed last Tuesday, as was cabled exclusively to the Associated Press."

72 "After gathering the news": Andrews, "A Chat with Miss Hamm." The timing dovetails with the three front-page stories published one after another over two columns of *The World* on Aug. 19, 1894, as the SS *China* docked in San Francisco ("Japan Was Cunning," "First Battle at Sea," and Meltzer, "Japan's New Envoy," *NY World,* all Aug. 19, 1894). All three have "via San Francisco, Aug. 18" appended to their datelines of Chemulpo, the port of Seoul; Nagasaki; and Yokohama. Neither of the first two stories is bylined. *The World* credited the third not to Hamm but to "Meltzer," identified as the "World's Correspondent in Yokohama." That same day, the *SF Examiner* quoted Hamm at length ("The Fighting Has Begun," *SF Examiner,* Aug. 19, 1894) as she debarked from the SS *China,* but with no mention of any major story of hers that dropped at the same time. (The *Examiner,* a Hearst paper, might well have been inclined to ignore an exclusive in Pulitzer's *World.*) So, credit to the unknown "Meltzer" aside, if the *World* stories of Aug. 19 are all or some by Hamm, which seems possible, even likely, what she produced is a more detailed reprise of events than had already been reported daily from a variety of sources for nearly a month.

72 No information of the trouble: Other early reports: "Corean King Missing," *NY World,* July 25, 1894, with datelines from Tacoma, Wash., London, and Washington, D.C.; "China Means to Fight," *NY World,* July 27,

1894; "Naval Fight Off Corea," *NY World,* July 28, 1894; "Japan Says This Is War," *NY World,* Aug. 2, 1894.

74 "All over the land": Elizabeth Phelps et al., *Our Famous Women: An Authorized Record of the Lives and Deeds of Distinguished American Women of Our Times* (Hartford: A. D. Worthington, 1884).

74 "supply a vacant niche": Frances Elizabeth Willard and Mary A. Livermore, *American Women: Fifteen Hundred Biographies with over 1,400 Portraits: A Comprehensive Encyclopedia of the Lives and Achievements of American Women During the Nineteenth Century,* vol. 2 (New York: Mast, Crowell & Kirkpatrick, 1897).

74 The authors omit: They omit, for example, Teresa Dean at Wounded Knee and Mary Hannah Krout from Hawaii during the revolution of 1893.

75 Several of them besides Crane: "The Journal's Great Journalists," *Buffalo Evening News,* May 8, 1897. Aside from this group, on May 9, the *Journal* filled the entire lead page of its Sunday supplement with battle and hospital scenes by Harriet Boyd. The story was widely reprinted or excerpted. Boyd was twenty-four, a graduate of Smith, fluent in Greek, and studying at the time at the American School of Classical Studies in Athens. In her piece, she reported that on April 27 she and eleven Greek nurses boarded the transport *Thrace* at the port of Piraeus. Like Crane's wife, she had no credentials, not even from the Red Cross, but she traveled anyway with only "a general air of curiosity and a rough tweed gown." The nurses arrived at Volo to treat the wounded. Boyd's command of Greek and familiarity with the country put her at a distinct advantage over most of the other U.S. correspondents. "Many correspondents from their ignorance of the language get their knowledge second hand," she sniffed in print. "It is well known here that almost all the English sources of information in Volo are notoriously corrupt." She first wrote for the *Journal* a couple of weeks earlier about her training to become a nurse volunteer. See Boyd, "A Journal Woman on the Battlefield in Greece: Harriet Boyd, the Only Woman War Correspondent at the Front Sends a Vivid Picture of Stirring Battlefield Episodes and Scenes in the Hospitals," *NY Journal,* May 9, 1897. Also, "Appeal for Greece," *Inter Ocean,* April 17, 1897.

75 "Imogene Carter's": "Imogene Carter's Pen Picture of Fighting at Velestino," *NY Journal,* May 10, 1897.

76 "As to what these few words": *Weekly Bee,* May 12, 1897; Imogene Carter, "War as Seen Through a Woman's Eyes," *NY Journal,* May 14, 1897.

77 *The Evening World* rolled out: Charles Garrett and Catherine King, "Girl Toilers in the City," *NY Evening World,* July 26, 27, 29, Aug. 1, 3, 8, 1898.

77 "Every beautiful newspaperwoman": Arthur Brisbane, "Great Problems in Organization: The Modern Newspaper in War Time," *Cosmopolitan,* Sept. 1898, as also cited in Charles Henry Brown, *The Correspondents' War: Journalists in the Spanish-American War* (New York: Charles Scribner's Sons, 1967), 210.

77 Carolyn Edy's count: See Edy, *Woman War Correspondent,* 21–26, and Joyce Milton, *The Yellow Kids: Foreign Correspondents in the Heyday of Yellow Journalism* (New York: Harper & Row, 1989), 271. Milton's count is 129 accredited correspondents, including Anna Northend Benjamin and the Canadian reporter Kit Coleman, whose real name was Kathleen Blake Watkins.

77 nurse volunteers: See "A Woman War Correspondent," Washington *Evening Star,* May 21, 1898. Fannie B. Ward, whom Alice Fahs dubbed an "invisible foreign correspondent," also reported from Cuba. See Fahs, *Out on Assignment,* 241–51; "Terrible Story of Cuba's Woes," *Lancaster Semi-weekly New Era,* March 19, 1898; "Fannie B. Ward Again in Cuba," *Lancaster Semi-weekly New Era,* July 27, 1898; "A Story of Heroism," *LAT,* Aug. 19, 1898; "Good Women," *Hartford Courant,* Feb. 11, 1899.

77 "freedom's poorest blade": Margherita Arlina Hamm, "Brown and Blue Boys," *WP,* July 31, 1898; "The Song of the Machete," *WP,* Aug. 21, 1898; "Margherita Arlina Hamm," *Windsor (Ont.) Star,* July 28, 1898.

77 recognition for their nursing: The other woman reporter to be so honored was Katherine Short White, wife of Trumbull White of the *Chicago Record.* See, for example, "One Woman's Work," *Wilmington Evening Mail,* July 30, 1898; *Terre Haute Evening Mail,* Aug. 6, 1898; "Good Women," *Hartford Courant,* Feb. 11, 1899.

78 "The swish": James Creelman, *On the Great Highway: The Wanderings and Adventures of a Special Correspondent* (Boston: Lothrop, Lee, Shepard, 1901), 336.

78 The two woman standouts: Anna Northend Benjamin, "Unique Decorations," *Rome (N.Y.) Semi-weekly Citizens,* Aug. 24, 1897; "Unique Keystones of the New Congressional Library at Washington," *Utica Sunday Journal,* Aug. 15, 1897; "Reindeer for Alaska," *Carlisle (Pa.) Sentinel,* Aug. 16, 1897; "Salem: Historical and Picturesque Features," *Outlook,* Nov. 6, 1897; "The Quick Proposal Record," *LAT,* Jan. 9, 1898; "Geese Wanted to Learn," *Boston Globe,* Feb. 6, 1898; "Women Polar Explorers," *LAT,* April 3, 1898; "The Innuit of Alaska," *Outlook,* April 24, 1898; "Arctic Factotum," *LAT,* April 24, 1898.

78 Until Benjamin could: Anna Northend Benjamin, "Hospital Work at the Front," *LAT,* June 19, 1898; "Horses and Mules for the Army," *Leslie's,* July 7, 1898; and "Yellow Fever at Key West," *Leslie's,* July 28, 1898.

Also see, "A Lady Correspondent," *NY Tribune,* June 28, 1898, and *NYT,* July 3, 1898, originally in the *London Daily Mail,* June 13, 1898.

78 From Guantánamo Bay: Anna Northend Benjamin, "A Woman's Point of View," *Leslie's,* Aug. 18, 1898.

79 To get home: "Burial of Miss Benjamin," *NY Tribune,* Jan. 25, 1902.

79 "not connected with the Red Cross": *NY Tribune,* Dec. 9 and 20, 1898.

79 reporting from the Philippines: *SF Chronicle,* June 4, 1899; "Transport Sheridan Reaches Manila," *SF Chronicle,* July 25, 1899.

79 "examining their cameras": Creelman, *On the Great Highway,* 326.

79 Up to a point: Ibid., 336. None of the other known American woman reporters in the Philippines fit either. See "To Be Married in Manila," *Marshalltown Evening Times Republican,* June 20, 1900; Margherita Arlina Hamm, *Manila and the Philippines* (New York: F. Tennyson Neely, 1898); "Absolute Divorce Given to Mrs. William E. S. Fales," *Brooklyn Eagle,* July 31, 1902; "Writer and Lecturer," *Boston Globe,* Dec. 18, 1907; "Death of Well-Known Writer," *SF Chronicle,* Dec. 18, 1907; "Margherita A. Hamm," *NY Tribune,* Dec. 19, 1907.

80 "They are as eager": Creelman, *On the Great Highway,* 336–37.

80 It turned out to be the eve: "Personal Notes," *LAT,* June 4, 1899.

80 "the effects of a tumor": "Death of Miss Benjamin," *NY Tribune,* Jan. 22, 1902; "Burial of Miss Benjamin," *NY Tribune,* Jan. 25, 1902.

80 "pushing, belligerent type": "Death of Miss Benjamin"; "Burial of Miss Benjamin." Among other obits: *Boston Globe,* Jan. 21 and 22, 1902; *NY World,* Jan. 22, 1902. Also, Anna Northend Benjamin, "A Siberian Evangeline," *Atlantic,* April 1902.

Chapter 5. New Thought

81 "her who is now": "Contributors' Club: A Reverie over a Book."

81 "a whole volume": Marian Ainsworth-White, "Higher Education of Women: Part II: Women in Journalism," *Arena,* June 1900.

81 Other articles focused: Eleanor Hoyt, "The Newspaper Girl in Fact and Fiction," *Collier's,* Jan. 31, 1903.

81 *The Ladies' Home Journal* asked: Edward Bok, "Is the Newspaper Office the Place for a Girl?," *Ladies' Home Journal,* Feb. 1901.

82 Edward Bok: Arrayed against Bok in the pro-suffrage camp were Brisbane of the *NY Journal;* John O'Hara Cosgrave, then of the New York *World;* Oswald Garrison Villard of the *Nation* magazine and the *New York Evening Post;* Ogden Mills Reid of the *NY Tribune;* William Dean Howells of *The Atlantic Monthly;* George Harvey and then Norman Hapgood of *Harper's Weekly;* S. S. McClure of *McClure's;* Frank Munsey of *Munsey's;* Erman J. Ridgway of *Everybody's;* Hamilton Holt of *The Independent;* and

W. E. B. Du Bois of *The Crisis.* See Brooke Kroeger, *The Suffragents: How Women Used Men to Get the Vote* (Albany: State University of New York Press, 2017), and Kroeger, "The Facilitators: Elites in the Victory of the Women's Suffrage Movement," in *Front Pages, Front Lines: Media and the Fight for Women's Suffrage,* ed. Linda Steiner, Carolyn Kitch, and Kroeger (Urbana: University of Illinois Press, 2020), 171–92.

82 "impressionable, emotional": Kate Masterson, "The Girl Problem: What the New Thought Has Done for Women," *Inter Ocean,* Oct. 1, 1905.

83 by 1900, more than 2,000: Linda Steiner, "Gender at Work: Early Accounts by Women Journalists," *Journalism History* 23, no. 1 (Spring 1997): 2–12. From 1890 to 1900, the number of men in the profession grew from 20,961 to 27,845; for women, the number went from 888 to 2,193.

83 "volcano of sensational feats": Kate Masterson, "The Newspaper Woman of Today," *Era,* Oct. 1902.

83 Sharp critical thinking: For example, Vassar was founded in 1861; Wellesley, in 1875. Oberlin admitted its first Black students in 1835 and granted its first bachelor of arts degree to a woman in 1841. The University of Kansas listed its first journalism course in 1891 and has offered journalism classes continually since 1903. The University of Missouri's, one of the oldest formal journalism schools, was established in 1908. See Maurine Beasley, "Good Women and Bad Girls," in *Journalism, 1908: Birth of a Profession,* ed. Betty Houchin Winfield (Columbia: University of Missouri Press, 2008), 162–80. See also Elizabeth McCracken, "Journalism for the College-Bred Girl," *Independent,* Aug. 29, 1912. By 1912, there were thirteen J-schools across the country, all admitting women as well as men. The first graduate journalism school at Columbia University, named for Joseph Pulitzer, would open that fall.

84 "exhausting toil": Ainsworth-White, "Higher Education of Women: Part II: Women in Journalism." See also Thomas R. Slicer, "The Choice of a Profession," *Cosmopolitan,* Aug. 1900; Foster Coates, "Women's Chances as Journalists," *Ladies' Home Journal,* Sept. 1890; "Chances for Women in Journalism," *Harper's Weekly,* Sept. 12, 1903; Anne Eliot, "Experiences of a Woman Reporter," *Collier's,* Aug. 21, 1909; Margaret Sangster, "My Girls," *Ladies' Home Journal,* June 1900; Susan B. Anthony, "The New Century's Manly Woman," *Leslie's,* March 3, 1900; Bok, "Is the Newspaper Office the Place for a Girl?"; E. Hovey King, "The Notable Newspaper Women of Washington," *Leslie's,* Dec. 5, 1904; Kate Masterson, "The Newspaper Woman of Today"; Hoyt, "Newspaper Girl in Fact and Fiction"; "Unusual Methods of Livelihood," *Current Literature,* March 1903; Helen Hamilton, "My Experiences as a Girl in New York," *Ladies' Home Journal,* Nov. 1903; Anna Couslich, "Southern Women Who Have Made

Their Mark in Journalism," *Leslie's,* Feb. 12, 1903; Helen Winslow, "The Confessions of a Newspaper Woman," *Atlantic,* Feb. 1905; Debon Ayr, "Hints to Women Who Would Be Newspaper Writers," *Leslie's,* Aug. 1, 1907; McCracken, "Journalism for the College-Bred Girl."

84 only Black member: "A Fine Musical Recital; Relative to Journalism, a New Drama; Personal Notes," *Cleveland Gazette,* June 7, 1888.

84 "novelty to be dreaded": Gertrude Mossell, *The Work of the Afro-American Woman* (Philadelphia: George S. Ferguson, 1908), 100–101.

84 No known barrier: For example, Bennett, *Journalism for Women.*

84 The number of women: Steiner, "Gender at Work." From 1900 to 1910, Steiner's figures also indicate that the number of men in the profession grew relatively slightly as the number of women nearly doubled.

84 Rheta Childe Dorr: As a struggling woman wage worker herself, she was keenly attuned to how different her white-collar circumstances were from theirs. "This gigantic swindle of women had been going on for centuries and would go on until the women themselves learned how to revolt," she later wrote. Woman factory workers seemed to be unquestioning, resigned to their fate. "No girl regarded her earnings as her own," Dorr wrote. "All handed in their pay-envelopes unopened and the pittance they received back for carfare and lunch they looked on as a gift from their fathers."

85 In need of more money: Rheta Childe Dorr, *A Woman of Fifty* (New York: Funk & Wagnalls, 1924), 98, 103, 311. Her editor was Hammond Lamont.

85 "when human character": Virginia Woolf, *Mr. Bennett and Mrs. Brown* (London: Hogarth Press, 1924).

86 "clever, impromptu": *Westminster (Md.) Democratic Advocate,* April 7, 1900, citing *Baltimore Telegram,* "Our Amateur Prize Photographic Contest—Washington Wins the Five-Dollar Prize," *Leslie's,* March 17, 1900.

86 Her nearly open access: Mrs. C. R. Miller files, Special Collections & Archives, Nimitz Library, U.S. Naval Academy at Annapolis. The file contains years' worth of separate agreements for photographs taken at Annapolis.

86 well-connected husband: Wallace L. Clapp, "Charles R. Miller," reprint of an article in the *Eastern Underwriter,* 1938, 4. Governor Warfield, like the Millers, attended Western Maryland and was a cofounder of Fidelity and Deposit Trust, where Miller, an attorney, worked his entire career, eventually rising to the rank of president.

86 "Because," she replied: L. M. "A Baltimore Woman's Success with Camera and Pen," *Baltimore American,* Oct. 20, 1907.

87 From 1900 to 1908 she wrote: For example, Mrs. C. R. Miller, "Fairyland Expo," *Leslie's,* Oct. 20, 1904; "Unique State Buildings at the St. Louis

Exposition," *Leslie's,* Oct. 27, 1904, centerfold; "Great Floral Clock," *Leslie's,* Nov. 17, 1904; "A Woman's Experience in the Wilds of Alaska," *Leslie's,* July 26, 1906; "Policing the Golden Mining Camps of the Yukon," *Leslie's,* Aug. 23, 1906; "What an American Found in Alaska," *Leslie's,* Sept. 27, 1906; "Found the Sun in Cuba," *Baltimore Sun,* March 21, 1907; Mrs. C. R. Miller, "With the American Army in Cuba," *Leslie's,* April 18, 1907; "Mrs. Charles R. Miller Home," *Baltimore Sun,* July 27, 1907; Mrs. C. R. Miller, "The World's Most Famous Leper Settlement," *Leslie's,* Jan. 30, 1908. Reporting from the Balkans and Turkey follows an item in the Westminster *Democratic Advocate,* Sept. 25, 1909, noting that the Millers had been traveling throughout Russia. Stories of hers from that part of the world follow soon after.

87 Great Baltimore Fire: Baltimore Fire Supplement, *Leslie's,* Feb. 18, 1904, with numerous "photographs by our special photographer, Mrs. C. R. Miller." More of her photographs appear in the issues of Feb. 25 and March 10, 1904.

88 the AP sent Egan to Japan: "Tale of Siege Told: Japanese Lift Veil," *NYT,* Nov. 4, 1904; "Martin Egan Dies," *NYT,* Dec. 8, 1938; "Port Arthur News Beat a Notable Achievement," *NYT,* Nov. 5, 1904; Melville Elijah Stone, *"M.E.S.," His Book* (New York: Harper and Brothers, 1918), 161, 164–65, 170. See also J. Anthony Lukas, *Big Trouble: A Murder in a Small Western Town Sets Off a Struggle for the Soul of America* (New York: Simon & Schuster, 1997), 679.

88 Eleanor Franklin arrived in Japan: Eleanor Franklin, "An American Woman Describes the Broadway of Yokohama," *Leslie's,* Aug. 11, 1904; "An American Girl's Plain Talk About the Japanese Girl," Sept. 8, 1904; "Tobacco's Prominent Part in Japan's Social Life," Nov. 10, 1904.

88 let the Japanese leader know: "Our War Correspondent Creates Consternation," *Richmond Times-Dispatch,* May 5, 1905; "Martin Egan Is Married," *Hawaiian Star,* Sept. 18, 1905.

88 "the only woman": "Our War Correspondent Creates Consternation."

89 Franklin and Egan: Martin Egan to Elizabeth Gignoux Baner, Aug. 8, 1905, Morgan Library & Museum, New York; "Martin Egan Is Married"; "Wedded in Tokio: Two Well-Known Newspaper People Become One," *New Orleans Times-Democrat,* Sept. 16, 1905.

89 "a bright American girl": Eleanor Franklin, "Russia Must Pay Cost of the War," *Boston Sunday Globe,* July 30, 1905; also carried the same day in such papers as the *WP,* the *Pittsburgh Post,* and the *Detroit Free Press.*

89 Katsura told her: Franklin, "Russia Must Pay Cost of the War." See "Martin Egan Is Married"; "Wedded in Tokio"; "Our War Correspondent," *Richmond Times-Dispatch,* May 5, 1905.

89 Miller, too, had her big moments: Mrs. C. R. Miller, "Peace of Europe Threatened by Events in the Balkans," *Leslie's,* Oct. 22, 1808; and "The Cholera Epidemic in Unsanitary Russia," *Leslie's,* Oct. 29, 1908.

89 she was in Barcelona: Mrs. C. R. Miller, "On the Spanish Firing Line in Melilla," *Leslie's,* Oct. 21, 1909; "My Adventures with the Spaniards in Melilla," Oct. 28, 1909; "The Camera's Story of Melilla," Nov. 11, 1909.

89 "who shall have their deeds": *Army and Navy Journal,* April 2, 1910.

89 In social notes: George Sheridan, "The World's Only Woman War Correspondent," *Leslie's,* Feb. 27, 1913. Other examples: "Baltimore Woman's Success with Camera and Pen," *Baltimore American,* Oct. 20, 1907; "Perilous Camera Trips of Woman Photographer," *Baltimore Sun,* Dec. 22, 1907; "An Artistic Woman's Unique Home," *Baltimore American,* Feb. 19, 1911; "Mrs. Miller: A Globe Trotter and Writer," *Baltimore Sun,* April 24, 1911.

90 for surgery: "Mrs. C. R. Miller Recovering," *Baltimore Sun,* Jan. 14, 1911.

90 Future assignments: Mrs. C. R. Miller, "Cuba's Queer Traveling Stores," *Leslie's,* Aug. 17, 1910; "My Adventures in the Dismal Swamp," *Leslie's,* June 8, 1911; *Westminster (Md.) Democratic Advocate,* June 9, 1911; Mrs. C. R. Miller, "The Panama Canal Rapidly Advancing Toward Completion," *Leslie's,* March 14, 1912, and "The Ill-Fated Warship 'Maine' Again," *Leslie's,* March 7, 1912; "A Leslie's Photographer's Strange Adventure," Dec. 19, 1912; "Women Playing Part in War of the Balkans," *NY Sun,* Nov. 17, 1912; Mrs. C. R. Miller, "With Our Naval Defenders at Guantanamo," *Leslie's,* May 1, 1913; Mrs. C. R. Miller, "Leslie's War Correspondent Visits Bulgarian Prisoners of War," Sept. 4, 1913; "The Florence Nightingales of Servia," Sept. 11, 1913.

90 "I am fighting": Mrs. C. R. Miller, "Pancho Villa Seen Through Woman's Eyes," *Leslie's,* Feb. 26, 1914.

91 Miller, for *Leslie's:* "Through Cuba on Motorcar," *Baltimore Sun,* March 9, 1907; "An American Woman Finds Traveling Safe in Cuba," *Leslie's,* April 11, 1907.

91 "Bullying the Woman": Rheta Childe Dorr, "Bullying the Woman Worker," *Harper's Weekly,* March 20, 1907.

91 Gertrude Mossell completed: Pennsylvania Trails of History, historical marker for Gertrude Bustill Mossell, 1423 Lombard Street, Philadelphia. See patrailsofhistory.com.

91 East Room of the White House: "In Honor of Congress," *WP,* Feb. 1, 1907. With thanks to the Theodore Roosevelt biographer Patricia O'Toole for a fuller explanation of this annual practice of the president.

92 "nerve and ingenuity": "Brilliant Women in Various Fields of Journalism," *Champaign (Ill.) News,* March 2, 1907.

92 " 'break in' where angels feared": "N.Y. World's Great Beat," *Hagerstown*

(Md.) Morning Herald, March 31, 1902; "Mrs. Astor on the Entertaining of Foreigners in New York Society," *NY World Extra Magazine*, March 9, 1902.

92 Mrs. John Jacob Astor: Ad, "First Interview on Record with Mrs. Astor by Nixola Greeley," *NY Evening World*, March 8, 1902; "Mrs. Astor on the Entertaining of Foreigners," March 9, 1902; Ross, *Ladies of the Press*, 86–87.

92 signed by "Nixola": Greeley-Smith, "Mrs. Astor on the Entertaining of Foreigners," Oct. 9, 1902.

93 "language not found": "N.Y. World's Great Beat."

93 "To be told": Mark Twain, "Mark Twain Says It's All Rubbish," *Santa Cruz (Calif.) Evening Sentinel*, March 13, 1902.

93 "cream-colored": "Newspaper Women: Horace Greeley's Granddaughter Who Prides Herself on Being a Cream-Colored Journalist," *NY Herald*, Sept. 1, 1906; Greeley-Smith, "Mrs. Astor on Entertaining." Also Ross, *Ladies of the Press*, 86–96.

93 "one true, sweet note": Dorothy Dix, "As a Woman Sees the Case Move Along," *Buffalo Enquirer*, via the Hearst Syndicate, Feb. 19, 1907; *Atchison (Kans.) Daily Globe*, Feb. 23, 1907.

94 "that woman shall supplement": Ada Patterson, "Ada Patterson Says Woman Is Best Juror in Trials Like Thaw's," *Vicksburg (Miss.) Evening Post*, Feb. 20, 1907.

94 "I wonder," she mooned: Winifred Black, "Like Bedraggled Kitten Before Fierce Bull Dog," *Lincoln Journal Star*, Feb. 21, 1907.

94 "The Vivisection": Nixola Greeley-Smith, "The Vivisection of a Woman's Soul," *NY Evening World*, Feb. 22, 1907.

94 "sob sister" became: See, for example, "'He'll be a Criminal for Life,' Sobs Sister," *Oakland Tribune*, Feb. 26, 1908; "As the Wind Blows," *Scranton Truth*, Sept. 10, 1910; "'Johnnie' Carroll, One of the Sells-Floto Performers on 'Denver,' a Trick Horse," *Detroit Free Press*, Aug. 28, 1911; "The Morning Hatchet," *Pittsburgh Post*, May 2, 1913; Sarah the Sob Sister, "'Why My Husband Left Me,'" *Reading (Pa.) Times*, Dec. 19, 1914.

94 "prowl around": Sarah Addington, "A Sob Traitor," *NY Tribune*, Sept. 5, 1918.

95 "In a world where women": Ibid.

95 deposed editor: "Woman-Run Paper No Failure," *Fourth Estate*, April 12, 1919. Chenoweth, who was educated but without any journalism experience, insisted that circulation and revenue increased on the women's watch. Another all-woman effort came about in 1919 after the weekly *Scarsdale Inquirer* went out of business in New York's Westchester County. The Scarsdale Woman's Club bought it for a dollar and turned

their service to the community into a healthy revenue source for the club. They ran the paper for the next forty years, until 1959, when they sold it for a handsome profit to finance the purchase of a new clubhouse. See "We Present to You Your Newspaper," *Scarsdale Inquirer,* Nov. 5, 1919; "Well-Known Woman Writer Appointed Editor of Scarsdale Inquirer," *Fourth Estate,* Jan. 13, 1923; "Club News," *San Bernardino Sun,* Aug. 16, 1934.

95 "Mary Miles Minter": For example: ad, "The Sob Sister," with Herbert Rawlinson and Anna Little, *Houston Post,* July 24, 1914; and ad, "Mary Miles Minter in 'The Heart Specialist,'" *Montgomery (Ala.) Advertiser,* May 17, 1922.

95 "natural offspring": Ed O'Malley, "Sob Sisters," *LAT,* Feb. 12, 1921.

96 at least forty of them: Edy, *Woman War Correspondent.* Edy's count for World War I is forty-one.

96 Shortly before Austria-Hungary: "The Servian Capital Taken by Austria," *Leslie's,* Aug. 13, 1914. Photos by Mrs. C. R. Miller.

96 husband-and-wife team: For example, Helen Johns Kirtland, "A Woman on the Battle Front," *Leslie's,* Aug. 24, 1918; "When the Sun Shines in Italy," *Leslie's,* Sept. 28, 1918; "Liberty Is in the Very Air in Europe," Nov. 16, 1918; and "Winning the War from the Clouds," Nov. 16, 1918; Helen Johns Kirtland and Lucian S. Kirtland, "A Tribute to Women War Workers They Have Done Their Bit," Nov. 30, 1918, and "They Have Done Their Bit," Dec. 28, 1918.

96 Yet the earliest historians: For example, Emmet Crozier, *American Reporters on the Western Front, 1914–1918* (New York: Oxford University Press, 1959).

96 President Woodrow Wilson presented: See Woodrow Wilson, "Equal Suffrage: Address of the President of the United States Delivered to the Senate of the United States on Sept. 30, 1918," senate.gov.

96 "There have been no great": Ross, *Ladies of the Press,* 4.

97 Attention focused on their pluck: See, for example, "Woman Picks Up Grenade and Is Killed Instantly," *Buffalo Courier,* Oct. 22, 1918; AP, "American Woman War Correspondent," *Boston Globe,* Aug. 19, 1926; "Cecil J. Dorrian Dies," *Brooklyn Times Union,* Aug. 19, 1926.

97 Roy Howard: Dorothy Schneider and Carl J. Schneider, *Into the Breach: American Women Overseas in World War I* (New York: Viking, 1991), 199.

97 Smaller client papers: Ross, *Ladies of the Press,* 369.

98 "valuable volunteer": George Creel, *How We Advertised America* (New York: Harper & Brothers, 1920), 300.

98 Edith Wharton: Edith Wharton, "The Look of Paris," *Scribner's,* May 1915; "In Argonne," June 1915; "In Lorraine and the Vosges," Oct. 1915; "In the North," Nov. 1915; "In Alsace," Nov. 20, 1915. Also, Edith Wharton,

Fighting France: From Dunkerque to Belfort (London: Macmillan, 1915). ("Tone of Paris," the last chapter of the book, was not previously published.) Also see "Mrs. Wharton and Kipling on the War," *NYT,* Dec. 5, 1915. For fuller treatment, see Edward J. Klekowski and Libby Klekowski, *Edith Wharton and Mary Roberts Rinehart at the Western Front, 1915* (Jefferson, N.C.: McFarland, 2018). "The Great Blue Tent," was one of Wharton's poems about the war. See Wharton, "The Great Blue Tent," *NYT,* Aug. 25, 1915.

98 Mary Roberts Rinehart: Mary Roberts Rinehart, *My Story* (New York: Farrar & Rinehart, 1931), 149–95; Mary Roberts Rinehart, *Kings, Queens, and Pawns: An American Woman at the Front* (New York: George H. Doran, 1915); Mary Roberts Rinehart, "A Talk with the King of Belgium," *Saturday Evening Post,* April 3, 1915; "For King and Country," April 17, May 1, 8, June 2, 26, 1915; "Queen Mary of England," June 19, 1915; "The Queen of the Belgians," July 3, 1915; "The Red Badge of Mercy," July 31, 1915. For fuller treatment, see Klekowski and Klekowski, *Edith Wharton and Mary Roberts Rinehart at the Western Front.*

98 Gertrude Atherton: Gertrude Atherton, "On France at War: Atherton," *NYT Sunday Magazine,* July 2, Aug. 27, Sept. 10, 17, 24, Oct. 1, 15, 1916. Also on whether the Germans intentionally infected French soldiers with tuberculosis: *NYT,* Sept. 25 and 27, 1916. Also Gertrude Atherton, "Women of France: What They Have Done in the Great War," *Delineator,* Feb., March, April 1917. Gertrude Atherton, *Life in the War Zone* (New York: courtesy of the *NYT,* 1916); *The Living Present* (New York: Frederick A. Stokes, 1917); *Adventures of a Novelist* (New York: Horace Liveright, 1932).

98 Inez Milholland: Inez Milholland, "Merrie England Hushed in Death Grip of War," *NY Tribune,* July 18, 1915; "Italy's Heroic Response Is Blind War Hysteria," July 24, 1915; "National Vanity Led Italy to Enter the War," July 26, 1915; "Everything German, Even Names, Taboo in Rome," July 31, 1915; "American Princess Aids Italian Soup Kitchen," Aug. 3, 1915.

98 Nellie Bly arrived: Nellie Bly, "Nellie Bly on the Firing Line," *NY Evening Journal,* Dec. 10, 1914. Bly's stories ran in the *Journal* from Dec. 3, 1914, until well into February.

98 "the first American-trained": Alice Rohe, "Once Gay Vienna Now City of Gloom," *Washington Times,* Oct. 23, 1914. That story of Rohe's, dated Oct. 6, was mailed to New York from Rome, delaying publication until Oct. 23.

98 Bly, though, was certainly ahead: Kroeger, *Nellie Bly,* 398.

99 "further into the war zone": Eleanor Franklin Egan, "Woman Tells of War Horrors and Terrors: Thrown into Jail; Escapes in Diver Attack,"

SF Examiner, Jan. 28, 1916; Eleanor Franklin Egan, "Behind the Smoke of Battle: How Turkey Is 'Dispersing' a Nation," *Saturday Evening Post,* Feb. 5, 1916.

99 At the behest of: Ida Tarbell, "Cardinal Mercier—Undaunted Soul," *Red Cross Magazine,* June 1918.

99 Rheta Childe Dorr: Dorr wrote for the New York *Evening Mail* and Bryant reported from "a woman's point of view" for the Bell Syndicate. Bryant went with her husband, the well-known journalist John Reed, who, on return to the United States in 1919, described himself in testimony before Congress as a "revolutionary socialist." With Reed during the same congressional appearance, Bryant said that although she went on assignment for Bell, she also was working for Philadelphia's *Public Ledger,* but for stories to be written only after her return to the United States. Chris Dubbs, *American Journalists in the Great War: Rewriting the Rules of Reporting* (Lincoln: University of Nebraska Press, 2017), 180; Dorr, *Woman of Fifty,* 320–43. For Bryant, see "Extols Bolshevik Rule," subhead: "Says She Tried to Shield Ledger," *Baltimore Sun,* Feb. 22, 1919.

99 "front-page girls": Genevieve F. Herrick, "The Newspaper Woman Joins Up," in *Journalism in Wartime,* ed. Frank Luther Mott (Washington, D.C.: American Council on Public Affairs, 1943), 126–28.

100 Nixola Greeley-Smith died: "Women in American Journalism," *SF Chronicle,* March 18, 1919.

100 Sadie Kneller Miller spent: "Mrs. Sadie K. Miller's Funeral Is Tomorrow," *Baltimore Sun,* Nov. 22, 1920; "Mrs. Sadie K. Miller, War Reporter, Is Dead," *NY Herald,* Nov. 22, 1920; "Mrs. C. R. Miller," *Westminster Sentinel,* Nov. 28, 1920; "Mrs. Sadie Kneller Miller," *NYT,* Nov. 23, 1920; "Former Citizen Dead," *Westminster Democratic Advocate,* Nov. 26, 1920.

100 Bly was in Vienna: Kroeger, *Nellie Bly,* 389–454.

101 "If this was bitter": Ross, *Ladies of the Press,* 59. Ishbel Ross joined the staff of the *NY Herald Tribune* in 1919.

101 "THE BEST REPORTER": Arthur Brisbane, "The Death of Nellie Bly," *NY Evening Journal,* Jan. 28, 1922.

101 Egan died: "Pearls and Pebbles," *Hawaiian Star,* March 2, 1908; "American Woman Has Thrilling Experiences in the War Zone," *Akron Beacon Journal,* Feb. 3, 1916.

101 *Herald Tribune* summarized: "Eleanor F. Egan, Writer of War and Peace, Dies," *NY Herald Tribune,* Jan. 18, 1925; "Rites for Mrs. E. F. Egan Will Be Held Tomorrow," *NY Herald,* Jan. 19, 1925; "Eleanor F. Egan Rites Attended by Noted Men," *NY Tribune,* Jan. 21, 1925.

101 a grief-stricken Martin Egan: "Funeral of Mrs. Egan," *NYT,* Jan. 21, 1925.

101 Kate Masterson would not become: *Indianapolis Journal,* May 4, 1904.

102 "at one time one of the best": "Mrs. Kate Masterson Was Prominent Newspaper Woman," *Brooklyn Eagle,* June 9, 1927.

102 both reported her breakdown: "Writer Sent to Bellevue," *NYT,* July 27, 1915; "Writer in Bellevue," *NY Tribune,* July 27, 1915.

102 "The tragic events of her life": "Kate Masterson," *NY Herald Tribune,* June 20, 1927.

Chapter 6. Janus-Faced

103 Editors, he reasoned: Burges Johnson, "Preparing College Women for Journalism," *Outlook,* Sept. 28, 1921.

103 The statistics told the story: Steiner, "Gender at Work."

103 As late as 1926: Catherine [*sic*] Brody, "Newspaper Girls," *American Mercury,* March 1926.

104 "We already have a woman": Ibid. Census figures do not quite square with the perception. The 33,773 total number of reporters and editors in 1910 rose only by around 600 people, to 34,382 by 1920. In that total, the increase in the number of women was slightly higher than the total, up by just over a thousand from 4,181 woman journalists to 5,273. By 1930, the number of women in the field jumped to 11,924, an increase of more than 100 percent.

104 "Women are usually": Ruth Brindze, "Journalism an Art Not a Calling, Says Talcott Williams," *Brooklyn Eagle,* Feb. 8, 1925.

104 Hurst's three-part series: Fannie Hurst, "Main Street—Russia," *McCall's,* Jan., Feb., March 1925. For a fuller treatment of Hurst's series and the critical response to it, see Brooke Kroeger, *Fannie: The Talent for Success of Writer Fannie Hurst* (New York: Times Books, 1999), 109–20.

104 a 1934 talk she gave: Fannie Hurst, "Are We Coming or Going?," *Vital Speeches,* Dec. 3, 1934; Kroeger, *Fannie,* 232–33.

104 "Ideal American College Girl": "Ideal Girls Stir Fannie Hurst's Ire," *NYT,* Sept. 16, 1938, later edition; "Call Shore Girl 'Ideal Co-ed,'" *Long Branch (N.J.) Daily Record,* Sept. 16, 1938.

105 Still others started late: McCormick had previous experience in journalism but came to note when she first wrote for the *NYT* ("New Italy of the Italians," *NYT,* Dec. 19, 1920; "Italy's Parliamentary Paradoxes," *NYT,* May 8, 1921). Bass published the *California Eagle,* Dunnigan came to journalism after a long career as a teacher, and Cooke worked for a U.S. senator after graduation from the University of Minnesota before becoming an assistant to W. E. B. Du Bois at *The Crisis.*

105 In *The American Mercury:* Brody, "Newspaper Girls."

106 Brody, born: Declaration of Intention, U.S. Department of Commerce and Labor, Bureau of Immigration and Naturalization, No. 39831, p. 345,

June 7, 1910. The application identifies her as Katia, born in 1900, the oldest of four children of Harris Mayer Borodowko. Also, Harris Mayer Borodowko, Petition for Naturalization, U.S. Department of Labor Naturalization Service, No. 39201, p. 101, including Katia, Isaac, Samuel, and Abraham, May 2, 1914. Also, 1940 U.S. Census, 877 South Avenue, Springfield, Mo., South Campbell Township, Ward 4-[6?], Block 456, Sheet Number 13A, April 13, 1940, notes her birthplace as Latvia. (Her identification is clear—magazine writer from New York—despite misspelled adopted last name as Broody.)

106 Brody felt secure enough: U.S. Passport application, No. 147556, New York, New York County, of Catharine Borodowko, "known professionally as Catharine Brody," Feb. 25, 1921. The spelling of Catherine shifts regularly in bylines and public records between the earliest Catharine and the later Catherine. The city editor who hired her was George T. Hughes.

106 When she returned: Brody, "Newspaper Girls"; Ross, *Ladies of the Press,* 116–17, 168.

106 In 1923, she persuaded: Catherine [*sic*] Brody, "What Happens When a Girl Goes Job Hunting in a Strange City," *Buffalo Morning Express,* Dec. 9, 16, 30, 1923, Jan. 6, 13, 1924; Brody, *Vancouver Sun,* Jan. 20, 27, Feb. 3, 17, March 2, 9, 23, 30, 1924.

106 Her fourteen-part series: See Walter A. Wyckoff, *The Workers: An Experiment in Reality* (New York: Charles Scribner's Sons, 1897); Whiting Williams, *What's on the Worker's Mind* (New York: Charles Scribner's Sons, 1920); Cornelia Stratton Parker, "Working with the Working Woman," *Harper's,* June, July, Aug., Oct., Nov., Dec. 1921. Others cited more fully at reference in previous chapter. Also, as a book, Parker, *Working with the Working Woman* (New York: Harper & Brothers, 1922). See also Brooke Kroeger, *Undercover Reporting: The Truth About Deception* (Evanston, Ill.: Northwestern University Press, 2012), 93–102. Also, search "other people's work" in the *Undercover Reporting* database, undercover.hosting .nyu.edu.

106 As a narrative construct: For more on Brody's career, see "Hope to Enlarge Scope of Service Main Reason for Coming 'Y.W.' Drive," *Lansing (Mich.) State Journal,* April 25, 1925; Ross, *Ladies of the Press,* 116–17, 168; Catherine Brody, "Wholesale Murder and Suicide: Do You Know the Menace of Reduceomania?," *Photoplay,* July, Aug., Sept. 1926; *Why Girls Go Back Home,* directed by James Flood, starring Patsy Ruth Miller, Clive Brook, and Jane Winton, scenario by Sonya Levien, story by Catherine [Brody], March 1, 1926, imdb.com. Also, Mordaunt Hall, "The Screen: The Conceited Actor," *NYT,* May 18, 1926.

106 "the susceptibility of men": Brody, "Newspaper Girls."

107 Brody's published call: Marguerite Moors Marshall, "The Woman of It," *St. Petersburg Times,* March 25, 1926.

108 "the feminine among the scribes": James Doherty, "Chaplain's Story—Woe," *NY Daily News,* Jan. 15, 1927.

108 "The three of us": "Women in Advertising and Journalism," *Editor & Publisher,* Jan. 22, 1927. The quotation is from Kuhn.

109 Maurine Dallas Watkins's: See Kori Rumore and Marianne Mather, *He Had It Coming: Four Murderous Women and the Reporter Who Immortalized Their Stories* (Chicago: Midway, 2019).

109 "Nobody ever heard": "Women in Advertising and Journalism."

109 She dismissed any claims: Catharine Brody, "She Gets a Job," *North American Review,* Aug. 1930; "Seen from the Hilltop," *Kane (Pa.) Republican,* July 19, 1930.

110 More than a score: O. O. McIntyre, "Blowing a Few Concrete Bubbles," *Richmond (Ind.) Palladium,* Sept. 17, 1932; Sam Love, "New York," *Springfield (Mo.) Press,* Oct. 28, 1932; Jack Stennett, "A New Yorker at Large," *Allentown (Pa.) Morning Call,* April 23, 1936.

110 *Nobody Starves:* Catharine Brody, *Nobody Starves* (New York: Longmans, Green, 1932); *Personne ne meurt de faim,* trans. Magdeleine Paz (Paris: Reider, 1936); "On the Ragged Edge," *Saturday Review,* Oct. 8, 1932; "Miss Brody's 'Nobody Starves' and Other Recent Works," *NYT,* Oct. 9, 1932; "Novel Shows Jobless Helplessly Milling About," *LAT,* Oct. 9, 1932.

110 Its book jacket: Rose Wilder Lane, who was close to Brody and to Lewis's wife, Dorothy Thompson, pressed Thompson hard for the endorsement on Brody's behalf. On the front cover of the jacket, Lewis's blurb adds, "Definitely important." Thompson to Lane, Twin Farms, June 8 and July 28, 1932, Dorothy Thompson Papers, George Arents Research Library, Syracuse University; Lewis to [Brody's publisher, Longmans, Green], July 16, 1932, Sinclair Lewis Collection, Port Washington Public Library, Port Washington, N.Y.

110 "the outstanding novel": *Springfield Leader & Press,* June 4, 1933; *Springfield (Mo.) News Leader,* July 23, 1933.

110 Brody spent a great deal: *Springfield (Mo.) News Leader,* July 23, 1933.

110 "Everyone in 'these parts'": *Springfield (Mo.) News Leader,* June 5, 1934.

110 Neither of her next: Gertrude C. Thomas, ed., "Famous Jewish Women Lauded at Institute," *Wilkes-Barre (Pa.) Times-Leader,* Jan. 4, 1938.

110 After that, Brody lay low: The known facts about her on record in the years that followed are few. In 1960, there is a paid death notice for Brody's mother in the *NYT,* yet her own death a mere two years later goes without one, even though her three younger brothers were all still alive

at the time. Obituary notice, "Borodovko—Sarah E.," *NYT,* April 28, 1960.

110 She died in May: Catherine [*sic*] Brody, New Jersey Death Index, 1901–2017, May 1962; Mount Zion Cemetery, Maspeth, Queens, date of death May 1962, findagrave.com.

110 Two years before: Julia Blanshard, "Woman Becomes Editor of New York Newspaper; Laura Vitray Is First of Her Sex to Win Post," NEA via *Camden (N.J.) Evening Courier,* June 23, 1930, among numerous other reprints. "Woman Journalist, 86, Dies of Heart Ailment," *LAT,* Oct. 21, 1948; John W. Leonard, "Mary Holland Kinkaid," *Woman's Who's Who of America* (New York: American Commonwealth, 1914–15), 1:459. There is no firm dating of Kinkaid's tenure at the *LA Herald,* thought to be in the early years of the twentieth century.

111 she cautioned any "girl reporter": Ross, *Ladies of the Press,* 9.

111 Legendary figures like: Stanley Walker, *City Editor* (New York: Frederick A. Stokes, 1934), 249, 255.

111 McDowell could thank: "Rachel McDowell Dies at Age of 69," *NYT,* Aug. 31, 1949.

112 "plump, energetic spinster": "She Sees the Pope," *Time,* Sept. 23, 1935.

112 "The Pure Language League": "Newsharks' Language," *Time,* Jan. 16, 1933; "She Sees the Pope"; "Rachel McDowell Leaves the Times," *NYT,* Jan. 1, 1949; "Miss McDowell Regrets," *Newsweek,* Jan. 17, 1949; "Rachel McDowell Dies at Age of 69"; "Speak No Evil," *Time,* Nov. 7 1949; Ross, *Ladies of the Press,* 149, 150, 152–61, 169.

113 Rachel Carson: Rachel Carson, "Undersea," *Atlantic,* Sept. 1937; Carson, *Under the Sea-Wind* (New York: Simon & Schuster, 1941). See, for example, William Beebe, "Of and About the Sea," *Saturday Review,* Dec. 27, 1941.

113 Ishbel Ross's move: The first was Emma Bugbee, whom the *Tribune* hired around 1911. See Ross, *Ladies of the Press,* 123; "Emma Bugbee, Reporter for 55 Years," *NYT,* Oct. 10, 1981; "Emma Bugbee Was Sitting at Her Desk," *Rochester Democrat and Chronicle,* April 22, 1966.

113 Pankhurst agreed to speak with her: Barbara A. Bannon, "Ishbel Ross," *Publishers Weekly,* Sept. 29, 1975; Marion Marzolf, *Up from the Footnote: A History of Women Journalists* (New York: Hastings House, 1977), 40.

113 featured twelve: Walker, *City Editor,* 261–323.

114 "a quiet, efficient, courageous": Ibid., 288.

114 "unflustered competence": Walker, foreword to Ross, *Ladies of the Press,* xi–xii.

114 From firsthand experience: Walker, *City Editor,* 248–64.

115 "startling variations": Walker, foreword to Ross, *Ladies of the Press,* xi–xii.

115 In the opening chapter: Ross, *Ladies of the Press,* 3–5, 11.

115 "City editors rarely take chances": Ibid.

116 shears and paste pots: Herrick, "Newspaper Woman Joins Up," 126–28.

116 front-page immigration series: "For Immigrants' Welfare," *NYT,* Nov. 2, 1921; "Advisory Group on Immigrant Welfare Meets," *Chicago Tribune,* Nov. 3, 1921; "Beg Your Pardon," Nov. 4, 1921; "Uncle Sam Oils Vacuum Cleaner for Ellis Island," Nov. 5, 1921; "Tribune Expose Aids Immigrants," Dec. 21, 1921.

117 On December 20: "Statement of Miss Genevieve Forbes, *Chicago Tribune,* Chicago, Ill." Hearing HRG-1921-IMN-0015, U.S. House of Representatives, Committee on Immigration and Naturalization, 67-2, Serial 1-B, Dec. 20, 1921, 257–81.

117 subhead of her obituary: Genevieve Forbes [Ireland to Ellis Island series], *Chicago Tribune,* Oct. 13, 14, 15, 16, 17, 18, 19, 21, 22, 23, 24, 25, 26, 1921; "Mrs. Herrick Dies; Wrote for Tribune," *Chicago Tribune,* Dec. 18, 1962. The labor secretary was James J. Davis.

117 Eleanor Roosevelt's clique: Maurine H. Beasley, "Eleanor Roosevelt's Press Conferences: Case Study in Class, Gender, and Race," *Social Science Journal,* Oct. 1, 2000. Also, for example, Eleanor Roosevelt, "My Day," United Features Syndicate, May 2, 1950.

117 She was fired in 1934: "Mrs. Herrick Dies; Wrote for Tribune." See also for dating, House ad, "Follow Congress Through the Tribune," *Chicago Tribune,* Jan. 6, 1934; " 'Here' Says Katharine Darst . . . ," *St. Louis Globe-Democrat,* July 19, 1934. Also, Emilie Le Beau Lucchesi, "The 'Girl Reporter' Who Exposed Terrors of Immigration," *Chicago Tribune,* April 16, 2016.

117 Charlotta Spears Bass: "Shocking Pink," *Time,* March 17, 1952.

118 Eleanor "Cissy" Patterson: Cissy Patterson was also the aunt of Alicia Patterson, who, after her rocky, libel-scarred days as a cub reporter for the family's *New York Daily News,* would go on to found and successfully publish Long Island's *Newsday,* starting in 1940, helped by the fortune of her husband, Harry Guggenheim.

118 From her power perch: Adela Rogers St. Johns, one of the best known of Cissy Patterson's protégées, became a journalist for the Hearst papers in 1912 with only two years of schooling at Hollywood High. She moved through the empire's properties in San Francisco, Los Angeles, and later Washington, D.C., with time out in between to write screenplays and books. See Adela Rogers St. Johns, *The Honeycomb* (New York: Doubleday, 1969), 97–98. Also, Adela Rogers St. Johns, "How Jobless, Hungry Girls Live Told by Adela Rogers St. Johns," *LA Examiner,* Dec. 20, 1931; "Penniless Woman," Dec. 21, 1931; "Any Woman Can Eat," Dec. 22, 1931;

"Suspicion's Gulf," Dec, 23, 1931; "Writer Forced to Charity," Dec. 24, 1931; "Jobless Women Hunger," Dec. 25, 1931; "By Six O'Clock," Dec. 28, 1931; "Present Facilities Can Aid Women," Dec. 29, 1931; "Associated Group of 100,000 Women," Dec. 30, 1931.

118 Patterson devoted: Eleanor Patterson, "Woman Editor Finds Einstein Taking Sun Bath, Beats Retreat," *St. Louis Star* via *Washington Herald*, Feb. 11, 1931; Arthur Brisbane, "In Energetic Chicago. The Woman Reporter. Crime's Jackals. Powerful Advertising," *St. Louis Times* via *NY American*, Feb. 12, 1931.

Chapter 7. Practice War

123 "the only American woman": Dorothy Thompson, "On Women Correspondents and Other New Ideas," *Nation*, Jan. 6, 1926.

123 Sigrid Schultz: George Seldes, "Blood Flows in Berlin Streets at Red Memorial," *Chicago Tribune*, Jan. 16, 1921. Schultz and Seldes are said to have remained friends for half a century, although he is not mentioned once in her oral history interview, conducted in 1972, when she was seventy-nine. Schultz to Seldes, n.d. [ca. late 1973], as cited in Helen Fordham, *George Seldes' War for the Public Good: Weaponizing a Free Press* (New York: Palgrave, 1975), 24, 31. Seldes traveled so much in the two years before his transfer to Mexico in 1927 that he only learned of his demotion when he and Schultz corresponded about it in the 1970s. Nancy Caldwell Sorel, *The Women Who Wrote the War* (New York: Arcade, 1999), 4, from Sigrid Schultz Papers, State Historical Society of Wisconsin, Madison.

124 "long before they came to power": Sigrid Schultz, Oral reminiscences, Oral Histories, 1972, box 70, no. 1, William E. Weiner Oral History Library, American Jewish Committee, Dorot Jewish Library, NY Public Library; Dorothy Thompson, "People in the News," WJZ, New York (Westinghouse/RCA) radio broadcast, March 8, 1938, cited in Peter Kurth, *American Cassandra: The Life of Dorothy Thompson* (New York: Little, Brown, 1990), 95, 483n101–2.

124 Ochs did not budge: The exceptions: The *Times*'s archives indicate that Mary Taft joined the staff to cover society and some city news around the time of the ownership transition, 1897 or 1898, and Midy Morgan's death preceded the Ochs purchase of the newspaper by six years. Nan Robertson, *The Girls in the Balcony: Women, Men, and "The New York Times"* (New York: Random House, 1992), 19.

124 Jane Grant: "Historic Data Regarding Minorities Employed by the New York Times; Staff Writers, Department Heads, Blacks and Female,

1862–1974," NY Times Archives, courtesy of Jeff Roth. Also, Jane Grant and Janet Flanner, *Ross, "The New Yorker," and Me* (New York: Reynal, 1965), 83–85.

124　She took leave: Jane Grant, "The Serious Opinions of Charles Chaplin," *NYT,* Sept. 18, 1921; "Geraldine Farrar's First Aid to Opera," Sept. 21, 1924; "Women's Influence Seen in Closed Car Comfort," Jan. 4, 1925.

125　"the first woman reporter": Grant and Flanner, *Ross,* 136. Ochs's statement was without reference to Midy Morgan because she covered livestock; Rachel McDowell because she covered religion (after twelve years on the staff of the *NY Herald* and six years before that with the *Newark Evening News*); Anne O'Hare McCormick in foreign and domestic correspondence (but not officially on staff until 1936); and certainly not Mary Taft, who covered the arts and women's clubs; or Marie Weldon, the society editor, or Anne Rittenhouse, who covered fashion.

125　any talk of women's "firsts": Thompson, "On Women Correspondents."

125　"Why Women Read": "Why Women Read the *Chicago Tribune,*" *Chicago Tribune,* Jan. 3, 1926.

126　"discipline my memory": Thompson, "On Women Correspondents." Also, Dorothy Thompson, unpublished memoir, Dorothy Thompson Collection, Special Collections Research Center, Syracuse University Libraries. Her parents had immigrated to the United States from Britain.

126　Before that, after college: For example, notices such as *Olean (N.Y.) Times Herald,* Feb. 25, 1915; *Buffalo Evening News,* Oct. 22, 1915, and Jan. 17, 1916; *Rochester Democrat and Chronicle,* Feb. 1, 1917. See also Johanna Neuman, *Gilded Suffragists* (New York: New York University Press, 2017); Kroeger, *Suffragents.* The period included the 1915 push for passage of the state suffrage amendment, which failed, and then the redoubled effort over the next two years that brought the pivotal victory of 1917. New York was the epicenter of the national movement. The success of its state amendment campaign revved the engine for the federal amendment's passage and then its ratification by three-quarters of the states in 1920.

126　"We were radicals": Thompson, unpublished memoir; Dorothy Thompson, "My First Job," *Ladies' Home Journal,* April 1957.

126　The battle for suffrage gave: In these years, Thompson also got to know Harriet Burton Laidlaw, Narcissa Cox Vanderlip, and Vira Boarman Whitehouse, all important "gilded suffragists" of the movement in New York state.

126　Thompson took a job: *Buffalo Times,* Aug. 2, 1918.

126　to save the $150: John Gunther, "A Blue-Eyed Tornado," *NY Herald Tribune,* Jan. 13, 1935. In the meantime, she wrote several features about the organization: Dorothy Thompson, "A Community Experiment Which Has Succeeded," *NYT,* March 16, 1919; Dorothy Thompson, "An Adventure in Americanism," *Leslie's,* Aug. 23, 1919.

127 "If I keep on": Thompson to Beatrice Sorchan, June 26, 1920, Thompson Collection; Kurth, *American Cassandra,* 49–50.

127 Sometimes at only a few paragraphs: For example, Dorothy Thompson, "Zionist Leaders Face Overthrow," *Washington Times,* July 10, 1920; "Zionists Uphold Man as Superior," *Salt Lake Telegram,* July 14, 1920; "Zionists Elect Justice Brandeis," *Oregon Daily Journal* (Portland), July 7, 1920; "Jews Fulfill Prophesy to Plant Million Trees," *Little Rock (Ark.) Daily News,* Aug. 17, 1920.

127 "(An American Girl)": For example, Thompson, "Artist Will Illustrate Bible in Palestine Home," *The Anaconda (Mont.) Standard,* Nov. 14, 1920.

127 "dug the toe": Dorothy Thompson, "Dead or Alive I Shall Be Free," *Chattanooga News,* Aug. 31, 1920; "Valera, Jr., Wants Dad," *Buffalo Enquirer,* Sept. 1, 1920.

127 While her Zionist conference: For examples, Dorothy Thompson, "II—The Hope of a New Palestine," *Outlook,* Sept. 8, 1920; "Can't Tell Who Is a Sein Feiner," *Miami Herald,* Sept. 16, 1920; "Cork Under Military Rule," *Charlotte (N.C.) News,* Sept. 17, 1920, first of six "pen pictures."

127 She accumulated many more bylines: For example, Dorothy Thompson, "Who's Boss in Italy, Employer or Employee?," *Wilmington (Del.) Morning News,* Nov. 26, 1920; "Workmen Guarding Industrial Plant They Have Seized from Operators," *Wichita Falls (Tex.) Times Record News,* Dec. 13, 1920.

128 "one must infer": Thompson, "On Women Correspondents."

128 "more attractive": Paul Scott Mowrer, *The House of Europe* (Boston: Houghton Mifflin, 1945), 392.

128 By December 1920: For example, Dorothy Thompson, "Says Vienna Is Beggars' City," *Washington Times,* Dec. 31, 1920.

128 "Richard Harding Davis": Don Wharton, "Dorothy Thompson," *Scribner's,* May 1937.

128 "cover a revolution": Susan Ware, *Seven Women Who Shaped the American Century* (New York: W. W. Norton, 1998), 53.

128 "amiable, blue-eyed tornado": "Woman of the Month—Dorothy Thompson," *Independent Woman,* Jan. 1939.

129 "traverse the 8 kilometers": Dorothy Thompson, "Charles Denies Intention to Seize Throne by Force," *WP,* Nov. 1, 1921.

129 "What a woman!": Margaret Case Harriman, "The It Girl," *New Yorker,* April 20 and 27, 1940; Jack Alexander, "The Girl from Syracuse," *Saturday Evening Post,* May 18, 1940, and "Rover Girl in Europe," May 25,

1940; H. R. Knickerbocker to Thompson and Sinclair Lewis, May 27, 1928, Thompson Collection; Peter Kurth, "Words of Warning," *Seven Days* (Burlington, Vt.), Oct. 27, 2004.

129 Imagine how such a comment: Kurth, *American Cassandra*, 85–87, citing a letter in Kurth's possession, from Schultz to Seldes, Nov. 9, 1975. See also Mowrer, *House of Europe*, 273–75. On the matter of "sex-attraction" as a feminine tool, Mowrer confessed his shame over the crush he developed on a beautiful reporter for a prominent weekly whom he called Gale Miller who, during World War I, had sought his advice about how to get to the front. Mowrer started taking her often to lunch at the Café de la Paix. One day, she begged off with a headache. Mowrer knew she did not speak French, so he insisted on going to her little furnished flat in Montmartre to see if there was anything she might need. There, he found her wrapped "in a silk dressing gown that ill concealed her shapeliness, lying on a couch in her living room, pale, but lovelier than ever." Mowrer was simply besotted. "I also loved my wife, but what had that to do with it?" he wrote. "Love was so wonderful, life so short." Not long after, without so much as a goodbye, she left for Spain with another correspondent. "This Gale Miller with her innocent eyes, was no more, I now perceived, than a common vampire who amused herself and exercised her power by going up and down the world bewildering men," Mowrer wrote. "What a fool I had been!"

129 Soon after the marriage: Dorothy Thompson, *The New Russia* (London: Jonathan Cape, 1929); Theodore Dreiser, *Dreiser's Russia* (Melbourne: Harry E. Longbridge, 1928).

129 "Bunk": Thomas F. Ford, "Did Dreiser Steal Dorothy's Thunder in Book on Russia? 'It's the Bunk,' He Asserts," *LAT,* Dec. 2, 1928.

130 The enmity festered: "Dreiser Slaps Lewis at Ray Long's Dinner After Rap at Book," *NY Evening Post,* March 20, 1931; AP, "Sinclair Lewis' Face Is Slapped by Dreiser," *Baltimore Sun,* March 21, 1931.

130 "to think that Hitler": AP, "Miss Thompson Says She Was Forced to Go," and "U.S. Won't Protest Thompson Ouster," *Minneapolis Star-Tribune,* Aug. 27, 1934; Dorothy Thompson, "Dorothy Thompson Says Crime Was She 'Blasphemed' Hitler," *Minneapolis Star-Tribune* via NANA, Aug. 27, 1934; Frances Davis, *A Fearful Innocence* (Kent, Ohio: Kent State University Press, 1981), 129.

130 class of 1898 valedictorian: Anne O'Hare McCormick, *NYT,* May 4, 1937. The information about McCormick's education in this profile is incorrect. It reports that McCormick earned a BA from the College of St. Mary's in Columbus and an LLD from the University of Dayton, but she never attended either school. Both of these were honorary degrees.

St. Mary's proffered the honor in 1928, the commencement year of its very first class as a college established in 1924. McCormick attended St. Mary's the academy, a high school (*Barquilla de la Santa Maria: Bulletin of the Catholic Record Society, Diocese of Columbus,* Dec. 2003). The honorary Dayton degree was awarded in 1929, a university archivist confirmed. (Amy Rohmiller, University of Dayton Archives, email to author, Oct. 23, 2020. Also, University of Dayton, 1929 Catalogue of Awards, 23.)

131 At the age of thirty: Anne O'Hare McCormick, "Anne O'Hare McCormick, Former Daytonian, Wins Pulitzer Prize," *Dayton Herald,* May 4, 1937.

131 "Only the hardiest": Robertson, *Girls in the Balcony,* 24.

131 "one of the best political": Anne O'Hare McCormick, "Italy and Popes and Parliaments," *NYT,* July 24, 1921.

131 "fired by the Napoleonic": Anne O'Hare McCormick, "Who'll Be Head of the Family?," *NYT,* Feb. 25, 1923.

132 "Mistress McCormick": Robertson, *Girls in the Balcony,* 28–33.

132 Nan Robertson: Ibid., 26–27.

132 "wisecracking, flirtatious": Arthur Gelb, *City Room* (New York: Berkley Books, 2014), 19.

132 Clifton Daniel: Robertson, *Girls in the Balcony,* 28.

132 And yet McCormick's name: See Clifton Daniel, *Lords, Ladies, and Gentlemen: A Memoir* (New York: Arbor House, 1984); James Reston, *Deadline: A Memoir* (New York: Random House, 1991); Arthur Krock, *Memoirs: Sixty Years on the Firing Line* (New York: Funk & Wagnalls, 1968).

132 "more and more experts": "Cartwheel Girl," *Time,* June 12, 1939.

132 "Anne had the map of Ireland": Iphigene Ochs Sulzberger and Susan W. Dryfoos, *Iphigene: Memoirs of Iphigene Ochs Sulzberger of the "New York Times" Family, as Told to Her Granddaughter, Susan W. Dryfoos* (New York: Dodd, Mead, 1981), 161.

133 One of Sulzberger's first acts: Robertson, *Girls in the Balcony,* 17–40.

133 *Independent Woman:* "Woman of the Month—Dorothy Thompson"; "Foreign Correspondent—Anne O'Hare McCormick," *Independent Woman,* July 1939.

133 "often had a good laugh": Kurth, *American Cassandra,* 278n.

134 In 1937, McCormick became: 1918 Pulitzer Prizes, pulitzer.org. That year, two Columbia journalism school students, one a woman, won the only "Newspaper History Award" the Pulitzer board ever offered for compiling a history of what the U.S. press had done for the public during 1917. Over the years, a number of women had been honored in the arts categories.

134 The announcement story: "'Idiot's Delight,' a Pulitzer Winner; 'Honey

in Horn' Gets Novel Prize; Sherwood Drama and First Work by H. L. Davis on 1936 List—Lauren D. Lyman, the Late Will Barber, and Cedar Rapids Gazette Receive Awards in Journalism," *NYT,* May 5, 1936; "Pulitzer Prize for Novel Won by 'Gone with the Wind'; 'You Can't Take It with You,' by Kaufman and Hart, Chosen as Best Play—Brooks's History, Nevins's Biography Named," *NYT,* May 4, 1937; "Wilder's Drama, 'Our Town,' Is Named Pulitzer Winner; Marquand's 'Late George Apley' Gets Prize for Novel—Journalism Awards to Raymond Sprigle, Arthur Krock, W. W. Waymack," *NYT,* May 3, 1938. See also pulitzer.org for winners, 1936, 1937, 1938.

134 It did not share: "Pulitzer Prize for Novel Won by 'Gone with the Wind' "; "Anne O'Hare McCormick," 20.

134 What a lackluster rendering: "Anne McCormick Award Medal for Journalism," *Dayton Herald,* May 15, 1937.

134 For this, there is some circumstantial evidence: See Krock to Mr. John H. Finley, Jan. 15, 1935, asking not to be nominated for the 1936 prize because he would not survive that year's Pulitzer advisory board; Krock to A. H. Sulzberger, May 7, 1937, saying that had Washington been the entry instead of foreign, he would have won; and Krock to Edwin L. James, April 8, 1938, suggesting his nomination for that year's awards for his interview with the president. All in Arthur Hays Sulzberger Papers, folder 2, New York Times Company Records, Manuscripts and Archives Division, NY Public Library.

135 The archives: In 1937, the only nomination the *Times* submitted was for the public service award, which went instead to the *St. Louis Post-Dispatch.*

135 all men: See the Pulitzer board members of 1937 at pulitzer.org.

135 To put McCormick's name forward: Heinz-Dietrich Fischer, *Outstanding International Press Reporting,* vol. 1, *1928–1945: From the Consequences of World War I to the End of World War II* (Berlin: de Gruyter, 1984), 79. ("The jury made a rather short statement by saying that the correspondence award should go to Anne O'Hare McCormick of the New York Times. The Board was of the same opinion and agreed to recommend the prize.") See also Herbert Brucker to Roger Howson, May 12, 1937, Pulitzer Prize Records. ("The nomination originated within the Advisory Board and was made after examination of our bound files of the Times.") Also, Report of the Secretary of the Advisory Board, April 29, 1937. ("Members of the Board agreed to recommend that the prize for foreign correspondence be awarded to Anne O'Hare McCormick of the New York Times for her dispatches and feature articles from Europe and Washington.") Sean Murphy of the Pulitzer staff explained that records for 1937 are scant for the jury reports and do not include the names of who

served. Sean Murphy, email exchange with author, Sept. 5, 2019. ("If a jury was indeed convened, it would have only consisted of tenured, tenure-track and part-time members of the Faculty of Journalism.")

135 A full-color portrait: "She Rides in the Smoking Car," *Time,* June 12, 1939.

135 The writer's lead: The honor conferred on Business and Professional Women's Day by the fair's Career Tours Committee.

136 "a plump pair of legs": "Cartwheel Girl."

136 "She appealed to women": Ibid.

136 "There are just as few": "Mrs. H. C. Bowing Hostess to St. Cloud Reading Room, Mrs. Shilplin Speaker," *St. Cloud Times,* March 26, 1937.

Chapter 8. Depressionistas

137 Martha Gellhorn's legacy: They are not the only woman journalists to achieve distinction in these years, but to give a sense of the place in time of those discussed so far: Anne McCormick was born in 1880, the same year as Rachel McDowell, the *NYT* religion writer, and the late Nixola Greeley-Smith, the *NY World*'s ace interviewer; Dorothy Thompson, born in 1893, was the same age as Sigrid Schultz; both were thirteen years younger than McCormick. Jane Grant, the early *NYT* reporter and *The New Yorker*'s cofounder, was born in 1894, as was another widely admired American woman in Europe, Janet Flanner, *The New Yorker*'s Paris columnist, better known as Genêt. Jane Grant brought Flanner to the magazine in 1926, soon after its founding. Also born in 1894 were Adela Rogers St. Johns of the Hearst empire and the *Chicago Tribune*'s Genevieve Forbes Herrick. Ishbel Ross was born in 1895.

137 Gellhorn led the front page: "Miss Martha Gellhorn," *St. Louis Star,* Aug. 25, 1926.

137 "put over the greatest": "This Will Introduce Mrs. George Gellhorn," *St. Louis Star,* April 21, 1919; and "Introducing Mrs. Gellhorn, St. Louis' Most Prominent Woman and Muskogee's Guest," *Muskogee (Okla.) Times,* Jan. 1, 1921.

138 The event Edna: Marguerite Martyn, "Men Took Women's Chairs and Crowded Them Out of Their Places in 'Golden Lane' of Suffragist 'Walkless Parade,'" *St. Louis Post-Dispatch,* June 15, 1916.

138 Martha, seven years old: "This Will Introduce Mrs. George Gellhorn"; "Introducing Mrs. Gellhorn, St. Louis' Most Prominent Woman and Muskogee's Guest."

138 During Martha's college years: Martha Gellhorn, unpublished memoir, n.d., 4–6, Martha Gellhorn Papers, Howard Gottlieb Archival Research Center, Boston University Collection.

138   She left Bryn Mawr: "To Visit East," *St. Louis Post-Dispatch,* May 18, 1932; "Society News," *St. Louis Star,* Sept. 7 and Dec. 5, 1929.

138   Bylines in the magazine: Martha Gellhorn, "Myopic Maidens," *New Republic,* July 31, 1929; "Rudy Vallée: God's Gift to Us Girls," *New Republic,* Aug. 7, 1929; "Contra 'Lady Chatterley's Lover,'" *New Republic,* Aug. 21, 1929.

138   By the fall, she was working: Ruth Reynolds, "Love Collaborate with Hemingway," *NY Sunday Daily News,* Dec. 8, 1940. The music critic was Fenton Moran.

138   Gellhorn's beat: Gellhorn, unpublished memoir, 4.

138   The managing editor: Caroline Moorehead, *Gellhorn: A Twentieth-Century Life* (New York: Henry Holt, 2003), 26–28. The managing editor who hired her was George O. Williams.

138   "a knight without armor": Marguerite Martyn, "St. Louis Girl Turns Author," *St. Louis Post-Dispatch,* Nov. 14, 1934.

138   "lousy": Reynolds, "Love Collaborate with Hemingway"; Martyn, "St. Louis Girl Turns Author."

138   Three days before Christmas: *St. Louis Post-Dispatch,* Dec. 23, 1931.

138   United Press hired her: "French Beauty Stage Darling Weds Egyptian," *Charles City Press,* June 9, 1930.

139   She traveled to North Africa: Moorehead, *Gellhorn,* 33.

139   She attributed the sacking: Gellhorn, unpublished memoir, 18.

139   Freed from the daily grind: Martha Gellhorn, "Geneva Portraits: Glimpses of the Women Delegates to the League of Nations" (headlines vary), *St. Louis Post-Dispatch,* Nov. 18, 20, and Dec. 5, 15, 18, 1930.

139   "Martha can't be more than 23": *LAT,* April 26, 1931.

139   She was in Paris: Martyn, "St. Louis Girl Turns Author"; Moorehead, *Gellhorn,* 56.

139   In 1934, Gellhorn published: In her unpublished memoir, her companion is identified as "B."

140   Gellhorn's reports for FERA: Martha Gellhorn in Eleanor Roosevelt, box 612, and Harry Hopkins, FERA, box 66, FDR Library Archives, Hyde Park, N.Y.

140   FERA dismissed her: Martha Gellhorn, "The Thirties," *Granta,* June 30, 1988.

140   when Gellhorn needed favors: Gellhorn to Eleanor Roosevelt, Feb. 7, 1936, FDR Library.

141   "ring as true": Mabel S. Ulrich, "The Courage of the Defeated," *Saturday Review,* Sept. 26, 1936. (Ulrich was a well-known physician and bookstore proprietor who was running the Minnesota office of the Federal Writers'

Project. See "Mabel Ulrich Gives Up Post," *Minneapolis Star,* June 30, 1938.) Gellhorn to Eleanor Roosevelt, Feb. 7, 1936, FDR Library. Also Martha Gellhorn, *The Trouble I've Seen* (New York: William Morrow, 1936). Later editions have an introduction by Gellhorn's biographer Caroline Moorehead.

141 "Going Home": Martha Gellhorn, "Going Home," *New Yorker,* Dec. 12, 1936.

141 This was just before: "Miss Gellhorn to Europe," *St. Louis Post-Dispatch,* March 17, 1937.

141 Gellhorn soon followed: In February, the St. Louis papers photographed Gellhorn marching on a picket line with local factory workers of the National Underwear Corporation. "Novelist Joins Picket Line," *St. Louis Post-Dispatch,* Feb. 11, 1937. She left for Spain the next month. "Miss Martha Gellhorn to Go to Spain to Write," *St. Louis Star-Times,* March 18, 1937.

141 Neither Anne O'Hare McCormick: From Anne O'Hare McCormick, "Affairs in Europe: Spain's 'Practice War' Tangle of European Aims," *NYT,* March 27, 1937. "They are not fighting for Spain. Nobody seems to be fighting for Spain, not even the Spaniards. One thinks of these legionaries and their mixed motives, their torn and wasted youth, because today another crisis among the non-interventionists reveals the equally mixed motives, the terribly tangled aims, of the governments involved in the Spanish struggle. To a greater or lesser degree all the national interests of Europe are somehow tied into this 'practice war' which, as it goes on, keeps on upsetting all outside calculations." From Dorothy Thompson, "On the Record: Women and Children First," *NY Herald Tribune,* April 30, 1937. "It is no longer possible for any human being with a heart in his breast or a head on his shoulders coolly to debate the pros and cons of Loyalists versus Rebels. For what is now happening there is the ruthless, cold-blooded vicious extermination of one of the rare peoples of the earth—the Basques. It is an extermination which beggars every description of war, which violates every convention which has been set by man as an inhibition against his own ruthlessness for 100 years or more. To sit by and not to protest with all the breath in one's body reads one out of the ranks of civilized and Christian society."

141 Gellhorn told stories: Gellhorn to Eleanor Roosevelt, Feb. 7, 1936, FDR Library: "Oddly, people don't enjoy nearly as much hearing about their own woes and therefore their own responsibilities as they do enjoy hearing about strangers' messes. Very normal. I'm constantly grateful to the U.S. Government, collectively and individually, for having had

the opportunity to get the material for this book. If no one else learns anything, I certainly consider that my post-graduate course is now completed, and I can start all over with the Kindergarten work."

141 For *Collier's:* Martha Gellhorn, "Men Without Medals," *Collier's,* Jan. 15, 1938; Martha Gellhorn, "A Reporter at Large: Madrid to Morata," *New Yorker,* July 24, 1937.

141 By the scholar Bernardo: See Bernardo Díaz Nosty, *Periodistas Extranjeras En La Guerra Civil: Periodistas, Fotoperiodistas, Colaboradoras de Prensa y Autoras de Memorias* (Seville: Renacimiento, 2022). Among the Americans writing for mainstream publications but not noted in the text were Anna Louise Strong and Josephine Herbst, both ardent pro-communists (While the Hemingway crew was still reporting, Strong was already in print with *Spain in Arms,* a book about her "travels through the sore spots and the danger zones." Herbst wrote at least one piece for *The Nation* about a Spanish village. See Josephine Herbst, "Spanish Village," *Nation,* Aug. 14, 1937). Elizabeth Deeble wrote for the *WP;* Anita Brenner for the *NYT* and the *Nation,* and Olga Kaltenborn for the *Brooklyn Eagle.* Nosty's count of 35 American women writers in Spain during the conflict includes memoirists, novelists, and reporters with no fixed affiliations. Nosty's total count of women contributing to the war narrative exceeds 180. The previously accepted count was 12.

142 "Blown by the wind": Davis, *Fearful Innocence,* 125.

143 "I was too full": Ibid., 145.

143 In *The Hartford Courant:* Ibid., 145–49; Frances Davis, "Calm, Horror Found in War," *Rochester Democrat and Chronicle,* Aug. 2, 1936; "Navarre Is with Rebels in Civil War: Woman Correspondent Describes Scenes in Spain," *Hartford Courant,* Aug. 11, 1936; "In the Spanish Rebel Camp," *Berkshire Eagle,* Aug. 14, 1936.

143 a nasty scratch: "Frances Davis Cohen," *NYT,* Nov. 6, 1982; "Girl Reporter," *Saturday Review,* Nov. 16, 1940; Davis, *Fearful Innocence,* 173–74.

143 "FROM ONE NEWSPAPER WOMAN": Davis, *Fearful Innocence,* 171.

143 Davis's condition: Ibid., 154–55, 171. See also Joseph W. Dauben, Mary Louise Gleason, and George E. Smith, "Seven Decades of History of Science: I. Bernard Cohen (1914–2003), Second Editor of *Isis,*" *Isis* 100, no. 1 (March 2009): 7n10–8n11, citing an author interview with Charles Gillespie, June 6, 2007; "Francis Davis Cohen," *NYT,* Nov. 6, 1982. *A Shadow in the Sun* received favorable reviews in such places as *The Boston Globe* and *The Saturday Review. Fearful Innocence* followed more quietly in 1981, the year before Davis died at seventy-four. Frances Davis, *A Shadow in the Sun* (New York: Carrick & Evans, 1940). "Boston Young

Woman Tells of Her Harrowing Experiences in Spain's War," *Boston Globe,* Oct. 4, 1940; John Hilton Smith, "Girl Reporter," *Saturday Review,* Nov. 16, 1940.

144 In Spain, the Packards: Eleanor Packard, "Rebels Drive to New Gains," *Honolulu Advertiser* via UP, Feb. 8, 1937; " 'Parade of Dead' Sickens Reporter," *Wilmington (Del.) Morning News,* April 23, 1937; "Webb Miller and Staff of Reporters Wait Bilbao's Fall," *Paterson (N.J.) Evening News,* June 16, 1937.

144 Gellhorn's great friend: Virginia Cowles, "Half of 300 U.S. Youths Fighting at Front in Spain Killed, N.Y. Socialite Discovers," *Pittsburgh Sun-Telegram,* July 4, 1937.

144 headline over her detailed: Martha Gellhorn, "Come Ahead, Adolf!," *Collier's,* Aug. 6, 1938.

144 Gellhorn stayed in Spain: *St. Louis Post-Dispatch,* Jan. 16, 1938.

145 Consider the early working lives: Worth mentioning for sports is Mary Standish on a lesser scale, who wrote Big Ten and bylined professional baseball for a couple of southern Illinois papers in the mid-1930s. For Standish, see, for example, "Russell Effective Despite Wickedly Wounded Foot," *Washington Star,* May 24, 1934, and "Dean Checks Red Legs as Giants Lose," *Decatur Herald and Review,* Oct. 1, 1934.

146 Agness Underwood: Joe Lewis, "Wiry City Editor Is No Lady but She's Top Newspaperman," *Raleigh (N.C.) News and Observer,* July 23, 1961; "Honor Press Woman," *Kansas City Star,* June 29, 1962; Associated Press, "To City Editor Post," *Kansas City Times,* Nov. 4, 1964; "Aggie Underwood, First Woman City Editor of Major Paper, Dies," *LAT,* July 4, 1984; "Did LA's Top Crime Reporter of the 1930s and '40s Crack the Black Dahlia Case?," *LA Magazine,* July 26, 2013; Agness Underwood, *Newspaperwoman* (New York: Harper, 1949).

146 "We didn't have parks": Kathleen Currie, "Women in Journalism: Marvel Cooke," Oct. and Nov. 1989 interviews, New York City, Washington Press Club Foundation Oral History Project. Also, entry for Madison Jackson, Registrar, Preparatory Department, vol. 1, Sept. 19, 1888, and entry for Madison Jackson, College Department, Sept. 17, 1890. Admission of attorney to State Bar, Upon Examination, Madison Jackson, et al., Supreme Court of the State of South Dakota, October 1895. As reported by Marvel Cooke in her oral history, he was unable to establish a law practice: too few Black inhabitants of the area and too few white people who would hire him.

147 Ultimately, she married: David L. Lewis, *W. E. B. Du Bois: A Biography* (New York: Henry Holt, 2009), 530, 670, 680.

147 "The Browsing Reader": Currie, "Marvel Cooke," 2, 50–53.

147 She moved on to become: See Oliver Ayers, "The 1935 Labour Dispute at the *Amsterdam News* and the Challenges Posed by the Rise of Unionism in Depression-Era Harlem," *Journal of American Studies* 48, no. 3 (Aug. 2014): 797–818.

147 Pauline Frederick: She was originally from the town of Gallitzin, where her father had been the postmaster. "College Honors Harrisburg Girl," *Harrisburg (Pa.) Evening News,* June 3, 1930. The article notes the award, accompanied by a $50 prize, honored her three years as associate editor of the school paper, her presidency of the poetry society, and her skill as a debater. She was also president of the Women's Student Government Association and the International Relations Club.

148 Frederick broke into journalism: Pauline Frederick, "Women of Diplomacy," *Washington, D.C., Sunday Star,* Oct. 16, 17, Nov. 1, 8, 15, 22, 29, Dec. 27, 1931; Jan. 3, 10, 31, 1932; "Pen Portraits," *Sunday Star,* Feb. 14, 21, 28, March 6, 1932; "Women of Official Life," *Sunday Star,* March 20, 27, April 3, 10, 17, 24, May 1, 8, 1932.

148 Frederick continued to draw: For example, Pauline Frederick, "Franco-American Policy Would Exchange People," *Muncie (Ind.) Star Press,* via NANA, May 4, 1945; "Russian Break with Japs May Speed War's End," *Cache (Utah) American,* June 18, 1945.

148 she would turn her interviews: Marilyn S. Greenwald, *Pauline Frederick Reporting: A Pioneering Broadcaster Covers the Cold War* (Lincoln: Potomac Books, an imprint of the University of Nebraska Press, 2014), 27.

148 "a regular reporter": Nancy H. MacLennan, "Only One of Her Kind," *NYT,* Dec. 5, 1948.

148 her byline appears over: Pauline A. Frederick, "Do You Have Achromaticitis?," *Tucson Citizen,* Sept. 20, 1933; "Autumn Plans the Bedroom," *Fall City (Neb.) Daily News,* Oct. 6, 1933.

149 "Ku Klux Klan country": Kathleen Currie, "Women in Journalism: Edith Evans Asbury," Aug. 8, 1988, Washington Press Club Foundation Oral History Project.

149 "Front-page girl": Ibid., 162.

149 By 1937, Edith Snyder Evans had outgrown: Ibid., 95, 99–100, 106–7.

Chapter 9. Home Front

151 Through the recommendation: Currie, "Edith Evans Asbury," 107, 114.

151 The War Department provided: "Ladies of the Army," *Time,* Aug. 11, 1941. U.S. Census counts indicate that the 14,750 woman reporters and editors of 1940 doubled to 28,595 by 1950, while the increase in the

number of men in those same ten years grew more slowly, from 43,503 to 61,730. This division's director was Oveta Culp Hobby, the executive vice president of *The Houston Post* and its publisher's wife.

152 "We women are no longer": "Fannie Hurst Sees Gains for Women," *NYT,* Feb. 6, 1942.

152 "four walls and a man": Fannie Hurst, "Women After Pearl Harbor," unpublished, Nov. 3, 1943, Fannie Hurst Collection, 190/1, Harry Ransom Center, Austin.

152 "None could dispute": "Press: Skirted," *Time,* March 13, 1944. The protest's leader and president of the Women's National Press Club was May Craig, who reported for four Maine papers.

153 "the bottom of the manpower": "Press: Skirted"; Flora Lewis, "U.S. Squeezes Spain," *Windsor (Ont.) Star,* Jan. 28, 1944; Associated Press, "U.S. Said to Cut Off Oil Going to Spain," *NYT,* Jan. 28, 1944; Flora Lewis, interview by Kathleen Currie, Paris, Nov. 30, 1990, 31, Washington Press Club Foundation Oral History Project.

153 "I was very proud": Currie, "Flora Lewis."

153 Eleanor Darnton: Six years earlier, the *Times* had done something similar for Ruby Hart Phillips in Cuba after her correspondent husband's death. She reported from the island for the next twenty-five years. See George James, "R. Hart Philipps, Times Reporter Who Covered Castro's Revolution," *NYT,* Oct. 30, 1985. Ruby's husband was the *Times*'s correspondent in Havana from 1931 until his death in an automobile accident in 1937. She left the *Times* in 1963 to become *Newsday*'s Latin America correspondent until she retired several years later.

154 "The news value": Memo, Eleanor Darnton to A. H. Sulzberger, April 9, 1945, Arthur Hays Sulzberger Papers, folder 25, New York Times Company Records Manuscripts and Archives Division, NY Public Library; John Darnton, *Almost a Family: A Memoir* (New York: Alfred A. Knopf, 2011), 127–32.

154 Women's National News Service: Her former assistant editor, Harriet Sweeney Crowley, was a cofounder.

154 "limped along": Darnton, *Almost a Family,* 127–32. Also, Lewis Wood, "Writers Who Quit OWI Charge It Bars 'Full Truth' for 'Ballyhoo,'" *NYT,* April 16, 1943, identifies Eleanor Darnton as "advertising expert and editor of *You* magazine." Examples of Washington, D.C., reporting and mentions: Eleanor Darnton, "Congress May Decide Who Works," *NYT,* Sept. 12, 1943; "Agencies to Widen Industry Feeding," *NYT,* Oct. 15, 1943. Dating: "Widow Sponsors the Byron Darnton," *NYT,* Dec. 17, 1943; "Liberty Ship Named for Newsman Launched," *WP,* Dec. 17, 1943 (identifies Eleanor Darnton as "women's editor of the *New York Times*"); "Newspaper

Women Elect," *NYT,* May 17, 1945 (identifies Eleanor Darnton as "of the Times"); "Newspaper Women Elect," *NYT,* May 16, 1946 (identifies Eleanor Darnton as "of the Women's National News Service"). By 1955, she appears to have been freelancing, first with a series on "Washington wives" and later with a focus on juvenile delinquency. "Eleanor Darnton Is Dead at 61; Writer on Juvenile Delinquency," *NYT,* May 16, 1968.

155 Flora Lewis had the highest: Representative byline searches via news papers.com for Flora Lewis for the AP, Pauline Frederick for NANA, and Aline Mosby for UP, with San Francisco, UN-related datelines, April–June 1945.

155 Hollywood celebrity beat: "Collier's Credits," *Collier's,* May 25, 1956; Kathleen Currie, "Women in Journalism: Aline Mosby," May 8–June 15, 1991, Meridale, N.Y., 17, Washington Press Club Foundation Oral History Project; Anne F. Siess, "Montana's Scoop" (master's thesis, University of Montana, 2003), 5.

155 kick-started the career: Aline Mosby, "Marilyn Monroe Admits She Is Girl on Calendar," *Kingsport (Tenn.) Times* via UP, March 13, 1952.

155 In one photo: For example, Aline Mosby, "Press: Uncovered Coverage," *Newsweek,* Aug. 24, 1953; "Woman Reporter Decides No Nudes Is Good Nudes," *El Paso Herald-Post,* Aug. 10, 1953; Mosby, "They Strip for Charity: Shivering Reporter Aids Nudists' Clothing Drive," *Wichita (Kans.) Evening Eagle,* Nov. 26, 1953.

155 "Listen, kid": Siess, "Montana's Scoop," 33.

156 "fat-faced, bullnecked, roughshod": "Press: The Women," *Time,* Oct. 26, 1942. The managing editor was William L. Ayers and the night editor, George Bradley.

156 "virtual revolution": "Women Are Writing the News," *Christian Science Monitor,* Sept. 25, 1943.

156 Her essay appeared: Frank Luther Mott, ed., *Journalism in Wartime* (Washington, D.C.: American Council on Public Affairs, 1943).

157 Herrick looked back: See Genevieve F. Herrick, "The Newspaper Woman Joins Up," in Mott, *Journalism in Wartime,* 126–28.

157 careful to speak respectfully: Ibid.

158 seen as novelties: See, generally, Underwood, *Newspaperwoman;* Jerry Belcher, "Aggie Underwood, First Woman City Editor of Major Paper, Dies," *LAT,* July 4, 1984.

158 married Herbert Asbury: "Newspaper Bride Gets Day's 'Grace' from AP Office," *Knoxville News-Sentinel,* April 1, 1945.

158 In 1946, her old Knoxville: "Ossoli Will Like This," *Knoxville News-Sentinel,* April 7, 1946.

158 As a result, by 1949: Currie, "Edith Evans Asbury," 133.

158 résumé-enhanching magazine assignments: In addition to the Bess Tru-
     man profile, see Edith Asbury, "Grand Old Lady of Johnstown," *Colliers,*
     Jan. 1, 1949, and "Futures by Fisher," May 21, 1949.

159 profile of Bess Truman: Edith Asbury, "Meet Harry's Boss, Bess," *Collier's,*
     Feb. 12, 1949.

159 Inez Robb: Over a nearly half-century-long career, Robb's national repu-
     tation was such that in 1962, when she was sixty-two, *Time* still fairly
     described her as "a whirling dervish," a "juggernaut in kid gloves." She
     kept up that pace for another seven years. See "Press: Juggernaut in Kid
     Gloves," *Time,* May 11, 1962.

159 Robb's piece challenged: Inez Robb, "And Maybe We Were Wrong About
     Her, Too," *Cosmopolitan,* Feb. 1, 1949.

159 "superenthusiastic rave": Katharine Graham, "The Magazine Rack," *WP,*
     Jan. 30, 1949.

159 She interviewed Sue Gentry: Sue Gentry, interview by Jim Williams,
     June 18, 1991, 43–44, Harry S. Truman National Historic Site, National
     Park Service, U.S. Department of the Interior, Independence, Mo. Gen-
     try's recollection of the visit is a case study in the influence of fame. The
     basic details are much as Asbury recalled them. Gentry correctly notes
     that the magazine was *Collier's* but attributes the authorship and the visit
     to Independence to the more famous writer Helen Worden Erskine, bet-
     ter known as Dorothy Dix, who came six years later. The as famous Robb,
     whom Gentry also recalled at a dinner in her honor at Judge Bundschu's,
     didn't come to Independence until 1952. Gentry remembered Robb was
     a "blonde" "pretty thing," dressed in a black taffeta dress so lovely that
     Gentry had the paper's photographer come to take her picture. Robb at
     that time wrote about Gentry in a column about how the national press
     had been besieging her little town, not mentioning that Asbury had been
     first in line three years earlier. See Inez Robb, "Assignment: America,"
     Franklin (Ind.) Evening Star, March 26, 1952; Helen Worden Erskine, "Tru-
     man in Retirement," *Collier's,* Feb. 4, 1955; Brian Burnes, "Famed Reporter
     Dies at 99," *Kansas City Star,* Oct. 12, 2004.

160 Judge Henry Bundschu: "This Week's Work," *Collier's,* Feb. 12, 1949.

160 Marvel Cooke covered: Marvel Cooke, "New Laurels for Marian Ander-
     son," *Amsterdam News,* April 5, 1939; Cooke, "Close to 100,000 at Lincoln
     Memorial Awed by Contralto," *Amsterdam News,* April 5, 1939.

161 "the Last Lady of the Land": "D.A.R. Refuses Auditorium to Hazel Scott;
     Constitution Hall for 'White Artists Only,'" *NYT,* Oct. 12, 1945; "Tru-
     mans to Defense of a Negro Pianist," *Springfield (Mo.) Leader and Press,*
     Oct. 12, 1945; "Criticize Mrs. Truman's Attendance of D.A.R. Tea," *Des
     Moines Register,* Oct. 13, 1945; "Race Discrimination Row Thwarts Bess

Truman's Hopes," *La Crosse (Wis.) Tribune,* Oct. 13, 1945. See also David McCullough, *Truman* (New York: Simon & Schuster, 1992), 576n1033; "DAR Irks Hazel Scott; She'd Like to Stay Here," *Minneapolis Tribune,* Oct. 13, 1945; "Has the D.A.R. Changed?," *Pittsburgh Courier,* May 4, 1945. Interestingly, seven months later, the DAR donated the hall for a United Negro College Fund benefit performance by the Tuskegee Choir. *The Pittsburgh Courier* welcomed that decision on behalf of the Black press, but cautiously, because it wondered about how permanent it would prove to be.

161 Asbury's article: Robb, "And Maybe We Were Wrong About Her, Too"; Asbury, "Meet Harry's Boss, Bess."

161 "Because I'm thorough": Currie, "Edith Evans Asbury," 124–29. The Katharine Graham "Magazine Rack" piece in the *WP* is dated Jan. 31, 1949, so Robb might have beaten Asbury to the newsstands after all. The issue of *Collier's* is dated Feb. 12, 1949, so even out a week earlier would be Feb. 5.

Chapter 10. Sidebars

162 "I have been moving": "Foreign Correspondent—Anne O'Hare McCormick."

162 In January, in Palestine: Anne O'Hare McCormick, "Palestine: Interests of Britain, Jews, and Arabs Are in Clash; Appearance of War Differences on Opinion Building a State," *NYT,* Jan. 7, 1939; "Europe: Rome Talks Gained Little, but Were a Good Gesture," Jan. 14, 1939; "Carpatho-Ukrainians Still Fight Despite Seizure by Hungarians: A Republic for a Day, Three Flags Fly over Its Capital in 27 Hours," March 17, 1939; "In Europe: British Are Calm in Decision to Face Any Threat; A Broad Commitment Now Capital of Europe," April 1, 1939. The district commissioner of Jerusalem was Edward Keith-Roach.

162 "too fantastic to be true": Martha Gellhorn, *The Face of War* (1959; New York: Grove Press, 2018), 52, cited in Moorehead, *Gellhorn,* 430.

163 "every assistance": Franklin D. Roosevelt to All American Foreign Service Officers, Sept. 11, 1939, FDR Library.

163 The articles for *Collier's:* Janet Somerville, *Yours, for Probably Always: Martha Gellhorn's Letters of Love and War, 1930–1949* (Buffalo: Firefly Books, 2019), 211.

163 They appeared: Gellhorn articles in *Collier's:* "Slow Boat to War," Jan. 6, 1940; "Blood on the Snow," Jan. 20, 1940; "Bombs for a Low Sky," Jan. 27, 1940; "Fear Comes to Sweden," Feb. 3, 1940.

163 *A Stricken Field: St. Louis Post-Dispatch,* March 16, 1940; "St. Louis Author," *St. Louis Post-Dispatch,* March 14, 1940.

163 The high commissioner: Martha Gellhorn, *A Stricken Field* (New York: Penguin Books, 1986), 308; G. E. R. Gedye, "Refugee Problem Disturbs Czechs," *NYT,* Oct. 11, 1938.

163 declared *A Stricken Field:* Benjamin Anastas, "Critic's Take: Martha Gellhorn's Greatest Novel Is Essential Reading for Today," *NYT,* May 25, 2017.

163 profiles of her: Harriman, "It Girl"; Alexander, "Girl from Syracuse"; "Rover Girl in Europe"; "Cartwheel Girl."

164 "the creation of the post-war": Kathleen Currie, "Flora Lewis," Paris, Nov. 30–Dec. 2, 1990, 35, Washington Press Club Foundation Oral History Project.

164 "with the AP woman": Currie, "Flora Lewis," 35. Cowan, a veteran reporter at forty-two, was no ingenue adventuress. Her shot at war corresponding came early enough in 1943 for Genevieve Herrick to acknowledge her in Herrick's symposium essay, along with Inez Robb of INS.

164 "a United Press newspaperman": Ann Stringer, "Bravo Amerikanski!," in *Yanks Meet Reds: Recollections of U.S. and Soviet Vets from the Linkup in World War II,* ed. Mark Scott and Semyon Krasilshchik (Santa Barbara, Calif.: Capra Press, 1988), 77–78.

165 "really changed me": Currie, "Flora Lewis," 6–8.

165 AP sent her to London: Ibid., 39, 44–45.

165 Higgins, obtained her credentials: Ibid., 37.

165 got to the library first: Antoinette May, *Witness to War: A Biography of Marguerite Higgins* (New York: Beaufort Books, 1983), 51.

165 One of her professors: John Chamberlain, "The Good Ones Die Young," *Pensacola News-Journal,* Jan. 11, 1966.

165 Higgins was from Oakland: Marguerite Higgins, *News Is a Singular Thing* (New York: Doubleday, 1955), 15.

166 "some of the pressures": Ibid., 46.

166 Higgins also got unsolicited aid: The women's editor was Dorothy Dunbar Bromley.

166 Beyond that, there was logic: Higgins, *News Is a Singular Thing,* 46.

166 Both figure in the most authoritative count: Mary Welsh for the London *Daily Telegraph,* and British women did the reverse, notably Clare Hollingworth, who added the *Chicago Daily News* to her list of strings, and Iris Carpenter, who wrote for *The Boston Globe.* At the end of Aug. 1939, the London *Daily Telegraph* took on Hollingworth to freelance from Warsaw. She borrowed the British consul's car to take a drive to the German border. There, in a German valley, she saw tanks massing but screened. She alerted the consul, who doubted her. She alerted the

British Foreign Office, which did not. She reported what she saw to the *Telegraph*, which published her eyewitness account on its front page, credited to "Our Correspondent" but without her name. A year later, for the London *Daily Express*, she eluded the Romanian Iron Guard censors to report the abdication of King Carol and the riots that quickly ensued. To avoid arrest, she pulled the diversionary tactic of stripping naked in front of the authorities who detained her, and then insisted that they let a friend at the British Legation collect her, which he did. See "Telegraph's Clare Hollingworth," *Daily Telegraph* (London), Jan. 11, 2017; James Beeson, "Journalist Who Broke Story of Nazi Invasion of Poland, Clare Hollingworth, Dies Aged 105," *Press Gazette* (London), Jan. 10, 2017; Anne Sebba, "Clare Hollingworth Obituary," *Guardian*, Jan. 10, 2017.

Nancy Caldwell Sorel, for *The Women Who Wrote the War*, counted 100 woman correspondents during the war years. Carolyn Edy, for *Woman War Correspondent*, used the figure 160. The article by Ann Burch, "Female Journalists Did Their Part in World War II," *Tampa Bay Times*, Jan. 4, 2002, has a higher figure, but it includes some errors and repetitions.

166 To put the figure: Michael Emery and Edwin Emery, *The Press and America: An Interpretive History of the Mass Media*, with Nancy L. Roberts (Boston: Allyn and Bacon, 1996), 261. The authors counted 500 recognized correspondents in 1915, augmented in 1917 when the United States entered the war. Put another way, in gross numbers, the World War II figure is greater than the combined total of all the women—the few—who reported during domestic or foreign conflicts for the entire century between the 1840s and the Spanish Civil War.

167 During World War II: See Carolyn M. Edy, "War Correspondents, Women's Interests, and World War II," in *Journalism's Ethical Progression: A Twentieth-Century Journey*, ed. Gwyneth Mellinger and John P. Ferré (Lanham, Md.: Lexington Books, 2020), 115–38; Edy, *Woman War Correspondent*, 136–42, 143–49; and Burch, "Female Journalists Did Their Part in World War II." Special thanks to Edy for sharing her vast expertise.

167 One reporter told Nancy Caldwell Sorel: Patricia Lochridge, interviewed by Sorel, May 17, 1995. During the war, Lochridge reported from Asia and the South Pacific for *CBS News* and *Woman's Home Companion*.

167 There was a side benefit: See Cynthia Enloe, in Michèle Midori Fillion's documentary *No Job for a Woman: The Women Who Fought to Write the War* (2011), nojobforawoman.com. In Enloe's words, "If women are excluded from one area, they sometimes use this almost as an unwanted opportunity to look elsewhere for the story."

168 "You ought to pay that cook": Martha Gellhorn and Virginia Cowles, *Love*

Goes to Press: A Comedy in Three Acts, ed. Sandra W. Spanier (Lincoln: University of Nebraska Press, 1946), 12.

169 Homer Bigart: Homer Bigart, *Forward Positions: The War Correspondence of Homer Bigart,* ed. Betsy Wade (Fayetteville: University of Arkansas Press, 1992), xx.

169 "sustained, careful": Herrick, "Newspaper Woman Joins Up," 127.

169 At the fifth annual: "Two News Women Honored for Work," *NYT,* Feb. 15, 1941. Kathleen McLaughlin's list of newspaperwomen who had been under fire in London included Eleanor Packard of UP; Helen Kirkpatrick of the *Chicago Daily News* and NY *Post;* Tania Long, then still with the *NY Herald Tribune,* who won the $100 prize for best story that year; Betty Wason for *PM,* honored for the "daring and courage she had shown in her coverage in Norway, Finland, Greece and elsewhere," but restricted to an honorable mention because she was not a club member; Marie Marlin of UP, who was with the Greek forces in Albania; and Virginia Cowles, writing for NANA, the feature syndicate, and occasionally for the *NYT.* McLaughlin omitted Mary Welsh, Hemingway's fourth wife after Gellhorn, who was working for the London *Daily Express,* but she did call out by name those who were back in the United States: Sigrid Schultz of the *Chicago Tribune;* Francis Davis, "still hospitalized in Boston"; Sonia Tomara; Hazel McDonald of the *Chicago Times;* and Anne O'Hare McCormick and Dorothy Thompson.

170 "Surely," said Eleanor: "Two News Women Honored for Work."

170 But beyond the celebration: Helen Kirkpatrick was a Smith graduate with graduate degrees in international law from the University of Geneva and the Graduate Institute of International Studies. She left a job in New York as an assistant buyer at Macy's to move to London, where she went to work for the *NY Herald Tribune,* then freelanced and copublished a newsletter. In 1939, the *Chicago Daily News* hired her, and she remained with the paper until 1946, when she left to cover the Nuremberg trials for the *NY Post.* Her outstanding work attracted not only Murrow's keen attention, but the admiration of the French and U.S. governments. In 1947, she was among nineteen war correspondents and the only woman singled out for the U.S. Medal of Freedom. The French government had already awarded her two medals, the Légion d'Honneur and the Médaille de la Reconnaissance Française. She was cited her for "exceptionally meritorious achievement," for never hesitating to face danger, and for providing "her objective interpretation of military operations," especially in France during its post-occupation period. She downplayed her honors, saying they were commonplace. See Helen Paull Kirkpatrick Papers, Sophia Smith Collection of Women's History, Smith College;

"Eisenhower Presents Medal to Editor of Atlanta Journal," *Dayton Daily News,* Nov. 19, 1947; Mary Van Rensselaer Thayer, "Lady War Scribe Cited. Dilatory Uncle Sam Honors Correspondent Kirkpatrick Years After French," *WP,* Sept. 22, 1949.

170 Shelley Mydans was frank: Shelley Smith Mydans, interview by Nancy Caldwell Sorel, Larchmont, N.Y., Dec. 9, 1991. Apropos, the lead of the *NYT* obituary for Shelley Mydans in 2002 does not mention any stories she covered as her major achievement, but focuses on her marriage to the more famous Carl, their wartime presence in Asia, their internment in Manila, and that she wrote a novel about it all. See also "Speaking of Pictures," *Life,* Feb. 23, 1942; "Shelley Mydans, 86, Author and Former P.O.W.," *NYT,* March 9, 2002. Also, Shelley Smith Mydans, *The Open City* (New York: Doubleday, 1945).

Sorel's interviews include the similar experiences of other war reporter wives as well. Annalee Whitmore was a Stanford graduate like Shelley Mydans and Melville Jacoby, whom Whitmore married. The Jacobys, too, were in Asia for *Time* and *Life.* Four months into their marriage, they reported from Bataan and Corregidor for six weeks, which forced them to undertake a twenty-day escape by sea, sailing only in darkness, to elude a Japanese blockade. See "The Press: Escape from Bataan," *Time,* April 13, 1942.

Tania Long, another European-educated polyglot, was based in Europe as an office assistant and translator in several bureaus of the *NY Herald Tribune* until a few months after her marriage in 1942 to Raymond Daniell, the London bureau chief of the *NYT.* "The Times didn't like married couples on their staff," she told Sorel, "so I wasn't put on the Times until six months after we were married." The bureau had a "very shorthanded" staff of five at the time, she said, plus the periodic visits of Anne O'Hare McCormick, making Tania Long the indisputable "low man on the totem pole." This status was not reflected in the legend under her byline, however; it was "By Wireless to the New York Times," just like her husband's. The difference, however, was clear in their story counts: between 1942 and 1946, Daniell signed more than 250 articles; she, fewer than 70. In those same four years, his stories appear on the front page 62 times; hers appeared only 5 times, and mostly on lifestyle topics. Indicative of the difference is the day they both made the front page, July 21, 1945. He leads the paper with President Harry Truman's renouncement in Berlin of any U.S. territorial or monetary ambitions. She has a feature below the fold, also from Berlin, about U.S., Russian, and British military police trying to stop Allied troops from selling food and cigarettes to Germans on the black market. On Sept. 29, under a

Frankfort on the Main dateline, she has the top center of the front page with a report on how U.S. troops were developing pro-German attitudes from sleeping with German women of all classes (and creating a spike in venereal diseases). His story appeared underneath hers, with the headline "Eisenhower Silent After Patton Talk." See Raymond Daniell, "Truman Says We Want No Territory, Ask Only Peace and World Prosperity with 'Mankind's Greatest Age' as Goal," *NYT,* July 21, 1945; Tania Long, "Allies Open War on Black Market and Army Goods Sales in Berlin," *NYT,* July 21, 1945; Long, "Pro-German Attitude Grows as U.S. Troops Fraternize," *NYT,* Sept. 29, 1945; Daniell, "Eisenhower Silent After Patton Talk," Sept. 21, 1945. See Tania Long Daniell, interview by Sorel, New York, Sept. 19, 1991, 6; and Reston, *Deadline.* Reston writes of this time in London: "We were all without our families, though Daniell dealt with this deprivation by marrying Tania Long of the *Herald Tribune* and adding her to the staff." In my attempt to determine her exact status when she joined the *Times,* Jeff Roth, who shepherds archives for the *Times,* produced a biographical summary of Long that indicates she became a staff member three months after her marriage to Daniell. I am especially grateful to Jeff Roth.

170 Pauline Frederick finally fulfilled: For example, "Pauline Frederick to Write on Europe's People," *Terril (Iowa) Record,* April 18, 1946 (and subsequently from Belgium, Denmark, and elsewhere); "Mrs. Crowding's Sister to Leave for Germany," *Sunbury (Pa.) Daily Item,* Nov. 2, 1945; "Blonde Aviatrix Arranged Suicide Plane Project for Germany Victory," *Freedom (Okla.) Call,* Feb. 21, 1946; "Woman Newspaper Writer Tells of Nuremberg Trials," *Sunbury (Pa.) Daily Item,* June 14, 1946.

170 She did an exclusive report: Pauline Frederick, "Hitler's Shame: Historic Church Altar Stolen by Germans, Returned to Poles," *St. Clair (Mo.) Chronicle,* July 11, 1946.

171 By 1946, Edward R. Murrow: "The GIs' Favorite Correspondent," pulitzer .org, n.d. Two years earlier, in 1944, Murrow won his first Peabody Award for outstanding war reporting in the previous year, and his first duPont followed in 1947. Newspapermen were also accumulating top awards during the war, among them, four apiece for war reporters for the AP and for the *NYT.* Ernie Pyle won for the Scripps-Howard Newspaper Alliance for his "distinguished coverage" in 1943, most noted for conveying the war experience through his empathic focus on the personal lives of the American soldiers.

171 CBS showed almost no enthusiasm: Mary Marvin Breckinridge, for instance, was a photographer and documentarian whom Murrow hired in Europe. She was a Vassar grad, a great-granddaughter of the U.S. vice

president John C. Breckinridge (under President James Buchanan), and a granddaughter of B. F. Goodrich. She had languages and sophistication. Professionally, she dropped her Mary in favor of Marvin and reported for the network from seven different countries, mostly on lifestyle topics. Murrow, whom she met at a conference while she was still a student, coached her in how to deepen her voice for the air. There were no postwar jobs with the network for her, for Helen Kirkpatrick, whose work he had admired, or for Betty Wason, whose reports from Greece and elsewhere CBS insisted a man read over the air. See Helen Paull Kirkpatrick Papers, Sophia Smith Collection of Women's History, Smith College; Leonard Miall, "Helen Kirkpatrick Milbank," *Independent* (London), Jan. 8, 1998 (republished in the *Independent,* Oct. 23, 2011). Also see Sorel, *Women Who Wrote the War,* 74–76, based on unspecified Sorel correspondence with Wason. Also, "Betty Wason—Indiana Journalism Hall of Fame," ijhf.org. Fillion, *No Job for a Woman.* Even earlier, the airwaves did carry women's voices doing news commentary for CBS, but always for broadcasts tagged as a woman's point of view. For example, *News Through a Woman's Eyes* was the program that Kathryn Cravens broadcast to St. Louis listeners in 1934 and that the network carried nationally from 1936 to 1938 as she logged thousands of miles to produce her show and came to be known as "the flying commentator." After that, Cravens wrote for newspapers until WNEW in New York City picked up her show in 1941. Four years after that, she was off to Europe. For the Cowles and Mutual Broadcasting networks, she reported from twenty-two countries. See "Kathryn Cravens, News Correspondent and Ex-actress, 92," *NYT,* Aug. 31, 1991; "The Life and Work of Edward R. Murrow: An Archives Exhibit," 2008, Digital Collections and Archives, Murrow Center, Tufts University.

171 He judged it "pleasing": Greenwald, *Pauline Frederick Reporting,* 55, citing Murrow to Robert Kennett, Aug. 27, 1946, and Kennett to Frederick, note, Aug. 29, 1946, box 38, folder 7, Pauline Frederick Papers, Sophia Smith Collection.

171 For reporters, the shiniest gold stars: See Higgins, *News Is a Singular Thing,* 95. Also, in this connection, Elizabeth M. Phillips, born Elizabeth Moss Murphy, was the one known woman the Black press sent to London. She was a later graduate of Marvel Cooke's alma mater, the University of Minnesota. She was the granddaughter of the founder and daughter of the publisher of the Baltimore *Afro-American* and the wife of one of its staff photographers. By 1942, she was the paper's city editor. On arrival in 1944, however, she suffered an attack of neuralgia that caused the temporary loss of the use of her left hand. Doctors recommended

her immediate return home. Nonetheless, she reported from her hospital bed about the preparations for the trip, her adjustment to war conditions, and the Black soldiers she met. The newspaper included her story in its book of war correspondent reporting. See Elizabeth M. Phillips, "Hospitals Are Nice—Phillips—First Woman Reporter in One Unexpectedly," Baltimore *Afro-American,* Dec. 2, 1944; Elizabeth M. Phillips, "3,000 Miles to a Hospital," in Ollie Stewart et al., *This Is Our War* (Baltimore: Afro-American, 1945), 205–12; Antero Pietila and Stacy Spaulding, "The *Afro-American*'s World War II Correspondents: Feuilletonism as Social Action," *Literary Journalism Studies* 5, no. 2 (Fall 2013): 49.

171 Sometimes there is politics: For more on this subject, see Ivor Shapiro, Patrizia Albanese, and Leigh Doyle, "What Makes Journalism 'Excellent'? Criteria Identified by Judges in Two Leading Awards Programs," *Canadian Journal of Communications* 31, no. 2 (2006): 425–45.

171 UP's Eleanor Packard: Packard, "Rebels Drive to New Gains"; " 'Parade of Dead' Sickens Reporter"; "Webb Miller and Staff of Reporters Wait Bilbao's Fall"; "Woman Reporter Scores Smash News Beat on Czech Fighting," *Nashville Banner,* Sept. 16, 1938.

171 Margaret Bourke-White: See, generally, Margaret Bourke-White, *Portrait of Myself* (New York: Simon & Schuster, 1963); Vicki Goldberg, *Margaret Bourke-White, a Biography* (Reading, Mass.: Addison-Wesley, 1987).

172 She predicted a second deluge: Sigrid Schultz, "Invasion Lies," *Collier's,* March 25, 1944.

172 Schultz had also divined: "As Sigrid Schultz Was Saying," *Collier's,* July 22, 1944.

172 Hemingway's D-day story: Ernest Hemingway, "Voyage to Victory," *Collier's,* July 22, 1944.

172 "commuter war": Martha Gellhorn, "Over and Back," *Collier's,* July 22, 1944.

172 The table of contents: "Collier's THIS WEEK, August 5, 1944," *Collier's,* Aug. 5, 1944.

173 no cover line for Gellhorn: Martha Gellhorn, "The Wounded Come Home," *Collier's,* Aug. 5, 1944. Hemingway's subsequent piece in *Collier's* also got the cover note and ran two pages inside. Ernest Hemingway, "London Fights the Robots," *Collier's,* Aug. 19, 1944.

173 "Her looks, her obvious courage": Moorehead, *Gellhorn,* 221.

174 On a Thursday in September: Ann Stringer, *"Bravo Amerikanski!": And Other Stories from World War II* (n.p.: 1st Books Library, 2000), 16–17.

174 "two-fisted competitor": Ibid., 157–58.

175 Her determination: Walter Cronkite, introduction to ibid., 2.

175 "That," he wrote: Ibid.

175 Stringer had crossed the ocean: Scott and Krasilshchik, *Yanks Meet Reds,* 77–83; Stringer, *"Bravo Amerikanski!,"* 25–62.

176 Two other woman correspondents: INS, International News Service, was a competing wire service that merged with UP in 1958 to become UPI.

176 "the Rhine Maidens": "The Rhine Maidens," *Newsweek,* March 19, 1945.

176 In response, SHAEF: Ibid.

177 "If the Army was": Stringer, *"Bravo Amerikanski!,"* 24.

177 "about half of them dead": For example, Ann Stringer, "Political Prisoners in Sorry Plight," *Latrobe (Pa.) Bulletin* via UP, April 14, 1945.

177 "The lampshade": For example, Ann Stringer, "Lampshade Made of Human Skin Examined by Writer," *Knoxville News-Sentinel,* April 23, 1945; "Nazis Use Skin of Humans for 'Ornaments,'" *Kenosha Evening News,* April 23, 1945.

177 She headed toward: Scott and Krasilshchik, *Yanks Meet Reds,* 77–83; Stringer, *"Bravo Amerikanski!,"* 25–62.

178 UP arranged for her to broadcast: Scott and Krasilshchik, *Yanks Meet Reds,* 77–83; Stringer, *"Bravo Amerikanski!,"* 25–62; "Kilgoround," *Kilgore (Tex.) News Herald,* April 27, 1945. See also, for example, "Yanks, Russians, Cheer and Drink Vodka as Allied Armies Meet," *Cincinnati Post* via UP, April 27, 1945.

179 "Perhaps I should have": Stringer, *"Bravo Amerikanski!,"* 177–78.

179 In this version of her account: Ibid., 179–81. See Iris Carpenter, *No Woman's World: From D-Day to Berlin* (Boston: Houghton Mifflin, 1946), 322–28. Yet in her entry in Stringer's *"Bravo Amerikanski!,"* Carpenter also wrote, "What made Ann's 'beat' supremely possible was that the First Army censors had put a twenty-four-hour hold on any linkup story. So my story (and of course, those of my colleagues) never saw the light of day until after Ann's was in print—and on the air!"

179 Back at the Scribe: Stringer, *"Bravo Amerikanski!,"* 70–71. The UP night manager was Gene Gillette.

179 Typically, it invited: Ann Stringer, "Russians Happy at Union of Armies; U.S. Girl Is Impressed," *Oroville (Calif.) Mercury Register,* April 27, 1945.

180 "I owned a private war": Lee Miller, "France Free Again: Saint Malo," *Vogue,* Oct. 15, 1944.

180 Lee Miller and David Scherman: Lee Miller, "'Believe It' Lee Miller Cables from Germany," *Vogue,* June 1, 1945; Sharon Sliwinski, "Visual Testimony: Lee Miller's Dachau," *Journal of Visual Culture* 9, no. 3 (Dec. 2010): 391.

180 Dachau would also provide: Marguerite Higgins, "33,000 Dachau Captives Freed by 7th Army," *NY Herald Tribune,* May 1, 1945.

180 "campaign ribbon": Higgins, *News Is a Singular Thing,* 95.

180 Miller spotted hot water: David Scherman, "Lee Miller in Hitler's
     Bathtub, Hitler's Apartment," *Vogue* (London), July 1945. With thanks
     for additional details supplied by Kerry Negahban of the Lee Miller
     Archives, East Sussex, U.K. Negahban, email exchange with author,
     Jan. 20, 2022.

Chapter 11. Bridges

185 It took until 1951: From the Pulitzer site: pulitzers.org by year. An ama-
     teur photo of a "thrilling rescue" in Redding, California, taken with a
     "Brownie" by Virginia M. Schau, won for photography in 1954; the 1955
     prize for local reporting went to Caro Brown of the *Daily Echo* in Alice,
     Texas, for coverage of a county corruption scandal; and in 1959, Mary
     Lou Werner of Washington's *Evening Star,* known later as Ludy Forbes,
     won for her yearlong series on the integration crisis in Virginia. In addi-
     tion, eight women won George Polk awards between 1949 and 1956, a
     few in shared honors by name but most as sole recipients. The winners
     by year are on the Polk site at liu.edu.
         1948: none; 1949: Foreign Reporting: A. T. Steele, Christopher Rand,
     Allen Raymond, Margaret Parton, and Dorothy Brandon, *NY Herald
     Tribune,* for series "Asia's Red Riddle"; 1950: Fern Marja, *NY Post;* Educa-
     tion Reporting: Fred Hechinger and Judith Crist, *NY Herald Tribune;* 1951:
     Foreign Reporting: Milton Bracker and Virginia Lee Warren, *NYT,* for
     stories on the government seizure of an Argentine newspaper; 1951: Reli-
     gious Reporting: Ann Elizabeth Price, *NY Herald Tribune,* for bringing
     unusual interest to an ordinarily quiet news beat; 1952: Foreign Report-
     ing: Marguerite Higgins, *NY Herald Tribune,* for articles from behind
     enemy lines in Korea and other nations; 1953: Community Service: Mar-
     garet Ryttenberg, *Newsday,* for a series "on the pressing need for medi-
     cal facilities in booming Long Island"; 1954: none; 1955: Metropolitan
     Reporting: Fern Marja, Peter J. McElroy, and William Dufty, *NY Post,* for
     a series leading to the exoneration of two youths imprisoned for rape;
     1956: Special Award: Endre Marton, AP, and his wife, Ilona Nyilas, UP,
     for defying a regime that had imprisoned them to report from Hungary;
     1958: Marya Mannes, *Reporter* magazine.
185 Edward R. Murrow's reject: "Personal Award: Pauline Frederick for 'Pau-
     line Frederick at the U.N.'" See peabodyawards.com and dupont.org.
185 "slick little chick": A ProQuest Search for 1954–55 shows extensive cov-
     erage throughout the country of Morrissy as sports editor of *The Cornell
     Daily Sun* and at the Yale Bowl. One example: Red Smith, "Move Over,
     Lady Godiva: Girl Writer Breaks Ivy Barrier Covering Yale Game,"
     Boston Globe, Oct. 17, 1954. See also Sam Roberts, "Anne Morrissy Merick,

a Pioneer from Yale to Vietnam," *NYT,* May 9, 2017; and Emma New-burger, "Anne Morrissy Merick '55, Vietnam War Reporter, Dies at 83," *Cornell Daily Sun,* May 9, 2017.

185 Smith did note: He did mention Mary Standish, who covered Big Ten sports for the *East St. Louis Journal* in the mid-1930s (and baseball for the *Decatur Herald and Review*) but left out the part where she was forbidden to enter the press box. See, for example, "Russell Effective Despite Wickedly Wounded Foot" and "Dean Checks Red Legs as Giants Lose," *Decatur (Ill.) Herald,* Oct. 1, 1934; Frisch, "Cards Irked by Loss of Second Tilt," *Decatur Review,* Oct. 5, 1934.

185 The case itself: The Torre case was the *NY Herald Tribune'*s second experience with the question; the earlier one, over a customs fraud exposé in 1914, did not result in jail terms for the reporter or the city editor, who both pleaded the Fifth Amendment. *Garland v. Torre,* 259 F.2d at 545, put Marie Torre, a television columnist, in the Hudson County Jail in Jersey City. A $1,393,000 defamation case filed by Judy Garland charged that Torre had unflatteringly characterized the star's temperament in print. Torre refused to disclose the source at CBS who had told her about a contract dispute with the singer. In an editorial the day Torre's sentence began, the newspaper asserted that its right to refuse to disclose its sources of information should be superior to the rights of an individual to obtain all the facts relative to an alleged injustice. This was, the paper argued, "not because any newspaper should be above the law or defy the law . . . but because the basic freedom of the press is the ultimate guaranty of all individual liberties, including those of Miss Garland to redressal of her injuries, if any." The paper said it was ready "to assist Miss Torre in every way to carry this case high enough—to the Supreme Court if necessary—to get this principle once and for all established." Torre served her ten-day term in full and, on return, produced a three-part exposé about her time in jail. See Robert Debo, "Ex-reporter Recalls His 40 Days in Jail," *Troy Record,* July 13, 1956; "Judy Tosses a Monkey Wrench," *NY Herald Tribune,* Jan. 10, 1957; "TV Writer Faces Jail for Silence," *Oakland Tribune,* Oct. 16, 1957; Don Ross, "Torre Case Parallel on Tribune in '14," *NY Herald Tribune,* Oct. 17, 1957; "Defending a Principle," Oct. 17, 1957 (for a contrarian view, see "A Network Executive Said," *Richmond News Leader,* Oct. 6, 1957); "Marie Torre Loses Plea in High Court, Faces Jail," Dec. 9, 1958; "Marie Torre Jail Term Is Set to Begin Today," Jan. 5, 1959; "Marie Torre Goes to Jail," Jan. 6, 1959; "Miss Torre Ends 10-Day Jail Term," Jan. 15, 1959; "Marie Torre's Own Story of Her 10-Day Stay in Jail," Jan. 25, 1959; "Unseen Bars Separate Inmate from Matron," Feb. 1, 1959; "Release Day, and Back

Home Again," Feb. 4, 1959; "Marie Torre, 72, TV Columnist Jailed for Protecting News Source," *NYT,* Jan. 5, 1997. See also "Suing for Age and Gender Discrimination, New York News Anchor Roma Torre Reflects on Late KDKA Anchor Marie Torre's Legacy," *Pittsburgh Post-Gazette,* Sept. 9, 2019.

186   Take, for example, a minor case: Kay Gardella, "A Couple of News Gals Talk About Their Work," *NY Daily News,* Aug. 23, 1958.

186   From 1930 to 1948: See Kleinberg, *Women in the United States,* 105; U.S. Government, *Population Comparative Occupation Statistics, 1870–1940,* 14, census.gov; and "Women in the Labor Force, Percentage of Civilian Labor Force by Sex 1948–2016," dol.gov.

187   In the field of journalism: Between 1940 and 1950, the number of woman reporters and editors practically doubled, growing from 14,750 to 28,595. The gross percentage of women in the field was also larger, rising from 25.3 percent of the total number of editors and reporters employed to 32 percent. Sourced from *Statistical Abstract of the United States,* prepared by the chief of the Bureau of Statistics, Treasury Department, retrieved from HathiTrust. Note the figures for 1960 are omitted because they include authors and the 1970 figures include authors, artists, and entertainers. Outside the totals, the abstracts include figures for people of color as follows: 1960, 2,218 men (includes authors); 1970, 20,000 (includes entertainers and authors and artists); 1972, 7,052; 1981, 10,045; 1991, 20,367; 2000, 13,122; 2010, 22,356 (includes news analysts, reporters, correspondents, and editors). The figures for people of color are outside the total employed numbers.

187   Murrow featured her: CBS aired *Person to Person* for eight years, from 1953 to 1961.

187   "I think it's because I'm interested": "Fannie Hurst," *Person to Person,* CBS, June 18, 1954.

187   "young, blond, and good-looking": "Collier's Credits," *Collier's,* May 25, 1956, in credits for Mosby's profile of Rod Steiger in the same issue. Aline Mosby, "The Weeper," *Collier's,* May 25, 1956.

188   She accepted payment: See, for example, "Clark Gable Linked to Mag's Party Girl by Scandal Witness," *NY Daily News,* Aug. 13, 1957; "Todd Joins List of Notables Denying Confidential Stories," *Wilmington (Del.) News Journal* via UP, Aug. 27, 1957. Also, Siess, "Montana's Scoop," 45–46, quoting Warren Sargent, interview by Dick Harnett, Nov. 6, 1995, corrected Feb. 17, 1996, 45–46, auburn.edu. See also Val Holley, *Mike Connolly and the Manly Art of Hollywood Gossip* (Jefferson, N.C.: McFarland, 2003), 29; and James P. O'Connell, "Subject: Mosby, Aline," Federal Bureau of Investigation, Security Support Division, Sept. 26, 1958,

accessed Sept. 4, 2022, maryferrell.org. The memo notes that UP fired Mosby for the *Confidential* leaks.

188 "the first truly professional":Whitman Bassow, *The Moscow Correspondents: Reporting on Russia from the Revolution to Glasnost* (New York: Paragon House, 1989), 312–13. Other women reporting from Moscow at the time included Collette Shulman and Priscilla Johnson (later McMillan).

188 "purely political reasons": For example, "Young Texan Wants to Be Red Citizen," *Bend (Ore.) Bulletin* via UPI, Oct. 31, 1959, and "Former Marine Wants to Become Soviet Citizen," *Streator (Ill.) Times* via AP, Oct. 31, 1959.

188 Two weeks later: Currie, "Aline Mosby," 56–57.

188 "like getting out of prison": Aline Mosby, "Ex-marine Explains His Choice to Live in Russia," *Coshocton (Ohio) Tribune* via UPI, Nov. 15, 1959, aarclibrary.org. Also, Mosby's recap after Oswald's arrest in Dallas: Aline Mosby, "Oswald's 1959 Interview with UPI," UPI, Nov. 23, 1963. Priscilla Johnson also interviewed Oswald in Moscow around the same time for NANA and wrote about it later as well. See Priscilla Johnson, "The Stuff of Which Fanatics Are Made," *Boston Globe* via NANA, Nov. 24, 1963.

188 Soon after, he called her: Currie, "Aline Mosby," 56–57.

189 "ruthless," "treacherous": These and more appear variously in Sorel's source interviews for *The Women Who Wrote the War* with Katherine Coyne, 40; Shelley Mydans, 28; Carl Mydans, 34, 37; Tania Long, 14; Patricia Lochridge, 8, 24, 29, 58; Helen Kirkpatrick, 10; Lael Wertenbaker, 18. (Provided courtesy of Carolyn Edy.) Also see May, *Witness to War,* 12, 22, 37, 39–40, 42, 52, 57–60, 62, 102–3, 114, 117–18, 184, 187, 189; and Kathleen Kearney Keeshen, "Marguerite Higgins: Journalist, 1920–1966" (PhD diss., University of Maryland, 1983), 9, 22, 28, 37, 38, 62, 79, 83, 86, 101, 108, 176, 132, 134, 140, 201, 204, 220, 222. Also, see generally, Peter Noel Murray, "Marguerite Higgins: An Examination of Legacy and Gender Bias" (PhD diss., University of Maryland, 2003).

189 One kinder response: Richard Kluger, *The Paper: The Life and Death of the "New York Herald Tribune,"* with the assistance of Phyllis Kluger (New York: Knopf, 1986), 440. Crist, incidentally, in 1950, at twenty-eight, won a joint George Polk for education coverage in the *NY Herald Tribune.*

189 "very hard-working": Currie, "Flora Lewis," 37–38.

189 "If I'd known then": As cited in May, *Witness to War,* 66.

189 "more front-page stories": Leonard Lyons, "The Lyons Den," *Montgomery Advertiser,* May 19, 1947.

190 "This attitude offers great": Higgins, *News Is a Singular Thing,* 155–57.

190 "If I was going to be married": Currie, "Flora Lewis," 40, 44–45.

190 By that time, the *Times:* From an email exchange Dec. 31, 2020, with David Dunlap of the *Times*'s staff, who works with the archives: "*Times*

history, as you know, is full of unorthodox exceptions to what everyone thinks is 'the rule,' so very little surprises me any longer. And spouses (wives, typically) played all kinds of roles as *Times* journalists." Also, Reston, *Deadline,* 88.

190 Once, in Israel: Currie, "Flora Lewis," 39–40, 47.

190 All paid "very little": Ibid., 41, 42, 47.

190 By November 1948: Flora Lewis, "President and 'Conscience' of Israel," *NYT Magazine,* Nov. 14, 1948.

190 "impossible": Currie, "Flora Lewis," 47.

191 "His job was more": Ibid., 40, 46.

191 She also wrote more frequently: In 1957, the Overseas Press Club presented her with its Mary Hemingway Award for foreign affairs reporting, and a year later Doubleday published her first book, *A Case History of Hope: The Story of Poland's Peaceful Revolutions,* which *The New Yorker* honored with an unsigned single-paragraph review. ("Miss Lewis . . . has spent enough time in postwar Poland to be able to evaluate the changes that occurred in this period. . . . She is clearly delighted by every scrap of liberty the Poles have won, and especially by the fact that they are now free at least to ask themselves whether a Communist society can be anything but a brutal, bloody nightmare.") *New Yorker,* Nov. 8, 1958.

191 She figured that having books: Flora Lewis, *A Case History of Hope: The Story of Poland's Peaceful Revolutions* (New York: Doubleday, 1958); Flora Lewis, "A Reporter at Large: On the Eve," *New Yorker,* Aug. 19, 1967.

191 "She was considered": Currie, "Flora Lewis," 37–38.

191 "Men didn't do that": The colleague Kluger quoted was Carl Levin.

191 On personal authority: A staffer came in from Europe to help out during a major invasion in the Middle East in 1982 at the request of the bureau chief, a woman. When the bureau chief announced she would be writing the day's lead story, as headquarters expected, he snapped, "If you can translate it, you can write it" and did not yield.

192 "antagonized sources": Kluger, *Paper,* 441–42. The colleague was Stephen White.

192 "very wearing and in many ways": Higgins, *News Is a Singular Thing,* 165.

192 "wit and intelligence": R.G., "Girl Reporter on the Loose," *Montgomery Advertiser,* June 18, 1950; Toni Howard, *Shriek with Pleasure* (New York: Prentice-Hall, 1950).

192 "I decided, what the hell": Currie, "Flora Lewis," 37–38.

192 transferred Higgins to Tokyo: Higgins, *News Is a Singular Thing,* 202–16.

192 "done distressingly well": Betty Barlow Long, "Herald Tribune Tokyo Bureau Chief Is Attractive Woman," *Honolulu Star-Bulletin,* May 15, 1950.

193 They barely got out: Keyes Beech, " 'I Have a Feeling It's the Start of

World War III,' Says Keyes Beech, Under Fire," *Chicago Daily News,* June 29, 1950; Burton Crane, "South Koreans Kill Own Troops by Dynamiting a Bridge Too Soon," *NYT,* June 29, 1950.

193 "The war got off": Keyes Beech, *Tokyo and Points East* (New York: Doubleday, 1954), 169.

193 For her front-page story: Marguerite Higgins, "Seoul's Fall: By a Reporter Who Escaped," *NY Herald Tribune,* June 29, 1950.

193 "telegraphic reporting": "Homer Bigart Goes to War," Pulitzer Prize site, pulitzer.org.

193 especially for his work: Bigart's move to the *NYT,* where he would be just as celebrated if not more so, would not come until 1955.

193 The biggest prize: Higgins, "33,000 Dachau Captives Freed by 7th Army"; "Miss Higgins to Speak," *Cincinnati Enquirer,* Jan. 9, 1952.

193 Only in retrospect: Higgins, *News Is a Singular Thing,* 95.

193 One of Bigart's first acts: Carl Mydans, "Girl War Correspondent," *Life,* Oct. 2, 1950; Mydans, "All About That Girl, Marguerite Higgins," *Boston Globe,* Oct. 1, 1950; Beech, *Tokyo and Points East,* 171, 173.

194 Beech, in his memoir: Beech, *Tokyo and Points East,* 173.

194 That very recklessness: Kluger, *Paper,* 448.

194 Bigart was by far: Mydans, "Girl War Correspondent"; Mydans, "All About That Girl, Marguerite Higgins." See Kluger, *Paper,* 448. In the spring of 1951, just in time for prize season, Higgins's book, *War in Korea,* came out. In one reviewer's estimation, it was "more about Marguerite than of the Korean war." "Books and Bookmen: It's More About Marguerite Than of the Korean War," *Fort-Worth Star-Telegram,* April 29, 1951.

195 Both Higgins and Bigart: The other winners were Fred Sparks, for the *Chicago Daily News,* and, for AP, Relman Morin and Don Whitehead.

195 "his outstanding reports": John Hohenberg, *The Pulitzer Prizes: A History of the Awards in Books, Drama, Music, and Journalism, Based on the Private Files over Six Decades* (New York: Columbia University Press, 1974), 192–94.

195 For Higgins, who had done: "Marguerite Higgins at Red Beach," n.d., pulitzer.org. The jury for the George Polk awards made a similar call in 1952. Bigart won for "the best consistent press reporting from abroad"; Higgins, for "courage, integrity, and enterprise above and beyond the call of duty." Also, "Marguerite Higgins Wins Polk Award," *Boston Globe,* April 30, 1951; "Miss Higgins to Get Press Club's Prize," *NYT,* April 30, 1951.

195 "Any one of her dispatches": Beech, *Tokyo and Points East,* 183.

195 "No way I can make": Harrison Salisbury, foreword to Bigart, *Forward Positions,* xvi.

196 "Wonderful, who's the mother?": Ibid., xxiii.

196 Some of the most successful: With thanks to Susan Akkad for pointing out the possibility that age was their asset. Also see Laura Hazard Owen, "Promoting Based on Potential: How the Atlantic Is Putting a Lot More Women in Charge," Nieman Lab, June 6, 2019.

196 All of them were women: Marvel Cooke was born in 1903; Alice Allison Dunnigan in 1906; Martha Gellhorn and Pauline Frederick in 1908; and Edith Evans Asbury in 1910. Soon after came Ethel Payne, born in 1911.

196 It came in the early 1950s: Frederick fared better in the young broadcast mediums of radio and television than Betty Wason, who took many risks for CBS during the war in Eastern Europe, Scandinavia, and Greece, but could not get hired thereafter. Wason overcame her stinging postwar snub from the network by writing cookbooks and a book about Greece under the Axis. She found work back in women's world, as an assistant food editor at *McCall's*, and as a women's editor for Voice of America and for *Woman's Home Companion*. Ruth Cowan stayed with the AP on her return to Washington, but still covered the women's angle of things.

196 "so-called women's news": Nancy H. MacLennan, "Only One of Her Kind," *NYT*, Dec. 5, 1948.

196 *Newsweek* featured: "Spinster at the News Mike," *Newsweek*, Oct. 27, 1947.

197 Her profile in the *Times:* MacLennan, "Only One of Her Kind."

197 The UN would quickly: United Nations Correspondents Association directories, New York, 1950–80. At no point do women represent less than 10 percent of the membership, and in later years the woman total is higher.

197 And yet for men: Throughout the 1950s and 1960s, Kathleen McLaughlin, Kathleen Teltsch, and Catherine Shea put in the better part of two decades covering the world body as the more permanent members of the *NYT* UN-based staff. The *Times*'s men, however, filter in and out after short terms. McLaughlin's career started at the *Chicago Tribune* in 1925, not long after Genevieve Forbes Herrick joined the staff, but she left the *Tribune* ten years later, in 1935, after a stint as its women's editor. Ten years after that, the *Times* sent her to London and Bonn, starting in 1944, and she remained with the paper throughout her UN assignment, which started in 1950 and lasted until close to her retirement at seventy in 1968.

197 After her stint: Currie, "Marvel Cooke," 90.

198 "not confined to 'Negro' news": For example, "First Negro Woman on New York Daily," *Alabama Tribune (Montgomery)*, May 12, 1950.

198 Sol Abraham: Currie, "Marvel Cooke," 97–98.

198 Almost immediately: See Maida Odom, "Remarkable Tale of Old-Time Reporter, Activist," *Philadelphia Inquirer*, Feb. 28, 1998; Glenda Cadogan, "Harlem's First Lady," *NY Daily News*, Feb. 10, 2000; Currie, "Marvel

Cooke," 107–9; Rodger Streitmatter, *Raising Her Voice: African-American Women Journalists Who Changed History* (Lexington: University Press of Kentucky, 1994), 85–94.

198 for her searing investigation: Marvel Cooke, "I Was a Part of the Bronx Slave Market," *NY Sunday Compass Magazine,* Jan. 8, 1950; Cooke, "Where Men Prowl and Women Prey on Needy Job Seekers," Jan. 9, 1950; "'Paper Bag Brigade' Learns How to Deal with Gypping Employers," Jan. 10, 1950; "'Mrs. Legree' Hires Only on the Street, Always 'Nice Girls,'" Jan. 11, 1950; "Some Ways to Kill the Slave Market," Jan. 12, 1950. Collected at undercover.hosting.nyu.edu.

198 "Negro women wait": Cooke, "I Was a Part of the Bronx Slave Market."

198 Cooke, in fact: For Cooke's earlier work on the subject, see Ella Baker and Marvel Cooke, "Bronx Slave Market," *Crisis,* Nov. 1, 1935. Also, for the *Amsterdam News:* Marvel Cooke, "'Modern Slaves,' Domestic Jobs Are Miserable in Hours, Pay. Union Is Seeking to Relieve Their Bad Situation," Oct. 16, 1937; "Bronx 'Slave Mart' Flourishes: Business Recession Is Blamed as Cause for Its Revival. Southern Girls Lured to New York by Racketeers," July 9, 1938; "Slavery: 1939 Style: Bronx Slave Mart Is Active as Ever," May 27, 1939; "Help Wanted for the Help: Sorry Plight of Domestics Sore Problem. Sad Is the Situation of New York's Workers in Homes of Rich," Oct. 7, 1939.

198 Colleagues bet Cooke: Paula Span, "Marvel Cooke's Tour of the Century," *WP,* Aug. 11, 1993.

198 "Occupation: Streetwalker": Marvel Cooke articles in *NY Compass:* "Occupation: Streetwalker," April 16, 1950; "Katie, 'Given Away' at 3, Turned to Streets at 15," April 17, 1950; "Katie's 'Not Ashamed Any More'—She Just Feels Helpless Now," April 18, 1950; "Katie Is Sent to the Reformatory on Her 1st Arrest," April 19, 1950; "How Vice Squad Operates," April 20, 1950; "Police Oldtimers Become Cynical About Prostitution," April 21, 1950; "'I Was Framed' Is Universal Cry in Woman's Court," April 23, 1950; "Chaneta's New Home: A Dingy, Heatless Flat," April 24, 1950; "It's Drab, Tawdry in Women's Court," April 25, 1950; "The Judge Is King in Women's Court," April 27, 1950; "A Trip Through Women's Prison," April 28, 1950; "A Plan to Deal with Prostitution," April 30, 1950; "What Can New York Do About Prostitution?," May 1, 1950. See also Odom, "Remarkable Tale of Old-Time Reporter, Activist"; Cadogan, "Harlem's First Lady"; Currie, "Marvel Cooke," 107–9; Streitmatter, *Raising Her Voice,* 85–94.

198 teenage narcotics addiction: Marvel Cooke articles in *NY Compass:* "What Can Happen to YOUR Child—a Study in Narcotics Addiction," May 20, 1951; "My Son, 20, Is a Hopeless Addict," May 21, 1951; "3-Way

Battle on Dope Proposed," May 21, 1951; "Southeast Bronx Narcotics Peddlers Found Wherever Children Gather," May 22, 1951; "Dope Area in Bronx Suddenly 'Quiet' as Compass Expose Turns Heat On," May 23, 1951; "Case History of a Teen Addict," May 24, 1951, 4.

198 The *Compass* folded: Other examples of failing publications where women got opportunity unusual for the times: Laura Vitray as city editor of the dying NY *Evening Graphic* from 1930 to 1932, or Jeane Hoffman, in 1949, as editor in chief of the once-flush but badly flailing "lad mag," the *Police Gazette*, as it turned 104. See *Austin-American Statesman*, Oct. 13, 1949; "Girl for the Gazette"; "Famous Woman Sports Writer Begins Series in Times Today"; *St. Louis Sporting News*, July 4, 1956; *St. Louis Sporting News*, Sept. 13, 1964; "Jeane Hoffman Is Dead at 47; Former Police Gazette Editor." Two years later, Hoffman was writing sports again for the *LAT* "from the feminine point of view," as the paper said in announcing it had hired the "Famous Woman Sports Writer."

199 Long after 1956: "Executive Sessions of the Senate Permanent Subcommittee on Investigations of the Committee on Government Operations," vol. 2, 83rd Cong., 1st Sess., 1953, Testimony of Marvel Cooke, Sept. 8, 1953, 1687–90, senate.gov. See also ad, "The First Line of Defense," *California Eagle*, Aug. 26, 1948; "Red Probers Win Army Aid," *Chicago Tribune*, Sept. 9, 1953; "Stevens to Review Curb by Army on Red Probe," *NY Herald Tribune*, Sept. 9, 1953. Also, Streitmatter, *Raising Her Voice*, 84–94; Currie, "Marvel Cooke," 41–42, 73–83, 128–38.

200 She joined the Women's National Press Club: The invitation was initially offered in 1947, but Dunnigan's discomfort at a club dinner party with Senator Margaret Chase Smith had been intense enough to keep her hesitant about membership. Streitmatter, *Raising Her Voice*, 106–17.

200 "If you have lived through": Kathleen Currie, "Women in Journalism: Ethel Payne," Washington, D.C., Aug. 27–Nov. 17, 1987, 49–50, Washington Press Club Foundation Oral History Project.

200 "The First Lady of the Black Press": Generally, ibid.; Streitmatter, *Raising Her Voice*, 118–28; and James McGrath Morris, *Eye on the Struggle: Ethel Payne, the First Lady of the Black Press* (New York: Amistad, 2017).

200 Edith Evans Asbury: Currie, "Edith Evans Asbury," 135–38. The reporter was Frank Adams, soon to replace Robert Garst (Asbury's future third husband) as city editor.

201 "For the first time": Ibid., 137–39.

201 She did a major five-part: Edith Evans Asbury, five-part series on aging in the *NYT*: "Growing Ranks of the Aged Pose Grave Social Problems," Feb. 21, 1955; "Sufficient Facilities Do Not Exist to Care for the Sick Aged," Feb. 22, 1955; "Rise in Aged Adds Burden on Young," Feb. 23,

1955; "Aids to Morale Needed for Aged," Feb. 24, 1955; "Europe Leads U.S. in Assisting Aged," Feb. 25, 1955.

201 She was the only woman: "Report on the South," *NYT,* March 13, 1956. The other nine reporters were John N. Popham, Luther A. Huston, George Barrett, Seth S. King, Damon Stetson, Peter Kihss, Gladwin Hill, Clarence Dean, and Russell Porter.

201 "stubborn curiosity": Gelb, *City Room,* 435–39, 475, 522–23.

203 "always probe far beyond": Ibid., 441, 478.

203 its 1926 house ad: House ad, "Why Women Read the *Chicago Tribune,*" *Chicago Tribune,* Jan. 3, 1926.

203 The *Newsweek* writer seemed: *Newsweek* cited Pat Leeds on the police beat and Gwen Morgan on finance. "Girls on the Tribune," *Newsweek,* March 25, 1957. The city editor was Tom Furlong.

203 Malcolm, after succeeding: "Donald Malcolm, Book Critic for the New Yorker, Dies at 43," *NYT,* Aug. 18, 1975.

Chapter 12. Foment

205 The 1960s: *The Feminine Mystique* was published Feb. 19, 1963. The Federal Drug Administration approved the birth control pill May 9, 1963. The Cuban missile crisis happened Oct. 16–28, 1962. President Kennedy signed the Equal Pay Act into law June 10, 1963, and Congress passed the Civil Rights Act July 2, 1964. On Aug. 28, 1963, the Reverend Dr. Martin Luther King gave his "I Have a Dream" speech during the March on Washington for Jobs and Freedom. John F. Kennedy's assassination was Nov. 22, 1963; Malcolm X's, on Feb. 21, 1965; Dr. King's, April 4, 1968, and Robert Kennedy's, June 6, 1968. The riots in the Watts neighborhood of Los Angeles occurred in 1965 and those during the Democratic National Convention in Chicago in Aug. 1968. *Hair* opened on Broadway April 29, 1968. The Woodstock music festival was Aug. 15–18, 1969.

205 A book published in 1963: For example, Betty Friedan, "We Drove the Rackets Out of Our Town," *Redbook,* Aug. 1955; Friedan, "The Happy Families of Hickory Hill," *Redbook,* Feb. 1956; Friedan, "Millionaire's Wife," *Cosmopolitan,* Sept. 1956; Friedan, "Day Camp in the Driveways," *Parents' Magazine & Family Home Guide,* May 1957; Friedan, "I Say Women Are People, Too!," *Good Housekeeping,* Sept. 1960; and an excerpt from the book, Friedan, "Have American Housewives Traded Brains for Brooms?," *Ladies' Home Journal,* Jan. 1963.

206 "What they said to me": Lynn Sherr, email exchange with author, Jan. 10, 2022.

206 "another exclusive men's club": Lynn Sherr, *Outside the Box: A Memoir* (Emmaus, Pa.: Rodale, 2006), 39–40.

206 By 1972, the percentage: The 28,595 woman reporters and editors of 1950 became 45,608 by 1960, and then reached its highest point yet at 67,896 of the journalism workforce by 1972, when the percentage of woman reporters and editors would jump to 47.4 percent on the way to better than parity—102,090 men to 102,910 women—by 1981. (The count of people of color among reporters and editors does not start until 1970 and is a tiny 7,052 in a total reporter and editor population of 164,000, or 4.3 percent.)

206 women at the weekly magazines: Helen Whitehead, "An Opinion: Helen Whitehead on the News Weeklies—and Women," *Mademoiselle,* Sept. 1970.

207 Lynn Povich's book: Lynn Povich, *The Good Girls Revolt: How the Women of "Newsweek" Sued Their Bosses and Changed the Workplace* (New York: PublicAffairs, 2016).

207 Povich joined the *Newsweek* staff: Ibid., 23.

207 "the back of the book": Lynn Povich, email interview by author, March 17, 2021.

207 Povich recalled the summer: Povich, *Good Girls Revolt,* xix.

207 Editors never nurtured: Whitehead, "Helen Whitehead on the News Weeklies—and Women."

207 Povich, in describing: Povich, telephone interview by author, Jan. 18, 2021.

208 "It was thrilling": Franny Heller Zorn in Povich, *Good Girls Revolt,* 18; Zorn, interview by author, Feb. 16, 2021.

208 Heller's contributions to the piece: The section editor was Jack Kroll. The page 3 cover note read, "Associate Editor Paul D. Zimmerman drew on files from the Paris and Los Angeles bureaus and on extensive coverage from reporter Frances Heller on Miss Deneuve in New York City."

208 "pieces of fluff": Zorn, email and telephone interviews by author, Feb. 16, 2021.

208 as he gave the assignment: "Catherine Deneuve—French Star over Hollywood Page 42," *Newsweek,* Aug. 26, 1968; Zorn, email and telephone interviews by author, Feb. 18 and March 9, 2021.

208 "Our 'problem that had no name'": Povich, *Good Girls Revolt,* xix; Povich, telephone and email interviews by author, Jan. 18 and Feb. 17, 2021.

208 Obviously, Povich said: Povich, telephone interview by author, Jan. 18, 2021.

208 The situation at *The New Yorker:* Thomas Kunkel, *Genius in Disguise: Harold Ross of "The New Yorker"* (New York: Random House, 1995), 171.

209 "simply could never": Ibid., 171; and Grant and Flanner, *Ross,* 251.

209 "was able to impart": Grant and Flanner, *Ross,* 258. In the memoir, neither

Grant nor Flanner makes note of having influenced the magazine's will-ingness to feature woman writers and entrust woman editors with major responsibility from the start. To me, this absence conveys the impres-sion that it was unremarkable for women at *The New Yorker* to have been given such outsized opportunity. Also, Ben Yagoda, telephone interview by author, June 7, 2021. Yagoda concurred with this view. See also Ben Yagoda, *About Town: "The New Yorker" and the World It Made* (New York: Scribner, 2000).

209 As a staff member in the 1960s: Calvin Trillin, email exchange with author, June 4, 2021.

209 Jane Kramer: Jane Kramer, *Off Washington Square: A Reporter Looks at Green-wich Village* (New York: Duell, Sloane & Pierce, 1963). She would become *The New Yorker*'s European correspondent.

209 Janet Malcolm moved on: New York City Directories and Records via ancestry.com show the birth date of Anne Olivia Malcolm as Dec. 17, 1962, ancestry.com.

209 published her poem: Janet Malcolm, "Thoughts on Living in a Shaker House," *New Yorker*, Nov. 2, 1963; "Children's Books for Christmas," Dec. 17, 1966; "Paley Park," Aug. 16, 1968. Malcolm's first husband, Don-ald, joined the staff of *The New Yorker* in 1958. See "Donald Malcolm, Book Critic for the New Yorker, Dies at 43."

209 Closer to the end of the decade: Ellen Willis and Jane Kramer are among the few women at *The New Yorker* who started out at the alternative weeklies of the 1960s and then found routes into mainstream careers. Claudia Dreifus, whose earliest experience was at labor papers and at *The East Village Other*, also had subsequent success at mainstream publi-cations, especially noted for her prowess with the Q &A format she has deployed for publications from *Playboy* to the science section of the *NYT*. Freelancing has many pluses in terms of freedom to develop the kinds of assignments that one wants to write, she said. But nearing her own eighth decade with no pension, the minuses have become more painfully apparent. Claudia Dreifus, telephone interview by author, Jan. 31, 2021.

210 "taken for granted": When Trillin joined the magazine staff, Janet Flan-ner had been writing her "Letter from Paris" for decades, Molly Painter-Downes was doing the "Letter from London," and Lillian Ross had been contributing distinctive pieces since the 1940s. The number of woman hires slowed in the years between 1930 and 1960, as the *New Yorker* his-torian Ben Yagoda pointed out in an interview with me, the exceptions being Andy Logan and Frances Scott Fitzgerald, the daughter of F. Scott and Zelda. Yagoda, interview by author, June 7, 2021.

210 At twenty-five, working in *Time:* For example, "Homemaker Winners

Announced," *Atlanta Constitution,* Feb. 16, 1959; "Suit Seeks Georgia Univ. Integration," *Bristol (Tenn.) Herald Courier,* Sept. 6, 1960; "U.S. Judge Orders U of Georgia to Admit 2 Negroes," *St. Louis Post-Dispatch,* Jan. 6, 1961; "First Negro Enrolls in Georgia College," *Grand Junction (Colo.) Daily Sentinel,* Jan. 7, 1961; "Charlayne Alberta Hunter," *NYT,* Jan. 16, 1961; Charlayne Hunter, "Our First Days at University of Georgia," *Jet,* Feb. 1961; Charlayne Hunter, "Charlayne Finds Friends at U. of GA," *Atlanta Inquirer,* Jan. 21, 1961; "Louisville Times Adds Negro to News Staff," *Louisville Courier-Journal,* March 16, 1961; "200 Newsmen of Many Media in Atlanta for School Integration," *Greenville (S.C.) News,* Aug. 31, 1961 (Hunter among them, interning at *The Louisville Times* and for *The Atlanta Inquirer*); Bruce Galphin, "Integration Boiled into Big Headlines," *Atlanta Constitution,* Jan. 1, 1962; item about Hunter's graduation from Georgia, *Tallahassee Democrat,* Jan. 1, 1963; Charlayne Hunter-Gault, "Georgia—of 25 Years Ago—on My Mind," *NYT,* June 14, 1988; Hunter-Gault, Zoom interview by author, April 16, 2021; Trillin, telephone interview by author, April 19, 2021.

210 "but never got any assignments": Charlayne Hunter-Gault, email exchange with author, Oct. 9, 2021.

210 While still in school: "Louisville Times Adds Negro to News Staff"; Charlayne Hunter, "We Want to Forget Past . . . Just Be Two Busy Students," *Jet,* Feb. 9, 1961; "200 Newsmen of Many Media in Atlanta for School Integration"; Hunter-Gault, Zoom interview by author, April 16, 2021; Trillin, telephone interview by author, April 19, 2021; Calvin Trillin, "An Education in Georgia," *New Yorker,* July 13, 20, 27, 1963; Calvin Trillin, *An Education in Georgia* (New York: Viking, 1964).

211 Trillin in turn arranged: Hunter-Gault, Zoom interview by author, April 16, 2021; Trillin, telephone interview by author, April 19, 2021; follow-up email from Trillin, April 22, 2021; Trillin, "Education in Georgia," July 13, 20, 27, 1963; Trillin, *Education in Georgia.*

211 Adlai Stevenson: Cover, "Adlai Stevenson," *Time,* Dec. 14, 1962; [Calvin Trillin], "The Administration: The Stranger on the Squad," *Time,* Dec. 14, 1962.

211 "An Education in Georgia": Hunter-Gault, Zoom interview by author, April 16, 2021; Trillin, telephone interview by author, April 19, 2021; follow-up email from Trillin, April 22, 2021; Trillin, "Education in Georgia," July 13, 20, 27, 1963; Trillin, *Education in Georgia.*

212 Hunter was so much: For example, *St. Albans (Vt.) Daily Messenger,* Sept. 2, 1963; Ray Goodall, "Let's Have More Mixed Marriages," *Vancouver Sun,* March 20, 1965; "Where Are the Seven Negroes Now Who Integrated Southern Colleges?," *El Paso Times* via AP, Aug. 22, 1965.

212 "no news or editorial work": "Georgia U. Negro Joins New Yorker," *Baltimore Sun* via AP, June 1, 1963; Susan Stovall, daughter of Walter Stovall and Charlayne A. Hunter, New York City Birth Index, Nov. 15, 1963, No. 43956.

212 one long unsigned paragraph: "Notes and Comments," *New Yorker,* Aug. 1, 1964. A long piece titled "Bedford-Stuyvesant" follows on the same page, but it is by a different, also unsigned, writer. Hunter-Gault, Zoom interview by author, April 16, 2021. See also Charlayne Hunter-Gault, *To the Mountaintop: My Journey Through the Civil Rights Movement* (New York: Roaring Brook Press, 2012), 111; and Hunter's articles in *The New Yorker:* "A Hundred Fifteenth Between Lenox and Fifth," Feb. 20, 1965; "A Trip to Leverton," April 24, 1965, classified as fiction but aside from a change in the name of the town, true (Hunter-Gault, Zoom interview by author, April 16, 2021); "The Black Student," March 18, 1966; "The Professor," Aug. 26, 1966; "Unlimited Visibility," Sept. 9, 1966; "The Corner," Dec. 30, 1966; "Representative," March 24, 1967; "Tiny Cards," Sept. 29, 1967; "Lull," Nov. 3, 1967; "Columbia's Long Overdue Apology to Langston Hughes," Dec. 30, 1967.

212 In 1968, she left: Ellen Schlafly, "Fellows Find Insight in Transaction with the Midwest," *St. Louis Post-Dispatch,* April 19, 1968; Hunter-Gault, Zoom interview by author, April 16, 2021.

212 the magazine *Trans-Action:* Charlayne A. Hunter, "On the Case in Resurrection City," *Trans-Action* 5 (Oct. 1968): 47–55.

212 "feet back in the street": Hunter-Gault, Zoom interview by author, April 14, 2021.

212 "into attitudes and issues": Display ad, "News4 Probe," *WP,* Nov. 14, 1968.

213 "the only civil rights movement": Martha Weinman Lear, "The Second Feminist Wave: What Do These Women Want?," *NYT Magazine,* March 10, 1968.

Chapter 13. Supernovas

214 Judges for several top: For example, six women were among the winners of awards from the Overseas Press Club during the decade, including a second OPC for Flora Lewis in 1962 for her *WP* coverage of meetings between the German chancellor, Konrad Adenauer, and the French president, Charles de Gaulle. Three OPCs went to women for their coverage of the Vietnam War: Liz Trotta for NBC and two freelancers in their mid-twenties, Frances FitzGerald, a 1962 cum laude graduate of Radcliffe, who wrote for the Sunday magazine of the *NY Herald Tribune* until the newspaper's demise, and Linda Grant Martin, who had worked briefly in junior positions at *The Saturday Evening Post* and *Newsweek.* She

had quit to accompany her new husband, Everett G. Martin, *Newsweek*'s new Saigon bureau chief, to Southeast Asia. FitzGerald wrote "The Tragedy of Saigon" on spec for *The Atlantic* and won the 1967 OPC for best interpretive foreign reporting. (See Frances FitzGerald, "The Tragedy of Saigon," *Atlantic,* Dec. 1966, and the next year, "The Struggle and the War: The Maze of Vietnamese Politics," *Atlantic,* Aug. 1967.) Greater awards would follow. Martin won the OPC's "Best Foreign Reporting of the Year" for her piece on a South Vietnamese village where the Americans had fruitlessly poured millions of dollars in aid. (Linda Grant Martin, "The Story of the 37-Year War of the Village of Tan An Hoi," *NYT Magazine,* Oct. 29, 1967.) She had been in Vietnam for a year at that point. Although *Newsweek* had not kept her on as a staffer, the magazine included her in the full-page national newspaper ad it ran to promote the many awards its full-time correspondents won in 1968. "Even the wife of one of our correspondents won an Overseas Press Club Award," the last entry read. As for the women in broadcast media, Liz Trotta's OPC is the decade's only notable award to a woman who worked in radio or television. There were no repeats in the 1960s of Pauline Frederick's 1953 duPont or her Peabody in 1954.

As for the George Polks, the count for woman winners fell from a high of eleven winners in the 1950s to only four throughout the 1960s. In 1962, Mary McGrory won for national reporting in the Washington *Evening Star* and Kitty Hanson, for a nursing home series in the *New York Daily News;* Susan Sontag won for criticism in 1965; and the French freelance photojournalist Catherine Leroy won for her arresting close-up, taken at Da Nang, of a navy corpsman as he tried to revive a dying U.S. marine in 1967. Leroy was a tiny twenty-two-year-old French freelancer, a daring, publicity-averse ace parachutist, and the first woman photographer and the first freelancer to win the prize. The photo is signature Leroy in the way it shows her close eye-to-eye interaction with her subjects, a way of incorporating her reaction to what she was seeing rather than standing outside it. This was the description the photographic historian Susan D. Moeller provided to Leroy's colleague Elizabeth Becker for her book about the women who reported from Vietnam. Leroy, Moeller said, "was doing things you weren't taught to do and that others weren't doing."

214 In 1960, Miriam Ottenberg: Ottenberg followed Mary Lou Werner, also of the *Star,* who won the year before for her yearlong coverage of the integration crisis in Virginia. The previous winners as already noted were Anne O'Hare McCormick, 1937; Marguerite Higgins, 1951; Virginia Schau, 1954; and Mrs. Caro Brown, 1955.

214 "that the two-layered look": Miriam Ottenberg, *The Pursuit of Hope* (New York: Rawson, Wade, 1978), 4.

215 She ventured into Mau Mau country: Ibid.

215 An epitaph described her: Rick Kogan, "Lois Wille, Trailblazing Chicago Reporter and Editorial Writer, Winner of Two Pulitzers, Dies at 87," *Chicago Tribune,* July 23, 2019; Katherine Q. Seelye, "Lois Wille, Twice a Pulitzer Winner in Her Beloved Chicago, Dies at 87," *NYT,* July 26, 2019. The third and final Pulitzer to a woman journalist in the 1960s went to Hazel Brannon Smith, a "white daughter of segregation," owner and editor of four Mississippi newspapers, for editorials "decrying white supremacy and all the violence wrought in its ungodly name." See Leonard Pitts, "Hazel Brannon Smith: 'A Product of Her Times'—and a Force for Change," Pulitzer Prizes, pulitzer.org.

216 "a terrier of an American reporter": John Miller, *All Them Cornfields and Ballet in the Evening* (Kingston upon Thames: Hodgson Press, 2010), 135.

216 In Mosby's version: Currie, "Aline Mosby," 48; Miller, *All Them Cornfields and Ballet in the Evening,* 135.

216 This was not the sort of thing: Currie, "Aline Mosby," 62–64, 134–35. Mosby tells the story twice during the oral history interview, with slight variations.

217 an article about the lunch: "Г-жа МОСБИ _В _ВЫТРЕЗВИТЕЛЕ" [Miss Mosby in a drunk tank], *Izvestia,* June 7, 1961. Translation courtesy of Aron Ouzilevsky, with gratitude. The "social parasite" was Igor Kholin, a Russian poet and fiction writer, and the "so-called painter" Lev Kropivnitski.

218 "Nepotism and her daddy's": Bassow, *Moscow Correspondents,* 312–13. Later, Mosby said she heard about indignant letters from Russians that *Izvestia* published, tsk-tsking the terrible behavior of Americans. And later still, she learned that another Western correspondent, a man, reporting in Georgia, had been similarly drugged. Bassow, a *Newsweek* bureau chief whom the Russians would expel in 1960, wrote in 1989 of how few women were sent in over the twenty years after Mosby. Of those, most worked for the wire services and ranged from novices on their first overseas assignment to experienced hands. The Soviets remained uncertain about how to treat them, but Bassow said this could be just as true for men. Experiences like Mosby's, from provocations and attacks to other bouts of extreme unpleasantness, were a given.

218 Random House published: Aline Mosby, *The View from No. 13 People's Street* (New York: Random House, 1962). See, for example, "Press: Over That Barrier," *Newsweek,* April 23, 1962.

218 *The New York Times* named Ada Louise: "Architecture Critic Appointed by the Times," *NYT,* Sept. 1963; Ada Louise Huxtable, *Classic New York: Georgian Gentility to Greek Elegance* (New York: Doubleday, 1964). See also David W. Dunlap, "Ada Louise Huxtable, Champion of Livable Architecture, Dies at 91," *NYT,* Jan. 7, 2013.

218 She had graduated: Adam Bernstein, "Ada Louise Huxtable, Pulitzer-Winning Architecture Critic," *WP,* Jan. 7, 2013; Dunlap, "Ada Louise Huxtable, Champion of Livable Architecture, Dies at 91."

219 Clifton Daniel: Daniel to Max Frankel, Jan. 4, 1982, Max Frankel Papers, box 1, New York Times Company Records.

219 "the most important pioneer": Paul Goldberger, "Tribute to Ada Louise Huxtable" (lecture, Museum of the City of New York, March 25, 1996).

219 When she died at ninety-one: Dunlap, "Ada Louise Huxtable, Champion of Livable Architecture, Dies at 91"; Michael Kimmelman, "A Critic of the Curb and Corner," *NYT,* Jan. 8, 2013.

219 "one of the most trenchant": Bernstein, "Ada Louise Huxtable, Pulitzer-Winning Architecture Critic, Dies at 91."

219 Gay Talese described her in his profile: Gay Talese, "The Perils of Pauline," *Saturday Evening Post,* Jan. 26, 1963; Carol Horner, "Pauline Frederick: Just a News Reporter," *Salt Lake Tribune* via Knight Ridder, Oct. 19, 1980.

220 He also brought up the younger: Talese, "Perils of Pauline." He mentioned Nancy Hanschman of CBS, soon to be better known in Washington as Nancy Dickerson, and Lisa Howard at ABC.

220 Frederick, Nancy Dickerson, and Lisa Howard: Lee Graham, "Women Don't Like to Look at Women," *NYT Sunday Magazine,* May 24, 1964.

220 "TV's Female Brain Trust": Claire Berman, "TV's Female Brain Trust," *Good Housekeeping,* July 1964. Lisa Howard was not on the subsequent list because she was about to lose her job for violating ABC's policy against engaging in a political campaign. "ABC Relieves Lisa Howard over Politics," *Lexington (Ky.) Leader,* Sept. 30, 1964.

221 "Marie Ochs": Gloria Steinem, "A Bunny's Tale," *Show,* May and June 1963, reprinted in *The Mammoth Book of Journalism,* ed. Jon E. Lewis (New York: Carroll, 2003), 346–52; also in Steinem, *Outrageous Acts and Everyday Rebellions* (New York: Henry Holt, 1983), 32–75, and vii, xix, 6, 16, 19–20; Carolyn G. Heilbrun, *The Education of a Woman: The Life of Gloria Steinem* (New York: Ballantine, 1996), 105–8.

221 Four techniques could land: Gloria Steinem, "Nylons in the Newsroom," *NYT,* Nov. 7, 1965.

221 Agness Underwood: Joe Lewis, "Wiry City Editor Is No Lady but She's a Top Newspaperman," *Raleigh News and Observer,* July 25, 1961; "Honor Press Woman," *KC Star,* June 19, 1962; [Underwood to AME], "To City

Editor Post," *KC Times,* Nov. 4, 1964; Belcher, "Aggie Underwood, First Woman City Editor of Major Paper, Dies."

222 "the gritty stuff ": James G. Bellows, *The Last Editor: How I Saved "The New York Times," "The Washington Post," and the "Los Angeles Times" from Dullness and Complacency* (Kansas City, Mo.: Andrews McMeel, 2002), 83, 105.

222 Curtis crashed the boundaries: Charlotte Curtis, "Black Panther Philosophy Is Debated at the Bernsteins," *NYT,* Jan. 15, 1970.

223 "She had the disposition": "Reporters: Sociologist on the Society Beat," *Time,* Feb. 19, 1965.

223 "The day after I was born": Patricia Bosworth, "Diane Sawyer Makes News," *Ladies' Home Journal,* Feb. 1985.

223 Clifton Daniel championed Curtis: Turner Catledge, *My Life and the "Times"* (New York: Harper Collins, 1971), 221. Also see, generally, Marilyn S. Greenwald, *A Woman of the Times: Journalism, Feminism, and the Career of Charlotte Curtis* (Athens: Ohio University Press, 1999).

223 Eleanor Darnton: "Eleanor Darnton Is Dead at 61; Writer on Juvenile Delinquency."

223 "also reflected a desire": Catledge, *My Life and the Times,* 221.

223 Curtis retained her position: "Women's Pages Used to Read Like Something Peeled Off a Sugar-Shot Cornflake Box. Now Charlotte Curtis Has Changed All That," *New York,* Oct. 6, 1969. By 1969, by then untethered from her original protectors, Julie Baumgold of *New York* magazine hearkened to the women who "have fallen under Charlotte's hatchet," to describe Curtis as a writer whose copy could be "killed but never cut" and whose prose "can cut but never kill."

223 Outstanding talent: Dunlap, "Ada Louise Huxtable, Champion of Livable Architecture, Dies at 91"; Robertson, *Girls in the Balcony,* 130.

224 "mod squad": "Lynn Sherr to Address AP Meeting in Vincennes," *Vincennes (Ind.) Sun-Commercial,* Oct. 9, 1969.

224 Jurate Kazickas: Sherr, *Outside the Box,* 44–46; Sherr, interview by author, East Hampton, N.Y., Dec. 22, 2019, and subsequent email exchanges.

224 a shrapnel wound: See Tad Bartimus et al., *War Torn: Stories of War from the Women Reporters Who Covered Vietnam* (New York: Random House, 2002), 121–53; Jurate Kazickas, "I Became a Feminist When the Officers Invited Me to Dinner but Not to the Front Lines," Veteran Feminists of America, Sept. 2018. (Interviewed by Penny Stoil; Dave Sperling, videographer.)

224 ABC hired Melba Tolliver: Her boss's name was Don Coe.

224 Before ABC: Jesse H. Walker, "Theatricals," *NY Amsterdam News,* Sept. 4, 1965; "Big City Queen," *NY Daily News,* Jan. 8, 1967; AP, "Secretary Doubles as 'Caster," *Austin Statesman,* Sept. 26, 1967; Robert E. Dallos, "TV

Strike, Burden for Some, Gives Others the Big Chance," *NYT,* Sept. 26, 1967; "ABC Secretary Fills In as Newscaster During Strike," *Jet,* April 13, 1967; Leo Penn, director, *A Man Called Adam.*

224 Decades later, she would point to 1963: Verne Gay, "What Ever Happened to Pioneering Reporter Melba Tolliver," *Newsday,* Jan. 31, 2020.

224 "Ten Negroes": The *Herald Tribune* reporter was Robert S. Bird.

225 "one of the bitterest, angriest": "From the *New York* (N.Y.) *Herald Tribune,* May 12, 1963, Robert S. Bird, 'The Negroes,'" Cong. Rec.—Senate, Proceedings and Debates of the 88th Cong., vol. 109, part 7, May 14–28, 1963, 8749–51; "Times Forum: Plea for a Traffic Light at Intersection" (letter to the editor from Flo Burke), *St. Petersburg Times,* June 24, 1963.

225 "rain-swollen river": This referred to Hurricane Beulah in Sept. 1967.

225 Tolliver's "big chance": Robert Mayer, "But Is Ted Mack a News Fan?," *Newsday,* March 30, 1967; Barbara Delatiner, "Not So Different AFTRA All," *Newsday,* March 31, 1967; Murry Frymer, "Melba Tolliver, Ex-celebrity, Looks Back Fondly on Fame," *Newsday,* April 13, 1967; "ABC Secretary Fills In as Newscaster During Strike"; Dallos, "TV Strike, Burden for Some, Gives Other the Big Chance"; "Secretary Doubles as 'Caster"; George Gent, "3 A.B.C. Newsmen Return to Work," *NYT,* Oct. 6, 1967; Barbara Campbell, "Melba? She's the Toast of the Town," *NYT,* Feb. 18, 1973; Gay, "What Ever Happened to Pioneering Reporter Melba Tolliver."

225 until ABC could create: Gay, "What Ever Happened to Pioneering Reporter Melba Tolliver."

225 That launched her: Pamela Newkirk, in-person and email interviews by author, East Hampton, N.Y., March 20–21, 2021.

226 "What happens when four": "In the Minneapolis Tribune Tomorrow," *Minneapolis Star-Tribune,* June 1, 1968.

226 "No other pop critic": Jon Michaud, "Q&A: Sasha Frere-Jones on Ellen Willis," *New Yorker,* May 8, 2011.

226 "enthralling and infuriating": Manohla Dargis and A. O. Scott, "Mad About Her: Pauline Kael, Loved and Loathed," *NYT,* Oct. 14, 2011.

226 "the most powerful": Laurence Van Gelder, "Pauline Kael, Provocative and Widely Imitated New Yorker Film Critic, Dies at 82," *NYT,* Sept. 4, 2001; Roger Ebert, "Knocked Up at the Movies," RogerEbert .com, Oct. 22, 2011.

227 "But for all his faults": Meg Greenfield, *Washington* (New York: Public Affairs, 2001), 126–28.

227 "dumb broad": Ibid., 128–29.

227 Hired as an editorial writer: J. Y. Smith, "Editorial Editor Meg Greenfield Dies," *WP,* May 14, 1999.

228 Atop the list is Rachel Carson's: Carson won the National Book Award for nonfiction in 1952 for *The Sea Around Us* and was nominated in 1956 for *The Edge of the Sea* and again for *Silent Spring* in 1963.

228 Carson posthumously drew: Rob Dunn, "In Retrospect: Silent Spring," *Nature,* May 30, 2012; Frank Graham Jr., "Fifty Years After Silent Spring, Attacks on Science Continue," *Yale Environment 360,* June 21, 2012; Elizabeth Grossman, "Rachel Carson's 'Silent Spring' Turns 50," *Atlantic,* June 25, 2012; Robert Isenberg, "The Book That Changed the World," *E: The Environmental Magazine,* Sept. 1, 2012; "How Important Was Rachel Carson's *Silent Spring* in the Recovery of Bald Eagles and Other Bird Species?," *Scientific American,* Aug. 31, 2012; "Legacy of Rachel Carson's Silent Spring," American Chemical Society, Oct. 26, 2012.

228 "changed the world": Isenberg, "Book That Changed the World."

228 In her own day: *Silent Spring* won the Schweitzer Medal of the Animal Welfare Institute; the Award for Distinguished Service from the New England Outdoor Writers Association; the Conservation Award for 1962 from Rod and Gun Editors of Metropolitan Manhattan; the Conservationist of the Year from the National Wildlife Federation; and the Annual Founders Award of the Izaak Walton League. Her women-specific honors include the 1963 Achievement Award from the Women's Division of Albert Einstein College of Medicine; a citation from the International and U.S. Councils of Women; and the Constance Lindsay Skinner Achievement Award for merit in the realm of books from the Women's National Book Association.

228 Hannah Arendt's: For example, Richard Brody, "'Hannah Arendt' and the Glorification of Thinking," *New Yorker,* May 30, 2013; Daniel Maier-Katkin and Nathan Stoltzfus, "Hannah Arendt on Trial," *American Scholar,* June 10, 2013; Roger Berkowitz, "Misreading 'Eichmann in Jerusalem,'" *NYT,* July 7, 2013; "Exercising Judgment in Ethics, Politics, and the Law: Hannah Arendt's *Eichmann in Jerusalem,*" Wesleyan University, Sept. 26–28, 2013, arendt.conference.wesleyan.edu; "Eichmann in Jerusalem: Fifty Years Later," Harvard Book Store, Oct. 4, 2013, harvard .com; "Panel Discussion on the 50th Anniversary of Arendt's Eichmann in Jerusalem," Yale Program for the Study of Antisemitism, Yale University, Nov. 18, 2103, ypsa.yale.edu; Adam Kirsch and Rivka Galchen, "Fifty Years Later, Why Does 'Eichmann in Jerusalem' Remain Contentious?," *NYT,* Nov. 26, 2013; "Hannah Arendt's Failures of Imagination," *New Yorker,* Dec. 3, 2013; "Before and After 'Eichmann in Jerusalem,'" *LA Review of Books,* Dec. 9, 2013.

228 That same year, the Schlesinger: For example, Janet Maslin, "Looking Back at a Domestic Cri de Coeur," *NYT,* Feb. 18, 2013; Eric Alterman,

"Remembering the 'Feminine Mystique,'" Center for American Progress, May 23, 2013; Michelle Bernard, "Betty Friedan and Black Women: Time for a Second Look?," *WP*, Feb. 21, 2013; Lynn Neary, "At 50, Does 'Feminine Mystique' Still Roar?," NPR, Feb. 10, 2013; "It Changed My Life," Radcliffe Institute Exhibition, Oct. 1, 2013.

229 "I have a photograph": Maslin, "Looking Back at a Domestic Cri de Coeur."

229 "unintentionally set us down": Bernard, "Betty Friedan and Black Women."

229 On that score, the suffrage: For further reading on the treatment of Black woman suffragists, see the relevant essays in Steiner, Kitch, and Kroeger, *Front Pages, Front Lines.*

229 The essays the book contains: For example, Hilton Als, "Joan Didion and the Granite of the Specific," *NY Review of Books,* Dec. 17, 2020; Nathan Heller, "What We Get Wrong About Joan Didion," *New Yorker,* Jan. 25, 2021.

230 "has claims to being": Heller, "What We Get Wrong About Joan Didion."

230 A year before she died: Als, "Joan Didion and the Granite of the Specific"; Roiphe quoted in William Grimes, "Joan Didion, 'New Journalist' Who Explored Culture and Chaos, Dies at 87," *NYT,* Dec. 23, 2021; Parul Sehgal, "Joan Didion Chronicled American Disorder with Her Own Unmistakable Style," *NYT,* Dec. 23, 2021.

Chapter 14. Vietnam

231 She wondered what: Aline Mosby, "Where Are the New Nelly Blys?," *Dateline* 9, no. 1 (1965).

231 Lynn Povich remembered Peer: Povich, *Good Girls Revolt,* 23.

231 Peer indeed covered: Povich, telephone interview by author, Jan. 18, 2021; W. H. Manville, "Boys and Girls (Foreign Reporting) Together," *Cosmopolitan,* June 1969.

232 Other women at *Newsweek:* United Nations Correspondents Association directories, New York, 1950–80; spot check of weekly *Newsweek* mastheads for those years. *Newsweek* had Barbara Woodman credentialed at the UN from 1952 to 1956, Ellen Lukas from 1961 to 1967, and Valerie Gerry in 1968 and 1969. All are described on the masthead as "senior editorial assistants" in their UN days. Only when Raymond Carroll had the top UN reporter spot during Lukas's UN tenure is the beat listed on the masthead as one of *Newsweek*'s full-fledged bureaus.

232 "Not heavy lifting": Povich, email interview by author, Feb. 18, 2021. For example, Masthead, *Newsweek,* Dec. 10, 1973. There are no women listed in top positions of editor, managing editor, executive editor, or senior

editor. Shana Alexander is the only woman among the contributing editors, and Elizabeth Peer, the only woman among the twenty-five general editors. Among the thirty-six associate editors, however, nearly half were women: Lucille Beachy, Mathilde Camacho, Rona Cherry, Linda Francke, Mariana Gosnell, Phyllis Malamud, Ann Ray Martin, Maureen Orth, Sandra Salmans, Helen Dimos Schwindt, Jean Seligman, Merrill Sheils, Sally W. Smith, Ellen L. Sullivan, Fay Wiley, and Lynn Young (Povich). Liz Peer, after Europe, continued to advance. In 1969, she was transferred to the Washington bureau, where she worked for the next five years. A 1973 masthead shows her with the rank of general editor, "a high title then," Povich said, even though "everyone had 'editor' in their titles on the masthead." Not for *Newsweek,* but a fit to that description was Kathleen McLaughlin in her *NYT* days after the *Chicago Tribune.* McLaughlin spent six years reporting from postwar Europe before her reassignment to many years at the UN.

232 "a good many years": A Flora Lewis award was established at the Overseas Press Club. For a full list of all OPC awards through the years, see opcofamerica.org.

232 Mosby named only Beverly Deepe: Mosby, "Where Are the New Nelly Blys?"; Bartimus et al., *War Torn,* xv–xxi.

232 When it did, Mosby went: "Newsmakers," *Philadelphia Inquirer,* Nov. 20, 1980.

232 By way of China: I traced Mosby's dates through her innumerable bylines
232 indexed in newspapers.com from the 1950s on. "Aline Mosby: Wire Service Reporter, Columnist," *LAT,* Aug. 21, 1998; "Journalist Mosby Dead at 76," *Missoulian* and AP, Aug. 16, 1998. Her obituary in the rival AP described her as "a journalist who covered everything from Hollywood gossip to world affairs for more than 50 years." AP, "Aline Mosby, Veteran Journalist," *New Philadelphia Times,* Aug. 16, 1998.

232 "today's real life girl reporter": Patricia E. Davis, "Lady on the Beat," *Mademoiselle,* May 1968.

233 Ellen Goodman followed: Ellen Goodman, email exchange with author, May 19, 2022.

233 Susan Brownmiller saw: See chapter 6 of Susan Brownmiller, *In Our Time: Memoir of a Revolution* (New York: Dial Press, 1999).

233 "ROMANCE. TRAVEL. ADVENTURE": Manville, "Boys and Girls (Foreign Reporting) Together."

233 "Getting a job": Craig R. Whitney, "Gloria Emerson, Chronicler of War's Damage, Dies at 75," *NYT,* Aug. 5, 2004.

234 Other than Liz Trotta: See, generally, Bartimus et al., *War Torn.* By the time Manville's story appeared in 1969, his list could have included

reporters like Ann Bryan Mariano for *The Overseas Weekly* since 1965; Denby Fawcett for KITV News (an ABC affiliate) in 1966; and, since 1967, Kate Webb for UPI, Anne Morrissy Merick for ABC, and Jurate Kazickas, who had freelance arrangements with NANA and several outlets before she joined the AP.

234 "The fastest way": Manville, "Boys and Girls (Foreign Reporting) Together."

234 "a new breed of newspaper woman": J. W. Cohn, "Women Cover the War News, Too," *WP* via *Women's Wear Daily*, Oct. 17, 1968. In the book *War Torn,* Kate Webb of UPI cites the article and identifies Cohn as a "he," but it's not clear from her text if or how she knew that. Bartimus et al., *War Torn,* 83.

234 Imagine the reaction: For example, Gerald R. Thorp, "She Covered War Better Than Many a Man," *St. Louis Post-Dispatch,* Jan. 10, 1966.

235 By 1968, Anne Morrissy: Bartimus et al., *War Torn,* 13–15, 104–5. It came about at a forward base, where General William C. Westmoreland encountered Denby Fawcett, the daughter of family friends of his from Honolulu, as she told the story in a memoir. They chatted and she told him offhandedly that she had been with the troops on the base for several days. The revelation so disturbed Westmoreland that, once back in Saigon, he issued an order that forbade woman reporters to remain with troops in the field overnight. In a guerrilla theater like Vietnam, "the field" could be just about anywhere. Westmoreland's arguments were reminiscent of those his predecessors had been applying for decades to keep woman correspondents out of the battle zones. The obedient ones, anyway. Women, he explained, might suffer emotional collapses or cause soldiers to lose focus as they rushed to the women's aid. Bartimus's co-authors were Fawcett, a political reporter for the ABC affiliate in Honolulu; Jurate Kazickas, freelancer; Edie Lederer, AP UN correspondent; Anne Morrissy Merick, freelancer; Tracy Wood, the investigative editor for the Orange County *Register;* and Kate Webb, formerly of UPI. See also Roberts, "Anne Morrissy Merick, a Pioneer from Yale to Vietnam"; and Laura Palmer, also a freelancer. See also Newburger, "Anne Morrissy Merick '55, Vietnam War Reporter, Dies at 83."

235 Ten women signed: Roberts, "Anne Morrissy Merick, a Pioneer from Yale to Vietnam"; Newburger, "Anne Morrissy Merick '55, Vietnam War Reporter, Dies at 83"; Elizabeth Becker, *You Don't Belong Here: How Three Women Rewrote the Story of War* (New York: PublicAffairs, 2021), 45–46.

235 more than four hundred women: Jerrold M. Starr, ed., *The Lessons of the Vietnam War* (Pittsburgh: Center for Social Studies Education, 1991); Becker, *You Don't Belong Here.* In a telephone interview, Feb. 18, 2021,

Becker said that a good number of the women in the larger count were credentialed as much "for access to the PX" as for anything else. Further, Elizabeth Becker, email exchange with author, May 28, 2022.

235 About seventy-five of them: Becker, book presentation via Zoom, Overseas Press Club, Feb. 12, 2021. The writer of the piece in *Women's Wear Daily* singled out the French photographer Catherine Leroy, by then with Black Star; Liz Trotta, still with NBC since May 1965; Kate Webb of UPI, a New Zealander from Australia who started as a stringer with the wire service in 1967 but became staff within a year and Saigon bureau chief soon after; Susie Kirk, the wife of Donald Kirk of *The Washington Star,* who had an arrangement with the German news agency Deutsche Presse; and Georgie Anne Geyer of the *Chicago Daily News,* whose earlier foreign assignments had included revolution in Latin America and stints in Russia and France. There was also mention of Beverly Deepe, who by then was preparing to leave journalism behind for marriage to a lieutenant colonel she met in Da Nang. *Cosmopolitan's* count of women in Vietnam in 1969 included only Nancy Dickerson, Frankie FitzGerald, Linda Grant Martin (by then in Hong Kong with her husband after the South Vietnamese expelled him), and Trotta, who, in the writer's estimation, was doing the "best work from abroad." See Mosby, "Where Are the New Nelly Blys?"; and Cohn, "Women Cover the War News, Too." With the folding of the *NY Herald Tribune* in 1966, Deepe moved on to report for *The Christian Science Monitor.* Also, Manville, "Boys and Girls (Foreign Reporting) Together."

236 "Most women listeners": Mary Lou Loper, "Newswomen Assess Nixon's 100 Days," *LAT,* May 25, 1969.

237 "flung themselves into a war": Bartimus et al., *War Torn,* xviii, xx.

237 "No woman is fat in France": Gloria Emerson, "French Find Easy Ways to Get Thin," *NYT,* Dec. 29, 1964.

237 And yet in Vietnam: Emerson's file of Saigon-datelined clippings in the *NYT* extends from March 5, 1970, to Sept. 19, 1971.

237 she called out bogus body counts: Patricia Sullivan, "Gloria Emerson Dies," *WP,* Aug. 8, 2004.

237 "because the war was supposed to be over": Whitney, "Gloria Emerson, Chronicler of War's Damage, Dies at 75."

237 Frances FitzGerald was: See Frances FitzGerald's articles in *The New Yorker:* "Vietnam—Fire in the Lake," June 23, 1972; "Vietnam II— Sovereign of Discord," June 30, 1972; "Vietnam III—A Cave on Karl Marx Mountain," July 7, 1972; "Johnson's Dilemma," July 14, 1972; "Vietnam V— Survivors," July 29, 1972; and Frances FitzGerald, *Fire in the Lake: The Vietnamese and the Americans in Vietnam* (New York: Little, Brown, 1972).

237 In magazine form: Frances FitzGerald, "The Struggle and the War," *Atlantic*, Aug. 1967. The magazine piece won an Overseas Press Club award for best interpretation of foreign affairs, opcofamerica.org. The George Polk was for "Annals of War: Vietnam, Fire In the Lake," *New Yorker*, July 1, 1972.

237 As a book: For FitzGerald's 1973 Pulitzer Prize, see nationalbook.org; pulitzer.org; and library.columbia.edu. In 2020, she won the first annual Tony Horwitz Prize from the Society of American Historians, sah .columbia.edu.

238 "If Americans read only": "Déjà-Vu I: On the Recent Re-issue of Frances FitzGerald's Fire in the Lake," *New Criterion*, Feb. 2021.

238 "enlightened decisions": Elizabeth Becker, "The Women Who Covered Vietnam," *NYT*, Nov. 17, 2017.

238 The lack of an official: Becker, *You Don't Belong Here*, 31. Becker explained that President Johnson relied on the powers granted him under the Gulf of Tonkin Resolution of 1964 instead of a formal declaration of war. That meant American journalists did not have to submit their reporting for review by military censors, nor was their access to the front tightly controlled the way it would be in the conflicts to come.

238 In Vietnam, to obtain local: Elizabeth Becker, Zoom interview by author, Feb. 18, 2021.

238 Becker's arrival: Reuters, "Cambodia Expels Reporter," *NYT*, April 21, 1973.

238 "pigeon out": Sylvana Foa, telephone and email interviews by author, March 22, 2021. Foa recalled she could not file from Phnom Penh "for several reasons, but mainly because the censor would never have let it pass. Under normal circumstances, I would have pigeoned the story to Hong Kong or Bangkok or even Saigon. But I did not have time."

238 Foa's reporting irritated: Reuters, "Cambodia Expels Reporter." See also Staff Report, "US Air Operations in Cambodia, April 1973" (prepared for the use of the Subcommittee on U.S. Security Agreements and Communists Abroad of the Committee on Foreign Relations, U.S. Senate, April 27, 1973), 2, which notes, "The UPI correspondent, an American named Sylvana Foa, who also reports for *Newsweek*, was subsequently presented with an order expelling her from Cambodia. We were told by Cambodian officials during the visit to Phnom Penh that American Embassy officials had been urging the Cambodian Government to expel her for some time."

239 "Miss Foa's critics": H. D. S. Greenway, "Facts Are Few, Reality Is Elusive in Cambodia," *WP*, April 29, 1973.

239 On May 11: Sydney Schanberg, "Embassy Still Controls Cambodia Raids," *NYT,* May 11, 1973.

239 "It is always necessary": Sydney Schanberg, "Credit Due on Deep Throat," *Village Voice,* June 29, 2005. The genesis of Schanberg's column was Michael Dobbs in the *WP* of June 20, 2005, failing to credit David Corn and Jeff Goldberg of *The Nation* for a story about the Watergate scandal they had broken a week earlier. Schanberg's own mea culpa was in the last paragraph of his column.

239 "I liked Sydney a lot": Foa, telephone interview by author, March 22, 2021.

239 To protest would have: Becker, *You Don't Belong Here,* profiled Frances FitzGerald, UPI's Kate Webb, and Catherine Leroy, the French free-lance photographer, and summons memory of the objectification and innuendo to which she and other women were so often subjected. Also, Becker, email and telephone exchanges with author, March 4, 2021.

239 What comes to mind: Currie, "Edith Evans Asbury," 154–55.

240 "No more Florence": Becker, *You Don't Belong Here,* 223; Becker, email and telephone exchanges with author, March 4, 2021.

240 A CIA agent: Foa, telephone interview by author, March 22, 2021. See also Becker, "Women Who Covered Vietnam," where she writes, "We had enough on our hands with the sexual politics of the day and the endless gossip about our personal lives."

240 "intrepid, bold": "A Times Reporter in Vietnam Wins a Polk Award: Gloria Emerson Is One of 12 Cited for Journalistic Work During 1970," *NYT,* Feb. 17, 1971.

240 Eight more Polks: That is more than twice the four Polks won by women in the 1960s, but the 1960s figure was down by half from the eight Polks won by women in the 1950s. See liu.edu, which includes in the lists for 1970–79—in addition to Emerson, FitzGerald, and the *New Yorker* critic Pauline Kael—Frances Cerra of *Newsday* for public service; Doris Ellen Olsten for local reporting on child abuse for the *Santa Maria Times;* Jean Heller of the AP for investigative work exposing the scandal surrounding the nontreatment of Black men for syphilis; Lesley Oelsner of the *NYT* for her reporting on changes in the U.S. justice system; Carol Talley and Joan Hayde for the *Dover Advance* on corrupt local officials; and Jane Shoemaker on a team with Thomas Ferrick and William Ecenbarger for *The Philadelphia Inquirer* with a public service award for exposing official corruption.

240 In fact, from the 1950s: Among the Pulitzer Prize inductees of the 1970s were the architecture critic Ada Louise Huxtable of the *NYT* in

1970—the first journalist of any gender to be honored for "distinguished criticism." In 1971, Lucinda Franks shared honors with Thomas Powers for their report "The Making of a Terrorist" for UPI. Franks broke free from having to gin up soft features as the only woman in UPI's London bureau in 1968 by borrowing a page from Dorothy Thompson. Early in 1970, Franks defied company policy and took herself to Belfast, where she covered the Troubles for the better part of the year. She distinguished herself enough to be called to New York that fall for the plum assignment that led to the Pulitzer in feature writing. She was twenty-four at the time, two years out of Vassar (where, likely not coincidentally, she helped found the local chapter of Students for a Democratic Society). The *NYT* hired her in 1974, and she remained on the paper for three years. More Pulitzers went to women in the 1970s. In 1972, Ann Desantis was among four *Boston Globe* reporters who won for exposing rampant corruption in Somerville, Massachusetts, and Margo Huston of *The Milwaukee Journal* won for her reporting on the elderly in 1977. Among the critics, Emily Genauer of the *Newsday* syndicate won for arts criticism in 1974, as did two star Washington-based political columnists: Mary McGrory of *The Washington Star* in 1975 and Meg Greenfield of the *WP* in 1978. The following year, Greenfield rose from deputy to the *Post*'s editorial page editor.

240 During the 1970s: See UPI, "Co-author Lucinda Franks Resident of Wellesley," *Boston Globe,* Sept. 14, 1970, and Katharine Q. Seelye, "Lucinda Franks Dies at 74; Prize-Winning Journalist Broke Molds," *NYT,* May 6, 2021. Franks went to the *NYT* from 1974 to 1977, until her marriage to the U.S. district attorney Robert Morgenthau, after which she freelanced. She joined the staff of *The New Yorker* from 1992 to 2006 and wrote several books, including Lucinda Franks, *Timeless: Love, Morgenthau, and Me* (New York: Sarah Crichton Books, 2014), 14–15; by year, pulitzer.org; J. Y. Smith, "Editorial Editor Meg Greenfield Dies," *WP,* May 14, 1999.

240 Gloria Emerson's book: Gloria Emerson, *Winners and Losers: Battles, Retreats, Gains, Losses, and Ruins from a Long War* (New York: Random House, 1976).

240 "Great Blue Heron": Frances FitzGerald, preface to *Winners and Losers,* reissued ed. (New York: W. W. Norton, 2014), ix.

240 "I don't know": Bartimus et al., *War Torn,* xiv.

241 headed to a children's hospital: Ibid., xvii. Martha Gellhorn, "Suffer the Little Children . . . ," *Ladies' Home Journal,* Jan. 1967, about Vietnam War casualties from 1957 to 1965. Also, Gellhorn, *Face of War,* 387–401. Also for the Vietnam years, Emerson singled out Frankie FitzGerald and the French photojournalist Catherine Leroy. In 1976, Leroy became the first

woman to win the Robert Capa Gold Medal, which honors the "best published photographic reporting from abroad requiring exceptional courage and enterprise." Emerson also named Liz Trotta of NBC and Marlene Sanders of ABC (but in Sanders's case to point out that she lasted only a month before being called home for personal reasons), and Kate Webb of UPI, whom North Vietnamese troops kidnapped in Cambodia and held for twenty-three harrowing days (she read her own obits). See Kate Webb, *On the Other Side* (New York: Quadrangle Books, 1972), and Bartimus et al., *War Torn,* 72–79. Emerson also mentioned Elizabeth Becker and the long-serving Beverly Deepe, who had inspired Emerson's own desire to go back to the country. Among the women arriving between 1972 and 1974 were Laura Palmer for ABC Radio, Tad Bartimus, Edith Lederer for AP, and Tracy Wood for UPI.

241 Beverly Deepe: Cohn, "Women Cover the War News, Too."

241 "hootch" maids: Gloria Emerson, "G.I.'s at Tayninh Just 'Kids' and 'Crazy' to a 41-Year-Old Maid," *NYT,* June 5, 1970. Also of related interest, Emerson, "G.I.s in Vietnam Get Heroin Easily," *NYT,* Feb. 25, 1971.

241 "The women received sexist treatment": Sherry Ricchiardi, "Women on War," *AJR,* March 1994.

Chapter 15. Collective Action

242 By the time the 1970s: For example, M.C.A. [Mary Clemmer Ames], "Washington Through New Spectacles"; Wingate, *Views and Interviews on Journalism,* 147; "Woman's Busy Life"; Brody, "Newspaper Girls"; "Women in Advertising and Journalism."

242 In the vanguard: Povich, *Good Girls Revolt,* 88.

243 It coincided with the publication: Cover note, "Women in Revolt," *Newsweek,* March 23, 1970.

243 When the issue appeared: Brownmiller, *In Our Time,* 136–66.

243 The inside cover note: Cover note, "Women in Revolt"; Povich, *Good Girls Revolt,* 3, 54, 87; Povich, telephone interview by author, Jan. 18, 2021.

243 Lynn Povich: The promotion of Lynn Povich, then Lynn Young, first appears on the masthead Feb. 15, 1971.

243 "one of the good guys": Povich, telephone interview by author, Jan. 18, 2021.

243 She had also seen: Povich, *Good Girls Revolt,* 23.

244 "I don't intend": "The Media: Male and Female," *Newsweek,* May 18, 1970. In Sept. 1978, eight years after the Time Inc. women filed their suit, Melissa Ludtke, who worked for *Sports Illustrated,* won her suit against the New York Yankees, the baseball commissioner, and the National League president, ending the exclusion of woman sports reporters from

the locker room of the Yankee clubhouse. See *Ludtke v. Kuhn,* 461 F. Supp. 86 (S.D.N.Y. 1978), No. 77, Civ. 6301, U.S. District Court for the Southern District of New York, Sept. 25, 1978.

244 *Reader's Digest, Newsday:* Gelb, *City Room,* 526. There were solo efforts as well. A frustrated *Chicago Tribune* staffer of four years filed an EEOC complaint of her own. (Author telephone interview with complainant, April 6, 2021.) Ruth E. Gruber, "on the desk" in Brussels for UPI in March 1977, her fourth year on staff, kept being passed over for choice assignments that went to men with less seniority. With no response from her editors in Europe, she wrote to the foreign editor in New York, Walter Logan, to tell him she had her visa in hand to travel to Zaire, as the Democratic Republic of the Congo was then named, to cover the Shaba War. Logan cabled back: "AT RISK OF SOUNDING LIKE A CHAUVINISTIC SOMETHING OR OTHER IT WAS DECIDED IT WOULD BE BETTER TO SEND IN A RUGGED MALE TO THAT RUGGED COUNTRY." Gruber called a Washington-based attorney who let UPI know at headquarters that despite Gruber's lack of Africa experience she had grounds for a case against the company's international division. Nothing directly came of it, but Gruber said it was after that exchange and the lawyer's follow-up that the number of women in the international bureaus proliferated. She herself got posted first to London, then to Belgrade, then to Warsaw (Poland expelled her on trumped-up espionage charges but later honored her with the country's Knight's Cross of the Order of Merit, the highest honor a foreigner can receive), then to Vienna. In those same years, from 1977 to 1983 and certainly beyond, women held the top positions and/or made up as much as half the staffs of UPI's prestige European posts. None was off-limits. (Ruth Gruber, email interview by author, March 12, 2021, with documentation sent later. Wire service back-channel exchanges between Gruber, UPI Brussels, and UPI Foreign Editor Walter Logan, UPI New York, March 27, 28, 1977. Ray Moseley was the Europe, Middle East, Africa editor, based in Brussels, and Charles Ridley was Moseley's deputy, the news editor.) Group emailed recollections from a number of Europe, Middle East, Africa Division colleagues, March 14, 2021. During this period, for UPI, I was stationed in Brussels, 1976–77; London, 1977–79; Tel Aviv, as staff in 1979 and as bureau chief in 1980–83; and London again as division editor for Europe, the Middle East, and Africa, 1983–84.

244 "I was not sensitive": Benjamin C. Bradlee, *A Good Life: Newspapering and Other Adventures* (New York: Simon & Schuster Paperbacks, 2017), 269.

244 Both at the *Post* and at the *Star:* "Adjectives Re-styled for Women in News," *Editor & Publisher,* July 25, 1970; "Sexist Journalism Out,"

Everywoman via the *Spokeswoman*, Sept. 11, 1970. The *Star*'s Charles Seib had a similar list of "don'ts" that ended with "Finally, avoid, please, the note of amused surprise that shows up so often in stories about successful women. It's a common failing of male feature writers."

245 But in April 1972: Woman news and editorial employees of the *WP* to Graham, Bradlee, and others, memo, April 4, 1972, courtesy of the curators of the exhibition *Cover Story: Katharine Graham, CEO,* Women's History Gallery, New-York Historical Society, July 1, 2021. At that time, the paper had 294 news and editorial employees, 40 of whom were women, making up 13.6 percent of the staff. With the next round of hires, the percentage of women was down slightly.

246 "they've let me ride my water buffalo": Robertson, *Girls in the Balcony,* 146. Robertson said Emerson made the comment to Betsy Wade, who, as Betsy Boylan, would become the lead plaintiff in the eventual case.

246 At the meeting, the discrepancies: Gelb, *City Room,* 525. Arthur Gelb put the average difference in pay at $59 less per week for women when they represented about 10 percent of the paper's 425 reporters and no women had yet reached masthead status.

246 For instance, Marilyn Bender: Katherine Q. Seelye, "Marilyn Bender Dies at 95; Journalist in a Male-Dominated Era," *NYT,* Nov. 5, 2020.

246 Twenty-two reporters, all men: Gelb, *City Room,* 478.

246 She never paid attention: Currie, "Edith Evans Asbury," 151–52.

247 "a fair amount": Max Frankel, *The Times of My Life and My Life with the "Times"* (New York: Random House, 1999), 455; Gelb, *City Room,* 526. Gelb recalled the caustic, amused reaction of the men on staff to the women's action. "They were quick to point out the irony of my having aggressively brought strong women onto the metropolitan staff only to see them treacherously join ranks with the lawsuit's instigators from other departments." At UPI in Chicago in those years, pay, assignments, and work schedules ("around the world, around the clock") were oppressive but uniformly fair, so far as we knew, but we women did think we could tell which of three successive bosses had hired each of us by our physical attributes.

247 The Gannett chain avoided: Kristin Gilger and Julia Wallace, *There's No Crying in Newsrooms: What Women Have Learned About What It Takes to Lead* (Lanham, Md.: Rowman & Littlefield, 2019), 56. "It wasn't just the right thing to do," Gracia Martore, a former Gannett company CEO, told the authors. "It was the right thing to do for business. We were in diverse communities across the country and it made an enormous amount of sense to reflect those communities." Also, Al Neuharth, *Confessions of an S.O.B.* (New York: Doubleday, 1989), 239–42. "You should

do it," Neuharth urged in a speech he gave around this time. "And if you do, your readers will benefit most of all because you will vastly improve those areas of the newspaper product which are designed primarily by men, but primarily for women." By 1973, he had named Gloria Biggs the publisher of the company's start-up paper in Melbourne, Florida. "Gloria Biggs, 89, Ex–Newspaper Publisher," *South Florida Sun-Sentinel,* June 17, 2001.

247 When Keegan died in 2011: Rick Kogan, "Anne Keegan, 1943–2011," *Chicago Tribune,* May 21, 2011.

247 Zekman, peerless over decades: Pamela Zekman, telephone interview by author, April 15, 2021.

248 The newspaper bought a tavern: See Pamela Zekman and Zay N. Smith, *The Mirage: A Tale of Cold Beer and Hot Graft, in Which a Team of Investigative Reporters Ran a Chicago Tavern to Probe Corruption—and Pulled Off the Greatest Sting in the City's History* (New York: Random House, 1979); Kroeger, *Undercover Reporting,* 257–80; and undercover.hosting.nyu.edu.

248 "could send journalism on a wrong course": See Myra McPherson, "Prizefights: The Pulitzer Donnybrook: The Rite of Spring and the Cries of Foul," *WP,* April 20 1979, for a recap of the brouhaha. McPherson includes quotations pro and con about undercover reporting and its importance from Eugene Patterson, editor and president of the *St. Petersburg Times;* Ben Bradlee of the *WP,* who led the opposition in the Mirage case; Clayton Kirkpatrick, editor and vice president of the *Chicago Tribune;* Jack Nelson of the *LAT;* and James Hoge, then of the *Chicago Sun-Times,* the presiding editor for the project. "The board's capriciousness and arbitrariness is mystifying and profoundly disappointing," Hoge said. "There was nothing in the board's advisory to indicate they were judging from a different set of rules than in the past. I just hate to say anything because it always looks like sour grapes."

249 In 1972, dozens of women: Sherr, *Outside the Box,* 49.

249 "A. J. Liebling Counter-Convention": Kevin M. Lerner, *Provoking the Press* (Columbia: University of Missouri Press, 2019), 6.

249 The "New Journalism" panel: Thomas Meehan, "The Time Renata Adler Didn't Dump Campbell's Soup on Tom Wolfe's Head," *Saturday Review,* June 3, 1972.

249 "How They Cover Me": The panelists with Curtis were Bella Abzug, Gore Vidal, Abbie Hoffman, Otto Preminger, Tony Randall, and Marvin Miller.

249 Lynn Sherr as moderator: Diana Loercher, "Women's Pages Take Hue of New Interest," *Christian Science Monitor,* May 5, 1972. On the panel as

moderator was Lynn Sherr, still at the AP but about to move on to television; Anne Roiphe, author of *Up the Sandbox;* Nancy Borman of the *Long Island Press;* James Brady, the editor and publisher of *Harper's Bazaar,* the lone man; Blair Sabol, contributor, *The Village Voice;* Ida Lewis, a former editor of *Essence,* then at *Encore;* Edith Nemy of the *NYT;* and Gloria Steinem, editor of *Ms.*

250 "No one seemed to know": Sally Quinn, "Countering the Publishers," *WP,* April 24, 1972; "Journalism's New Nation," *WP,* April 26, 1972; Sherr, email exchange with author, Jan. 10, 2022; Loercher, "Women's Pages Take Hue of New Interest."

250 At the next year's *MORE* event: Sally Quinn, "Media: (More) Party," *WP,* May 4, 1973; Thomas Collins, "A More Subdued Journalism Jamboree," *Newsday,* May 11, 1973; Robert S. Van Fleet, "Reporters Also Warned," *Daily Item (Sunbury, Pa.),* May 8, 1973.

250 "Images of Women in the Media": "Much More for Women This Year at the More Convention," *NOW Newsletter,* June 1974.

250 At the *Times,* for instance: "The Times Settles Sex-Bias Suit Filed by Female Workers in U.S. Court," *NYT,* Nov. 21, 1978; Frankel, *Times of My Life,* 455; Margalit Fox, "Nan Robertson, Pulitzer-Winning Times Reporter, Dies at 83," *NYT,* Oct. 14, 2009.

251 The *Times* promoted: Richard Sandomir, "Le Anne Schreiber, 73, Dies; a First Among Sports Editors," *NYT,* June 4, 2019.

251 "I was, depending on one's view": Ibid. Schreiber agreed to take the job but only for two years. Her obituary quotes from her memoir, Le Anne Schreiber, *Midstream: An Intimate Journal of Loss and Discovery* (New York: Viking, 1990): "If *The New York Times* was ready to appoint a female head of a hugely male department for the first time in its history, I had no right to refuse the position." She then became a deputy editor on the *NYT Book Review* but left the paper in 1984. She died of lung cancer in 2019.

251 She went straight to "the rim": Carolyn Lee, interview by author, New York City, Feb. 20, 2020, email Dec. 2, 2021.

Chapter 16. Star Power

252 "believed to be": Masthead, *Louisville Courier-Journal,* July 27, 1974. Sutton's name appears on the masthead under the publisher and editor, Barry Bingham Jr. and Robert P. Clark, as executive editor. As Carolyn Lee, who worked there at the time, explained, Bingham almost entirely confined himself to business matters and the editorial page. Clark oversaw both the afternoon *Louisville Times* and *The Courier-Journal.* Sutton, as the replacement for George Gill, had the hands-on, day-to-day

news operation as her brief, which was why the appointment attracted so much attention.

252 "Women of the Year": An article on the front page of the *WSJ* is often cited as being about her appointment, but in fact it is a one-sentence "believed to be first" mention in a much longer piece about *The Courier-Journal* itself. However, the *WSJ* did carry an inside four-paragraph announcement of her appointment in much the way other papers across the country did. See "Louisville Courier Names Woman Managing Editor," *WSJ*, July 6, 1974, and David Garino, "'Messrs. Clean' Louisville Newspapers Cherish Independence, Guard It Jealously," *WSJ*, July 11, 1974; "Woman of the Year: Great Changes, New Chances, Tough Choices," *Time*, Jan. 5, 1976. *Time* said in addition to being first, she had "brightened the editorial content" of *The Courier-Journal*.

253 Before Sutton reached: Susan E. Tifft and Alex S. Jones, *The Patriarch: The Rise and Fall of the Bingham Dynasty* (New York: Summit Books, 1991), 306–10. *The Patriarch* has a copy of the memo Sutton wrote to Bingham as soon as "the blood stopped flowing" from the wound in her back. A word search of "Carol Sutton" and "1974" in newspapers.com lists several pages of newspaper accounts of her appointment as news from June 27 through July 30, 1974.

253 Keith Runyon worked: Keith Runyon, "The First Woman Senior Editor at a Major Newspaper Worked in Louisville," WFPL.org, May 16, 2014; Andrew Wolfson, "Courier Journal First to Name a Woman as Managing Editor," *Louisville Courier-Journal*, Nov. 19, 2018; Ann Cooper, interview by author, New York City, Dec. 13, 2021. Also, Kimberly Voss, "The Burden of Being First," *American Journalism* 27, no. 1 (2010): 117–43. Sutton stayed at the paper until her death at fifty-one in 1985, bringing credit in other ways. The National Association of Black Journalists made her its first white member. Also, "Carol Sutton, Ex–Managing Editor of CJ Dies," *Louisville Courier-Journal*, Feb. 20, 1985; Robert D. McFadden, "Carol Sutton, Ranking Editor in Louisville, Ky., Dead at 51," *NYT*, Feb. 20, 1985.

253 Mary Anne Dolan had: Bellows, *Last Editor*, 174.

254 Dolan told an AP reporter: Linda Deutsch, "New Boss in the Newsroom Points to Changing Trends," *Fort Worth Star-Telegram* via AP, Jan. 1, 1982.

254 In 1977, Dolan followed Bellows: Ibid.

254 He also knew how close: Frank Lalli, telephone interview by author, April 17, 2021. He attributed the revelation to Don Forst, who had been Bellows's executive editor at the *Herald Examiner*. Deutsch, "New Boss in the News Room Points to Changing Trends"; Dolan clip file in newspapers.com at *The Evening Star*, 1971–77. Lalli became the associate editor for

business at the *New York Daily News*, then chief editor of Time Inc.'s *Money* magazine, and then the editor of John F. Kennedy Jr.'s magazine, *George*.

254 The managerial prowess of Kay: Suzanne Wilding, "Kay Fanning: The Lady Is a Newspaperman," *Town & Country*, Jan. 1986; "Monitor Editor to Lead US Editors' Group," *Christian Science Monitor*, April 10, 1987; David T. Cook, ed., "Katherine W. Fanning: A Pioneer in American Journalism," *Christian Science Monitor*, Oct. 23, 2000; Edward Wong, "Katherine W. Fanning, 73; Pioneering Newspaper Editor," *NYT*, Oct. 23, 2000. Fanning's previous marriage, which ended in divorce, was to Marshall Field IV, the heir to a large publishing empire that included the *Chicago Sun-Times*. At the paper in Alaska, where she moved with her three children after the divorce, she started as a librarian and then bought the paper with her second husband, Larry Fanning, a former editor of the *Sun-Times*, in 1967.

254 Women, as emerging stars: Toki Schale Johnson, "Toki Types," *Pittsburgh Courier*, Feb. 24, 1968; Charlayne Hunter, "To Mr. and Mrs. Yesterday," *NYT Book Review*, March 24, 1968 (review of *Soul on Ice* by Eldridge Cleaver); Ellen Schlafly, "Fellows Find Insight in Transaction with the Midwest," *St. Louis Post-Dispatch*, April 19, 1968; display ad, "News4 Probe," Charlayne Hunter, Ben Holman, and Jean Smith featured for work that "delves into attitudes and issues of social significance," *WP*, Nov. 14, 1968.

255 "We'd never had a bureau": Hunter-Gault, Zoom interview by author, April 16, 2021. Also see, Gelb, *City Room*, 546.

255 "one of the best jobs": John J. Goldman and Siobhan Flynn, "Correspondent of the Hour," *Washington Journalism Review*, Sept. 1985, 40–44.

255 It told of Walter Vandermeer: Gelb, *City Room*, 545.

255 The byline went to Lelyveld: Joseph Lelyveld, "Obituary of a Heroin User Who Died at 12," *NYT*, Jan. 12, 1970.

255 Both reporters received: "Two Times Reporters Win Byline Awards," *NYT*, March 31, 1970.

255 Gelb made a point: Gelb, *City Room*, 544.

255 "It seems that being Black": Hunter-Gault, Zoom interview by author, April 16, 2021. The rest of her quotation is "because I don't believe in objectivity. That's for my computer. I believe that you bring all of you to what you do, and yet you try to be fair and balanced. That's my phrase in lieu of objectivity."

256 Ava Thompson Greenwell's book: Ava Thompson Greenwell, *Ladies Leading: The Black Women Who Control Television News* (Jefferson, Ind.: BK Royston, 2020), 8–10.

256 It was she who persuaded: Charlayne Hunter, "200 Black Women 'Have Dialogue,'" *NYT,* Jan. 10, 1972.

256 "I went ballistic": Hunter-Gault, Zoom interview by author, April 16, 2021.

257 "She turned me down": Gelb, *City Room,* 545; Hunter-Gault, Zoom interview by author, April 16, 2021.

257 By 1978, after nearly a decade: Charlayne Hunter-Gault, "Minority Contractors Losing Jobs over Bonding: Lack of Bonding Is Said to Be a Major Impediment to Growth Among Minority Contractors," *NYT,* Dec. 25, 1977. Earlier front-page *NYT* articles that turned up in a Pro-Quest byline search for the years 1970 to 1979 included Charlayne Hunter, "Closed Hospitals' Workers Still on New York Payroll," July 24, 1976; "Summer Job Program Arouses Hope and Criticism," Aug. 14, 1976; "Young Doctor at Lincoln: Disillusion and Departure," Aug. 16, 1976; "Black Muslim Temple Renamed for Malcolm X," Feb. 2, 1976; "Blacks Organizing in Cities to Combat Crimes by Blacks," Feb. 22, 1976; "Black Intellectuals Divided over Ideological Direction," April 28, 1975; "Slump Killing Black Teen-Agers' Hopes," May 19, 1975; "Woman Expected to Head N.A.A.C.P.," Jan. 13, 1975; "Election Delays Plan for Harlem," Nov. 2, 1974; "State Office Building in Harlem Is Dedicated," May 21, 1974; "Beame to Appoint Dinkins, Gribetz," Nov. 28, 1973; "Blacks Call Post for Dinkins a Milestone," Nov. 29, 1973; "School Job Feud Roils Harlemites," April 18, 1972; "Harlem Crime Toll Is Put at $2 Billion," April 27, 1971; "People's Needs Shape a Growing Harlem Hospital," Aug. 11, 1971; "Harlem Prep and Academies Periled," Feb. 16, 1971; "Huge Renovation of Apartments Starts in Harlem," Aug. 6, 1970; "Community Dispute Cuts Service at City Hospital," Aug. 26, 1970.

257 She liked that the format: Hunter-Gault, Zoom interview by author, April 16, 2021. The entire quotation is: "I did things to increase my own experience and résumé, so to speak, and the *NewsHour* offered something that was challenging, but also provided maybe a different audience. It was the one news organization that dug really deep, because when it first went on the air, it was a half hour at the time, and it would be on one subject. I wanted to expand and see what I could do in that field because even then, in electronic media, while there were some African Americans, there were not many."

257 Why, for instance, were there no Black: Deirdre Carmody, "Survey Found No Minority Employees at Most U.S. Newspapers, Editors Are Told," *NYT,* April 13, 1978.

258 "Unfeminine" was what: Gay, "What Ever Happened to Pioneering Reporter Melba Tolliver."

258 Someone leaked the story: Campbell, "Melba? She's the Toast of the Town."

258 "But believe me": Gay, "What Ever Happened to Pioneering Reporter Melba Tolliver."

258 Asked about the problems: Campbell, "Melba? She's the Toast of the Town."

259 "discussing an article about racial strife": Frankel, *Times of My Life,* 464, 465.

259 "Over my dead body": Currie, "Flora Lewis," 57–58.

259 "a skilled journalist": "Short Takes," *Time,* June 19, 1972.

259 "I would be wary": John and Nina Darnton, interview by author, March 30, 2020.

260 The trouble started with John Hess: Currie, "Flora Lewis," 69–70. Hess repeated all of his accusations against Lewis in his book *My Times: A Memoir of Dissent* (New York: Seven Stories Press, 2003), published after her death.

260 Two years in as bureau chief: Linda Fannin, "NY Times Paris Bureau Chief Ascribes Job to Climate," *Austin American-Statesman,* Nov. 13, 1974.

260 Rosenthal wanted her to stay: Currie, "Flora Lewis," 69–70.

260 On September 26, 1973: "Mrs. Huxtable on Editorial Board," *NYT,* Sept. 26, 1973; Paul Goldberger, "Paul Goldberger Reflects on Vincent Scully's Legacy," *Architectural Record,* Dec. 1, 2017, architecturalrecord .com; Paul Goldberger, email interviews by author, Feb. 7 and 8, 2021. His first piece for the magazine was pitched before he graduated from high school and published the month he started at Yale. Goldberger, "Tony Imperiale Stands Vigilant for Law and Order," *NYT Magazine,* Sept. 29, 1969. During college, his byline appeared in *Senior Scholastic* and the *NYT* and, in that first year, in the *Times, ARTnews,* and *Architectural Forum.*

260 Pulitzer Prize for distinguished criticism: See paulgoldberger.com. See the Pulitzer Prize lists: pulitzer.org.

261 "It's difficult to know": Goldberger, email interviews by author, Feb. 7 and 8, 2021.

261 "Because there is no better reporter": Lenora Williamson, "CATCH-lines," *Editor & Publisher,* Dec. 15, 1973, quoting from Salisbury, interview by Margaret Kreiss for the *Modesto (Calif.) Bee.*

261 Pauline Frederick stayed: Nancy Randolph, "Pauline Frederick Bride in Caribbean," *NY Daily News,* April 1, 1969.

261 The UN would remain: Carol Horner, "Pauline Frederick: Just a News Reporter," *Salt Lake Tribune* via Knight Ridder, Oct. 19, 1980, 139.

261 Linda Wertheimer: See Lisa Napoli, *Susan, Linda, Nina, and Cokie: The*

Extraordinary Story of the Founding Mothers of NPR (New York: Abrams Press, 2021).

261 Cokie Roberts: Gerald Fraser, "17 Win duPont-Columbia Broadcast-News Awards," *NYT,* Feb. 7, 1979.

262 As if in testament: Tom Sowa, "Reporter Doesn't Mind Political Grind," *Spokesman Review* (Spokane), April 24, 1989. In 1978, Wertheimer received a special citation from the duPont award jurors for being the first and only reporter allowed on the floor with a live microphone during the U.S. Senate's thirty-seven-day debate over the Panama Canal Treaties.

262 In these years, Barbara Walters: "Barbara Walters' Biggest Bloopers," ABC News, Nov. 15, 2006.

262 "36 WOMEN with Real Power": Donna Israel Berliner and David C. Berliner, "36 Women with Real Power Who Can Help You," *Cosmopolitan,* April 1975.

262 The justification for her positioning: Barbara Walters, *Audition: A Memoir* (New York: Alfred A. Knopf, 2008), 305.

262 Walters's early days at ABC: Judy Flander, "Women in Network News," *Cosmopolitan,* July 1985.

263 When Radner died: Barbara Walters, "Ms. Walters Reflects," *Vanity Fair,* June 2008.

263 Walters's memoir credited: Walters, *Audition,* 340–41; Walter Cronkite, *A Reporter's Life* (New York: Alfred A. Knopf, 1996), 312. Walter Cronkite of CBS initially broke the news of Sadat's willingness to go to Jerusalem, but Sadat first made the overture about his willingness to meet with Begin to Peter Jennings of ABC. Jennings was without a camera crew when he heard it, so Cronkite got the beat. In memory, Walters's televised joint interview stands out the most.

263 Connie Chung got her start: Michel Martin, "Connie Chung: On News, Family, Fighting with Humor," *Wisdom Watch,* NPR, June 8, 2011; Douglas Brinkley, *Cronkite* (New York: HarperCollins, 2012), 485, citing Chung, interview by Brinkley, July 28, 2011. Stahl and Chung both started at CBS in 1971, Stahl as a producer who became a correspondent three years later and then rose further, thanks to her role in reporting Watergate. Cronkite mentored Chung, plucked by Bill Small, the CBS Washington bureau chief at the time, from the local affiliate. Cronkite saw her potential to be a star and advised her never to "get a big head" or to break news on the say-so of a second- or third-tier source. Chung might also have mentioned Catherine Mackin, who spent years at newspapers before moving on to television, garnering national attention as a floor reporter at the 1972 presidential conventions. By 1976, at thirty-seven, she had become a regular solo anchor on a network evening newscast

after Arledge hired her away to work for ABC in 1977 for $100,000 a year in a national correspondent position, remarkable for the times. In the Senate, Mackin competed with NBC's Jessica Savitch, who also exuded skill from the anchor chair in the 1970s until her death in a car accident in 1983.

263 Carole Simpson came: Two years later, NBC hired her as a network general assignment reporter in Washington. Also in these years, two eventual top executives at CBS, Marcy McGinnis, who started as an administrative assistant in 1970, and Susan Zirinsky, who arrived as an intern in the network's Washington bureau in 1972, began their respective climbs.

263 In the magazine world, Janet Malcolm: Janet Malcom [*sic*], "Help! Homework for the Liberated Woman," *New Republic,* Oct. 10, 1970.

264 From 1970 to 1973: Grant and Flanner, *Ross,* 213.

264 In the meantime, not long after: Katherine Q. Seelye, "Janet Malcolm, Provocative Journalist with a Piercing Eye, Dies at 86," *NYT,* June 17, 2021.

264 At the newspapers, young women: In this group was Laura Foreman, whom the *Times* hired to cover politics from its Washington bureau in 1977 but abruptly forced her resignation seven months later. An ethics scandal erupted over her relationship with a Pennsylvania state senator. Foreman was thirty-four at the time, having distinguished herself over three and a half years on the staff of *The Philadelphia Inquirer,* first as one of the paper's fastest and most able rewrite artists (she had split six years between the wire services AP and UPI before that) and then on the city politics beat, where she was considered "unusually gifted." A tax evasion investigation of the legislator Henry J. Cianfrani, which brought to light the gifts he gave her while she covered politics—some valued at more than $10,000—brought about her downfall. Rumors of the affair had reached the *Inquirer*'s editors in the spring and summer of 1975, but without proof of her involvement, coupled with Foreman's own denials, the editors took no action. In fact, confirmation did not come until the late winter or spring of 1976, after her move to Washington. The *Inquirer* reported that it had no prior knowledge of the gifts—among them, furniture, a fur coat, and a 1964 Morgan sports car. The editor, Gene Roberts, stated the paper's policy against the acceptance of gifts from subjects or sources of news stories and against any relationship or intense personal involvement between a reporter and a subject or news source that might be construed as a conflict of interest. Foreman issued her own statement at the time, saying she did not believe she had done anything wrong. The revelations prompted the *Inquirer* to deputize its

top two investigative reporters to conduct a major internal investigation, one of the first of this nature. In seventeen thousand words presented like a fable, the reporters offered the results of their inquiry, describing the relationship between "a sultry 31-year-old Inquirer reporter who speaks in a soft southern drawl" and "a 52-year-old politician who speaks in the dialect of the south Philadelphia streets" and how the paper had committed a serious lapse of editorial vigilance by ignoring the conflict of interest and ethical problems the affair posed. See "An Inquirer Conflict in the Cianfrani Case," *Philadelphia Inquirer*, Aug. 28, 1977, and Donald L. Bartlett and James B. Steele, "The Full Story of Cianfrani and the Reporter," *Philadelphia Inquirer*, Oct. 16, 1977. See also Katherine Q. Seelye, "Laura Foreman, Reporter Whose Romance Became a Scandal, Dies at 76," *NYT*, July 23, 2021.

264 In 1976, Molly Ivins: David Jones, email exchange with author, June 4, 2022; Grace Lichtenstein, email exchange with author, June 5, 2022.

264 "vastly overqualified dictationist": Bellows, *Last Editor*, 181.

265 "He always had a sparkle": Maureen Dowd, email exchange with author, Jan. 10, 2022.

265 Anna Quindlen got her start: Anna Quindlen, email exchange with author, Jan. 3, 2022.

265 Jill Abramson and Jane Mayer: Jill Abramson, telephone interview by author, Oct. 22, 2021.

265 The same would prove true: ProQuest search for Lesley Visser bylines in *The Boston Globe*, Aug. 1976 to Feb. 1977. See also Ernie Roberts, "Draft Nets Kapstein $500,000," *Boston Globe*, Dec. 4, 1976.

266 "Women of the Year": "Women of the Year: Great Changes, New Chances, Tough Choices," *Time*, Jan. 5, 1976.

Chapter 17. Not Quite

269 Although women had long served: The president of the University of Chicago was Hanna Gray. See Pulitzer Prize winner listings for 1980 and 1981, which also list the board: pulitzer.org. The chief editorial writer for the *Monitor* was Charlotte Saikowski.

269 the same year Mary Anne Dolan: "Jim Bellows Dies at 86; Legendary Editor of the L.A. Herald Examiner," *LAT*, March 7, 2009; Associated Press, "Paper Names Woman Editor," *Tucson Citizen*, Nov. 20, 1981.

269 *Ladies' Home Journal*: Shirley James Longshore and Donna P. Conley, "Women to Watch," *Ladies' Home Journal*, Nov. 1984.

269 Suddenly that seemed: Deutsch, "New Boss in the Newsroom Points to Changing Trends."

270 "the only female managing editor": "Dateline," *LAT*, April 18, 1980.

270 The series was the work: Merle Linda Wolin, email exchanges with author, April 14–16, 2021. See also Kroeger, *Undercover Reporting,* 118–24, 138, 274–77.

270 The proposal to go undercover: Frank Lalli, telephone interview by author, April 17, 2021, and subsequent email exchange, May 22, 2021.

271 Lalli guided the project: Lalli, telephone interview by author, April 17, 2021; "Felker to Head News' Afternoon Edition," *NY Daily News,* July 18, 1980.

271 "editor, sounding board": Wolin, email exchange with author, March 25, 2021.

271 Once published: "Latter-Day Sweatshops," *Hanford (Calif.) Sentinel,* Feb. 13, 1981.

271 Wolin brought these proposals: For the Merle Linda Wolin series "Sweatshop: Undercover in the Garment Industry," see undercover.hosting.nyu.edu.

271 The radio versions: Wolin, email exchange with author, March 25, 2021; Lalli, telephone interview by author, April 17, 2021. Lalli, by then ensconced in New York City, watched the rollout with displaced pride. Dolan's editing of the project, he said, was simply masterful.

271 The paper sold out: Wolin, email exchanges with author, April 14–16, 2021.

271 The series not only brought national attention: For example, Roger Gillott, "Reporter Exposes Filth, Intimidation in the Garment Industry," *Sheboygan Press* via AP, Jan. 31, 1981.

271 earned Dolan and Wolin an invitation: Thomas B. Rosenstiel, "Dolan Quits as Herald Examiner Editor: Departure Leaves Newspaper with Two Key Positions Vacant," *LAT,* July 27, 1985; "Reemergence of Sweatshops and the Enforcement of Wage and Hour Standards: Hearings on H.R. 6103, Before the Subcommittee on Labor Standards of the Committee on Education and Labor, 97th Cong. 169 (1981–82)" (statement of Merle Linda Wolin, reporter, and Mary Anne Dolan, managing editor, *LA Herald Examiner*). See also Kroeger, *Undercover Reporting,* 124, 138, 277.

272 "at the midnight hour": "Here's Why a Cheyenne Native Missed Out on Pulitzer Prize," *Casper Star Tribune,* April 26, 1982. Hanna Gray and Charlotte Saikowski were still Pulitzer board members in 1982.

272 Dolan responded: McPherson, "Prizefights"; John J. Goldman, "Times' Bernheimer Wins Pulitzer for Music Criticism," *LAT,* April 13, 1982.

272 In surveys, readers expressed: As a response to diminishing trust in the press, saying a hard no to would-be truth tellers engaging in reporting for which they did not entirely tell the truth became an easy way for some papers to symbolize their commitment to doing better, even

though it did not address the issues that caused reader complaints. Early investigations that involved undercover techniques included probes of government bureaucracy, Medicaid, and accident fraud (undercover .hosting.nyu.edu). The Pulitzers would take another decade and a half before they again awarded a prize to a deserving nominee with an undercover dimension to the project, as they had so many times before Mirage.

272 *Newsday*'s publisher at the time: "Here's Why a Cheyenne Native Missed Out on Pulitzer Prize."

272 A generation later: For Tony Horwitz and the *NYT*'s "How Race Is Lived in America" winners, see pulitzer.org. In 2008, Anne Hull, Dana Priest, and Michel Du Cille of the *WP* won for their investigation of Walter Reed Hospital, which involved some surreptitious techniques. See also Brooke Kroeger, "Why Surreptitiousness Works," *Journal of Magazine and New Media Research* 13, no. 1 (Spring 2012).

273 "arguably the toughest, most tenacious": Linda Witt, "Dig She Must," *Chicago Tribune,* June 23, 1985. See also dupont.org for 1988.

273 More broadly, the women's discrimination suits: "The Associated Press Agreed Wednesday to Pay $2 Million," UPI, June 15, 1983; "Gloria Biggs, 89, Ex–Newspaper Publisher."

273 Responding to the settlement: Kay Mills, *A Place in the News: From the Women's Pages to the Front Page* (New York: Columbia University Press, 1990), 308–9. See also Gilger and Wallace, *There's No Crying in Newsrooms,* 26. Mills quotes Neuharth saying, "It took a hell of a lawsuit to convince those damned male chauvinists on that board and their management that they could no longer do this." Informed that all of the AP complainants had since left the company, Neuharth replied, "All of them? Is that a fact? Well, it serves AP right."

273 *The New York Times* cited a survey: Anthony DePalma, "Women Gaining in Journalism," *NYT,* Aug. 23, 1981; Anthony DePalma, email interview by author, April 13, 2021. DePalma did not recall who conducted the survey, but said it was neither he nor the *Times.* In addition to Cunningham, in management at smaller papers the survey found a woman publisher; a woman copublisher; three woman managing editors; five woman city editors or news editors; a woman editorial page editor; and a woman sports editor.

273 By 1987, three more women: Wilding, "Kay Fanning: The Lady Is a Newspaperman"; "Monitor Editor to Lead US Editors' Group"; Cook, "Katherine W. Fanning"; Wong, "Katherine W. Fanning, 73; Pioneering Newspaper Editor."

274 She held the position: Sandy Mims Rowe, email exchange with author, Oct. 28, 2021. In 1986, Barbara Henry began leading Gannett's *Rochester*

Democrat with its circulation of 222,637. "Landers Named Editor of Reno Gazette-Journal," AP News, May 25, 1986 (replacing Henry, who moved on to be editor of the Rochester paper).

274 On her watch: Mark Lisheron, "Riding High," *AJR*, March 2000. On Rowe's watch, *The Oregonian* won Pulitzers for explanatory writing in 1999, feature writing and the public service medal in 2001, editorial writing in 2006, and breaking news in 2007. Author exchanges with Rowe, Oct.–Nov. 2021.

274 A "landmark event": Tom Rosenstiel, "Journalism History Made: A Woman Lands the Top Newsroom Job at Major Daily," *LAT,* June 12, 1987, correction adding Sandra Rowe appended.

274 It is hardly surprising: Ibid.

274 "Just watch": Rowe, telephone interview by author, Nov. 3, 2021.

275 Of twenty copy editors listed: Jean Ward, "Check Out Your Sexism," *CJR,* March 1, 1980. See also Stephen Hess, "The Sex Test," *CJR,* March 1986. This second sexism quiz was conducted by Stephen Hess, an expert in media and government, who tested the assertions of unnamed Washington-based reporters for the *NYT* ("The news will not change until the people covering the news change") and the *WP* ("If you're going to operate in some wonderland, you can say that your background doesn't color your story"). Hess gave copies of four articles with bylines removed to the seven women and five men in one of his graduate seminars at Harvard and asked them to identify the gender of each article's writer. Collectively, they got 71 percent of their answers wrong. Hess attributed this in part to the test-taking skills of this "smart bunch." Among them were a state senator, a university administrator, a radio news editor, a consumer advocate, and several government officials. Erroneous assumptions got in their way, like their incorrect identification of a writing style as feminine or the hunch they played that a *WSJ* reporter in 1986 was surely a man. "My interpretation, however, is that the press reflects where the society is at," Hess said. "In a sense, the test is a confirmation of the success of feminism. The students could not correctly detect sexism in these articles because it wasn't there."

275 By 1980, the appositive for Flora: "People Are Talking About," *Vogue,* March 1, 1980. Previous: Gardella, "Couple of News Gals Talk About Their Work." The rest of the *Vogue* appositive: reporter of "interpretive journalism that goes beyond reporting of facts—accurately, vividly, precisely—to give shape and meaning to illusive, chaotic events, without sensationalism and with purposeful restraint."

275 Ben Bradlee named Karen DeYoung: John Darnton remembered DeYoung from her freelance days in Africa as "terrific," "definitely a

competitor." She joined the *Post* as a metro reporter in 1976, then became Latin America correspondent and bureau chief, then London bureau chief (with Middle East bylines), then deputy foreign editor in 1980, before taking the foreign editor post for five years the following year. She then became national editor, assistant managing editor for national news, and, at seventy-one, associate editor and senior national security correspondent. At seventy-two, she was still in that position on staff. See washingtonpost.com. Also, Darnton, telephone interview by author, March 30, 2020.

275   In junior executive roles: Arthur O. Sulzberger, telephone interview by author, Jan. 11, 2022. See Robertson, *Girls in the Balcony,* 229–33. Robertson tells of "the speech" the young Sulzberger gave to middle and upper-level managers in his days as deputy publisher and his father's heir apparent. He emphasized a U.S. Census prediction that by the end of the 1990s some 80 percent of all new American employees would be women, minorities, or first-generation immigrants. In other words, recruiting and promoting widely was as good for business as it was the right thing to do.

275   In 1984, six years after the suit: Chira, text exchange with author, May 30, 2022: "I majored in history and East Asian studies, took immersive Japanese language classes, etc. BUT I was also very young, among the youngest foreign correspondents so, in this case they also took a chance on me." True, but her skills were a solid risk-lowering edge. Experience and skills, yet again, the tried-and-true women's catapult.

275   Rule viewed her experiences: Rule, email exchange with author, June 13, 2022.

276   From memory she summoned: Rowe, telephone interview by author, Nov. 3, 2021.

276   Nationally, by 1983, the number: David H. Weaver and G. Cleveland Wilhoit, *The American Journalist: A Portrait of U.S. News People and Their Work,* 2nd ed. (Bloomington: Indiana University Press, 1991), 16–19. From 20.3 percent of reporters, editors, and producers in 1971, the number of women had grown to 33.8 percent in 1982–83, lower than the average number of women in the workforce generally, which had risen to 42.5 percent. Minority journalists, the authors said, tended to be significantly younger than others and more likely to be working in the faster-growing fields of radio and television than for newspapers, newsweeklies, or news services.

276   When Roberts took charge: Gene Roberts, telephone interview by author, May 26, 2022.

277 She spoke to *The New York Times:* DePalma, "Women Gaining in Journalism." Any number of woman journalists based at home or abroad could recount experiences as egregious or far more egregious than the insult Cunningham shared for publication. In the roiling Middle East, from 1979 to 1983, when I served as a reporter and then chief of UPI's bureau in Tel Aviv (and after that, for 1983–84, as the company changed hands, as the London-based chief division editor for Europe, the Middle East, and Africa), men commonly dined out on sex and body gossip about the few—very few—woman journalists who came and went among them. They were quick to disparage a woman's sense of fair play if her copy showed up on top of theirs in a telex operator's yet-to-send pile (an accusation familiar from Marguerite Higgins's glory days in Europe and Korea) or if she landed a hard-to-get exclusive interview with one of the region's political or military strongmen.

278 It turned out: Runyon, "First Woman Senior Editor at a Major Newspaper Worked in Louisville."

278 Sylvana Foa stayed: Foa then took the new top editor's job at Univision and then became chief spokesperson to the UN High Commissioner for Refugees and then to the UN secretary-general, Boutros Boutros-Ghali.

278 Her UPI files contain a plea: Foa, Bangkok, to Al Kaff, New York, Oct. 31, 1981, Personal Papers of Sylvana Foa.

278 Only 120 of the country's 1,700: Wilding, "Lady Is a Newspaperman." This profile of Fanning also noted two early managing editors, Gloria B. Anderson, managing editor of *The Miami News* from 1978 to 1981 and the Knight News wire from 1976 to 1977, and Sue Ann Wood, who became managing editor of the *St. Louis Globe-Democrat* for the years 1983–84 until the paper changed ownership. See "Gloria Brown Anderson Named Managing Editor of the News," *Miami News,* Dec. 30, 1977, and her résumé on LinkedIn, accessed Nov. 4, 2021; Tim O'Neil, "Sue Ann Wood, Reporter and Editor at Two St. Louis Papers, Dies at 85," *St. Louis Post-Dispatch,* March 12, 2016. John Darnton said during the years he served as city editor of the *NYT,* from 1986 to 1990, under the editor Max Frankel, the paper was "sort of in trouble," meaning in financial straits, and was not really hiring in his department. The *Times* did loosen restrictions for minority targets of opportunity, and Darnton quickly recalled the hire of Dean Baquet, whom the *Times* lured away from the *Chicago Tribune* in those years, not long after Baquet, William Gaines, and Ann Marie Lipinski won the 1988 Pulitzer Prize for investigative reporting.

278 At *The New York Times:* Robertson, *Girls in the Balcony,* 232.

279 Why describe her suit: Quindlen, email exchange with author, Jan. 3, 2022. First expressed in Joan Konner and Barbara Rick, *She Says: Women in News,* directed by Barbara Rick, PBS, Dec. 19, 2001.

279 Carolyn Lee said: Lee, interview by author, New York City, Feb. 20, 2020.

279 "I don't doubt": Max Frankel, email interview by author, May 24, 2021.

279 "It made economic sense": Brooke Kroeger, "The Road Less Rewarded," *Working Woman,* July 1994. Coincidentally, Lynn Povich, of the *Newsweek* suit, by then had become *Working Woman*'s editor. She assigned the story. See also Barbara F. Reskin and Patricia A. Roos, *Job Queues, Gender Queues: Explaining Women's Inroads into Male Occupations* (Philadelphia: Temple University Press, 1990). From 1976–84, when I worked for UPI in Europe and the Middle East after four years in Chicago, women at various points served as bureau chiefs in London, Paris, Rome, Madrid, Belgrade, Athens, Tel Aviv (myself, 1980–83), and Vienna.

280 "My guess is the *'Times'* absolute": Scott, email exchange with author, May 19, 2022.

280 Carolyn Lee, whom Abe Rosenthal: Lee, telephone interview by author, May 24, 2022.

280 When he became national editor: Jones, telephone interview by author, June 4, 2022; Lichtenstein, email exchange with author, June 5, 2022. Actually, Jones said, the woman who was supposed to have succeeded him as school newspaper editor left school because she became pregnant and the job ultimately went to a man, but that did mean that Jones's wife-to-be moved up a rung to become the next year's managing editor. Jones too would get the Phil Spitalny moniker and a poster proclaiming it as a fiftieth birthday gift. It listed all the members of his "All-Girl Orchestra" from 1972 to 1982 and their respective chairs, among them, Lee on the siren, Wade as tub thumper, Lichtenstein on the pipes, and Ivins for occasional notes.

281 The picture for women in broadcasting: Terri Schultz-Brooks, "Getting There: Women in the Newsroom," *CJR,* March 1, 1984. The article included photographs of Carol Kleiman, associate financial editor of the *Chicago Tribune;* Marlene Sanders, by then a correspondent for CBS; Eileen Shanahan, late of the *NYT* and by then senior assistant managing editor of the *Pittsburgh Post-Gazette;* Carole Ashkinaze, columnist and first woman member of the editorial board of *The Atlanta Constitution;* Peggy Simpson, economic correspondent for the Hearst newspapers and Washington columnist for *The Boston Herald;* Mary Lou Butcher, former reporter for *The Detroit News;* Christy Bulkeley, vice president, Gannett Central

and publisher, the Danville, Illinois, *Commercial-News;* Helen Thomas, White House reporter, UPI; Joan Cooke, metro reporter, the *NYT.*

281 For the successful women of the medium: Flander, "Women in Network News."

281 title of her memoir: Christine Craft, *Too Old, Too Ugly, and Not Deferential to Men* (Rocklin, Calif.: Prima Pub. and Communications, 1988).

281 In 1984, ABC had no woman correspondents: Sheila Weller, *The News Sorority: Diane Sawyer, Katie Couric, Christiane Amanpour—and the (Ongoing, Imperfect, Complicated) Triumph of Women in TV News* (New York: Penguin Press, 2014), 156–57. See also Judith Marlane, *Women in Television News Revisited: Into the Twenty-First Century* (Austin: University of Texas Press, 1999), 127.

281 "caution, submission, hurt": Flander, "Women in Network News." Lynn Sherr, also forty-two, wondered what would happen when they all got wrinkles. "There has to be strength in numbers," she said. "They can't get rid of all of us at once, can they?" Sherr remained a regular presence with Barbara Walters on ABC's newsmagazine *20/20* until she turned sixty-six in 2008. Andrea Mitchell, then thirty-eight and another enduring presence, found it impossible to believe the ax might fall on so many talented women with such solid credentials. "That would be bad management, not to mention the morality factor," she said, adding in self-deprecation that she thought she often didn't count in "people's calibrations." Ann Compton, also thirty-eight, had managed to have three children on her network's clock by 1985, taking brief leaves for each birth so as not to be gone so long the bosses might think her irrelevant. Marlene Sanders remained on the air until 1989, moving at the end from ABC to public television.

282 Carole Simpson was forty-seven: Weller, *News Sorority,* 156–57. See also Marlane, *Women in Television News Revisited,* 127.

282 "Dazzling, Dynamic": Chris Chase, "Dazzling, Dynamic Diane Sawyer," *Cosmopolitan,* Dec. 1986.

282 In the world of magazines: For example, *Arizona Republic,* Jan. 5, 1984; *Tampa Tribune,* Jan. 5, 1984; Edwin McDowell, "New Editor Is Chosen for Vanity Fair," *NYT,* Jan. 5, 1984; "US Job for Tina Brown," *Guardian,* Jan. 5, 1984.

283 Not long after her arrival: Jill Gerston, "Putting New Flair in Vanity Fair," *Philadelphia Inquirer,* Feb. 24, 1984.

283 In the universe of major awards: Pulitzer prizes between 1980 and 1989 went to Madeleine Blais, Shirley Christian, Edna Buchanan, and Carol Guzy of the *Miami Herald;* Joan Vennochi, Joan Fitz-Gerald,

and Ellen Goodman, *Boston Globe;* Bette Swenson Orsini and Lucy Morgan, *St. Petersburg Times;* Loretta Tofani, *WP;* Nan Robertson, *NYT;* Manuela Hoelterhoff and Karen Elliott House, *WSJ;* Jackie Crosby, *Macon (Ga.) Telegraph and News;* Alice Steinbach, *Baltimore Sun;* Mary Pat Flaherty, *Pittsburgh Press;* Katherine Ellison, *San Jose Mercury News;* Ann Marie Lipinski and Lois Wille, *Chicago Tribune;* Jacqui Banaszynski, *St. Paul Pioneer Press Dispatch;* Jane Healy, *Orlando Sentinel;* and Karen Blessen, *Dallas Morning News.* In 1981, the board regifted the award for feature writing to Teresa Carpenter of *The Village Voice.* This came two days after the *WP* returned the prize Janet Cooke initially received on revelation that she had fabricated the eight-year-old third-generation heroin addict at the center of her reporting. The episode lives in journalistic infamy. See pulitzer.org. Between 1980 and 1984, only one Overseas Press Club award went to a woman, House of the *WSJ,* but the numbers grew in the decade's second half. Among the winners were Barbara Walters, who received two OPC President's Awards; Janet Knott of *The Boston Globe,* who won the 1987 Robert Capa Award for her photo series from Haiti in crisis; and Gannett's Margaret Ellen Hale, whose coverage of the AIDS crisis won the Hal Boyle Award. See opcofamerica.org.

283 Of the old guard: Dunlap, "Ada Louise Huxtable, Champion of Livable Architecture, Dies at 91."

284 All the same, considering the climate: Curtis died of breast cancer. "Charlotte Curtis, a Columnist for the Times, Is Dead at 58," *NY Times,* April 17, 1987.

284 "The Times now believes that 'Ms.' ": "Editor's Note," *NYT,* June 20, 1986; Amisha Padnani and Veronica Chambers, "Examining the Meaning of 'Mrs.,' " *NYT,* May 15, 2020.

284 Janet Malcolm was in her late forties: Malcolm's stories for *The New Yorker* include "I—The Impossible Profession," Nov. 16, 1980; "II—The Impossible Profession," Nov. 23, 1980; "I—Trouble in the Archives," Nov. 27, 1983; and "II—Trouble in the Archives," Dec. 4, 1983.

284 "For people who rarely": Tom Zito, "Shrinks and Slim Tops and Flops in Print," *WP,* Jan. 8, 1981.

284 Three years later came: Robert S. Boynton, "Till Press Do Us Part: The Trial of Janet Malcolm and Jeffrey Masson," *Village Voice,* Nov. 28, 1994.

285 "Every journalist who is not": Janet Malcolm, "I—The Journalist and the Murderer," *New Yorker,* March 13, 1989.

285 "The literary set": "Literary Fight," *Philadelphia Inquirer,* March 16, 1989. See also, for example, Linnea Lannon, "When Writers Abuse Those Who Talk to Them," *Detroit Free Press,* March 26, 1989; Charles E. Claffey, "The Talk of the Town," *Boston Globe,* March 23, 1989.

285 The headline over: Eleanor Randolph, "The Critic and the Criticized,"
     WP, March 18, 1989. Garry Abrams weighed in with "Moral Debate
     Rages over Writers Who Exploit Human Tragedy," *LAT*, March 30, 1989.
     The *NYT* carried four items about the two-part series over eleven days:
     once as an editorial; once as commentary; once as an editor's note that
     took issue with the unsourced, unattributed generalizations in Albert
     Scardino's analysis of the debate over journalism ethics that Malcolm
     unleashed; and once with corrections to two of Scardino's erroneous
     characterizations of Malcolm's position in Masson's lawsuit. *Newsday*
     gave space to Joe McGinnis to make his case that a writer's responsibility
     was to his reader, not to his subject. And in late April, *The Miami Herald*
     recapped the entire story with a two-and-a-half-page explainer, starting
     with the murders of Captain Jeffrey MacDonald's pregnant wife and two
     daughters straight through McGinnis's cultivation of MacDonald for his
     book and Malcolm's cultivation of McGinnis for hers.
285 "about anything and everything": Jon Katz, telephone interview by
     author, May 24, 2021.
286 "Do the best you can": Quindlen, email exchange with author, Jan. 3,
     2022; Robertson, *Girls in the Balcony*, 216–18.
286 "only the first of many": Frankel, *Times of My Life*, 455.
287 In 1988, Jill Abramson: Abramson, telephone interview by author,
     Oct. 22, 2021.
288 Flora Lewis, by then a *Times:* Craig R. Whitney, "Flora Lewis, Astute
     Observer of World Affairs for the Times and Others, Dies at 79," *NYT*,
     June 2, 2000.
288 When Colvin first got to Paris: Lindsey Hilsum, *In Extremis: The Life and
     Death of the War Correspondent Marie Colvin* (New York: Picador, 2019).
288 The virtuous circle: *Martha Gellhorn: On the Record*, narrated by Marie
     Colvin, BBC, 2003, youtube.com.
288 In conflict after conflict: Among many such references, Lyse Doucet, "It's
     What We Do," *Prospect* (London), Jan. 25, 2019.
289 At the helm of the *Herald Examiner:* Mary Anne Dolan, "When Feminism
     Failed," *NYT Magazine*, June 26, 1988.
290 In 1985, Dolan, exhausted: Rosenstiel, "Dolan Quits as Herald Examiner
     Editor."

Chapter 18. Power Coupling

291 Darnton, remember: Eleanor Darnton was the *NYT* women's editor, 1944
     to 1945. Also, Currie, "Flora Lewis," 57–58.
291 accompanied by his wife: "John Darnton Marries Nina Lieberman,"
     NYT, Aug. 22, 1966.

291 Rosenthal saw a Nina Darnton credit: Fay Willey, Nina Darnton, and Tony Clifton. "Would the Polish Army Fight?," *Newsweek,* June 15, 1981.

292 Whitney wrote to Darnton: John Darnton and Nina Darnton, telephone interviews by author, March 30, 2020.

292 The next letter: Rosenthal to John and Nina Darton, July 14, 1981, courtesy of John Darton. Rosenthal allowed as how an exception was being made for a wife who was a stringer for a competing publication before her husband joined the *Times* and that with his next posting elsewhere, the wife had agreed to give the position up.

293 "It didn't seem to be that unreasonable": Darntons' telephone interviews by author, March 30, 2020.

293 Nina shared her story: Ibid.

293 "A husband-and-wife team": Ibid.

293 She was not put on the *Times*'s payroll: Ibid.

294 It was a tremendous opportunity: David Shribman, telephone interview by author, July 6, 2021.

294 "You know, I have a wife who works": Ibid.

296 "No one," he said: Ibid.

297 "I don't condone this": Ibid.; Steven R. Weisman, email exchange with author, Oct. 7, 2021.

298 At the *Post,* Felicity Barringer: Felicity Barringer, telephone interview by author, May 4, 2021.

299 "It had nothing to do with me": Ibid.

299 "As I look back on it": Ibid.; Felicity Barringer, "Craft Sweeps by Halley's Comet," *NYT,* March 7, 1986.

300 As reporters, she and Weisman: Elisabeth Bumiller, telephone interview by author, May 17, 2021; John Darnton, telephone interview by author, March 30, 2020; Barringer, telephone interview by author, May 4, 2021.

300 More than that, Weisman said years later: Weisman, email exchange with author, Oct. 7, 2021. The *Post* bureau chief in New Delhi at the time was Bill Claiborne.

300 In a later recounting: For two stories with versions of these and related accounts of working couples: David Shaw, "Foreign Correspondents: Job Abroad Often Fatal to Marriage," *LAT,* July 8, 1986; Howard Kurtz, "Married . . . with Press Pass," *WP,* Nov. 3, 1991.

300 The arrangement pleased her: Bumiller, telephone interview by author, May 17, 2021; John Darnton, telephone interview by author, March 30, 2020; Barringer, telephone interview by author, May 4, 2021.

301 "Abe never denied": Weisman, email exchange with author, Oct. 7, 2021.

301 More than three decades later: Geraldine Baum, speech, Columbia

Alumni Awards ceremony, April 27, 2019, courtesy of Baum. See jour
nalism.columbia.edu. Baum went from *Newsday* to the *LAT* in its Washington, New York, and Paris bureaus and served as bureau chief in Paris
and New York.

Chapter 19. Moving Up

303 The choice of Max Frankel: Frankel, *Times of My Life*, 445–49.

303 In February 1989: "For Women Like Barbara Walters, a Man Who Can't
Be Intimidated Comes Along About as Often as an Unknown Picasso,"
Manhattan, Inc., Feb. 1989.

303 "undesirable competition, collusion": Frankel, *Times of My Life*, 449.

304 In the cases of Barringer and Bumiller: John and Nina Darnton, telephone
interviews by and email exchanges with author, March 30, 2020; Barringer, telephone interviews by and email exchanges with author, May 4,
Aug. 26, Oct. 9, 2021; Bumiller and Weisman, telephone interviews by and
email exchanges with author, May 17, Oct. 7, 2021; Shribman, telephone
interviews by and email exchanges with author, July 6, Nov. 5, 2021.

304 Even his initial masthead appointees: Frankel, *Times of My Life*, 432–33,
455–56. His quotation about women: "We were still not comfortably
integrated in the upper ranks."

304 "Max felt this himself": Sulzberger, email exchange with author, May 19,
2022.

304 And yet despite the strong obligation: Frankel, *Times of My Life*, 432.

305 Yet by the time Frankel took charge: Mark Lisheron, "Riding High," *AJR*,
March 2000.

305 a one-word reaction: Rowe, email exchange with author, Nov. 6, 2021.

306 Most listed Carolyn Lee: "Carolyn Lee Is Named Times's Picture Editor," *NYT*, Feb. 23, 1984.

306 Soma Golden's name: Confidential memoranda to Frankel from Craig
Whitney, John M. Lee, Arthur Gelb, Allan M. Siegal, and Peter Millones,
Oct.–Nov. 1986, Frankel Papers.

306 Lee had been picture editor: Frankel, email exchange with author,
May 24, 2021.

306 She was admired: Robertson, *Girls in the Balcony*, 234.

306 Frankel personally brought Soma: Frankel, email exchange with author,
May 24, 2021.

306 "determined to give an encouraging signal": Frankel, *Times of My Life*,
432–33; "Times Editors Named to Senior News Posts," *NYT*, Jan. 16,
1987.

306 Under Rosenthal, her relegation: Lee, interview by author, New York
City, Feb. 20, 2020; "Carolyn Lee Is Named Times's Picture Editor";

"Lelyveld of the Times Is Named Managing Editor as Gelb Retires," *NYT,* Dec. 31, 1989; "The Times Promotes 2 to Senior Editor Posts," *NYT,* Dec. 10, 1988.

307 In 1988, Geneva Overholser: Overholser's other experience was as a reporter at the *Colorado Springs Sun* and as a freelancer in Kinshasa and Paris.

307 "Horseflesh!": Geneva Overholser, interview by author, New York City, Oct. 26, 2021. Overholser said the executive was Brian Donnelly.

307 The woman peers around the country: Dennis Hevesi, "Janet Chusmir, Executive Editor of the Miami Herald, Dies at 60," *NYT,* Dec. 23, 1990.

308 In 1993, the year Rowe: Rowe, email exchange with author, Oct. 28, 2021. She retired in 2010.

308 The byline belonged to: Geneva Overholser, "Why Hide Rapes?," *NYT,* July 11, 1989.

308 "to turn a spotlight": Overholser, interview by author, March 17, 2022.

308 "a critically important topic": Overholser, interview by and follow-up email exchanges with author, Oct. 26–27, 2021.

308 Schorer recalled: "Pulitzer Prize Winner Jane Schorer Meisner," Iowa PBS, Dec. 19, 2016, youtube.com.

309 *Register* won: Overholser, as a member of the Pulitzer board at the time, recused herself during the deliberations but, once the decision was made, urged that Schorer be credited by name along with the paper.

309 "faced strong headwinds": See genevaoverholser.com with links to all the relevant articles, including Overholser, "Why Hide Rapes?"; Overholser, "American Shame: The Stigma of Rape," *Des Moines Register,* July 11, 1989; Jane Schorer, "It Couldn't Happen to Me: One Woman's Story," *Des Moines Sunday Register,* Feb. 25, 26, 27, 28, March 1, 1990 (reprints at documentcloud.org and archive.org/stream); Overholser, "How This Story Came to Be," *Des Moines Sunday Register,* Feb. 25, 1990; pulitzer.org.

309 "'protect this poor woman'": Overholser, email to author, Oct. 27, 2021, and March 19, 2022; Overholser, interview by author, March 17, 2022. Overholser does see the work's reflection in the current outrage over sexual assault and the "languishing of rape kits in police departments across the land."

309 "Best Editor": "Best Editor, Best Newspaper, Best of Gannett," *Editor & Publisher,* Nov. 24, 1990.

310 "the liquor flowed": Cohen, email exchange with author, Nov. 1, 2021; Overholser, interview by author, New York City, Oct. 26, 2021.

310 She spoke for three minutes: Overholser, interview by author, New York City, Oct. 26, 2021.

310 "Here's my dream": Gilbert Cranberg, "A Swan Song in Des Moines," *CJR*, May–June 1995. See also, generally, Gene Roberts, Thomas Kunkel, and Charles Layton, *Leaving Readers Behind: The Age of Corporate Newspapering* (Fayetteville: University of Arkansas Press, 2001), and Roberts and Kunkel, *Breach of Faith: A Crisis of Coverage in the Age of Corporate Newspapering* (Fayetteville: University of Arkansas, 2002).

310 In the instant after: Cohen, email exchange with author, Nov. 1, 2021. Cohen said at around the same time, there was interest in finding a top slot for another editor and Cohen's "rabbi" in the company had retired, leaving him somewhat vulnerable. He remained with the company in the lesser position of national editor of the Gannett News Service until he retired late in 2001. See also Geneva Overholser, "Profit Pressures over Time," Poynter Institute, April 6, 2004, which also appeared as Overholser, "Good Journalism and Business," *Newspaper Research Journal* 25, no. 1 (2004).

310 The *Register*'s 1991 Pulitzer: The other six named woman winners that year were Susan Headden (with Joseph T. Hallinan), investigative, *Indianapolis Star*; Sheryl James, feature writing, *St. Petersburg Times*; Natalie Angier, science reporting, *NYT*; Marjie Lundstrom and Rochelle Sharpe, national reporting, Gannett; Caryle Murphy, international reporting, *WP*. See pulitzer.org.

311 *Backlash*: Susan Faludi, *Backlash: The Undeclared War Against Women* (New York: Crown, 1991), 379–89. Faludi tells of a 1986 meeting of the Journalists' Trade Group of the National Writers Union at which each attendee told a story of the sexist treatment she had received but then all disavowed feminism and expressed no interest in forming a woman's caucus for 1970s-style collective action.

311 For the decade: The other women named as individual or team winners of the 1990s were Mary Ann Gwinn, *Seattle Times*; Tamar Stieber, *Albuquerque Journal*; Lorraine Adams, *Dallas Morning News*; Deborah Blum, *Sacramento Bee*; Maria Henson, *Lexington (Ky.) Herald-Leader*; Eileen Welsome, *Alberquerque Tribune*; Stephanie Saul, *Newsday*; Laurie Garrett, *Newsday*; Alix Freedman, *WSJ*; Stephanie Welsh, Newhouse News Service; Deborah Nelson, *Seattle Times*; Lisa Pollak, *Baltimore Sun*; Eileen McNamara, *Boston Globe*; Annie Wells, *Press Democrat* (Santa Rosa, Calif.); Martha Rial, *Pittsburgh Post-Gazette*; and Linda Greenhouse, *NYT*. See pulitzer.org.

311 It is also worth noting: Balmaseda, whose heritage was Cuban, won in 1993 for her commentary in *The Miami Herald* on the city's Cuban Americans and the deteriorating situation in Haiti. The other four woman winners of color all worked for the *NYT*. Wilkerson won for feature

writing in 1994 and Jefferson for criticism in 1995. Both are Black; in fact, Wilkerson, the *Times*'s Chicago bureau chief at the time, was the first African American woman to be so honored. WuDunn and Kakutani are both of Asian descent. WuDunn's 1990 trifecta—Pulitzer, George Polk, and an Overseas Press Club award—were for her reporting with Nicholas Kristof on the riots in China's Tiananmen Square. They were the first married couple to be so honored. Kakutani, the *Times*'s imposing book reviewer, won the 1998 Pulitzer for criticism.

311 Wilkerson's recruitment: Robertson, *Girls in the Balcony*, 218, confirmed in Quindlen, interview by author, Jan. 23, 2022.

311 precocious pile of bylined articles: A ProQuest search from 1978 to 1988 includes twenty-eight stories by Wilkerson in the *WP* between the summer of 1982, in her second and third year at Howard, and her first byline in the *NYT,* a profile of Fritz Winfred Alexander II, "the first black named to a full term on the New York State Court of Appeals," published Jan. 3, 1985. She graduated from Howard in the spring of 1984. Misha Cornelius, "Howard Alumna Isabel Wilkerson Receives Inaugural NYU/Axinn Foundation Prize," *Howard Newsroom*, Dec. 8, 2020, newsroom.howard.edu.

312 Her column called "Liberties": "Quindlen Leaving the Times to Be a Full-Time Novelist," *NYT,* Sept. 10, 1994.

312 At last there were signs: Corrine Dufka, who covered the war in Bosnia and in El Salvador, won a Robert Capa for her photojournalism from Liberia. As for the decade's named George Polk winners, the woman count was also strong. More than 40 percent of the prizes went to women, among them Tracy Wilkinson of the *LAT* for her reporting from Kosovo; Amy Goodman of *Democracy Now!* for documenting Chevron's role in the murder of two environmentalists in Nigeria; the much-lauded Laurie Garrett of *Newsday* for a twenty-five-part series on rampant AIDS and tuberculosis in the former Soviet Union; Christiane Amanpour and Anita Pratap for their reporting from Afghanistan for CNN; and Amanpour again for "putting herself at risk in first hand reports on the war in what had once been Yugoslavia."

312 Between 1970 and 1992: Stephen Hess, *International News and Foreign Correspondents* (Washington, D.C.: Brookings Institution, 1995), 11–29. See also Heidi Dietrich, "Women in War Zones," *Quill,* Oct. 2002.

312 "sit around talking about 62mm mortars": Ricchiardi, "Women on War." The "better than sex" quotation is from Janine di Giovanni.

312 Yet others pointed to the work: See pulitzer.org.

312 This they attributed: Ricchiardi, "Women on War." All the same, Maggie O'Kane, Britain's Journalist of the Year that year for her work from the

Balkans, told Ricchiardi that most of the woman conflict reporters she knew still had to start as freelancers to "prove they can do it." In 1991, she covered the Persian Gulf War for *The Irish Times* with lowly stringer status. Janine DiGiovanni spoke of how hard she had to lobby London's *Sunday Times* to get sent to Bosnia, despite her prior conflict reporting from Nicaragua and the Israeli-occupied West Bank.

313 Caryle Murphy: Caryle Murphy, "Angola Expels Correspondent," *WP,* Aug. 17, 1976.

313 By Labor Day: Murphy, telephone interview by author, July 31, 2021.

313 Fourteen months later: Caryle Murphy, "South African Court Refuses to Probe Biko Coverup Charges," *WP,* Nov. 19, 1977.

313 then Cairo: Starting with Nora Boustany and Caryle Murphy, "Lebanon Battles Demonstrate Syria-Iran Rivalry," *WP,* Jan. 7, 1990.

313 During her five years: Murphy's Middle East–based colleagues in those years included Carol Morello for *The Philadelphia Inquirer,* Kim Murphy for the *LAT,* Laurie Kassman for VOA, Gayle Young for CNN, Susan Sachs for *Newsday,* and Carol Rosenberg for *The Miami Herald.* The change in the staffing profile Murphy describes from a decade earlier is significant. I served in the region, for UPI from 1979 to 1983, the last three years as Tel Aviv bureau chief. Trudy Rubin, also an American, now a *Philadelphia Inquirer* columnist, was then on contract for *The Christian Science Monitor,* based in Israel. I know of no other American women who were bureau chiefs in the region at that time. In the Middle East, UPI had several excellent woman hires in our Beirut bureau in those earlier years, all local women, and our local stringer in Amman was a woman.

314 She filed a story: Caryle Murphy, "Iraq Expands Force Near Kuwaiti Border," *WP,* July 31, 1990.

314 As negotiations: Caryle Murphy, "Iraq Takes Hard Line as Talks Open," *WP,* Aug. 1, 1990.

314 "vivid tableau": Caryle Murphy, "We Are Under Foreign Occupation!," *WP,* Aug. 3, 1990.

314 Murphy managed to keep filing: Howard Kurtz, "Washington Post Wins Two Pulitzer Prizes," *WP,* April 10, 1991.

314 "Everywhere we looked": Caryle Murphy, "26 Days in Kuwait: Chaos, Fear, and Tears," *WP,* Aug. 29, 1990.

315 Murphy's reports from hiding: "Post Reporter Murphy Wins Polk Award," *WP,* March 15, 1991, and liu.edu; Murphy, telephone interview by author, July 31, 2021. At the time, Michael Getler was the *Post*'s assistant managing editor for foreign news.

315 Sonni Efron: Dietrich, "Women in War Zones." See also author telephone interview with Efron, July 7, 2022.

315 "We not only deplore it": Memorandum, Frankel to the staff of the New York Times newsroom, Oct. 15, 1991, box 8, folder 3, Frankel Papers.

316 "No silver bullet": Totenberg in Konner and Rick, *She Says.*

316 "No," Rowe told her colleagues: Rowe, telephone interview by author, Nov. 3, 2021.

316 Narda Zacchino: See Marlene Cimons, "The Click! Heard 'Round the Nation," *LAT,* Oct. 18, 1991. The attorney Gloria Allred told Cimons that since Hill's televised appearances began, her law firm had been logging three hundred calls a day from women seeking advice about the pursuit of sexual harassment complaints.

316 "in light of recent reports": Petition signed by twenty-two *Times* women to Arthur Sulzberger and copied to Max Frankel, Joe Lelyveld, and Carolyn Lee, July 7, 1993, box 8, folder 3, Frankel Papers.

317 "While it is not always easy": "Sexual Harassment Policy," Memo, Sulzberger to Staff, Sept. 10, 1993, box 9, folder 8, Frankel Papers.

317 "extensive political machinery": David Brock, *Blinded by the Right: The Conscience of an Ex-conservative* (New York: Crown, 2002), 95–131.

317 The months of reporting: Abramson, telephone interview by author, Oct. 22, 2021. See also John Koblin, "Bill Keller and Jill Abramson Ride the Times Publicity Caravan," *NY Observer,* June 23, 2009, repurposed from the *Observer* in Megan Garber, "The Grey Lady Exposed," *CJR,* June 23, 2009, and Zeke Turner, "Maureen Dowd and Jill Abramson Bond over Genitalia," *Mediaite,* June 23, 2009.

317 Dowd and Mayer: Mayer and Dowd, email exchanges with author, Jan. 10–14, 2022.

317 In 1978, ASNE's human resources committee: William H. Freivogel, "Study: Women's Quotes, Bylines Increased Little," *St. Louis Post-Dispatch,* April 4, 1990. The study found that 32 percent of front-page photos featured women in Feb. 1990 compared with 24 percent the year before; 14 percent of news sources were women compared with 11 percent the previous year; and women's bylines virtually stagnated at 28 percent in 1990 over against 27 percent in 1989.

318 Betsy Carter, the editorial director: Paula Span, "Between the Covers," *WP,* Dec. 30, 1998; Andy Grove, "Taking On Prostate Cancer," *Fortune,* May 13, 1996.

318 Frankel denounced the "mischievous publicity": Frankel, *Times of My Life,* 456–57; Freivogel, "Study: Women's Quotes, Bylines Increased Little"; Eleanor Randolph, "The Newspaper Editors, at a Loss for Words," *WP,* April 4, 1990.

318 "self-inflicted crises": Frankel, *Times of My Life,* 456–57.

318 Claudia Payne: "Judy Mann: Progress Tempers Anger," *WP,* April 11,

1990; Payne, email exchange with author, May 30, 2020; Frankel, *Times of My Life,* 456–57; additional author exchanges with Susan Chira and Suzanne Daley, both of whom participated, and Deborah Sontag, who helped with sourcing, as did Charlie Kaiser, who came up with a photograph of the teapot button via Anne Mancuso.

319 Suzanne Daley: Daley, email exchange with author, May 23, 2022; Frankel, *Times of My Life,* 456–57.

319 "Tough Times Cut": Alex S. Jones, "Tough Times Cut Opportunities for Minority Journalists," *NYT,* Nov. 19, 1990.

320 "I left behind": Frankel, *Times of My Life,* 468. Also, Freivogel, "Study: Women's Quotes, Bylines Increased Little"; Randolph, "Newspaper Editors, at a Loss for Words." The survey showed that gays and lesbians found newspapers "largely hospitable" to them as employees, but that they nonetheless continued to experience an undercurrent of bias along with subjection to derogatory comments.

320 In *The New Yorker:* James Wolcott, "Hear Me Purr," *New Yorker,* May 20, 1995.

321 Christopher Hitchens: Christopher Hitchens, "Top Dowd," *Vanity Fair,* June 1995.

321 "The Opinion Shaper": The Editors, "America's 100 Most Important Women," *Ladies' Home Journal,* Nov. 1999.

321 Tina Brown, "the brash": Brown replaced Robert Gottlieb, who succeeded William Shawn, who followed the magazine's cofounder Harold Ross.

321 In all, Brown would win: Howard Kurtz, "Tina Brown Quits the New Yorker," *WP,* July 9, 1998.

321 Not on the *Journal* list: Malcolm, "II—Trouble in the Archives"; Malcolm, "The Morality of Journalism," *NY Review of Books,* March 1, 1990 (afterword to Knopf publication of *The Journalist and the Murderer*).

321 "Who's Afraid": Robert S. Boynton, "Who's Afraid of Janet Malcolm?," *Mirabella,* Nov. 1992, robertboynton.com.

322 A reputation for coldness: Katie Roiphe, "Remembering Janet Malcolm," *Paris Review,* June 21, 2021; and Katie Roiphe, "Janet Malcolm, the Art of Nonfiction No. 4," *Paris Review* (Spring 2011).

322 "signifier for some": Boynton, "Till Press Do Us Part."

322 "received wisdom": Douglas McCollam, "You Have the Right to Remain Silent: Toward Interviewing with Honor," *CJR,* Jan.–Feb. 2003.

322 "Was she perceived as harsh": Janet Malcolm, *The Last Interview, and Other Conversations* (Brooklyn: Melville House, 2022).

323 "something on everyone's mind": Roberts, telephone interview by author, May 26, 2020.

323 "an indelible mark": "Science Editor Appointed," *NYT,* Nov. 14, 1996 (the story says her post as deputy metropolitan editor was to begin early in 1997); "Times Names 4 to Senior Positions on the News Staff," *NYT,* May 24, 1997 (Purnick appointed metropolitan editor); Paul Tharp, "Landsman to Succeed Purnick as Times Metropolitan Editor," *NYT,* July 21, 1999.

323 There had also been: Author in-person interview, July 10, 2021, with two staffers at the time, email exchanges with a third, and an email exchange with Oreskes, Sept. 14, 2021; Lewin, telephone interview by author, June 1, 2022. Lewin said Elissa Gootman had a similar arrangement.

323 It might have been coincidental: Oreskes, email exchange with author, Sept. 14, 2021.

323 "It was not a pure": Ibid.

324 "There is no way in an all-consuming profession": William H. Honan, "Commencements: At a Poignant Return, Cosby Praises Teachers," *NYT,* May 20, 1998.

324 "Where do these people live?": Sara Rimer, "Having It All: The Truth and the Myth Don't Match," *Baltimore Sun,* May 31, 1998. See also Richard Cohen, "The Parenting Trap," *WP,* July 12, 1998; Joan Beck, "When Kids Get in the Way of Careers," *Chicago Tribune,* May 28, 1998. Richard Cohen of the *WP* wrote of the conundrum that the "parenting trap" had become for career journalists, but Joan Beck in the *Chicago Tribune* countered by citing a new book by Susan Chira, Purnick's colleague at the *Times* and another stalwart destined in time for senior posts. Chira wrote of the accommodations the newspaper granted her so that she could fulfill her obligations as a mother, especially during the two lengthy life-threatening illnesses of one of her two children. In Chira's view, not only was it possible to manage both career and children, but it could be done to the benefit of both.

325 Wow, she thought: Margaret Sullivan, telephone interview by author, July 5, 2021, and subsequent calls and email exchanges, 2021–22. Special thanks to her.

Chapter 20. Moving On

326 "pioneering": Christi Harlan, "Role Models in Transition: Highly Visible Women Leaving Business in Better Shape Than They Found It," *Quill,* July 1, 1995.

326 Joann Byrd: "Editor at West Coast Paper Is Post's New Ombudsman," *WP,* Dec. 24, 1991. See also bio of Joann Byrd, University of Oregon School of Journalism, journalism.uoregon.edu; Julie Muhlstein, "Advice

from Longtime Journalist: 'Challenge Everything,' " *Everett (Wash.) Daily Herald,* Jan. 29, 2017.

326 And *Talk* magazine: AP, "New Magazine Talk of the Town," *Newport News (Va.) Daily Press,* Aug. 4, 1999.

326 Her publisher: AP, "Editors, Publishers Discuss Higher Paper Prices, Making Money While Meeting Ideals," *Alamogordo Daily News,* April 7, 1995. A clue to the reason for her ouster was in her comments at the ASNE meeting, two months after her dismissal. The AP quoted her acknowledging the importance of profits to a newspaper's economic independence but saying at the same time that editors devoting more time to business and marketing issues cut into the time they had to spend on the journalism.

326 One day before: Beyond the 1990 Pulitzer gold medal, the numerous awards and honors on Geneva Overholser's curriculum vitae include being named one of the country's "Fifty Most Powerful Women" by *Ladies' Home Journal;* the Gannett company's "Best Editor" of 1990; "Best Newspaper Editor" of 1992 by the *Washington Journalism Review;* and "Editor of the Year" in 1993 by the National Press Foundation.

327 shocked her staff: The *Des Moines Register* articles about the Overholser-Westphal resignations not cited below: "A Business Like No Other," Feb. 18, 1995; Chuck Offenburger, "A Lot of That Going Around," Feb. 16, 1995; Dale Kasler, "Resignations Raise Questions About Paper's Course," Feb. 26, 1995; "Editors Leave the Register: What It Means," Feb. 26, 1995; "Register's Westphal Joining McClatchy," March 10, 1995; Dale Kasler, "Ryerson Returns to Iowa to Become Register Editor," March 15, 1995; "The Register's Readers Say Overholser's Statements Hypocritical," Oct. 6, 1995. See also Howard Kurtz, "A Tale of Two Editors," *WP,* Sept. 30, 1995; Alicia C. Shepard, "An Editor Finds Her Personal Life on Page One," *AJR,* Nov. 1995.

327 "decision after decision": John Carlson, "Top Register Editors Quit; News Staff Expresses Shock," *Des Moines Register,* Feb. 14, 1995.

327 "reopened a bitter debate": William Glaberson, "Departures at Paper Ignite a Debate on News vs. Profit," *NYT,* Feb. 15, 1995 (reprinted in the *Register,* Feb. 17, 1995).

327 She had often spoken: Ron Cohen, email exchange with author, Nov. 1, 2021; Geneva Overholser, interview by author, New York City, Oct. 26, 2021.

327 The story quoted Jim Squires: Glaberson, "Departures at Paper Ignite a Debate on News vs. Profit."

327 "burnout syndrome": Howard Kurtz, "Top Editors Give Up Paper Chase," *WP,* Feb. 15, 1995.

327 The *Tribune* likened Gannett: Tim Jones, "When Headlines, Bottom Lines Bump," *Chicago Tribune,* Feb. 17, 1995.

327 *American Journalism Review:* John Morton, "Are Bean Counters Taking Over?," *AJR,* April 1995.

327 "If I'm so optimistic": Geneva Overholser, "Editor's Job: Great Demands vs. Rich Rewards," *Des Moines Register,* Feb. 19, 1995.

328 Within a month: Howard Kurtz, "Ex–Des Moines Editor Is Named Post Ombudsman," April 4, 1995; "Geneva Overholser Takes Job with Washington Post," *Des Moines Register,* April 4, 1995; "Ex-editor Named Ombudsman," *NYT,* April 5, 1995.

328 In June 1995: "Former Register Editor Seeks to End Marriage," *Des Moines Register,* June 9, 1995.

328 "Because I'm a loudmouth": Alicia C. Shepard, "Geneva Talks," *AJR,* Sept. 1995.

328 It quoted Overholser: Thomas A. Fogarty, "Personal Reasons Played a Role in Editor's Departure," *Des Moines Register,* Sept. 26, 1995.

328 Three days later, with a thumbnail: Patrick M. Reilly, "Nothing Stings Like a Spurned Employer with a Printing Press," *WSJ,* Sept. 29, 1995.

329 "none of that holds": Geneva Overholser, "When the Tables Are Turned," *WP,* Oct. 1, 1995, and "Regretting the Quote on 'Personal Life,'" *Des Moines Register,* Oct. 3, 1995.

329 "What happened in Des Moines": Overholser, interview by author, New York City, Oct. 26, 2021; Len Downie, email exchange with author, March 17, 2022.

329 "a new approach and a new mindset": Harlan, "Role Models in Transition," 39.

329 The story named sixteen: "Lelyveld of the Times Is Named Managing Editor as Gelb Retires"; "Times Names Editors to Senior Posts," *NYT,* July 14, 1993.

330 That brought Suzanne Daley: Suzanne Daley, email exchange with author, May 23, 2022.

330 "one of the strongest reporters": Roberts, telephone interview by author, May 26, 2022.

330 Swarns next went to Washington: Rachel L. Swarns, *American Tapestry: The Story of the Black, White, and Multiracial Ancestors of Michelle Obama* (New York: HarperCollins, 2013).

330 And yet, significantly: On the editorial page side, Charlotte Curtis, the paper's formidable women's page editor from 1965 to 1974, made the masthead when she ran the op-ed page, from 1974 to 1982, carrying the title of associate editor. But this was not a news-side appointment.

330 Lee, when asked long after: Lee, telephone interview by author, Sept. 12

and 20, 2021; Sulzberger, telephone interviews by author, Oct. 27, 2021, and subsequent email exchanges.

331 Golden, adjusting: Soma Golden Behr, email exchange with author, March 2, 2022. (Career path aside, on hearing her response, March 10, 2022, Lelyveld, in a brief in-person exchange, indicated he thought Golden might have had this potential. Lee thought the same.)

331 *Quill* did list: Harlan, "Role Models in Transition." Among the women in upper but not uppermost management cited in the *Quill* piece were Barbara Gutierrez, managing editor of *El Nuevo Herald* in Miami; Ann Marie Lipinski, then managing editor of the *Chicago Tribune;* and Monica Lozano-Centanino, associate publisher and editor of *La Opinión* in Los Angeles. Lesley Stahl was still at CBS News on *60 Minutes,* and the *LAT* could count three women in senior positions: Narda Zacchino, associate editor; Carol Stogsdill, senior editor; and Karen Wada, assistant managing editor. Joan Motyka, the reporter recruitment manager at *The New York Times,* pointed out how many more women were "in the pipeline," "coming up" at the *Times* than ever before.

331 "very much bone and muscle": Ibid. Other women the article named who were in top positions by 1995 were Jennifer Allen, publisher of *The Ironton Tribune* in Ohio; Sandra Rowe, executive editor of the Portland *Oregonian;* Betty Liddick, executive editor of the Stockton *Record* in California; Karin Winner, editor of *The San Diego Union-Tribune;* Sharon Rosenhause, managing editor of the *SF Examiner;* and Margaret Downing, managing editor of the *Clarion-Ledger* in Jackson, Mississippi.

331 "My sense is like Jill's": Abramson and Mayer, email exchanges with author, May 19, 2022.

331 "Girls don't do throw weight": Mayer, email exchange with author, Nov. 3, 2021. Anecdote first suggested in Sarah Cristobal, "In Conversation with Julie K. Brown and Jane Mayer, Two Reporters Exposing Corruption All the Way to the Top," *InStyle,* July 24, 2019.

332 Phillips, fired in 2002: Keith J. Kelly, "Ex-editor Claims Bias at Journal," *NY Post,* July 2, 2004; Richard Prince, "Suing the Wall Street Journal," *Journal-isms,* Aug. 22, 2011, and "Black Women's Daily Indignities," *Journal-isms,* March 30, 2017.

332 In 1995, Gail Collins: "Times Names a Columnist," *NYT,* June 15, 1999.

332 "strong eye for talent": Oreskes, email exchange with author, May 18, 2022.

332 "In all three jobs": Linda Fannin, "NY Times Paris Bureau Chief Ascribes Job to Climate," *Austin American-Statesman,* Nov. 13, 1974. Separate author email exchanges with Janny Scott, Lelyveld, Sulzberger, May 19, 2022,

and with Oreskes, May 18, 2022, and numerous telephone exchanges with Alison Smale, 2019–22.

332 Abramson responded: Abramson, telephone interview by author, Oct. 22, 2021; Baum, telephone interview by author, March 5, 2022. First reported in Howard Kurtz, "Jill Abramson: New York Times' Executive Editor on How to Stop the Brain Drain," *Daily Beast*, updated July 13, 2017.

332 A *Village Voice* writer: Cynthia Cotts, "Press Clips: Jill of All Trades," *Village Voice*, March 9, 1999.

333 Much of Abramson's management: Abramson, email interview by author, Oct. 23, 2021.

333 Her promotion: "Times Appoints 2 Editors to Senior News Positions," *NYT*, Dec. 5, 2000; Paul D. Colford, "E-Editor at Times," *NY Daily News*, Dec. 5, 2000; Howard Kurtz, "New York Times Ventures into TV News, Programming," *WP*, Dec. 5, 2000.

333 In a lengthy look: Ken Auletta, "The Howell Doctrine," *New Yorker*, June 10, 2002; Howard Kurtz, "The Times, a-Changing; Howell Raines Shakes Up His Staff," *WP*, June 3, 2002; Kurtz, "Jill Abramson: New York Times' Executive Editor on How to Stop the Brain Drain."

333 Krenek's elevation: Marilyn W. Thompson, "In the Maelstrom," *AJR*, Dec. 1, 1998.

334 At the century's close: The NYU professor Mitchell Stephens conceived of the project and chaired the effort, this time and twice again with "ten best" lists in the first two decades of the twenty-first century. See journalism.nyu.edu. The members of the 1999 committee, led by Stephens, were Madeleine Blais, Alan Brinkley, David Brinkley, Lydia Chavez, Karen Durbin, Clay Felker, Jeff Greenfield, Pete Hamill, Nancy Maynard, Mary McGrory, Eric Newton, Dorothy Rabinowitz, Gene Roberts, Morley Safer, David Shaw, George Will, and Ben Yagoda, and from the NYU faculty David Dent, Todd Gitlin, Lamar Graham, Brooke Kroeger, Susie Linfield, Michael Ludlum, Robert Manoff, Anne Matthews, Pamela Newkirk, Michael Norman, Richard Petrow, Mary Quigley, Marcia Rock, Jay Rosen, Stephen Solomon, Mitchell Stephens, Carol Sternhell, Jane Stone, and Ellen Willis.

Chapter 21. Assessment

337 At the start of the new millennium: "The Changing Newsroom: Meet the American Daily Newspaper of 2008," Pew Research Center, July 21, 2008.

338 These included the counting: With thanks to the NYU professor and press critic Jay Rosen for help with this list.

338 In the 2000s, the Pulitzer count: Of 130 named individual or team re-

cipients of Pulitzer prizes for journalism between 2000 and 2009, the number of women honored totaled 38, or 29 percent, the highest percentage for a given decade to date. See pulitzer.org.

338 In 2001, Gail Collins: Gelb, *City Room,* 526. In addition to Lee and Golden, four business-side women were on the list, led by Janet Robinson, by then promoted to company president and general manager. When Jill Abramson became one of two managing editors in 2003, the numbers remained the same because Lee retired. See, for example, comparative *NYT* mastheads of March 9, 2003, and of Oct. 1, 2003. Seven of twenty-two remained the count.

338 Kathleen Carroll: "The Associated Press Names Executive Editor," *Hattiesburg (Miss.) American,* May 25, 2002; AP, "AP Executive Editor Kathleen Carroll to Step Down as Year Ends," news release, July 20, 2016. A search of newspapers.com and ProQuest shows not more than a handful of papers picked up the announcement, compared with, say, the appointments of women to the executive editor job, many years later, at the *NYT* and the *WP.* Sally Buzbee was succeeded at the AP by a third woman, Julie Pace. See also "Sally Buzbee Named Associated Press Executive Editor," AP, Nov. 17, 2016; "Julie Pace Named New Associated Press Executive Editor," AP, Sept. 1, 2021. Compared with the coverage of AP appointments generally, the media attention paid to Buzbee's hiring by the *Post* was enormous.

338 As Buzbee started: Private email exchanges among former *WP* women seeking signatories to a draft letter to Buzbee, May 16, 2021.

338 Between 1970 and 2000: Mark Lisheron, "Riding High," *AJR,* March 2000. Despite the bad economic climate of the first decade of the twenty-first century, *The Oregonian,* with Sandy Rowe in charge from 1993 to 2010, was an unusually bright light. She had ample resources for a good part of the period and a talented staff that brimmed with energy and optimism. "All I had to do," Rowe told Lisheron, "was figure out a way not to screw it up."

339 Melissa Ludtke's 1978 lawsuit: Emma Baccellieri, "The Everlasting Legacy of Melissa Ludtke, Who Dared to Join the Boys Club of the Baseball Press," *Sports Illustrated,* Sept. 28, 2018. The *Sports Illustrated* managing editor was Bill Colson.

339 *Columbia Journalism Review:* Tracy McNamara, "'You're a Dumb Broad'—and That's Progress," *CJR,* Jan.–Feb. 2000. For profile information, see lesleyvisser.com. All of these Visser displays on her website among a total of twenty-two items that appear as her "Trailblazing Legacy of Firsts."

339 "I wasn't at the dawn": Sally Jenkins, "Who Let Them In?," *Sports Illustrated,* June 17, 1991. By 1990, Visser had left *The Boston Globe* for CBS,

where, after three years in which she covered major events in all sports, including the World Series, the network made her a regular presence on *NFL Today*, actually the second woman on the show since Phyllis George left back in 1984. When NFL television rights passed out of CBS's hands, Visser moved on to ABC Sports and then to ESPN, where she covered Super Bowls XXIX and XXXIV and got her regular assignment on *Monday Night Football*.

339 Rectification took another thirty years: Ahiza Garcia, "Meet the First Woman to Call an NFL Game in 30 Years," CNN Business, Sept. 11, 2017. This was when Beth Mowins landed that assignment from ESPN during a *Monday Night Football* doubleheader.

339 In 2006: CBS Sports, "Lesley Visser Previews Indianapolis-Tennessee Game with Visit with Titans Quarterback Vince Young for Week 13 of 'The NFL Today,' on Sunday, Dec. 3," press release, Nov. 29, 2006.

339 "She Made It" roster: Visser twice received Hall of Fame honors: one from the Sports Museum and one from the Pro Football Hall of Fame, which chose her for its Pete Rozelle Radio-Television Award.

339 "tripping over themselves": McNamara, "'You're a Dumb Broad.'"

340 "this unique bizarre thing": Ibid.

340 Harpaz, on the campaign trail: Andie Tucher, "Books: Move Over, Boys," *CJR*, Sept.–Oct. 2001. Tucher compared and contrasted the two books published more than thirty years apart. Unfortunately, with women dominant in the Clinton press corps, pack journalism and all its negatives still ruled the coverage. Tucher also said Harpaz missed the chance to emphasize the holistic approach to the profession that women were in a position to bring as wives and mothers who treated their work as one part of their lives, not life itself. Such a posture, Tucher argued, had the potential to make women more perceptive and understanding, less isolated, and thus better human beings who were better at their jobs.

340 The documentary *She Says:* See "PBS Dominates News and Documentary Emmys with 14 Awards," PBS Publicity, Sept. 11, 2002; see also imdb .com.

340 The ten women: Konner and Rick, *She Says*.

341 Carole Simpson was still: Ibid.; Mariya Mosely and Susan Schwartz, "Broadcast Legend Carole Simpson Reflects on Shaping History," ABC News, Feb. 8, 2021. Simpson remained the weekend anchor at ABC until 2003 and retired from the network three years later.

341 In the film: Konner and Rick, *She Says*. See also Audrey Edwards, "Seeing 20/20 with Deborah Roberts," *Essence*, March 2002. Simpson and the Atlanta-based Monica Kaufman, the first Black anchor at WSB-TV, inspired the career of Deborah Roberts, another high-powered Black

broadcaster, also in the weekend news anchor slot at ABC along with her correspondent post on the network's newsmagazine *20/20*. *Essence* magazine adoringly profiled her in 2002 as a "captivating blend of southern gentility and tough-minded professionalism," "a dark-skinned beauty in an industry that prefers its women fair, if not blond." Edwards made a point of explaining what women like Simpson, Kaufman, and Roberts had faced and overcome in the fiercely competitive atmosphere of television news "when we know who tends to succeed on such playing fields."

342 Dramatic gender imbalance: Geneva Overholser, "After 9/11: Where Are the Voices of Women? (Newspapers)," *CJR*, March–April 2002. By that point, Overholser was holding a named faculty chair at the Washington outpost of the University of Missouri journalism school and then went on to direct the journalism department at the University of Southern California, a position she held until 2013.

343 "These folks don't want": Ibid., citing Sharon Peters, "Gen X in the Newsroom: Expectations, Attitudes Don't Fit with Traditional Culture," Northwestern University Media Management Center.

343 Margaret Sullivan was prominent: Sullivan, telephone interview by author, July 5, 2021.

343 Sullivan's most pressing: Ibid. Also, "Sullivan Is Named Editor of the News," *Buffalo News*, Aug. 11, 1999; Sarah Lundy, "Orlando Sentinel Editor Charlotte Hall Retires," *Orlando Sentinel*, Sept. 1, 2010. In 2003, the Tribune Company, which still owned *Newsday* at the time, favored Howard Schneider over Hall for editor of *Newsday*, but moved Hall to *The Orlando Sentinel*, where she did get the top job in 2004.

344 Shortly before Hall's move: Mark Jurkowitz, "More Women in J-School Doesn't Translate into Jobs," *Boston Globe*, Aug. 27, 2003.

344 In 2003, Bill Keller: Keller and his team came to power in 2003, after the fabrication scandal of the young reporter Jayson Blair and the resignations in its wake of Howell Raines, who had been executive editor for only two years, and his managing editor, Gerald Boyd. Geddes held the deputy managing editor title through the successive editorships of Joe Lelyveld, Raines, and Lelyveld again in the immediate Raines aftermath. Keller's appointment of Abramson and Geddes as managing editors lasted all eight years of Keller's tenure.

344 "a rising star": Howard Kurtz, "Times Names Jill Abramson as News Managing Editor," *WP*, Aug. 1, 2003.

344 "to see where progress for women": Ellen Goodman, "Women and News: Expanding the News Audience, Increasing Political Participation, and Informing Citizens" (keynote speech, Joan Shorenstein Center

Conference on Press, Politics, and Public Policy, Nov. 29–30, 2007);
Goodman, email exchange with author, May 19, 2022.

345 *Politico* credited: Luke O'Brien, "How to Lose $100 Million: The Undoing
of Tina Brown," *Politico,* May–June 2014; Tina Brown, *The Diana Chronicles* (New York: Random House, 2007). In the five years between *Talk* and
The Daily Beast, Brown wrote a column for the Style section of the *WP*
for about a year and a half as she worked on the Diana book. A ProQuest
search shows columns under Brown's name on a range of topics appeared
regularly in the *WP* throughout 2004 and in all but the summer of 2005.
As the decade ended, Brown was engaged with her annual Women in
the World Summit, an ongoing for-profit venture, which declared as its
mission "to discover and amplify the unheard voices of global women
on the front lines of change. Women in the World shares unflinching
narratives that illuminate the long march for gender equality, shine a
light on places where women's voices are never heard, and celebrate the
women who live with courage and passion both in the spotlight and on
the margins."

345 Dana Priest and Anne Hull: Kroeger, *Undercover Reporting,* xiii, 3–7, 56,
188, 263–65, 293–94, 297, and notes.

346 But the composition of the Pulitzer board: In 2008, the woman board
members were Danielle Allen, a sociologist, and the journalists Amanda
Bennett, Joann Byrd, Kathleen Carroll, and Ann Marie Lipinski. The
women on the board in 1982 were the University of Chicago president
Hanna Gray and *The Christian Science Monitor*'s Charlotte Saikowski;
pulitzer.org.

346 In 2009, Jessica Bennett: Lynn Povich's *Good Girls Revolt* would not be
published until 2012; its one-season television series for Amazon Prime,
which prompted renewed attention, was released in 2016.

346 Bennett, Jesse Ellison: Jessica Bennett, Jesse Ellison, Sarah Ball, "Are We
There Yet?," *Newsweek,* March 19, 2010; Povich, *Good Girls Revolt,* ix–xx;
Maria Shriver, "The Battle of the Sexes Is Over," *Forbes,* Oct. 16, 2009.

347 At almost the same time: "Women in Leadership: Journalism," National
Archives, March 15, 2010, youtube.com.

347 Diane Rehm spoke: See also Marsha Mercer, "Americans Hardly Flinch
Now at Electing a Man of Lusty Appetites," *Tampa Tribune,* Dec. 1, 1996.

348 The figures for NPR: Alicia C. Shepard, "Where Are the Women?," NPR,
April 2, 2010. The "constructed week" sampling technique reviewed
NPR shows from April 13, 2009, to Jan. 10, 2010.

349 In 2010, women claimed: For the full list, see "Top Ten Works of Journalism of the Decade, 2000–2009," Arthur L. Carter Journalism Institute, New York University, journalism.nyu.edu. The women honored for

the decade were Adrian Nicole LeBlanc for *Random Family: Love, Drugs, Trouble, and Coming of Age in the Bronx;* Jane Mayer for *The Dark Side: The Inside Story of How the War on Terror Turned into a War on American Ideals;* Barbara Ehrenreich for *Nickel and Dimed: On (Not) Getting By in America;* and Anne Hull and Dana Priest of the *WP,* with the photographer Michel du Cille, for their Walter Reed Army Medical Center investigation.

Chapter 22. The More Things Change

350 *The Guardian:* Annalena McAfee, "Women on the Front Line," *Guardian,* April 15, 2011. McAfee highlights Margaret Fuller, Jessie White, Anna Northend Benjamin, Cora Stewart Taylor (a.k.a. Imogene Carter a.k.a. Cora Crane), Mary Roberts Rinehart, Nellie Bly, Ishbel Ross, Martha Gellhorn, Clare Hollingworth, Virginia Cowles, Marguerite Higgins, Janet Flanner, and, more recently, Anna Politkovskaya, Lara Logan, and Lynsey Addario. See also Susan Douglas, *Enlightened Sexism: The Seductive Message That Feminism's Work Is Done* (New York: Henry Holt, 2010), which points out the cognitive dissonance created by television's alternating depictions of women, some in high-powered men's jobs and others who are "shallow and materialistic," "obsessed with guys they barely knew, involved in catfights." See also Sarah Seltzer, "USA: Are Women on Prime Time TV Really Prime?," Women's Feature Service, New Delhi, June 6, 2011, which mentions Barbara J. Berg, *Sexism in America: Alive, Well, and Ruining Our Future* (Chicago: Chicago Review Press, 2009), and Jessica Valenti, *The Purity Myth: How America's Obsession with Virginity Is Hurting Young Women* (New York: Seal Press, 2009).

350 In the early part: Margaret Sullivan told me that most of the people of color she brought on at *The Buffalo News* were women. "I'm not sure why that was," she said. "When I brought Dawn Bracely from the Rochester paper to be an editorial writer, she gave our board (and community) not only her perspective as a Black person but as a woman. And she was the first woman of color to join the board; she remains there today, doing important work. Similarly, when I promoted Lisa Wilson to be executive sports editor, she made two kinds of history for us: the first woman and the first Black person to run the sports department—that combination was a rarity in the country. I'll add that she was clearly the best candidate, did an excellent job, was beloved in the department, and has gone on to a top position at *The Athletic.* She also is a past president of APSE." Sullivan, email exchange with author, Feb. 25, 2021.

350 "when sophisticated reporting": "Media and Tech News," civilrights.org, Oct. 6, 2010.

350 The appointment received little: Ross called her new firm Boss Ross

Media LLC. Sonya Ross LinkedIn curriculum vitae: linkedin.com. Also see Branden Campbell, "AP, Ethnicity Editor Strike Deal on Race Bias Suit," *Law360,* March 29, 2019, and "Ross Leaves AP, Settles Lawsuit, Starts Project," *Tennessee Tribune,* Sept. 26, 2019. Ross had accused an unnamed Washington bureau chief of discriminating against her and of not being given a promised raise when she took on the race and ethnicity responsibilities. She also charged that the company took retaliatory action after she sued.

351 In fact, the only news: Jeremy W. Peters, "Abramson Named Executive Editor at the Times," *NYT,* June 2, 2011; Patricia Sullivan, "Jill Abramson—a Breakthrough at the NY Times, Decades in the Making," Women's Media Center News & Features, June 8, 2011.

351 Thirteen years had passed: Marilyn W. Thompson, "In the Maelstrom," *AJR,* Dec. 1, 1998.

351 Ann Marie Lipinski: Steve Rhodes, "Ann Marie's World," *Chicago Magazine,* April 2, 2001. At forty-five, Lipinski became the *Tribune*'s editor in Jan. 2001. Both Krenek and Lipinski are two years Abramson's junior.

351 In 2006, Abramson herself: Jill Abramson, "When Will We Stop Saying 'First Woman to ——'?," *NYT,* April 9, 2006.

351 Remember Clifton Daniel: Robertson, *Girls in the Balcony,* 238.

351 "Anything that happens": Abramson, interview by author, Oct. 22, 2021.

351 With news of Abramson's appointment: See Sullivan, "Jill Abramson— a Breakthrough at the NY Times." For the earlier *Newsweek* suit, the women's first attorney, Eleanor Holmes Norton, stepped aside to accept the mayor's appointment as chair of the New York City Commission on Human Rights, and Rabb took her place. See Povich, *Good Girls Revolt,* 105.

351 Betsy Wade: The *Times* suit was filed under Wade's married name, *Elizabeth W. Boylan v. New York Times Company.* See "Women Charge the Times with Sex Discrimination," *NYT,* Nov. 8, 1974. Named were Elizabeth Boylan (a.k.a. Betsy Wade), Louise Carini, Joan Cook, Nancy Davis, Grace Glueck, and Andrea Skinner.

351 "very long, thin pipeline": Sullivan, "Jill Abramson—a Breakthrough at the NY Times."

351 Susan Chira, the *Times*'s foreign editor: Ken Auletta, "Changing Times," *New Yorker,* Oct. 17, 2011.

352 all the key people: Abramson, email exchange with author, Oct. 23, 2021. Abramson's managerial positions: *Legal Times,* editor, 1984–87; *WSJ,* deputy bureau chief, 1993–97; *NYT,* Washington editor and then Washington bureau chief, 1998–2003; *NYT,* managing editor, 2003–11.

352 Certainly, the publisher: Jill Abramson, *Merchants of Truth: The Business of News and the Fight for Facts* (New York: Simon & Schuster, 2019), 194–224.

352 "I was seen as playing favorites": Ibid., 199.

352 "heiress apparent": Gabriel Sherman, "Times Two: Jill Abramson, the Times' First Heiress Apparent," *NY,* Oct. 4, 2010.

352 She had been successful: Abramson, interview by and email exchanges with author, Oct. 22, 23, 31, 2021; Amy Chozick, "Times Chief Is to Retire at Year-End," *NYT,* Dec. 15, 2011.

352 He ticked off her faults: Abramson, *Merchants of Truth,* 216.

352 those who had been friends: See ibid., 200–201; Abramson, interview by and email exchanges with author; Sulzberger, informal conversations with author, 2021 and years previous.

353 It was somewhat curious: Sulzberger, telephone interview by author, Oct. 27, 2021. Masthead, *NYT,* May 1, 2014, shows Bill Keller, executive editor; Jill Abramson and John M. Geddes, managing editors; William E. Schmidt, deputy managing editor; and assistant managing editors Dean Baquet, Tom Bodkin, Susan Edgerley, Glenn Kramon, Gerald Marzorati, Michele McNally, and Jim Roberts.

353 "'Tough and abrasive?'": Ben McGrath, "Times Talk," *New Yorker,* May 19, 2014.

353 When Sulzberger asked Abramson: Sulzberger, telephone interview by author, Oct. 27, 2021. In *Merchants of Truth,* 201, Abramson wrote that she readily agreed because she loved Baquet, but had in mind and first suggested Richard L. Berke, who had been her deputy when she was Washington bureau chief. In the months before her promotion, women held four of twelve positions on the news section masthead: Arthur Ochs Sulzberger Jr., publisher; Bill Keller, executive editor; Abramson and John Geddes, managing editors; William E. Schmidt, deputy managing editor; and, as assistant managing editors, Dean Baquet, Tom Bodkin, Susan Edgerly, Trish Hall, Glenn Kramon, Gerald Marzorati, and Michele McNally. For the opinion pages, Andrew Rosenthal was editorial page editor and Carla Anne Robbins and David Shipley were his deputies.

353 The commentariat: Abramson, telephone interview by author, Oct. 22, 2021. See, for example, Peters, "Abramson Named Executive Editor at the Times"; John Hudson, "Meet Jill Abramson: The New Editor of the New York Times," *Atlantic* via *Wire,* June 2, 2011; Jason Horowitz and Paul Farhi, "Turning a Page at the New York Times," *WP,* June 3, 2011; Jane Mayer, "Abramson and Anita Hill," *New Yorker,* June 3, 2011; Auletta, "Changing Times"; Dana Goldstein, "Jill Abramson, Feminist

Journalist," *Nation,* June 2, 2011; Ed Pilkington, "Jill Abramson: I'm a Battle-Scarred Veteran," *Guardian,* June 7, 2011; Kurtz, "Jill Abramson: New York Times' Executive Editor on How to Stop the Brain Drain."

353 For *The New Yorker:* Mayer, "Abramson and Anita Hill." Mayer added, "In her one bylined piece in *The New Yorker*"—meaning the review they cowrote of David Brock's Anita Hill takedown, which he later self-condemned as a "'witches' brew' of deception"—"readers got a glimpse of a future top editor at the *Times* intent on defending not Anita Hill but journalism itself."

353 Ken Auletta: Abramson, interview by author, Oct. 22, 2021.

353 His piece ran six weeks: Auletta, "Changing Times"; Jill Abramson, *The Puppy Diaries: Raising a Dog Named Scout* (New York: St. Martin's Griffin, 2012).

354 Abramson, on Baquet's suggestion: Chira, after five years in Tokyo and before she became foreign editor in 2004, served as education correspondent in 1990; deputy foreign editor from 1997 to 1999; editor of the "Week in Review" from 1999 to 2002; and editorial director of book development from 2002 to 2004.

354 one of six assistant: Abramson, interview by author, Oct. 22, 2021; Mayer, "Abramson and Anita Hill"; Auletta, "Changing Times"; Peters, "New Editor of the Times."

354 Michele McNally: Sam Roberts, "Michele McNally, Who Elevated Times Photography, Dies at 66," *NYT,* March 1, 2022; "Michele McNally Is Retiring from the New York Times," *NPPA: The Voice of Visual Journalists,* Feb. 22, 2018.

354 Susan Edgerley: Around the same time, Edgerley, a former metro editor, was taken off the masthead after six years, first to become an aide-de-camp to Abramson for six months until Abramson settled on a good next post for her, one Edgerley liked. She became dining editor, capitalizing on her interest in food, wine, and restaurants, a side interest she had developed over the years. When she was assistant managing editor, her charge had been news hiring, training, and development and the early uphill efforts to integrate the *Times*'s then totally separate print and web reports, a role that diminished as the newsroom edged closer to full embrace of its new digital-first reality. Edgerley, telephone interview by author, Nov. 12, 2021; masthead and Edgerley's résumé on LinkedIn, linkedin.com. Also, "The New York Times Chooses New Editor for the Metro Section," *NYT,* Oct. 17, 2003; "Talk to the Newsroom: Assistant Managing Editor Susan Edgerley," *NYT,* May 5, 2008, which notes her promotion to AME in 2006.

354 "Divine Sisterhood": "The Divine Sisterhood: All Hail 40 Women Who

Changed the Media Business in the Past 40 Years," *CJR,* July–Aug. 2012. The names on the list: Jill Abramson, Christiane Amanpour, Tina Brown, Betsy Carter, Connie Chung, Gail Collins, Katie Couric, Christine Craft, Anthea Disney, Nora Ephron, Arianna Huffington, Charlayne Hunter-Gault, Molly Ivins, Dorothy Kalins, Geraldine Laybourne, Frances Lear, Ellen Levine, Carol Loomis, Susan Lyne, Rebecca MacKinnon, Sonia Nazario, Martha Nelson, Asra Q. Nomani, Peggy Orenstein, Geneva Overholser, Lynn Povich and the other women who sued *Newsweek* for sex discrimination, Anna Quindlen, Maria Elena Salinas, Diane Sawyer, Liz Smith, Lesley Stahl, Susan Stamberg, Gloria Steinem and the *Ms.* crew, Martha Stewart, Kara Swisher, Betsy Wade and the women who sued the *NYT* for sex discrimination, Barbara Walters, Ruth Whitney, Oprah Winfrey, and Susan Zirinsky.

354 known as Z: Caroline Que, "Taking CBS News to 'a Better Place,'" *NYT,* June 17, 2019; David Bauder, "Zirinsky Leaving as CBS News Chief, amid Industry Change," AP, April 14, 2021. Zirinsky remained with the network with a producing deal after her run in full charge.

354 That fall, *The Buffalo News:* Gene Warner, "Sullivan Is Leaving News for Post at N.Y. Times, Will Be Public Editor; Legacy Here Notes," *Buffalo News,* July 17, 2012; Sullivan, interview by author, New York City, Oct. 18, 2021; Abramson, email exchange with author, Oct. 31, 2021. In Abramson's words, "I picked her."

355 Sullivan had hardly warmed: Margaret Sullivan, "Times Must Aggressively Cover Mark Thompson's Role in BBC's Troubles," *NYT,* Oct. 24, 2012; Joe Coscarelli, "Incoming New York Times CEO Gets Cold Welcome from Public Editor," *Intelligencer,* Oct. 23, 2012; "NYT Editor Questions Ex–BBC Boss Thompson's 'Integrity to Be CEO' After Pedophile Scandal," *Asian News International,* Oct. 25, 2012; Richard Reeves, "Will the Times Take Us to War?," *Charleston Sunday Gazette,* July 6, 2014.

355 "Simple, really": Jay Rosen, email exchange with author, Nov. 14, 2021.

355 "troubled history": Margaret Sullivan, "Covering New War, in Shadow of Old One," *NYT,* June 29, 2014.

355 "There was this prurient": Noreen Malone, "Slow Burn, Episode 7, The Road to the Iraq War," *Slate,* June 10, 2021; Judith Miller, *The Story: A Reporter's Journey* (New York: Simon & Schuster, 2015), 89.

356 It bothered James Risen: Malone, "Slow Burn, Episode 7."

356 "Judy was a very, very": Engelberg, telephone interview by author, Nov. 29, 2021.

356 Margaret Sullivan won plaudits: Reeves, "Will the Times Take Us to War?" Reeves wrote, "The *Times* may be the best newspaper in the world, it may try like hell to avoid being used by people in power, but there is a

reason that many people outside the United States consider it the official voice of the United States. That power, which is very real, is the reason Sullivan's candor is so important right now."

356 She also pointed to the lack: Sullivan, "Covering New War."

356 "I think it's not an exaggeration": Jill Abramson and Ken Auletta, New Yorker Festival, Oct. 5, 2013, newyorker.com.

356 Auletta did not ask: Keith Kelly, "Tricky Times Target," *NY Post*, Jan. 25, 2013.

357 the senior staff members: Abramson, *Merchants of Truth*, 215.

357 About halfway into: Dylan Byers, "Turbulence at the Times," *Politico*, April 23, 2013.

358 "not exactly the image": Abramson, *Merchants of Truth*, 211.

358 The story did include: Byers, "Turbulence at the Times"; Abramson, *Merchants of Truth*, 211.

358 attacked it as a "hatchet job": Emily Bell, "Jill Abramson and the Wholly Sexist Narrative of the Woman in Power," *Guardian*, April 24, 2013.

359 "Likability": Abramson and Auletta, New Yorker Festival.

359 Three months later: Margaret Sullivan, "The Times, from the Top: Looking Ahead," *NYT,* Jan. 11, 2014.

359 "point of pride": On that date, Jan. 11, 2014, the news-side masthead of the *NYT* read: Jill Abramson, executive editor; Dean Baquet, managing editor; Tom Bodkin, Janet Elder, and Lawrence Ingrassia, deputy managing editors; Susan Chira, Rebecca L. Corbett, Ian Fisher, Michelle McNally, and Matthew Purdy, assistant managing editors.

359 She named three other women: Pamela Paul as editor of the *NYT Book Review* in April, Alison Mitchell as editor of the national desk in July, and Carolyn Ryan as Washington bureau chief in Nov. See Andrew Beaujon, "New York Times Names Pamela Paul Editor of Book Review," Poynter, April 9, 2013; Christine Haughney, "New York Times Names a New National Editor," *NYT,* July 12, 2013.

359 Abramson had encouraged Jodi Kantor: Jodi Kantor, email exchange with author, Jan. 3, 2022.

359 Kantor's effort: Jodi Kantor, "Harvard Business School Case Study," *NYT,* Sept. 7, 2013; "Working Anything but 9 to 5," *NYT,* Aug. 13, 2014. The latter was published after Abramson's departure.

360 "scoop machine": Abramson, *Merchants of Truth*, 210–11; Kantor, email exchange with author, Jan. 3, 2022.

360 Sullivan asked: Sullivan, "Times, from the Top."

360 mentioned the recent hires: The third hire was Matt Apuzzo from the AP.

360 That year's personnel evaluation: Abramson, telephone interview by author, Oct. 22, 2021.

360 "In shockingly personal terms": Abramson, *Merchants of Truth*, 216.

360 By April: Abramson, telephone interview by author, Oct. 22, 2021; Sulzberger, telephone interview by author, Oct. 27, 2021.

360 Margaret Sullivan devoted: Margaret Sullivan, "Still Talking About It: 'Where Are the Women?,'" *NYT,* May 12, 2014. See also "The Status of Women in the U.S. Media 2014," WMC Reports, Women's Media Center, Feb. 18, 2014, womensmediacenter.com.

361 "Women are running things": Sullivan, "Still Talking About It."

362 "Times Ousts Jill Abramson": David Carr and Ravi Somaiya, "Times Ousts Jill Abramson as Executive Editor, Elevating Dean Baquet," *NYT,* May 14, 2014.

362 "the idea of having a true partner": Abramson, *Merchants of Truth,* 220–21.

362 According to Carr: Carr and Somaiya, "Times Ousts Jill Abramson."

363 Friday morning, May 9: Abramson, *Merchants of Truth,* 220–21.

363 Over the coming days, speculation mounted: Susan B. Glasser, "Editing While Female," *Politico,* May 16, 2014; Rebecca Traister, "I Sort of Hope We Find Out That Jill Abramson Was Robbing the Cash Register," *New Republic,* May 15, 2014; Kristen Hare, "'Brilliant,' 'Respected,' and 'Uniquely Powerful': Some Different Words About Jill Abramson," Poynter, May 15, 2014; Tracie Powell, "A Complicated First: A Black Editor Takes the Helm at the Gray Lady," *AllDigitocracy,* May 15, 2014.

363 This poured more fuel: Amy Joyce, "Jill Abramson's Dismissal Reignites Equal Pay Discussion," *WP,* May 15, 2014.

363 Sulzberger maintains: Sulzberger, interview by author, Oct. 27, 2021. For Abramson's account of the compensation issues, see Abramson, *Merchants of Truth,* 217.

363 Adding to the cacophony: David Carr, "Abramson's Exit at the Times Puts Tensions on Display," *NYT,* May 18, 2014.

364 In the New York newsroom: Author interviews with a *Times* colleague of Abramson's who did not wish to be named and with Ethan Bronner, April 11, 2022, and a subsequent email exchange, May 22, 2022.

364 "lost the support": Carr, "Abramson's Exit."

364 "Mom's badass new hobby": Cornelia Griggs (@cornelialg), Twitter, May 15, 2014, 12:14 p.m.

364 "How did our workplace": Carr, "Abramson's Exit."

364 In the following days: A sampling of the numerous stories that followed the *Times*'s announcement of Abramson's ouster: Ken Auletta, "Why Jill Abramson Was Fired," *New Yorker,* May 14, 2014; Erik Wemple, "Jill

Abramson 'Unexpectedly' Out at New York Times," *WP,* May 14, 2014; Brian Stelter, "Why Did the New York Times Really Sack Its Editor?," CNN, May 15, 2014; Leslie Kaufman and Ravi Somaiya, "Times Seeks to Reassure Its Staff," *NYT,* May 16, 2014; Ken Kurson, "Source Confirms Abramson's Higher Profile Annoyed Sulzberger," *NY Observer,* May 16, 2014; Kara Bloomgarden-Smoke, "Jill Abramson's Newsroom Management Style Wasn't a Surprise," *NY Observer,* May 15, 2014; Traister, "I Sort of Hope We Find Out That Jill Abramson Was Robbing the Cash Register"; Hare, "'Brilliant,' 'Respected,' and 'Uniquely Powerful'"; Joyce, "Jill Abramson's Dismissal Reignites Equal Pay Discussion"; Glasser, "Editing While Female"; Monica Anderson, "As Jill Abramson Exits the NY Times, a Look at How Women Are Faring in Newsrooms," Pew Research Center, May 16, 2014; Geneva Overholser, "Abramson and Sulzberger: The Two Who Couldn't Tango," genevaoverholser.com, May 17, 2014; Carr, "Abramson's Exit"; McGrath, "Times Talk"; Ken Auletta, "Summing Up the Firing of Jill Abramson," *New Yorker,* May 26, 2014; Nikki Usher, "It's Not Just Jill Abramson: Women Everywhere Are Getting Pushed Out of Journalism," *WP,* May 28, 2014.

364 In Auletta's summation: Auletta, "Summing Up the Firing of Jill Abramson."

364 Abramson was conscious: Abramson, *Merchants of Truth,* 197.

365 "I was a less than stellar": Ibid., 224.

365 "I never said to anyone": David Folkenflik, "'Period of Turmoil' Preceded Abramson Firing, Says Top Editor at the 'Times,'" *Morning Edition,* NPR, May 29, 2014.

366 "Dean," she said: Abramson, telephone interview by author, Oct. 22, 2021, and subsequent emails, Oct. 23 and 31, 2021.

366 The story reverberated: Anderson, "As Jill Abramson Exits the NY Times, a Look at How Women Are Faring in Newsrooms."

366 In 2004, the number: Anna Griffin, "Where Are the Women?," *Nieman Reports,* Sept. 11, 2014. With Abramson gone, the three were Debby Henley at *Newsday,* Nancy Barnes at *The Houston Chronicle,* and Kathy Best at *The Seattle Times.*

366 The writer did note: Reference is to Overholser, "After 9/11."

367 Of the millennials: Griffin, "Where Are the Women?"

367 "two talented journalists": Carr, "Abramson's Exit."

Epilogue: #MeToo, You, Too

368 Three years into: Carly Sitrin, "Narrative Conference Focuses on Long-Form Journalism," BU News Service, April 2, 2016; Andrea Asuaje,

"Talese Stumbles over Question on Female Journalists," BU News Service, April 2, 2016. HBO released the documentary *Everything Is Copy—Nora Ephron: Scripted and Unscripted,* written and directed by her son Jacob Bernstein, 2015, air date Oct. 2, 2016, hbo.com.

368 He did not mention: Gay Talese, "Frank Sinatra Has a Cold," *Esquire,* April 1966; and, about Pauline Frederick, Talese, "Perils of Pauline."

368 "This keynote": Amy Littlefield (@amylittlefield), Twitter, April 2, 2016, 12:44 p.m.

369 "Gay Talese was all good": Hannah-Jones's tweets no longer retrievable were screen captured in Sridhar Pappu, "Gay Talese Goes Through the Twitter Wringer," *NYT,* April 6, 2016.

369 Michelle García: Michelle García, "Me and Gay Talese in the Middle," *Guernica,* April 12, 2016.

369 Among journalists: "Oregonian Reporter Joins ProPublica's Newsroom," ProPublica, Dec. 16, 2011; Engelberg, telephone interview by author, Nov. 29, 2021.

370 Engelberg remembered: Engelberg, telephone interview by author, Nov. 29, 2021. For Hannah-Jones's reportage during her ProPublica years, see propublica.org.

370 "a reporter's reporter": Jake Silverstein, "Nikole Hannah-Jones Joins the New York Times Magazine," NY Times Company Announcement, April 1, 2015.

370 "chronicling the persistence": "Nikole Hannah-Jones," MacArthur Foundation, macfound.org.

370 Another decision at the *Times:* Margaret Sullivan, "In a Time of Racial Turmoil, Why Change Course on Covering Race?," *NYT,* Jan. 29, 2015; Chris Ip, "What Will Happen to the New York Times' Race Beat?," *CJR,* Jan. 28, 2015.

370 Tanzina Vega: "On Creating a Race Beat," *NYT,* July 8, 2014, reports that the beat was created "six months ago"; Abramson, email exchange with author, March 19, 2022. The editors moved Vega to metro to cover the Bronx courts. She resigned soon after.

370 Baquet and Susan Chira: Sullivan, "In a Time of Racial Turmoil."

371 In March 2015: Jessica Bennett, "Monica Lewinsky Is Back, but This Time It's on Her Terms," *NYT,* March 19, 2015.

371 "It prompted what we are now": Jessica Bennett, telephone interview by and subsequent email exchanges with author, Nov. 19, 20, 21, 2021.

371 Through the grapevine: Ibid.

371 In an interview: Laura Bult, "Gay Talese Couldn't Name a Female Journalist of His Generation Who Inspired Him at Talk, Sparking Outrage

on Social Media," *NY Daily News,* April 3, 2016. The faculty member, Mitchell Zuckoff, had been onstage with Talese, along with the college's dean, Tom Fiedler.

371 "I'm talking about ancient history": Ryu Spaeth, "Gay Talese Says Twitter Is 'Wicked, Restless,'" *New Republic,* April 7, 2016.

371 That history, for Talese: Buchanan citation, Pulitzer Prize for general reporting, 1986: pulitzer.org.

371 On Monday, April 4: Katie Roiphe, "Gay Talese, the Art of Nonfiction No. 2," *Paris Review,* no. 189 (Summer 2009).

371 He also mentioned: Shirley Leung, "Gay Talese on Lack of Female Role Models: 'I Misunderstood the Question,'" *Boston Globe,* April 4, 2016.

371 "I'm just getting started": Susan Orlean (@susanorlean), Twitter, April 4, 2016, 10:43 a.m.

371 The *Globe* column came down hard: Leung, "Gay Talese on Lack of Female Role Models."

372 "He asked again": Amy Littlefield, "Meet the Poet Who Inadvertently Took Down Gay Talese, and the Journalist Talese Insulted," *Rewire News Group,* April 5, 2016; and Littlefield, telephone interview by author, March 18, 2022.

372 "résumé check": Touré, "The 'Resume Check': On Gay Talese, Racism, and Sexism in the Press Room," *HuffPost,* April 9, 2016.

372 As Hannah-Jones told Littlefield: Littlefield, "Meet the Poet"; Littlefield, telephone interview by author.

372 As the reception ended: Littlefield, "Meet the Poet"; Littlefield, telephone interview by author.

372 García, as a conference speaker: García, "Me and Gay Talese." Author email exchanges with Michelle García, Aug. 21, 2022.

373 The tweets, the stories, the blog posts: For example, Ellen McCarthy, "Gay Talese Can't Name a Single Female Writer Who Inspired Him. Thankfully, Twitter Has a Few Suggestions," *WP,* April 2, 2016; Dayna Evans, "Gay Talese Asks Prominent New York Times Magazine Writer if She's Off to Get Her Nails Done," *Cut,* April 6, 2016; L. V. Anderson, "Gay Talese Demands to Know How a Black *New York Times* Staff Writer Got Her Job," *Slate,* April 6, 2016; Spaeth, "Gay Talese Says Twitter Is 'Wicked, Restless'"; Ricky Riley, "White Veteran Journalist Asks Award-Winning Black Journalist About Her Credentials," *Atlanta Black Star,* April 8, 2016; Touré, "'Resume Check'"; Richard Prince, "Baquet: 'Flawed' Story on Gay Talese Points to Diversity Issues at New York Times," *Root,* April 11, 2016.

373 To a journalist reporting: Laura Hazard Owen, "Promoting Based on

Potential: How the Atlantic Is Putting a Lot More Women in Charge," Nieman Lab, June 6, 2019.

374 "Has anyone told Jeffrey": Andi Zeisler (@andizeisler), Twitter, June 6, 2019.

374 In Talese's case: Pappu, "Gay Talese Goes Through the Twitter Wringer."

374 Talese said his now infamous: Recall the "crusading cupcakes" in Red Smith, "Move Over, Lady Godiva," *Boston Globe,* Oct. 17, 1954.

374 He echoed the list: Pappu, "Gay Talese Goes Through the Twitter Wringer."

374 Gail Sheehy: Bellows, *Last Editor,* 83.

374 Consider the superb: Gay Talese, *The Kingdom and the Power: Behind the Scenes at "The New York Times": The Institution That Influences the World* (New York: Random House, 1966). A word search for the word "woman" or "women" is revealing, as are name searches for editors and reporters of any gender at the time.

374 On Thursday, Margaret Sullivan: Margaret Sullivan, "A 'Flawed Story' on Gay Talese, and 'Clumsy' Handling of Race and Gender," *NYT,* April 7, 2016.

375 "Too often," he wrote: Ibid.

375 At around the same time: "The New York Times Is Looking for an Editor to Cover Gender," NY Times Interactive Job Listings, Aug. 26, 2016.

375 In the spring of 2016: Pulitzer Prizes, 2016, pulitzer.org.

375 In May, Megan: Michael Barbaro and Megan Twohey, "Crossing the Line: How Donald Trump Behaved with Women in Private," *NYT,* May 14, 2016.

375 For Twohey: Jodi Kantor and Megan Twohey, *She Said: Breaking the Sexual Harassment Story That Helped Ignite a Movement* (New York: Penguin Press, 2019), 14.

375 To do the work properly: Jim Rutenberg, telephone interview by author, Nov. 29, 2021.

375 After Roger Ailes resigned: John Koblin, Emily Steel, and Jim Rutenberg, "Roger Ailes Leaves Fox News and Rupert Murdoch Steps In," *NYT,* July 22, 2016.

375 Steel and Michael Schmidt: Rutenberg, telephone interview by author, Nov. 29, 2021.

375 Baquet made Joe Kahn: Sydney Ember, "New York Times Reinstates Managing Editor Role and Appoints Joseph Kahn," *NYT,* Sept. 16, 2016.

375 Susan Chira moved: Susan Lehman, "Gender Issues in Sharp Focus at the Times," *NYT,* Oct. 4, 2016. Povich's book brought Povich's daughter, Sarah Shepard, into Bennett's life in a group they formed called the

Feminist Fight Club. That became the basis for and the title of Bennett's book, *The Feminist Fight Club: A Survival Manual (for a Sexist Workplace)* (New York: Harper Wave, 2016).

376 "What's going on?": Lehman, "Gender Issues in Sharp Focus at the Times."

376 Was the gender focus: Ibid.

376 "Then the election happened": Bennett, telephone interview by and subsequent email exchanges with author, Nov. 19, 20, 21, 2021.

377 In December, the new public editor: Liz Spayd, "Preaching the Gospel of Diversity, but Not Following It," *NYT,* Dec. 17, 2016.

377 On January 10, 2017: Emily Steel and Michael S. Schmidt, "Fox News Settled Sexual Harassment Allegations Against Bill O'Reilly, Documents Show," *NYT,* Jan. 10, 2017.

377 "Without O'Reilly": Rutenberg, telephone interview by author, Nov. 29, 2021.

377 In March, Spayd bemoaned: Liz Spayd, "The Declining Fortunes of Women at the Times," *NYT,* March 4, 2017.

378 As millennials entered: Katherine Goldstein, "Where Are the Mothers?," *Nieman Reports,* July 26, 2017, updated Feb. 25, 2020.

378 Bennett got the gender editor: Jon Levine, "Washington Post Names Monica Hesse as Paper's First 'Gender Columnist,'" *Wrap,* May 23, 2018. These stories note gender editors already in place: "Ghana: Girls' Education Campaign," *Africa News,* Oct. 11, 2004; "Q&A: Activist Hopes for End to War Trauma Among Women," Inter-Press Service, Dec. 26, 2009; "The Herald Beefs Up Squad," *Herald* (Harare), Nov. 9, 2013; "TV News," BBC News, May 16, 2014.

379 Bennett's start date: Shortly after Bennett, Alicia Pin-Quon Wittmeyer took a similar job on the *Times*'s opinion section. The Weinstein story first broke Oct. 5, 2017. The announcement of Bennett's appointment came Oct. 10, 2017, but she had been in place for some weeks before that. Bennett, telephone interview by and subsequent email exchanges with author, Nov. 19, 20, 21, 2021.

379 The tagline: Sandra E. Garcia, "The Woman Who Created #MeToo Long Before Hashtags," *NYT,* Oct. 20, 2017. A good decade before 2006, Burke's reaction at a youth camp to the deeply affecting details of a thirteen-year-old's story of her own childhood abuse was "I couldn't even say, 'me, too.'" It gave the movement its tagline.

379 Later, Julie Brown: Cristobal, "In Conversation with Julie K. Brown and Jane Mayer."

380 She mentioned the public attacks: See Alan Dershowitz, "Dershowitz: Julie Brown Doesn't Deserve a Pulitzer," Newsmax, July 17, 2021.

380 "You have to fight": Cristobal, "In Conversation with Julie K. Brown and Jane Mayer."

380 The gold medal: See the Pulitzer Prize winners lists, 2018, pulitzer.org.

380 At the *Times,* Jessica: "Jessica Bennett Named Gender Editor," NY Times Company Announcement, Oct. 10, 2017.

381 "For the first time in history": Jessica Bennett, "A Newsletter for the #MeToo World," *NYT,* Dec. 1, 2017.

381 Top figures lost their jobs: "262 Celebrities, Politicians, CEOs, and Others Who Have Been Accused of Sexual Misconduct Since April 2017," *Vox,* n.d., vox.com.

381 "Not even close": Alexis Okeowo, "Nikole Hannah-Jones Keeps Her Eyes on the Prize," *Vanity Fair,* Dec. 2020–Jan. 2021.

382 To NBC, she said: Claretta Bellamy, "Nikole Hannah-Jones on the 1619 Project Book, Harsh Truths of the Black Experience," NBC News, Nov. 18, 2021.

382 New Rules Summit: See "Women & Power," at nytimes.com.

382 Bennett and Chira staged: Jessica Bennett and Susan Chira, "The Rules of the Workplace, Then and Now," *NYT,* Sept. 30, 2018.

384 Among the journalists present: Caroline Que, "Susan Zirinsky on Leading a Reset at CBS News," *NYT,* June 17, 2019. Zirinsky stepped down to take a new producer role at the network. Joe Peyronnin, email exchange with author, Feb. 25, 2022.

384 Elisabeth Bumiller: "Harassment, Equality, Power: What Leaders Said at the New Rules Summit," *NYT,* June 17, 2019.

384 This was a far cry: Engelberg, telephone interview by author, Nov. 29, 2021. See also "Marjorie Hunter, 78, a Pioneering Washington Correspondent for the Times," *NYT,* April 11, 2001.

384 In the first years of the 2020s: Mason Walker, "U.S. Newsroom Employment Has Fallen 26% Since 2008," Pew Research Center, July 13, 2021. From 114,000 in 2008, the drop by 2020 was 30,000 workers combined in newspapers, radio, broadcast television, cable, and "other information services" (the best match for digital publishers).

384 There was evidence in the third of NYU's: For the full list, see journalism .nyu.edu. Those whose reportage was selected among the ten best of the decade between 2010 and 2019 are Isabel Wilkerson for *The Warmth of Other Suns;* Jodi Kantor and Megan Twohey for *She Said,* about the reporting of the Harvey Weinstein abuse scandal; Katherine Boo for *Behind the Beautiful Forevers;* Michelle Alexander for *The New Jim Crow;* Julie K. Brown for "How a Future Cabinet Member Gave a Serial Sex Abuser the Deal of a Lifetime," in *The Miami Herald;* Sheri Fink for *Five Days at Memorial: Life and Death in a Storm-Ravaged Hospital;* and Nikole

Hannah-Jones and colleagues for the *NYT Magazine*'s "1619 Project." Wilkerson, Alexander, and Hannah-Jones are Black.

385 As expected, *The New York Times:* Ravi Somaiya, "New York Times Expands Newsroom Leadership to Address Shifts in Industry," *NYT,* Sept. 24, 2014. This eliminated the managing editor title and made Susan Chira, Janet Elder, Matthew Purdy, and Ian Fisher all deputy executive editors. Baquet eliminated the deputy executive editor position in 2016 (Fisher by then was gone), reviving the position of managing editor and putting Joe Kahn in the role. Ember, "New York Times Reinstates Managing Editor Role and Appoints Joseph Kahn." On the Kahn, Lacey, and Ryan appointments, see Michael M. Grynbaum and Jim Windolf, "Joe Kahn Is Named Next Executive Editor of the New York Times," *NYT,* April 19, 2022, and Michael M. Grynbaum, "New York Times Names Marc Lacey and Carolyn Ryan as Managing Editors," *NYT,* April 20, 2022.

385 Four behavioral scientists: Aneeta Rattan et al., "Tackling the Underrepresentation of Women in Media," *Harvard Business Review,* June 6, 2019.

385 online harassment of woman journalists: Hanaa' Tameez, "This Is What It's Like to Be a Media Company's First-Ever Online Safety Editor," Nieman Lab, Jan. 19, 2022; Margaret Sullivan, "Online Harassment of Female Journalists Is Hard to Endure," *WP,* March 14, 2021; Leah Fessler, "Workplace Harassment in the Age of Remote Work," *NYT,* June 8, 2021.

385 At around the same time: Meg Heckman, "What's the Future of the Gender Beat in U.S. Newsrooms?," Nieman Lab, Nov. 18, 2021, summarizing Heckman, "Constructing the 'Gender Beat': U.S. Journalists Refocus in the Aftermath of #MeToo," *Journalism Practice,* Nov. 15, 2021.

385 Its most recent report: "The Status of Women in the U.S. Media 2021," Women's Media Center, 2021, 11–12.

386 In its "Toward Parity" conclusion: Ibid., 259–60.

386 The 19th*: Gary Dinges, "Women-Focused Texas Media Outlet Set for Debut," *Austin American-Statesman,* Jan. 28, 2020.

387 Margaret Sullivan pointed all of this: Margaret Sullivan, "It's Been One Pivot After Another for the 19th—the Start-Up News Site About Gender and Politics," *WP,* Aug. 4, 2021.

387 In May 2022: Ramshaw, Zoom interview by author, May 11, 2022, and telephone exchange, May 31, 2022.

388 At the suggestion of Errin Haynes: Ramshaw, Zoom interview by author, May 11, 2022, and telephone exchange, May 31, 2022.

INDEX

Page numbers in *italics* refer to photographs.

ABC, 196, 197, 220, 221, 224, 225, 235, 257–58, 262, 281, 282, 290, 326, 340, 341

abolition, *see* slavery and abolition

abortion, 387

Abraham, Sol, 198

Abraham Lincoln Brigade, 141

Abramson, Jill, 265, 287, *287,* 317, 331–33, 344, 351–54, 356–67, *357, 365,* 370, 378, 383, 521n, 523n, 526–28n

Acosta, Alex, 379

Addario, Lynsey, 525n

Adenauer, Konrad, 132, 473n

Adler, Renata, 209, 249

Adolfo, 331

Adzhubei, Alexei, 216

ageism, 281–82, 505n

Aguilar, Alberto, 270–71

Aguinaldo, Emilio, 79

Ailes, Roger, 375

Alabama Tribune, 198

Albany *Times Union,* 138

Alexander, Fritz Winfred, II, 512n

Alexander, Michelle, 537n

Alexander, Shana, 481n

Algeria, 218

AllDigitocracy, 363

Allegheny College, 48

Allen, Danielle, 524n

Allen, Jeff, *248*

Allen, Jennifer, 519

Allred, Gloria, 514n

almshouses, 15, 16

Als, Hilton, 230

Altgeld, John Peter, 58

Amanpour, Christiane, 282

American Academy of Arts and Letters, 284

American Civil Liberties Union, 243

American Institute's Farmers' Club, 45

American Journalism Review, 241, 312, 327, 328, 334, 351

American Lawyer, 287

American Mercury, 105, 106, 109

American Newspaper Publishers Association, 249

American Scholar, 230

American Social Science Association, 61

American Society of Newspaper Editors (ASNE), 257, 273, 276, 305, 308, 317, 319, 326, 343

American Tapestry (Swarns), 330

American University, 147–48, 155

American Women (Willard and
    Livermore), 74, 420n
American Women and the World War
    (Clarke), 96
Ames, Daniel, 27, 29
Ames, Mary Clemmer, *see* Clemmer,
    Mary
Amsterdam News, 147, 160, 197
Anchorage Daily News, 254
Anderson, Gloria B., 503n
Anderson, Marian, 160
Angier, Natalie, 511n
Angola, 313
Anthony, Susan B., 58, 74, 185
AOL, 345
*Appeal in Favor of That Class of
    Americans Called Africans* (Child),
    8–9
April Fools, The, 208
architecture, 218, 219
Arena, 81
Arendt, Hannah, 228, 334
Argus, 64
Arizona Republic, 64
Arledge, Roone, 262–63, 282, 497n
Army, U.S., 151–52, 200
Army and Navy Journal, 89
Arnett, Peter, 241
Around the World in Eighty Days
    (Verne), 57
Asbury, Edith Evans, 145–46, 148–50,
    151, 158–61, 200–203, *202,* 240,
    246–47, 466n
Asbury, Herbert, 158
Ascoli, Max, 226–27
Ashkinaze, Carole, 504n
ASNE (American Society of
    Newspaper Editors), 257, 273, 276,
    305, 308, 317, 319, 326, 343
Associated Negro Press, 199
Associated Press (AP), 72, 88, 128,
    151, 153, 154, 158, 164, 165, 179, 188,

190, 195, 201, 212, 221, 224, 244,
    260, 273, 338, 340, 350–51
Astor, Mrs. John Jacob, 92–93
asylums, 15, 16, 54–56, 402n
Athenaeum, 21
Atherton, Gertrude, 98
Atlanta Constitution, 45, 72, 276
Atlanta Inquirer, 210
Atlantic, 26, 31, 34, 35, 80, 81, 113, 353,
    373
Atlantic City Evening Union, 95
atomic bomb, 193
Auletta, Ken, 333, 353–54, 356–59,
    357, 364
Austin American-Statesman, 49, 326
Austria, 89, 98

Backlash (Faludi), 311
Back Street (Hurst), 187
Bailey, Gamaliel, 23–26, *24,* 31
Baker, Ray Stannard, 47
Balkans, 89, 312
Ball, Sarah, 346
Balmaseda, Liz, 311, 511n
Balough, Maggie, 326–27
Baltimore, Md., Great Fire in, 87
Baltimore Sun, 113, 244, 324, 348
Baltimore Telegram, 59, 86
Banaszynski, Jacqui, 506n
Bancroft Prize, 237
Baquet, Dean, 352–54, 357–58,
    362–67, 368, 370, 371, 374–75, 378,
    385, 503n, 527n, 538n
Barbaro, Michael, 375
Barnard, Anne, 361
Barnard College, 265, 324
Barnett, Claude A., 199
Barnett, Ferdinand Lee, 51
Barringer, Felicity, 294, 298–99, *299,*
    303–4
Barstow School, 160
Bartimus, Tad, 482n, 487n

Barton, Clara, 74, 77, 79
baseball, 59, 60, 85, 86, 415n, 446n, 461n
Bass, Charlotta Spears, 105, 117–18, *118*, 431n
Bass, Joseph, 117
Bassow, Whitman, 188, 475n
Baukhage, H. R., 154, 171
Baum, Geraldine, 301–2, 323
Baumgold, Julie, 477n
BBC, 288, 355
Beach, Moses Yale, 21
Beachy, Lucille, 481n
Beals, Jessie Tarbox, 85–86, *85*
Beck, Joan, 516n
Becker, Elizabeth, 235, 238–40, 474n, 482–84n, 487n
Beech, Keyes, 192–95
Begin, Menachem, 263, 496n
Bell, Emily, 358–59
Bellows, Jim, 221–22, 253–54, 264, 265, 269, 270, *270*
Belmont, Alva, 135
Belmont, Mrs. August, 44
Bender, Marilyn, 246
Benjamin, Anna Northend, 78–80, *78*, 85, 86, 234, 421n, 525n
Bennett, Amanda, 276, 524n
Bennett, James Gordon, 43
Bennett, Jessica, 346, 370–71, 376–81, 382, 383, 385, 535–36n
Berke, Richard L., 527n
Berlin, 123–25, 128, 129, 189–90, 192
Bernard, Michelle, 229
Bernstein, Leonard, 222
Best and the Brightest, The (Halberstam), 237
Bigart, Homer, 169, 193–96, 203, 246, 465n
Bigelow, John, 44
Biggs, Gloria, 490n
Bingham, Barry, Jr., 253, 491n

Bisland, Elizabeth, 57
Blabey, Eugene, 279
Black, Ella, 415n
Black, Winifred, 91, 93, 94
Black Dahlia, 158
Black Panthers, 203, 222
Blacks, 4, 42, 48, 117, 118, 224–25
  Civil War service of, 42
  lynching of, 49–51
  as reporters and editors, 257–59, 275, 307
  segregation and, 200, 201, 210, 211, 224
  slavery and, *see* slavery and abolition
  use of "Negro" and "black" terms for, 256
  women, 4, 48, 84, 229, 256, 258
  women in journalism, 185, 199, 200, 210–11, 255–58, 275
Blackwell's Island, 15, 16, 54–56, 402n
Blaine, James G., 31, 35, 70
Blaire, Jayson, 523n
Blais, Madeleine, 505n
Blanco, Ramón, 76, 77
Blessen, Karen, 506n
Bloomer, Amelia, 185
Bloomingdale Asylum, 16, 54
Bly, Nellie, xii, 49, 51–58, *55*, 60, 61, 66, 73, 74, 81, 96, 98–101, 107, 116–19, 129, 167, 206, 231, 347, 414n, 525n
  Cuba and, *63*, 64–65, 67–69, 75, 77
  entry into journalism, 49
Bodkin, Tom, 527n
Bogart, Humphrey, 155
Bogert, Carroll, 387
Bok, Edward, 82
Bonaparte, Napoleon, 49
Bond, Julian, 210
Boo, Katherine, 537n
Booth, Mary L., 74

Borman, Nancy, 491n
Boston Courier, 14
Boston Evening Transcript, 4
Boston Globe, 78, 89, 176, 195, 233, 265, 297, 320, 344, 371–72
Boston Herald, 70
Boston Herald American, 348
Boston Traveller, 35–36
Boston University (BU), 142, 368, *369,* 370, 372, 375
Botsford, Gardner, 264
Bourke-White, Margaret, 140, 171, 334
Bowen, Henry C., 29
Bowles, Samuel, 26–27
Boxer Rebellion, 80, 87
Boyd, Gerald, 333, 523n
Boyd, Harriet, 420n
Boynton, Robert, 321
Boys on the Bus, The (Crouse), 340
Bracely, Dawn, 525n
Bracker, Milton, 460n
Bradlee, Ben, 244, 245, 248, 275, 296, 300–302, 327, 367
Brady, James, 491n
Brandon, Dorothy, 460n
Breckinridge, John C., 457n
Breckinridge, Mary Marvin, 456–57n
Brenda Starr, Reporter (Messick), 207, 210
Brenner, Anita, 445n
Breslin, Jimmy, 222
Briggs, Charles Frederick, 17
Brill, Steven, 287
Brisbane, Arthur, 58, 76–77, 98, 100–101, 118–19, 129, 422n
Broadway Journal, 17
Brock, David, 317, 528n
Brody, Catharine, 105–7, 109–11, *109,* 111, 123, 233, 431–32n, 433–34n
Bromley, Dorothy Dunbar, 452n
Bronner, Ethan, 364

Brook Farm, 6, 19
Brookings Institution, 312
Brooklyn Eagle, 102
Brooklyn Times-Union, 149
Brooklyn Union, 29
Brown, Caro, 460n, 474n
Brown, Julie K., 379–80, 537n
Brown, Tina, 283, 321, 326, 345, 524n
Browning, Norma Lee, 203
Brownmiller, Susan, 233, 346
Bruce, Georgina, 402n
Brussels World's Fair, 188
Bryant, Louise, 99, 430n
Bryn Mawr College, 137, 138, 148
Buchanan, Edna, 371, 505n
Buchanan, James, 457n
Buffalo Courier, 86
Buffalo News, 324, *337,* 354
Bugbee, Emma, 434n
Bulkeley, Christy, 504n
Bumiller, Elisabeth, 294, 298–302, *301,* 303–4, 378, 384
Bundschu, Henry, 160
Burch, Ann, 453n
Burke, Tarana, 379
Burr, Aaron, 400n
Burton, Julie, 386
Business Week, 306
Butcher, Mary Lou, 504n
Buzbee, Sally, 338, *338,* 521n
Byline Award, 255
Byrd, Joann, 326, 328, 524n

Cabanos Prison, 66, 67
Café de Flore, 142
Calderón, Felipe, 373
California Eagle, 117
Camacho, Mathilde, 481n
Cambodia, 238–39, 278, 484n
Cameron, Denis, *236*
Campbell, Helen, 46, 411n
Canadian Press, 165

Capper, Charles, 19
Carnegie Foundation, 265
Carpenter, Iris, 176, 179, 452n, 459n
Carpenter, Teresa, 506n
Carr, David, 362–64, 367
Carroll, John, 362
Carroll, Kathleen, 338, 351, 524n
Carroll, Raymond, 480n
Carson, Lee, 176
Carson, Rachel, *112,* 113
  Silent Spring, 113, 228, 334, 479n
Carter, Betsy, 318
Carter, Jimmy, 347–48
Cary, Alice and Phoebe, 28
Cary, Mary Ann Shadd, 30, *31,* 33,
  41–42, 50, 74, 407n
Case History of Hope, A (Lewis), 464n
Castro, Fidel, 221
Catholic Universe Bulletin, 131
Catholic University, 265
Catledge, Turner, 223, 259, 291
Catt, Carrie Chapman, 135
Cazneau, Jane McManus Storm, 4, 5,
  10, *11,* 13, 19–22, 74, 400n, 403–4n
CBS, 148, 171, 174, 187, 220, 248, 263,
  282, 326, 354, 384
CBS Evening News, 351
CBS Reports, 341
Cerra, Frances, 485n
Chamberlain, Neville, 162
Chambers, Julius, 54, 55
Channing, William Henry, 14–15, 21
Chapelle, Dickey, 241
Chaplin, Charlie, 108, 155
Chaptal, Marie, 139
Charles, Cecil, 418n
Chase, Sylvia, 263
Chatham University, 113
Chautauqua, 48
Chautauquan, 46–48, 52
Cheetah, 226
Chenoweth, Mary North, 95, 427n

Cherry, Rona, 481n
Chicago (Watkins), 109
Chicago Daily News, 128, 143, 192, 195,
  215, 371
Chicago Defender, 200
Chicago Journal of Commerce, 156
Chicago Sun-Times, 215, 247–48, *248,*
  272, 345
Chicago Tribune, 68, 71, 99, 109, 116–18,
  123–26, 129, 157, 169, 177, 203, 215,
  247, 248, 272, 318, 327, 343, 351,
  352
Child, David, 8, 11, 17, 21
Child, Lydia Maria, 4, 5, 7–14, *12,*
  16–17, 19–22, 23, 34, 54, 74, 399n,
  402n
China, 71–72, 80, 87, 512n
  Boxer Rebellion in, 80, 87
  Japan's war with, 70–72, 88–89
China, SS, 71
Chira, Susan, 275, 351–52, 354, 370,
  371, 375–77, 380, 382–85, 387,
  516n, 528n, 538n
Christian, Shirley, 505n
Christian Science Monitor, 156, 250,
  254, 269, 273
Chung, Connie, 263, 282, 326, 496n
Churchman, 78
Chusmir, Janet, 274, 307–8
CIA, 240
Cianfrani, Henry J., 497–98n
Cincinnati Commercial Gazette, 65,
  67, 68
Cincinnati Times-Star, 149, 201
City Editor (Walker), 113, 233
City News Bureau, 247
civil rights, 117, 147, 200, 206, 242,
  243
Civil Rights Act, 206
Civil War, 26, 28, 42, 65, 89, 406–7n
  Harpers Ferry battle in, 27–28, 72,
  74, 80

Clapper, Raymond, 157
Clark, Michele, 263
Clark, Robert P., 491n
Clarke, James Freeman, 21
Clay, Henry, 15
Clemmer, Mary, vii, 23, 25–30, 27,
    32, 34–36, 41, 45, 72, 74, 80
Clinton, Bill, 371
Clinton, Hillary, 321, 340, 376, 522n
CNN, 282, 313, 340, 353
Coates, Foster, 42, 53, 58–62
Coates, Ta-Nehisi, 381
Coats, Janet, 276
Cockerill, John, 43, 53
Cohen, Frances Davis, 141–43, 445n,
    454n
Cohen, Ron, 309–10, 511n
Cold War, 189
Coleman, Kit, 78, 421n
Collier's, 141, 144, 145, 158, 159, 162, 163,
    171–74, 187
Collins, Gail, 286–87, 287, 332, 338
Columbia Daily Telegraph, 24, 25
Columbia Journalism Review, 274, 281,
    322, 339–40, 342, 354
Columbia University, 104, 135, 153,
    158, 165, 187, 191, 207, 226, 232,
    287, 298, 301, 358, 423n
Columbus Citizen, 223
Columbus Dispatch, 68, 69
Colvin, Marie, 287–89, 288
Committee on Public
    Information, 98
communism, 118, 199, 464n
Compton, Ann, 505n
concentration camps, 175, 177, 180,
    181, 193
Condé Nast, 283
Confidential, 187–88, 218
Congress, U.S., 152, 199, 271, 384
    House Un-American Activities
    Committee, 118, 146

Senate Committee on Foreign
    Relations, 238
Senate Subcommittee on
    Investigations, 199
Women's Caucus in, 343
Congressional Record, 224
Constitutional amendments, 4, 42
    Nineteenth, 96, 173, 386, 388, 437n
Constitutional Hall, 160
Conversations seminars, 7, 9, 13, 34
Cooke, Cecil, 147, 197
Cooke, Janet, 506n
Cooke, John, 505n
Cooke, Marvel, 105, 145–47, 146, 148,
    160, 197–99, 431n, 446n, 457n, 466n
Cooper-Church Amendment, 238
copyreaders, 156
Corbett, Rebecca, 359, 377
Corn, David, 485n
Cornell Daily Sun, 185
Cosgrave, John O'Hara, 422n
Cosmopolitan, 57, 159, 233–34, 262,
    281–82
Couric, Katie, 321, 351
Cowan, Ruth, 164, 452n, 466n
Cowles, Virginia, 141, 144, 144, 169,
    234, 454n, 525n
    Love Goes to Press, 168, 168, 191, 240
Cox, Donald, 222
Craft, Christine, 281
Crane, Burton, 192–93
Crane, Cora Stewart Taylor, 75–78,
    525n
Crane, Stephen, 75, 77–78
Cravens, Kathryn, 457n
Creel, George, 98
Creelman, James, 78–80, 144
Crichton, Judy, 341
Crisis, 147, 197
Crist, Judith, 189, 220, 460n, 463n
Croly, Jane Cunningham, 32–33,
    35–37, 42, 46, 71

Cronkite, Walter, 174–75, 186, 351, 496n

Crosby, Jackie, 506n

Crouse, Timothy, 340

Crowley, Harriet Sweeney, 448n

Cuba, 91, 162–63
  War of Independence in, 64–69, 74–79, 82, 83, 85, 167

Cunningham, Linda Grist, 273, 277, 503n

Curley, John, 329

Currie, Kathleen, 146, 149, 164, 165, 188, 190, 192, 198, 201, 216

Curse of the Good Girl, The (Simmons), 346–47

Curtis, Charlotte, 222–23, *222*, 246, 249, 250, 261, 284, 286, 477n, 506n, 518n

Cushman, Charlotte, 44

Czechoslovakia, 144, 162, 171

Dachau, 180, 181, 193

Daily Beast, 345, 353

Daily Compass, 197–99

Daily Express, 190

Daily Mail, 143

Daily South Carolinian, 24

Daily Telegraph, 151

Daley, Suzanne, 319, 330

Dallas Morning News, 340

Dallas Times Herald, 285, 334

Dana, Charles, 42

Daniel, Clifton, 132, 219, 223, 351

Daniell, Raymond, 174, 455n, 456n

Darnton, Byron "Barney," 153, 154

Darnton, Eleanor, 153–54, 223, 291, 448–49n

Darnton, John, 153–54, 259, 291–93, *292*, 300, 303, 501–3n, 508n

Darnton, Nina, 291–93, *292*, 303, 508n

Dateline, 231, 232

Daughters of the American Revolution (DAR), 160

Davis, Frances, 141–43, 445n, 454n

Davis, Rebecca Harding, 408n

Davis, Richard Harding, 69, 128

Davis, Sammy, Jr., 224

D-day, 171–73, 176, 178

DDT, 228

Dean, James, 155

Dean, Teresa Howard, 414–15n, 420n

de Beauvoir, Simone, 233

Deeble, Elizabeth, 445n

Deepe, Beverly, 232, 241, 483n, 487n

de Gaulle, Charles, 231, 473n

Delmonico's, 32

Democratic National Convention, 138

Deneuve, Catherine, 208

DePalma, Anthony, 500n

Depew, Chauncey, 92

De Porte, Barbara, 127

Depression, Great, 103–5, 110, 140, 141, 145, 148, 164, 167, 196, 198

Dershowitz, Alan, 380

Desantis, Ann, 486n

Des Moines Register, 307–10, 327–29

de Staël, Madame Germaine, 7, 9, 399n

Detroit Free Press, 32, 233

Detroit News, 244, 272

de Valera, Eamon, 127, 131

de Valera, Eamon, Jr., 127

DeYoung, Karen, 275, 501–2n

Dial, 10–12, 14

Díaz Nosty, Bernardo, 141

Dick, Elsie, 209

Dickens, Charles, 16, 32, 54

Dickerson, Nancy, 220, 221, 483n

Didion, Joan, 203, 204, 229–30, *229*, 334, 343, 368, 371, 374

DiGiovanni, Janine, 513n

digital journalism, 345, 366, 378

Diller, Barry, 345

Dix, Dorothy, 91, 93, 450n
Dobbs, Michael, 485n
Dolan, Mary Anne, 253–54, 265,
    269–72, *270,* 274, 289–90, 499n
Dolnick, Sam, 364–65
Dominus, Susan, 376
Donaldson, Sam, 282
Dooley, Nancy, 243
Dorr, Rheta Childe, 84–85, 91, 99,
    424n, 430n
Dowd, Maureen, 264–65, 285–86,
    286, 311–12, 317, 320, 321, 332,
    365
Downie, Len, 296, 300, 329
Downing, Margaret, 519n
Dramatic Mirror, 66
Draper, Muriel, 209
Dreifus, Claudia, 471n
Dreiser, Theodore, 129–30
Du Bois, W. E. B., 118, 147, 197, 423n,
    431n
du Cille, Michel, 525n
Dudar, Helen, 243
Dufka, Corrine, 512n
Dufty, William, 460n
Dunnigan, Alice Allison, 105,
    199–200, 431n, 466n, 468n
duPont Award, 185, 272–73, 354
Dylan, Bob, 226

E: The Environmental Magazine,
    228
Earhart, Amelia, 146
Easter Rising, 127
Ebert, Roger, 226
Ebony, 224
Ecenbarger, William, 485n
Economist, 190
Edgerley, Susan, 354, 527n, 528n
Edison, Thomas Alva, 66
Editor & Publisher (E&P), 108, 109,
    309

Education in Georgia, An (Trillin),
    211–12
Edwards, Charles, 307, 310, 327
Edy, Carolyn, 77
EEOC (Equal Employment
    Opportunity Commission), 242,
    243, 252, 275, 316, 488n
Efron, Sonni, 315
Egan, Eleanor Franklin, 87–91, *88,* 96,
    99, 101, 234
Egan, Martin, 87–91, 99, 101
Egypt, 313
Ehrenreich, Barbara, 320, 525n
Einstein, Albert, 118–19
Eisenhower, Dwight, 200
Elder, Janet, 361, 538n
Elizabeth II, 220
Ellison, Jesse, 346
Ellison, Katherine, 506n
Emerson, Gloria, 233–34, 236–37,
    236, 240–41, 246, 371, 485–87n,
    489n
Emerson, Lidian Jackson, 6, 9, *10,* 18
Emerson, Ralph Waldo, 3, 5–7, 9–11,
    10, 13–15, 20–22
Emerson College, 70
Emmy Award, 273, 340, 354
Engelberg, Stephen, 356, 369–70,
    384
Enloe, Cynthia, 453n
Ephron, Nora, 233, 249, 289, 321,
    343, 368, 374
Epstein, Jeffrey, 379, 380
Equal Employment Opportunity
    Commission (EEOC), 242, 243,
    252, 275, 316, 488n
Equal Pay Act, 206
Equal Rights Amendment, 173
Esquire, 233, 298, 318
Ethiopia, 144
Evans, Harold, 283
Evers, Medgar, 224

Face of War, The (Gellhorn), 334
Fahs, Alice, 421n
Fales, William E. S., 70–71
Faludi, Susan, 311, 321, 511n
Fanning, Kay, 254, 273, 274, 308,
    493n
Fanning, Larry, 493n
Farnham, Eliza, 402n
Farrow, Ronan, 380
Fatal Vision (McGinnis), 284–85
Fawcett, Denby, 482n
Fawcett Publications, 149
FBI, 118
Federal Communications
    Commission (FCC), 263, 275
Federal Emergency Relief
    Administration (FERA), 140,
    141
Fein, Esther, 323
Feminine Mystique, The (Friedan),
    205–6, 212, 228–29, 334
feminism, *see* women's rights and
    feminism
Ferber, Edna, 110
Ferraro, Geraldine, 279
Ferrick, Thomas, 485n
Field, Kate, 408n
Field, Marshall, IV, 493n
Fifteenth Amendment, 42
Fillmore, Millard, 30–31
film, 226
Financial Times, 190
Fink, Sheri, 360, 537n
Finland, 162, 170
Finland, SS, 126–27
Fire in the Lake (FitzGerald), 237
Fish and Wildlife Service, 113
Fisher, Ian, 538n
Fisk University, 48
FitzGerald, Frances, 237–38, *237,*
    240, 473n, 474n, 483–86n
Fitzgerald, Frances Scott, 471n

Fitz-Gerald, Joan, 505n
Flaherty, Mary Pat, 506n
Flanner, Janet (Genêt), 174, 189, 209,
    334, 442n, 470–71n, 525n
Fleming, J. L., 50, 51
Flood, Theodore L., 47–48
Floyd, George, 387
Flynn, Errol, 155
Foa, Sylvana, 238–40, 278, 484n,
    503n
Foer, Franklin, 355, 356
football, 339, 522n
Forbes, Genevieve, *see* Herrick,
    Genevieve Forbes
Forbes, Ludy, 460n
Ford, Christine Blasey, 382
Ford Foundation Fellowship, 232,
    369
Foreman, Laura, 497–98n
Forst, Don, 492n
Fortune, 140, 150, 318
Fortune, Timothy Thomas, 51
Fortune 500 companies, 382
Fourteenth Amendment, 4, 42
Fox News, 375, 377
France, 191
France-Soir, 190
Francke, Linda, 481n
Franco, Francisco, 141, 144, 171
Franco-Prussian War, 65
Frankel, Max, 247, 258, 279, 286,
    303–7, 315, 317–20, 322, 330, 332,
    353, 361, 503n, 514n
Franklin, Eleanor, *see* Egan, Eleanor
    Franklin
Franks, Lucinda, 486n
Frederick, Pauline, 145–48, *147,*
    154–55, 170–71, 173, 185, 186,
    196–97, 219–21, 235–36, 261, 262,
    347, 447n, 449n, 466n, 474n
Frere-Jones, Sasha, 226
Freud, Sigmund, 128, 284, 321

Friedan, Betty, 229, 317
  The Feminine Mystique, 205–6, 212, 228–29, 334
front-page girls, 96, 99, 103, 113, 115, 149, 169
Frugal Housewife, The (Child), 8
Fugitive Slave Act, 30
Fulbright Scholarship, 219
Fuller, Margaret, 3–22, *6*, 23, 29, 30, 32, 34, 43, 50, 54, 74, 93, 136, 234, 398n, 399n, 400n, 404n, 525n
  asterisk sign of, 14, 18, 388–89
Fuller, Timothy, 5–6
Furness, Betty, 281
Furst, Peter, 180

Gaines, William, 503n
Galaxy, 33, 43
Gallagher, Wes, 164
Gallardo, Adriana, 373
Gallup, 220
Galveston News, 64
Gangs of New York, The (Asbury), 158
Gannett, 247, 273, 307, 309–10, 327–29
García, Michelle, 369, 372–73
Garibaldi, Giuseppe, 18
Garland, Judy, 186, 461n
Garrett, Laurie, 512n
Garrison, William Lloyd, 9, 21
Gay, Eva, 56
Geddes, John, 344, 353, 523n, 527n
Gelb, Arthur, 132, 201–3, 255–57, 299, 489n
Gellhorn, Edna Fischel, 137–39
Gellhorn, Martha, 137–42, *140*, 144–45, 147, 148, 162–63, 167, 169, 172–74, 196, 234, 241, 288, 334, 371, 444–45n, 454n, 466n, 525n
  Love Goes to Press, 168, *168*, 191, 240
Genauer, Emily, 486n

Generation X, 343, 367, 379
Genêt, *see* Flanner, Janet
Gentry, Sue, 159–60, 450n
George, Phyllis, 522n
George Polk Award, 237, 240, 312, 315, 321, 354, 380
George V, 90
Germany, Nazi, *see* Nazi Germany
Gerry, Valerie, 480n
Geyer, Georgie Anne, 371, 483n
Gibbons, Sheila, 349
Gibney, Frank, 193
Gibson, Janine, 362, 365
Gill, George, 253, 491n
Gingold, Judith, 243
Girls in the Balcony, The (Robertson), 132, 306
Girls in the Van, The (Harpaz), 340
Glasser, Susan, 363
Godey, Louis Antoine, 4, 24–25
Godey's Lady's Book, 4, 17, 24–25
Godiva, Lady, 185
Goebbels, Joseph, 172
Goethe, Johann Wolfgang von, 6, 14
Goldberg, Jeffrey, 373–74, 485n
Goldberger, Paul, 261
Golden, Soma, 306, 323, 329–31, 338, 521n
Goldman, Emma, 58
Goldman, Peter, 243
Good Girls Revolt, The (Povich), 207–8, 350, 524n
Good Housekeeping, 220
Goodman, Amy, 512n
Goodman, Ellen, 233, 320, 344–45, 506n
Good Morning America, 321
Goodrich, B. F., 457n
Gorbachev, Mikhail, 299
Gosnell, Mariana, 481n
Gottlieb, Robert, 515n
Gould, Eleanor, 209

Graham, Katharine, 159, 245, 301, 302, 347

Grant, Jane, 124–25, *125,* 209, 442n, 470–71n

Graves, Ralph, 125

Gray, Hanna, 498n, 524n

Great Baltimore Fire, 87

Great Depression, 103–5, 110, 140, 141, 145, 148, 164, 167, 196, 198

"Great Lawsuit, The" (*Woman in the Nineteenth Century*) (Fuller), 12, 14, 15–17, 19

Greece, 75, 78, 420n

Greeley, Horace, 6, 10–21, *13,* 23, 25, 30, 44, 60, 92, 388, 404n

Greeley, Mary Young Cheney, 12–14, *13,* 18

Greeley-Smith, Nixola, 91–94, *92,* 100, 442n

Greene, Melissa Fay, 334

Greenfield, Meg, 226–27, *226,* 486n

Greenhouse, Linda, 384

Greenway, David, 239

Greenwell, Ava Thompson, 256

Greenwood, Grace, 23–26, *24,* 29, 31, 34, 35, 41, 45, 136, 405n, 406n

Greenwood Leaves (Greenwood), 24, 25

Grey, Lita, 108

Gridiron Club, 342

Griggs, Cornelia, 364

Grimké, Sarah, 16

Griswold, Rufus Wilmot, 19

Grove, Andrew, 318

Gruber, Ruth E., 488n

Grunwald, Henry, 244

Gruson, Sydney, 165, 190, 191, 232, 259, 260, 291

Guardian, 350, 353, 358, 362

Guernica, 373

Guggenheim, Harry, 435n

Guggenheim Fellowship, 188, 219

Gutierrez, Barbara, 519n

Gutman, Roy, 312

Guzy, Carol, 311, 505n

Haberman, Maggie, 384

Haines, Errin, 388

Halberstam, David, 237

Hale, Margaret Ellen, 506n

Hale, Sarah Josepha, 4, 25

Hall, Charlotte, 343–44, 523n

Hall, Trish, 527n

Hallinan, Joseph T., 511n

Hallinan, Vincent, 118

Halstead, Murat, 65, 68, 69

Hamilton, Eva, 58

Hamilton, Gail, 23–26, 29, 31, 32, *32,* 34, 35, 41, 45, 136

Hamm, Margherita Arlina, 69–73, *71,* 74, 77, 89, 90, 419n

Hannah-Jones, Nikole, 369–70, *369,* 372, 373–75, 381–82, *382,* 537–38n

Hansen, Liane, 339

Hanson, Kitty, 474n

Hapgood, Norman, 422n

Harbinger, 19

Harding, Warren G., 101, 117

Harlem Renaissance, 147

Harpaz, Beth, 340, 522n

Harper's Bazaar, 29, 34, 74

Harpers Ferry, Battle of, 27–28, 72, 74, 80

Harper's Magazine, 25, 221

Harper's Weekly, 91

Hart, Gary, 294, 296

Hartford Courant, 143

Harvard Business Review, 385

Harvard Business School, 359

Harvard University, 228, 265

Harvey, George, 422n

Hassard, John R. G., 43

Hawthorne, Julian, 76

Hawthorne, Nathaniel, 6, 76

Hayde, Joan, 485n

Headden, Susan, 511n
Healy, Jane, 506n
Hearst newspapers, 65, 66, 76, 91, 93,
    118, 141, 254, 289
Hechinger, Fred, 460n
Hefner, Hugh, 221
Heller, Frances, 208
Heller, Jean, 485n
Heller, Nathan, 230
Hemingway, Ernest, 141, 145, 162,
    172–73, 445n, 454n, 458n
Hepburn, Katharine, 130
Hepworth, George, 43
Herbst, Josephine, 445n
Herrick, Genevieve Forbes, 99,
    116–17, *116*, 125, 156–57, 169, 452n,
    466n
Hess, John, 260
Hess, Stephen, 501n
Higgins, Marguerite, 153, 154,
    165–66, 169, 173, 180, 187–96, *194*,
    220, 231, 234–35, 240, 355, 460n,
    465n, 474n, 503n, 525n
Hill, Anita, 315–17, 341, 353, 382,
    514n, 528n
Hillman Prize, 380
Hiroshima, 193
His Girl Friday, 132
Hitchens, Christopher, 321
Hitler, Adolf, 104, 130, 131, 144, 164,
    172, 175, 180–81, 334
Hoelterhoff, Manuela, 506n
Hofeller, Leo, 211
Hoffman, Jeane, 468n
Hoge, James, 272, 490n
Hoge, Warren, 306
Hokinson, Helen, 209
Holiday, 230
Hollingworth, Clare, 452–53n, 525n
Holman, Ben, 493n
Holman, Carl, 210
Holmes, Hamilton, 210

Holt, Hamilton, 422n
home economics, 46
Honolulu Star-Bulletin, 192
Hoover, Herbert, 101
Hopkins, Harry, 140
horse racing, 44
Horwitz, Tony, 272
Hosmer, William, 14
House, Karen Elliott, 506n
House Un-American Activities
    Committee, 118, *146*
Houston Chronicle, 285
Howard, Johnette, 339
Howard, Joseph, Jr., 52, 55–56
Howard, Lisa, 220, 221
Howard, Roy, 97–98, 129
Howard University, 42, 311
Howells, William Dean, 422n
Huffington, Arianna, 345, 367
Huffington Post, 345
Hughes, Howard, 155
Hull, Anne, 345, 525n
Hunter, Maggie, 384
Hunter College, 152, 218
Hunter-Gault, Charlayne, 210–12,
    210, 224, 255–57, 493n, 494n
Hurst, Fannie, xii, 104–5, 110, 152, 187
Hussein, Saddam, 314
Hussein of Jordan, 356
Huston, Margo, 486n
Hutchinson, Nelly Mackay, 33–35,
    43, 53, 56, 408n
Huxtable, Ada Louise, 218–19, *219*,
    223, 246, 259–61, 283–84, 485–86n

Ideal American College Girl
    competition, 104–5
Ifill, Gwen, 347, 348, *348*
Imitation of Life (Hurst), 187
immigrants, 53, 85, 116–17, *116*
Independence *Examiner*, 159
Independent, 24–25, 28, 29, 34, 61, 79

Independent Woman, 133
India, 300–301
Industrial Revolution, 3
In Our Time (Brownmiller), 346
InStyle, 331, 379
integration, 200, 201, 210, 211, 224
International Herald Tribune, 332, 344
International News Service (INS),
    127, 128, 159, 164, 176, 177, 188
International Olympic Committee,
    339
Inter Ocean, 71
inventors, 47
Iraq, 314, 344, 355, 356
Ireland, 127, 486n
Isaacs, Norman, 211
Italy, 18, 44, *95,* 98, 104, 123, 124, 131,
    144, 162, 404n
I've Got a Secret, 215
Ivins, Molly, 225–26, *225,* 264, 281,
    283, 285, 504n
Izvestia, 216, 217, *217*

Jabir Ahmed Sabah, Sheik, 314
Jackson, Allan, 177
Jackson, Amy, 147
Jackson, Madison, 146, 446n
Jackson, Marvel, *see* Cooke, Marvel
Jackson, Stonewall, 27
Jacoby, Melville, 455n
James, Sheryl, 511n
Japan, 80, 88–89, 164, 170, 200
    atomic bombing of, 193
    China's war with, 70–72, 88–89
    Russia and, 87, 89
Jarrín, Jaime, 271
Jefferson, Margo, 311, 320, 512n
Jennings, Peter, 496n
Jerome, Leonard, 44
Jerome, William Travers, 94
Jerusalem, 162
Jet, 211, 224

Jews, 127, 175
Johns Hopkins University, 113
Johnson, Lyndon B., 224, 238, 484n
Johnson, Priscilla, 463n
Jonas, Gerry, 211
Jonas, Joan, 211
Jones, David, 280–81, 504n
Jordan, Elizabeth, 66, 416n
Journalism for Women (Bennett), 61–62
Journalist, 48, 70, 71
Jouvenel, Bertrand de, 139–41
Jouvenel, Henri de, 139
J. P. Morgan and Company, 99
Judge, 66
Jumel, Eliza, 400n
Jungle, The (Sinclair), 45
Jurgensen, Karen, 321
Juvenile Miscellany, 8

Kael, Pauline, 209, 226, 249, 334,
    485n
Kahn, Joe, 375, 385, 538n
Kaiser Health News, 387–88
Kakutani, Michiko, 311, 512n
Kaltenborn, H. V., 157
Kaltenborn, Olga, 445n
Kansas City Call, 147
Kantor, Jodi, 359–60, 377, *377,* 379,
    380, 537n
Kaplan, Bernard, 234
Karl I, 128–29
Kassman, Laurie, 513n
Katsura Tarō, 88, 89
Katz, Jon, 285
Kaufman, Monica, 522–23n
Kavanaugh, Brett, 382
Kazickas, Jurate, 224, 482n
Keegan, Anne, 247
Keller, Bill, 344, 352, 523n, 527n
Kelly, William J., 102
Kennedy, Jacqueline, 220
Kennedy, John F., 189, 342

Kihss, Peter, 203, 246
Killing Fields, The (Schanberg), 239
King, Florence, 320–21
King, Martin Luther, Jr., 255
Kingdom and the Power, The (Talese), 374
Kinkaid, Mary Holland, 434n
Kintzel, Roger, 326
Kirk, Donald, 483n
Kirk, Susie, 483n
Kirkpatrick, Helen, 170, 454n, 457n
Kirtland, Helen Johns, *95*, 96, 144
Kirtland, Lucian Swift, 96, 144
Kleiman, Carol, 504n
Kluger, Richard, 189, 191–92
Knight-Ridder, 276
Knott, Janet, 506n
Knoxville News-Sentinel, 149, 201
Korea, 72, 80
Korean War, 192–95, *194,* 234, 235, 241, 460n, 465n
Kovach, Bill, 294–97
Kowshing, SS, 72
Kramer, Jane, 209, 334, 371, 471n
Kramon, Glenn, 527n
Krenek, Debby, 333–34, 351, 526n
Kristof, Nicholas, 512n
Krock, Arthur, 133–35
Krout, Mary Hannah, 415n, 418n, 420n
Kuhn, Irene, 108–9
Ku Klux Klan, 51, 118, 149
Kunkel, Thomas, 209
Kuwait, 313–15

Lacey, Marc, 385
Ladies' Home Journal, 58, 136, 241, 269–70, 321
Ladies Leading (Greenwell), 256
Ladies of the Press (Ross), 96, 113–15
Lady Chatterley's Lover (Lawrence), 138

La Flesche, Susette, 59, *59,* 74
LaFrance, Adrienne, 373
Laidlaw, Harriet Burton, 437n
Lalli, Frank, 254, 270, 271, 492–93n, 499n
Lane, Rose Wilder, 110, 433n
Lange, Dorothea, 140
Lansing, Sherry, 269
Laurie, Annie, 56
Laventhol, David, 272
Lawrence, D. H., 138
League of Nations, 139, 163
LeBlanc, Adrian Nicole, 525n
Lederer, Edith, 482n, 487n
LeDuff, Charlie, 272
Lee, Carolyn, 251, 279–81, 306–7, *306,* 329–31, 338, 491n, 504n, 514n, 521n
Leeds, Pat, 469n
Legal Times, 287
Lelyveld, Joe, 203, *210,* 255, 322–23, 330, 332, 333, 514n, 523n
Lemmon, Jack, 208
Leopold, Nathan, 203
Lerman, Leo, 283
Leroy, Catherine, 474n, 483n, 485n, 486n
Leslie's Weekly, 78, 79, 86–88, 90, 91, 96, 100, 144
Letters from New York (Child), 14, 16
Letters on the Equality of the Sexes, and the Condition of Woman (Grimké), 16
Levin, Carl, 464n
Lewin, Tamar, 323
Lewinsky, Monica, 371
Lewis, Flora, 153–55, *153,* 164–66, 173, 186, 187, 189–92, 223, 232, 234, 259–60, 275, 288, 291, 293, 320, 332, 449n, 464n, 473n, 481n, 495n
Lewis, Ida, 491n
Lewis, Sinclair, 110, 129, 130, 433n
Lewis Institute, 126

LGBTQ+ community, 350, 376, 388
Liberator, 9
Library of American Literature, A
    (Stedman and Hutchinson,
    eds.), 56
Lichtenstein, Grace, 264, 281, 504n
Liddick, Betty, 519n
Life, 140, 149, 170, 171, 179, 195, 206,
    207, 244
Light, Murray B., 324–25
Lincoln, Abraham, 44, 49
Lincoln Memorial, 160
Lipinski, Ann Marie, 343–44, 351,
    503n, 506n, 519n, 524n, 526n
Lipsey, Stanford, 325
Literary Journal, 9
Littlefield, Amy, 369, 372
Little House on the Prairie (Wilder), 110
Livermore, Mary A., 74, 420n
livestock, 44–46, 111, 272, 437n
Living Way, 48
Lochridge, Patricia, 453n
Locke, John, 7
Logan, Andy, 471n
Logan, Lara, 525n
Logan, Walter, 488n
London *Weekly Times,* 71
Long, Lois, 209
Long, Tania, 174, 454–56n
Longmans, Green & Co., 110
Look, 207
Lopez, Andy, 174
López, J. Gerardo, 271
Lorimer, George Horace, 101
Los Angeles Herald, 110, 158
Los Angeles Herald Examiner, 221, 254,
    269–72, 270, 274, 289–90, 346
Los Angeles Herald-Express, 146
Los Angeles *Record,* 146
Los Angeles Times, 78, 95, 139, 270,
    274, 280, 293, 300, 313, 315, 316,
    318, 323, 342, 352, 362

Los Angeles Times Company, 259
Louisville *Courier-Journal,* 251,
    252–53, 278
Louisville Defender, 199
Louisville Leader, 199
Louisville Times, 211, 253
Love Goes to Press (Gellhorn and
    Cowles), 168, *168,* 191, 240
Lozano-Centanino, Monica, 519n
Luce, Henry, 171, 206, 207, 244
Ludtke, Melissa, 339, 487n
Lukas, Anthony, 203, 246
Lukas, Ellen, 480n
Lundstrom, Marjie, 511n
Luong, Nguyen Ngoc, *236*
lynching, 49–51

MacArthur, Arthur, Jr., 79
MacArthur, Douglas, 194, *194*
MacArthur Foundation, 283, 370
MacDonald, Jeffrey, 284–85, 507n
MacFarquhar, Larissa, 371
Mackin, Catherine, 496–97n
MacNeil/Lehrer Report, 257
MacSwiney, Terence, 127
Mademoiselle, 206, 207, 209, 232–33
Madison, Paula, 341–42
Maine, USS, 76
Malamud, Phyllis, 481n
Malcolm, Donald, 203–4
Malcolm, Janet, 203–4, 209, 263–64,
    264, 283–85, 321–22, 371, 374,
    506n, 507n
Malcolm X, 255
Man Called Adam, A, 224
Mandela, Nelson, 330
Manhattan, Inc., 303
manifest destiny, 20, 404n
Manila Times, 99
Mannes, Marya, 460n
Man Ray, 179
Manuel, Ralph N., 296

Marble, Manton, 44
Margaret Fuller (Marshall), 22
Mariano, Ann Bryan, 482n
Marja, Fern, 460n
Marlin, Marie, 454n
Marsh, George Perkins, 44
Marshall, Marguerite Moors, 107–8
Marshall, Megan, 22
Marshall Project, 385, 387
Martin, Ann Ray, 481n
Martin, Everett G., 474n
Martin, Linda Grant, 473–74n, 483n
Marton, Endre, 460n
Martore, Gracia, 489n
Marzorati, Gerald, 527n
Maslin, Janet, 228–29
Massachusetts Journal, 8
Masson, Jeffrey, 284, 321–22, 507n
Masterson, Kate, 65–69, *70*, 74, 75,
     82–85, 91–92, 101–2, 167, 418n
Mayer, Jane, 265, 287, *287*, 317, 326,
     331, 353, 361, *365*, 379–80, 525n,
     528n
*May You Be the Mother of a Hundred
     Sons* (Bumiller), 301
Mazzini, Giuseppe, 18
McCall's, 104
McCarthy, Joseph, 199
McCarthy, Mary, 368
McClatchy, 254, 328
McClure, S. S., 422n
McClure's, 47, 49
McCormick, Anne O'Hare, 105, 106,
     123, 124, 129–36, *133*, 137, 141, 151,
     162, 169, 197, 223, 231, 234, 260,
     293, 320, 431n, 437n, 439n, 441n,
     442n, 444n, 454n, 455n, 474n
McCormick, Francis J., 131
McCullers, Carson, 374
McDaniel College, 60
McDonald, Hazel, 454n
McDougall, Walt, 55

McDowell, Rachel Kollock, 111–12,
     111, 437n, 442n
McElroy, Peter J., 460n
McGinnis, Joe, 284–85, 507n
McGinnis, Marcy, 497n
McGrory, Mary, 474n, 486n
McLaughlin, Kathleen, 125, 169–70,
     454n, 466n, 481n
McMillan, Priscilla, 463n
McNally, Michele, 354, 527n
Media Report to Women, 349
Media Watch, 317, 319
Medill, Joseph, 118
Memoirs of Margaret Fuller Ossoli
     (Fuller et al.), 21–22, 32
Memphis Free Speech, 47, 50–51
Men's League for Woman
     Suffrage, 82
Merchants of Truth (Abramson), 352,
     358, 360, 362, 365
Mercier, Désiré Cardinal, 99
Merick, Anne Morrissy, 185, 235,
     482n
#MeToo movement, 377, 379, 383,
     536n
Metropolitan Club, 130
Mexican-American War, 4, 404n
Mexican Revolution, 90
Miami Herald, 274, 298, 308, 313, 330,
     371, 379
Middle East, 313–15, 513n
Middleton, Drew, 179, 197
Miles, Dixon S., 27
Miles, John DeBras, 68
Milholland, Inez, 98
millennials, 366–67, 378, 379
Miller, Charles R. (husband of
     Sadie), 60, 86–87, 89, 90, 424n,
     425n
Miller, Charles Ransom, 43
Miller, Judith, 355–56
Miller, Lee, 179–81, *181*

Miller, Sadie Kneller (Mrs. C. R. Miller), 59–60, 85–87, *87*, 89–91, 96, 98, 100, 424n, 425n
Mills, Kay, 500n
Milton, Joyce, 421n
Minneapolis Tribune, 225–26, *225*
minority hiring and promotion, 257–59, 275, 307, 317, 319–20, 323, 341, 350
Mirabella, 321
Mirage tavern project, 248–49, *248,* 272, 345
Miramax, 321
Mitchell, Alison, 530n
Mitchell, Andrea, 263, 505n
Moeller, Susan D., 474n
Monde, 366
Monroe, Marilyn, 155
Montreal Star, 234
Moore, Garry, *215*
Moore, Roy, 380
Moorehead, Caroline, 173
MORE, 249–50, *249*
Morello, Carol, 513n
Morgan, Gwen, 469n
Morgan, J. P., 101
Morgan, J. P., and Company, 99
Morgan, Lucy, 506n
Morgan, Midy, 43–46, *45,* 51, 61, 111, 136, 410n, 436n, 437n
Morgenthau, Robert, 486n
Morin, Relman, 465n
Morocco, 89, 218
Morris, Joe Alex, 157
Morris, Robert G., 42
Morrissy, Anne, 185, 235, 482n
Mosby, Aline, 154, 155, *155,* 187–89, 231–33, 288, 449n, 481n
  in Russia, 216–18, *217,* 475n
Mossell, Gertrude Bustill, 74, 84, *84,* 91
Mott, Frank Luther, 157

Motyka, Joan, 519
Moulton, Louise Chandler, 408n
Mowrer, Paul, 128, 439n
Mrs. Herndon's Income (Campbell), 46
"Ms.," use of, 284
Munich Conference, 164
Munsey, Frank, 422n
Munsey's, 78
Murdoch, Rupert, 283
Murphy, Caryle, 313–15, *313,* 511n
Murphy, Kim, 513n
Murrow, Edward R., 148, 171, 185–87, 454n, 456n, 457n
Museum of Modern Art, 218
Museum of Television and Radio, 339
Museum of the City of New York, 219
music, 226
Mussolini, Benito, 104, 131, 162, 164
"Mx," use of, 284
Mydans, Carl, 170, 194–95, 455n
Mydans, Shelley Smith, 170, 173, 455n

NAACP, 147
NANA (North American Newspaper Alliance), 117, 148, 154, 170, 215
Napoleon I, 49
Nashville Banner, 171
Nation, 123, 125, 128, 353, 369
National Anti-Slavery Standard, 11–12, 402n
National Archives, 347
National Book Award, 228, 237–38, 240, *287*
National Book Critics Circle Award, 311
National Era, 23–26, 31
National Magazine Award, 321
National Organization for Women (NOW), 250

National Press Club, 342, 380
National Press Foundation, 315
National Public Radio (NPR), 261, 292, 293, 348–49, 365–66
National Woman Suffrage Association, 42
Native Americans, 59, 68, 74
Nazi Germany, 124, 130, 162, 163, 170–72, 174, 175, 177, 180, 452–53n
  concentration camps of, 175, 177, 180, 181, 193
  Hitler in, 104, 130, 131, 144, 164, 172, 175, 180–81
  Nuremberg trials and, 170, 174
NBC, 148, 197, 212, 219, 220, 234, 235, 261–63, 265, 281, 348, 382
Nelson, Nell, 56
Nemy, Enid, *249,* 491n
Nervi, Pier Luigi, 219
Nesbit, Evelyn, 91, 93, 94
Neuharth, Al, 247, 273, 489–90n, 500n
Newark Evening News, 112
New Century for Woman, The (Women's Centennial Committee), 35
Newell, Eleanor, 144
New Haven Register, 244
New Journalism, 249
New Republic, 138, 204, 209, 263, 363, 371
New Rules Summit, 382
New Russia, The (Thompson), 129
news agencies (wire services), 97, 151, 175
  AP, 72, 88, 128, 151, 153, 154, 158, 164, 165, 179, 188, 190, 195, 201, 212, 221, 224, 244, 260, 273, 338, 340, 350–51
  Associated Negro Press, 199
  Canadian Press, 165
  City News Bureau, 247
  INS, 127, 128, 159, 164, 176, 177, 188

Reuters, 174
UP, 97, 123, 129, 138, 139, 144, 152–55, 164, 169, 171, 173–75, 178–79, 187–88
UPI, 188, 216–18, 232–33, 238, 239, 247, 277–79, 287, 288, 342
Women's National News Service, 154
Newsday, 244, 250, 258, 259, 272, 301, 312, 313, 332, 339, 344
News Four Probe, 212
Newspaper Guild, 112, 198
Newspaper Reporters Association of New York City, 255
News Through a Woman's Eyes, 457n
Newsweek, 155, 176, 188, 196–97, 203, 206–8, 231–33, 238, 242–44, 291–93, 346, 350, 351, 370, 383
News with the Woman's Touch, 225
New Thought, 82
New York, 249, 352
New York Age, 51
New York American, 118
New York Amsterdam News, 147, 160, 197
New York City, 103
  Harlem, 255
  Lower East Side, 85
  "slave market" job sites in, 198
  slums in, 46
New York Daily Mirror, 108
New York Daily News, 108, 109, 118, 186, 271, 287, 332–34, 339, 351, 371
New Yorker, 124, 141, 163, 174, 189, *202,* 206, 208–12, 224, 226, 228, 230, 237, 249, 261, 264, 284, 317, 320, 321, 326, 333, 334, 351, 353, 371, 380
New-Yorker (Greeley publication), 13
New Yorker Festival, 356, *357,* 358
New York Evening Graphic, 110

New York Evening Journal, 58, 65, 66, 68, 75–77, 82, 93, 98, 100, 108, 118

New York Evening Post, 27–28, 85, 129

New York Evening Telegram, 42

New York *Evening World,* 77

New York Family Story Paper, 57–58

New York Globe, 106

New York Herald, 11, 43, 66, 93, 100, 112

New York Herald Tribune, 101, 102, 108, 111, 119, 135, 153, 165, 169, 180, 185, 189, 191–93, 196, 220, 221, 224, 232, 254, 374

New York *Mail and Express,* 42, 53, 58

New York Newsday, 287

New York Newspaper Women's Club, 169–70, 180, 193

New York Observer, 353

New York Post, 149–50, 201, 233, 243, 265, 364

New York Press Association, vii, 36

New York Review of Books, 230

New York Star, 197

New York Sun, 11, 21, 42, 112

New York Times, 25, 33, 61, 88, 100–102, 110, 112, 128, 152–54, 163, 169, 174, 196, 210, 221, 228–30, 232, 237, 239, 258, 264, 265, 269, 273, 275–76, 283, 285, 286, 288, 308, 311–12, 326, 331, 332, 338, 342, 348, 355, 370–71, 374, 380, 381, 384–86

Abramson at, 333, 344, 351–54, 356–67, 378, 383

Asbury at, 201–3, *202*

Baquet at, 352–54, 357–58, 362–67, 368, 370, 371, 374–75, 378, 385, 503n, 538n

Curtis at, 222–23, 284

editorial board of, 133, *133,* 134

Emerson at, 233–34

Frankel at, 303–7, 317–20, 330

Grant at, 124–25

Hunter at, 255–57

Huxtable at, 218, 219

journalist couples and, 291–302, 303–4, 508n

Lewis and, 190–91, 259–61

McCormick at, 123, 129, 131–35, *133*

Morgan at, 43–44

"Ms." term used at, 284, *see also* "Mx.," use of

"Negro" and "black" terms used at, 256

Rosenthal at, 197, 201, 260, 275, 279, 291–302, 303, 306, 327, 353

sexual harassment and, 277, 315–17

1619 Project at, 381–82

women's discrimination charges against, 244, 246–47, 250–51, 279, 293, 304, 330, 351

women's positions and salaries at, 278–81, 304, 305, 318, 322–24, 329–30, 377–78

New York Times Magazine, 212, 219, 220, 261, 289, 370, 372

New York Tribune, 6, 11–16, 18, 20, 29, 30, 33, 34, 43, 46, 54, 56, 80, 92, 94, 98, 113, 388

New York University (NYU), 70, 218, 334, 349, 384–85

New York Woman, 318

New York Women's Press Club, 33

New York *World,* 32, 43, 44, 49, 53–58, *63,* 64–65, 66, 72, 76, 91–94, 100, 106, 110, 116

New York World's Fair, 135, 162

New York World-Telegram, 161, 200, 201

New York Yankees, 339

Nieman Foundation, 366–67

Nieman Reports, 378

Nightingale, Taylor, 50

19th*, The, 386–89

Nineteenth Amendment, 96, 173, 386, 388, 437n

Nixon, Richard, 235, 282

Nixon, Tricia, 257–58
Nobel Prize, 110, 129, 130
Nobody Starves (Brody), 110
North American Newspaper
    Alliance (NANA), 117, 148, 154,
    170, 215
North American Review, 8–9, 109
Northcott, Kaye, 264
Northwestern University, 257, 324,
    342, 343
Norton, Eleanor Holmes, 526n
Nougayrède, Natalie, 366
NOW (National Organization for
    Women), 250
NPR (National Public Radio), 261,
    292, 293, 348–49, 365–66
Nuevo Herald, 308
Nuremberg trials, 170, 174
Nyilas, Ilona, 460n

Obama, Barack, 342, 355, 376
Obama, Michelle, 330
Oberlin College, 423n
Oberlin Herald, 64
Observer, 190
Ochs, Adolph, 124, 132, 203, 436n,
    437n
Oelsner, Lesley, 485n
Office of War Information, 153
Off Washington Square (Kramer), 209
Ohio State University, 146
oil industry, 49–50
O'Kane, Maggie, 512–13n
O'Keeffe, Georgia, 135
Olson, Lisa, 339–40
Olsten, Doris Ellen, 485n
Olympic Games, 339
Omaha World-Herald, 59
O'Malley, Ed, 95
Opinión, 271
Oregonian, 274, 308, 369
O'Reilly, Bill, 375, 377

Oreskes, Michael, 323–24, 332, 333
Oriental News Service, 88
Orlando Sentinel, 344
Orlean, Susan, 371, 374
Orsini, Bette Swenson, 506n
Orth, Maureen, 481n
Osnos, Peter, 300–301
Ossoli, Giovanni Angelo, 19–20
O'Sullivan, John, 404n
Oswald, Lee Harvey, 188–89
Ottenberg, Miriam, 214–15, *215*
Our Famous Women (Phelps et al.), 74
Outcault, Richard F., 64
Outlook, 78, 79, 127
Overholser, Geneva, 307–10, *309*,
    327–29, 342–43, 367, 510n, 517n,
    523n
Overseas Press Club, 321, 354
Overseas Weekly, 235

Pace, Julie, 521n
Packard, Eleanor, 169, 171, 173, 234,
    454n
Packard, Reynolds, 144
Painter-Downes, Molly, 471n
Palestine, 127, 162
Pall Mall Gazette, 45
Palmer, Laura, 487n
Panic of 1873, 41
Pankhurst, Emmeline, 113
Paris, 48, 99, 106, 128, 130, 138, 139,
    142, 176, 178, 190, 207, 218, 231–34,
    237, 243, 259–60, 288, 330, 332
Paris Review, 322, 371
Parker, Dorothy, 209
Partisan Review, 320
Parton, Margaret, 460n
patents, 47
Patriarch, The (Tifft and Jones), 253,
    492n
Patterson, Ada, 91, 93–94
Patterson, Alicia, 435n

Patterson, Eleanor "Cissy," 77, 118–19, 435n
Patton, George, 180
Paul, Alice, 173
Paul, Pamela, 530n
Pauley, Jane, 263, 339
Payne, Claudia, 318–19
Payne, Ethel, *199*, 200, 466n
PBS, 257, 340, 348
PBS NewsHour, 348
Peabody Award, 185, 273
Pederson, Rena, 340
Peer, Elizabeth, 207, 231, 233, 481n
Penn State, 280
Pennsylvania College for Women, 113
People's Voice, 197–99
Perón, Juan, 173
Persian Gulf, 315, 513n
Person to Person, 187
Pew Research Center, 366
Philadelphia Inquirer, 276–77, 283, 285, 313, 322
Philadelphia *Public Ledger,* 123, 124, 128
Philippines, 79–80, 83, 85, 87, 99, 170
Phillips, Carolyn, 331, 332
Phillips, Elizabeth M., 457–58n
Phillips, Ruby Hart, 448n
photojournalism, 85, 86, 96, 140, 171, 179, 253, 354, 474n, 487n
Pileggi, Nick, 368
Pilnyak, Boris, 130
Pine Ridge Reservation, 59
Pinkham, Lydia, 185
Pittsburg Dispatch, 42, 43, 49, 52
Pittsburgh Gazette, 32
Pittsburgh Post-Gazette, 279, 297
Plath, Sylvia, 206
Playboy Club, 221
Plume d'Or, 232
PM, 197

Poe, Edgar Allan, 17, 403n
Poland, 191, 291–93, 464n
Politico, 345, 353, 357–59, 363
Politkovskaya, Anna, 525n
Pollitt, Katha, 320
Poor People's Campaign, 212
Port Arthur, 87, 88
poverty, 46
Povich, Lynn, 207–8, 231, 232, 242–44, 350, 481n, 504n, 524n, 535n
Povich, Shirley, 207
Powell, Adam Clayton, 160–61, 197
Powers, Thomas, 486n
Prague, 163
Pratap, Anita, 512n
Presbyterian Church, 111
presidential campaigns and elections, 340, 341, 376, 387
PressThink, 355
Price, Ann Elizabeth, 460n
Priest, Dana, 345, 525n
Primetime, 282
prisons, 14, 15, 146, 402n
ProPublica, 369–70, 373
Progressive Party, 118
Prose Writers of America (Griswold), 19
prostitutes, 14, 15, 198
Provincial Freeman, 30
Pry, Polly, 56
psychoanalysis, 264, 284
Publishers Award, 255, 257
Puck, 66
Pulitzer, Joseph, 57, 64, 65, 76, 91, 423n
Pulitzer Prize, 22, 51, 134–35, 185, 193, 195, 214, 215, 227, 237, 240, 247–49, 253, 254, 260–61, 269, 271–72, 283, 291, 293, 297, 308–12, 315, 320, 322, 338, 344–46, 352, 354, 358, 360, 371, 375, 380
Punch, 283

Purdy, Matthew, 538n
Purex, 225
Purnick, Joyce, 303–4, 323, 324, 361,
    516n
Pyle, Ernie, 456n

Queen Elizabeth 2, 207
Quill, 315, 326, 329–31
Quindlen, Anna, 265, 279, 286, *286,*
    311–12, 320, 326, 342
Quinn, Sally, 250, 300, 301

Rabb, Harriet S., 351
Radcliffe College, 228
Radner, Gilda, 263
Raines, Howell, 333, 344, 353, 354,
    523n
Ramshaw, Emily, 387, 388
Rand, Christopher, 460n
Randolph, Eleanor, 285, 318
Random House, 218, 300
rape victims, 308–9
Rather, Dan, 326
Raymond, Allen, 460n
Raymond, Henry J., 44
Reader's Digest, 244
Reagan, Nancy, 331
Reagan, Ronald, 275, 276, 331
Real Anita Hill, The (Brock), 317,
    528n
Real Paper, 280
Reasoner, Harry, 262
Recktenwald, Bill, *248*
Reconstruction, 50, 258
Record, 280
Red & Black, 210
Red Cross, 79, 101, 129, 420n
Red Cross Magazine, 99
Red Record, A (Wells), 51
Reed, John, 99, 430n
Reeves, Richard, 222, 529–30n
Rehm, Diane, 347–48

Reid, Helen Rogers, 119, 126, 135, 140,
    166, *166*
Reid, Ogden Mills, 422n
Reid, Whitelaw, 43, 46
Reitsch, Hanna, 170
religion, 111–12, 437n, 460n
Reporter, 226
Republican, 26
Republican National Convention,
    138
Republican Party, 118
Reston, James "Scotty," 132, 456n
Reuters, 174
Rewire, 372
Rex, Margery, 108
Ridgway, Erman J., 422n
Rinehart, Mary Roberts, 98, 525n
Risen, James, 356
Rittenhouse, Anne, 437n
Robb, Inez, 159, 160, 164, 450n,
    452n
Robbins, Carla Anne, 527n
Roberts, Cokie, 261, 262, 347–49
Roberts, Deborah, 522–23n
Roberts, Gene, 276–77, 280, 319,
    322–23, 330, 497n
Robertson, Nan, 132, 223, 246, 306,
    489n, 502n, 506n
Robeson, Paul, 118
Robinson, Janet, 333, 352, 355, 521n
Robles, Frances, 360
Rochester Democrat and Chronicle, 143
Rockefeller, John D., 50
rock music, 226
Rocky Mountain News, 71
Roe v. Wade, 387
Rohe, Alice, 97–99, *97,* 123, 129
Roiphe, Anne, *249,* 491n
Roiphe, Katie, 230, 322, 371
Roland, Madame, 49
Roosevelt, Eleanor, 117, 135, 140, 160,
    161, 162, 163, 170, 220

Roosevelt, Franklin D., 117, 135, 140, 159, 163, 178
Roosevelt, Theodore, 91
Rosen, Jay, 355
Rosenberg, Carol, 513n
Rosenhause, Sharon, 519n
Rosenstiel, Tom, 274
Rosenthal, Abe, 197, 201, 260, 275, 279, 280, 303, 306, 327, 353, 508n
  journalist couples and, 291–302
Rosenthal, Andrew, 527n
Rosenthal, Elisabeth, 323, 387
Ross, Harold, 124, *125*, 209, 515n
Ross, Ishbel, 96, 97, 101, *107*, 108, 111, 113–16, 145, 222, 233, 442n, 525n
Ross, Lillian, 334, 371, 374, 471n
Ross, Sonya, 350–51, 525–26n
Roth, Jeff, 456n
Rowe, Sandy Mims, 273–74, 276, *276*, 305, 307, 308, 316, 343, 369, 519n, 521n
Royall, Anne Newport, 11, 136, 347, 401n
Rubin, Alissa J., 375
Rubin, Trudy, 513n
Rudoren, Jodi, 361
Rule, Sheila, 275
Runkle, Lucia Gilbert, 408n
Runyon, Keith, 253, 278
Russell, Rosalind, 132
Russia, 89, 104, 118, 130, 166, 171, 188, 192, 298–99
  Finland and, 162, 170
  Japan and, 87, 89
  Mosby in, 216–18, *217*, 475n
  revolution in, 99, 100
  soldiers from, 177–79, *176*
Rust College, 48
Rutenberg, Jim, 375, 377
Rutland Herald, 265
Ryan, Carolyn, 385, 530n
Ryttenberg, Margaret, 460n

Saarinen, Aline, 220, 221
Sabin, Lawrence, 174
Sabol, Blair, 491n
Sachs, Susan, 513n
Sacramento *Weekly Bee*, 76
Sadat, Anwar, 263, 496n
Saikowski, Charlotte, 524n
St. Cloud Times, 136
St. Johns, Adela Rogers, 118, 435n, 442n
St. Louis Post-Dispatch, 139, 144
St. Louis Star, 137
St. Louis World's Fair, 86, 87
St. Mary's of the Springs Academy, 130, 131
Salisbury, Harrison, 174, 195–96, 261
Salmans, Sandra, 481n
Sanders, Marlene, 220, 221, 225, 281, 487n, 504n, 505n
Sand War, 218
San Francisco Call, 70
San Francisco Chronicle, 79, 87
San Francisco Examiner, 99
Saturday Evening Post, 25, 37, 101, 163, 219, 230
Saturday Night Live, 263
Saturday Review, 140–41
Saturday Visiter, 30
Savitch, Jessica, 497n
Sawyer, Diane, 223, 282, 321
Scardino, Albert, 507n
Schanberg, Sydney, 239, 485n
Schau, Virginia M., 460n, 474n
Scherman, David E., 179–81
Schlesinger, Arthur M., Jr., 238
Schlesinger Library, 228
Schmidt, Michael, 375, 377
Schmidt, William E., 527n
Schneider, Howard, 523n
Schorer, Jane, 308–9, 510n
Schreiber, Le Anne, 251, 306, 491n
Schulman, Bob, 253

Schultz, Sigrid, 123–25, *124*, 129, 169, 171–72, 436n, 442n, 454n
Schwindt, Helen Dimos, 481n
Scott, A. O., 226
Scott, Hazel, 160
Scott, Janny, 280, 323
Scripps Company, 97
Seale, Bobby, 203
segregation and integration, 200, 201, 210, 211, 224
Sehgal, Parul, 230
Seib, Charles, 489n
Seldes, George, 123, 129, 436n
Seligman, Jean, 481n
Senate Committee on Foreign Relations, 238
Senate Subcommittee on Investigations, 199
Seneca Falls Convention, 19
September 11 terrorist attacks, 342
sexism quiz, 274–75, 501n
sexual harassment and assault, 277–78, 315–17, 340–41, 375, 380–82, 384, 514n
  #MeToo movement and, 377, 379, 383, 536n
SHAEF (Supreme Headquarters Allied Expeditionary Force), 176–77, 179
Shanahan, Eileen, 279, 504n
Shapiro, Henry, 218
Sharpe, Rochelle, 511n
Shawn, William, 209, 211, 515n
Shea, Catherine, 466n
Sheehan, Susan, 209
Sheehy, Gail, 221–22, 249, 265, 374
Sheils, Merrill, 481n
Shepard, Sarah, 535n
Sheppard, Eugenia, 222
Sheridan, 79
Sherr, Lynn, 206, 221, 224, 249–50, *249*, 490–91n, 505n

She Said (Kantor and Twohey), 380, 537n
She Says, 339, 340–41
Shipley, David, 527n
Shipstead, Henrick, 147
Shoemaker, Jane, 485n
Show, 221
Shribman, David, 294–97, 303
Shriek with Pleasure (Howard), 192
Shriver, Maria, 346
Shulman, Collette, 463n
Silent Spring (Carson), 113, 228, 334, 479n
Silverstein, Jake, 370
Simmons, Rachel, 346–47
Simmons College, 348
Simpson, Carole, 263, 282, 341, *341*, 497n, 522–23n
Simpson, Peggy, 504n
Sinclair, Upton, 45, 110
Sing Sing, 14
Sinn Féin, 127
Sino-Japanese War, 70–72
Sivam, Seetharams, *288*
1619 Project, 381–82
60 Minutes, 248, 282
Skrzycki, Cindy, 294–97
Slate, 355, 363
slavery and abolition, 4, 8, 9, 11, 14, 17–18, 20, 21, 23–25, 30, 51
Slouching Towards Bethlehem (Didion), 229–30, 334
slums, 46
Smale, Alison, 332
Small, Bill, 496n
Smith, Hazel Brannon, 475n
Smith, Jean, 493n
Smith, Margaret Chase, 220, 468n
Smith, Red, 185, 374
Smith, Richmond, 88
Smith, Sally W., 481n
Smith, Zay, *248*

Smith College, 204, 205, 226

Snyder, Edith F., *see* Asbury, Edith Evans

sob sisters, 94, 95, 109

Society of Professional Journalists, 315, 329

Somaiya, Ravi, 362

Sontag, Susan, 334, 374, 474n

Sorbonne, 48

Sorel, Nancy Caldwell, 167, 170, 453n, 455n

Sorosis, 32–33, 46, 411n

South Africa, 330

Southern Literary Messenger, 20

Soviet Union, *see* Russia

Spain, 89, 153, 167, 293
   civil war in, 141–44, 164, 169–71, 444n, 445n, 453n
   Cuba's war of independence from, 64–69, 74–79, 82, 83, 85, 167
   U.S. war with, 86, 97

Spain in Arms (Strong), 445n

Span, Paula, 318

Sparks, Fred, 465n

Spayd, Liz, 377–78

sports, 185, 265, 339–40, 461n, 487–88n, 522n
   baseball, 59, 60, 85, 86, 415n, 446n, 461n
   football, 339, 522n
   women's, 339

Sports Illustrated, 244, 339

Springfield Press, 110

Springfield Republican, 34

Squires, Jim, 327

Stahl, Lesley, 263, 282, 339, 496n, 519n

Stalin, Joseph, 131, 199

Stamberg, Susan, 261

Standard Oil, 49–50, 334

Standard Union, 71

Standish, Mary, 446n, 461n

Stanton, Elizabeth Cady, 74

Stars and Stripes, 180

State Department, 148, 153, 164, 199

Stead, W. T., 61

Steel, Emily, 375, 377

Steele, A. T., 460n

Steer, Sarah, 406–7n

Steffens, Lincoln, 47, 110

Steinbach, Alice, 506n

Steinem, Gloria, 203, 204, 221, 249, 491n

Stephens, Mitchell, 520n

Stevenson, Adlai, 211

Stewart, Martha, 321

Stogsdill, Carol, 519n

Stone, Melville, 88

Story of Cuba, The (Halstead), 69

Stoss, Veit, 171

Stowe, Harriet Beecher, 24, 74

Strange Justice (Mayer and Abramson), 317

Stricken Field, A (Gellhorn), 162, 163

Stringer, Ann, 164, 169, 173–79, *176,* 234

Stringer, William J., Jr., 173–74

Strong, Anna Louise, 445n

Stuart, Reginald, 329

Su, Varatharajah, *288*

suffrage movement, 4, 43, 58, 73–75, 82, 96, 113, 126, 137–38, 173, 205–6, 212, 213, 229, 388, 437n

Sullivan, Ellen L., 481n

Sullivan, Margaret, 324–25, *337,* 343, 354–56, 359–63, 374, 387, 409n, 525n

Sullivan, Margaret F., 409n

Sulzberger, A. G., 362, 364

Sulzberger, Arthur Hays, 132, 133, 223

Sulzberger, Arthur Ochs, Jr., 275, 304, 316–17, 332, 352–54, 358, 360, 362–64, 366, 367, 514n, 527n

Sulzberger, C. L., 293
Sulzberger, Iphigene Ochs, 132–33, 223
Sunday Times (London), 288
Supreme Court, U.S., 50, 199, 346, 384
 Kavanaugh's nomination to, 382
 Roe v. Wade, 387
 Thomas's nomination to, 315–17, 353
Sutton, Carol, 252–53, 269, 274, 278, 491–92n
Swarns, Rachel, 330
sweatshops, 270–72, 345–46
Swisshelm, Jane Grey, 30–31, *31*
Syracuse University, 126
Syria, 288–89, *288*

Taft, Mary, 436n, 437n
Talese, Gay, 219–20, 249, 368–69, 371–74
Talk, 326, 345
Talley, Carol, 485n
Tampa Tribune, 276
Tarbell, Ida, 41, 46–52, *47, 52,* 60, 61, 74–75, 99, 135, 234, 334, 413n
Tatler, 283
Taubman, Phil, 294, 298–99, *299*
Taylor, Bayard, 404n
Taylor, Breonna, 387
television, 263, 281–82, 338–39, 341, 525n
Teltsch, Kathleen, 466n
Ten Days in a Mad-House (Bly), 54
Texas Observer, 285
Texas Tribune, 387
Thaw, Henry K., 91, 93, 94
Thirteenth Amendment, 42
Thomas, Clarence, 315–17, 353
Thomas, Helen, 342, 505n
Thompson, Dorothy, 105, 106, 123–30, 132–36, 137, *137,* 138,

141–43, 151, 163, 165–66, 169, 197, 231, 334, 433n, 437n, 442n, 444n, 454n, 486n
Thompson, Jack, 177–79
Thompson, Mark, 352, 355, 362, 365
Thoreau, Henry David, 6, 20
Time, 112, 118, 132, 135, 136, 152–53, 156, 163, 190, 193, 206, 207, 210, 211, 223, 244, 252, 253, 259, 265, 266, 275, 285, 298
Time Inc., 244
Time-Life Books, 244
Time Life Inc., 206
Times (London), 283
Title IX, 339
Today, 220, 262, 263, 321
Tofani, Loretta, 506n
Toledo Blade, 64
Tolliver, Melba, 224–25, *224,* 257–58
Tomara, Sonia, 454n
Topping, Seymour, 294–95
Torgau, 177–79, *176*
Toronto Mail and Empire, 78
Torquato Tasso (Goethe), 6
Torre, Marie, 461n
Totenberg, Nina, 261, 262, 316
Touré, 372
Tracy, Spencer, 130
Train of Powder, A (West), 174
Traister, Rebecca, 363
Trans-Action, 212
transcendentalists, 6, 19, 21, 93
Trillin, Calvin, 209–12, 249, 471n
Trotta, Liz, 234–36, *234,* 241, 473n, 474n, 483n, 487n
Trouble I've Seen, The (Gellhorn), 140–41
Truman, Bess, 159–61
Truman, Harry, 159–61, 186, 199, 200, 455n
Trump, Donald, 375–77, 379, 384
trust in the press, 272, 499n

Tucher, Andie, 522n
Turkey, 75, 89
Twain, Mark, 93
20/20, 321
Twitter, 373
Two Gentlemen of Verona, The
  (Shakespeare), 34
Twohey, Megan, 375, 377, *377,* 379,
  380, 537n

Ulrich, Mabel S., 443–44n
Uncle Sam's Diary, 148
Uncle Tom's Cabin (Stowe), 24
undercover reporting, 77, 116–17, *116,*
  198, 215, 221, 247–49, 270–72, 500n
Under the Sea-Wind (Carson), 113
Underwood, Agness, 145–46, *145,* 148,
  158, 185, 187, 221
United Nations (UN), 154, 170, 197,
  232, 261, 294–96
United Press (UP), 97, 123, 129, 138,
  139, 144, 152–55, 164, 169, 171,
  173–75, 178–79, 187–88
United Press International (UPI),
  188, 216–18, 232–33, 238, 239, 247,
  277–79, 287, 288, 342
*United States Magazine and Democratic
  Review,* 20, 21
United States News, 148
University of California, Berkeley,
  165, 204
University of California, Los Angeles
  (UCLA), 165
University of Chicago, 99, 269
University of Dayton, 134
University of Georgia, 210
University of Kansas, 68, 423n
University of Massachusetts at
  Amherst, 286
University of Michigan, 204
University of Minnesota, 147
University of Missouri, 157, 423n

University of Montana, 154
University of Texas at Austin, 173
University of Wisconsin, 46
USA Today, 321
U.S. Federal Emergency Relief
  Administration, 140, 141
U.S. Fish and Wildlife Service, 113
U.S. News & World Report, 148, 294,
  295
U.S. Patent Office, 47

Vallée, Rudy, 138
Van Anda, Carr, 131
Vanderlip, Narcissa Cox, 437n
Vandermeer, Walter, 255
Vanity Fair, 26, 283, 321, 381
Vassar College, 103, 207, 223, 423n
Vega, Tanzina, 370
Vennochi, Joan, 505n
Verne, Jules, 57
Victor Emmanuel III, 131
Victoria Times, 88
Vietnam War, 206, 214, 224, 232,
  234–41, 242, 247, 312, 473–74n,
  482n, 483n, 484n, 486n
Villa, Francisco "Pancho," 90, 100
Village Voice, 209, 239, 322, 332
Villard, Oswald Garrison, 422n
Virginian-Pilot, 305, 316
Visser, Lesley, 265, 339, 521–22n
Vital Speeches, 104
Vitray, Laura, 468n
Vogue, 139, 179, 180, 204, 230
Vox, 381

Wada, Karen, 519n
Wade, Betsy, 169, 196, 279, 281, 351,
  489n, 504n
Walesa, Lech, 291
Walker, Stanley, 111, 113–15, 233
Walker, Walton II., 194
Wallace, George, 224

Wallace, Julia, 276
Wall Street Journal, 259, 272, 287, 297, 311, 317, 326, 328–29, 331, 332, 344, 353, 361
Walnut Hills High School, 149
Walter, Cornelia, 4–5, *5*, 22, 398n
Walter, Lynde, 398n
Walter Reed National Military Medical Center, 345
Walters, Barbara, 220, 221, 262–63, 281, 282, 321, 366, 496n, 505n, 506n
war correspondents, 64–80, 89, 90, 96–97, 312–13, 418n, 454n, 513n
  number of, 166
  see also specific wars
Ward, Fannie B., 418n, 421n
Ward, Samuel G., 22
War Department, 151, 157
Warfield, Edwin, 86, 424n
War in Korea (Higgins), 465n
War Labor Board, 199
Warren, Virginia Lee, 460n
Warren Commission, 188
War Torn (Bartimus et al.), 236–37, 240, 482n
Washington, Booker T., 50
Washington, D.C., 152–53, 185, 212, 227, 384
Washington *Evening Star*, 148, 214
Washington Herald, 118
Washington Journalism Review, 255, *309*
Washington Post, 59, 60, 77, 159, 191, 200, 207, 219, 229, 232, 239, 240, 250, 284, 285, 294, 296, 298, 300–302, *303*, 311, 318, 321, 326, 327–28, 338, 342, 344, 345, 347, 348, 353, 379, 380, 387
  Greenfield at, 226, 227
  Murphy at, 313–15
  women's discrimination charges against, 244–45, 275

Washington Post Company, 243
Washington Star, 244–45, 253–54, 264–65, 285
Washington State University, 148
Washington Times, 118
Washington Times-Herald, 118
Washington University in St. Louis, 212
Washington Week in Review, 348
Wason, Betty, 454n, 457n, 466n
Watkins, Maurine Dallas, 109
Webb, Kate, 482n, 483n, 485n
Webster, Daniel, 30
Weinstein, Harvey, 321, 326, 377, 379, 536n, 537n
Weisman, Steve, 294, 298–301, *301*
Weizmann, Chaim, 190
Welch, Margaret, 61
Weldon, Marie, 437n
Wellesley College, 206, 423n
Wells, H. G., 140
Wells, Ida B., 47–51, *48*, 57, 60, 74, 234, 347
Welsh, Mary, 452n, 454n
Werner, Mary Lou, 460n, 474n
Wertheimer, Linda, 261–62, 496n
Wesleyan University, 228
West, Rebecca, 105, 174
Western College for Women, 149
Westmoreland, William, 235, 238, 482n
Westphal, David, 327–29
Weyler y Nicolau, Valeriano, 64–69, 76
Weymouth, Katharine, 347
Wharton, Edith, 98
What Mad Pursuit (Gellhorn), 139
White, Jessie, 525n
White, Katherine Angell, 209
White, Katherine Short, 421n
White, Stanford, 91
White, Stephen, 464n

White, Trumbull, 421n
Whitehead, Don, 465n
Whitehouse, Vira Boarman, 437n
White House Correspondents'
    Association, 152, 289, 342
Whitman, Walt, 18
Whitmore, Annalee, 455n
Whitney, Craig, 292
Wilder, Gene, 263
Wilder, Laura Ingalls, 110
Wiley, Fay, 481n
Wilkerson, Isabel, 311, *311,* 320,
    511–12n, 537n
Wilkins, Roy, 147
Wilkinson, Tracy, 512n
Willard, Frances, 74, 420n
Wille, Lois, 215–16, *215,* 506n
Willis, Ellen, 209, 226, 320, 471n
Wilson, Alex, 200
Wilson, Lisa, 525n
Wilson, Woodrow, 96, 98–100
Winfrey, Oprah, 321
Winn, Marcia, 203
Winner, Karin, 519n
Winners and Losers (Emerson), 240
wire services, *see* news agencies
Wittmeyer, Alicia Pin-Quon, 536n
Wolcott, James, 320–21
Wolfe, Tom, 222
Wolin, Merle Linda, 270–72,
    345–46
womanhood, new image of, 81–83
Woman in the Nineteenth Century ("The
    Great Lawsuit") (Fuller), 12, 14,
    15–17, 19
Woman of the Year, 130
Woman's Press Club of New York
    City, 102
women in journalism
    acceptance of, 83, 109, 151, 185, 209
    accusations against, 107–8, 114–16
    advice given to, 83–84

age discrimination against, 281–82,
    505n
attributes of, 83–84, 105
Black, 185, 199, 200, 210–11, 255–58,
    275
collective responses to
    discrimination against, 242–46,
    250–51, 252, 273, 307, 351
"firsts" and, 73, 86, 134
front-page girls, 96, 99, 103, 113, 115,
    149, 169
implicit or legacy bias and, 186
invisibility of, 25, 73
with journalist husbands, 291–302,
    303–4
late bloomers, 196
in management positions, 117–19,
    274, 278, 279, 289, 305, 307, 342,
    344, 366
motherhood and, 265–66, 323–24,
    361, 378, 505n, 516n
number of, 42, 60, 66, 83, 84, 90,
    103, 151, 156, 166, 187, 206, 213, 276,
    278, 317–18, 344–45
pay disparities and, 34, 36, 56, 60,
    109, 247, 278–79, 366
physical attractiveness of, 106–7, 111,
    129, 439n
smears on reputations of, 192
sob sisters, 94, 95, 109
young women and journalism
    careers, 60–61, 81–82, 131
women in the workforce, 3, 28, 47, 81,
    85, 152, 186–87, 279, 311
    underpaying of, 46, 77, 81, 85, 206,
    382
Women in the World Summit, 524n
Women's Caucus in Congress, 343
Women's Centennial Committee, 35
Women's Committee of the Council
    of National Defense, 99
Women's History Month, 347

Women's Media Center, 351, 360,
    385–86
Women's National News Service,
    154
Women's National Press
    Association, 84
Women's National Press Club, 152,
    200
women's rights and feminism, 4, 5,
    17, 73, 104, 205–6, 213, 228, 229,
    242–43, 250, 265, 320, 350, 374,
    501n, 511n
  labor rights, 28
  #MeToo movement, 377, 379, 383,
    536n
  Seneca Falls Convention, 19
  suffrage, 4, 43, 58, 73–75, 82, 96, 113,
    126, 137–38, 173, 205–6, 212, 213,
    229, 388, 437n
Women's Wear Daily, 234
Women Who Wrote the War, The (Sorel),
    167, 453n
Wood, Amy, 147
Wood, Sue Ann, 503n
Wood, Tracy, 482n, 487n
Woodman, Barbara, 480n
Woodruff, Judy, 263, 340–41, 348
Woodward, Josephine Miles, 67–69,
    70, 74, 75, 418n
Woolf, Virginia, 85
Work of the Afro-American Woman, The
    (Mossell), 91
World's Fairs
  Brussels, 188

  New York, 135, 162
  St. Louis, 86, 87
World War I, 96–101, 123, 124, 144,
    152, 157, 166, 167
World War II, 151–53, 155–59,
    162–64, 167–81, 193, 199, 231, 234,
    235, 241, 260, 347, 453n
  D-day invasion in, 171–73, 176, 178
  see also Nazi Germany
Worthington & Co., 73–74
Wounded Knee Massacre, 59, 74
WuDunn, Sheryl, 311, 512n

Yagoda, Ben, 471n
Yale Bowl, 185, 235
Yale University, 228, 265
yellow journalism, 64, 67, 76, 91,
    93, 95
Yellow Kid, The (Outcault), 64
You Don't Belong Here (Becker), 235,
    239
Young, Gayle, 513n

Zacchino, Narda, 316, 519n
Zamora, Amanda, 387
Zeisler, Andi, 373–74
Zekman, Pamela, 247–48, 248,
    272–73, 345
Ziegenmeyer, Nancy, 308–9
Zionism, 127
Zirinsky, Susan, 354, 384, 497n
Zita of Austria, 128–29
Zorn, Franny Heller, 208
Zuckerman, Mort, 333, 334

A NOTE ABOUT THE AUTHOR

Brooke Kroeger is a journalist, author, and professor emerita at NYU, where she was the founding director of the Arthur L. Carter Journalism Institute and of the institute's joint graduate program in global studies. Earlier in her career, she was UN correspondent for *Newsday* and deputy metropolitan editor for *New York Newsday* after eleven years with United Press International, most in leadership roles in Chicago, Brussels, London, and Tel Aviv. Her earlier books are *Nellie Bly: Daredevil, Reporter, Feminist* (1994), one of NPR's 1994 Best Books of the Year; *Fannie: The Talent for Success of Writer Fannie Hurst* (1999), one of the *St. Louis Post-Dispatch*'s Best Books of the Year for 1999; *Passing: When People Can't Be Who They Are* (2003), a *Post-Dispatch* Best Book of the Year for 2003; *Undercover Reporting: The Truth About Deception* (2012), a finalist for the Frank Luther Mott/Kappa Tau Alpha Research Award; and *The Suffragents: How Women Used Men to Get the Vote* (2018), recipient of the Independent Publisher Gold Medal in U.S. History. Links to her work can be found on her website at brookekroeger.com.

A NOTE ON THE TYPE

This book was set in Janson, a typeface long thought to have been made by the Dutchman Anton Janson, who was a practicing type-founder in Leipzig during the years 1668–1687. However, it has been conclusively demonstrated that these types are actually the work of Nicholas Kis (1650–1702), a Hungarian, who most probably learned his trade from the master Dutch typefounder Dirk Voskens. The type is an excellent example of the influential and sturdy Dutch types that prevailed in England up to the time William Caslon (1692–1766) developed his own incomparable designs from them.

Composed by North Market Street Graphics
Lancaster, Pennsylvania

Printed and bound by Berryville Graphics,
Berryville, Virginia

Designed by Betty Lew